		1853		Franklin Pierce
J. Neely Johnson, Amer.	2nd Vigilance Committee in San Francisco	1856		
		1857		James Buchanan
John B. Weller, Dem.		1858		
	Discovery of Comstock Lode	1859		
Milton S. Latham, Lec. Dem. John G. Downey, Lec. Dem.		1860		
		1861	Civil War	Abraham Lincoln
Leland Stanford, Rep. Frederick F. Low, Union		1862	Pacific Railroad Act	
	Building of the Central Pacific	1863		
		1864	Pacific Railroad Act	
		1865		Andrew Johnson
Henry H. Haight, Dem.		1867		
	University of California chartered Depression in California	1868		
		1869		Ulysses S. Grant
Newton Booth, Rep.		1871		
		1873	Panic of 1873	
Romualdo Pacheco, Rep. William Irwin, Dem.		1875		
		1877		Rutherford B. Hayes
	New constitution Battle of Mussel Slough	1879		
George C. Perkins, Rep.		1880		
		1881		James A. Garfield, Chester A. Arthur
George Stoneman, Dem.		1883		
		1885		Grover Cleveland
Washington Bartlett, Dem. Robert W. Waterman, Rep.		1887		
		1889		Benjamin Harrison
Henry H. Markham, Rep.	Stanford University opened	1891		
		1893	Panic of 1893	Grover Cleveland
James H. Budd, Dem.		1895		
		1897		William McKinley
Henry T. Gage, Rep.		1899		
	Ruef and Schmitz in power	1901		Theodore Roosevelt
George C. Pardee, Rep.		1903		
	San Francisco Graft Prosecution Lincoln-Roosevelt League formed	1906		
James N. Gillett, Rep.		1907		
		1909		William H. Taft
	Republican Progressives sweep the state elections	1910		
Hiram W. Johnson, Rep.		1911		
	Los Angeles Aqueduct	1913		Woodrow Wilso
Hiram W. Johnson (as Prog.) William D. Stephens, Rep.		1915		
		1917	United States in World War I	
		1921		Warren G. Har Calvin Coolidg
Friend W. Richardson, Rep. Clement C. Young, Rep.		1923		
		1927		
		1929	Stock market crash Great Depression	Herbert C. Hoo
James Rolph, Jr., Rep.		1931		
		1933		Franklin D. Ro
Frank F. Merriam, Rep. Culbert L. Olson, Dem.	Merriam defeats Sinclair	1934		
		1939		
		1941	United States in World War II	
	Japanese evacuation	1942		
Earl Warren, Rep.		1943		
		1945		Harry S. Trum
		1950	Korean War	
Goodwin J. Knight, Rep. Edmund G. Brown, Dem.		1953		Dwight D. Eis
		1959		
	California Water Bonds	1960		
		1961		John F. Kenne Lyndon B. Johnson
		1963		
Ronald Reagan, Rep.		1967		
		1969		Richard M. Nixon

D0482454

CALIFORNIA: An interpretive history

Klamath R.
Mt. Shasta
Pit R.
Trinity R.
Eureka
Shasta Lake
395
Redding
10
Mt. Lassen
Susanville
Eel R.
Sacramento R.
Feather R.
99
Yuba R.
Ukiah
Clear Lake
Marysville
80
S I E R R A N E V A D A
American R.
L. Berryessa
50
Placerville
Lake Tahoe
Santa Rosa
Napa
Sacramento
Pt. Reyes
Vallejo
San Rafael
Berkeley
San Francisco
Oakland
Stockton
San Mateo
Mono Lake
Redwood City
Modesto
Palo Alto
San Jose
San Joaquin R.
Merced
Santa Cruz
Bishop
Monterey
Salinas
Kings R.
Fresno
Mt. Whitney
Salinas R.
99
Kern R.
395
San Luis Obispo
Bakersfield
Tehachapi Mts.
Santa Maria
Mojave Desert
15
Pt. Arguello
Barstow
Santa Barbara
66
San Miguel Is.
101
Pasadena
Santa Rosa Is.
San Bernardino
Santa Cruz Is.
Los Angeles
Riverside
Palm Springs
Long Beach
60-70
Santa Catalina Is.
Salton Sea
San Clemente Is.
Imperial Valley
San Diego
80

CALIFORNIA

AN INTERPRETIVE HISTORY *Second Edition*

WALTON BEAN

Professor of History
University of California, Berkeley

McGRAW-HILL BOOK COMPANY

New York San Francisco St. Louis Düsseldorf Johannesburg
Kuala Lumpur London Mexico Montreal New Delhi
Panama Rio de Janeiro Singapore Sydney Toronto

To BETH, my wife, with love

CALIFORNIA: AN INTERPRETIVE HISTORY

This book was set in Fairfield by Holmes Typography, Inc. The editors were Robert P. Rainier and Ronald Q. Lewton, the designer was Ronald Q. Lewton, and the production supervisor was Michael A. Ungersma. The maps were done by Nancy Fouquet. The printer and binder was Kingsport Press, Inc.

Copyright © 1968, 1973 by McGraw-Hill, Inc. All rights reserved. No part of this publication may be reproduced, stored in a retrieval system, or transmitted in any form or by any means, electronic, mechanical, photocopying, recording, or otherwise, without the prior written permission of the publisher. Printed in the U.S.A.

Library of Congress Cataloging in Publication Data

Bean, Walton.
California; an interpretive history.

1. *California–History.*
F861.B4 1973 917.94'03 72-3670
ISBN 0-07-004224-1

34567890 KPKP 7987654

PREFACE

WHEN THE FIRST EDITION of this book went to the printer in 1967, its preface remarked that California's massive growth in the 20th century had made it the most populous of the states by the mid-1960s, and that in annual production and income it ranked "sixth among the *nations* of the world, after the United States, Russia, West Germany, Britain, and France, and slightly ahead of Japan." Five years later, California's rate of growth has slowed, while Japan's economy has passed not only California's but also those of West Germany, Britain, and France. Yet it is still as true as ever that the story of California's dynamic growth is a major part of modern history. Even in the earliest years after its admission to the Union one of its first senators, William M. Gwin, described it accurately as "this unprecedented state." Today, the interest of Californians in their own history is clearly increasing, not declining, because they are more concerned than ever before with the forces that have formed and will form their environment.

The persistence of inaccurate clichés about California's history has tended to prevent a full realization of the recency and swiftness of its emergence upon the modern scene. A highly respected national magazine, for example, recently spoke of "history-rich Monterey, where Spanish grandees were dining off damask before the Pilgrims set foot on Plymouth Rock." The writer of the article was reasoning from the fact that Vizcaíno entered and named the Bay of Monterey in 1602. But Monterey was not actually founded until 1770, a full 150 years after the landing of the Pilgrims; and life in that tiny Spanish outpost never faintly resembled the life of grandees. As late as 1846, just before the American conquest, Mexican California had only about 7,000 inhabitants other than the Indians. California's Spanish, Mexican, and early American periods will always retain their fascination, and this book does justice to their color and adventure. Much more fully than any previous volume, however, it also analyzes the fabulous and vital developments of the 20th century.

California's achievements have been tremendous and spectacular, and they receive full recognition here. Balanced treatment also demands recognition of faults and failures. The book offers fresh interpretations of many of California's most controversial and persistent problems, such as racism, vigilantism, and the maltreatment of agricultural labor.

I wish to make special acknowledgement for the help I have received from Earl Pomeroy; and from Gunther Barth, Robert H. Becker, Don E. Fehrenbacher, Raymond W. Hillman, Robert V. Hine, Harry L. Knight, Rudolph M. Lapp, Christopher Paige, Ray Stafanson, Edward F. Staniford, Paul S. Taylor, John Barr Tompkins, Robert Trempy, and Gerald T. White.

I am also indebted to the researches of graduate students, many of whose theses are cited in the "selected bibliographies." A still larger list may be found in Pamela A. Bleich, "A Study of Graduate Research in California History in California Colleges and Universities," *California Historical Society Quarterly*, XLIII–XLIV, from September 1964 through December 1965.

WALTON BEAN

Berkeley, California

CONTENTS

MAPS

Chapter I

INTRODUCTION: GEOGRAPHY AND HISTORY

CALIFORNIA is a notoriously extraordinary place. Three elements in its geography have played especially crucial parts in its history: its extreme isolation, its extraordinary climate, and the great diversity among its various subregions.

The rise of a modern civilization began remarkably late in California because of its extreme geographical remoteness from Europe and Asia, and even from the original Spanish and British colonial settlements in the Western Hemisphere. The Spanish founded their first settlement on the Pacific Coast in 1519, at Panamá. Not until 1769, two and a half centuries later, did they found their first settlement in Alta California at San Diego. Throughout the Spanish and Mexican periods the difficulties of getting to California prevented any substantial number of settlers from going there; and despite the American conquest and the tremendous lure of the gold discovery, California's isolation continued to retard its growth until, and even after, the opening of the first transcontinental railroad in 1869.

Once the barriers of geographical remoteness had been overcome, the unique and gentle climate of California became a greater attraction than gold had been. As James J. Parsons has pointed out, "It so happens that California's arbitrarily conceived boundaries outline the only area of winter rain and summer drought in North America." Except on the northwest coast, where the average annual precipitation ranges up to 109.43 inches (at Monumental in Del Norte County), rainfall in California ordinarily occurs only between late October and early May. In the state as a whole, the average yearly precipitation is 23.88 inches; but throughout the late spring, the entire summer, and the early autumn, there is very seldom any precipitation at all. California's climate is often called "Mediterranean," although its summers are more comparable to those of North Africa than to those of Italy, where occasional summer rainfall does occur.

For all but a few of the Indian tribes of California, the dry summers made agriculture impossible before the coming of the white man. But in the American period, when irrigation was developed on a vast scale, the uniqueness of the climate gave California a virtual monopoly on the production of many highly valuable agricultural crops, and the invention of the refrigerated railway car made it possible to market them throughout the country. Climate was also a vital factor in the location of other major industries in California, notably the production of motion pictures and aircraft.

Within the common pattern of summer drought, California's climatic conditions vary widely, and it has many climates rather than one. General discussions of "the California climate" have usually described only the coastal or marine climate, with its relatively cool summers and warm winters and its relatively humid atmosphere throughout the year. In the Great Central Valley, and other interior valleys, the variations in temperature are much wider; and in the vast desert areas they are extreme. The foothill climate, with its advantage of relative freedom from fog, also requires separate classification; and the mountain climate at some points in the Sierra Nevada is much like that of the Alps.

In many other respects, also, California's physiographic diversity is striking and historically significant. California is huge—the third largest of the states, after Alaska and Texas. It extends over nearly 10° of latitude, with a coastline of 1,264 miles, and its land surface is 158,693 square miles, or 99,898,880 acres. Within this vast area, the profusion of varying landscapes offers some of the world's most inspiring adventures in scenery and some of its finest opportunities for recreation. Altitudes vary from 14,495 feet at the top of Mt. Whitney, the highest point in the United States outside Alaska, to −282 feet at Badwater in Death Valley, though these two points are only 60 miles apart.

Among California's many rich natural resources, its many varieties of forests and soils have contributed vitally to its economic development. Coal and iron are lacking, but gold, oil, and other minerals are present in great quantities. So is water for irrigation and power, though getting the water from regions of excess to regions of shortage is one of the state's greatest problems.

SELECTED BIBLIOGRAPHY

James J. Parsons, "The Uniqueness of California," *American Quarterly*, VII (Spring 1955), 45–55, is a good introduction to the effects of California's geography on its history. Norman E. A. Hinds, *Evolution of the California Landscape* (1952), William J. Miller, *California through the Ages; the Geologic Story of a Great State* (1957), and Gordon B. Oakeshott, *California's Changing Landscapes: A Guide to the Geology of the State* (1971), describe the geological background. Robert D. Durrenberger, *Patterns on the Land* (1957,

1960), is a collection of geographical, historical, and political maps of California. On climate, see Ernest L. Felton, *California's Many Climates* (1965); and Harry P. Bailey, *The Climate of Southern California* (1966). Paul F. Griffin and Robert N. Young, *California, the New Empire State: A Regional Geography* (1957); David W. Lantis, Rodney Steiner, and Arthur E. Karinen, *California: Land of Contrast* (1963); David N. Hartman, *California and Man* (1968); and Elna Bakker, *An Island called California: An Ecological Introduction to the Natural Communities* (1971), are useful surveys of California's geography, which make clear the remarkable diversity of its climate, landforms, vegetation, soils, and other resources.

Chapter II

THE ORIGINAL CALIFORNIANS

BEFORE THE COMING of the white man, the way of life of the California Indians had remained virtually static for thousands of years. It was a survival of the Stone Age. But the causes and the meaning of this fact have been much misunderstood, largely because of the persistence of rather primitive ideas about the nature of primitive man, and particularly the persistence of racism—the belief that some races are biologically, morally, and intellectually inferior to others, and the use of this belief to justify the oppression of some races by others. Among competent ethnologists, the race theories underlying this pattern of thought have long been discredited.

The survival of a Stone Age culture in California was not the result of any hereditary biological limitations on the potential of the Indians as a "race." They had been geographically and culturally isolated. The vast expanse of oceans, mountains, and deserts had sheltered California from foreign stimulation as well as from foreign conquest, and even within California the Indian groups were so settled that they had little contact with each other. On the positive side, there was something to be said for their culture just as it was. California supported a much larger number of Indians than did any other region of comparable size in North America north of Mexico. The California Indians had made a successful adaptation to their environment and they had learned to live without destroying each other.

Food and population. The nature and extent of the food supply deeply influenced the culture of the Indians of California, and determined the size of their population. They produced no food through agriculture, except in the extreme southeastern portion along the lower Colorado River, but their natural sources of food were remarkably diverse and often ingeniously obtained. They lived by hunting, fishing, and gathering. The great staple was the acorn, which because of its high fat content has a higher caloric value than wheat. When washed free of tannic acid, acorn flour was made into porridge or bread. In many desert areas, mesquite pods took the place of acorns. Deer and small game were generally available. Insects were a widely accepted source of nutriment. The rattlesnake was a particular delicacy to some groups, though most others rejected snakes entirely. Fish were abundant in the streams, notably salmon in the Northwest. Fish and meat were often dried. Along the coast, shellfish were consumed in quantities, and many shellmounds as much as 30 feet high, which accumulated as heaps of kitchen refuse over periods of 3,000 years, provide important archaeological clues to Indian life.

The term "Digger" as applied to the California Indians is a misnomer, based on the mistaken idea that they lived largely by grubbing up roots. American pioneer immigrants, seeing Indian women busy with digging sticks, were unaware that they wanted root fibers for basketmaking more often than for food. The diet of the California tribes did include certain roots and bulbs, but perhaps the real reason the Digger legend persisted was that it was easier to deprive the Indians of their lands and their lives if it could be believed that they were only miserable and subhuman creatures anyway.

The most distinctive method used in preparing food was the process of leaching the tannic acid from acorn flour. The flour produced by pounding husked acorns with a stone mortar and pestle was winnowed by tossing in a shallow basket. Then it was spread out in a sandy shallow depression or basin and repeatedly doused with water to wash away the acid. Bread might then be baked in an earth oven, but much more commonly the flour was placed in a basket with water brought to a boil by throwing in hot stones. This produced a gruel or porridge, which was eaten either plain or flavored with berries, grass seeds, nuts, or bits of meat or fish.

The cooking basket might be caulked with pitch or tar, but it was often so tightly woven that it would hold boiling water without caulking. As this suggests, the California Indians were remarkably skilled in basketmaking. In this art they had no equals anywhere in the world, either in the utility of the product or in the beauty of the designs. They had developed basketry to such a point that potterymaking was hardly necessary and was confined mainly to the southern region, which was influenced by Southwestern Indian culture. Metals, on the other hand, were entirely unknown. In common with all the other Indians of North America north of Mexico, those of California lacked any technique for extracting metals from ores.

Hunting was mainly with the bow, which was often backed with sinew for extra strength. Arrows were cleverly feathered, and the heads were made of obsidian, which is sharper than flint and more readily shaped by flaking. Knives were also of obsidian. Fishing was done with nets or hooks; with harpoons, particularly for salmon; or by poisoning, accomplished by throwing buckeyes into small pools at the edge of a stream.

The ordinary tools of gaining a living, such as stones, arrows, harpoons, and knives, also served as the only weapons. Only the Colorado River Indians and a few of the Northwest tribes had a weapon as such, the war club. The hunting and fishing was done mainly by men, the gathering of plant foods and the cooking by women. In general, everyone worked hard and the division of labor was fair and effective. The picture of the Indians as lazy is the result of the demoralization that set in after the coming of the white man, who treated the Indian as if he were an inferior being and, seemingly, proved that he was.

The Mojaves and the Yumas practiced agriculture to the extent of dropping corn, bean, and pumpkin seeds in the mud left by the annual flood waters along the lower Colorado; farther west, there is some evidence that agriculture existed among the Cahuilla. But with such partial exceptions, the Indian agriculture of the American Southwest did not spread into California. One essential explanation of this is that the aboriginal California Indian population was in a Malthusian equilibrium. The natural food supply was moderately abundant and fairly well assured. The attempt to divert labor from hunting and gathering to the unfamiliar and risky techniques of agriculture would have produced a net loss from the disruption of the existing system.

The actual number of persons supported by this system in California, before the coming of the Spaniards, can never be precisely determined, but a reasonable estimate is that there were at least 275,000 Indians within the present boundaries of the state when the first Spanish settlement was founded in 1769. There have been extremely wide variations among the estimates of the aboriginal population of North America as a whole; but Indian population density in California before the coming of the white man was probably much greater than the average for other areas of North America north of Mexico.

Aspects of material culture. Dwellings were generally rude and simple, and conical, or dome-shaped, except in the Northwest, where they were often solid frame structures built of redwood planks and in rectangular form. In central California poles and brush were the most common building materials, and many houses were partly underground or banked with earth.

The sweat house, or *temescal,* was a distinctive institution. Its use was confined to men. An open fire, not steam, was used to produce heat; and since the upper part of the *temescal* was likely to be full of smoke, the men had to lie on the floor. While they were still perspiring freely they would rush to a nearby stream or lake and plunge into the usually chilly water. This was not done for any supposedly health-giving purpose, but rather as a social habit. The *temescal* had some of the aspects of a men's club, and in some tribes the men customarily slept there. Women and children were expected to do their bathing less ceremoniously, and in the early morning before the men were awake.

The most common boat was the *tule balsa,* merely a raft made of rushes but often bound into a boatlike shape. Seagoing dugout canoes, carved from

Interior of a temescal. (Courtesy of the Bancroft Library)

half of a redwood trunk, were used in the northwest; the Chumash of the Santa Barbara Channel region also made seaworthy canoes, though of plank rather than dugout construction.

Men ordinarily wore no clothing at all; the standard garment for women was a short skirt in two pieces, front and back. This was made of plant fibers, or skin, in which case the lower part was slit into fringes for decoration and freedom of movement. When the weather forced a degree of protection from cold, both sexes wore blankets made of furs. The sea otter was most prized, but deer and rabbit skins were more common.

Location, linguistic groups, "tribes." The pattern of availability of plant and animal foods, and the complete reliance upon them, tended to delimit not only the number of people but also their location. The California Indians lived in settled village communities of about 100 to 500 inhabitants, usually groups of kindred families; the location of these communities was determined very precisely by the availability of food.

Another culture-determining factor was the babel of tongues. Language barriers combined with the localized nature of food supplies and food seeking to discourage mobility and to intensify isolation and provincialism. Of the five main language stocks in California, four were common to other parts of North America, suggesting that there had been a vast jumble of migrations in very ancient times, before the mixture hardened. These five main stocks were subdivided into 21 language families, which in turn were subdivided into numerous dialects, most of which were mutually unintelligible. For example, the Indians of San Diego could not understand those of San Luis Rey, a few miles to the north, for the Diegueño spoke a dialect of the Yuman language family, while the Luiseño spoke one of the dialects of Shoshonean. Indian California was the region of greatest linguistic diversity in the world, excepting, according to some scholars, only the Sudan and New Guinea.

Typically, the California Indian knew that he had been born and would die in a little town on the bank of a certain stream, and that the land in the immediate vicinity belonged to his people. Just across certain hills, on another stream, were other people whom he might visit and with whom, if he could converse, he might intermarry, but on whose proprietary rights he should not infringe.

Anthropologists have attempted various definitions of the "tribe" in California. It may be considered as a body of people who shared a group name, a dialect, and a territory; on this basis there are said to have been 105 such tribes. But many of the groups so defined had no known group name for themselves, so that names have been supplied by the Spaniards or by the anthropologists. Other tribes had names that meant no more than "people" in the original. Moreover, the tribe was usually merely a linguistic group. Politically it was likely to be a mere congeries of tribelets, each of them no more than a group of neighboring villages, perhaps with a principal village in a permanent location and three or four smaller ones that were periodically moved a short distance, when the houses had deteriorated.

Elsewhere in North America a tribe was ordinarily a nation of several thousand people, having a strong and militant national consciousness. With the exception of the Mojaves and the Yumas on the southeastern margin, no such breadth of organization or political consciousness existed among the California Indians. The village community was usually the highest political unit. It is easy to see why the California Indians found it impossible to organize any widespread and effective resistance even to a handful of Spaniards, let alone to a horde of Anglo-Americans.

Social culture. The most extraordinary diversity prevailed not only among the languages spoken but also in nearly all other aspects of culture. Elements of culture occurring only in part of California, most of them only in a small part, greatly outnumbered those that were universal. The Northwest cultural province had many of the characteristics of the tribes to the north of it, and the culture patterns of Southeastern California bore some resemblance to those of tribes to the east. The Central culture province was the most distinctively "Californian." Even within these broad subdivisions, there was great diversity. Meaningful generalizations can be made about California Indian culture only if it is understood that there were exceptions to almost every general statement.

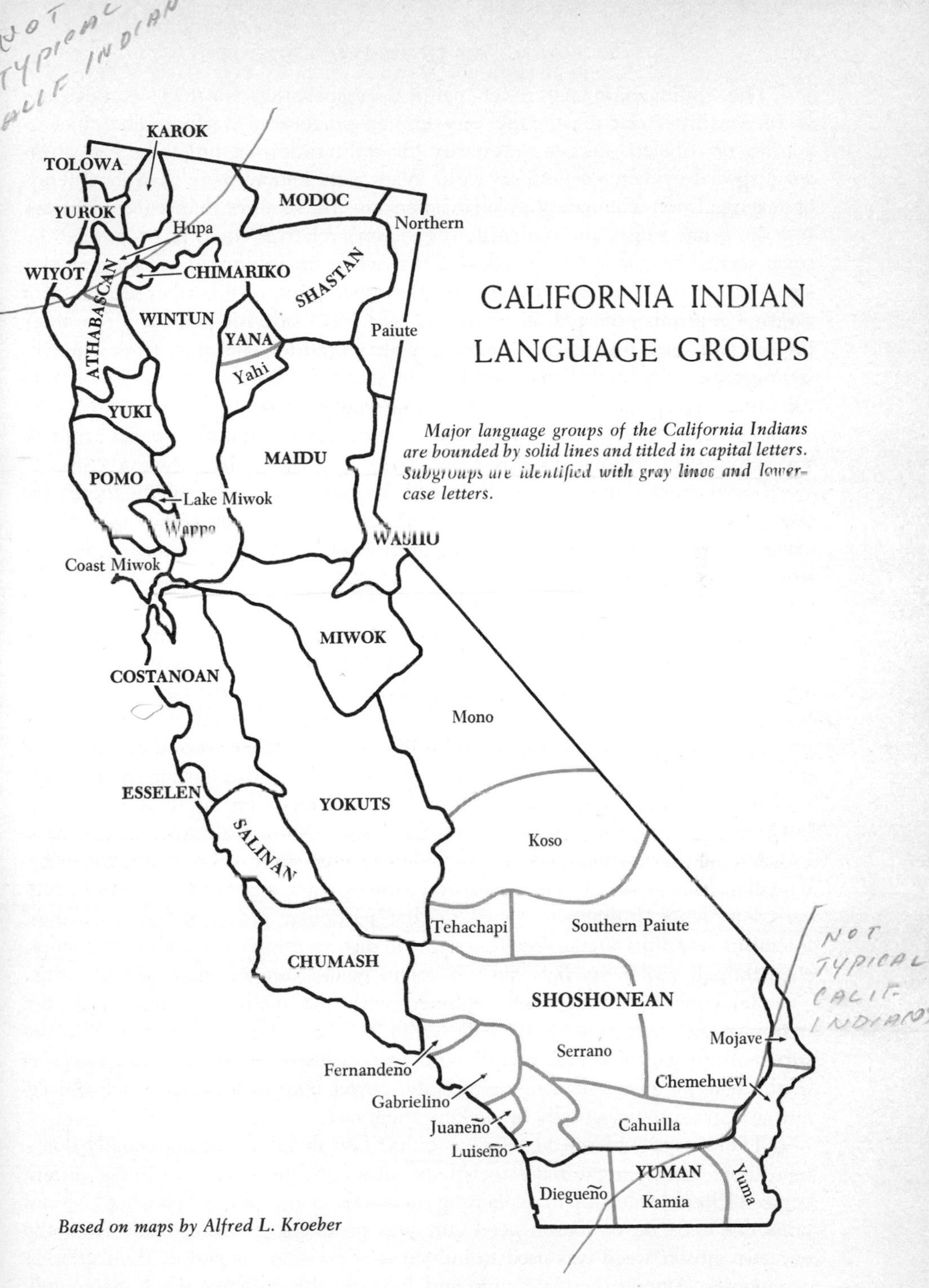

CALIFORNIA INDIAN LANGUAGE GROUPS

Major language groups of the California Indians are bounded by solid lines and titled in capital letters. Subgroups are identified with gray lines and lower-case letters.

Based on maps by Alfred L. Kroeber

The rudimentary nature of political organization, in fact its near absence, was interrelated with the very limited practice of warfare. The chief of a tribe, or tribelet, was not necessarily the military leader, unless he had given some special evidence of military skill. Wars were seldom more than local feuds of revenge, more commonly involving persons and families than tribes. Murder was the prime cause, and ordinarily the victim's relatives could be propitiated by some sort of payment for their loss. Even when an intertribal offense led to a small battle, one side would often pay the other to prevent further attacks. If a series of reprisals occurred, it might end with each side compensating the other for the damages. But when a death was attributed to witchcraft from a neighboring tribe, this tended to create a more stubborn dispute that might become inherited. Trespassing and food poaching were also occasional causes of war. Although there was no individual land ownership, the concept of tribal property was rather strongly developed.

Social classes hardly existed, except in the Northwest, where there was the greatest interest in acquiring wealth and personal property, and where slavery, based on debt, was commonly practiced. Indians in other areas were not uninterested in wealth, however. Gambling was widespread. Money was in the form of strings of beads made of dentalium shells or clam shells.

The family was by far the most important social institution, and in general a highly effective one. Marriage was by purchase, and polygamy was allowed if the husband could afford it. Adultery was regarded as an economic injury to the woman's husband, for which he might be paid; prostitution was unknown. In the Central region a kinship taboo forbade conversation with one's mother-in-law. One interpretation sometimes placed on this custom, however, is erroneous: it actually resulted not from a fear of meddling by the spouse's parents, but rather from great respect for them. Most California tribes were exogamous; that is, marriage was outside the immediate clan within the tribe. The clan usually had a totem, a natural kind or class, especially of animals, conceived as being intimately related to that particular group of human beings; totemism was thus a convenient system of distinguishing such kinship groups, even though visible symbols, such as totem poles, were not used in California.

Religious leadership was combined with the medical profession in the person of the shaman, who was believed to be in direct communication with the supernatural world. Illness was thought to be caused by foreign disease-objects in the body, and the shaman claimed the power both to introduce such objects and to remove them, usually by sucking them out.

There were widespread religious cults. The shamans did not usually dominate these loosely organized associations, although they might assume a certain degree of local leadership in explaining their rites. South of the Tehachapi Mountains the *toloache* or jimson-weed cult was prevalent. A drink made from the narcotic jimson weed was used to induce sacred visions as part of the initiation ceremonies. Among the Gabrielino and Juaneño this cult was much elaborated, and related to belief in a deity called Chinigchinich. In Central California the Kuksu cult placed more emphasis on esoteric rites that included dancers impersonating several deities. The "world-renewal" cult was a major aspect of religious life on the Northwest Coast. Its rites were designed to renew abundant food supplies and to prevent calamities.

Ceremonial observances were everywhere associated with adolescence and with mourning, and there were many first-fruit, first-salmon, or acorn-harvest ceremonies, comparable to our own Thanksgiving. The religious ideas of some of the California Indians were more elaborate than commonly supposed. For example, the belief in a prehuman race, rather than an anthropomorphic creator, was an interesting foreshadowing of the idea of evolution. The exact form of religious observance was often regarded as less important than its substance. Some of the beliefs of the Spanish missionaries, such as the idea that man was a sinful and fallen creature, were essentially foreign to Indian religious beliefs.

The California Indians had no system of writing beyond the use of very simple designs and symbols in the decoration of rocks, or in ground-painting as a part of religious ceremony and instruction in the southern region. Thus they were prehistoric in that they left no written records. In this sense, we must speak of California as having been first "discovered" by the Spaniards, and of its "history" as having begun at that time.

SELECTED BIBLIOGRAPHY

For the general reader and student, the best introductory volumes are Robert F. Heizer and Mary Ann Whipple, editors, *The California Indians, a Source Book* (1971); Theodora Kroeber, *Ishi in Two Worlds, a Biography of the Last Wild Indian in North America* (1961); and Jack D. Forbes, *Native Americans of California and Nevada* (1969). Alfred L. Kroeber, *Handbook of the Indians of California* (1925, reprinted 1953), is a very valuable reference work in the form of an extensive and remarkable series of tribal descriptions. An excellent summary account is R. F. Heizer, "The California Indians: Archaeology, Varieties of Culture, Arts of Life," *California Historical Society Quarterly*, XLI (March 1962), 1–28. See also Heizer, *Languages, Territories, and Names of California Indian Tribes* (1966).

The best of the Spanish missionary writings was Father Gerónimo Boscana's "Chinigchinich," on the religious and social customs of the Juaneño. This appeared in English translation in Alfred Robinson's *Life in California* (1846, reprinted 1947). Stephen Powers, *The Tribes of California* (1877), was first published in *The Overland Monthly*, 1872–1875. Powers was an extremely clever journalist and amateur ethnologist, and his work, making allowance for its many inaccuracies, is vividly colorful and readable. *The Native Races of the Pacific States of North America* (five volumes, 1875–1876), written mainly by Henry L. Oak and others, contains an immense amount of detailed information, as do all the volumes of *Bancroft's Works.* Volume I,

Wild Tribes, and volume III, *Mythology and Languages*, include material on the California Indians. Twentieth-century anthropology has added much scientific knowledge and many more accurate interpretations, notably in the numerous volumes of the University of California *Publications in American Archaeology and Ethnology* and *Anthropological Records.*

For evidence that Indian agriculture extended somewhat farther west of the Colorado than historians have traditionally supposed, see Harry W. Lawton and Lowell J. Bean, "A Preliminary Reconstruction of Aboriginal Agricultural Technology among the Cahuilla," *The Indian Historian*, I (Winter 1968), 18–24, 29.

The first reasonably reliable estimate of the number of Indians in Alta California before the coming of the Spaniards was made by C. Hart Merriam, "Indian Population in California," *American Anthropologist*, n.s., VII (1905), 594–606. Extrapolating from mission records, Merriam reached a figure of 260,000. A. L. Kroeber, in his *Handbook* (1925), estimated the number at only 133,000, but in later years Kroeber came to agree with other students of the subject that the actual figure was closer to Merriam's, and probably even higher; see Sherburne F. Cook, "The Aboriginal Population of Upper California," *XXXV Congreso Internacional de Americanistas: México* (1962), 397–403; and Martin A. Baumhoff, *Ecological Determinants of Aboriginal California Population* (1963). For the area of the United States as a whole, estimates have varied much more widely.

Some of the many works on various aspects of culture include A. L. Kroeber, *The Religion of the California Indians* (1907), and his *California Culture Provinces* (1920); Stanislaw Klimek, *Culture Element Distributions, I: the Structure of California Indian Culture* (1935); E. W. Gifford and G. H. Block, *California Indian Nights Entertainment* (1930); Theodora Kroeber, *The Inland Whale* (1959), a collection of California Indian tales; and James R. Moriarty, "A Reconstruction of the Development of Primitive Religion in California," *Southern California Quarterly*, LII (December 1970), 313–344.

Comparisons with other parts of the continent may be found in J. R. Swanton, *The Indian Tribes of North America* (1952), and Harold E. Driver, *Indians of North America* (1961).

Chapter III

DISCOVERY AND EARLY EXPLORATION

THE STORY of California in the days of the Spaniards is one of great color and fascination, even though the Spaniards themselves were disappointed in California and in general did not regard it as a very important part of their empire.

The "northern mystery" in the time of Cortés. Hernán Cortés, the conqueror of the Aztec empire in central Mexico, was also chiefly responsible for the discovery by the Spaniards of the lower part of what they ultimately called "the Californias."

In his urge to explore northwestward from the lands of the Aztecs, Cortés was following the lure of various tales of magnificent wealth. Some of these derived from Marco Polo's accounts of Cathay, for Cortés at first believed that Asia might be reached by a short sea voyage from Mexico. Spaniards of his time also put their trust in the ancient and medieval legends of the Terrestrial Paradise and the Amazon Island, and in such American Indian tales as those of the Seven Cities, and of El Dorado, "the Gilded Man," a king whose subjects covered him with gold dust every morning and washed it off every night. These were largely the same tales that had led to the discovery of the treasure of Montezuma. As applied to the lands north of Mexico, however, such stories led to bitter disillusionments for Cortés and for his followers, rivals, and successors.

As early as 1522, the year after his successful siege of the Aztec capital, Cortés established a shipyard at Zacatula on the Pacific coast of Mexico as a base for a series of attempts to send out exploring expeditions. These plans were repeatedly interrupted. Ship construction without local supplies was fantastically difficult, and when the first vessels were finally ready in 1526 the King of Spain ordered them sent to the Moluccas in the South Pacific. The royal government had become suspicious of the great conquistador, even as it had become suspicious of Columbus a generation earlier. Nuño de Guzmán, a jealous rival of Cortés, accused him of various crimes of which Guzmán himself was guilty, including a desire for power as an independent ruler. Cortés had to return to Spain for two years to defend himself against such charges.

At last, in 1532, Cortés was able to send two small ships northwestward under Diego Hurtado de Mendoza. One of these vessels was wrecked on the coast of Guzmán's province of Nueva Galicia, which then included most of New Spain north of Mexico City. The fate of the other vessel is unknown.

Nevertheless, in the following year, 1533, Cortés dispatched the expedition that discovered Lower California, first assumed to be an island rather than a peninsula. The original commander of this expedition, Diego Becerra, was killed in a mutiny at sea, and the actual discoverer was the pilot Fortún Jiménez, leader of the mutineers. He landed at the bay which was later named La Paz, but peace did not attend this first Spanish landing. Jiménez and 20 others were killed in a battle with the Indians.

When the survivors returned with reports of pearls at La Paz, Cortés determined to go there in person and to found a colony. Arriving in 1535, he gave to the bay and the supposed island the name of Santa Cruz. Neither the settlement nor Cortés's name for it endured. The Indians were primitive and hostile. The desolate land itself seemed hostile, and navigation to and from it was treacherous because of the sudden and prolonged windstorms.

Spanish dreams of treasure in the North might then have languished if they had not been promptly revived by the appearance in northern Mexico of Álvar Núñez Cabeza de Vaca and his companion, the Christianized Moor Estevánico. These two were survivors of a disastrous Spanish expedition to Florida. After making their way around the northern shores of the Gulf of Mexico they heard from the Indians of the Southwest a new version of the story of the Seven Cities, now identified as the Seven Cities of Cíbola. This became the core of the collection of legends known in New Spain as "the northern mystery," which periodically raised hopes of "another Mexico" or "new Mexico" of fabulous riches.

Antonio de Mendoza had been sent out as the first viceroy of New Spain, partly to restrain the power of Cortés. In 1539 Mendoza sent a northward exploring expedition guided by Estevánico and led by Fray Marcos, a Franciscan friar who was apparently chosen as leader on the theory that his reports could be relied upon. Estevánico was killed by Indians, and Fray Marcos returned with an account of having seen, in the distance, a city of silver shining in the sun.

In 1540, overruling the claims of Cortés, Viceroy Mendoza placed Francisco Vásquez de Coronado in command of a large and lavishly equipped expedition. For two years, and all the way to western Kansas, Coronado followed a series of imaginative Indian suggestions. Some of these, including the mythical Gran Quivira, were deliberate attempts to send him and his men to their deaths in the

Don Fernando Cortés. (Courtesy of the Bancroft Library)

desert. He returned to Mexico heartbroken and disgraced. As for Cíbola, the silver city of Fray Marcos, it had proved to be of whitewashed adobe.

In the meantime Cortés had organized another expedition, in 1539, commanded by Francisco de Ulloa and designed to reach the Seven Cities by sea. In this, of course, Ulloa failed, but he did discover, by sailing to the head of the gulf, or Sea of Cortés, that "California" was a peninsula and not an island. This was Cortés's last attempt to unlock the northern mystery. He returned to Spain again in 1540, and died there after several years of fruitless efforts to reestablish his power.

Ulloa's voyage was followed by that of Hernando de Alarcón, sent by Mendoza in 1540 to cooperate with the land expedition of Coronado. Alarcón sailed to the mouth of the Colorado River and ascended the river for an unknown distance. In the same year Melchor Díaz, in command of a branch of the Coronado expedition, reached the Colorado River by land, hoping but failing to make a junction with Alarcón. It is probable that Alarcón came far enough up the river to make him the first European to see any part of Upper California. It is also probable that Melchor Díaz was the first European to set foot on it, for accounts of his expedition seem to indicate that he crossed the river at a point considerably north of the modern boundary. If he did so, he may also have been the first Spaniard to die on the soil of Upper California, for he was killed in an accident somewhere in this region.

The next year, 1541, Francisco de Bolaños was sent to continue Alarcón's efforts to find the Seven Cities and to join the men of Coronado, but one of the frequent storms in the gulf blew him far off course, and his chief distinction was in exploring both sides of the peninsula and in attaching the present name of *Cabo de San Lucas* to the lower tip of it.

The naming of California. All these exploring expeditions involved extreme hardships, and several ended in complete disaster. In some cases, only fragmentary records of them exist. Many details are uncertain, and one of these is the question of the identity of the explorer who first applied the romantic name, California. Much ingenious reasoning has been used to support the various guesses, the best of which range from Jiménez in 1533 to Bolaños in 1541.

The earliest authenticated record of the use of the name by explorers is in the journal of the Cabrillo expedition in 1542, but there it appears as a name already in common usage. It may be argued that Jiménez could not have been the one who applied it to the land he discovered, because Cortés subsequently gave the name of Santa Cruz to the same place, but this is not conclusive. Cortés is known to have ignored other names bestowed by Jiménez, and to have refused to accord any honor whatever to the memory of that mutineer, whom he hated for the murder of his commander, Becerra, a kinsman of Cortés himself. The case for Bolaños as the possible christener of California rests on the fact that several of the names that he gave to points on the peninsula are still in use.

For centuries the derivation of the name was even more uncertain than the question of who first applied it. Of the many fanciful notions, the most prevalent was that it came from the Latin *calida fornax,* or "hot furnace," and originated in some explorer's opinion of the climate of Lower California. In 1862, however, Edward Everett Hale discovered what is undoubtedly the correct explanation. Hale was a Boston Unitarian minister and writer, otherwise best known for his story, "The Man without a Country." In the course of his wide readings he came across an old Spanish novel, *Las Sergas de Esplandián* ("The Exploits of Esplandián"), written about 1500 by Garcí Ordóñez de Montalvo. In it there were several references to an Amazon island called California.

Montalvo's *Sergas de Esplandián* was a sequel to his translation into Spanish of the Portuguese novel, *Amadís de Gaula.* It was an inferior sequel; as Hale remarked, the *Sergas* was deservedly forgotten for 300 years, and its role as the source of the name of California was thus forgotten with it. In the early years of the 16th century, however, Montalvo's story went through several editions, and there can be little doubt that Cortés and his captains, if they had not read it, had at least heard it described. In 1524, in a letter to the King, Cortés reported his expectation of finding an island of Amazons a few days' sail to the northwest.

Amadís of Gaul had been the late-medieval ideal of the perfect knight. Montalvo's Esplandián was introduced as the son of Amadís. In the course of a siege of Constantinople in which father and son were leading the defense of the city against a motley army of pagans, there suddenly appeared among the besiegers a certain Calafía, Queen of California. This, wrote Montalvo, was an island "on the right hand of the Indies" and "very near to the terrestrial paradise." It was inhabited by black women "without any men among them, because they were accustomed to live after the manner of Amazons." Their weapons were of gold, "for in all the island there is no other metal." In California "there were many griffins, on account of the great ruggedness of the country." When the griffins were small, "the women went out with traps to take them to their caves, and brought them up there. And being themselves quite a match for the griffins, they fed them with the men whom they took prisoners, and with the boys to whom they gave birth." For battle, these monstrous birds were trained to seize men from the ground and drop them from great heights. At Constantinople Calafía turned loose her griffins, but the maneuver failed because the creatures attacked the men of both armies indiscriminately. Later the Amazon queen became converted to Christianity, gained a proper respect for men, married a relative of Esplandián, and returned with him to California. "What happened after that," wrote Montalvo, "I must be excused from telling." The reader may doubt that the marriage was an entirely happy one.

Several scholars have participated in a lively controversy over the suggestion that the name of California may have been derisively bestowed. Ruth Putnam wrote that she could almost hear the jeering tone in which Spanish explorers would have given, to a barren and hostile place, the name of the fabled land of gold they had hoped to find. Others, including Charles E. Chapman, have opposed this theory on the ground that when the Spaniards wished to give a place a name that reflected their displeasure with it, they did so directly and not derisively. For example, there was Ulloa's name for the *Cabo del Engaño* (Cape Disappointment) on the west coast of Lower California. Another instance was *El Camino del Diablo,* for the Devil's highway through northern Sonora to the Colorado River. Such discussions, however, have overlooked the alternative explanation, that to Spanish soldiers of the time of Cortés the "California" of contemporary parlance would in itself have been a highly opprobrious name, directly suitable for a land of desolation and terror—a land in which women were the soldiers and in which women despised men and set griffins on them.

Since California's actual history has so often resembled romantic fiction, it is not entirely inappropriate that it got its name from a novel.

Cabrillo and the discovery of Alta California. The evidence that Alarcón or Melchor Díaz first sighted Upper (or Alta) California by land, near its southeast corner, is not quite substantial enough to take the traditional honor of discovery away from Juan Rodríguez Cabrillo, who first sighted it from the sea in 1542. This brilliant navigator was of Portuguese birth. Language purists have pointed out that his father's name was undoubtedly Rodríguez, and that Cabrillo was merely the name of his mother, but nevertheless he has usually been known to historians as Cabrillo. The main purpose of his expedition, sent out under the orders of Viceroy Mendoza, was a search for the long-rumored though mythical Strait of Anián, later sought by the English under the name of the Northwest Passage. For more than two centuries the dream of a water route to Asia through North America would continue to lure the explorers of several nations.

Cabrillo sailed from the port of Navidad on the west coast of Mexico on June 27, 1542. His two small ships, the *San Salvador* and the *Victoria,* were poorly built, manned by conscripts, and wretchedly provisioned. On September 28 he discovered and entered the fine harbor of San Diego. His name for it was San Miguel, but this and the names of all the other points he discovered were changed by later explorers, particularly by Vizcaíno.

After spending six days at San Diego, the little vessels made a series of anchorages at Catalina Island, San Pedro, and Santa Monica, and then at Ventura and several other points along the Santa Barbara Channel. They could make no landings north of Point Conception, because of the powerful northwest winds. They next found refuge in a harbor on San Miguel Island, but there, unfortunately, Cabrillo fell and broke his arm. He insisted upon continuing the voyage, and for weeks his ships beat their way northward in the heavy seas, unable to find a safe landing place. He decided to spend the winter at San Miguel Island and there, in January of 1543, he died, apparently from an infection resulting from the broken arm which he had suffered on the same island three months earlier.

In obedience to Cabrillo's dying wish, and in spite of their pitiful hardships, his men agreed to continue their explorations under the leadership of the chief pilot, Bartolomé Ferrelo. Before they turned back on March 1 they had actually reached a point off the coast of southern Oregon, but again they could find no new anchorages. In April they reached their home port of Navidad, nearly starved and desperately sick with scurvy. They had found no straits and no rich cities, and they could hardly have appreciated the future value of what they did find. But it is clear that the discoverers of Upper California were men of admirable courage and extraordinary devotion to duty.

Francis Drake and Nova Albion. More than a generation elapsed between the Cabrillo expedition and the next landing by Europeans on the coast of Upper California. This was the visit of Francis Drake and the *Golden Hind* in 1579. It occurred by accident in the course of a three-year voyage around the world, a voyage intended partly to open up English trade with the Moluccas, and partly to "anoy" the King of Spain in "his Indyes" by engaging in what the English regarded as privateering and the Spaniards regarded as piracy. In this period Queen Elizabeth suspected King Philip of complicity in a series of plots on her life, and relations between England and Spain were seldom very far short of outright war. Another and incidental purpose of the voyage was a search for the Northwest Passage.

Nearly a year and a half after he sailed from England, Drake had to make an emergency landing on the coast of California to careen and repair his ship. The *Golden Hind,* originally named the *Pelican,* was a vessel of only 100 tons burden, and by this time she was carrying about 30 tons of captured Spanish treasure, mostly silver. The seams in her hull had begun to open. On June 17, 1579, Drake found "a conuenient and fit harborough" where he stayed for five weeks. It is probable that this was actually what is now called Drake's Bay, although the location of the landing has long been in dispute. American scholars and scientists at first supposed that it was on the Marin shore of San Francisco Bay. The geographer George Davidson discredited this theory, and concluded that Drake landed at Drake's Bay, just behind Point Reyes. The historian Henry Raup Wagner, on the other hand, insisted in his detailed study of the entire voyage that Drake had landed at Trinidad Bay, more than 200 miles farther north, and may also have visited Bodega Bay—but that he never saw Drake's Bay at all. In view of the ambiguity of the geographical evidence, however, the anthropological evidence is especially significant. The Indians were the feature of the visit that Drake's men found most interesting, and to which their accounts of it devoted the greatest detail. From the descriptions of the houses, the feathered baskets, the ceremonies, and the language of these Indians, anthropologists have clearly identified them as the Coast Miwok, whose country included both Drake's Bay and Bodega Bay, about 20 miles to the north. The culture described bears no resemblance to that of the Yurok, the Indians of the Trinidad Bay region, and thus Trinidad Bay could not have been the place. Moreover, only Drake's Bay has the "white bancks and cliffes" whose resemblance to the cliffs on the English Channel contributed to Drake's naming the place Nova Albion, or New England.

In claiming the country for Queen Elizabeth, Drake erected a plate of brass with a chiseled inscription and a hole for a sixpence bearing Her Majesty's picture. The finding of this fascinating relic, minus the sixpence, was announced in 1937, and it is on display at the Bancroft Library of the University of California in Berkeley. Its original location cannot be identified with certainty from the circumstances of its finding, since there is no way of knowing how far or how many times it may have been carried about in the interim. The authenticity of the plate has also been a subject of some controversy in itself, but on this point the favorable evidence, both historical and metallurgical, is more substantial and convincing than are the doubts expressed by the skeptics.

Drake's landing on the California coast was a chance occurrence, and as an incidental result of it he "took possession" in case England should ever want the region. There is no sound evidence, however, that Drake or any other Englishmen of his time ever seriously intended to plant a colony there. This notion was largely created by the English more than two centuries later as a part of their claim to the Oregon country; it was revived by Americans, after

Drake's Plate of Brass. (Courtesy of the Bancroft Library)

they acquired California, as a kind of sentimental foreshadowing of Anglo-American possession. Drake's men did assume, incorrectly, that the Indians in placing a feathered crown on Drake's head were turning over the sovereignty of their country to him. The Indians also cried pitifully and tore their cheeks with their fingernails until the blood ran, and the English supposed this to be a kind of sacrifice to them as gods. The facts are that these were the mourning practices of the Coast Miwok, and that the Indians undoubtedly regarded the Englishmen as relatives who had returned from the dead.

The main significance of the voyage of the *Golden Hind* was that she was the second ship to sail around the world, the first English ship to do so, and the first ship of any nation to make the entire voyage under one commander (Magellan had been killed in the Philippines). Drake's title of knighthood, granted after his return, was a modest recognition of so great an achievement. The significance of his landing in California, however, has sometimes been misunderstood and exaggerated.

The Manila galleon and the California coast. The Philippine islands were added to the Spanish colonial empire by a gradual process of conquest beginning with the voyage of Legazpi in 1565, and they were governed as a part of the Viceroyalty of New Spain until the end of Spanish control in Mexico. By the time of the Drake expedition the Spaniards had already estab-

Francis Drake and the California Indians. An engraving published in 1599 as part of a collection compiled by Theodore and John De Bry. (Courtesy of the Bancroft Library)

lished a profitable trade route between Mexico and the Philippines, and for many decades Spanish interest in the coast of California was largely the result of the fact that the ships from Manila sailed past it, with their rich cargoes from the Orient, on the last leg of their long trans-Pacific voyage to Acapulco.

In the hope of finding a port of call to ease the hardships of that voyage, Francisco Gali, in 1584, searched in vain for the mythical Strait of Anián, and also made reports on some points he had sighted on the California coast, though he did not land there. In 1587, Pedro de Unamuno landed at what was probably Morro Bay, north of San Luis Obispo; but after a short march inland his party suffered several casualties in an Indian attack, and he gave up the attempt at further exploration of California.

Manila was a very convenient gathering point for luxury goods from many parts of East Asia, to be exchanged for silver and gold from the mines of Mexico, and the trade became so large that merchants in Spain were in danger of losing their Mexican markets. Under the prevailing mercantilistic system of discriminating against the colonies and in favor of the mother country, the King decreed in 1593 that the Manila galleons must be limited to one a year, and their cargoes to a value of 250,000 pesos. At the demand of the silk manufacturers of Seville, oriental silks were to be excluded entirely. Nevertheless the profits were extremely high, and since they were now concentrated in a single annual voyage, there was great temptation to crowd extra cargo into space that should have been reserved for food and water. The voyage from Manila usually took six or seven months, during which the crews suffered horribly from starvation, thirst, and scurvy. They also had to fear English pirates, ever since the forays of Drake, and particularly those of Thomas Cavendish, who captured one of the galleons off Lower California in 1587. There was, it seemed, a growing need for a port on the California coast where the annual Manila galleon could get fresh food and water and perhaps an escort vessel.

The Spanish authorities entrusted the galleon of 1595 to the Portuguese merchant-adventurer Sebastián Rodríguez Cermeño, on condition that the voyage should include an exploration of the California coast in search of the best site for a port of call. After an especially harrowing passage across the Pacific, Cermeño sighted land somewhere north of Cape Mendocino. There his ship, the *San Agustín*, was nearly wrecked by a storm, and several of the officers, submitting a written petition that he should keep away from the coast and sail directly to Acapulco, took every step short of mutiny in the effort to persuade him to give up the projected explorations. He refused, and on November 6, rounding Point Reyes, he anchored in Drake's Bay, which he called the Bay of San Francisco.

The Cermeño expedition reported no evidence that Drake had landed in the same bay 16 years earlier, but this does not answer the question of whether Drake had actually done so. Cermeño's men and the Indians did not get into very effective verbal communication with each other. As for material relics, it is recorded that the Indians had returned every present the Englishmen gave them, and it is doubtful that Drake's plate of brass had remained very long on its wooden post.

On shore, the Spaniards assembled a launch that had been brought along for use in exploring coastal areas. This little vessel was to be their salvation, for on November 30 a great gale from the southeast, the direction in which the bay is completely exposed, drove the *San Agustín* aground. The breakers pounded her to pieces in a few hours, and strewed her cargo, provisions, and timbers along the beach. To the amazement and outrage of his crew, not even this disaster persuaded Cermeño to abandon his interest in exploration. With 70 men crowded into the open launch, the *San Buenaventura*, he found excuses for many landings; and although he sailed past the Golden Gate without seeing it, he described many other points with remarkable accuracy considering his difficulties.

Vizcaíno and Monterey. Cermeño had found no new harbor that was safe, and the viceregal government doubted the thoroughness and accuracy of his charts. The fact that he had lost the *San Agustín* with her rich cargo disgraced him unfairly, and also dissuaded the authorities from risking any more of the valuable and heavily laden galleons in coastal explorations.

The further search for a good harbor in Northern California was now entrusted, after long negotiations, to another *adelantado,* or merchant-adventurer, Sebastián Vizcaíno. On the understanding that he would be rewarded with various concessions including the future command of one of the Manila ships, Vizcaíno invested a considerable amount of his own capital in an elaborate expedition in 1602. Setting out from Acapulco with two ships and a launch, he permanently renamed many of the places along the California coast, and on December 16 he entered a bay that he named for the viceroy, the Conde de Monterey. Vizcaíno announced himself as the discoverer of this bay, although he was not. Cermeño had seen it seven years earlier, and his description of it, though not detailed, was actually far less misleading than that of Vizcaíno, who made absurdly exaggerated claims for its value as a harbor.

Vizcaíno seems to have feared that if he did not return with a favorable report he would not receive the rewards he hoped for. The result was that he described the bay to the viceroy not only as having an abundance of fine timber for shipbuilding, but as being "sheltered from all winds"—a claim that can only be described as positively fraudulent, since the bay actually includes no proper harbor at all.

Viceroy Monterey, pleased with the idea that a fine port would bear his name, awarded Vizcaíno the command of the next Manila galleon. Shortly afterward, however, Monterey was promoted to the viceroyalty of Peru. His successor as Viceroy of New Spain, the Marqués de Montesclaros, completely distrusted Vizcaíno, revoked the award of the galleon, and went so far as to have the expedition's mapmaker, Martínez Palacios, convicted of forgery and hanged.

Montesclaros ridiculed and blocked the whole project of a California port of call. He pointed out, correctly, that when the galleons sighted California they had only a few days' voyage left, since the strong prevailing winds and currents along the coast almost always bore them swiftly southward. In this judgment history vindicated him, for even after Upper California was finally settled, more than a century and a half later, the annual ships from Manila almost never stopped there. Nevertheless, it was generally felt that Montesclaros had acted out of jealousy and spite, as in part he undoubtedly had. Many did not share his disbelief of Vizcaíno's story that there was a splendid harbor at Monterey. This legend became generally accepted as a fact, and played a central part in occasional plans for settlement in Upper California. No such plan was actually carried out until the time of the Portolá-Serra expedition of 1769. When Portolá saw the Bay of Monterey he failed to recognize it as such.

The lapse of 60 years between Cabrillo and Vizcaíno, and of another 167 years between Vizcaíno and Portolá, emphasizes the utter isolation of California and the low regard in which the Spaniards held it. California was a place that should have contained gold, but apparently did not; a place where a strait should have been, but was not; a barren and dangerous coast that a ship sailed past once a year. Getting to it from Mexico was far more trouble than it was worth. Just as the winds and currents made the southward voyage brief and easy, they made the northward voyage long, difficult, and sometimes impossible. Land travel seemed even more forbidding. Lower California was on the very rim of Christendom during the whole of the Spanish colonial period in America, which lasted more than three centuries, and for all but the last half century of that period, Upper California remained beyond the rim.

SELECTED BIBLIOGRAPHY

Charles E. Chapman, *History of California; the Spanish Period* (1921), maintained that the Chinese had discovered California, and even established a regular trade with it, in ancient times. See, however, Douglas S. Watson, "Did the Chinese Discover America? A Critical Examination of the Buddhist Priest Hui Shen's Account of Fu Sang, and the Apocryphal Voyage of the Chinese Navigator Hee-Li," *California Historical Society Quarterly,* XIV (March 1935), 47–58. Watson pointed out that Chapman relied partly on modern elaborations of an ancient fable, and partly on a New York newspaper article of 1890 that was obviously a mere hoax, intended to poke fun at Chicago's plans for its Columbian Exposition. But in spite of these mistakes, and his equally lamentable misinterpretations of the California Indians, Chapman's books are still valuable.

Important works on the discovery and early exploration of California are Henry R. Wagner, *Spanish Voyages to the Northwest Coast of America in the Sixteenth Century* (1929) and *Cartography of the Northwest Coast of America to the Year 1800* (two volumes, 1937); and Maurice G. Holmes, *From New Spain by Sea to the Californias 1519–1668* (1963). See also Jack D. Forbes, "Melchor Díaz and the Discovery of Alta California," *Pacific Historical Review,* XXVII (November 1958), 351–358; and H. R. Wagner, *Juan Rodríguez Cabrillo, Discoverer of the Coast of California* (1941).

Ruth Putnam, in *California, the Name* (1917), elaborated a suggestion in Hubert Howe Bancroft's *History of California* (vol. I, 1884, chap. III), that the name was derisive. Charles E. Chapman disagreed in his *History of California, the Spanish Period* (1921). A translation of the parts of Montalvo's *Las Sergas de Esplandián* relating to Queen Calafía, with commentary, may be found in Edward Everett Hale, *The Queen of California; the Origin of the Name of California* (first published in 1864; reprinted in 1945). See also Donald C. Cutter, "Sources of the Name 'California,'" *Arizona and the West,* III (Autumn 1961), 233–243.

On Drake's landing in California, works of special interest include H. R. Wagner, *Sir Francis Drake's Voyage around the World, Its Aims and Achievements* (1926); California Historical Society, *The Plate of Brass; Evidence of the Visit of Francis Drake to California in the Year 1579* (1953); Robert F. Heizer, *Francis Drake and the California Indians, 1579*

(1947); and Joseph R. Ellison, "True or False?" *Saturday Evening Post*, CCXV (April 3, 1943), 32–36. Walter A. Starr argued that "Drake Landed in San Francisco Bay in 1579," *California Historical Society Quarterly*, XLI (September 1962), appendix; so did Robert H. Power, mainly for different reasons, in "Portus Novae Albionis Rediscovered?" *Pacific Discovery*, VII (May–June 1954), 10–12. Arguments for Drake's Bay are in Chester W. Nimitz, "Drake's Cove—a Navigational Approach to Identification," *Pacific Discovery*, XI (March–April 1958), 12–20; and Adolph S. Oko, "Francis Drake and Nova Albion," *California Historical Society Quarterly*, XLIII (June 1964), 135–158.

William L. Schurz did justice to the historical importance of *The Manila Galleon* (1939). On the Cermeño expedition, see Henry R. Wagner, "The Voyage to California of Sebastián Rodríguez Cermeño in 1595," *California Historical Society Quarterly*, III (April 1924), 3–24; and Robert F. Heizer, "Archaeological Evidence of Sebastián Rodríguez Cermeño's California Visit," in the same journal, XX (December 1941), 315–328. W. Michael Mathes, *Vizcaíno and Spanish Expansion in the Pacific Ocean, 1580–1630* (1968), considerably enhances Vizcaíno's reputation and the significance of his explorations.

Chapter IV

THE SPANISH COLONIAL FRONTIER

PART OF THE PLAN of the Vizcaíno expedition had been that its leader would ultimately found a kind of semiproprietary colony in California. This approach to the formidable problems of colonization was permanently abandoned after Vizcaíno's failure. New Spain lacked the manpower for the settlement of her remote and unprofitable northern frontiers. When the colonization of these areas finally came, it was largely through an ingenious plan intended to transform the Indians into colonists by the use of that remarkable institution, the Spanish mission.

Spain's Indian policies. The Spanish attitudes toward the Indians grew from an interesting blend of religious, economic, military, and political motives.

The Indians were officially regarded not only as subjects of the Spanish monarchy with rights to its protection, but also as human beings with souls to be saved. The Pope had assigned Brazil to Portugal and the rest of America to Spain on condition that the inhabitants be Christianized; and the Pope had delegated to the Spanish crown the extraordinary right to appoint all bishops, parish priests, and missionaries in Spanish America, and to collect tithes for their support. Their Most Catholic Majesties, the Spanish monarchs, made frequent references to their duty of Christianization, and the missionaries were untiring in their efforts to carry it out.

There were others, however, who were primarily interested in the Indians because they could be made to labor for the profit of their conquerors. Legal provisions under which this purpose was interrelated with the religious one were first worked out for the island of Hispaniola, or Haiti. There, under the rule of Columbus and his successors, the Spaniards exploited the Indians so ruthlessly and shortsightedly that this maltreatment, combined with disease, entirely exterminated the native labor supply, an outcome that shocked not only the clergy but also the most coldly realistic of the ministers of government. The Laws of Burgos and the later Laws of the Indies sought to prevent such abuses.

The manorial system of labor embodied in these regulations could be applied more or less effectively to Spanish rule over the Aztec empire in central Mexico, because by a remarkable coincidence it strikingly resembled the feudal system that the Aztecs, the previous conquerors, already had in operation. In many ways, the Spaniards had only to put themselves into the places of the former Aztec overlords, and to add the justification that in return for the salvation of their souls the Indians might be required to contribute the labor of their bodies.

In one variant of the Spanish system, an *encomendero,* often originally a soldier but presumably also a devout Catholic layman, was given Indians in trust. The *encomienda* plan had first developed in Spain as a temporary grant by the Crown of manorial rights over lands conquered from the Moors, made to a knight as a reward for military services. The discovery of the New World came in the same year that the capture of Granada ended the centuries of the Reconquest. Many of the Spaniards who came to America were soldiers who might otherwise have been out of employment. Because his profession was the bearing of arms, each tended to consider himself a nobleman for whom manual labor should be done by serfs and who should therefore be "given Indians."

The *repartimiento,* or allotment, was theoretically a more advanced device. A part of the male population of any Indian community could be called upon to work for wages for a certain time at a specified task judged necessary to the public interest. Naturally this system was often abused, for wages were microscopic and any task might meet the definition. Outright slavery was recognized in the case of Indians captured in "just wars," that is, Indians who had resisted the Spaniards. In later times these systems were generally replaced by that of debt peonage.

The most essential key to the Spanish colonial plan for the Indian, however, was that the Indian was to be made Spanish—in religion, in language, and in the gradual intermixture of blood. He was to be required to work; he was also to be permitted to live. All this was in sharp contrast with the views of the English colonists, of whom it is said that on arriving on the new shore they fell first upon their knees and then upon the aborigines. The Spanish conquest was largely a conquest of native labor; but there was no comparable plan for assimilating the Indian into the Anglo-American scheme of things, and displacement or extermination were almost the only alternatives. As for racial intermarriage, the Anglo-Americans were usually intolerant of it. They were generally able to secure wives of English descent, whereas the Spanish American colonies were extremely unattractive to Spanish women. Hubert Howe Bancroft argued that the English policies were morally superior, and charged that the Spanish attitude toward the Indians consisted of wanting their sons as serfs and their daughters as concubines. But this, like most criticism of Spaniards by Anglo-Americans on the score of treatment of the Indians, came with bad grace and out of a bad collective conscience.

The most tragic effect of Spanish colonization on the Indians of New Spain was one that had nothing to do with the intentions of anyone—the deadly effect of the white man's diseases on a population entirely without immunities to them. Mexico had originally had far more people than Spain itself. The population of central Mexico before the landing of Cortés has been estimated as no less than 11 million and possibly as much as 17 million. A century later it had fallen to about two million, a dreadful decline of 80 or 90 percent, attributed in large part to epidemics of smallpox and typhus.

Spanish scholars have often denounced what they called the "black legend" that Spanish cruelty was responsible for such declines. The decimation of the Indians of Mexico in the first century of Spanish possession was one of the greatest catastrophes of history, but the chief cause was not cruelty; it was disease, over which no one had any control.

The mission as a frontier institution. After the population had stabilized and begun to increase again in the early 17th century, the *encomienda* and the *repartimiento* continued to be workable devices for the organization of Indian life and labor on the great plateau of central Mexico. There, under their Aztec masters, the Indians had for centuries been successful hoe-culture farmers, skillfully terracing their lands and irrigating their crops of corn, beans, potatoes, squash, and cotton. On the far northwestern frontiers, however, the Indians were unaccustomed to serfdom, and those of Lower and Upper California were unaccustomed to any sort of agriculture at all. Only the zeal of the missionaries offered hope of bringing the Indians of northwestern New Spain, and the regions in which they lived, under Spanish organization and control. For this worldly reason, as well as because of its official interest in spreading the Catholic faith, the crown was willing to provide funds for the expenses of the missions. The royal revenues were limited, however, and the frontiers were vast. Consequently the work of the missions often depended in part upon private gifts to the religious orders that conducted them.

As a method of advancing and consolidating a frontier, the mission had its roots in the long struggle against the Mohammedan Moors in Spain. The cross and the sword had moved forward together, in forcible conversion of the infidel. In Spanish America, each mission had a small guard of two or more soldiers, and there was usually a larger garrison at a *presidio* or military post nearby. Cooperation between padres and soldiers was seldom cordial, but it was always indispensable. The missionaries were typically men of tremendous courage and faith; but with the exception of those who actively sought martyrdom, they were usually aware that the strength of their own personalities had to be supplemented by the soldier's weapons, even though they were constantly anxious lest the soldiers corrupt the Indian neophytes, or apprentices in Christianity.

The mission was not only a church, but also an agricultural *pueblo* or town, in which hundreds or even thousands of Indians were concentrated after they had been brought there with the aid of presents and kept there with the aid of the soldiers. There were cultivated fields, gardens, orchards, and vineyards, often fenced with nearly impenetrable hedges of prickly pear, and watered from irrigation ditches with stone dams. The mission was also a kind of industrial school, instructing some of the Indians in various handicrafts. At a little distance, each mission had its rancho, and eventually large herds of cattle.

Theoretically every mission was temporary. If the plan had worked as the Spanish government hoped, each mission would have been secularized 10 years after its founding. That is, the pueblo would receive a grant of 4 square leagues of land; the fields, town lots, and other property would be parceled out among the Indians; and community government would pass to native officials who had been trained for the purpose. The mission church would be turned over to parish priests, known as "secular" clergy, as distinct from the missionaries, who were called "regular" clergy because they were under the regulations and vows of a particular order. The missionaries were then supposed to begin their work all over again farther on, in a continuous process of frontier expansion.

In practice, however, the schedule was never met. Most missions continued for decades, and some for more than a century. Although the Laws of the Indies provided that mission Indians should receive real training for self-government, in practice they received little or none. The missionary fathers made the basic mistake of regarding the Indians as children whose minds were incapable of development beyond the child's level. They turned them into helpless dependents and kept them in that condition. Every detail of work, play, clothing, and even the choice of a mate, was rigidly controlled. So far as possible the missionaries kept their charges from contact with any Europeans but themselves, and did not prepare them to take a place in any kind of society but that of the mission. When secularization finally came, the whole community simply disintegrated. There are many viewpoints concerning the effect of mission life itself on Indian morale. The Spanish missionaries often spoke of the "temporal and spiritual conquest" of new provinces. The phrase is apt. Very often, no real conversion took place after the Indians' own gods were destroyed. The Indian was spiritually as well as physically conquered, his spirit broken.

The Jesuits in northwestern New Spain. The black-robed missionaries of the Society of Jesus were in charge of the frontier regions of northwestern Mexico for 176 years, beginning in 1591, under the terms of a contract given them for this purpose by the King. Their work never extended into Upper California, nor did any Spanish settlement during the period of their tenure, but for the last 70 years of that period they conducted the missions on the Baja California peninsula. The Jesuits were the most disciplined and militant of all the Spanish missionaries. Their order had been deliberately organized along quasi-military lines. The founder, Saint Ignatius of Loyola, was a Spaniard of noble birth who had been a soldier of the King before he became a soldier of Christ.

By 1687 the Jesuit frontier had been extended northwestward on the mainland as far as the country of the Pimas, and in that year Father Eusebio Kino began the building of the missions in Pimería Alta—northern Sonora and southern Arizona. Kino, born in Italy, was the greatest of all the Jesuits of New Spain, a man who combined a scholar's training and interests with a generally vigorous personality. He was also a skilled ranchman and an incredibly indefatigable traveler on horseback. Before coming to Pimería, Kino had been the cosmographer for an expedition to Baja California. This expedition was a failure, but it left him with an intense feeling of the need for missions there. Later, when he rediscovered the forgotten fact that Baja California was a peninsula and not an island, he dreamed of extending the chain of missions from Pimería Alta to establish a land route around the head of the gulf. Although this was never accomplished, it was Kino's constant pressure on his superiors that led to the establishment of the missions on the peninsula in 1697. Before this time there had been many pearlfishing expeditions, but no attempt at settlement had been successful. In recognition of the great difficulties they would face in Baja California, the Jesuits were given complete control over all soldiers and civilians, as well as the privilege of soliciting in Spain and elsewhere for the Pious Fund, a special private endowment.

Under such leaders as Father Juan María de Salvatierra and his assistant and successor, Father Juan de Ugarte, the Jesuits maintained their Baja California missions until 1767, when the King issued an order expelling them from all the Spanish dominions. This sharp reversal of policy toward the Jesuits grew partly out of European court politics. The Kings of Portugal, France, and Spain were successively persuaded that the Black Robes had become a menace. Most of the charges against them were grossly exaggerated, and some were fantastic. The Jesuits were said to be very wealthy; but, though it was true that they had been quite successful in the business management of many of their enterprises, their frontier missionaries certainly lived in the strictest poverty, most of all in Baja California. It was also charged that the Jesuits were or soon would be engaged in various seditious conspiracies; and although Charles III of Spain refused to inform the Pope of his reasons for the decree of expulsion, he hinted that he believed his very life to be in danger from Jesuit plots.

José de Gálvez and the plan for Alta California. The expulsion of the Jesuits from New Spain was entrusted to Visitor-General José de Gálvez. He found that the Baja California missions, supposedly prosperous, were sadly run-down and almost depopulated. They were turned over to military administrators under Captain Gaspar de Portolá, and then to the Franciscans under

Father Junípero Serra. The names of these three remarkable men soon became important in the story of the founding of Alta California.

Gálvez was the most effective visitor-general in the history of New Spain, though not the first. The *visita* was a distinctively Spanish administrative technique for investigations and reorganizations, and a *visitador-general* was a special deputy of the King, with extraordinary powers overlapping and sometimes transcending those of the viceroy.

The *visita* of Gálvez, which began in 1765, was primarily intended to reform the finances and increase the revenues of New Spain as a part of the energetic attempts to reorganize the Spanish government under Charles III after the expensive and disastrous Seven Years War. The expulsion of the Jesuits was an added assignment. But the consolidation of the northwestern frontier and its extension to Alta California were Gálvez's own projects, and seem to have been the result of his intense personal ambitions. He had risen from rather humble origins, and although he was a brilliant, forceful, and generally successful administrator, he was also unusually vain, selfish, ruthless, deceitful, and unstable. It was, indeed, because of Gálvez's possession of this very combination of qualities that the occupation of San Diego and Monterey, long considered and periodically given up as hopeless, actually materialized. New Spain had been decaying, and he now made it appear to be flourishing and expanding. This was the sort of achievement which, along with others, later led to his being made Minister of the Indies.

Gálvez proposed a scheme for the consolidation and development of the whole of the far northwest under a vast new governmental unit to be called a *commandancy-general,* and to include the areas of Sinaloa, Sonora, Chihuahua, and the Californias. To justify this plan, he made use of the old and perennial fear that some other European power would establish itself on the Pacific Coast and menace New Spain from the north. It was long believed that the Spanish colonization of Upper California occurred because of a diplomatic report that Russia was about to move in the direction of Monterey. The truth was that Gálvez's plan was already well advanced when this absurdly exaggerated report reached him, and that he merely added it to the rumors he himself had been spreading about various alleged intentions of the English and the Dutch. Another argument used by Gálvez in support of his plans was that the development of Alta California would ultimately provide a great source of royal revenue, although, as it turned out, the result was an annual deficit during most of the period of Spanish rule.

As a naval and supply base for the Californias, Gálvez ordered the founding of the new port of San Blas on the coast of Mexico several hundred miles northwest of Acapulco. The site of San Blas was badly chosen; the harbor was small, shallow, and constantly filling with silt, and the air was full of mosquitoes from the neighboring swamps. The location had been recommended by a merchant who also secured from Gálvez the contract for construction of buildings.

In 1768 Gálvez sailed from San Blas for Baja California, where he completed the planning of the "sacred expedition" that would colonize Alta California in the following year. The various divisions of this expedition, two by land and three by sea, were to be launched from the peninsula.

The mainland approach was blocked by Indian rebellions in Sonora. These had been going on unchecked for many years, but Gálvez was sure that a determined military campaign could quickly suppress them. That campaign, however, proved to be as maddeningly unsuccessful and frustrating as a number of its predecessors had been. Once, while visiting Sonora, Gálvez actually suffered a temporary attack of insanity. He had been increasingly given to the belief that he received divine instructions, and now for a brief time he was convinced that he was God Himself. At one moment he proposed to reduce the Indians to submission by importing 600 Guatemalan apes as soldiers. Soon afterward he ordered the treasury opened to the troops of the local garrison. Not until his return to Mexico City did he recover his health.

From the viewpoint of the United States, it is fortunate that the Spaniards occupied Alta California when they did. Tenuous as that occupation was, it may ultimately have forestalled the acquisition of the territory by some nation strong enough to have delayed or even prevented its later acquisition by the United States. But at the time and under the circumstances in which it was undertaken, the Spanish occupation of Alta California was impractical and unnecessary, and largely a result of the mental instability of Gálvez, who conceived and ordered it. From the beginning, Captain Portolá had very grave doubts about the whole enterprise, but he was a good professional soldier and he went where he was ordered. As for Father Junípero Serra, although he also was not asked whether he wished to go, it fortunately happened that he was eager to do so.

SELECTED BIBLIOGRAPHY

Spain's Indian labor policies are described in Lesley Byrd Simpson, *The Encomienda in New Spain* (1950) and *The Repartimiento System* (1938). The great population decline is dealt with in Sherburne F. Cook and L. B. Simpson, *The Population of Central Mexico in the Sixteenth Century* (1948); Woodrow Borah, *New Spain's Century of Depression* (1951); and S. F. Cook and Woodrow Borah, *The Indian Population of Central Mexico, 1531–1610* (1960).

The mission system appears in a very favorable light in Herbert E. Bolton, "The Mission as a Frontier Institution in the Spanish American Colonies" and "The Black Robes of New Spain," in his *Wider Horizons in American History* (1939). Clarence H. Haring, *The Spanish Empire in America* (1947), and Bailey W. Diffie, *Latin American Civilization, the Colonial Period* (1945), are somewhat more critical. Impressive accounts of the missionary work of the Jesuits are Peter M. Dunne, *Pioneer Black Robes on the West Coast* (1940), *Pioneer Jesuits in Northern Mexico* (1944), and *Black Robes in Lower California* (1952); and H. E. Bolton,

Padre on Horseback (1932) and *Rim of Christendom* (1936), respectively a sketch and a full biography of Father Kino. See also Theodore E. Treutlein, editor, *Pfefferkorn's Description of Sonora* (1949). Colorful descriptions of Baja California in fiction are in Antonio de Fierro Blanco [Walter Nordhoff], *The Journey of the Flame* (1933), and, from a very different viewpoint, in John Steinbeck, *The Pearl* (1947).

Herbert I. Priestly, *José de Gálvez, Visitor-General of New Spain* (1916), and Charles E. Chapman, *The Founding of Spanish California; the Northwestward Expansion of New Spain, 1687–1783* (1916), deal with backgrounds of the colonization of Alta California. Michael E. Thurman, *The Naval Department of San Blas, 1767 to 1798* (1967), tells the story of the supply base.

Chapter V

SPANISH SETTLEMENT OF ALTA CALIFORNIA

A HANDFUL of Spanish officers and missionaries and a scarcely larger number of mestizo and mulatto soldiers and sailors carried out the founding of the colony of Alta California under fantastic difficulties. The military men and the missionaries had quite different ideas of what they were doing and why, and they were often at cross-purposes. But their joint achievement is an impressive tribute to human courage in the face of adversity.

The Franciscans and Father Junípero Serra. St. Francis of Assisi had founded the Order of Friars Minor, oldest and largest of his orders, more than three centuries before the founding of the Society of Jesus. The Franciscans were the first missionaries in the New World, where their work began with Columbus's second voyage and continued vigorously in many parts of Spanish America through the later period when the Jesuits and other orders shared the missionary field. The name of Gray Friars was sometimes given to the Franciscans, because their robes were woven of white and black wool; the color of their habit was still gray at the time of the founding of Alta California, though later it was changed to brown.

The Franciscans were not given the full control over military and civil matters that the Jesuits had held in Baja California. The decision to entrust the California missions to the Franciscans was the result of the belief that they were not only more obedient to the vows of poverty than were the Jesuits, but also less disposed to subordinate the interests of their country to those of their order. This had become the prevailing opinion in the Spanish government. It was inaccurate, and it was unfair to both of the orders concerned. Certainly the relations between the Franciscans and the governmental officials in California were to include a long series of sharp disputes. Father Junípero Serra, in particular, vigorously subordinated everything to his conception of religious duty.

Father Junípero, the first and most famous of the missionaries in Alta California, was a Spanish farmer's son, born in the village of Petra on the island of Majorca in 1713. The family name, Serra, is the Catalonian form of the Castilian word *sierra.* Upon joining the Franciscan order, Miguel, as he was originally called, exercised the privilege of choosing a name by which he wished to be known "in religion." Junípero had been the name of one of St. Francis' closest companions, whose devotion was said to have inspired the founder to wish "that I had a whole forest of such Junipers."

Serra became a professor of philosophy at the University of Majorca, but at the age of 35 he determined to give up this quiet and relatively comfortable position for the strenuous life of a foreign missionary. He also hoped for martyrdom, as had St. Francis himself, although in neither case was this hope fulfilled. According to Father Francisco Palóu, Serra's former pupil and later companion, assistant, and biographer, Serra once spoke of martyrdom as the true "gold and silver of the Indies" for which they would search.

As prospective missionaries, Serra, Palóu, and Juan Crespí, another of Serra's former students, were first assigned to the apostolic College of San Fernando in Mexico City. This establishment was both a headquarters for Franciscan missionaries in New Spain and a special training center to accustom them to privation, fatigue, mortification, and penance.

In manifestations of zeal, no one excelled Serra. Upon his arrival in Mexico he had chosen to walk all the way from Vera Cruz to the capital. Early in the course of the journey he suffered an insect bite that became infected. He neglected medical care for it, and his leg and foot remained swollen and ulcerous for the rest of his life, a condition that he alternately ignored and regarded as a blessing. While delivering missionary sermons he would sometimes scourge his own shoulders with a chain; or, holding a cross in one hand, beat his breast with a stone held in the other; or burn his bared chest with lighted candles. He slept on a narrow bed made only of hard wooden boards. Hanging on the wall beside the bed he kept a thong of sharp-pointed iron links, for scourging himself when thoughts that he regarded as sinful came in the night. St. Francis had practiced mortification of the flesh, and it was not uncommon among the missionaries of Serra's time, although regulations of the apostolic college provided that it should never go so far as to be permanently incapacitating.

After an impressive record in missionary work in the Sierra Gorda and other parts of Mexico, Serra became Father-president of the missions in Baja California, and then of the prospective new missions in Alta California. At the time of his appointment to the latter post, he was 55 years old. He held it until his death in 1784 at the age of 70. Throughout his life he was a vigorous, hard-driving man, never turning back from a task he had begun, always demanding the full measure of work from others as well as from himself. In physical stature, Serra was short, not more than 5 feet 2 or 3 inches in height—but in courage and determination, he was a giant.

The sacred expedition. Supplies and men for the first missions and presidios to be founded in Alta California came in part from the peninsula and in part from the mainland by way of San Blas. The Pious Fund of the Californias, transferred from the custody of the Jesuits to that of the Franciscans, was extended to the new ventures in the north, and Gálvez and Serra agreed that church furniture, ornaments, vestments, and utensils, as well as livestock and other supplies, were to be drawn from the Baja California missions.

It had always been proper to call upon old missions to contribute to the establishment of new ones, and any objection that might have arisen was obviated by the fact that at this time Father Serra was in charge of both. He had not been in Baja California long enough to become greatly attached to the missions there, and the plan provided that he would continue as Father-president in the old California until the day he left it for the new, and then turn over the Baja missions to his faithful understudy, Father Francisco Palóu.

As was customary in founding new establishments, a number of Christianized Indians from the peninsula were taken along with the expedition in order to serve as, so to speak, bellwethers for the new flock. In addition to soldiers from the garrison at Loreto under Capt. Fernando Rivera y Moncada, 25 Catalonian volunteers, light infantry under Lt. Pedro Fages, were detached from their previous assignment to the campaign in Sonora. There were also several blacksmiths, cooks, and carpenters, along with Miguel Costansó, military engineer and cartographer, and Dr. Pedro Prat, army surgeon of French ancestry.

The expedition as a whole was under the command of Capt. Gaspar de Portolá. When settlements had been established at San Diego and Monterey, Portolá and Rivera were to return to duty on the peninsula, leaving Lieutenant Fages in charge of the military and civil government of the new colony.

Three ships were provided for the expedition, the *San Carlos,* the *San Antonio,* and the *San José,* all less than 200 tons, and all hastily and imperfectly constructed under the difficulties that still hampered shipbuilding on the Pacific Coast. All three vessels reached Baja California from San Blas in leaky condition, even before the beginning of the longer voyage, and all three had to be careened and repaired. Visitor-General Gálvez personally superintended the repairs and the loading of the flagship, the *San Carlos,* and carried some of the mission furniture on board with his own hands. When she sailed from La Paz, on January 9, 1769, he accompanied her in a launch to see her round Cape San Lucas. Her captain was Vicente Vila, an officer of the Spanish royal navy; the passengers included Fages and his 25 Catalan soldiers, the engineer Costansó, and Doctor Prat. The *San Antonio,* a smaller supply ship, sailed from Cape San Lucas on February 15 under Juan Pérez. The third vessel, the *San José,* named for the saint whom Gálvez proclaimed patron of the expedition, was lost with all on board somewhere on her way toward San Diego.

Of the two land parties, the first was under Captain Rivera, with 27 *cuirassiers.* On the frontier the cuirass was a sleeveless jacket of tough leather, made by quilting several thicknesses of deerskin or sheepskin, and usually arrowproof. Father Crespí, chaplain and diarist of the expedition, noted quite accurately that these *soldados de cuera,* or leather-jacket soldiers, were the best light cavalry in the world and were equally skilled as cowboys. Driving a large herd of cattle, horses, and mules, this party set out from the northernmost Spanish outpost in Baja California on March 24.

The second land contingent, including Portolá and Serra, left the same point on May 15. Following the trail made by Rivera, and less encumbered with livestock, it could move somewhat more rapidly, but the journey over deserts and gullies was a hard one. When Serra's ulcerated leg threatened to disable him completely, he asked a muleteer to treat it as he would a sore foot on one of his animals. The muleteer's poultice of mud and herbs had an almost miraculous effect, and Serra was able to continue, much relieved.

The first objective of the whole expedition was the founding of a presidio and a mission at San Diego as a way station for the journey to Monterey. The *San Antonio* was first to arrive at San Diego, on April 11, after a relatively easy voyage of 54 days. Her commander, Juan Pérez, formerly a pilot on the Manila galleon route, was probably the best Spanish navigator in the Pacific during this period. True, he had first sailed beyond his objective and as far as the Santa Barbara Channel, but that was the fault of miscalculations of latitude by the Vizcaíno expedition.

The *San Carlos,* although she had started a month earlier, did not arrive until nearly three weeks later, after 110 days at sea. The effects of scurvy had advanced so far that no one was able to lower a boat, and Pérez's men had to board her in order to do so. The first Spanish settlement in Alta California was a sail-tent hospital. Doctor Prat was himself so ill that he could be of little help to the others. He later became insane.

The first land party, under Rivera, arrived on May 14, and Rivera ordered the tents moved several miles northward to the foot of the hill where the presidio would later be built. Portolá rode in a little ahead of his men on June 29, and Serra and the others reached the stricken camp on July 1. Of about 300 men in the various branches of the "sacred expedition" of 1769, not more than half survived to reach San Diego, many died of scurvy there, and for months half the survivors were too sick to travel farther. All but a handful of the Christianized Indians who had been brought with the land contingents had died or deserted; the military officers had felt compelled to deny them rations from the dwindling food supplies.

Of the sailors, 38 had died. The *San Antonio,* with a truly skeleton crew of eight men, had to be sent back to San Blas to bring new supplies for the whole expedition and new crews for both ships. The *San Carlos* was left at anchor in the bay with two men on board to keep her from being stripped by the Indians. The whole situation was stark and desperate. Nevertheless, two weeks after his arrival at San Diego Portolá set out toward his main objective, the legendary harbor of Monterey, taking with him Rivera, Fages, Costansó, Father Crespí, and nearly all the others who were still able to travel, leaving Serra at San Diego to care for the more than 50 invalids.

On the way north the expedition felt several earthquakes near the river called the Santa Ana, or *Río de los Temblores.* Four days later the *Río de Porciúncula,* site of the future pueblo of Los Angeles, was named by Crespí for the day of its discovery and crossing, August 2. This was the day of the festival of Our Lady the Queen of the Angels, one of the many titles of the Virgin Mary. For the Franciscans, in particular, an important shrine of the Virgin was the chapel of Porciúncula, near Assisi. There St. Francis had worshiped, and around that chapel the great church of St. Mary of the Angels had later been built.

Continuing northwestward on a route that would become El Camino Real (the King's Highway), remarkably close at most points to the route of the modern Highway 101, the expedition was delayed north of San Luis Obispo until a way could be found through the rugged Santa Lucias. After the group had found its way to what is now called the Salinas Valley the going was much easier, but in following the Salinas River Portolá made the unfortunate mistake of supposing that it was the Carmel, which Vizcaíno had described. Thus when Portolá reached the shore of the Bay of Monterey, the peninsula and Point Pinos lay to the south, and not to the north as they should have. To add to the confusion he could see nothing resembling the fine harbor, praised by Vizcaíno and subjected in the interim to 167 years of idealized imagination. Moreover, Portolá and his half-starved men had managed to convince themselves that they would find the *San José,* with abundant food supplies, riding at anchor in that harbor.

After a few days' search the party pushed on northward along the coast. At the end of October they reached Point San Pedro and looked across the Gulf of the Farallons toward Point Reyes and Drake's Bay, which to them was Cermeño's "Bay of San Francisco." Although Point Reyes was 40 miles away, and they could not be sure of its identity from that distance, they saw enough to increase their fears that they must have passed Monterey without finding it. Sergeant José Ortega understood some Indians to be trying to tell him that a ship was anchored somewhere to the north. Heading a party of scouts, Ortega found his advance blocked by a vast and unknown bay. On November 2, 1769, a party of soldiers hunting deer also sighted this bay from the hills west of the present city of Millbrae. Whether Ortega or the deer hunters saw it first cannot be known.

A more significant question is that of why it had so long remained unnoticed by Spanish navigators. Part of the answer probably lies in the fogs that so often shroud the Golden Gate, and part in the fact that Angel Island lies behind it in such a position as to give, from any distance at sea, the impression of a continuous coastline.

Neither Portolá nor anyone else in the expedition seems to have regarded the discovery of the great bay as anything but an obstacle, except for Father Crespí, who wrote in his diary: "It is a very large and fine harbor, such that not only all the navy of our most Catholic Majesty but those of all Europe could take shelter in it."

Considering how long Spaniards had been searching for the Strait of Anián, it is surprising that no one speculated that it might now have been discovered; but for weeks the attention of these men had been desperately concentrated on the search for a harbor with a ship in it, and food on the ship. An attempt was made to get around the bay, and Ortega and his scouts got just around the southern end of it, but on November 11 the whole expedition gave up and turned back the way it had come.

At this time the great bay was not even given a name. There was some confused speculation that it might be the estuary of the Bay of San Francisco (that is, of Drake's Bay) as recorded by Cermeño. Portolá was so discouraged as to write in his diary that the expedition had "found nothing." The next objective became that of getting back to San Diego alive. The group arrived there on January 24, 1770, after subsisting on 12 of the mules.

Nothing encouraging had happened at San Diego during their absence. Serra had founded the mission of San Diego de Alcalá at a temporary location in a hut on Presidio Hill, on July 16, 1769, but there was not yet a single convert. The language barrier was at first impenetrable because the Baja California Indians were of no use as interpreters. The Diegueño were more than willing to come into the Spanish camp to receive presents, but the soldiers were too few and too weak from hunger and scurvy to attempt to hold any of them there by force. The Indians were greatly attracted to any form of cloth, which had been unknown to them, and they soon took to stealing it, even from the bodies of the sick. Fortunately the Diegueño would not touch the food supplies of the Spaniards, to which, correctly in a way, they attributed the sickness. In August they had attacked the camp with a shower of arrows, but the killing of several of them by musket fire made them more respectful. At last one Indian baby was offered for baptism, but Serra's joy turned to grief when the Indians suddenly snatched it from his arms and ran off before the ceremony could be completed. Yet nothing, it seemed, could discourage the indomitable Father-president.

On February 10, 1770, Portolá sent Rivera and 40 men on the long journey back to Baja California for supplies. A month later, when there was still no sign of the *San José* or of the return of the *San Antonio*, Portolá announced that if no relief came by March 19, the feast of St. Joseph, the patron of the expedition, he and his men would march south the next morning. Serra and Crespí protested, refused to turn back, and arranged with Vicente Vila that they would be taken on board the *San Carlos,* still anchored in the bay, to await the coming of a supply ship. After nine days of prayer, the *San Antonio* was sighted on the very afternoon of March 19. The danger of abandonment had passed.

In the admiring biography of Serra written years later by Francisco Palóu, who was not in San Diego to observe these events, the episode of the deadline is so dramatized that some historians have doubted that it ever really occurred. It seems to be confirmed in eyewitness accounts, however, including not only one by Crespí but also one by Portolá himself.

Portolá now sent the *San Antonio* carrying Serra, Costansó, and Fages, on to Monterey. Portolá himself set out for the north again by land, with 12 soldiers, leaving eight to guard San Diego. This time, at last, Portolá fully realized that what he had previously seen of the harbor of Monterey was all there was of it—at best a roadstead with no shelter from the north wind. But he had his orders, and so a presidio of poles and earth was constructed at Monterey under the direction of Costansó, and a mission was built nearby under the direction of Serra. Both were formally established on June 3, 1770. Leaving Fages in charge of the government of Alta California, Portolá then sailed for Mexico.

There was great formal rejoicing in Mexico City over the establishment of the new province, even though the reports of Portolá to the visitor-general and the viceroy were more candid than they cared to hear. Portolá was of the opinion that if the Russians wanted Alta California, which he doubted, they should be allowed to have it as a punishment for their aggressive designs. The Spanish occupation of Monterey could never prevent the Russians from establishing themselves at some other point on the coast. It was impossible, Portolá wrote, "to send aid to Monterey by sea, and still more so by land, unless it was proposed to sacrifice thousands of men and huge sums of money." For example, he attributed the disappearance of the supply ship *San José* to the probability that at the end the scurvy had left not a single sailor able to steer her against the constant and terrible headwinds from the northwest.

Bucareli, Anza, and the founding of San Francisco. The Spanish occupation of Alta California now consisted of two pinpoints on the coast, 450 miles apart. Differences of opinion between Serra and Fages deepened into a feud. In 1771 Serra moved the mission of San Carlos Borromeo from Monterey to the Carmel River, named long before by the Vizcaíno expedition in honor of its chaplains, three friars of the Order of Our Lady of Mount Carmel. This mission became Serra's headquarters for the arduous struggle to establish the others. Ultimately there would be 21 missions in Alta California, nine of them founded during his lifetime, but at the beginning only Serra himself foresaw such a degree of success. Repeatedly Fages vetoed his requests for new missions because there were not enough soldiers to protect them. The earliest attempts at agriculture failed, and food supplies remained desperately low. In 1772 the California settlements were saved from starvation by the meat which Fages provided from a grizzly-bear hunt in a valley north of San Luis Obispo.

Visitor-General Gálvez returned to Spain in 1771, and a new viceroy, Antonio de Bucareli, arrived in the same year. At first Bucareli was too busy with other duties to take much interest in Gálvez's new colony. In 1773, however, he turned his attention to it, and for several years he gave it enough care and support to bring it through its precarious infancy. Again the fear of foreign encroachments reinforced Spanish interest in California, the English now rivaling the Russians as objects of concern. Bucareli particularly detested the English. He had once been captain-general at Havana, and he keenly felt the humiliation of all Spaniards at the ease with which the English had captured that port during the Seven Years War. In the 1770s, moreover, the voyages of Capt. James Cook were indicating a renewed English interest in the Pacific.

In 1773 Serra made a journey to Mexico City to plead for more support for new missions and the substitution of Sergeant Ortega for Lieutenant Fages as governor of Alta California. Instead, Bucareli replaced Fages with Captain Rivera, although this would soon involve Serra in more disputes with the new governor than with the old one.

About the same time, Capt. Juan Bautista de Anza submitted a proposal for an expedition to open a land route from northern Sonora to Monterey. The land route from the peninsula was now useless because the impoverished Baja California missions had already contributed as much as they could, and besides they had just been turned over to the Dominicans. A mainland route from Sonora was now much more practicable than before because recent mining discoveries and the subsequent increase in the Spanish and mestizo population of that province had done more than all the military campaigns to overcome the Indian insurrections there.

With eager encouragement from Serra, Bucareli resolved not only to adopt Anza's project of a new land route to Monterey, but also to empower him to extend Spanish settlement to the strategic bay of San Francisco. Fages had made further explorations of the eastern shores of that great bay, and further unsuccessful attempts to get around it, in 1772. It was clear that it was no mere "estuary" of the smaller bay to the north, and usage now gradually shifted the name of *Bahia de San Francisco* to its permanent location.

Anza was an ideal leader for the project he proposed. Like his father and grandfather before him, he was a soldier of long experience on the northern Sonora frontier. The opening of a trail from Sonora to Alta California had been the dream of his family for three generations. He led two expeditions to California, one to explore the trail and the other to bring settlers, including some for the new San Francisco site.

On the first of these expeditions, Anza rode out from Tubac, a presidio south of Tucson, in January of 1774. The party of 34 men was poorly mounted because the Apaches were constantly running off the best horses from the presidio herds.

One of the men with Anza was Father Francisco Garcés. This remarkable Franciscan had already extended Kino's earlier explorations of the Colorado River region, and had won the confidence of Salvador Palma, chief of the Yumas. The goodwill of the Yumas was a vital factor in the success of Anza's expeditions, and when that goodwill came to a tragic end a few years later, in the Yuma massacre of 1781, the trail to California which Anza blazed was to be cut off for nearly half a century.

Ferried across the Colorado River with the aid of the Yumas and their tule rafts, Anza and his men struck out westward across the sand dunes of the Colorado Desert, became lost, and finally struggled back to the river after 10 days. After leaving much of their baggage with Chief Palma, they traveled southward to get around the dunes, turned west again in the region of the present Mexican boundary, traversed what would later flourish as the Imperial Valley, moved northward along the eastern slopes of the mountains through the Anza Desert and the Borrego Valley, and crossed the mountains into the Cahuilla Valley by way of the Royal Pass of San Carlos.

On March 22, 1774 they reached the Mission of San Gabriel, founded three years earlier. Continuing to Monterey, and returning over his former route, Anza reached Tubac in May, and a few months later went to Mexico City to make a full report to the viceroy.

Greatly encouraged by the opening of the new route from Sonora to California, Viceroy Bucareli promoted Anza to the rank of lieutenant colonel, and planned a new group of expeditions for 1775. In the previous year Juan Pérez, sent to look for Russian establishments, had discovered Nootka Sound (off the coast of British Columbia) in the course of his voyage of exploration of the northwest coast. It was on this discovery that the United States later based its claims to the region in succession to Spain's. In the expeditions by sea in 1775, Bruno Hezeta discovered the Columbia River; Juan de Bodega reached the 58th parallel, and on his return voyage discovered the bay that bears his name; and the expedition under Juan Manuel de Ayala, in the *San Carlos,* made the first passage by ship through the Golden Gate, known to the Spaniards merely as *La Boca,* or the mouth. The Ayala expedition to explore San Francisco Bay had begun under Miguel Manrique, but this commander lost his mind a few days after leaving San Blas and had to be put ashore. He had left several loaded pistols about his cabin, and one of these accidentally exploded, wounding his successor, Ayala. The lateness of Spanish settlement of Upper California can be vividly seen in the fact that this unfortunate pistol shot occurred within a few days of "the shot heard round the world," fired at Lexington, Massachusetts, on April 19, 1775, and signaling the beginning of the American Revolutionary War.

A launch made at Monterey and piloted by Ayala's subordinate, José Cañizares, was actually the first vessel through the Golden Gate, on August 5;

the *San Carlos* followed on the evening of the same day. Ayala's wound confined him to the ship, but his men spent several weeks in making a thorough exploration of the arms of the bay with the launch. The names of Angel Island and of Alcatraz, the *Isla de los Alcatraces,* or island of the pelicans, date from the Ayala expedition, although the name of Alcatraz was then applied to the island now called Yerba Buena.

The second Anza expedition also began in 1775, and was responsible for the founding of the presidio and mission at San Francisco in the following year. Except for Anza's own small escort, this expedition consisted almost entirely of settlers who would remain in California as *pobladores,* or populators. There were about 30 soldier-colonists and their families, and four civilian settlers and their families, recruited mainly in Sinaloa. The need for married soldiers in California came from both the need for future citizens for the province and the desire to reduce the difficulties with the Indians repeatedly caused by soldiers who were either unmarried or living far from their families in Mexico. For example, in 1773 three soldiers at San Diego were accused by one Indian girl of having killed another after assaulting them both. The men were sent to Mexico for trial. After the proceedings against them had dragged on for five years, their lives were spared on the ground that the evidence against them was a transcript of the testimony of a child through an interpreter. However, they were sentenced to spend the rest of their lives as citizens of California, a somewhat paradoxical verdict reflecting the evil reputation the new colony had in Mexico.

The time when people would want to go to California was very far in the future; only those in the direst poverty were willing to go, and then only on the promise of the government to outfit them completely and to pay all their expenses for years to come. Upon Anza's warning to Viceroy Bucareli, however, all such payments were in the form of clothing, food, equipment, and supplies, and not in cash, which might have been gambled away immediately. With the second Anza expedition went a large herd of cattle and horses to serve as breeding stock.

Following his previous route Anza reached San Gabriel with his second expedition in January 1776. There he learned that the Indians had attacked and destroyed the mission at San Diego in the previous November, killing Father Luis Jayme and two soldiers, and mutilating the body of Father Jayme.

Governor Rivera had only 70 soldiers in the whole province, scattered among five missions and two presidios. He was on his way from Monterey to San Diego to punish the offenders, and Anza was induced to join forces with him for that purpose. Their arrival at San Diego, coinciding with those of a supply ship from San Blas and a small land force sent up from the peninsula, completely overawed the Indians; but Rivera was excommunicated by the padres for entering the improvised church to seize an Indian chief who had sought the right of asylum, but who was suspected of being the main instigator of the revolt.

In March, Anza's party of colonists reached Monterey, and Anza himself proceeded to the San Francisco peninsula to choose the sites for the new presidio and mission. Governor Rivera, in spite of orders from the viceroy, had done nothing to prepare for the founding of San Francisco, and was in fact bitterly opposed to it. He was now 65 years old, and had repeatedly requested retirement. He was still a captain, and part of his irritation at this time was undoubtedly the result of his belief that Anza, who was only 41, had gained promotion to a higher rank for services no greater than his own. It was Rivera, after all, who had led the first overland party of Spanish colonists into California. A few years later, during the Yuma massacre, he would be killed while leading the last one, at the age of 70.

For the site of the new presidio, Anza chose a point near the northernmost tip of the San Francisco peninsula. Rivera had noted, and it was one of his objections, that the whole northern part of the peninsula consisted largely of sand dunes. About three miles to the southeast of the presidio site, however, Anza found a little oasis on a creek, and here, on March 29, 1776, he marked the site of the mission. He named the creek *Laguna de Nuestra Señora de los Dolores* because, as Father Font recorded in his diary, March 29 in the religious calendar "was the Friday of Sorrows," referring to Our Lady of Sorrows, the Virgin Mary. From this there later arose the popular name of Mission Dolores for what was officially the Mission of San Francisco de Asís.

Various obstacles, including some set up by Governor Rivera, delayed the actual founding of the new establishments for several months. In the meantime Anza departed for Mexico and left Lt. José Moraga in charge of the new colonists. On June 27 a group of 193 persons, mostly soldier-settlers and their families, arrived at the site of the San Francisco mission. The presidio was formally established under the command of Lieutenant Moraga on September 17, and Father Palóu formally opened the mission on October 9.

Neve and the pueblos of San José and Los Angeles. The new California was now regarded as more important than the old one, and this was reflected in the reorganization of their joint government in 1776. Felipe de Neve was now appointed governor of both the Californias, with headquarters at Monterey, where he arrived to replace Rivera early in 1777. Rivera's pleas for retirement were again denied, and he was again placed in charge of Baja California, this time as lieutenant governor under Neve's superior authority. Neve was another army officer, and probably the best administrator among the Spanish governors of California. In his *Reglamento* of 1779, revising and enlarging an earlier decree of Viceroy Bucareli, Neve established the code of law that remained in effect until the end of Spanish rule.

Neve had been ordered to try to solve the food supply problems of the presidios by establishing agricultural towns or pueblos. The missions were beginning to be agriculturally self-supporting, but the padres protested against

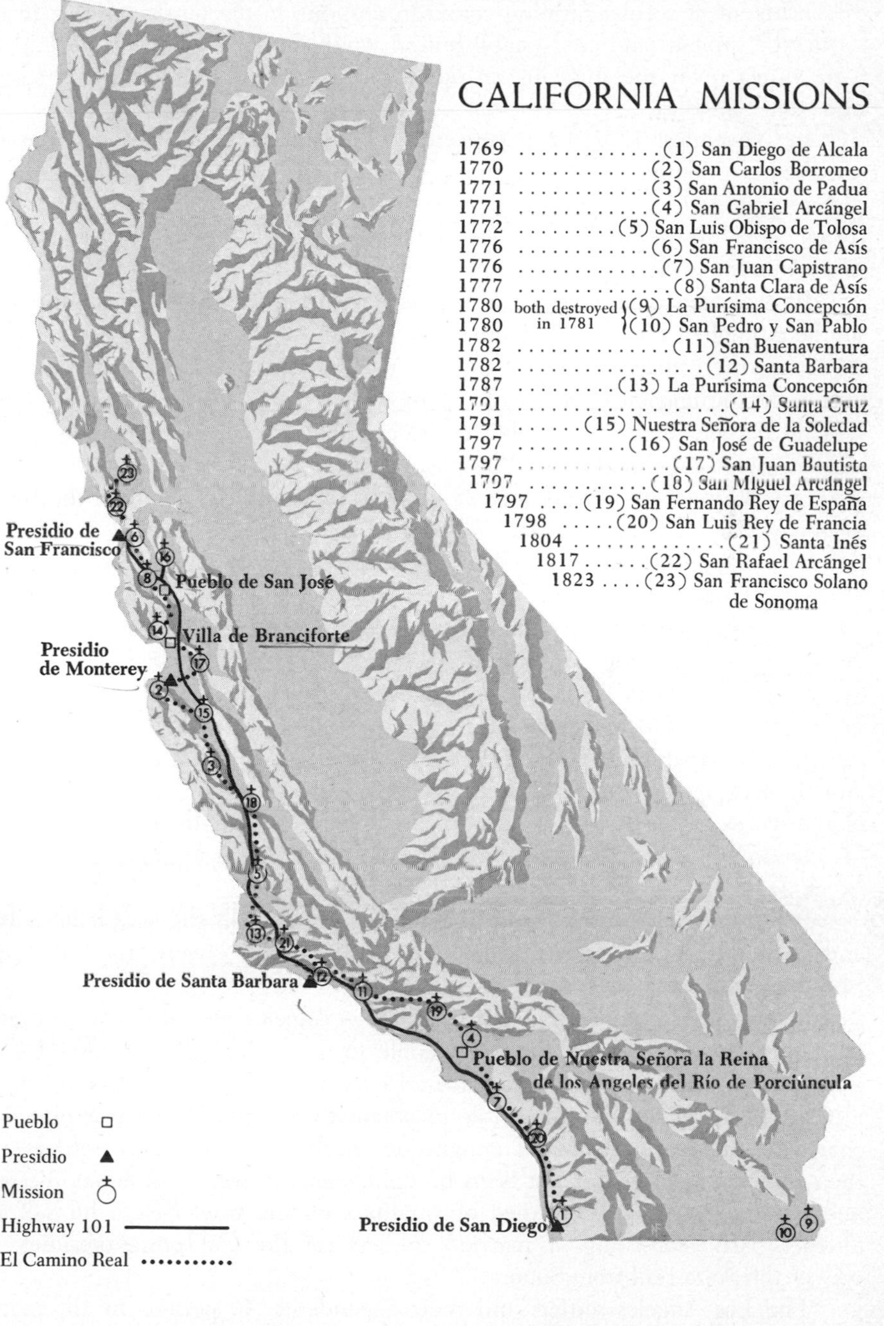

CALIFORNIA MISSIONS
1769 ....(1) San Diego de Alcala
1770 ....(2) San Carlos Borromeo
1771 ....(3) San Antonio de Padua
1771 ....(4) San Gabriel Arcángel
1772 ....(5) San Luis Obispo de Tolosa
1776 ....(6) San Francisco de Asís
1776 ....(7) San Juan Capistrano
1777 ....(8) Santa Clara de Asís
1780 both destroyed in 1781 (9) La Purísima Concepción
1780 (10) San Pedro y San Pablo
1782 ....(11) San Buenaventura
1782 ....(12) Santa Barbara
1787 ....(13) La Purísima Concepción
1791 ....(14) Santa Cruz
1791 ......(15) Nuestra Señora de la Soledad
1797 ....(16) San José de Guadelupe
1797 ....(17) San Juan Bautista
1797 ....(18) San Miguel Arcángel
1797 ....(19) San Fernando Rey de España
1798 .....(20) San Luis Rey de Francia
1804 ....(21) Santa Inés
1817 ......(22) San Rafael Arcángel
1823 ....(23) San Francisco Solano de Sonoma
Presidio de San Francisco
Pueblo de San José
Villa de Branciforte
Presidio de Monterey
Presidio de Santa Barbara
Pueblo de Nuestra Señora la Reina de los Angeles del Río de Porciúncula
Presidio de San Diego
Pueblo
Presidio
Mission
Highway 101
El Camino Real

requisitions on their crops and herds to provide food for the garrisons. With the establishment of secular farming communities, one in the north and one in the south, the military and civil establishment would no longer have to depend for food either upon the missions or upon the expensive and hazardous supply line from San Blas.

In November 1777 Neve collected 14 men and their families from the presidios of Monterey and San Francisco and settled them at the new pueblo of San José de Guadalupe, the first town to be founded in Spanish Alta California. It lay to the southeast of the mission of Santa Clara de Asís, established a few months earlier.

In the same year Neve made a personal survey of possible locations for a southern pueblo. He chose a point near the *Río de Porciúncula,* not far from the site of the Indian village of Yang-Na, most of whose former inhabitants now resided in the mission of San Gabriel about nine miles to the northeast. There was no harbor, and no navigable river, but that was of no importance for a small agricultural community. The place was on a plain extending 16 miles to the west, 60 miles to the east, and 25 miles to the south. Its name, in the fullest of the versions in early official documents, was to be *El Pueblo de Nuestra Señora la Reina de los Angeles del Río de Porciúncula,* or The Town of Our Lady the Queen of the Angels by the River of Porciúncula. That this would soon be abbreviated was rather obviously inevitable, but the part of it to be chosen by popular usage was a matter of accident. It might have been *Pueblo;* or it might have been *Porciúncula,* which, since it means "little portion," would be more than a little incongruous today. It turned out to be *Los Angeles,* or rather, in the Spanish and Mexican periods, usually simply *Angeles.* The modern American expression, "the City of the Angels," often imagined to be a translation of the name, is inaccurate in more than one respect. The town was not named for the Angels, except indirectly; nor was the name meant to imply any particular characteristic of the prospective inhabitants.

It is ironic that San Francisco and Los Angeles, hardly the least materialistic and self-indulgent of modern cities, were named, respectively, for the ascetic St. Francis of Assisi and for the Virgin Mary.

Like the San Francisco colonists, the Los Angeles *pobladores* were drawn from the poorest classes of Sinaloa, people to whom any change offered some hope of improvement. Neve asked for 24 experienced farmers "without known vice or defect." It proved impossible to obtain that many. Rivera was placed in charge of the recruitment and emigration. Early in 1781 the 12 settlers and their families, who had at last been brought together, were sent across the gulf and up the peninsula. One died of smallpox on the way. Rivera himself led another party, consisting of married soldiers for the California presidios, by way of the Anza trail from Sonora.

The Los Angeles settlers and their dependents, 46 persons in all, arrived at San Gabriel mission in August. Their origins, as Hubert Howe Bancroft puts it, were a mixture of Indian and Negro with here and there a trace of Spanish.

The San José colonists were ahead of them not only in priority of founding but also in educational matters. That is, of the nine heads of families now at San José, there was one who could read and write. This was José Tiburcio Vasquez, said to be the ancestor of the famous bandit.

After a few weeks under smallpox quarantine at some distance from San Gabriel, the *pobladores* moved to the spot Neve had chosen for them, about three-fourths of a mile west of the river of Porciúncula, and a little to the northwest of the present plaza. Neve set the date of September 4, 1781, for the founding of the pueblo, and it has served as the official birthday even though there were no ceremonies on that day, or indeed until five years later when the lands were formally allotted.

Although the government had undertaken to supply all the needs of the settlers, and although Neve's regulations provided an extreme form of paternalistic control for the pueblos, the situation was far from that of a welfare state. Early in 1782, by order of the Governor, three men were "sent away as useless to the pueblo and themselves," and their property was confiscated. One of these was Josef Lara, the only one of the original settlers of Los Angeles who claimed to have been born in Spain.

The padres considered the pueblo settlers to be a lazy and dissolute lot, good for nothing but drinking, gambling, and the pursuit of Indian women. Yet somehow, within a few years, irrigated agriculture and cattle raising at Los Angeles developed far enough to ensure the survival of the community, although its crops and herds could not yet rival those of San Gabriel, the "mother of agriculture in California" and the most productive of the missions.

Father-president Serra found Governor Neve even more determined than his predecessors to maintain the authority of the government over that of the missionaries. The governors had been so instructed, because it was the policy of the entire Spanish government at this time to treat the church as essentially an arm of the state. Of his many disputes with Neve, the one that disturbed the Father president most arose from Neve's insistence that there was a technical flaw in the papers authorizing Serra to administer the sacrament of confirmation. At the height of this long argument, Serra confided to Father Lasuén that he was suffering from insomnia, caused, he said, not by his bad leg but by the trouble given him by the Governor.

The Yuma massacre. José de Gálvez, having become Minister of the Indies in the royal government at Madrid, was finally able to put into effect his earlier plan to reorganize the higher administration of the frontiers of New Spain. In 1776 the entire group of frontier provinces from Sinaloa, Sonora, and the Californias to New Mexico and Texas was detached from the control of the viceroy at Mexico City and placed under a commandant-general of the "Interior Provinces" with headquarters at Arispe in Sonora.

Teodoro de Croix, first commandant-general of the *Provincias Internas,* took little interest in the Californias, which he never visited. His attention was mainly on the defense of the frontiers to the east, where he hoped to crush the Apaches and end their perpetual raids. The Indians of Alta California, except for those at San Diego, had given very little trouble, and the concern of Croix with the California establishments was largely in reducing their expenses. Unfortunately he failed to realize that the Yumas, whose location on the Colorado River was so strategic, were much more warlike than other California tribes. They had become accustomed to generous presents, and they were angry when these were reduced to a trickle. In 1780 two missions were founded in Yuma territory on the California side of the Colorado River, but, over the protests of the padres, both establishments were peculiar mixtures of mission, presidio, and pueblo. This novel economy measure failed dismally, although in any case the Yumas would probably have proved to be the least amenable to missionization of all the California Indians.

In June 1781 Captain Rivera and his party of married soldiers reached the Colorado on their way to California. Some went ahead to San Gabriel, but about half of the party including Rivera camped on the eastern bank of the river to rest. Their cattle destroyed part of the Indians' supply of mesquite beans, and Rivera's men generally succeeded in antagonizing the Yumas even more than the Spaniards at the new missions had done. On July 17 the Yumas destroyed both missions, and the next day crossed the river to surprise and kill Rivera and all his soldiers. The women and children with the Spaniards were enslaved. Altogether, 30 soldiers and four padres, including Garcés, were put to death. Capt. Don Fernando Rivera y Moncada, the weary and irascible old veteran who had felt condemned to interminable service in some of the most difficult roles ever demanded of a soldier or a colonial administrator, was released from duty at last.

The Yuma massacre was one of the worst disasters in the whole history of the Spanish frontier. Some of the captives were later ransomed, but no serious attempt was made to punish the Yumas or to reopen the Colorado River route. The Anza Trail remained cut off until the 1820s, and in the meantime there was virtually no land communication at all between Mexico and California.

SELECTED BIBLIOGRAPHY

The first California biography was Francisco Palóu's *Relación Histórica de la Vida y Apostólicas Tareas del Venerable Padre Fray Junípero Serra,* published in Mexico in 1787; it was translated and edited by Maynard J. Geiger as *Life of Fray Junípero Serra* (1955). Zephyrin Engelhardt, *The Missions and Missionaries of California* (four volumes, 1908–1915), and his separate volumes on several of the individual missions, contain a mass of information, but their defensive tone becomes wearisome. In pleasing contrast, Maynard J. Geiger, *The Life and Times of Fray Junípero Serra* (two volumes, 1959), is a work of urbane scholarship, although it takes no less satisfaction in Franciscan achievements. Of the several shorter biographies of Serra, it will suffice to mention Theodore Maynard, *The Long Road of Father Serra* (1954), and Omer Englebert, *The Last of the Conquistadors, Junípero Serra* (translated from the French by Kartherine Woods, 1956).

Theodore E. Treutlein, "The Portolá Expedition of 1769–1770," *California Historical Society Quarterly*, XLVII (December 1968), 291–314, is illuminating. On the discovery of San Francisco Bay and the beginnings of San Francisco see Treutlein, *San Francisco Bay: Discovery and Colonization, 1769–1776* (1968); and Frank M. Stanger and Alan K. Brown, *Who Discovered the Golden Gate?* (1969).

Much of the primary material on the early years of Alta California has been published. Important examples are Palóu's *Noticias de la Nueva California*, completed in 1783, published in 1857, and translated by Herbert E. Bolton as *Historical Memoirs of New California* (four volumes, 1926); accounts of the Sacred Expedition by Portolá, Costansó, Fages, and Vila, in the first two volumes of the *Publications* of the Academy of Pacific Coast History (1910–1911); Bolton, *Fray Juan Crespí, Missionary Explorer* (1927); H. I. Priestley, *A Historical, Political, and Natural Description of California by Pedro Fages* (1937); and Douglas S. Watson, *The Spanish Occupation of California* (1934).

Bernard E. Bobb, *The Viceregency of Antonio Maria Bucareli in New Spain, 1771–1779* (1962), includes a description of Bucareli's policies toward California. Herbert E. Bolton, *Anza's California Expeditions* (five volumes, 1930), exhaustively chronicles the two expeditions and the founding of San Francisco; the first volume, also published separately as *Outpost of Empire* (1931), is Bolton's summary of the story; the other four volumes are documentary. John Galvin, editor, *The First Spanish Entry into San Francisco Bay, 1775* (1971), is a narrative of the Ayala expedition.

Edwin A. Beilharz, *Felipe de Neve, First Governor of California* (1971), is a valuable study. Documents on the founding of Los Angeles were included in the Historical Society of Southern California's annual *Publication* of 1931, the year of the sesquicentennial. On the Afro-American ancestry of a number of the founders of Los Angeles and of other early settlers of California, see Jack D. Forbes, *Afro-Americans in the Far West: A Handbook for Educators* (1967). The name of the town is discussed in Francis J. Weber, *El Pueblo de Nuestra Señora de Los Angeles: An Inquiry into Early Appellations* (1968).

Chapter VI

OUTPOSTS OF A DYING EMPIRE

FOR THE NEXT 40 years, from the Yuma massacre in 1781 to the final collapse of Spanish rule over Mexico in 1821, New Spain made little effort to strengthen its outposts in Alta California. There, as elsewhere, the over-extended Spanish colonial empire was on the defensive, and crumbling. The mission system continued to expand, but it did not succeed in turning the Indians into genuine colonists. Other than the native Indians, there were about 600 persons in Alta California in 1781, and about five times as many in 1821, but the increase was almost entirely from the birth of descendants of the earlier colonists rather than from the arrival of new ones. The numbers of cattle and horses grew much more rapidly, and a fourth institution, the private rancho, began to develop along with the presidios, missions, and pueblos. Nellie Van de Grift Sánchez and other writers have called Spanish California an "Arcadia." Like that isolated mountain kingdom in ancient Greece, it was quiet, simple, and pastoral. But life in it was by no means as ideal as this analogy would imply.

Don Pedro Fages and Doña Eulalia. Upon the departure of Felipe de Neve in 1782, Pedro Fages again became governor. This irritated Father Serra, who had engineered Fages's earlier removal. But by far the liveliest disputes of Fages's second administration resulted from the arrival of his wife, Doña Eulalia, the first Spanish lady of quality to attempt to make a home in California. The story of her sojourn at Monterey was an impressive example of the difficulty of persuading Spanish ladies to come to the more rustic and isolated of the colonial capitals, and to remain in them.

The Governor's lady was then in her 20s, less than half the age of her husband. She came from a much wealthier family than his, and was entirely unprepared for the hardships of the frontier. When she was finally persuaded to join Don Pedro in Alta California, he traveled happily to Lower

California to meet her and they began what was supposed to be a triumphal journey overland to Monterey.

Things went wrong from the beginning. Doña Eulalia was so deeply touched by the nakedness and poverty of the Indians who greeted her along the way that she made them presents of clothing from her wardrobe, as well as from the Governor's, until he warned her that it would not be possible to replace these articles in California. The revelation that there were no dressmakers in Monterey came as a shock. She had not been long in the cramped and bare *adobe* which served as the gubernatorial residence when she began to demand that they return to civilization. When Fages refused, she barred the door of their bedroom against him for months, and when this failed to change his mind she publicly accused him of infidelity with an Indian girl, and demanded a divorce. For a time the scandalized padres were no more successful than her husband in quieting her tantrums. Then she seemed to relent, and a reconciliation was effected; but shortly thereafter the Governor had to try to intercept a letter in which she begged his superiors to recall him on the ground that the climate was ruining his health. After several years of such marital discord, which was quite possibly the greatest of the many hardships of his post, Fages gave in and was granted retirement.

In all her years in Alta California the life of its first First Lady seems to have been brightened only once, and briefly, by an event that occurred in 1786. This was the visit to Monterey of a European nobleman, the Comte de La Pérouse, who was engaged in a global voyage of scientific exploration for the French government. Other than those of the Spaniards themselves, the two vessels under La Pérouse were the first ships to visit Alta California since the voyage of Drake, more than two centuries before.

La Pérouse was a perceptive and sympathetic observer of conditions in the province. He felt that its importance lay in the distant future, and that no substantial development of it would occur under Spanish rule. He had the highest admiration for the character of the missionaries—"these men, truly apostolic, who have abandoned the idle life of a cloister to give themselves up to fatigues, cares, and anxieties of every kind." But he doubted that they were accomplishing anything of permanent value. Under their theocratic system the Indian was "too much a child, too much a slave, too little a man," and in the resort to stocks, irons, and the lash, and the use of soldiers to hunt down those who tried to escape, there was a distressing resemblance to the slave plantations he had seen in Santo Domingo.

A few weeks before the final departure of Pedro Fages from Monterey in the autumn of 1791, the little capital was visited by another scientific exploring expedition, this time Spanish, under the command of Alejandro Malaspina. Among its instructions was the order to put to final rest the question of whether there was a Strait of Anián. In the crew of one of Malaspina's two ships was the first American who came to California and stayed—John Green, a sailor from Boston who had signed on at Cádiz as a gunner. Green died of dropsy a few hours after the expedition arrived at Monterey, on September 13, and on the following day he was given a Roman Catholic burial at the presidio chapel. According to the padre who officiated, Green had "abjured his heretical opinions and received the Holy Sacraments of Baptism, Penance, and Absolution" shortly before he died.

During the 12 days of the Malaspina expedition's visit, its artists produced some remarkable sketches, notably views of Monterey and Carmel and portraits of local Indians. The expedition did not become as well known as that of La Pérouse, partly because Malaspina ran afoul of court intrigue soon after his return to Madrid. As a result, he was exiled and his extensive records consigned to gather dust in the Spanish naval archives for generations.

Attempts at reinforcement. Spain was now beginning to experience a long series of international difficulties in which she would gradually drift from humiliation into utter disaster. In 1778 Capt. James Cook had visited Nootka Sound, a harbor on Vancouver Island, and claimed the rights of discovery, although four years earlier Juan Pérez had discovered the place and claimed it for Spain. The publication of Captain Cook's account of the potential riches of the fur trade in the Nootka region led to an international race to exploit it. In 1789 Esteban José Martínez was sent to take possession of Nootka Sound for Spain, and to build a fort. Upon his arrival he found five ships anchored there—two American, one Portuguese, and two British. The British commander, Capt. James Colnett, had also come with orders to take possession of the harbor, and to build a fort and a trading post. Martínez arrested Captain Colnett and seized his ships as prizes. The news of this act led England to threaten war. Spain appealed to France for help, but the French Revolution had begun, and the National Assembly was not disposed to honor the Family Compact between the Bourbon monarchs. Thus in 1790, in the first Nootka Sound treaty, Spain was forced to give up its claims to exclusive rights on the Pacific Coast north of California.

George Vancouver was appointed as a British commissioner to work out details of the application of the treaty, and in 1792 and the following year he visited several points in California, with special interest in the presidios. (The fourth and last of the presidios, at Santa Barbara, had been established in 1782.) Vancouver was amazed at the weakness of these establishments: at the time of his visits there were two cannon at the presidio of San Francisco, neither of them serviceable, and three at San Diego, none of them even mounted. Santa Barbara had two cannon, and Monterey eight. The Spanish authorities, worried because the extent of this weakness would now be known to the British government, made plans to try to strengthen their feeble hold on the province as best they could. Orders were given for the construction of new batteries, but there were only token results. Moreover, the guns installed at Fort Point, San Fran-

"Presidio de Monterrey" from sketches of the Malaspina Party. Donald C. Cutter, Malaspina in California. *(Courtesy of the Bancroft Library)*

cisco, were found to have been rendered unusable by exposure and neglect a few years later.

In 1796 the viceroy, the Marqués de Branciforte, and the Governor, Diego de Borica, made plans for a new type of pueblo to be colonized by retired soldiers and their families. These ex-soldiers would not only be self-supporting but would provide a ready reserve in case of foreign incursions. The project had the advice of Miguel Costansó, the military engineer who had been in California with Portolá. The attempt to put it into practice illustrated the able planning that so often characterized Spanish colonial administration, and the typical frustration of such planning by hopeless difficulties.

The site of the new pueblo, to be called the Villa de Branciforte, adjoined the lands of the Mission Santa Cruz—to the bitter objections of the padres. The funds available for founding the new town were sadly inadequate. Not a single ex-soldier could be found in Mexico who would go there voluntarily, and nearly all the colonists who finally arrived in 1797 were men convicted of petty crimes, now sentenced to live in a Spanish version of Botany Bay. It is not surprising that the Villa de Branciforte did not flourish, although it struggled along for many years as a collection of huts. Such was the last attempt under Spanish rule to found any new civil or military establishment in California, with the exception of a few cattle ranchos on lands granted mainly to noncommissioned officers retired from garrison duty.

A dismal impression of Spanish prospects in California must remain, even though Governor Diego de Borica, a jovial Basque who was an early California booster, did his best to brighten the picture in a number of his reports. "This is a great country," he wrote soon after his arrival at Monterey, "the most peaceful and quiet country in the world; one lives better here than in the most cultured court of Europe." The climate he described as "healthful, between cold and temperate," and in general "so good that all are getting to look like Englishmen." There was "good bread, excellent meat, tolerable fish; and good humor which is worth all the rest. Plenty to eat, but the most astounding is the general fecundity, both of rationals and irrationals."

This last was a significant reference to the Spanish way of distinguishing the two main groups of the colonial population. The *gente de razón,* the people of reason, included all who were not full-blooded Indians. Literacy was much too rare to be a requisite. This idea of "civilized" or "rational" persons was also used interchangeably with "whites." Any admixture of white ancestry, mestizo or mulatto, was counted as white, and also qualified a person as rational. This distinction was itself irrational. In essence it was a distinction between "human" and subhuman. Among the rationals, the very few "pure-blooded Castilians," or rather those who could pass themselves off as such, were at the top of the colonial heap, and degrees of admixture often effectively determined social status.

Toward the end of his governorship (1794 to 1800), Borica was still interlarding his reports with such glowing remarks as "To live much, and without care, come to Monterey." But in view of the fact that ill health was causing him to beg for retirement, as Rivera, Fages, and Neve had done before him, we must suspect that his continued praise of life in California may have been designed to help in finding a willing and competent replacement. This was not easy. The governorship of California was not one of the most desirable posts in the Spanish colonial service.

In these years only the missions were showing any degree or kind of prosperity, and even that prosperity was deceptive and ultimately doomed. Under the leadership of Serra's equally able if slightly less colorful successor, Fermín Francisco de Lasuén, Father-president from 1785 to 1803, the number of Alta California missions doubled, from 9 to 18. Their Indian population more than doubled, rising to about 20,000, nearly as large as it ever became. Lasuén's presidency ended with his death, at the age of 83 years. His work was in many respects as remarkable as Serra's, although his historical reputation has suffered unfairly because he was one of the later Father-presidents and not the first, and from the lack of such a biographer as Serra's Palóu. It was Lasuén who supervised the building of the beautiful churches that replaced the rude structures of Serra's time. In the inevitable conflicts with the secular officials, Lasuén was no less firm than Serra had been, but he was less inclined to flamboyancy in argumentation.

The coming of the Russians. Count Nikolai Petrovich Rezanov made his famous visit to San Francisco in the spring of 1806. He came as an official of the Russian American Fur Company, seeking supplies to relieve the danger of starvation in its colony at Sitka, and incidentally investigating the possibilities of the fur trade in Northern California itself. The Spaniards were aware that the Russian position in the Pacific Northwest was almost as weak as their own, and they were concerned lest it be strengthened. Trade between Spanish colonies and foreigners was illegal. In the face of such difficulties, Rezanov's mission seemed doomed to failure.

At this point, "seeing that our situation was not getting better," he decided to improve it by a proposal of marriage to Doña Concepción Argüello, the 15-year-old daughter of the commandant of the San Francisco presidio.

Apart from the international political complications, there was a further impediment to granting Rezanov's request for the young lady's hand: he was of the Orthodox Eastern faith, whereas she was Roman Catholic. But her tender pleas moved the hearts of her father, the Governor, and the padres, and permission was given subject to ultimate approval in Rome. Rezanov then explained that he also would have to secure permission, and that this would require him to consult the religious authorities in St. Petersburg, as well as the Czar himself. Thus the wedding was postponed until his next visit to San Francisco, and in the meantime he was permitted to gather a cargo of supplies from the missions. Rezanov never returned to California, having died in the course of his journey to Russia. It was several years before the news of his death reached his fiancée.

Inevitably, accounts of this poignant episode have varied in their estimates of the sincerity of Rezanov's intentions. His own account suggests that he contemplated an honorable marriage, although one of diplomatic convenience. Interpretations of the lady's feelings have also varied. Bret Harte, in his poem "Concepción Argüello (Presidio de San Francisco, 1800)" [*sic*], invited his many readers to "listen to the simple story of a woman's love and trust." Others have pointed out that the story was not that simple. In fact it appears that Concepción's youthful love for Nikolai Petrovich, a man 35 years older than herself, was inspired in part by the contrast between the impoverished life of the presidio and her dreams of life at the court of St. Petersburg. As for Bret Harte's portrait of the lady, in her later years, as a "trembling, . . . wasted figure" who considered herself to have "died too" when Rezanov did, the actual evidence indicates that in middle age she became a stout and rather jolly woman who found much pleasure in acts of kindness and charity.

Rezanov had secured only a temporary trading concession. In 1812 the Russian American Fur Company built a fortified village which they called Ross, a name derived from the same root as that of Russia. Located on the coast about 18 miles north of Bodega Bay, Fort Ross had several purposes. It was intended to produce food not only for itself but for the company's operations in Alaska, to serve as a headquarters for the hunting of sea otter in northern California waters, and also to serve as a station for the trade which the Russians hoped to open on a regular basis with the Spanish Californian settlements. Though such trade was still forbidden by the Spanish government, locally it was very much needed and wanted, and at this time Spain and Russia were on friendly terms. The Russians insisted that their new settlement carried no hostile intent, and professed to have believed that San Francisco was the northernmost limit of Spain's legal possession of the coast. They knew that the Spaniards had no force available that could drive them out, and they politely disregarded the formal Spanish protests. On one occasion the garrison at San Francisco had to borrow powder from a visiting Russian ship in order to fire a salute from the only cannon in the presidio that could still be fired with any safety.

Exploration of the Central Valley. Had the Spaniards chanced upon the treasure of the Sierra Nevada, the history of California and even of the modern world might be incalculably different. But it is not surprising that the very few Spanish explorers who traversed parts of the Central Valley as far as the foothills of the Sierra should have failed to notice bits of gold in the streambeds or in outcroppings of quartz. The Spaniards had no pressing reason to explore the vast range itself, and to have discovered the gold in its foothills they would have had to be a great deal luckier than the Spaniards generally were in California. In Mexico and Peru they had known that gold and silver were present because the Indians had already discovered them and learned to use them. The California Indians had not discovered precious metals; they had had no acquaintance with any metal whatever.

Spanish settlement in Alta California was confined to a thin coastal strip. Except for the two short-lived establishments on the Colorado which were wiped out by the Yuma in 1781, the farthest inland Spanish settlement was Mission Soledad—only 30 miles from the sea. Following the discovery of the Central Valley by Pedro Fages during his exploration of the northeastern reaches of San Francisco Bay in 1772, there were periodic efforts to find places suitable for missions in various parts of the great interior region.

No missions were actually founded there, however, and the purposes of most of the Spanish expeditions into the valley were no more than those of pursuing escaped neophytes, punishing occasional raiders, and recovering stolen cattle and horses. The frequent raids on the livestock of the coastal settlements were carried on mainly by Indians who had once lived in the coastal areas but had fled to the interior to avoid missionization. The Spaniards had eliminated dozens of Indian villages near the coast in order to concentrate their populations in the missions.

The outstanding figure among Spanish explorers of the Central Valley was Lt. Gabriel Moraga. His father, José, the first commandant of the Presidio of San Francisco, had brought Gabriel to California as a boy with the second Anza expedition. Between 1805 and 1817 the younger Moraga led a large number of expeditions into the great valley. He was responsible for such names as those of *El Río de Nuestra Señora de la Merced,* the river of Our Lady of

Mercy; *El Río de Los Santos Reyes,* the river of the Holy Kings; the San Joaquin and Sacramento Rivers; *Mariposa,* from the many butterflies seen there in 1806; and *Calaveras,* a place of skulls. *El Río de las Plumas* was named by Lt. Luis Argüello, from the feathers of wild fowl seen floating on its waters. Plumas County gets its name from the Spanish word, while the name of Feather River has been anglicized from it.

The last years under the Spanish flag. Some of the little scenes that were being enacted in the frontier colony of California during this period were colorful and admirable; others were pitiful and drab. In any case, they received very little attention from the Spanish government, which was in an increasingly tragic situation. During most of the stormy era of the French Revolution and Napoleon, Spain was under the befuddled rule of Charles IV. It was characteristic of that monarch that he was almost the only person in Madrid who did not seem to know that his favorite adviser and chief minister, Manuel Godoy, a former captain of the royal guard, was the Queen's lover. Partly as a result of Godoy's policies, Spain was in alliance with France and almost continuously at war with England from 1796 to 1808, and consequently trade between Spain and her American colonies was largely cut off by the British navy.

In 1807 Napoleon became impatient with the way the Spanish regime was being conducted. He lured Charles IV, his Queen, and the crown prince, Ferdinand, to France for a visit, threw them into prison there, and announced that his brother, Joseph Bonaparte, would be the new King of Spain. In the spring of 1808 the Spanish people rebelled against this French regime, and for five years Spain was locked in one of the bitterest struggles in history, until the French armies were finally driven from the Iberian peninsula in 1813. Meanwhile Spain had little strength to spare for ruling her colonies, and their long and sporadic Wars of Independence set in. Amid the surging tides of world events, California remained a stagnant backwater.

The Mexican Revolution began in 1810 when the creole priest, Miguel de Hidalgo, published his famous outcry against tyranny, from his parish in the village of Dolores. In all the years until the news of Mexico's final independence reached California in 1822, few people in that isolated colony other than the governors and a few of the padres had any understanding of the issues in the terrible internal strife that was taking place in Mexico and in Spain. Nor was there much interest in those struggles except for complaints that because of them the supply ships from San Blas came even less often than before, and for several years did not come at all. The people of the presidios and pueblos suffered not only from the absence of all the little extra comforts of life, but even from the absence of clothing other than the crude homemade articles. They became intensely jealous of the self-sustained and growing wealth of the missions. The padres were enjoying the fruits of choice lands and well-irrigated gardens—oranges and grapes, wines and brandies. Padres, as well as others, were increasingly inclined to engage in contraband trade with foreign vessels, exchanging cowhides and tallow for cloth and other luxuries.

The most sensational events of the period, so far as California was concerned, were the brief raids on its capital and two other points on its coast, conducted in 1818 by two privateering vessels sailing under the flag of Buenos Aires and commanded by the Frenchman Hippolyte de Bouchard. California was loyal to Spain; hence the military justification for these acts of pseudopatriotic piracy. On November 20 Bouchard's vessels appeared in Monterey Bay. Governor Pablo Vicente de Solá and the other local inhabitants retreated to the area of Salinas. Bouchard and his men evacuated the capital after a few days, having set fire to whatever they could not carry away. They next landed at Refugio, about 30 miles from Santa Barbara, and succeeded in burning some ranch buildings.

The other object of the privateers' attentions was San Juan Capistrano, which they looted and burned. Their departure ended California's only participation in the Wars of Independence. Three years later the tattered flag of Spain was lowered for the last time at Monterey, and the new banner of Mexico, bearing an eagle and a snake, was raised in its place.

SELECTED BIBLIOGRAPHY

The *History of California,* volume I, 1542–1800, and volume II, 1801–1824, written by Henry L. Oak (volumes XVIII [1884], and XIX [1885], of *The Works of Hubert Howe Bancroft,* binder's title *Bancroft's Works*), remain the most important books on the period of this chapter. The authorship of *Bancroft's Works* is discussed in Chapter XXI. Also useful are Edith Buckland Webb, *Indian Life at the Old Missions* (1952); Kurt Baer and Hugo Rudinger, *Architecture of the California Missions* (1958); Engelhardt's volumes on the missions; Chapman's *History of California*; and M. J. Geiger, *Franciscan Missionaries of Alta California, 1769–1848: A Biographical Dictionary* (1969). The many books that dwell on the romantic aspects include *California Pastoral* (1888), written actually as well as nominally by Bancroft; Nellie Van de Grift Sánchez, *Spanish Arcadia* (1929); Alberta Johnston Denis, *Spanish Alta California* (1927); Irving B. Richman, *California under Spain and Mexico* (1911); and Richard F. Pourade, *Time of the Bells* (1961), volume II of his *History of San Diego.*

For the accounts of distinguished visitors, see Jean Francois Galaup, Comte de La Pérouse, *Voyage round the World* (two volumes, translation, 1798–1799); Donald C. Cutter, *Malaspina in California* (1960); George Vancouver, *A Voyage of Discovery to the North Pacific Ocean* (three volumes, 1798); and Francis J. Weber, "The California Missions and Their Visitors," *The Americans,* XXIV (1968), 319–336.

"The Establishment of the Villa de Branciforte" is well described by Florian Guest in the *California Historical Society Quarterly* XLI, (March 1962), 29–50.

Accounts of the coming of the Russians include T. C. Russell, editor, *The Rezanov Voyage to Nueva California in 1806* (1926); *Langsdorff's Narrative of the Rezanov Voyage to Nueva California in 1806* (1927); and "The Russians in California," *California Historical Society Quarterly*, XII (September 1933), a special issue. The prevalent notion that Doña Concepción was then 16 years old, rather than 15, stems largely from Gertrude Atherton. Although Mrs. Atherton was considered a daring writer in her day, her sense of propriety constrained her to add a year to her heroine's age in her historical novel *Rezánov*. She also supplied the acute accent, which does not exist in Russian.

"Spanish Exploration of California's Central Valley" is the subject of Donald C. Cutter's Ph.D. thesis, University of California, Berkeley (1950).

Chapter VII

A MARGINAL PROVINCE OF A TROUBLED REPUBLIC

AS ONE OF THE MOST isolated and least valued of all the colonial possessions of Spain, California had grown used to being neglected. The independent nation of Mexico, periodically torn with revolutionary disturbances and established as a republic after a brief and tragic interlude under the "empire" of Agustín Iturbide, was even less able than Spain had been to concern itself seriously or effectively with the distant northern region.

Government and politics in theory and practice. The most influential framers of the "Federal Constitution of the United Mexican States," adopted in 1824, were liberal idealists who modeled their country's new organic law in part on that of the United States of America. But there were great differences between the political, economic, and social backgrounds of the two countries. In Mexico, not even the upper class had acquired any substantial experience in self-government under Spanish colonial rule, and only a tiny fraction of the people were literate and prosperous enough to take an informed part in public affairs. Nevertheless, on paper the constitution of 1824 guaranteed both complete political equality and complete racial equality. Indians were not only entitled to vote and to hold office, but like all other citizens they were supposed to enjoy full freedom of person and property. In this respect, indeed, the Mexican constitution went far beyond its American counterpart, to which the Thirteenth, Fourteenth, and Fifteenth Amendments, abolishing Negro slavery and seeking to establish the civil rights of the Negro, had not yet been added.

The liberal Mexican constitution-makers of 1824 were not unaware of their country's limitations, and they dreamed of developing a civil society and a prosperous economy in which republican government and equal rights for all men could become more than empty forms and phrases. As applied to the remote province of California, these vague hopes led to several new policies. Governors of California were now authorized to permit freer trade with foreigners, subject only to import duties; to move toward secularization of the missions; and to increase rancho land grants, including grants to foreigners willing to be naturalized and to accept Roman Catholicism.

Under the first Mexican constitution, California was only a territory, not a state, although it was promoted to the rank of a "department" under the constitution of 1836 and the laws of 1837. Governors were appointed by the government of Mexico. There was a provincial legislative branch, of sorts, in the form of an elected *diputación,* but in practice it functioned only occasionally when the governor chose to convene it, and then merely as an advisory rather than a legislative body. In effect, the governor was not only the civil and military executive; he could usually control the provincial lawmaking process also, and he exercised nearly all of the judicial authority in the more important matters. In other words, there was no real separation of powers and no effective legal limitation of executive power. The general government of California remained what it had been under Spain, a petty military despotism. Control from Mexico City, however, was greatly weakened because the government could provide few soldiers of any sort, and none competent or reliable, for service in California; it lacked the money to pay them.

During California's Mexican period, one important substitute for a system of checks and balances did arise: the comic-opera "revolution," a political device characterized by bombastic "pronouncements," chesslike marches and countermarches, and noisy but bloodless artillery duels, just out of range, in which both sides retrieved each other's cannonballs and fired them back.

As the power of the Mexican governors and the Franciscan missionaries weakened, the real authority in California, insofar as there was any, gravitated into the hands of a small group of *ranchero* families, mostly California-born. The fact that these families were so closely intermarried was one reason that there was so little actual killing in battles between revolutionary factions. There was too much risk of killing a brother-in-law.

The main political motives of the leaders of this little ranchero oligarchy were, first, the hope of taking over from the missions their lands, their cattle, and their skillful cowboys, and second, the desire for political power and glory. In their struggles to achieve these objectives, the *californios* were badly divided by personal, factional, and sectional disputes. In the rivalry between *norteños* and *sureños,* such Northern California leaders as Juan Bautista Alvarado, Mariano Guadalupe Vallejo, and José Castro were aligned against Southern California politicos like José Antonio Carrillo, Pío Pico, and Juan Bandini. Confronted by the restless ambitions of these volatile native sons of California, governors sent up from Mexico had an increasingly difficult time.

Josiah Royce later maintained that the bloodless revolution, given the limitations of its social and historical context, was really a comparatively civilized method of settling internal political differences. In certain obvious respects it was infinitely preferable to the American Civil War, for example. The numerous Californian insurrections were, in part, merely a fairly harmless form of public entertainment. On the other hand, the Californians were capable of fighting with skill, courage, and deadly effectiveness when they thought it appropriate. They would prove this spectacularly against General Kearny's unfortunate American dragoons at the battle of San Pascual in 1846.

Government by mock revolution had serious defects, however, and one of these was that the resulting decisions were likely to be temporary. In one five-year period, from 1831 to 1836, Mexican California had 11 distinct gubernatorial administrations, not counting three men who were appointed to the governorship by Mexico but whom the Californians did not permit to take office. By contrast, there had been only 10 governors in the whole period of more than half a century of Spanish rule.

The secularization problem. By far the most important political issue in the province during the 1820s and 1830s was the question of the secularization of the missions, or rather, and more realistically, the question of who was to profit from the acquisition of their lands and herds. This troublesome problem so far overshadowed all others that the whole story of the political and quasi-military events can best be understood in connection with it.

As early as 1749, by royal order, the Spanish government had made an attempt to secularize the missions of Mexico—that is, to turn the properties over to the Indians and to replace the missionaries with secular parish clergy under the jurisdictions of the bishops. This attempt was abandoned largely because there were not enough secular priests available. In California, Governor Neve's *Reglamento* of 1779 had tried to limit new missions to the purpose of religious instruction, given in the Indians' own native villages; but Father Serra succeeded in blocking this radical departure from the regular mission system because he believed, probably correctly, that very few of the Indians would have accepted conversion unless forced to do so.

In 1813 the liberal Spanish Cortes of Cádiz issued a sweeping decree of secularization, but the restored Bourbon monarchy revoked this order. The liberals revived it after the Spanish revolution of 1819, and in 1820 the viceroy of New Spain proclaimed it to be in effect. In California, when Father-president José Señán received this news, he offered to turn the missions over to the Bishop of Sonora, since California was still a part of that diocese. The Bishop declined the responsibility, and thus the decree, as a Spanish government measure, was neatly circumvented.

The California missionaries generally viewed the results of Mexican independence with foreboding. They were particularly shocked to learn that during the revolutionary disorders under Emperor Iturbide the Franciscan apostolic College of San Fernando in Mexico City was made to serve as a cavalry barracks. Most of the missionaries were Spaniards, and as such they were targets for the hostility of Mexican revolutionary nationalists. For centuries the creoles had hated the *gachupines.* A "creole," or *criollo,* was a person who had been born in the Spanish American colonies; sometimes the word meant a person of entirely European ancestry, sometimes it was used without regard to racial origin. The Mexican word *gachupines,* meaning men born in Spain, had originally meant "those who wear spurs," and it implied, usually correctly, that the Spanish-born regarded themselves as superior beings. That feeling was bitterly resented in Mexico, and ambitious men born in California were also beginning to feel the same kind of resentment, not only against Spaniards but against Mexicans, particularly officials.

For centuries the Spanish church had been an integral part of Spain's authoritarian system of colonial control. Inevitably, republican theories were often anticlerical. Such theories, however, were often rationalizations for avarice. There was rising criticism of the missions for their temporal wealth and for their exploitation of the Indians. Unfortunately these were privileges that many an eloquent anti-clerical wanted to appropriate for himself.

The question of whether the Indians in the California missions were exploited and wretched or contented and appreciative will long remain a moot one. It has been said that "the preponderant testimony" describes the mission Indians as happy and well adjusted, preferring mission life to their previous freedom, and grateful for close supervision, hard work, colorful rituals, and the salvation of their souls. This is, to say the least, an extremely questionable conclusion. The bulk of the evidence has been the writings of the missionaries, who naturally tended to believe what they deeply yearned to believe about a matter so vital to their consciences. It is significant that the padres always applied the term "neophytes," or apprentices in Christianity, even to Indians who had been born in the missions and spent their entire lives there. The belief that any group of human adults could be happy under a system that treated them as if they were hopelessly retarded children was a very questionable one.

The picture of the missions as ideal communities also failed to note their terrifying death rate. The California mission registers recorded more than twice as many deaths as births, mainly because of disease. Not only did the Indians lack immunities, but confinement within the adobe walls of the missions deprived them of the modicum of sanitation they had enjoyed in their own villages, from their *temescals* and their practice of occasionally burning their old huts and building new ones.

The best evidence of how the Indians actually felt about the missions would be the testimony of the Indians themselves, and unfortunately very few of them had any opportunity to get their testimony into the historical record.

One who did was Victoria, an Indian girl who grew up in the Mission of San Gabriel and later married the "Scotch *paisano*," Hugo Reid. Her Christian name was the same as that of a young woman who had once jilted Reid in Scotland. It should also be noted that it was Reid who recorded his wife's recollections, and that his non-Catholic background, along with his status as the recipient of the Rancho Santa Anita, carved out of San Gabriel mission lands, gave him a viewpoint that was particularly hostile to the missionaries. The Franciscan historian Father Zephyrin Englehardt described Hugo Reid as "that embittered Scotchman" who "lied about religious matters."

Nevertheless, it is clear that Victoria regarded life in the mission as a life of misery, humiliation, and terror. The alliance of the padres and the soldiers, she told her husband bitterly, had turned even Indian chieftains like her own father into humble, confused, awkward, and shamefaced men. She could not entirely understand why her people, the Gabrielino, who had once given good accounts of themselves in occasional battles with neighboring tribes, had offered so little resistance to the Spaniards; but she remembered how the soldiers, armed with muskets, had come to her village when she was six years old, and taken its people to the mission. At first the Indians had been filled with surprise and astonishment; then a strange lethargy set in. They were told to fear a Hell that was lacking in their own religion. Corporal punishment, also, was something that had been unknown to them before.

One stark episode that Victoria remembered from her mission childhood occurred when an Indian woman who had a miscarriage was charged with infanticide and punished by having her head shaved, by being flogged every day for 15 days, by wearing irons on her feet for three months, and by "having to appear every Sunday in church, on the steps leading up to the altar, with a hideous painted wooden child in her arms." This took place while San Gabriel was under the regime of Father José María Zalvidea, a particularly stern disciplinarian. In Hugo Reid's opinion, Zalvidea "must . . . have considered whipping as meat and drink to [the Indians], for they had it morning, noon and night."

Like Serra, Zalvidea was as stern with himself as with his Indian wards. He often lashed his own shoulders and back, and under his coarse robe he always wore a belt with iron points pressing into his flesh. He made San Gabriel "the Pride of the Missions," yet to a man of his faith pride was the first of the seven deadly sins. Perhaps this conflict was one of the things that unbalanced his mind. In 1826 he suffered a nervous breakdown and was transferred to San Juan Capistrano for hospitalization.

Among the strongest critics of the mission system was Juan Bautista Alvarado. The missionaries, in his opinion, had "found the Indians in full enjoyment of their five senses, valiant in war . . . far-sighted in their own way"; but when the padres departed, "they left the Indian population half-stupefied, very much reduced in numbers, and duller than when they found them." It may be relevant that Alvarado, even more than Hugo Reid, was personally interested in the disposal of mission lands. As a native of California who became one of its governors, Alvarado would secure extensive land grants for himself and his political followers.

The missionaries, on their side, argued that the Indians were not ready for secularization, and this was certainly true. That the missions had failed to make them ready after more than a half a century, and showed no signs of ever making them ready, were facts that the padres blamed on the alleged inherent defects of the Indians rather than on the defects of the mission system or on their own desire to perpetuate it.

Apart from the question of where the fault lay, the missionaries predicted very accurately the fate that was in store for the Indians when secularization came. For example, as Father-president Durán pointed out, the Indians living in the pueblo of Los Angeles were forced to labor for the merest pittances and were subjected to frightful punishments for trivial misdeeds; they were given no security of any kind, and were in every way "far more wretched and oppressed than those in the missions."

From Echeandía to Figueroa. The first governor of California under the Mexican republican constitution, or more precisely and officially the first *jefe político superior* and *comandante general militar,* was José María Echeandía, a lieutenant colonel of engineers. He arrived in 1825 with instructions to proceed cautiously and gradually toward ultimate secularization; but although he drafted various plans for this eventuality, a number of formidable difficulties stood in the way. The missions were still the chief source of supplies for the presidios. In effect, these supplies were obtained free of charge because the only payment made for them was in drafts on the federal treasury in Mexico City—which never honored the drafts. Cash revenues for the territorial government depended on duties levied on the goods imported in exchange for Californian cowhides and tallow, and the missions were still the chief producers of the hides and tallow.

To add to the Governor's troubles, he was in poor health, and spent much time in San Diego to escape the fogs of the North. This, at least, was the reason he gave for his protracted absences from Monterey. Another motive was his love for a young lady of San Diego, Señorita Josefa Carrillo, who finally disappointed him by eloping with another suitor, the American sea captain Henry Delano Fitch.

In 1829 the unpaid soldiers at Monterey revolted under the leadership of Joaquín Solís, an ex-convict who was living in California as a part of his sentence. The revolt was suppressed after a bloodless "battle" near Santa Barbara; but later in the same year, in deep discouragement, Echeandía submitted his resignation.

Early in 1830 a conservative and proclerical "centralist" faction gained control of the government in Mexico. Its appointee as governor of California was a reactionary politician and army officer, Lt. Col. Manuel Victoria, a vigorous opponent of secularization and a stern believer in the virtues of military authority. Shortly before the centralist coup, the previous Mexican regime had appointed the radical republican José María Padrés as governor, but before he could take office his appointment was superseded by Victoria's. Padrés remained in California in his earlier position of adjutant inspector of troops. He despised both the personality and the ideas of the man who would now hold the higher office. Padrés was not only a bitter critic of the missions, but also a man of considerable ability and personal magnetism, and several young Californians, including Vallejo and Alvarado, became his disciples. He taught them, as Bancroft put it, "to theorize eloquently on the rights of man, the wrongs of the neophytes, and the tyranny of the missionaries."

Shortly before Victoria arrived at Monterey, Padrés induced the outgoing Governor Echeandía to issue an order for general secularization. When Victoria reached the capital early in 1831 he promptly suspended this decree, and soon afterward proclaimed a number of repressive measures. For opposition to his policies he banished several prominent men, including Padrés, and imprisoned several more. The result was an insurrection in Southern California, led by José Antonio Carrillo and ex-Governor Echeandía.

When a small force under Governor Victoria met the rebels north of Cahuenga Pass, near Los Angeles, on December 4, 1831, hostilities might have been confined to the verbal level if the Governor had not made a slurring remark about the fighting qualities of his own men. One of his aides, Lt. Romualdo Pacheco, was so goaded by this sarcasm that he drew his saber and rode out ahead of the Governor's troops. On the rebel side, young José María Ávila was burning with resentment at having been imprisoned in Los Angeles for sedition. He suddenly charged at Pacheco and killed him with a pistol, then spurred toward Victoria and wounded him with a lance thrust. A soldier shot Ávila with a musket, and Victoria, though badly wounded, killed Ávila with his sword. Forty-three years later a son and namesake of Romualdo Pacheco, born a month before his father's death, would become one of the American governors of California.

By provoking actual bloodshed, Governor Victoria had violated the rules of the California political game. He was packed off to Mexico on the next ship, and there was a chaotic scramble for power. For about a year the South was ruled by Echeandía and the North by Agustín Zamorano. (Zamorano is better known for having imported California's first printing press, used mainly for the publication of official documents.)

The ouster of Governor Victoria was a deathblow to the mission system. Although the conservative faction was still precariously in power in Mexico City, it recognized the need to conciliate the rebellious Californians by permitting secularization of the missions and by appointing a governor who could be trusted to carry it out in the fairest way possible. The man selected was Brevet Brig. Gen. José Figueroa, governor from early in 1833 until his death in 1835.

Figueroa and secularization. In terms of both ability and character, Figueroa was far the best of all the officials sent up by the Mexican republic. The tragedy was that no governor could have arranged the assignments of the mission lands to private ownership in an orderly and satisfactory manner under the conditions that existed.

In August 1833 the Mexican Congress adopted an immediate general secularization law which was extremely vague about procedures for carrying it out. In the following year, however, it became clear that this law was the work of that vocal champion of freedom for the Indians, José María Padrés, and that Padrés had also engineered the Mexican government's approval of an ambitious "colonization" scheme under which he and a group of his Mexican friends were to take over the lands of the missions. His close associate José María Híjar, a wealthy Mexican whom he had persuaded to finance the project, was to be not only the "Director of Colonization," but also the new governor of the territory.

A substantial number of colonists actually arrived from Mexico to occupy their new estates. Governor Figueroa, however, had already appointed the administrators or *comisionados* who were to supervise the disposal of mission lands, and his appointees were all Californians. A notable example was Mariano Guadalupe Vallejo. When Vallejo, Alvarado, and other former Californian admirers of Padrés heard that among his colonists there were 21 prospective mission administrators from Mexico, and when they recalled that there were just 21 missions, their feelings toward their erstwhile intellectual leader underwent a sharp and sudden change. Fortunately, from their point of view, the credentials of Padrés and Híjar were canceled from Mexico City when Gen. Antonio López de Santa Anna took power in another of the kaleidoscopic shifts of Mexican politics. As for the Padrés-Híjar colonists who chose to remain in California, Vallejo arranged for their settlement in the frontier region which was now under his control as a kind of feudal barony. Figueroa had made Vallejo not only the administrator of the Solano mission and grantee of the Petaluma rancho, but also the military commander of the whole northern frontier district.

Figueroa's proclamation of August 9, 1834, defined the general terms under which the process of secularization was to be conducted. It was planned for ten missions in 1834, six in 1835, and the other five in 1836. Half of the property was supposed to go to the Indians, and the law forbade them to dispose of it, but these provisions were not effectively carried out. Some Indians tried to make a living by farming their small allotments of land near the mission buildings, but none of them retained these lands more than a few years. Many never realized that they were supposed to have been given any land at all. The law attempted to limit the killing of cattle, but as the time of secularization approached, the missionaries slaughtered much of the stock in order to salvage, from the sale of the hides, as much wealth as possible for the Pious Fund. As a result, the missions were surrounded with thousands of skinned carcasses rotting in the sun.

For several years the morale of the padres had been declining. Many of them were old men who had lived so long in the missions that they regarded them as their only homes. Some, on the other hand, looked forward to relief from their responsibilities. Shortly before secularization one padre wrote that there was "hardly anything of the religious left in me. . . . I made the vows of a Friar Minor; instead I must manage temporalities, sow grain, raise sheep, horses, and cows. . . . These things are as disagreeable as thorns . . ., and they rob me of time, tranquility, and health both of soul and body."

Because there were no secular parish priests to replace them, the Franciscans remained at the mission churches to continue their religious duties. For a time many of the neophytes remained huddled around the padres. Indians who had been trained as *vaqueros,* or cattle wranglers, found employment on the private ranchos into which the mission lands were gradually subdivided. Others were able to gain a living as laborers in the towns. Many sank into vice and drunkenness. Some left the coastal area to try to find homes with alien tribes in the interior.

Alvarado and provincial autonomy. Figueroa was deeply disturbed by the failure of his secularization policies to protect the legal and moral rights of the Indians. In any event his efforts were cut short when, in the fall of 1835, he died of an apoplectic stroke. His passing removed a brake from the rapacity of the mission administrators and their friends and relatives, and again plunged California into noisy "revolutionary" struggles for control of the governorship. After the brief terms of José Castro and Nicolas Gutiérrez as acting governors, Mexico sent up a new champion of centralism, Col. Mariano Chico, who repeated most of the blunders of Governor Victoria and lasted only three months before he too was expelled.

Juan Bautista Alvarado, the clever and eloquent young president of the *diputación,* now emerged as the hero of the Californians, particularly the northerners. With the aid of about 30 riflemen led by Isaac Graham, a Tennessee backwoodsman who had come to California to operate a whisky distillery, Alvarado seized control of Monterey. He brought an end to the second provisional administration of the Spanish-born Gutiérrez and deported him along with most of the other Mexican officials.

On November 7, 1836, California was proclaimed "a free and sovereign State," until Mexico should repudiate centralism and restore the principles of the federalist constitution of 1824. Alvarado became provisional governor, and Vallejo, already in charge of the northern frontier, now became the military commander of the whole California "department." Vallejo was Alvarado's uncle, though only two years his senior and also less than 30 years old.

An act of the Mexican Congress in 1835 had promoted Los Angeles from a pueblo to a city (*ciudad*) and ordered the capital transferred there. This federal law was a result of the efforts of California's congressional delegate, José Antonio Carrillo, a Southern Californian and an expert in political intrigue. As one of his first official actions, Alvarado proclaimed that the capital would continue at his native Monterey, but he was forced to placate the southerners by permitting them to choose a subgovernor with considerable regional authority.

Even if Mexico had not had its hands full with the Texan War of Independence, it would probably have been disposed to compromise with Alvarado by appointing him as the legal governor of California under the Mexican republic. He accepted this arrangement in 1837 and continued to hold the office for five years.

In the period before the last fragments of the mission holdings passed into private hands at the end of 1845, the administration of these properties grew steadily more corrupt, incompetent, and generally disgraceful. In 1839 Alvarado made a belated and perfunctory effort at reform by appointing a visitor-general of missions, the naturalized Englishman, William E. P. Hartnell; but Hartnell's efforts were futile, partly because mission administrators such as Vallejo for San Rafael and Sonoma, and Pío Pico for San Luis Rey, had too much power in their respective districts. When Hartnell tried to make changes in some of Vallejo's plans for San Rafael, Vallejo actually arrested him. Hartnell could do no more than make a partial record of the disintegration and spoliation that were going on. He was paid no salary for his disheartening year's work; but he received two land grants from Alvarado in appreciation of his efforts.

Alvarado and Vallejo soon fell to quarreling with each other, and by 1842 they were both so disillusioned with the anarchic state of affairs in the province that they willingly turned over the political and military commands to the last governor from Mexico, Brig. Gen. Manuel Micheltorena. He was an amiable man, but his administration was no better than those of most of his predecessors. The army of 300 soldiers he brought with him consisted almost entirely of ex-convicts, and since as usual they failed to receive their pay, they obtained food and other items by a highly informal process of foraging, to the outrage of the local population. Alvarado and José Castro led still another revolt, and there was a new "battle of Cahuenga Pass" in February 1845. It was a repetition of the encounter on almost the same spot in 1830, except that this time the only casualties were a horse and a mule; but it was enough to induce Governor Micheltorena to follow the examples of Governors Victoria, Chico, and Gutiérrez by departing for Mexico, along with his ragged and thieving soldiers.

This marked the failure of the last attempt to reestablish any more than nominal Mexican control over California. Pío Pico assumed the governorship with Los Angeles as the capital, but having no influence much farther north than Santa Barbara he had to compromise with the *norteños* by recognizing José Castro as military commandant. This gave Castro the *de facto* control of the Monterey customs house and consequently of most of the governmental income. This arrangement, made on the eve of the Mexican War, left the province as weak and divided as it had ever been.

The heyday of the rancheros. Throughout the Mexican period the potential resources of California remained not only undeveloped but largely unsuspected. The most substantial economic activity was cattle raising, and the chief commercial products were hides and tallow for export. The local processing of these commodities went no farther than the staking out of the hides to dry in the sun, and rendering of the fat into tallow by melting it in kettles, after which it was poured for storage into bags called *botas,* made out of whole hides.

After the missions disintegrated there was virtually no manufacturing. Rawhide was used as a local makeshift for all sorts of purposes, but the manufacture of hides into shoes and other leather products was done in New England. Even the simple processes of making soap and candles out of the tallow were done in Chile or Peru. The missions, for their own use, had made such things as coarse woolen blankets, crude shoes, the leather parts of saddles, soap, candles, and coarse pottery. They had also developed irrigated agriculture to the point of producing a remarkable variety of grains, vegetables, and fruits, and some wine and brandy. All these skills disappeared after secularization. The diet of the rancheros and their families consisted largely of fresh or dried beef. Not even milk was widely used, and little or no butter or flour was produced. Even such ordinary articles as brooms had to be imported.

There were about 20 private rancho land grants during the Spanish regime, and about 500 during the Mexican period, of which the great majority were made after secularization and especially by Governors Alvarado, Micheltorena, and Pico. Under the liberal Mexican "colonization" provisions of 1824 and 1828, the maximum legal limit for a private rancho grant in California was 11 square leagues—about 50,000 acres, or 76 square miles. Not even this generous limit was always applied, because in many cases several different grants were made to the same individuals.

In a ranching country where a dozen acres of grassland might be required to pasture a single cow through the long dry summer season, such vast grants were not regarded as too large, and minor discrepancies in boundary measurements were of no importance. The boundaries were laid out without the aid of surveying instruments, and the methods of measuring distance ranged between pure guesswork and paying out lengths of a lasso from the back of a horse. As corners of the grant, the *diseño* or map might show markers no more permanent than a pile of stones, a steer's skull tossed on a bush, a notched tree trunk, or a clump of cactus. The whole process was accomplished with an easy informality which was very convenient at the time but which would later contribute to the maddening and almost endless confusion of efforts to establish land titles in American courts.

Except for a few grants in the Central Valley, held mainly by naturalized foreigners, the ranchos were located where the missions had been, in a narrow strip along the coast. Cattle were driven on the hoof to the *matanzas,* or slaughterings, as near as possible to the coastal points where the hides and tallow were stored to await the foreign trading ships. Other than the horse and the mule, the only form of land transportation was the lumbering, springless, spine-jarring *carreta,* an oxcart with wheels sliced from a big log. Excellent horses, however, were so numerous that they were allowed to run and graze freely, dragging lassos for easy catching. Walking was a lost art. It was much easier to catch a passing horse, ride it where one wished to go, and turn it loose again. To Richard Henry Dana, all Californians in the 1830s seemed to be centaurs; and John Bidwell, in 1846, heard a local proverb to the effect that no Californian with a claim to any trace of Spanish blood would do any work that he could not do on horseback.

The plentitude of cheap Indian labor also contributed to the ranchero's reluctance to work. Californians, wrote Sir George Simpson of the Hudson's Bay Company in 1841, seemed to have been drawn "from the most indolent variety of an indolent species," and the people of Monterey were "a community of loungers." A recurring phrase in conversation was "*poco tiempo,*" or "too little time," meaning that there was not time enough today to do anything that could be done tomorrow.

In the pursuit of pleasure the Californians showed remarkable vigor. Parties often consisted of three days of dancing and drinking in which the hosts' energies invariably exceeded those of their foreign guests. There was prodigal hospitality in the entertainment of strangers, perhaps as an excuse for procrastination of more serious matters. Singing and dancing were passions with Californians of all ages. Favorite dances were the *jota,* the *borrego,* the *fandango,* the *jarabe,* the *bamba,* and the somewhat more dignified *contradanza.* The *bamba* required a señorita to perform its lively and intricate steps with a full glass of water on her head. In one of the easier variations, while constantly tapping the floor with her feet she had to step into a silken hobble, raise it to her knees, lower it again, and give two or three whirls, all without spilling the water and all to the accompaniment of swift strumming of the guitar and many shouted comments intended to distract her.

Apart from weddings, which also occasioned three-day celebrations, the chief social event was the annual *rodeo* or roundup. Since there were no fences, the cattle that roamed over the thousand hills of several neighboring ranchos had to be annually segregated, and the calves branded. Then the families of the district would gather for days and nights of fiesta, with much dancing, brilliant displays of horsemanship, cockfighting, gambling, and sometimes bull and bear baiting.

The absence of education was almost incredible. Only two of the Spanish governors, Borica and Solá, and only one Mexican governor, Figueroa, made any genuine efforts to establish schools, and the results were pitifully short-lived and ineffective. With few exceptions, the missionaries had opposed the teaching of reading either to Indians or to others because it might increase unruliness and discontent. Occasionally the padres had held ceremonial burnings of "prohibited books." Now and then, for a few days or weeks, a retired soldier with almost no knowledge, and with no idea whatever of how to impart what little he had, would be given a pittance to try to operate a "school" at Monterey or at one of the other towns. Instruction was administered alternately with a cat-o'-nine-tails and a catechism. Vallejo, one of the few literate Californians, recalled with bitterness how one of these incompetent schoolmasters had nearly succeeded in destroying his boyhood interest in learning. In their adolescent years Vallejo and Alvarado had the good fortune to be protégés of Governor Solá, who taught them from books in his personal library. For about a year William E. P. Hartnell conducted a boy's school near Monterey under the patronage of Governor Figueroa, but it had to be closed soon after Figueroa's death for lack of funds and pupils. These few efforts, except for the teaching of manual arts and church music to the Indians in the missions, represented very nearly the entire history of formal education in California as a Spanish colony and a Mexican province.

California's population in 1845, other than the full-blooded native Indians, was only about 7,000. Of these, less than 1,000 were adult males. The number of native Californians who were literate, even by the loosest definition, was probably no more than 100. Many of the largest landholders could not write their own names.

Perhaps no period of history has ever been more extremely romanticized than have "the halcyon days of the dons" in California. The colorfulness of those days was sadly superficial, even for the landed ruling class, in spite of their gay costumes and their desperate attempts to live the good life.

SELECTED BIBLIOGRAPHY

Henry L. Oak's third and fourth volumes of "Bancroft's" *History of California* are indispensable for this period. Woodrow James Hansen, *The Search for Authority in California* (1960), is a valuable analysis of political and social problems from about 1820 to 1849. Gerald J. Geary, *The Secularization of the California Missions* (1934), is useful and enlightening even though consistently biased. See also Manuel P. Servín, "The Secularization of the California Missions; a Reappraisal," *Southern California Quarterly*, XLVII (June 1965), 133–150; and C. Alan Hutchinson, "The Mexican Government and the Mission Indians of Upper California, 1821–1835," *The Americas*, XXI (1965), 335–362.

Susanna Bryant Dakin, *A Scotch Paisano: Hugo Reid's Life in California, 1832–1853* (1939), and her volume on *The Lives of William Hartnell* (1949), add notably to the story of secularization and landholding. Other biographical treatments are Madie Brown Emparan, *The Vallejos of California* (1968); George Tays, "Mariano Guadalupe Vallejo and Sonoma—a Biography and a History," *California Historical Society Quarterly*, XVI–XVII (1937–1938), 99–121, 216–255, 348–372, 50–73, 141–167, 219–242; and George L. Harding, *Don Agustín V. Zamorano* (1934). Robert G. Cleland, *The Cattle on a Thousand Hills* (1951), is a good picture of the ranchos, of which a fairly typical example is described in Cleland's *The Irvine Ranch of Orange County* (1952). This was revised with an epilog by Robert V. Hine (1962).

C. Alan Hutchinson, *Frontier Settlement in Mexican California: The Híjar-Padrés Colony and Its Origins, 1769–1835* (1969), is sympathetic with the colonization scheme and critical of Figueroa.

Chapter VIII

AMERICAN INFILTRATION: TRADERS, TRAPPERS, AND SETTLERS

THE COSMOPOLITANISM of modern California was notable even in the period of tenuous Mexican rule. Of the foreigners who came, the most important historically were the Americans. Very few of these, however, came with any original intention of Americanizing the province.

The Yankee traders. American interest in California began in the late 18th century when New England merchants discovered that there was a lucrative market in China for the fur of the sea otter. These animals flourished, in what were thought to be inexhaustible numbers, along the Pacific Coast from the Aleutian Islands to Lower California, and particularly along the Alta California shores. The skin of a full-grown sea otter was 5 feet long and more than 2 feet wide, with a thick, black, glossy fur, and its value when shipped to the Chinese port of Canton was about $300. The fur seal was more numerous, but less valuable. Although the Spaniards forbade foreigners to obtain furs in California, they could not prevent them from doing so, and ships from New England gained the greatest share of the trade in competition with the British and the Russians.

One such voyage produced the first impressions of California to be published in the United States. In 1803 the *Lelia Byrd,* out of Salem, entered the Bay of San Diego on the pretext of needing fresh food. Captain William Shaler and First Mate Richard Cleveland tried to make a clandestine agreement with the port commander for the acquisition of a stock of otter skins, a type of arrangement they had succeeded in making with the officials of other Spanish ports in the region. This time, however, Cleveland was thrown into jail and had to be forcibly rescued by his shipmates. The *Lelia Byrd* escaped from the harbor only after an exchange of shots with the little battery on Point Loma. Five years later Captain Shaler told his side of the story in his "Journal of a Voyage between China and the Northwest Coast . . .," published in the *American Register*. He regarded the violation of Spanish colonial trade restrictions as a kind of patriotic duty for enterprising Yankees, and his article not only advertised the possibilities of the California fur trade but also advocated American acquisition of the province. "It would be as easy to keep California in spite of the Spaniards," he wrote, "as it would be to win it from them in the first place."

By the end of the Spanish period both the sea otter and the fur seal had been almost exterminated along the coast of California. New England whalers began to pay increasingly frequent visits to the Coast, but the main American trading interest in the region now shifted to cowhides and tallow. In 1821 a decree of the Mexican revolutionary regime opened the ports of Monterey and San Diego to foreigners and the spring of 1822 saw the arrival of the *John Begg*, the first foreign ship to be openly welcomed by California port authorities. Among the passengers on this ship was William E. P. Hartnell, newly appointed resident manager at Monterey for the partnership of Hugh McCulloch and himself, California agents for the British trading firm of John Begg and Company. "Macala and Arnel," in the hispanicized form of the partners' names, secured a three-year contract to take all the hides the missions could furnish, at one dollar each.

The advantage to the British was short-lived. Within a few weeks of Hartnell's coming, William A. Gale arrived on the *Sachem* from Boston, with a cargo of notions. By bidding up the price of hides to two dollars, which was still a remarkable bargain, he seems to have persuaded some of the padres to evade their contract with the British agency. Gale became the resident agent of the Boston firm of Bryant and Sturgis, which soon had such a large share of the hide and tallow trade that for years the United States was commonly known in California as "Boston." During the Mexican period this one firm was responsible for the export of about half a million hides, or about four-fifths of the total. Hides were called "California banknotes," and were in fact the province's main form of currency.

Import duties were substantial, ranging at various times from about 25 percent to almost twice that figure. Often these duties were at least partially evaded. Customs officials were paid a commission for keeping their eyes open, but there were Yankee captains who were willing to pay them larger sums to keep their eyes closed. Sometimes the duties were assessed and paid at Monterey on only a fraction of the imported cargo, much of it having been hidden temporarily in some neighboring cove. Even if duties were fully paid, however, the profits of bringing out a shipload of New England manufactured goods and returning to Boston with a cargo of hides were as high as 300 percent.

The classic description of the hide and tallow trade was written by Richard Henry Dana, in *Two Years Before the Mast*. Though it is usually thought of as a portrayal of life at sea and as a tract intended to reform the working conditions of seamen, much of the book was devoted to Dana's observations ashore in California; for the crew, in the employ of Bryant and Sturgis, spent most of the two-year voyage in collecting hides along the California coast.

The Danas of Cambridge were one of the oldest and most distinguished families of New England. As a Harvard undergraduate, Richard Henry had suffered a temporary breakdown of his eyesight, attributed to a case of measles. At the age of 19, in 1834, he signed on as a common sailor for the long voyage to California in the hope that it would improve his health, a purpose which it seems to have accomplished remarkably well almost from the time the ship left Boston harbor.

The outward-bound cargo of "everything under the sun" was quickly disposed of at Monterey, where boatloads of eager purchasers were rowed out to the ship as if she were a floating department store. Dana's pride in his New England heritage was reinforced by what he saw of the Californians, "an idle, thriftless people" who could "make nothing for themselves." The country abounded in grapes, he wrote, "yet they buy, at a great price, bad wine made in Boston and brought round by us, and retail it among themselves at a real (12½ cents) by the small wine glass." Their cowhides, "which they value at two dollars in money, they barter for something which costs seventy-five cents in Boston; and buy shoes (as like as not made from their own hides, which have been carried twice around Cape Horn) at three and four dollars, and 'chicken-skin boots' at fifteen dollars a pair."

Loading the hides was a strenuous operation. Except for San Diego, none of the chief depositories of hides along the coast had an adequate harbor, and the ship had to be anchored as much as 3 miles offshore. A hide would spoil if it got wet, and each one, stiff and heavy and as broad as the arms could reach, had to be tossed up and balanced on the sailor's head so that he could wade through the surf and put it into a swaying small boat.

The hide and tallow trade was significant not only in the economic history of New England and of early California, but also because it increased the interest of Americans in a distant region with which for many years it formed almost their only contact. *Two Years Before the Mast*, published in 1840, brought Americans the same message that Captain Shaler's journal had carried more than three decades earlier, but Dana's message was more substantial and convincing. "In the hands of an enterprising people," he wrote, "what a country this might be!"

The beaver trappers. Just as American seagoing commerce with California had begun in the quest for the skin of the sea otter, so the history of overland contact had its beginnings in the search for beaver pelts. The trapper was the spearhead of the American landward advance, particularly in the Far West; and the first American overland expedition to California was conducted in 1826 by a young beaver hunter named Jedediah Strong Smith. It was he who deserved the title of "the Pathfinder," a title bestowed in later years upon a more publicized and less authentic hero, John C. Frémont.

The Smiths, and Jedediah's mother's family, the Strongs, were of old New England stock, but his father chose to move westward, and Jedediah was born in southern New York and grew up in Ohio and Illinois. In 1826, in partnership with David Jackson and William Sublette, Smith purchased the Rocky Mountain Fur Company from William Ashley of St. Louis, and set out with 17 men to traverse the unexplored desert region between the Great Salt Lake and California. His objectives were the opening of a virgin beaver country and the establishment of a place of deposit on the Pacific for the furs of this new empire. He was driven also by his own adventurous curiosity.

Traveling by way of the Sevier, Virgin, and Colorado Rivers and then across the Mojave Desert and the San Bernardino Mountains, Smith and his men reached San Gabriel Mission on November 27, 1826. San Gabriel was then at the height of its temporal prosperity, and from Father José Bernardo Sánchez, the jovial successor of the gloomy Zalvidea, the Americans received a full measure of hospitality which they remained to enjoy for several weeks.

In the words of his biographer Dale L. Morgan, Jedediah Smith was "an unlikely sort of hero for the brawling West of his time, that West about which it has been said that God took care to stay on his own side of the Missouri River." The "mountain men" have been portrayed in stereotype as murderous brawlers, given to drunken orgies at their periodic rendezvous. Actually, though there were many such men among them, the personalities and backgrounds of the trappers were remarkably diverse. Smith was a quiet young man who never used tobacco or profanity, partook of wine or brandy only sparingly and on formal occasions, and was deeply imbued with a Calvinist religious faith. Harrison G. Rogers, the clerk of the expedition, was a staunch Presbyterian who on New Year's Day in 1827 delivered a quite erudite "Address to the Rev. Father of San Gabriel Mission" on the early history and missionary activities of the Christian Church. Sánchez listened with impeccable politeness to this effort to correct his theology and save his soul, and for thus allowing his guests "full liberty of conscience," as well as for setting a bountiful table and being generous with all sorts of supplies, Rogers recorded the good padre as "the greatest friend I ever met with in all my Travels," and as "worthy of being called a Christian." A few months later Smith gave the entire Sierra Nevada the name of "Mount Joseph" in honor of "old Father Sanchus."

In December, Smith journeyed to San Diego in the hope of securing Governor Echeandía's permission to travel in California, but the Governor, lacking a full realization of the unlimited energies of American business enterprise, found it difficult to believe that Smith was not a spy. Echeandía seemed never to have heard of beaver hunting, and he doubted the truth of Smith's explanation that he had been forced to come to California because his supplies had run out on the Colorado. He was inclined to send Smith and his men to Mexico for trial, but he compromised and ordered them to leave California by the way they had come.

Smith chose to define "California" as being merely the coastal strip of missions and presidios. Thus he felt that he had complied with the Governor's orders when he recrossed the San Bernardino Mountains in January 1827; and instead of returning to the Colorado, he then moved northwestward across the Tehachapis into the San Joaquin Valley. This he found to be a trapper's paradise, and he had accumulated a large number of pelts by the time he reached the river known thereafter as the American. He still believed that the legendary Buenaventura River flowed, somewhere, from the Rockies westward to the Pacific. Failing to find this nonexistent gateway, he tried during the first week in May to get his party over the Sierra by way of the rugged American River canyon, but the snow was too deep and he had to turn back. On May 20, with two men and seven horses, leaving the rest of the party in a base camp on the Stanislaus with Rogers in charge, Smith set out again, apparently by way of the north fork of the Stanislaus River and Ebbetts Pass, and soon accomplished the first recorded crossing of the mighty Sierra. The journey across central Nevada and on to the Great Salt Lake was full of epic hardships, but Smith finally managed to reach his headquarters in northern Utah on July 3, although it was necessary to sacrifice their horses for food.

Within 10 days he was on his way back to California with 18 men, but his luck was worse than in the previous year. At the Colorado crossing the Mojaves attacked the party and killed 10 of its members. In September the survivors reached the camp of the first expedition in the northern San Joaquin Valley; but when Smith sought assistance at the Mission San José, about 15 miles north of the pueblo of the same name, Father Narciso Durán arrested him, and only released him to go to Monterey for another conference with Echeandía. The Governor was even more disposed than before to make Smith stand trial for illegal entry into the province, an offense of which he was at least technically guilty; but uncertainty about the consequences of such strong action led to a renewal of permission for the trappers to depart. Early in 1828 they made another search for a good passageway through the great barrier of the Sierra Nevada. Again failing to find one, they made instead the first recorded journey by land up to the northwestern coast of California into Oregon. There the Umpquas killed most of the men. With only two others Smith finally reached the Hudson's Bay Company headquarters at Fort Vancouver. Three years later he was killed by Comanches on the Santa Fé Trail.

While Smith was pioneering the routes between the Great Salt Lake and California, other adventurous American trappers and traders had been making their way from Missouri into New Mexico. The most notable of these was James Ohio Pattie, who pressed on from Santa Fé to California by way of the Gila Valley. Pattie's father, Sylvester, was a product of the Kentucky and

Missouri frontiers who had taken his son with him to the Southwest. The younger Pattie proved to be a very enterprising but intensely conceited and hotheaded boy. In the fall of 1826 he and a party of other fur hunters trapped along the Gila River to the Colorado. Moving northward, they got into a quarrel and then a bloody battle with the Mojaves. In warfare with the Indians, Pattie and his companions committed atrocities as vicious as those of the "savages" themselves, and it is probable that the reason the Mojaves attacked the 1827 expedition of Jedediah Smith, although they had been peaceful during his previous journey through their country, was that they had had dealings with the Pattie expedition in the meantime.

When Pattie returned to Santa Fé, the Governor of New Mexico confiscated all his furs because they had been gathered in Mexican territory without a license. Undaunted, he set out again along the Gila in the fall of 1827, this time in a group under the command of his father. They traveled down the Colorado all the way to the tidewater, under the mistaken impression that there was a Mexican town at the river's mouth. Running out of food, except for a little dried beaver meat, they struggled westward through Baja California to the Dominican mission of Santa Catalina, and in March 1828 they were sent to San Diego under guard. Governor Echeandía, already irritated by the unauthorized incursions of Jedediah Smith, put these new intruders in jail, where Sylvester Pattie died.

At this time an epidemic of smallpox broke out in the northern missions. Fortunately, James Ohio Pattie had brought along a supply of smallpox vaccine and he was released in order to undertake a vaccination tour. According to his own account, he immunized more than 20,000 persons, mostly Indians, as far north as Fort Ross. In payment, he was then offered a grant of land and cattle on condition that he become a Mexican national and a Roman Catholic, but he denounced this insult to his patriotism and principles and traveled to Mexico City to seek payment in money. Failing to receive it, he returned by ship to the United States.

It should be emphasized that historical knowledge of these events comes largely from *The Personal Narrative of James O. Pattie*. The editor of that remarkable volume, and also, to an unknown extent, the writer of it, was Timothy Flint, a missionary and author of many works about the West in which fact and fiction were seldom clearly distinguishable, and time sequences often confused. Pattie was a braggart, and it is impossible to be sure how much Flint's embellishments may have added to Pattie's own. *The Personal Narrative,* first published in 1831, was the original "Western," the prototype of uncounted thousands of writings that have since fed the public appetite for the vicarious enjoyment of adventure and violence.

Other trappers soon improved upon the routes of Smith and Pattie. The expeditions of Ewing Young and William Wolfskill blazed trails from Taos and Santa Fé to Los Angeles. In 1833 Joseph Reddeford Walker, a fur trapper from Tennessee and Missouri, made the first westward crossing through the center of the Sierra Nevada. Walker's expedition from the Rockies to California was a branch of the operations of Capt. Benjamin Bonneville, who was on a two-year furlough from the United States Army. Ostensibly, this leave was granted so that Bonneville could engage in the fur business, but one purpose of it may have been the encouragement of explorations, of potential military value, in Mexican territory. Walker's men discovered what was later the main wagon-train route through central Nevada, along the Humboldt River, which they called more appropriately the Barren. Though their trail over "the dark and deathlike wall" of the Sierra is partly a matter of speculation, it probably lay somewhere between the headwaters of the East Walker River and those of the Tuolumne. They have often been credited with being the first white men to see the Yosemite Valley. Cold, hunger, and exhaustion dulled their appreciation of it that day in the fall of 1833, and indeed, some historians have maintained that what they really saw was Hetch Hetchy. Be that as it may, when Walker died half a century later, after a long career as an explorer and guide over the whole of the Far West, it was the discovery of Yosemite that he wanted engraved on his tombstone at Martinez. Walker went on to Monterey, wintered in the San Joaquin Valley, and in 1834 crossed the southern Sierra by way of the Kern River and Walker Pass. After moving up the Owens Valley, he retraced his route along the Humboldt.

Early settlers. The first foreigners to settle permanently in Spanish California did so by accident. In 1814 John Gilroy, a Scotch sailor on an English ship, was left at Monterey because of sickness. He married a daughter of the Ortegas, acquired a part of their lands, and lived to see a flourishing American town, bearing his name, on the site of his rancho. Like so many holders of Mexican titles, however, he would finally lose his property to American land lawyers and squatters.

The first American settler in California, or rather the first one around whose name any substantial body of fact and legend has gathered, was Joseph Chapman, sometimes called "the unwilling pirate." A member of the Bouchard expedition, he was captured at Monterey in 1818, but claimed that Bouchard had shanghaied him in Honolulu. In any case, his skills as a millwright and boatbuilder soon made him a welcome and useful resident.

The next few years saw the arrival of several remarkable Yankees who came as traders and remained to gather a great share of the profits of merchandising into their own hands, an easy achievement in view of the lackadaisical attitudes toward business matters on the part of most of the natives, as well as their ignorance of the outside world. William Goodwin Dana and Alfred Robinson at Santa Barbara and Abel Stearns at Los Angeles became the chief merchants of their communities and, partly by marriage, large landowners as well; Thomas O. Larkin became the most important merchant in Monterey.

William G. Dana arrived at Santa Barbara from Boston in 1826. Although he was a relative of the more famous Richard Henry, there was no direct reference to him in *Two Years Before the Mast,* and this has given rise to much interesting speculation. It was said that Richard refused to see William at the time of his visit to Santa Barbara. The reason, apparently, lay in the story of William's eager espousal of the Roman Catholic faith, of Mexican citizenship, and of young Josefa Carrillo of Santa Barbara, with no more regret than that the formalities of naturalization delayed the marriage for two years (by which time the bride was 16 years old). It seems probable that Richard, so much more bound to the Calvinist religion, the inherited patriotism, and the racial pride of the family, had his kinsman in mind when he wrote that certain Americans in California had "left their consciences at Cape Horn."

Don Abel Stearns was also the bearer of an old and distinguished Massachusetts family name. He went first to Mexico, and had already become naturalized when he arrived in California in 1829, hoping for a land grant. Instead, Governor Victoria suspected him of some political plot and banished him. He returned in 1831 to join in the movement that overthrew Victoria, and soon became a leading figure in the politics as well as the economy of Los Angeles. As a prosperous trader in hides and liquors he was as flagrant a smuggler as most of his competitors, yet in 1836 he was appointed *síndico* or fiscal agent of the village. Nicknamed *Cara de Caballo,* or Horseface, he was a homely man even before he acquired a scar about the mouth, left by the knife of a disgruntled customer in his store. Nevertheless, his appearance did not prevent his marriage to the beautiful Doña Maria Francisca Paula Arcadia Bandini, and with the added influence of his wife's relatives he began to acquire the estates that soon made him the largest landowner and cattleman and the wealthiest citizen of Southern California. He had no children, which was most unusual among those who married "native daughters." Don Guillermo and Doña Josefa Dana, for example, had 21.

The title of "Don," derived from the Latin *dominus,* or "lord," was applied in Mexican California to almost any man of more or less substantial means, particularly a landowner. In baptism and naturalization a foreign first name was officially changed to its Spanish equivalent, if there was one, as in the case of Don Juan Warner, for example. In polite address this might also be done unofficially, as in the case of Don Tomás Larkin, one of the few foreign residents who managed to rise to positions of wealth and importance in California without embracing Roman Catholicism, Mexican nationality, and a local lady.

Thomas Oliver Larkin, another Massachusetts Yankee, came to Monterey in 1832 at the suggestion of his half-brother, John Cooper, who was already engaged in trade there. One of Larkin's fellow passengers on the long voyage around the Horn was Mrs. Rachel Hobson Holmes, on her way to join her husband at Hilo. There she discovered that she was a widow, and a few months later Larkin proposed to her by correspondence. A civil marriage ceremony between two non-Catholic foreigners would have been questioned by the Mexican authorities, and consequently the ceremony was performed on board a ship off the Santa Barbara coast, by the ship's owner and captain, John C. Jones, United States consul at Honolulu. Mrs. Larkin was the first American woman to live in California.

Larkin opened a general store at Monterey, and for a number of reasons his business as a middleman between ranchers and traders was soon flourishing remarkably. The ranchers and their families were glad to be freed of their dependence on the uncertain arrivals of the trading ships; Larkin had, as Bancroft put it, "no inconvenient veneration for the revenue laws," and he offered a tempting charge-account system. The chief officials of the province, among others, became heavily indebted to him. He did a thriving business in redwood lumber, largely for export to the Sandwich Islands and Mexico. And in his designs for his own home, the customs house, and other buildings, he established the "Monterey style" of architecture.

All these early American immigrants had come by sea and taken up residence in the coastal strip. In addition, there were those who came overland and settled mainly in the interior; the term "pioneer" has sometimes been reserved, rather arbitrarily, for these overland settlers. Except for a number of men who came as beaver trappers and decided to stay, the first important settler in this American overland migration was "Dr." John Marsh. Still another son of Massachusetts, Marsh had graduated from Harvard with the class of 1823.

That a Harvard graduate of Marsh's generation should have committed his life to the outer fringes of the West was the result of a series of extraordinary circumstances. He first came to the frontier as a tutor of officers' children at what was later called Fort Snelling, in Minnesota. There he "read medicine" under the post surgeon, and planned to return to Harvard to enter the medical school. However, the post surgeon died shortly before Marsh had completed the planned two-year program of study, and at about the same time Marsh fell in love with a young woman of mixed French-Canadian and Sioux parentage. They had a child. Fearing that his family would never accept a grandson with Indian blood, Marsh felt that he could not return to Massachusetts. He was appointed a subagent to the Sioux, but his partiality for his wife's people and against their tribal enemies led to his discharge from this position. Unwisely, Marsh also sold guns to the Sioux in violation of Federal law. In flight from a warrant for his arrest on this charge, and deeply depressed by the death of his Indian wife, he lived for a time in Independence, Missouri, then drifted on by way of Santa Fé to Los Angeles.

When Marsh arrived in Los Angeles in 1836 he was destitute, and to earn money he secured permission to practice medicine. For credentials he offered his Harvard Bachelor of Arts diploma, correctly suspecting that he was the only person in the town who could read the Latin in which the diploma was printed. Any qualifications were better than none at all, and thus Marsh became the first American doctor to open an office in California. Because his fees were paid almost entirely in cowhides, his little adobe soon resembled a warehouse rather than an office. After a few months, in order to purchase a ranch, he sold his stock of hides for $500, and accepted Roman Catholicism and naturalization.

Marsh was now a morose, greedy, and indeed miserly man, determined to acquire wealth in compensation for his many bitter disappointments. In 1837 he bought a huge tract near the Sacramento–San Joaquin delta at the foot of Mount Diablo. The original grantee, José Noriega, had found the place too isolated and too exposed to Indian cattle thieves, but Marsh made it the first successful rancho in the great Central Valley. This he accomplished largely by taking payment in cattle for his medical services throughout the Northern California settlements. He customarily exacted a fee of 50 head.

Two years after Marsh settled in the region of the San Joaquin delta, John Sutter arrived with his ambitious designs for the Sacramento Valley. Sutter, originally Johann August Suter, was a German Swiss, and in the history of the American movement overland into California he and his New Helvetia were to play a significant role.

Sutter, like Marsh, was a fugitive from tragedy and from justice. In Switzerland he had been married only one day before the birth of his first son, and the marriage was unhappy even though it finally produced five children. Sutter always lived extravagantly, and in 1834, faced with debtor's prison after the failure of his dry-goods business, he deserted his family and absconded to America. After interludes in St. Louis and Santa Fé, he went with a trapping expedition to Oregon, and then by ship to Honolulu, Sitka, Yerba Buena, and Monterey, where he arrived in July 1839. In the meantime his powers of romantic imagination had made him "Captain" Sutter, formerly of "the Royal Swiss Guard of France." In Oregon he had heard of the Sacramento Valley, and there he now sought the wide open spaces where a man could plan things as he would like them to be.

The quarrel between Governor Alvarado and Comandante Vallejo was at its height, and Alvarado thought he saw a chance to use Sutter, and his grandiose colonization scheme, as a check upon Vallejo's power and pretensions. With the Governor's blessing, Sutter selected a tract on the Sacramento River at its junction with the American. After one year, the minimum period of legal residence, the glamorous newcomer received not only Mexican citizenship and a grant of 11 square leagues but also the status of a regional official. He was authorized "to represent in the Establishment of New Helvetia all the laws of the country, to function as political authority and dispenser of justice, in order to prevent the robberies committed by adventurers from the United States, to stop the invasion of savage Indians and the hunting and trapping by companies from the Columbia."

Beginning with beaver pelts and wild-grape brandy, Sutter went on to establish a cattle ranch and farm, using the labor of Indians and vagabond

John A. Sutter. (Courtesy of the Bancroft Library)

foreigners, and succeeding remarkably, for a time, in obtaining credit. In 1841, for example, when the Russian American Fur Company abandoned Fort Ross, Sutter's note for $30,000 secured the purchase of its implements and livestock with only $2,000 paid down. Several cannon from Ross strengthened the defenses of Sutter's own fort. That establishment would soon be a focal point for early American overland migration.

Covered wagons, 1841 to 1846. The first organized group to cross the Rockies for the purpose of settlement in California was the Bidwell-Bartleson party of 1841. The previous year, John Marsh had written a letter to some friends in the neighborhood of Independence, Missouri, praising the lands and climate of California and minimizing the difficulty of getting there. Soon after this letter was received, and while it was being avidly circulated, a trapper named Antoine Robidoux made a speech to a gathering in the same

Sutter's fort. (Courtesy of the Bancroft Library)

district. In California, said Robidoux, the illnesses so common in Missouri were unknown, while the "Spanish" authorities were "most friendly," and the people "the most hospitable on the globe." Lured by these rosy testimonials, more than 500 persons organized a Western Emigration Society and pledged to assemble near Independence in the following spring. During the winter, however, Missouri newspapers and merchants, interested in preventing an exodus of their readers and customers, circulated stories that painted a sharply different picture. One of these concerned the harsh treatment accorded to some Americans at Monterey during the "Graham affair" in 1840.

Governor Alvarado had come to regret his shortsighted use of the help of Isaac Graham and his band of American riflemen in the little revolution of 1836. They complained that the Governor was not sufficiently grateful to them. "I was insulted at every turn," Alvarado told Alfred Robinson, "by the drunken followers of Graham." It would be appropriate to call Isaac Graham a barefaced scoundrel, despite his unkempt beard; and the American ex-trappers and ex-sailors who hung around his distillery, though some of them made an honest living by cutting redwood for Larkin's lumber business, were no great credit to the country of their origin. Their alcoholic boasting led to rumors that they were plotting a Texan-style revolution. As a result in April 1840 Graham and 38 other foreigners, mostly Americans, were arrested, packed into Monterey's one-celled jail, and then sent to Mexico. Later they were set free.

In Missouri, however, the news of the episode so discouraged the members of the Western Emigration Society that only one of the original signers appeared at the appointed place in May 1841. This was John Bidwell, a young former schoolteacher, originally from Chautauqua County, New York. In addition to Bidwell, 68 new prospects appeared. John Bartleson was elected captain, solely because he insisted that otherwise he would not go. As Bidwell later put it, very generously, Bartleson "was not the best man for the position," but "he had seven or eight men with him, and we did not want the party diminished."

No one in the group had ever been West, and their only maps were ridiculously inaccurate. By good luck they fell in with a party of missionaries and trappers, bound for Oregon and guided by Thomas ("Broken Hand") Fitzpatrick, one of the best of the mountain men. When the time came to leave the Oregon Trail and strike out across the Great Basin for California, about half the emigrants prudently decided to go to Oregon with Fitzpatrick, and several others turned back toward Missouri. The rest managed to find the Humboldt River, but had to abandon their wagons. Near the Humboldt Sink, Bartleson and eight other men took the best horses, deserted the party, and rushed on ahead. They failed to find a pass and returned shamefacedly, begging a share of the little food that remained. Bidwell quietly readmitted them to the group. It did not need to be said that he and not Bartleson was now the captain. At the end of October, miraculously, they found their way over the Sierra and down to the Stanislaus, and on November 4, 1841, they arrived at Marsh's ranch.

On the first evening Marsh treated the gaunt and impoverished pioneers with hospitality, but within a day his miserliness reasserted itself; he demanded high prices for supplies, and fees for his help in getting passports. By contrast, when Bidwell visited Sutter's Fort a few weeks later he was most cordially welcomed, as nearly all newcomers were. Bidwell became Sutter's secretary, and wrote to friends in Missouri that while Marsh was "perhaps the meanest man in California," Sutter was the emigrant's benefactor and friend—as indeed he was. New Helvetia was to be the headquarters for several rescue parties sent to help stranded travelers over the Sierra. On the other hand, legend has somewhat exaggerated Sutter's generosity. The goodness of his heart was not the only consideration. He saw the early American migrants as potential assets to his colonial establishment—as workers for his increasingly varied enterprises and as ultimate buyers of some of the vast lands he had received for the asking.

In the fall of 1841 an emigrant party including William Workman, John Rowland, and Benjamin D. Wilson, traveled from Santa Fé to Los Angeles. In 1843 Lansford W. Hastings, a frontier lawyer with filibustering ambitions, led a group into California from Oregon. Several of its members, including Hastings, had the perverted desire to shoot down an Indian, and the unprovoked murders they committed in the upper Sacramento Valley stored up trouble for them and for future pioneers. In the same year Joseph B. Chiles, who had been with the Bidwell expedition, organized another Missouri group. Guided by Joseph Reddeford Walker, most of its members got through to the San Joaquin Valley by way of Walker Pass, but only after they had abandoned their wagons in Owens Valley. The Stevens party, coming from Missouri in 1844, was the first to succeed in getting wagons over the Sierra, and also the first to make use of what would later be the main route, Donner Pass, though that name was not acquired until the tragedy that was to follow two years later.

The year 1845 saw the beginning of a somewhat more substantial annual migration. Reports from Thomas O. Larkin, John Marsh, and John C. Frémont were stirring up interest in California. Lansford W. Hastings, through speechmaking and the publication of his dangerously misleading *Emigrant's Guide*, was pursuing his dream of leading hordes of Americans to the western paradise, and hoping that their gratitude would make him a new Sam Houston, president of a Pacific republic or governor of a new American state. The largest emigrant party of 1845, the Grigsby-Ide group, had more than 100 members, and the total for the year was more than 250 persons.

More than twice as many came in 1846. In a sense they were in a new category, for although their plans were made before the outbreak of war between the United States and Mexico, California was under the American flag when they reached it. The worse than worthless advice of Lansford W. Hastings was a cause of dangerous delays for many of them, and it led the Donner party into the worst disaster in the history of the California Trail.

The Donner party was organized at Springfield, Illinois. It passed through Independence on time, in May, but instead of taking the established route by way of Fort Hall, north of the Great Salt Lake, it followed "Hastings' Cutoff" to the south of it. Winter set in early. On November 2 the main party decided to rest overnight only a few miles short of the Sierra summit. That night a snowstorm blocked the pass. Most of the party was snowed in near Donner Lake until February, and many survived only by eating the flesh of the dead. Of 87 persons in the original group, 40 perished.

There was heroism as well as horror. When a rescue party arrived from Sutter's Fort, Tamsen Donner refused to leave her husband, George, who was too weak to travel. Their three daughters were saved, but George and Tamsen died.

Any one of the days the Donner party had wasted along the trail would have saved it, and thus the fault was not all Hastings'. As the tension had grown worse, days had been squandered on bitter quarreling. There was the day in early October when John Snyder hit James Reed a staggering blow on the head with his whip, and Reed responded by fatally stabbing Snyder with his hunting knife. A faction demanded that Reed be lynched, and at last a compromise banished him from the train. Yet Reed, who went on ahead, became one of the most compassionate of the rescuers.

Alfred Robinson had written to Larkin urging all possible efforts to publicize California, so that "the American population will be sufficiently large to play the Texas game." But California before the gold rush was less attractive to American settlers than either Texas or Oregon; the emigrants to California were primarily interested in trying to advance their own fortunes rather than their country's, and many were so discouraged that they drifted north to Oregon or back to "the States." Nevertheless, overland emigration would undoubtedly have made a change to American sovereignty inevitable in a few more years. It had not yet accomplished this by 1846, but other and related historical forces had been in motion.

SELECTED BIBLIOGRAPHY

Adele Ogden's *The California Sea Otter Trade* (1937) is the best treatment of its subject. Significant memoirs are William Shaler, "Journal of a Voyage from China to the Northwestern Coast of America Made in 1804," *American Register... for 1808*, pages 136–175, edited and with an introduction by Lindley Bynum (1935); and Richard Cleveland, *Narrative of Voyages and Commercial Enterprises* (1842). See also Magdalen Coughlin, "Boston Smugglers on the Coast (1797–1821): an Insight into the American Acquisition of California," *California Historical Society Quarterly*, XLVI (June 1967), 99–120. The hide and tallow trade is best described in Richard Henry Dana, *Two Years Before the Mast* (1840, with many reprintings); Alfred Robinson, *Life in California* (1846); and Doyce B. Nunis, Jr., editor, *The California Diary of Faxon Dean Atherton, 1836–1839* (1964).

Robert G. Cleland, *This Reckless Breed of Men: The Trappers and Fur Traders of the Southwest* (1952), is readable and reliable. Hiram M. Chittenden, *The American Fur Trade of the Far West* (three volumes, 1902), is an important work on the larger area. Dale L. Morgan, *Jedediah Smith and the Opening of the West* (1953), is a brilliant biography; the journal of Harrison Rogers is in Harrison C. Dale, editor, *The Ashley Smith Explorations and the Discovery of a Central Route to the Pacific, 1822–1829* (1941). *The Personal Narrative of James O. Pattie* (1831, with several editions by Timothy Flint) is described in the text of the chapter. The Walker expedition was recorded in the *The Adventures of Zenas Leonard*, edited by John C. Ewers (1959); and in *The Life and Adventures of George Nidever*, edited by William H. Ellison (1937). LeRoy R. Hafen, editor, *The Mountain Men and the Fur Trade of the Far West* (ten volumes, 1971), provides 300 biographical sketches.

On the American and other immigrants to California before 1849, both by sea and by land, an indispensable source is the *"Pioneer Register,"* an alphabetical biographical dictionary appended to volumes II-V of the Bancroft *History of California. The Larkin Papers*, edited by George P. Hammond (10 volumes, 1951–1964), also have references to a remarkable number of persons. The biography of Larkin by Reuben L. Underhill, *From Cowhides to Golden Fleece* (1939), is often misleading. *John Marsh, Pioneer* (1930) and his biographer, George D. Lyman, were both medical men with far-ranging interests. James P. Zollinger, *Sutter, the Man and His Empire* (1939); and Richard Dillon, *Fool's Gold: The Decline and Fall of Captain John Sutter of California* (1967), are good biographies. *Sutter's Own Story*, edited by Erwin G. Gudde (1936), is his story as he told it orally to Bancroft. Andrew F. Rolle, *An American in California: The Biography of William Heath Davis* (1956), traces the career of an American trader and settler in the San Francisco Bay region.

Good accounts of the overland migration are in George R. Stewart, *The*

California Trail (1962), and in Irving Stone, *Men to Match My Mountains: The Opening of the Far West, 1840–1900* (1956). Rockwell D. Hunt, *John Bidwell, Prince of California Pioneers* (1942), is useful biography. There were many memoirs, including Bidwell's *A Journey to California in 1841* (1842); Nicholas (Cheyenne) Dawson's *California in '41, Texas in '51* (1894); *Josiah Belden, 1841 California Pioneer*, edited by Doyce B. Nunis, Jr. (1962); and Edwin Bryant, *What I Saw in California: Being a Journal of a Tour by the Emigrant Route through California in the Years 1846, 1847* (1848). On the Donner tragedy, see Charles F. McGlashan, *History of the Donner Party* (1879), and George R. Stewart, *Ordeal by Hunger* (1936).

A well-balanced view of this period may be found in John A. Hawgood, "The Pattern of Yankee Infiltration in Mexican Alta California, 1821–1846," *Pacific Historical Review*, XXVII (February 1958), 27–38.

Chapter IX

THE AMERICAN CONQUEST

Overtures, diplomatic and undiplomatic. Official American efforts to acquire California had an inauspicious beginning in 1835, as an extension of President Andrew Jackson's earlier plans for the purchase of Texas. These schemes originated largely in the fertile brain of Col. Anthony Butler, an American speculator in Texas lands and an old friend of Jackson's, to whom the President had unwisely entrusted the ministry to Mexico. Butler disgraced himself and his government by letting it be known in Mexico City that he expected to purchase the republic's northern territories by buying some of its political leaders. When Butler later tried to implicate Jackson in his schemes for bribery, Old Hickory denounced him as a liar.

President Jackson was interested in California mainly because the acquisition of San Francisco Bay as a port for American commerce and whaling in the Pacific might reconcile the North to the annexation of Texas as a slave state. Early in 1837 Gen. Santa Anna came to Washington, after his release by Sam Houston, to request American mediation between Texas and Mexico. Jackson then unsuccessfully offered 3½ million dollars for Mexican recognition of a southwestern boundary of the United States extending along the Rio Grande and thence westward to the Pacific along the 38th parallel. He was unaware that this line would have left the entrance to San Francisco Bay about 12 miles south of the border. He was equally unsuccessful in urging the Texans to bring California within their own boundaries, though Sam Houston dreamed of doing so.

Martin Van Buren of New York, Jackson's chosen successor in the Presidency, privately deplored some of the more headlong tendencies of his illustrious old chief. He opposed the annexation of Texas, and any territorial expansion of slavery. Moreover, the panic of 1837 began a few weeks after his inauguration, and his single term as President was one long period of depression in which the Treasury was in no condition to provide for purchasing any new territory.

With economic recovery in the '40s, the United States began to assert its Manifest Destiny to extend its borders to the Pacific. Early in the Tyler administration, Daniel Webster as Secretary of State and Waddy Thompson as minister to Mexico warmly advocated a plan to secure California in exchange for cancellation of American financial claims against the Mexican government. Thompson wrote to Webster that California would be an even more desirable acquisition than Texas because it would not merely provide a splendid port, but in American hands would soon become "the granary of the Pacific." Although Thompson had never been in California, he described it as "the richest, the most beautiful, the healthiest country in the world."

But again, as in the Anthony Butler episode, an American blunder raised an outcry in Mexico City that made any peaceful cession of territory to the United States politically impossible. Early in September 1842, Commodore Thomas ap Catesby Jones, commander of the American Pacific squadron, received a false report at Callao, Peru, that the United States and Mexico were at war, and that Mexico intended to cede California to Great Britain rather than see it fall into American hands. Admiral Thomas and his British Pacific squadron had just left Callao, reportedly under sealed orders from England. Jones, who had received instructions in Washington a year earlier to act quickly in just such an eventuality, promptly sailed for California in what he supposed to be a race with Thomas. He anchored at Monterey on October 18, and on the next day demanded the peaceful surrender of the port and the district. This was concluded on the 20th, the American flag was raised, and Jones proclaimed California under armed but courteous and benevolent American occupation. This proclamation remained in force only one day. On the 21st, when Jones landed in person and examined the latest official communications from Mexico, he realized that he had been completely and regrettably misinformed.

Governor Micheltorena was in the South. Jones sent him a letter of explanation, offering to continue his now entirely friendly sojourn at Monterey in order to apologize in person upon the Governor's next visit there. On receiving the news of the seizure, Micheltorena had issued, for the record, a bombastic call to arms to repel the invader. With obvious relief, but well aware that the government in Mexico City would take a much more irritated view of the matter than did anyone in California, Micheltorena advised Jones to come to him at Los Angeles. There he received the commodore and his explanations with courtesy and hospitality, but sent reports to Mexico City in an entirely different tone. The Mexican government conveyed an angry protest to Washington demanding extreme punishment for Jones; but although the United States disavowed his actions, he suffered only a temporary removal from his command.

As the Jones incident clearly shows, American suspicions of the designs of Great Britain on California played a large part in American thinking, and incidentally provided a very useful rationalization of American designs. The fact was that Her Majesty's Government had no intention whatever of trying to acquire California. Sir Robert Peel, Prime Minister from 1841 to 1846, and the Earl of Aberdeen as his Foreign Secretary, were well aware that such an attempt would have involved a costly and hazardous war with the United States. The same view prevailed with regard to British-American rivalry in Texas and Oregon. But it was not until the early 20th century, when the British Foreign Office records were opened to historians, that the actual attitudes of the British government became known. In the years before the Mexican War, there were outward appearances of a designing nature, quite sufficient to provide fuel for American fears.

In 1839, for example, a London publisher brought out the first book in English entirely devoted to California. This was a *History of Upper and Lower California* written by Alexander Forbes, a British merchant at the Mexican town of Tepic. The book advocated a plan for the colonization of vast tracts of land in California, to be granted as payment to the British holders of 50 million dollars worth of Mexican government bonds. Richard Pakenham, British minister to Mexico, recommended such a scheme to Aberdeen in 1841; but the Foreign Secretary, in the secrecy of diplomatic correspondence, was emphatic in his rejection of any design that would involve either the outright acquisition of a colony or the activities of "companies of British adventurers."

A few months earlier, Sir George Simpson of the Hudson's Bay Company had visited California and admired the Bay of San Francisco. He concluded quite correctly that some native Californians were so afraid of American control that they would welcome a British protectorate. Sir George's enthusiasm for such a development was obvious, and Americans had no way of knowing that the British government did not support his views.

The French, also, had some degree of interest in California dating all the way back to the visit of the Comte de La Pérouse. In 1842 the French agent Eugène Duflot de Mofras, as well as the American explorer, Navy Lt. Charles Wilkes, reported that California was certain to pass to some power other than Mexico, and soon. French hopes were faint, based on little more than the idea that Mexico might prefer to see California in the friendly hands of a Latin and Catholic nation, rather than under Anglo-Saxon Protestants.

The weakness of Mexican control of California had been so apparent to any observer for so long that a spate of foreign designs was inevitable. One was a stillborn proposal that Prussia acquire California. Since Prussia had no merchant marine to speak of, and no navy whatever, the backers of the scheme went so far with their lively imagination as to suggest that the Danes might be willing to lend the services of some of their ships.

Plans of the Polk administration. James K. Polk of Tennessee was a political disciple of Andrew Jackson, who lived to congratulate him on his inauguration as President in March 1845. Polk, like his mentor, was always ready to believe any rumors of fell designs on the part of the British. Jackson, as a 14-year-old prisoner of war in the American Revolution, had received a saber cut on the forehead for refusing to clean a British officer's boots, and he never forgot it. Polk also shared some of the anti-British views of Senator Thomas Hart Benton of Missouri, powerful chairman of the Senate military affairs committee. Benton firmly though incorrectly believed that perfidious Albion had intended to acquire California ever since Drake claimed and named New Albion in 1579, and that she was now determined to have San Francisco Bay in order to strengthen her naval power in the Pacific.

On coming into office, President Polk confided to Secretary of the Navy George Bancroft that the acquisition of California would be one of his most cherished goals. Within the month of Polk's inauguration, Governor Micheltorena and his *cholo* troops were virtually deported from California, and this ended the last desperate effort to assert any effective control over the province from Mexico City. When the news of this development reached the East Coast in June 1845, several American newspapers pointed out the ridiculous ease with which it had been accomplished, the apparent absence of any strong government at all in California, and the danger that Great Britain would take advantage of the situation. Before 1845, American newspaper references to California had been few. Now a chorus of editorials began to call for American acquisition.

During this same period, Polk received reports from Mexico City of the startling proposal of a young Irish priest named Eugene McNamara, to bring 2,000 families, 10,000 colonists altogether, to a grant of 3,000 square leagues in California. McNamara gained the approval of the Archbishop of Mexico, and then addressed a burning appeal to the Mexican President: "Your Excellency knows too well that we are surrounded with a vile and skillful enemy, who loses no means, however low they may be, to possess himself of the best lands of that country, and who hates to the death your race and your religion." If his plan were not adopted, the young priest warned, "before another year the Californias will form a part of the American Nation. Their Catholic institutions will become the prey of the Methodist wolves; and the whole country will be inundated with these cruel invaders." The McNamara scheme was wildly impracticable, but many Americans regarded it with genuine alarm as being somehow simultaneously a British and a popish plot.

Having determined to acquire California, Polk would have preferred to purchase it. Duff Green had reported a few months earlier that all the Mexican factions were so eager to ruin their opponents and confiscate their property that the slightest appearance of willingness to sell a foot of territory to the United States would cause any administration to be disgraced and overthrown as treasonable. Although this analysis would soon prove all too accurate, Polk nevertheless sent John Slidell on a special mission to Mexico with an offer of as much as 40 million dollars for Upper California and New Mexico.

"Money," said Slidell's instructions, "would be no object when compared with the value of this acquisition." This was Polk's own view, but he was well aware that the prospects of success were dim, and therefore he put an alternative plan into operation simultaneously. This involved secret instructions to Thomas O. Larkin, consul at Monterey since the previous year, to try to persuade the Californians to secede from Mexico and seek American protection.

Larkin had been highly successful in his business pursuits in California, but he had not become a *californio*. He also took great pride in the fact that his were the first children born in California of parents who had both been born in the United States. He had been reporting to Washington every suspicion and rumor of sinister British intentions toward California, and in some instances he seems to have exaggerated his reports beyond what he himself believed, so great was his yearning for American annexation at this time. His letter of July 10, 1845, made a particularly strong impression on President Polk. In it he maintained that the appointment of a British vice consul for Upper California was extremely suspicious, and undoubtedly a cover for an appointment as a secret agent. The official in question was James Alexander Forbes (not Alexander, author of the *History of . . . California*). Actually, James Forbes told Larkin that although British diplomatic and consular officials had suggested some kind of British political involvement in California, their government had flatly forbidden them to engage in anything of the sort. Other letters by Larkin indicate no real doubt that Forbes was telling him the truth, as we now know that Forbes was.

Consul Larkin, however, was soon commissioned to do what it was convenient to assert that Vice Consul Forbes might be doing. On October 17, 1845, a secret dispatch signed by James Buchanan, the Secretary of State, appointed Larkin "confidential agent in California." He was instructed to warn the Californians against any attempt to bring them under the jurisdiction of "Foreign Governments." Further, he was to "arouse in their bosoms that love of liberty and independence so natural to the American Continent." In the disputes between Mexico and California, Buchanan wrote to Larkin, "we can take no part," unless Mexico "should commence hostilities against the United States; but should California assert and maintain her independence, we shall render her all the kind offices in our power as a Sister Republic." Still further, "Whilst the President will make no effort and use no influence to induce California to become one of the free and independent States of this Union, yet if the People should desire to unite their destiny with ours, they would be received as brethren, whenever this can be done, without affording Mexico just cause of complaint."

The plan had real possibilities. Larkin was on friendly terms with officials at Monterey, whom he had supplied for years with most of their provisions and merchandise. The government had reached a state of truly insufferable confusion, and almost everyone admitted the need for some decisive change. Since the departure of Micheltorena, the capital and the assembly had been at Los Angeles under Don Pío Pico as Governor, while the customs and the treasury remained at Monterey, with Col. José Castro as military commander. Mariano Guadalupe Vallejo was frankly reconciled to American annexation because he considered it both inevitable and preferable to the alternatives. Colonel Castro, though he bristled at any suggestion of American military force, was confidentially circulating a plan for "declaring California independent in 1847–1848, as soon as a sufficient number of foreigners should arrive." Larkin also enlisted the cooperation of Jacob P. Leese, of Sonoma; Don Abel Stearns, of Los Angeles; and J. J. Warner, near San Diego; and all three became not only active in the scheme but also convinced that it would work.

The promising Polk-Larkin plan for winning the province by peaceful conciliation of the *paisanos* was impeded by resentment of the blustering actions of Capt. John C. Frémont in California in March 1846. A few weeks later the scheme was entirely nullified by the Bear Flag Revolt—in which Frémont also had a part—and by the outbreak of the Mexican War.

John Charles Frémont. Frémont was one of the most controversial figures not only in the history of California but in the history of the United States. His mother, the young wife of a wealthy and elderly citizen of Richmond, had run away with a young French *émigré*. In Virginia a divorce could only be obtained from the state legislature, which refused to pass the necessary act. Frémont's parents lived together as man and wife until the death of the father, which ocurred when John Charles was five years old. The circumstances of his birth seem to have given him, as in the analogous case of Alexander Hamilton, a feeling of extraordinary need to establish his place in the world. He was like the young Hamilton, too, in that he was a precocious lad, and in the fact that his promising qualities attracted the sympathy of influential men who helped him to gain an education. But there was also a side of Frémont's personality that made him impulsive, unstable, and erratic throughout his life. He was ever the impatient opportunist and adventurer, and there was hardly a single action of his whole sensational career that did not produce some troublesome set of complications, and interminable disagreement among biographers and historians about his motives and conduct.

As a lieutenant in the Corps of Topographical Engineers, Frémont met

John Charles Frémont. (Courtesy of the Bancroft Library)

Senator Thomas Hart Benton, who inspired the younger man with his own fiery enthusiasm for the vast possibilities of westward exploration and expansion, and with his dream of extending American territory to the Pacific. At Benton's home Frémont met the Senator's daughter Jessie, an extraordinary girl of 16 whose great intellectual gifts had been developed by her father's intensive and devoted tutoring. Frémont's first opportunity to court Jessie came when he invited the Bentons to view the funeral procession of President William Henry Harrison from rooms which he had borrowed, overlooking the procession's route. They were secretly married a few months later, and after stormy protests Benton was reconciled to the marriage. Frémont gained a brilliant and beautiful wife and a brilliant and influential father-in-law, and both became his invaluable though highly possessive allies.

Frémont then led a series of Western exploring and scientific expeditions, authorized by Congress at the prompting of Senator Benton. The first of these followed the Oregon Trail as far as South Pass in the Rockies. The final report of this expedition—combining Frémont's own genius for publicity with his wife's sparkling literary style, and also borrowing something of the flavor of Washington Irving's *Adventures of Captain Bonneville*—was widely circulated throughout the country, and established Frémont as a national hero.

His second expedition, in 1843 and 1844, proceeded to Oregon, then south along the eastern side of the Cascades and the Sierra Nevada, and across the Sierra into California by way of Carson Pass in the dead of winter. After a month's rest at Sutter's Fort, Frémont and his men traveled southward through the San Joaquin Valley and over Tehachapi Pass, then eastward by way of the Old Spanish Trail and Utah. The expedition's return was hailed with rejoicing since it had been gone so long it was presumed lost. There was a temporary flurry over Frémont's setting out with a howitzer, which the War Department had specifically ordered him not to take on the grounds that the expedition was supposed to be scientific and not military. It had to be explained that Mrs. Frémont had intercepted this dispatch and had taken it upon herself to suppress it, but her father defended this action successfully in the Senate.

With the second expedition already well publicized, the Frémonts' collaborative prose soon described it in even more fascinating terms than the first. Understandably the report was another bestseller, and became the most widely read description of the Far West.

In Washington, D.C., in the spring of 1845, Frémont became convinced that war with Mexico was imminent, that his third expedition should be prepared for military rather than merely scientific activities, and that with it he should play an important role in conquering California. In this idea he received some private encouragement from Senator Benton and from Secretary of the Navy Bancroft. The Senator, however, had no executive authority, nor was the Secretary of the Navy Frémont's official superior.

There is no evidence that Frémont received authorization for military operations in Mexican territory either from President Polk or from the War Department. Nevertheless he recruited 60 armed men, all expert marksmen, and arrived in California in December 1845. Early in 1846 he appeared at Monterey. He had come, he said, merely to survey a route to the Pacific, and his men were not soldiers. They would remain "on the frontier," away from the coast, and he was in Monterey merely to procure supplies so that he might continue on his way to Oregon. In February, however, his 60 armed men arrived from the interior and encamped a few miles east of Monterey itself. Colonel Castro then peremptorily ordered Frémont and his armed force out of California. In angry and headstrong defiance, Frémont entrenched his men on Hawk's Peak (now Frémont Peak) in the Gabilán Mountains overlooking the Salinas Valley, and raised the American flag. Castro called for volunteers, and raised a force of about two hundred. Larkin mediated, and Frémont, after three days on his mountaintop, retreated to the Sacramento Valley. Obviously playing for time, he moved slowly northward—"slowly and growlingly," as he put it in a letter to his wife.

On May 9, 1846, he was overtaken near Klamath Lake in southern Oregon by Lt. Archibald H. Gillespie of the Marine Corps, who had come to California disguised as a merchant traveling for his health, under instructions from Polk and Buchanan to cooperate as a secret agent with Larkin in the plan of peaceful persuasion. Gillespie, like Frémont, was a rash and high-spirited young man.

Arriving in California in April, he had heard reports that war with Mexico was imminent, and these reports he brought to Frémont along with a packet of letters from Senator Benton. The two young officers seem to have convinced each other that the plan for peaceful conciliation was now out of date, that British intervention was to be feared, that bold initiative was called for, and that Frémont's force should return to California prepared for military action.

Whether Gillespie brought Frémont any secret official authorization to proceed in this way has been hotly debated. There is no reliable documentary evidence for this claim. Frémont probably acted, as he had already acted several weeks earlier at Hawk's Peak, on his own imagination of what the interests of the United States required him to do under particular circumstances, and on his own guess at what orders he might have received from the War Department if it had been able to communicate with him at the time. Thus his own ambitions and impulses had free rein.

One event that illustrates Frémont's character occurred on the night after his talks with Gillespie; in his excitement Frémont forgot to post sentries, and more surprisingly, his guide, Kit Carson, failed to notice this oversight. A band of Klamath Indians attacked the camp and killed three men. Before the return to California there was a brief delay while Frémont and his party wiped out the adult male inhabitants of the nearest Indian village and destroyed its accumulated food supply. In encounters between whites and Indians, there were those on both sides who followed the dismal practice of taking revenge upon the innocent when the guilty were not readily available.

The Bear Flag Revolt. In the meantime, a fantastic crop of frightening rumors had circulated among the American immigrants recently settled in the Sacramento and Napa Valleys. Frémont and his men had spread some of these rumors on their way northward. In particular, it was falsely reported that Colonel Castro would soon follow up his order expelling Frémont with an order for the forcible expulsion of all the American settlers. Color was given to this rumor when, after Frémont's return from Oregon to the Sacramento Valley, Castro again raised a militia force with headquarters at Santa Clara and sent two lieutenants to the region of Sonoma to gather supplies and horses for his troops.

The origins of the Bear Flag Revolt were confused, and the evidence, especially on Frémont's part in it, is often contradictory. The American settlers in the area were a miscellaneous group of people in a very insecure situation. Nearly all of them were rough frontiersmen. Some were roving hunters and trappers, or runaway sailors. Most were squatters who could acquire no title to the lands they occupied unless they became Mexican citizens and Roman Catholics. Most of them probably believed the rumors that they would soon be attacked and driven out of California. Emboldened by the return of Frémont, on June 10 a group under the rough and ready Ezekiel Merritt began the revolt by seizing the herd of horses intended for Castro's militia. Some further and more formal action was needed, lest the rebels remain merely horsethieves. Thus on the morning of Sunday, June 14, a party of more than 30 armed settlers descended upon the village of Sonoma.

There were no longer any soldiers at this former military post, and Col. Mariano Guadalupe Vallejo was no longer on active duty, but the filibusters surrounded his home and informed him that he was a prisoner of war. He invited the leaders in to explain what war he was a prisoner of, and when this proved a difficult question he brought out bottles of *aguardiente* to aid in the discussion. Ezekiel Merritt, William Knight, and Robert Semple had entered first. The rest waited outside for several hours, then elected John Grigsby to go in and investigate. After another interval, they sent in William B. Ide, who, according to his own account, found the previous commissioners befuddled by Vallejo's brandy. Ide, a teetotaler, finally arranged the terms of capitulation, with Jacob P. Leese, Vallejo's brother-in-law, acting as translator.

Colonel Vallejo was probably the most widely respected citizen of California. He had no objection to being arrested because as an advocate of American annexation he was thus relieved of his embarrassing trust as a Mexican officer. The sensible course would now have been to parole him, and he was given some assurance that this would be done, but instead he was taken under arrest to Sutter's Fort. Frémont, who now placed the fort virtually under his own command, committed the foolish outrage of ordering Vallejo into a cell where he was imprisoned for two months. Frémont, feeling that Castro had humiliated him, now acted as if it were Castro and not Vallejo who was his prisoner. He sternly reprimanded Sutter for trying to make Vallejo's bare cell more comfortable.

At Sonoma, Ide and his associates declared themselves a republic and devised a flag. It was a piece of white cotton cloth, with a star and a stripe. In the upper left-hand corner a large lone star, obviously suggesting an analogy with the history of Texas, was painted in red. To the right of the star, and facing it, was what was intended as a grizzly bear, passant. Under these emblems, CALIFORNIA REPUBLIC was lettered in black ink. A broad stripe of red flannel, made from an article of used clothing variously recalled as either a petticoat or a man's shirt, was sewn along the bottom of the cotton. This was the original of the banner which the California Legislature adopted in 1911 as the state flag, and which since then must be flown over all state buildings.

Ide had once been a Yankee schoolteacher, and he loved the traditions of the embattled farmers at Lexington and Concord. He wrote a flowery and somewhat eccentric proclamation, solemnly though not deliberately misrepresenting most of the circumstances. He remained under the impression that he had "conquered California."

In later years Ide and Frémont made rival claims, both considerably exaggerated, for credit in the matter of the Bear Flag Revolt. Frémont's connection with the beginning of it was highly equivocal and opportunistic. He helped to foment the rebellion by encouraging the American settlers to goad the *californios* into attacking them so that he and his men could come to their defense.

Castro sent about 50 men northward across the bay, under Joaquín de la Torre, to try to retake Sonoma. On June 24, there was a skirmish north of San Rafael, later magnified into the "Battle of Olompali." In the entire "Bear Flag War," two Americans and five or six *californios* were killed. Torre's men soon evacuated the area north of the bay.

Frémont, having now assumed command of the Bear Flaggers and informally merged his force with theirs, crossed from the Marin peninsula on July 1. Entering the long-ungarrisoned little ruin of the San Francisco presidio, he spiked its 10 old Spanish guns. This was a typically Frémontian act—dashing in appearance but superfluous in reality. Those venerable cannon had been cast in Lima about 1625. They had never been fired in anger, and for at least 40 years they had been incapable of firing so much as a salute.

In a more notable and enduring achievement, also described in his *Memoirs,* Frémont gave the entrance to the bay "the name of Chrysopylae, or Golden Gate, for the same reasons that the harbor of Constantinople was called Chryoceros, or Golden Horn."

Frémont joined a Fourth of July celebration at Sonoma, and the next day he more or less formally organized the "California battalion" of American volunteers, with himself in command and Lieutenant Gillespie as adjutant. On the 7th, however, Commodore Sloat raised the American flag at Monterey. It was raised at Yerba Buena and Sonoma on the 9th, and replaced the Bear Flag at Sutter's Fort on the 11th. The life of the Bear Flag "republic," a rather romantic and later fantastically romanticized period of a little less than a month, was thus ended. The revolt would probably have made a war between the United States and Mexico inevitable if that war had not already broken out on the disputed southern border of Texas.

By instigating the filibustering activities known as the Bear Flag Revolt, and by participating in them, Frémont actually accomplished only two things. One was an unnecessary embitterment of feelings between Americans and *californios,* in violation of the United States government's policy and best interests. The other was an enhancement of his own somewhat spurious popular reputation as a patriot and hero.

The Mexican War and California. The causes of the Mexican War were complex and are still disputed. Only a brief sketch of its general background is necessary here. In the 10 years since the establishment of the Republic of Texas in 1836, Mexico had never recognized it as independent. In February 1845 the American Congress passed a joint resolution inviting Texas to join

THE AMERICAN CONQUEST

1846-1847

the American Union, and President Tyler signed the resolution on March 1, three days before the inauguration of Polk. Mexico regarded the prospective American annexation of Texas as a hostile act, and broke off diplomatic relations with the United States, threatening war but not declaring it. President Herrera prudently feared that a war would not only fail to regain Texas but would lose California and New Mexico as well. He hinted that he would receive an American minister. After Slidell had reached Mexico City, Herrera changed his mind, but the report that he had even considered receiving an American negotiator led to his overthrow by General Paredes.

Mexico was particularly bitter at the claim of Texas that its southern boundary was the Rio Grande, rather than the Nueces River, some distance to the north. On April 7, 1846, President Polk learned of Mexico's refusal to receive Slidell. The next day Gen. Zachary Taylor was ordered to cross the Nueces and occupy the disputed zone. Soon several Americans were killed in skirmishes with Mexican troops. With this news in hand, Polk asked Congress to declare that a state of war existed by hostile action of Mexico. Congress did so, and Polk signed the declaration on May 13, 1846.

Several months earlier, Secretary of the Navy Bancroft had instructed

Commodore John D. Sloat of the Pacific squadron that in the event of war with Mexico he was to occupy such ports in California as he considered necessary for the establishment of American authority in the province. He was also to make every effort to establish friendly relations with the people and to avoid hostilities with them. In June, at Mazatlán, Sloat received definite but still unofficial reports that the United States and Mexico were at war. On July 2 he anchored at Monterey, but hesitated lest he repeat the embarrassing mistake of Commodore Jones. He offered to fire a salute to the Mexican flag, an honor which the port authorities declined because they lacked the powder to return it. As Lieutenant Wilkes had reported in 1841, the presidio at Monterey had been demolished; there were three guns, no two of them of the same caliber; and the California navy consisted of one small vessel with no guns, so unskillfully manned that she could not make headway against the wind.

Larkin advised caution, but when Sloat learned of the operations of Frémont and the Bear Flaggers he feared that complications might develop, especially if the British squadron should arrive before the American flag had been raised. After five days' delay, Sloat made up for his hesitancy by issuing on the 7th a proclamation which went so far as to declare that "henceforward California will be a portion of the United States." Although he came "in arms with a powerful force," it was not as an enemy to the people of California but "as their best friend." He painted a glowing picture of the benefits that would follow, including greater political freedom and stability, honest and efficient administration, and "a great increase in the value of real estate." With "the great interest and kind feelings I know the government and people of the United States possess toward the citizens of California, the country cannot but improve more rapidly than any other on the continent of America."

On July 23, Sloat, who had been in ill health for some time, turned over his command to Commodore Robert F. Stockton, and the tone of the occupation changed sharply. Stockton, like Frémont and Gillespie, was eager to distinguish himself by vigorous action. Like Frémont, Stockton had strong political ambitions, though these feelings had a somewhat different background. His grandfather, Richard Stockton, had been a signer of the Declaration of Independence, and his father had been a United States Senator. The commodore himself had been offered the secretaryship of the Navy under Tyler. In the 1850s he would be a Senator from New Jersey and would seek the presidential nomination of the superpatriotic and anti-Catholic American or Know-Nothing party.

As one of his first acts after assuming command, Stockton mustered the "California Battalion of Mounted Riflemen" into United States service (apparently the naval service, though this has never really been clear), commissioning Frémont as major and Gillespie as captain. Stockton then issued a new, bombastic, and offensive proclamation to the people, drawn up with the advice of Frémont and Gillespie. Colonel Castro at Santa Clara and Governor Pío Pico at Los Angeles announced that resistance was hopeless, and both satisfied their honor by leaving for Mexico. In August Los Angeles was occupied without resistance. Stockton was now able to announce that California was "entirely free from Mexican dominion," but he irritated the Angeleños by unwisely and unnecessarily ordering martial law, and then made the further mistake of leaving Gillespie in charge with a small garrison.

The inhabitants of Los Angeles were not accustomed to any very strict maintenance of order, and Gillespie's rules were oppressive and arbitrary. The order for a curfew, for example, was highly unrealistic. When some of the more disorderly elements behaved with their customary exuberance, Gillespie began to treat them as rebels before they had actually thought of rebellion. They soon thought of it, and Capt. José María Flores and several other officers broke their paroles to lead a revolt that spread rapidly throughout Southern California.

On September 24 Gillespie was besieged on Fort Hill near the Los Angeles plaza, but his courier Juan Flaco (Lean John) Brown managed to get through, and rode 500 miles in five days to inform Stockton at San Francisco. On the 27th the rebels captured Benito Wilson and a group of other Americans at the Chino Rancho of Isaac Williams, about 25 miles east of Los Angeles. Soon afterward Gillespie surrendered under terms that permitted him to march his men to San Pedro for embarkation. At San Pedro, however, they met a relief force of marines and sailors who had arrived from San Francisco, and who now joined them for a march back toward Los Angeles. The march was hot and dusty and by foot since the rebels had rounded up all the horses in the region.

About 15 miles inland, at Domínguez Rancho on October 8, the Americans encountered a force led by José Antonio Carrillo, well mounted, and equipped with a surprisingly effective cannon. This had long been used to fire salutes at the Los Angeles plaza on festive occasions. Before the town's surrender to Stockton it had been buried in the garden of Señora Inocencia Reyes. Dug up and lashed to the running gear of a wagon, fired with homemade powder and a cigarette, and moved rapidly about by skilled horsemen, it proved a deadly weapon, and the "Battle of the Old Woman's Gun" was a brilliant little victory for the *californios*. The Americans, trying to pursue this mobile artillery on foot, suffered a number of casualties and withdrew to San Pedro.

Los Angeles remained in rebel hands for three months more, while Stockton went to San Diego for horses and supplies and Frémont moved down from the north with the California Battalion, suppressing minor branches of the insurrection on the way. At this same time Gen. Stephen W. Kearny was crossing the desert from New Mexico.

In June, at Fort Leavenworth, General Kearny had received instructions from Secretary of War William L. Marcy to occupy New Mexico and then proceed to California to organize a military and civil government there. Kearny occupied Santa Fé without resistance, and set out for California with 300 dragoons. On the way, unfortunately, he met Kit Carson, whom Stockton had sent eastward in August with the premature news that California was peacefully and firmly in American hands. Kearny sent most of his force back to Santa Fé, and continued with only about a hundred men. When they reached Southern California they had come 2,000 miles in one of the longest and most difficult marches in American Army history. They were exhausted and half-starved, and most of their mounts had been worn out and replaced with mules or unbroken horses.

Several hours before dawn on December 6, Kearny was encamped near the Indian village of San Pascual, about 35 miles north-northeast of San Diego, when he learned that a rebel detachment was in the village. Kit Carson assured him that the Californians were cowards who would not and could not fight; and hoping to capture their horses, Kearny roused his men for an immediate advance in the darkness, cold, and fog. The wretched mounts of the dragoons moved with widely varying speeds, and the rebels, under Andrés Pico, lured them into a pursuit until they were widely strung out, then suddenly turned to attack them.

The American cavalry sabers were hopelessly ineffective against the Californian lances, wielded by men whom Kearny well described as "admirably mounted and the very best riders in the world; hardly one that is not fit for the circus." Practically all the casualties were on the American side—22 killed, including several officers, and 16 wounded, including Kearny himself. After 10 minutes of fighting, Don Andrés's men withdrew. On the basis of remaining in possession of the battlefield, Kearny reported the battle of San Pascual as a victory, and Army historians later certified it as "not . . . a defeat," but this verdict is open to question, to say the least. Kearny was in a desperate predicament, but Kit Carson and Lt. Edward F. Beale managed to get through to San Diego. Stockton sent out a relief force, and with its help Kearny reached San Diego on December 12.

The rebel cause was weakened by the usual chronic dissensions, by a shortage of powder, and by the gradual abandonment of the hopes of Flores and others that they could hold out until Mexico should be victorious over the United States in the main theaters of war. A joint force under Stockton and Kearny recaptured Los Angeles on January 10, 1847, after minor skirmishes. Flores now fled to Sonora, and Andrés Pico chose to surrender the rebel forces to Frémont, who had reached the San Fernando Valley from the north. Andrés Pico had heard of the clemency Frémont had recently shown to Jesús Pico, another of the officers who had broken parole by joining the rebellion, and whom Frémont had captured at San Luis Obispo. Military law would have permitted his execution by a firing squad, but the tearful pleas of the wife and the 14 children of Jesús Pico led Frémont to spare his life. Frémont was flattered at being the officer who now received the final surrender, and by the terms of the Capitulation of Cahuenga on January 13, 1847, he extended full pardon to all the rebels.

The *californios* had acquitted themselves with honor. Kearny later reported to the adjutant general that they rebelled because they had been "most cruelly and shamefully abused by our people. Had they not resisted they would have been unworthy the name of men."

The surrender at Cahuenga ended organized resistance to the American occupation. It also marked the beginning of a series of bitter disputes between Kearny and Stockton, and between Kearny and Frémont, over the question of who was now in command and who was authorized to act as military and civil governor. Stockton's instructions from the Navy Department on this point were vague, while Kearny's instructions from the War Department were quite explicit. Nevertheless, Stockton still considered himself in charge. Before sailing for further operations on the west coast of Mexico, he appointed Frémont his successor as governor of California. Kearney refused to recognize this appointment, and regarded Frémont, who had recently been promoted to lieutenant colonel, as under his own command. Frémont was able to persuade himself that authority he had received from a commodore in the Navy should prevail over the orders of a brigadier general in the Army who was now his own immediate superior. On this basis Frémont rashly assumed the powers of governor, and repeatedly defied military orders from General Kearny. Further orders from Washington clearly sustained Kearny's side of the argument.

The question that now arose, as seen by Kearny and by nearly all the officers under his command except Frémont, was that of the effect on the discipline and morale of the Army if mutiny were to be condoned because the mutinous officer was a son-in-law of the chairman of the Senate Committee on Military Affairs. The feeling among most of Frémont's brother officers was such that if Kearny had ordered a court-martial in California, Frémont might have been shot. Instead the court-martial of Frémont was conducted in the National Capital. During the proceedings Frémont, and Benton as his counsel, did everything they could to impugn Kearny's integrity and destroy his reputation. Nevertheless, in January 1848 Frémont was found guilty of disobedience of orders and sentenced to dismissal from the service. President Polk approved the verdict but remitted the penalty. Bitterly, Frémont refused this executive clemency and resigned his commission. Popular opinion generally supported Frémont. In the eyes of the American people in the 1840s, insubordination was not a very serious offense.

Jessie Benton Frémont was of the opinion that "Our house—our library and my father's committee room—were the real war department." She seems to have done much to encourage her husband in this same view, and in other highly questionable opinions as well. One of these was that he was not sufficiently aggressive. In later years Frémont was one of the first two Senators from California, temporarily a millionaire from the mineral proceeds of his Mariposa land grant, the first candidate of the Republican party for the presidency in 1856, and temporarily a major general in the Civil War. None of this satisfied his wife. She once told one of his aides: "Oh, if my husband had only been more positive! But he never did assert himself enough. That was his great fault." She seems to have felt that if Frémont had only been as vigorous as she was, he and she would have been President of the United States and Commander-in-Chief of the Army and Navy.

Jessie Frémont's aggressive impulses arose in part from being a woman in a society that offered gifted women very limited scope. Throughout the early American period, California attracted the most adventurous and reckless Americans, with the male sex overwhelmingly predominant, both numerically and otherwise.

SELECTED BIBLIOGRAPHY

American projects for peaceful acquisition are described by Robert Glass Cleland, in "The Early Sentiment for the Annexation of California," *Southwestern Historical Quarterly*, XVIII (1914–1915), 1–40, 121–161, 231–260; George P. Hammond, editor, *The Larkin Papers*, volumes III and IV; John A. Hawgood, editor, *First and Last Consul: Thomas Oliver Larkin and the Americanization of California* (1970); Norman A. Graebner, *Empire on the Pacific* (1955); Charles G. Sellers, *James K. Polk, Continentalist* (1966); and Frederick Merk, *Manifest Destiny and Mission in American History* (1963). On rival aspirations see Merk, *The Monroe Doctrine and American Expansionism, 1843–1849* (1966); Abraham P. Nasatir, *French Activities in California* (1945), and "The French Consulate in California, 1843–1856," *California Historical Society Quarterly, XI-XIII* (1932–1934), *passim*; E. D. Adams, "British Interest in California," *American Historical Review*, XIV (July 1909), 744–763; George B. Brooke, "The Vest Pocket War of Commodore Jones," *Pacific Historical Review*, XXXI (August 1962), 217–233; and Russell M. Posner, "A British Consular Agent in California: The Reports of James A. Forbes, 1843–1846," *Southern California Quarterly*, LIII (June 1971), 101–112.

The biographies of John C. Frémont that were published in 1856 were at least as worshipful as most presidential campaign biographies of the period. Their judgments were sharply reversed in the 1880s by three important works: the second volume of Theodore H. Hittell's *History of California* (1885); Josiah Royce's *California, from the Conquest in 1846 to the Second Vigilance Committee in San Francisco, a Study of American Character* (1886; new edition with an excellent introduction by Earl S. Pomeroy, 1971); and Oak's fifth volume of "Bancroft's" *History of California* (1886). Among other criticisms, Royce, Oak, and Bancroft openly questioned Frémont's veracity, especially in his claim to have had secret authorization for his filibustering activities. Frémont's *Memoirs of My Life*, of which only the first volume was published (1887), reasserted the claim. The explanation is probably that both Frémont and his wife were unusually addicted to the human foible of deceiving themselves on embarrassing issues.

The most extensive biography of Frémont, by Allan Nevins, is generally sympathetic. The first edition of this work bore the title *Frémont, the West's Greatest Adventurer* (two volumes, 1928). Cardinal Goodwin, in *John Charles Frémont, an Explanation of his Career* (1930), asserted that Nevins had placed too much reliance on Frémont family papers. Nevins, in turn, complained that Goodwin's work, though able, was "studiously hostile" to its subject. In the later editions of Nevins's biography, some of its most favorable judgments were slightly modified, and the title was changed to *Frémont: Pathmarker of the West* (rather than "Pathfinder," which had been used in the long subtitle of the original edition). Bernard De Voto, in *The Year of Decision, 1846* (1942), deplored all adulation of Frémont, past, present, and future. But Irving Stone, with the license of the novelist, exalted Jessie and her husband in *Immortal Wife* (1944). Dwight L. Clarke, in *Stephen Watts Kearny, Soldier of the West* (1961), sought to rescue Kearny from the "historical eclipse" to which he was consigned by Frémont and his admirers. See also Kenneth M. Johnson, *The Frémont Court Martial* (1968).

Donald Jackson and Mary Lee Spence, editors, *The Expeditions of John Charles Frémont* (three volumes and Map Portfolio, 1970–), makes the original documents available.

A *Biography of William B. Ide*, by his brother Simeon, also appeared under the title *Who Conquered California?* (1880). See also Fred B. Rogers, *William Brown Ide, Bear Flagger* (1962); Werner H. Marti, *Messenger of Destiny* (1960), on Archibald Gillespie; and John A. Hawgood, "John C. Frémont and the Bear Flag Revolution: a Reappraisal," *Southern California Quarterly*, XLIX (June 1962), 67–96. John A. Hussey, "The United States and the Bear Flag Revolt," Ph.D. thesis, University of California, Berkeley (1941), is substantial and well balanced. Numerous articles and documents on the subject have appeared in various issues of the *California Historical Society Quarterly*. The chief engagement during the "conquest" is thoroughly described in Arthur Woodward, *Lances at San Pascual* (1948). On a less bloody but equally interesting conflict, see John Douglas Tanner, Jr., "The Campaign for Los Angeles—December 29, 1846, to January 10, 1847," *California Historical Society Quarterly*, XLVIII (September 1969), 219–242.

Chapter X

THE GOLD RUSH

THE DISCOVERY of gold in the foothills of the Sierra Nevada occurred on January 24, 1848. This was only nine days before the signing of the Treaty of Guadalupe Hidalgo, and thus the discovery was unknown to the signers of that agreement, in which Mexico ceded California to the United States.

The knowledge could have made no critical difference in the negotiations. Mexico had been overrun by American troops, and was in no position to quibble over terms of peace, even though California would now be considerably more valuable than it had yet appeared to be.

That the Spaniards had found so much treasure in other parts of the hemisphere but entirely failed to find gold in California was ironic but understandable. They had seen little reason to explore the approaches to the Sierra, and even less reason to settle there, and the local Indians, if they noticed any gold, had had no interest in it. During the Mexican period a minor discovery was made, in March 1842, by Francisco López, a *ranchero* who pulled up some wild onions and found particles of gold among the roots. This was at Placerita Creek, about 35 miles northwest of Los Angeles. The first gold ever sent from California to the United States Mint, 20 ounces forwarded by Alfred Robinson for Abel Stearns, came from that area, but the placers there were of trifling importance, received little attention, and soon played out.

Marshall's discovery at Sutter's Mill. The crucial discovery was the result, although the accidental and indirect result, of an American's ingenuity. James Wilson Marshall was a moody and somewhat eccentric master carpenter who had come from Missouri to Oregon in 1844 and then south to California with the Clyman-McMahon party in 1845. His mechanical skills made him one of the most valued employees of John A. Sutter; but the scarcity of lumber in the Central Valley was frustrating to a carpenter,

James Wilson Marshall, by Peter Van Valkenburgh. (Courtesy of the Bancroft Library)

and had discouraged a number of other Americans who had thought of making their homes there. In August 1847 Marshall contracted with Sutter to build a sawmill in the foothills in order to provide lumber both for Sutter's own use and for sale to immigrants. Marshall chose a site on the south fork of the American River, where there was an abundance of timber and a flow of water that looked ideal for diversion into a millrace. The site was about 45 travel miles east-northeast of Sutter's Fort, at a place called Coloma from the Indian name Culloomah or "beautiful vale." With a crew including several Mormons, construction proceeded remarkably well considering the isolated location and the crudity of the materials and methods available. In January it appeared that the tailrace needed to be further deepened and its bottom cleared of obstructions. It was while Marshall was inspecting the progress of this work that he saw a glittering particle, caught behind a riffle of stone beneath the water. The tailrace was, in effect, a sluice cut through a sandbar at a bend of the river, and if Marshall had actually been searching for placer gold he could hardly have hit upon a better way of finding it.

With his glittering discovery, Marshall rode down to New Helvetia. There, behind a locked door, Sutter put the samples to several tests in the light of what he knew of the properties of the metal and what he could learn from the *American Encyclopedia*. When Sutter concluded that "It's gold—at least twenty-three-carat gold," Marshall got into such a state of feverish excitement that he insisted on riding back to Coloma in the rain in the middle of the night—the first victim of the gold mania. Sutter's behavior was somewhat less erratic; his primary concern was that the discovery would greatly endanger the completion of his sawmill. At Coloma he persuaded the workmen to continue with their task and to confine their prospecting to Sundays.

Efforts to keep the news from spreading were in vain. For example, one of the children of Mrs. Wimmer, the cook at Coloma, talked of the discovery to a teamster; then, to save her boy from being ridiculed as a liar, the good women showed the teamster some nuggets. Sutter himself, anxious as he was to keep the matter quiet, could not resist some boasting about it. He made an agreement with some Indians for a lease on the land around Coloma, and in dispatching a messenger to Col. Richard B. Mason, the military governor at Monterey, asking for validation of this agreement, Sutter not only revealed the discovery but sent along 6 ounces of gold to prove it.

Although the news leaked out quickly enough, it attracted very little attention for several months. There had been idle rumors of gold ever since the expeditions of Drake and Vizcaíno. None had actually been found until the trivial Placerita discovery of 1842, and this suggested that while there was some gold in California there was not enough to make it worth digging. Brief news reports of gold near New Helvetia, written with obvious lack of conviction, appeared in the two little weekly newspapers of San Francisco—one item in the *Californian* on March 15, 1848, and another in the *California Star* 10 days later—without creating any notable excitement.

The '48ers. The gold fever did not begin to be epidemic until May 12. On that day, in San Francisco, the mania that would eventually spread over the whole world was touched off deliberately and for purposes of revenue by the enterprising merchant, manipulator, real estate speculator, and Mormon elder, Samuel Brannan.

Brannan had arrived in 1846 as the leader of the California Mormons. A remarkably vigorous young man of Irish ancestry, articulate, ingenious, and highly opportunistic, he began his career as a molder of opinion and emotion by editing a journal published in New York for the Mormons of the Atlantic seaboard. When the leaders at Nauvoo, Illinois, determined in 1845 that the Latter-Day Saints should "flee out of Babylon," Elder Brannan, then 26 years old, was delegated to lead a party of more than 200 by ship around the Horn to California. They sailed from New York in the ship *Brooklyn* on February 4, 1846, which happened to be the same day that the main body of Mormons set out from Nauvoo across the ice of the Mississippi River. As flights from the sovereignty of the United States, these migrations were frustrated by the Mexican War. When the *Brooklyn* anchored in San Francisco Bay, on July 31,

1846, she found herself alongside the U.S.S. *Portsmouth,* whose commander, Capt. John B. Montgomery, had landed on the 9th to raise the American flag over Yerba Buena.

The arrival of the Brannan party tripled the population of that village. The first buildings had been erected there in 1835, when William A. Richardson, an English deserter from a whaler, had put up a shanty of rough boards, and the American, Jacob P. Leese, had built a slightly more substantial structure out of redwood planks brought by boat from Monterey. Early in 1847, by his authority as *alcalde,* Lt. Washington Allon Bartlett of the *Portsmouth* changed the name of Yerba Buena to San Francisco. Otherwise, the town's history had not yet been very eventful. No one there was as yet especially prosperous, with the exception of Samuel Brannan, who was already its leading citizen.

Brannan engaged in an assortment of business activities and investments, flagrantly putting Mormon funds to his own use and profit. Charged with embezzlement, he was the defendant in one of the first jury trials ever held in California, but the jury disagreed. He continued to gather in the tithes and to decide what should be done with the proceeds. When Brigham Young sent down a deputation from Salt Lake City to bring back "the Lord's money," Brannan said that he would turn over the money when he got a receipt signed by the Lord. He repeatedly urged the Salt Lake Mormons to come to the paradise of California, and he never understood Brigham Young's decision that the Saints could maintain their integrity and solidarity only by concentrating in Utah. Finally Brannan's superiors "disfellowshipped" or excommunicated him, though for some time he denied the validity of this proceeding.

One of Brannan's enterprises was a general store at Sutter's Fort, operated in partnership with Charles Smith. In March 1848, after customers at this store had begun to offer gold in payment for whisky and other commodities, Brannan became aware of the reality of the discovery and of the uses to which he could put it. He spent the next several weeks in quietly purchasing every article of merchandise he could get hold of in Northern California that would be in demand by gold seekers, then moving these articles to his store at New Helvetia. Then, on May 12, he came down to San Francisco, waved a bottle of gold dust in one hand and his hat in the other, and shouted "Gold! Gold! Gold from the American River!"

The symptoms of the craze which the sight of gold now began to produce in many men have often been described, but perhaps never more vividly than by James H. Carson: "I looked on for a moment; a frenzy seized my soul; unbidden my legs performed some entirely new movements of polka steps—I took several—houses were too small for me to stay in; I was soon in the street in search of necessary outfits; piles of gold rose up before me at every step; castles of marble, dazzling the eye with their rich appliances; thousands of slaves bowing to my beck and call; myriads of fair virgins contending with each other for

View of San Francisco, 1847. (Courtesy of the Bancroft Library)

my love—were among the fancies of my fevered imagination. The Rothschilds, Girards, and Astors appeared to me but poor people; in short, I had a very violent attack of the gold fever."

The most confirmed skeptics quickly succumbed. The editor of the *California Star,* Edward C. Kemble, a young man not yet out of his teens, continued to maintain as late as the issue of May 20 that the whole thing was a sham, "a supurb [*sic*] take-in as was ever got up to guzzle the gullible." The owner of the *Star* was none other than Brannan himself, and obviously he had not taken his young editor into his scheme. In any event, Kemble soon reversed himself and went off to join the gold rush.

Within a short time nearly every town in California lost a majority of its population. On May 29 the *San Francisco Californian* complained that "The whole country, from San Francisco to Los Angeles, and from the sea shore to the base of the Sierra Nevadas, resounds with the sordid cry of gold, GOLD, GOLD! while the field is left half-planted, the house half built, and everything neglected but the manufacture of shovels and pickaxes." The paper also announced that it was suspending publication; it had no choice, in view of the departure of its staff, subscribers, and advertisers. A few days later the *California Star* also suspended for the same reason.

At San Jose the jailer, Henry Bee, had 10 Indian prisoners in custody, two of them charged with murder. He tried to turn them over to the alcalde, but that official had already left. Bee solved the problem by taking all 10 prisoners

The steamboat landing at Sacramento in the early 1850s. (From the Honeyman Collection, Brancroft Library)

with him to the diggings, where they worked for him until he had made a fortune, then escaped to prospect on their own account.

Soldiers and sailors deserted by the hundreds. Colonel Mason reported that he was powerless to stop desertions, especially after a soldier on a three weeks' furlough found $1,500 worth of gold, more than his Army pay for five years. Mason toured the diggings in July. Some Mormon miners asked him whether they must turn over to Sam Brannan the tithes of their findings which he was soliciting from them, to which the Governor replied that they were required to pay as long as they were fools enough to do so.

The French consul, describing the situation in California in August, reported that "Never, I think, has there been such excitement in any country of the world." During the summer months the contagion began to spread to Hawaii, Oregon, and Utah, and in the fall to Mexico, Peru, and Chile. Altogether probably about six thousand gold seekers came to California from these areas in 1848. The main gold rush from "the States" did not begin until the year of the discovery was almost over.

The '49ers. In September 1848 Lt. Edward F. Beale arrived in Washington with reports and also with some actual specimens of gold, sent by Larkin. This led to many newspaper comments and to fairly wide discussion, but as yet few planned to leave for California. The spread of the gold craze over the whole country came after the sending of President Polk's annual message to Congress on December 5. Polk welcomed the news as a justification of his policies in acquiring the Mexican cession. "The accounts of the abundance of gold," he wrote "arc of such an extraordinary character as would scarcely command belief were they not corroborated by the authentic reports of officers in the public service." In evidence, the President appended Colonel Mason's report of his personal tour of the diggings, in which Mason asserted that there

Monterey in 1856. The growth of population and commerce in the gold rush years came elsewhere. From Journal and Drawings of Henry Miller. *(Courtesy of the Bancroft Library)*

was enough gold "in the country drained by the Sacramento and San Joaquin rivers" to pay the cost of the Mexican War "a hundred times over."

Two days later Lt. Lucien Loeser arrived at the Capital with a tea caddy crammed with 230 ounces of gold. Placed on display at the War Department, this drew excited crowds, and the Philadelphia Mint soon announced that samples of it had a degree of fineness equal to the standard of United States gold coins.

The mania for sudden wealth now pervaded all classes, and the urge to be off to the goldfields stimulated many related industries. One of these was the marketing of fanciful devices for gold mining, practically all of them destined to be junked. Another was the hasty publication of alleged guidebooks of varying degrees of fraudulence, most of them derived, at best, largely from Mason's report, along with some fragments of the writings of Larkin, Frémont, and Lansford W. Hastings. One such opus, published in New York in December, 1848, was *The Emigrant's Guide to the Gold Mines*..., 30 pages long and selling for 25 cents, or 12½ cents without the map; the latter alternative was the better buy, since the map was entirely worthless. Another item, of 1849 vintage, was *The Digger's Handbook and Truth about California* by one D. L. Sydney. In penciled insertions on the title page of a surviving copy of this work, some disillusioned purchaser identified the author's initials, D. L., as "Damn Liar." Tin Pan Alley provided accompaniment, with "The Gold Digger's Waltz," "The San Francisco Waltz," "The Sacramento Gallop," and a pirated adaptation from Stephen Collins Foster, which emerged as

> O Susanna! don't you cry for me!
> I'm going to California with my wash-bowl on my knee.

There were three main routes to the goldfields: by way of the Isthmus of Panama, around Cape Horn, or overland. The sea routes drew the heavy traffic in the first months of the great rush in the winter and early spring of 1849 because they were open all year round, although in the long run more than twice as many gold seekers would go to California by land as by sea. Before '49 the Cape Horn route had been the most traveled one, but it covered a distance of about 18,000 nautical miles and took five to eight months, and thus the Panama shortcut suddenly became attractive to thousands who feared that all the gold might be gone before they could arrive to claim their share of it.

Moreover, it happened that a new passenger service on the Panama route was just becoming available. In 1847 Congress had granted subsidies to two new merchant steamer lines, the United States Mail Steamship Company for the voyage between New York and Chagres on the Atlantic side of the isthmus, and the Pacific Mail Steamship Company for the Panama-California-Oregon run. Three 1,000-ton paddle-wheel steamers were built for the Pacific. The first of them, the *California,* left New York in October 1848 with almost no passengers, on her way around the Horn toward the Pacific port of Panama. When she arrived there in January, she found 700 Americans clamoring to get aboard. They had traveled by ship to Chagres, by small boat up the fever-infested Chagres River, and by mule the rest of the way across the isthmus. The *California's* rated capacity was not more than 250, and she had taken on 69 Peruvians who refused to get off. Among the Americans waiting in Panama was Gen. Persifor F. Smith, on his way to relieve Colonel Mason as military commander in California. Hard-pressed by his angry compatriots, Smith issued a kind of proclamation, in which he asserted incorrectly that American law forbade foreigners to dig gold on American soil. The *Panama Star,* a newspaper founded by some of the Americans temporarily stranded for lack of transport, published the general's statement in its first issue, along with an equally ungenerous editorial: "If foreigners come [to California] let them till the soil and make roads, or do any other work that may suit them . . ., but the gold mines were reserved by nature for Americans only, who possess noble hearts." After days of intensive ticket scalping, the *California* sailed with about 400 on board. During most of 1849, because of delays at Panama, the average time from New York to San Francisco by this route was three to five months, though by 1850 increased service in the Pacific had reduced it to six or eight weeks.

Of the Argonauts who chose to travel around the Horn, many were organized in joint stock companies, both for the voyage and in the expectation of working together in mining operations after their arrival. These companies usually purchased old ships, which they fondly supposed they could sell in California. Actually, most of these vessels joined the fleet of several hundred hulks that were abandoned to settle gradually into the mud along the San Francisco waterfront, and nearly all of the companies disintegrated into smaller groups more suitable for prospecting. The removal from service of the hundreds of obsolescent old vessels now consigned to the ghost fleet, at the same time that the gold rush was stimulating the building of the clipper ships, made the early 1850s the golden age of the American merchant marine. The new California clippers were twice as large as the China clippers designed in the '40s,

Donald McKay's Flying Cloud. (*Courtesy of the Bancroft Library*)

and with freight at $60 a ton, each of them paid for itself with its first cargo. In 1851 the maiden voyage of Donald McKay's *Flying Cloud* set a record of 89 days from New York to San Francisco, a record which no other sailing ship has ever excelled. The clippers were designed to carry premium freight at maximum speed. They were much less important for carrying passengers, who found them highly uncomfortable. Inevitably, too many were built, and a few years later some were reduced to carrying guano, while others could get no cargoes at all.

A majority of the '49ers traveled overland, especially those from the Ohio and Mississippi Valleys. The main route was the California Trail, by way of the Platte, South Pass, and the Humboldt. This route was already well established by the earlier emigrants, but for each person who followed it in 1848 there were 50 in 1849, some of them in wagon trains miles long. Between the Rockies and the Sierra the loss of oxen and horses was dreadful because the great trek used up all the grass within easy reach of the trail, even along the stretches where there had ever been any grass. Men, women, and children had to walk in order to spare the strength of such animals as were still alive to draw the wagons, and some families had to fry the last of their bacon for axle grease. By the time they reached the 40 miles of unbroken desert southwest of the Humboldt Sink, many were no longer concerned to save their property, but only their lives, and the trail was littered with an almost incredible miscellany of discarded articles. There was very little danger from hostile Indians at this time, but there was a major epidemic of Asiatic cholera. The disease was not only agonizing and usually fatal, but also peculiarly terrifying because medical science had not yet discovered that it was transmitted mainly through the contamination of drinking water, and those who tended the sick or came anywhere near them imagined that the ghastly affliction might be spread in various other ways.

Besides the three main arteries of travel, a number of alternate routes attracted smaller contingents. Some crossed the isthmus by way of Nicaragua rather than Panama. There were several fairly important southern trails, not only across Texas and New Mexico but also across old Mexico to Mazatlán or San Blas or to the Gila. A number of '49ers branched off from the main California Trail by going southwest from Salt Lake to Southern California, and for some who rashly attempted a shortcut from this route, notably the Manly and Jayhawker parties, Death Valley earned its name. Others turned off from the Humboldt River into Black Rock Desert, to swing far north of the Sierra and into the upper end of the Sacramento Valley by way of the Pit River. This roundabout way, known as Lassen's Cutoff, was as outrageously misnamed as Hastings', and in general Peter Lassen and Lansford Hastings were about equally incompetent as guides. The majority chose a direct route through the central Sierra, though many were frightened by the reputation of Donner Pass and instead used Carson Pass about 20 miles south of Lake Tahoe.

The diggings. Before the end of 1849, miners were swarming over the foothill region between the Yuba River in the north and Mariposa in the south, the region now appropriately traversed by California State Highway 49. Within this area lay the Mother Lode, in a continuous belt extending about 120 miles from a point north of Coloma to a point near Mariposa, and varying in width from a few hundred feet to 2 miles. This network of thousands of veins of gold was formed when the Cordilleran revolution produced the Sierra Nevada by cracking the earth's surface and thrusting up a great tilted block of the earth's crust. A long ribbon of molten gold ore flowed up into fissures in the granitic rock. Erosion then tore loose particles of gold and washed them into the rivers, where they lodged on sandbars, behind stones, or in "pot holes" in the banks or streambeds. These particles were known as *placer* gold, from a Spanish word meaning a place near the bank of a stream where alluvial gold could be found.

The miners spoke loosely of the "Mother Lode country" as including not only the great vein of ore still embedded in the rocks, but also the larger area where placer gold had been deposited. The Mokelumne River, separating Amador and Calaveras Counties, was the approximate boundary between the "northern mines" and the "southern mines." There were also some fairly important gold-bearing areas in other parts of California, particularly in the regions of Mt. Shasta and the Trinity and Klamath Rivers, where a new rush began in 1850. Popular terminology lumped these with the northern mines, though they

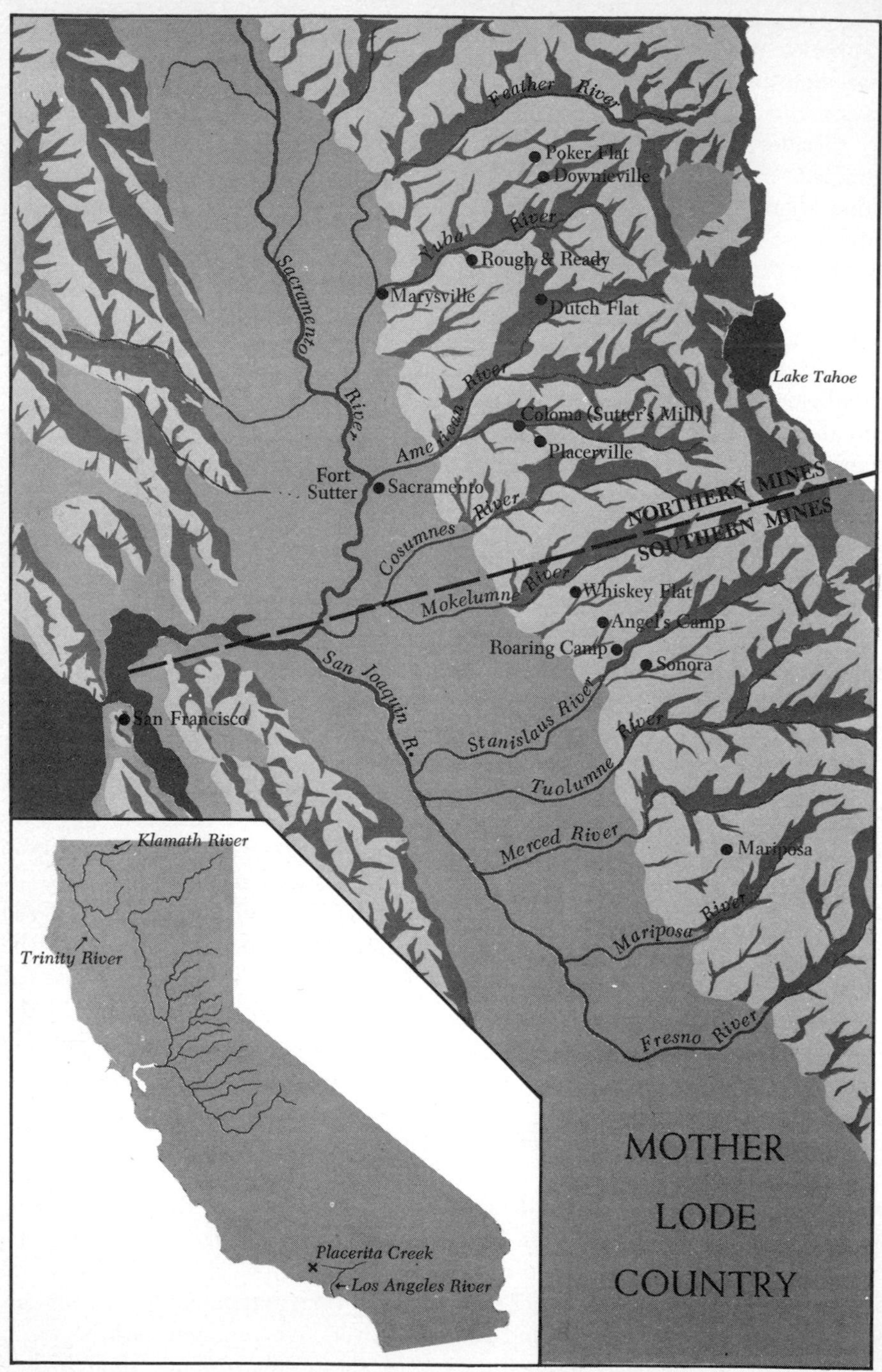
Feather River
Poker Flat
Downieville
Yuba River
Rough & Ready
Sacramento River
Marysville
Dutch Flat
Lake Tahoe
American River
Coloma (Sutter's Mill)
Placerville
Fort Sutter
Sacramento
Cosumnes River
NORTHERN MINES
SOUTHERN MINES
Mokelumne River
Whiskey Flat
Angel's Camp
Roaring Camp
Sonora
San Joaquin R.
San Francisco
Stanislaus River
Tuolumne River
Merced River
Mariposa
Mariposa River
Fresno River
Klamath River
Trinity River
Placerita Creek
Los Angeles River
MOTHER
LODE
COUNTRY

would be better described as in a separate "northwestern" group. Lesser discoveries were also made in several isolated parts of Southern California.

Early mining methods. Very few Americans had any previous experience in gold mining. New Spain had a major gold rush at Zacatecas in 1548, three full centuries earlier. Although the Spaniards in Mexico and Peru had at first sought gold largely with the sword from Indians who were already in possession of it, or with the whip through forced Indian labor in the mines, they had also developed a number of the more advanced techniques of the mining industry. In fact, there were dozens of Spanish-Mexican mining terms which had no English equivalents and which were soon put to use by the Americans in California. *Placer* was only the most familiar of these; other examples included *bonanza,* or rich ore, and *borrasca,* or barren rock. In the United States, there was a gold-mining industry of modest importance in Georgia and the Carolinas during the first half of the 19th century, and several veterans of these southern-Appalachian diggings brought important knowledge of mining methods to California. The first was Isaac Humphrey, from Georgia, who was at Sutter's Fort at the time of the discovery. Arriving at Coloma a few weeks later and finding the early prospectors still using nothing more than their knives and spoons, he introduced them to the pan and then to the rocker or cradle.

Of the various devices for using the movement of water to separate particles of gold from sand, gravel, and clay, the simplest was a flat-bottomed pan, made of iron or tin. A quantity of what was hoped to be "pay dirt," obtained with the pick and shovel, was tossed into the pan, thoroughly wetted and stirred, and the rocks or pebbles picked out of it. Then the miner held the pan under the surface of a pool or stream and swirled it about with a gently rotating motion for at least 10 minutes, one side of the pan held a little higher than the other, until the clay and nearly all of the sand were washed away. Gold being heavier, particles of it remained in the bottom.

The lure of the gold rush was the prospect of acquiring wealth quickly and easily—by lucky chance rather than hard work. But panning for gold turned out to be one of the most exhausting forms of manual labor ever devised. To the hard work with pick and shovel, panning added the necessity of squatting or stooping in the burning sun, either beside the icy water or in it, for hours, while moving the wrist, arm, and shoulder muscles and concentrating attention very carefully on the overflow.

The first improvement on the pan was the rocker, an oblong box without a top, several feet in length, mounted on rockers like a child's cradle, and placed in a sloping position. It was open at the lower end, while above the upper end there was a hopper with a sieve. Three men usually worked together, one shoveling dirt into the hopper, another pouring buckets of water to wash

"A Primitive Outfit." After a sketch from life in 1850 by John W. Audubon. (Courtesy of the Bancroft Library)

the dirt down through the trough, and a third vigorously rocking the cradle. Thus the gold was trapped behind the cleats or "riffles" nailed at intervals along the bottom. No part of the operation of a rocker was as uncomfortable as panning, and some relief from the monotony of the labor could be had by exchanging jobs. Although much of the finer gold slid over the cleats and was lost, the average return was higher than in panning because a much larger quantity of dirt could be processed in a day.

Near the end of 1849 the "long tom" appeared as an enlargement and a considerable improvement of the rocker. The tom was usually about 12 feet long, stationary, and placed where a stream of water could be run through it from a ditch or a wooden flume. This eliminated both the pouring of water and the rocking of the cradle. About a year later the long tom evolved into the sluice, a whole series of riffle boxes fitted together into a continuous string, sometimes as much as several hundred feet in length. This device, though commonly employed even in ancient times, seems to have been reinvented in California. In an important related development, a wing dam was built part way across a stream to divert a flow of water into a sluice; sometimes an entire river was dammed and turned aside to expose the pay dirt in a section of the streambed. The reason such relatively efficient methods were so slow in appearing was that they required fairly large groups of men to work together, and in the first two years the miners were so intensely individualistic that the industry was still at most a small-business operation.

The final separation of gold from the sand and other dross was often accomplished by the use of mercury, or quicksilver, which has the property of amalgamating with gold. When this amalgam is heated in a closed vessel, the mercury vaporizes. Thus separated from the gold, the mercury can also be recovered, as soon as it cools again from vapor to liquid. Fortunately, quicksilver had been found in 1845 at New Almaden in the hills a few miles south of San José.

Mining-camp law. The primary concern of the early California miners with legal problems was in the regulation of mining claims. Because the mining camps had sprung up beyond the reach of any established law, they had to adopt their own regulations. Practically none of the land in the gold region had passed into private hands, and the rights of the Indians were ignored. California was in the midst of a peculiarly awkward transition from Mexican to American sovereignty. Congress had not provided for the extension of American territorial government to any part of the Mexican cession, and even if it had, there was no Federal mining law that would have been relevant to the California mining camps, because no precious metal had ever been discovered before on public lands of the United States.

In devising their own mining codes the Argonauts were acting in a tradition of American frontier self-government that went all the way back to the Mayflower Compact. In each camp there was a mass meeting to organize a "mining district" and elect a committee to draw up a set of regulations. Eventually more than 500 camps adopted such codes, so similar to each other as to rule out the possibility that they were separately and spontaneously invented. Spanish-Mexican mining codes and customs had a considerable influence, as did the experience of '49ers from the lead and tin mines of Cornwall and other parts of England. Each code defined the permissible size of a claim and required that it be continuously worked if it was to remain valid. Thus the title was merely usufructuary, not a title to ownership of the land but merely to the use of it for mining purposes. Each district elected a recorder, variously called an alcalde, arbitrator, or chairman, and often its only officer. His duties were to keep the register of claims and to settle disputes arising from charges of claim jumping, sometimes with the assistance of a panel of arbitrators chosen by the contestants.

As described thus far, the plan was highly reasonable and highly democratic. A far less admirable aspect of the codes was that many of them included "restrictive covenants" barring Mexicans, Asiatics, or other foreigners. Still other problems of the mining camps arose from the extemporized administration of criminal justice, the resort to lynching and vigilantism. But racial oppression directed against foreigners and Indians in early American California, and extralegal methods for the punishment of crime, are the subjects of other chapters.

The historical significance of the gold rush. The traditional view of this remarkable migration describes it as the most fortunate as well as the most significant factor in the whole of California's history. It can be cogently argued, however, that in the long run the state would have been better off if it had contained no gold at all, that because of its other advantages it would eventually have become just as populous and prosperous, and that in the meantime its social evolution would have been not only more gradual but also far more orderly and civilized.

Obviously the lure of sudden wealth brought an early and rapid influx of population. At the end of 1848 about six thousand miners had obtained about 10 million dollars worth of gold. In 1849 the amount produced was two or three times as large, but there were more than 40,000 miners to share in it, and thus the individual miner's average daily return declined radically. In 1852, the peak year, the output was about 80 million dollars and the number of miners about 100,000. During the hundred years after the beginning of the gold rush, the output of California gold totaled about two billion dollars. All the gold produced in a century was worth less than the value of one year's agricultural output of the state in the 1960s, and much of the gold was ultimately destined to be put back into the ground, in the Treasury Department's hoard at Fort Knox.

It may be granted that if there had been no gold discovery, Oregon would probably have been ready for admission as a state before California was. The first transcontinental railroad might have been built to Oregon. But if California's first transcontinental had been built later, it might have been in the hands of a somewhat less rapacious group of men, and it might have obtained less of a stranglehold on the state's economy and politics.

What sort of people did the gold rush bring to California? Bancroft's famous description is interestingly balanced: ". . . the toiling farmer, whose mortgage loomed above the growing family, the briefless lawyer, the starving student, the quack, the idler, the harlot, the gambler, the hen-pecked husband, the disgraced; with many earnest, enterprising, honest men and devoted women." The women were few, however, and the honest and devoted women still fewer, and in general, the notion that the Argonauts came to California as pioneers and commonwealth builders is a myth. The great majority of them came in the hope that they could quickly plunder California of her treasure and return to their homes. It is true that the penniless adventurer was excluded by the necessity of having an original stake of several hundred dollars for the expenses of the trip, and that many of the '49ers were young married men hoping to make enough to return to their wives and children with financial security. But most of those who remained in California did so because they failed to accumulate even enough to get them back home. On the whole they were unsuccessful, disillusioned, embittered men.

The hard labor, the shockingly inflated prices of food, the badness and monotony of their own cooking, the prevalence of sickness and of homesickness, all added to the widespread sense of desperation that so many of the diaries record. Hinton R. Helper, for example, took as dim a view of the gold rush as he later expressed concerning the institution of slavery and its impending crisis in his native South. Often there were efforts to find relief in a desperate kind of humor, as in the naming of such camps as Hell's Delight, Gouge Eye, Poker Flat, Devil's Retreat, Murderers' Bar, Poverty Hill, and Gomorrah, and in the organization of the Ancient and Honorable Order of E Clampus Vitus, or "the Clampers." The derivation of the name of this miner's fraternal society is unknown; there are no records of its early meetings, it is said, because they were devoted so largely to hard drinking that no one was ever in condition to keep minutes, or able the next day to recall what had happened. The constitution provided only that all members were officers and "of equal indignity," although some, such as the Clampatriarch and the Noble Grand Humbug, seem to have been more equal than others. The members were pledged to take care of widows and orphans, especially widows. In general, however, there was tragedy rather than humor or romance in the drinking, gambling, and vice in which many miners sought escape from the hardships and anxieties of "seeing the elephant," as the experience of mining came to be called.

The gold rush was the product of a kind of mass hysteria, and it set a tone and created a state of mind in which greed predominated and disorder and violence were all too frequent.

SELECTED BIBLIOGRAPHY

John W. Caughey, *Gold Is the Cornerstone* (1948), is a useful general volume on the gold rush. Rodman W. Paul, *California Gold* (1947), stresses the technological, economic, and legal aspects; see also his later work, *Mining Frontiers of the Far West, 1848–1880* (1963). Valeska Bari, *The Course of Empire* (1931), is a good collection of first-hand accounts. John W. Caughey, editor, *Rushing for Gold* (1949, also published as the February 1949 issue of the *Pacific Historical Review*), is a collection of excellent secondary studies.

California Gold Discovery: Centennial Papers of the Time, the Site and Artifacts (1947), includes a treatment of "Sutter's Sawmill" by Aubrey Neasham. See also Theressa Gay, *James Marshall, Discoverer of California Gold* (1967); and Rodman W. Paul, editor, *The California Gold Dis-*

covery (1966). Paul Bailey, *Sam Brannan and the California Mormons* (1953), deals with Brannan's role. Ralph P. Bieber, "California Gold Mania," *Mississippi Valley Historical Review,* XXXV (June 1948), 3–28, describes the excitement in the East. Hundreds of diaries or memoirs dealing with the gold rush have been published. E. Gould Buffum, *Six Months in the Gold Mines* (1850), and James H. Carson, *Early Recollections of the Mines* (1852), describe the days of '48.

John H. Kemble, *The Panama Route, 1848–1869* (1943) and Bayard Taylor, *El Dorado, or Adventures in the Path of Empire* (two volumes, 1850), deal with the isthmian approach. Oscar Lewis, *Sea Routes to the Gold Fields* (1949), also includes Cape Horn. Octavius T. Howe, *Argonauts of '49* (1923), is a history of the emigrant companies from Massachusetts. On the overland routes, see George R. Stewart, *The California Trail* (1962); Owen C. Coy, *The Great Trek* (1931); Irene D. Paden, *In the Wake of the Prairie Schooner* (1943); Walker D. Wyman, editor, *California Emigrant Letters* (1952); Archer B. Hulbert, *The Forty-niners* (1931), a synthetic diary; Alonzo Delano, *Life on the Plains and among the Diggings* (1854); and Ralph P. Bieber, *Southern Trails to California in 1849* (1937).

Some of the best descriptions of life in the diggings are in *The Shirley Letters from the California Mines, 1851–1852* (1949); Frank Marryat, *Mountains and Molehills* (1855, 1962); Sarah Royce, *A Frontier Lady* (1932); Josiah Royce, *California . . . a Study of American Character* (1886, 1948); and Charles H. Shinn, *Mining Camps* (1885, 1948). Hubert Howe Bancroft's social history of the gold rush, *California Inter Pocula* (1888), explains its title in its opening words: "Drunk! aye, drunk with avarice! Behold . . . California in her cups"—though an alternative translation might be "California between drinks." Views of the darker side include George Payson, *Golden Dreams and Leaden Realities* (1853); and Hinton R. Helper, *The Land of Gold; Reality Versus Fiction* (1855), also edited by Lucius Beebe and Charles M. Clegg under their title of *Dreadful California—Being a True & Scandalous Account of the Barbarous Civilization, Licentious Morals, Crude Manners and Depravities, Inclement Climate and Niggling Resources, together with Various Other Offensive & Calamitous Details of Life in the Golden State* (1948). J. S. Holliday, "The Gold Rush in Myth and Reality," Ph.D. thesis, University of California, Berkeley (1959), is ungilded but sympathetic.

See also Ralph J. Roske, "The World Impact of the California Gold Rush," *Arizona and the West,* V (Autumn 1963), 187–232; and Jay Monaghan, *Australians and the Gold Rush* (1966).

Chapter XI

THE ESTABLISHMENT OF STATE GOVERNMENT

THE CONGRESS of the United States, deadlocked over the future of slavery in new territories, provided no legal form of government whatever for California from the end of the Mexican War in 1848 until its admission into the Union on September 9, 1850. During this period the confused conditions of the gold rush intensified the confusion that resulted from California's undetermined and very peculiar legal and political status.

Military governments. From the outbreak of the war until the ratification of the treaty of peace, California was governed under the customs of international law which provided that in conquered territory under military occupation the previous system of local law remain in effect with such modifications as the military commander considered necessary. Thus the American commanders were also ex officio governors; but there was much uncertainty about their legal status, powers, and responsibilities, both in Washington, D.C., and on the part of the commanders themselves.

Further confusion arose from the changes of personnel. When the "governorship" had passed from Commodore Sloat to Commodore Stockton to Colonel Frémont to General Kearny to Colonel Mason—five governors in the first 10 months—Captain DuPont of the U.S.S. *Cyane* wrote that "The Californians think . . . we cannot be much better than Mexico for they connect the appearance of every new commander-in-chief with the result of some new revolution."

The prevailing system of local government in Mexican California, which the American military governors necessarily adopted, was based on the powers of the alcalde, an office derived from the Arabian and Moorish *Al-Cadi*, or village judge. Under Spain and Mexico, alcaldes were usually elected by the citizens of the town, subject to confirmation by the governor, but often the governor had simply appointed them when he considered it necessary or preferable. The alcalde was traditionally regarded as the father of the village. His duties were many and remarkably varied, and his jurisdiction, sometimes extending for hundreds of miles into the country, was ill-defined and unclear. He performed the functions of mayor, sheriff, and judge, often arresting a person, presiding over his trial, passing sentence, and enforcing the sentence. He combined the judicial and executive powers, and he often exercised the legislative power as well—by extemporizing legislation, and by serving as the presiding and dominating officer of the town council or *ayuntamiento* if his town happened to have one.

The patriarchal aspects of the office and the absence of the separation of powers were shocking to many Americans. Walter Colton, appointed and later elected as the first American alcalde of Monterey in 1846, wrote that "such an absolute disposal of questions affecting property and personal liberty never ought to be confided to one man. There is not a judge on the bench in England or the United States whose power is so absolute as that of the alcalde of Monterey."

The provisional government movement. From the beginning the American military governors assumed that the ultimate annexation of California to the United States was a foregone conclusion, and this view was strengthened in March 1847 by the arrival of Col. J. D. Stevenson's regiment of New York Volunteers, recruited with the understanding that they would be disbanded in California at the end of the war and would thus provide not merely a garrison but a body of permanent American settlers. Even before the end of the technical state of war, there were many protests against "the inefficient mongrel military rule," as a writer in the *California Star* described it, and against alcalde rule.

With the news of the ratification of the treaty, the question of how California was supposed to be governed became extraordinarily difficult and embarrassing. The situation was complicated both by the onset of the gold rush and by the fact that Congress failed to agree on any system of civil government. Congress provided for a territorial government in Oregon in the spring of 1848, but all such plans for New Mexico and California bogged down in the national political struggle which had raged since the introduction of Representative David Wilmot's proposal that slavery be forbidden in any territory acquired from Mexico.

The treaty signed at Guadalupe Hidalgo was ratified in May 1848, and the official news of the ratification reached California on August 6. Thereafter, military government had to be continued *de facto,* with no other legal basis than the law of necessity. Colonel Mason understood the problem at least as well as did any of his critics. He reminded the Adjutant General in Washington that the only duly constituted civil officers in California were "the alcaldes appointed or confirmed by myself. To throw off upon them or the people at large the civil management and control of the country, would most probably lead to endless confusion, if not to absolute anarchy; and yet what right or authority have I to exercise civil control in time of peace in a territory of the United States? or if sedition and rebellion should arise where is my force to meet it?" The discharge of the impatient New York Volunteers reduced the military force in California to two companies of Regulars, and desertions to the mines were rapidly thinning their ranks.

In December 1848 the Americans in what were now the largest towns in Northern California embarked on plans to provide for themselves the institutions of representative government which Congress had failed to provide for them. Meetings in San Jose and San Francisco initiated this movement. Early in January 1849 Peter H. Burnett presided over two meetings in Sacramento which discussed "the necessity and propriety of organizing a Provisional Government for the Territory of California." Burnett had been a leader in the formation of such a government in Oregon, and a member of its supreme court. According to his *Recollections* "at least two-thirds of the population of Oregon capable of bearing arms" came to California in the gold rush, himself among them.

On February 12, 1849, a public meeting in Portsmouth Square created a "Legislative Assembly for the District of San Francisco," with 15 elected members. This was done with the encouragement of a letter to the people of California from Senator Thomas Hart Benton, published in the *Alta California,* in which Benton argued that military government derived its power from war and that with the end of the war the only right to govern lay in the consent of the people themselves. San Francisco's "Legislative Assembly" met early in March and sought recognition of its authority from Gen. Persifor F. Smith. That officer had recently succeeded Colonel Mason in his capacity as military commander, though not in his capacity as governor, the functions having been separated as a gesture toward the demands for civil government. General Smith refused to recognize the Assembly, and against the "Benton" or "Settlers' theory" of the situation he asserted the "Administration theory"—that the government could be changed only by the proper authority, which was Congress. Each side maintained, quite accurately, that the claims of the other to the right to operate a *de facto* government were illegal. But the settlers' position was too uncertain to allow them to proceed in defiance of the military authorities, and although several Northern California towns made joint plans for a constitutional convention, they repeatedly postponed it.

Gen. Bennett Riley succeeded Colonel Mason as "civil" Governor in April 1849. Late in May he received the news that Congress had again adjourned without agreement on a territorial organization for California, and on June 3 he issued his own call for a constitutional convention to meet at

Monterey on September 1. He had no real authority to do this, but it was a wise and necessary solution of the problem. It placated the settlers, retained and repaired his prestige as *de facto* governor, and gave unity, organization, and strength to the project for a convention. It was also consistent with the attitude of President Zachary Taylor, a Southern unionist who felt that California might help to break the congressional deadlock over the territorial expansion of slavery if it would confront the rest of the country with an accomplished fact, by drawing up a state constitution that would settle the explosive issue so far as California was concerned.

The President could make this suggestion only informally and unofficially, because all the legal authority in the matter lay with Congress. Under the normal procedure, patterned roughly on that of the Northwest Ordinance, Congress would first have established a territorial government; then, when the territory had enough inhabitants, Congress would have passed an "enabling act," authorizing an elected convention (or sometimes the territorial legislature), to prepare a constitution and submit it for congressional approval of the admission of the state. All but four new states, since the original thirteen, had evolved through the territorial stage in this way. California would skip that stage entirely—as Vermont, Kentucky, Maine, and Texas had done—but under circumstances that differed from those prevailing in any of them.

President Taylor sent T. Butler King of Georgia as his personal and confidential emissary to California. In the sweltering summer of 1849, King traveled throughout the mining regions, urging the busy miners to take an interest in the forthcoming elections of delegates to the convention. His formal dress and pompous manner evoked some derision in the mining camps. Moreover, he insisted on traveling in the hottest part of the day, and thus deeply irritated General Smith, who personally commanded his military escort.

The steamer on which King had arrived from Panama also carried another politician of even greater importance to California's future. This was William M. Gwin of Tennessee, a Democrat who had served one term in Congress and had been appointed to various minor Federal offices by Presidents Jackson and Polk. Early in March 1849, as the Presidency passed to a Whig, and after Congress had adjourned with no solution of the California tangle, Gwin realized that California would soon form its own state government. He left Washington with the announced intention of assisting in that process and then of returning as one of the first United States Senators from the new state. He achieved both of these ambitions. Obviously, not all of California's golden opportunities were in its mines.

The constitutional convention and its problems. Early in September the convention assembled at Monterey, in Colton Hall, a substantial building that the first American alcalde had erected as a town hall and schoolhouse.

Of the 48 delegates who attended, only 11 came from the southern districts: San Diego, 2; Los Angeles, 5; Santa Barbara, 2; San Luis Obispo, 2. Thirty-seven came from the northern districts: Monterey, 5; San Jose, 7; San Francisco, 8; Sonoma, 3; Sacramento, 8; and San Joaquin, 6. The newly populous mining districts of Sacramento and San Joaquin elected a number of other delegates who did not attend, primarily because they were unwilling to interrupt their search for gold.

The constitutional convention of '49 was not mainly a convention of '49ers, although the latter were now the bulk of the electorate. A large majority of the delegates at the convention had been in California more than three years—in contrast with Gwin "of San Francisco," who had been there only three months. About half the members were less than 35 years old. Eight were native Californians, of whom the most important were Mariano Guadalupe Vallejo of Sonoma and José Antonio Carrillo of Los Angeles. Of the Americans, a substantially larger number had come from Northern states than from Southern. The 14 lawyers formed the largest single occupational group. One delegate, B. F. Moore, from Florida and San Joaquin, gave his occupation as "elegant leisure."

General Riley's proclamation had left open the question of whether the new government should be that of a state or of a territory, and this was one of the first questions the convention settled. On a motion introduced by Gwin, who could not become a senator from a territory, the vote was decisively for a state government, even though every Southern California delegate who was present voted otherwise. The landowners of what would soon be the southern "cow counties" were well aware that the taxation of ranch land would be the main source of early state revenues, since the miners, though now a large majority of the citizens, generally owned no land on which to pay taxes. The administrative expenses of a territory, on the other hand, would have been paid by the Federal government. Naturally the Southern Californians would have preferred that alternative, but they were hopelessly outnumbered. Carrillo proposed a compromise by which the part of California north of San Luis Obispo would be a state and the southern part a territory, but the idea was not seriously considered.

To the surprise of many, the question of slavery was easily decided by a unanimous vote. However, the overwhelming sentiment for the exclusion of slavery from California was not based on humanitarian considerations. The question had come to a head in the mines when Col. Thomas Jefferson Green and a group of other Texans had appeared at Rose's Bar on the Yuba River with a number of Negro slaves. In Texas politics Green had been an unsuccessful rival of Sam Houston, who once maintained that Green had all the characteristics of a dog except fidelity. On the Yuba, Green and his fellow Texans appropriated a large number of claims and set their slaves to working them. The Argonauts, whether from the North or from the South, were sensitive on the matter of the dignity of hard manual labor, or rather of their particular form of it; they were outraged at the imputation that goldmining was work appropriate for Negro slaves. On Sunday, July 29, a mass meeting resolved "that no slave or negro should own claims or even work in the mines," and served notice that the slaves must be out of the district by the next morning. Three days later the same miners elected William E. Shannon as their delegate to the convention at Monterey. It was Shannon who introduced the provision that "Neither slavery nor involuntary servitude, unless for the punishment of crimes, shall ever be tolerated in this state."

A few of the members of the convention held liberal views on racial matters, but the majority did not. This was clear in the debates on a proposal to exclude free Negroes, as well as slaves, from California—debates that brought forth angry feelings. The proposal to exclude free Negroes was introduced by M. M. McCarver, from Kentucky and Sacramento. Many owners of slaves, he said, were planning to bring them to California, and free them there, on condition that they work in the mines as indentured servants. Moreover, McCarver asserted, free Negroes were "idle in their habits, difficult to be governed by laws, thriftless and uneducated," and their presence in California would be an evil "greater than that of slavery itself." At one point the free-Negro exclusion clause was actually adopted, and it would have remained in the document except for a growing fear that Congress might consider it in violation of the Federal Constitution and therefore reject the California constitution as a whole. Negroes were citizens in some of the states in the North, and the Federal Constitution declared that citizens of each state should be "entitled to all privileges and immunities of citizens in the several states." The overriding consideration was the fear of anything that might delay the full establishment of "a proper form of state government" and its full national recognition.

At this time the power to deny suffrage on the ground of race was still within the constitutional authority of a state. Here, the chief complication was that the former Mexican citizens of California had the right to become American citizens under the treaty of peace. Most Mexican Californians had some admixture of Indian ancestry, and Mexican law had not formally denied suffrage to Indians. In an uneasy compromise the California constitution extended the suffrage only to white male citizens, but authorized the state legislature by a two-thirds vote to extend it to Indians or the descendants of Indians. That the legislature would do this was most unlikely; the provision was mainly to prevent Congress from considering that the proposed constitution was in violation of the treaty with Mexico, and thus find additional cause to delay California's admission as a state.

The problem that gave the convention most trouble was the question of the eastern boundary. Should this be based on the Sierra Nevada and the Colorado River, or should there be a much larger California extending several hundred miles farther east? Under Spain and Mexico, California had never had any definite eastern boundary at all, and each mapmaker had been forced to make his own guess. On the maps in most common use at the time of the Mexican War, and notably on the one used in the official negotiation of the treaty, Mexican California had included not only the present area of Nevada, but most of what are now Utah and Arizona as well. The convention's committee on boundaries proposed a Sierra-Colorado River line. Gwin, supported by Henry W. Halleck, Secretary of State under Mason and Riley and delegate from Monterey, favored the much larger unit, with a boundary east of the Great Salt Lake. The convention, changing its mind repeatedly, almost broke up over this question.

A legend perpetuated by several historians, including Hubert Howe Bancroft and Josiah Royce, long maintained that the idea of an extreme eastern boundary was a plot to create a California so large that in a later division of the state the southern part would be opened to slavery. But in the convention at Monterey, the men from Southern states more often voted for the smaller boundaries, and the men from Northern states for the larger ones. As usual, the delegates were primarily concerned with the possible reactions in Washington, D.C. Some argued that Congress might reject the constitution and postpone the admission of California if its boundaries were too large. Others argued the opposite. Robert Semple quoted T. Butler King as saying, in his capacity as confidential agent of President Taylor, "For God's sake leave us no territory to legislate upon in Congress." On the other hand, it was pointed out that the greater area was too large to be fairly represented in a state legislature, and that it would be particularly unfair and impractical to try to include the Mormons of the Salt Lake region when they were not represented in the convention. They had, in fact, already held a convention of their own in March 1849, and formulated a provisional constitution for a "State of Deseret."

In the end the decision was for the present boundaries of California: on the north, the 42d parallel; on the east, the 120th meridian southward to its juncture with the 39th parallel (a point in Lake Tahoe); thence in a straight southeasterly line to the intersection of the 35th parallel and the Colorado River; then down the middle of the channel of that river to the Mexican border, at the point where the Gila flows into the Colorado.

Like most state constitutions drawn up in the years after the panic of 1837, that of California made a strenuous effort to prevent the organization of banks, although, as we shall see, their rise was inevitable.

Equally futile was the provision forbidding dueling. Gwin, one of the leading advocates of this provision, would fight a duel himself in 1853, and a few years later another United States Senator from California would be killed in one.

California was the first American state to include in its constitution a provision for the separate property of married women. All property of the wife, owned by her before marriage or acquired afterward by gift or otherwise, should remain her property. Such had been the law in Mexican California, and the Americans were under some obligation to preserve it—but an argument offered by Halleck was probably more effective. He advised all his fellow bachelors to vote for this section because it would attract not only prospective wives, but wealthy prospective wives, to California. In vain did some of the married delegates protest that nature had made men the protectors of women and that the constitution should not tamper with this relationship.

For public education, California made the usual provisions of a frontier state. That is, it announced its acceptance of the land grants that the Federal government customarily made to new states for the support of public schools and for a "seminary of learning," or university. "The Legislature," said the constitution, "shall encourage by all suitable means the promotion of intellectual, scientific, moral and agricultural improvements"; and "as soon as may be," it should create a university "with such branches as the public convenience may demand." Robert Semple, president of the convention, exuberantly asked his colleagues: "Why should we send our sons to Europe to finish their education? If we have the means here we can procure the necessary talent; we can bring the President of Oxford University here by offering a sufficient salary." But even if Oxford had had an official with the title of president, the University of California could not easily have attracted him, even 20 years later when that institution was actually opened. Until the 20th century it would remain small and isolated.

Some other uninformed statements were also made in the convention, as when a delegate objected to the phrase "a jury of his peers" on the ground that there was no house of peers in democratic America. But in general the convention did a fairly creditable job under difficult circumstances. It is true that not much of the constitution of 1849 was original. A majority of its provisions were taken from the constitution of Iowa, of which Gwin had arranged to have copies printed for the use of every delegate. Much of the rest of it came from the constitution of New York.

The design accepted for the state seal, on the other hand, was quite original and distinctive, if somewhat cluttered. Minerva, the Roman goddess of political wisdom and of handicrafts and the guardian of cities, appears in the foreground. At her feet crouches a grizzly bear feeding on bunches of grapes. A miner works with rocker and bowl, ships ply the Sacramento River, and the snowy peaks of the Sierra Nevada are seen in the distance. The Greek motto "Eureka," and 31 stars, the last one for the new state of California, are at the top of the design.

One point of dissension was raised: General Vallejo objected to the bear. It reminded him of the indignities he had suffered in the Bear Flag Revolt, and he proposed that it be removed from the seal unless it were shown as

secured by a lasso in the hands of a *vaquero*. In the end he accepted the assurances of Anglo-American delegates that this particular bear signified no offense to the native Californians.

The first legislature. A month after the convention adjourned, the first state officials were elected, on November 13, 1849, the same day on which the constitution was ratified by a light vote, 12,061 in favor and 811 against. Peter H. Burnett was elected Governor, and John McDougal, Lieutenant Governor. On December 15 the legislature began to assemble at the first state capital, San Jose. In joint session of the two houses, it elected Frémont and Gwin as United States Senators; Frémont had the larger number of votes, but a drawing by lot gave him the short term, ending March 3, 1851, while Gwin drew the term extending four years longer.

The permanent location of the state capital was left open to future bids from rival towns, in order to insure that land and buildings would be provided without cost to the state government. The fact that California had not yet been admitted to the Union made the prospects of obtaining state funds uncertain, and because the first legislature failed to establish a permanent location, the capital was hawked about in a most undignified manner. Within five years the seat of government would be moved from San Jose to Vallejo; back to San Jose; back to Vallejo; to Sacramento; back to Vallejo; to Benicia; and at last, in 1854, permanently to Sacramento.

The first state legislature of California, though not a very distinguished body, did not entirely deserve the name that it acquired, "The Legislature of a Thousand Drinks." The appellation seems to have grown out of a phrase repeatedly used by Thomas Jefferson Green. That irrepressible political adventurer from Texas, unabashed when the miners excluded him and his slaves from the Yuba diggings, had secured election as state senator from Sacramento. Moreover, he became chairman of the senate finance committee, and was seeking election to one of the four new major-generalcies of the state militia. A number of the candidates for various offices to be filled by the legislature maintained bars from which they dispensed hospitality to the members in the hope of receiving their votes in return. At the end of each day's session, at least until the one that elected him as a militia commander, Green loudly invited the legislators to have "a thousand drinks" at his expense; journalists could not resist the temptation to apply the phrase as a description of the legislature generally.

The compromise of 1850 and the admission of California to the Union. Congress nearly rejected the new government of California. The new state's admission would upset the equal balance in the number of free and slave states and in the number of their United States Senators, a balance that had long given the South a veto against Federal laws inimical to its "peculiar institution." In the great debates in the national Capital, Southern senators demanded an extension of the Missouri Compromise line of 36°30′ to the Pacific Coast. This line would have bisected California just south of Monterey, and the portion to the south of it would have been organized as a territory open to slavery. The "great compromise" proposed, instead, that California be admitted as a free state, as its people desired, but that the territories of Utah and New Mexico be organized without the ban of the Wilmot Proviso against slavery. Daniel Webster, in his famous speech in the Senate on the 7th of March, argued for this solution and tried to allay the protests of Northern abolitionists and opponents of the expansion of slavery. Slavery, he said, had been perpetuated mainly for its usefulness in the production of cotton. Nature itself had excluded slavery from California and New Mexico, by making their lands so arid that cotton could never be grown there, "and I would not take pains uselessly to reaffirm an ordinance of nature, nor to re-enact the will of God." Webster could hardly have foreseen that with the help of irrigation California would one day produce more cotton than any other state but Texas.

At last, when the South had been further mollified by a stringent new law regulating the return of slaves who had escaped into Northern states, the "omnibus" provisions of the great compromise were approved. The President signed the bill for the admission of California on September 9, 1850. The news reached San Francisco on October 18 and was celebrated with colorful parades; but the new state government had already been operating for nearly a year, exactly as if it had been authorized by Congress. Californians were showing a strong disposition to take things into their own hands.

SELECTED BIBLIOGRAPHY

Theodore Grivas, *Military Governments in California, 1846–1850* (1962), does much to dispel the confusion that has surrounded its subject. The official *Report of the Debates in the Convention of California, on the Formation of the State Constitution* (1950) was well prepared by J. Ross Browne. Cardinal Goodwin, *The Establishment of State Government in California, 1846–1850* (1914), is still a basic work on this period. Also valuable are William H. Ellison, *A Self-governing Dominion; California, 1849–1860* (1950); Woodrow J. Hansen, *The Search for Authority in California* (1960); James A. B. Scherer, *Thirty-first Star* (1942); and William E. Franklin, "Peter H. Burnett and the Provisional Government Movement," *California Historical Society Quarterly*, XL (June 1961), 123–136. Important memoirs are Walter Colton, *Three Years in California* (1850); Samuel H. Willey, *The Transition Period of California* (1901); William H. Ellison, editor, "Memoirs of Hon. William M. Gwin," *California Historical Society Quarterly*, XXI (1940), 1–26, 157–184, 256–277, 311–367; and Charles A. Barker, editor, *Memoirs of Elisha Oscar Crosby* (1945). Robert G. Cowan, *The Admission of the 31st State by the 31st Congress* (1962), is an annotated bibliography of the congressional speeches.

Chapter XII

CRIME AND PUNISHMENT

ONE OF THE most striking and significant evidences of the chronic social disorganization in post-gold rush California was the outbreak of a rash of "vigilance committees." Most historical treatments of these bodies have condoned their actions, and many have even glorified them. The present account takes a different view.

The nature of vigilantism. Richard Henry Dana, in the chapter that he added to his *Two Years Before the Mast* after his return visit to California in 1859, described San Francisco as having been rescued from

> its season of heaven-defying crime, violence, and blood . . . and handed back to soberness, morality, and good government, by that peculiar invention of Anglo-Saxon Republican America, the solemn awe-inspiring Vigilance Committee of the most grave and responsible citizens, the last resort of the thinking and the good, taken to only when vice, fraud, and ruffianism have entrenched themselves behind the forms of law, suffrage, and the ballot.

Several historians, writing in the same tone of defensive righteousness, have perpetuated the racist notion that vigilantism was one of the evidences of Anglo-Saxon superiority, a proof of American ingenuity in adapting self-government to the special conditions of the frontier.

The truth is, first, that vigilantism was not a superior institution, and second, that there was nothing exclusively Anglo-Saxon about it, except perhaps the use of the rope instead of the bullet. *Vigilante* is a Spanish word meaning a watchman or a guard, and the first "committee of vigilance" in California was not in San Francisco in 1851. Rather it was the one described in a manuscript called *"Vigilantes de Los Angeles, 1836,"* by its president, Victor Prudon, a naturalized Mexican of French birth. This *"junta defensora de la seguridad pública"* seized a man and a woman from the custody of the alcaldes and shot them for the murder of the woman's husband.

The true and great contributions of "Anglo-Saxon" jurisprudence have been on the side of the due process of law, while the methods of the vigilance committees were parodies of due process. Their methods were generally more organized and elaborate than those of mere lynch mobs. But the "committees" did not hold their "trials" in open court. They acted in anger and in haste. They did not consider motions for change of venue. Witnesses for the defendants were usually afraid to testify, or even to appear. The committees often resorted to hanging because they had no way of enforcing a sentence of long-term imprisonment. And there was no provision for appeal or for executive clemency.

Taking the law into one's own hands, particularly after regular courts had been established, was itself a criminal action. Yet, remarkably enough, the early American historians of California almost unanimously applauded it. Even the idealistic philosopher, Josiah Royce, in spite of his personal detestation of violence and bullying, strongly praised "popular justice" as exercised by the vigilance committees of San Francisco, although at the same time he condemned lynching in the mines as barbarous and futile. Hubert Howe Bancroft indulged in the most elaborate defenses and rationalizations of "popular tribunals" on such grounds as the sacred right of revolution. He maintained that the vigilantes were "the people," and that the people (especially the self-appointed "best" people) were above all law. These apologistic viewpoints have too often gone unchallenged.

Men who form lynch mobs and vigilance committees, like all other men, are themselves inwardly tortured by assorted feelings of guilt. Samuel Brannan, who did more than anyone else to instigate vigilantism in San Francisco, was building the first great California fortune on money that he had diverted from church property and tithes to his personal use and profit, a practice not far from the robbing of almsboxes. Apostate though he was, he was not unaffected by the knowledge that his former church regarded him as the supreme example of the corrupting influence of money on the human soul. Clearly, Brannan was subconsciously seeking freedom from his own guilt in arrogating to himself the punishment of others.

The emotion of guilt is essentially the fear of punishment. Gratification in inflicting pain, humiliation, and even death and destruction upon someone else results from the subconscious, irrational feeling that thereby one somehow achieves escape from punishment, or even assures one's own survival. In varying degrees and circumstances the latent existence of this sadistic pattern is universal among human beings. Because it is the least admirable of human traits, and also because rational recognition of it defeats its hidden irrational purpose, men resort to extreme sanctimoniousness in order to disguise it, in their own minds most of all. This element accounts for the strange air of righteous solemnity often noted in a number of the public ceremonies sponsored by the San Francisco committees of vigilance. The rank and file of these organizations included a substantial contingent of the worst and most guilty, who joined for the conscious purpose of saving themselves from hanging. But the leadership included some of the "best" men, who joined for more subtle and obscure but not entirely different reasons. Vigilantism was a manifestation of moral self-delusion and righteous sadism.

Early lynching in the mines. During the summer and fall of 1848 there was very little crime in the mining camps because the great wave of gold seekers, with its large criminal element, had not yet arrived. Late in the fall, near the Calaveras River, a sailor who had deserted his ship was flogged and his ears were cropped for a robbery, and the miners who heard of the episode generally asserted that it had had a good effect on the conditions of public safety. At Sutter's Fort in December a merchant named C. E. Pickett killed a man in self-defense. Brannan, who had himself been the defendant in one of the first jury trials in American California, and who was a business competitor of Pickett's, insisted that he be tried for murder. The first and second alcaldes and the sheriff resigned rather than conduct a trial. Because no one else was willing to serve as either prosecutor or judge, Brannan served in both capacities, but the jury balked and the prisoner was acquitted.

The first of the gold-rush mob actions that resulted in hanging occurred in the middle of January 1849 in a mining camp only 9 miles from the site of the discovery at Coloma. Thus Dry Diggings gained the name of Hangtown, later to be changed again to Placerville. Of five men who were whipped for robbery, three were then hanged by a mob that also threatened to hang E. Gould Buffum for trying to oppose the proceedings.

The "Hounds" in San Francisco. Congress left California almost literally lawless from 1846 to 1850. Within this vacuum there began to appear, in San Francisco, a form of organized lawlessness and terrorism. When Colonel Stevenson's regiment of New York Volunteers was disbanded, a group of its members led by Lt. Sam Roberts formed an organization called the Regulators, or more commonly, the Hounds, allegedly dedicated to maintaining public order, and especially devoted to hounding Spanish Americans and other "foreigners" out of California. Alcalde Leavenworth tried to use them as deputy policemen, but he could not control them. They held drunken parades and levied tribute, bullied merchants by day and looted foreign settlements by night. In the evening of July 15, 1849, they paraded to an attack upon Little Chile, a tent community at the foot of Telegraph Hill, where some of them murdered a mother and criminally assaulted her daughter.

The next morning Sam Brannan addressed a crowd from the roof of the

"Hounds" attacking Chileans. (Courtesy of the Bancroft Library)

alcalde's little office on the Plaza. A counterorganization called the Law and Order party was formed and its members deputized, a charitable fund for the Chileans was collected, and by sunset Roberts and 18 other Hounds had been caught and imprisoned in a ship in the bay.

Nine men were more or less legally convicted of crimes, but the penalty was banishment, and this proved unenforceable. Many of the Hounds continued their depredations, though no longer openly. In such activities they were joined by some of the "Sydney Ducks," ex-convicts or escaped convicts from Australia. The Australian immigrants were thus given a bad name that most of them did not deserve.

The San Francisco committee of 1851. The beating and robbery of C. J. Jansen, a prominent merchant, in his shop in the heart of town on February 19, 1851, produced another outburst of popular excitement. Two Australians, Berdue and Windred, were arrested, and mistakenly identified by Jansen as the men who had assaulted and robbed him. Berdue was wrongly believed to be James ("English Jim") Stuart, another Australian who had escaped from jail at Marysville while awaiting trial for the murder of a sheriff.

A mob incited by Brannan was preparing to seize and hang the two prisoners without a trial when a young merchant named William Tell Coleman managed to catch the ear of the crowd and to persuade it to organize a "people's court." This procedure, with Coleman acting as prosecutor, resulted in a hung jury. The two men were then returned to the jurisdiction of the regular authorities.

On May 4, 1851, there occurred the fifth and greatest in a series of fires that had repeatedly devastated the city. The fact that this fifth fire occurred on the anniversary of the second intensified the growing suspicion that all the fires were incendiary, set by Hounds and Sydney Ducks in revenge and defiance and to facilitate looting. Loot was found hidden in the "Sydney Town" district, and criminals were thought to be emboldened by the failure to hang the supposed robbers of Jansen. A volunteer night patrol was organized, and on Sunday, June 8, the *Alta California* published a proposal for a "committee of safety" or "committee of vigilance." That afternoon a meeting in Sam Brannan's office determined to call a larger meeting of other responsible citizens, and on June 9, in Brannan's building, that meeting adopted a constitution for the first San Francisco "Committee of Vigilance."

The very next evening, taps on a fire bell summoned the committee to pass judgment on John Jenkins, who had been caught stealing a small safe and was dragged to the committee's headquarters instead of the police station. Jenkins was insolent, and threatened that his friends were organizing to rescue him and destroy the committee. The decisive moment came when William A. Howard, a sea captain, cried, "Gentlemen, as I understand it, we came here to hang somebody." Coleman opposed hanging a man at night, and suggested waiting until dawn, when Jenkins would "rise with the sun." But Brannan secured the approval of the crowd in the Plaza, and there, from a beam at the south end of the "Old Adobe," Jenkins was hanged by moonlight. Thus the committee began its work by hanging the first criminal it apprehended, within a few hours after his crime, and for a rather petty robbery rather than a murder. The death penalty for robbery and grand larceny had been adopted by the California legislature early in 1851, and remained in effect until 1856. But hanging men for stealing meant that there was no greater penalty for murder, and over the state as a whole it had the net effect of greatly increasing the number of murders committed by robbers to prevent identification or pursuit.

A coroner's inquest into the death of Jenkins identified nine vigilantes as parties to it, but the committee made their arrest impractical by releasing the names of all its members. In July the committee chanced to apprehend the real James Stuart, and thus secured the exoneration of the innocent Berdue, who was then awaiting execution by action of the legally constituted courts. This episode, though the result of mere accident, won the committee many admirers whom it would not otherwise have gained. After securing a highly picaresque confession from Stuart, the committee hanged him, and in August it also hanged two other Sydney Ducks, McKenzie and Whittaker, whom Stuart's confessions had implicated in various robberies.

Seal of the San Francisco Vigilance Committee. (Courtesy of the Bancroft Library)

In the meantime the executive committee had deposed Sam Brannan as its president, and replaced him with the less impulsive and less erratic Stephen Payran. The roster shows that along with Brannan the founders and early members of the vigilance committee of 1851 were predominantly commission merchants and sea captains—two groups who disliked government, courts, lawyers, and politicians as forces that threatened interference with their own freedom of action. It was a peculiar base on which to rest a claim that the leading vigilantes were "the best citizens" of the community; but this claim was made, and has been periodically repeated ever since.

It is significant that no lawyers whatever were members of the committee of vigilance. The committee would not have welcomed their membership, even had they wished to join it.

Before its extrajudicial activities ended in September, the vigilance committee of 1851 had made nearly 90 arrests. Besides its four hangings, it had whipped one man, sentenced 28 to deportation, remanded 15 to the authorities for trial, and released 41.

Statewide vigilance. San Francisco's example inspired the formation of several local vigilance committees in other towns, and a further increase of less formal lynching in the mining communities. Of dozens of such cases, perhaps the most infamous was the hanging of the Mexican woman Juanita by a

The execution of John Jenkins. (Courtesy of the Bancroft Library)

mob of miners at Downieville on July 5, 1851. They had gathered to hear a Fourth of July oration by United States Senator John B. Weller, and afterward had celebrated far into the night. In the early hours of the morning Juanita killed one of them with a knife. The friends of her victim, one Joseph Cannan, asserted the theory that he had not intended to harm her, and that his purpose in entering her cabin was only to apologize to her for having broken her door down, which had happened only because he was intoxicated.

Within a few hours Juanita was brought to "trial" by what one observer, David P. Barstow, called "the hungriest, craziest, wildest mob that ever I saw anywhere." After saying that she would defend herself again in the same way under the same circumstances, Juanita adjusted her own noose and stepped from the improvised scaffold. Barstow was certain that "the hanging of the woman was murder. No jury in the world, on any principle of self-defense or protection of life and property, would ever have convicted her."

At Napa in May of 1851 a group of citizens lynched Hamilton McCauley, largely as a matter of local pride and as an incident in their political feud with neighboring Benicia. Napa was a town of Northerners, Benicia a town of Southern Chivalry Democrats. McCauley, of Benicia, had tried to chastise a freed Negro on the street in Napa. The Negro not only struck back but beat McCauley severely in the fight that followed. The local justice of the peace taunted McCauley, who stabbed him to death. For this crime McCauley was legally sentenced to execution. His friends persuaded Governor John McDougal to commute the sentence to life imprisonment, but residents of Napa hanged the prisoner before the sheriff could arrive from Benicia to deliver the commutation paper.

In the riotous cow town of Los Angeles in the 1850s there were more executions, both legal and extralegal, than in the much larger city of San Francisco. It was sometimes difficult to distinguish the legal executions from the lynchings in Los Angeles because of the tendency of the constituted authorities to authorize vigilantism. In 1851, the mayor and the city council created a vigilance committee by formal action. Among those it hanged were three men charged with the murder of Maj. Gen. J. H. Bean of the California militia. One of the men hanged was later proved innocent. In 1854, Mayor Stephen C. Foster dispersed a mob bent on lynching the gambler and killer Dave Brown, by promising that if the regular authorities did not succeed in convicting and executing him he would resign as mayor and join the vigilantes. When Brown's lawyers secured a stay of execution, Mayor Foster kept his promise, directed the lynching, and resumed his office after it was over.

The most famous case in the southern mines occurred at Columbia on October 10, 1855. This was the hanging of John S. Barclay for killing an intoxicated man who had laid violent hands on Barclay's wife. There was a mock trial in which only the prosecutor, a local political idol who had just been elected to the state senate, was permitted to speak at any length. The drunken viciousness of the mob, the extreme courage of the sheriff in risking his life to try to take the prisoner away from it, and the fact that by that time the legal courts in the area were well organized, produced some local reaction against lynching in general.

The San Francisco committee of 1856. The Committee of Vigilance formed in 1851 has been known as the "first" such body in San Francisco, and that of 1856 as the "second." This is misleading. It should be recalled that both the Regulators (or Hounds) of 1849, and the Law and Order party formed to combat them, were previous instances of self-constituted vigilance organizations in the city.

The organization or rather the revival of the Committee of Vigilance in 1856 followed two highly sensational shootings, the killing of Gen. William H. Richardson by the gambler Charles Cora, and the shooting of James King of William, crusading editor of the *Daily Evening Bulletin,* by the politician James P. Casey. Richardson, then serving as United States Marshal, had become extremely angry when Cora and his mistress, the wealthy Arabella Ryan, keeper of a notorious house of prostitution, attracted attention by sitting directly behind Richardson and his wife in a box at the opening of the new American Theater. The next evening Richardson, clearly intoxicated, accosted

Cora on the street and drew a derringer pistol. Cora drew his own derringer and fired a fatal shot. Arabella Ryan, who called herself Belle Cora, then secured the services of Col. Edward D. Baker, and in the subsequent trial Baker's forceful plea on the ground of self-defense led to a hung jury.

Cora was in jail awaiting a second trial when the shooting of James King of William occurred on May 14, 1856. James King had added the name of William, his father, to distinguish him from other James Kings in the District of Columbia, where he was born. He came to San Francisco in 1848, and in the early 1850s became wealthy as a banker. The sudden loss of his fortune, however, embittered him, and he became a newspaper editor in order to attack the various men upon whom he blamed his own troubles and those of the city. His editorship of the *Bulletin* was a sort of journalistic vigilantism. The pen, he felt, could be mightier than the rope or the whip, the printing press a mightier punisher of evil than the gallows. He denounced the Tammany-style political machine of David C. Broderick, and accused him of having imported James P. Casey from New York City as an expert ballot-box stuffer. Casey was elected a county supervisor in an election widely denounced as corrupt. King published in the *Bulletin* the fact that Casey had served a term in the New York state penitentiary at Sing Sing.

A great many men had come from the older parts of the country to escape their pasts, so many that it was often considered a necessary convention in California that a man's past was nobody's business. A popular song of the period was

> Oh, what was your name in the States?
> Was it Thompson or Johnson or Bates?
> Did you murder your wife and flee for your life?
> Oh, what was your name in the States?

King's exposure of his prison record deeply disturbed Casey and made him almost incoherent. He threatened King in the *Bulletin* office and shot him on the street an hour later.

That evening a group of former members of the vigilance committee of 1851 determined to reactivate the movement, under the leadership of William Tell Coleman, now the most respected of the group. Coleman was a man of handsome and commanding appearance who had come to Sacramento in 1849 at the age of 25. The early lynchings in the region had impressed him as demonstrations of the great value of "prompt and summary punishment." He was consistently successful in business from his first transaction, in which he found one merchant who promised to buy as many bottles of a certain patent medicine as he could deliver at 5 dollars a bottle, and another who sold him nearly 300 bottles at 3 dollars each. Since then, William T. Coleman & Company, with headquarters in San Francisco, had become one of the country's leading mercantile firms.

The *Herald*, then the largest newspaper in the city, was the only one that opposed the revival of the vigilance movement. Most of the merchants had promptly joined the committee. They ceremoniously burned a large number of copies of the *Herald* on Front Street, and nearly ruined it by withdrawing their advertisements.

The committee began to collect arms and to form a military unit. On the other hand, a number of prominent citizens formed the Law and Order party, denouncing the vigilantes and adopting the name of the organization of 1849, which had taken all its actions against the Hounds in full cooperation with the legal authorities. Among the Law and Order leaders were Mayor Van Ness, Sheriff Scannell, and Gen. William Tecumseh Sherman, whom the Governor of the state had recently appointed commander of the San Francisco district of the California militia.

On May 16 Governor J. Neely Johnson came down from Sacramento to confer with Coleman. Few state executives have ever been more bitterly denounced than Johnson was for his role in these conferences and in the events that followed them. He was only 28 years old at the time—California in the 1850s was a young man's country—and he was in an extremely explosive situation. Having been swept into office only the year before, in the sudden and brief triumph of the American or Know-Nothing party in California, he was painfully inexperienced. In his discussion with Coleman he believed that he had secured a promise that the vigilantes would not attack the jail to seize Cora and Casey. Coleman later maintained that he had merely promised to give notice before moving to seize the two men, and that a condition even of this promise was that the governor guarantee *"an immediate trial and instant execution"* by the public authorities. Four days after the shooting, 2,500 armed vigilantes advanced on the county jail and removed Cora and Casey to the committee's headquarters. The sheriff's 150 deputies made no attempt to resist, and thus a self-appointed committee had virtually taken over the government of San Francisco at a time of almost hysterical public excitement.

Two days later, on the 20th, while Cora was being tried before the vigilance tribunal, word came that James King of William had died. The emotional effect of this announcement ensured the hanging not only of Casey but also of Cora, although Cora was condemned by a bare majority of the vigilante tribunal while Casey was condemned unanimously.

Both men were hanged with great public ceremony on the 22d, the day of King's funeral. Cora had just been quietly married to Arabella Ryan. He died with outward composure and without comment. Casey made a brief and excited speech, denying that he was guilty of murder.

The Law and Order leaders had hoped that the committee, having "hanged somebody," would now disband. Instead it made further arrests and strengthened the defenses of its headquarters building, known as Fort Gunnybags. A Law and Order committee urged Governor Johnson to call out the state militia to suppress insurrection. One leader of this Law and Order group was John McDougal, Governor in 1851, whose popularity and reputation in the state had

A membership certificate of the San Francisco Vigilance Committee of 1856, suggesting the self-congratulation and self-righteousness that characterized the organization. (*Courtesy of the Bancroft Library*)

been destroyed when he had issued proclamations criticizing the earlier Committee of Vigilance.

Before calling out the militia, Governor Johnson and General Sherman secured a promise of arms from Gen. John E. Wool, commandant of the

Federal Army on the Pacific Coast and of the Federal arsenal at Benicia. Justice David S. Terry of the state supreme court issued a writ of habeas corpus for the release of Deputy Sheriff William Mulligan, keeper of the county jail, who was being held prisoner by the vigilance committee. The committee defied the writ. Sheriff Scannell telegraphed the Governor that a large body of armed men was defying the authority of county and state government, and asked for help from the militia. On June 2 Governor Johnson ordered General Sherman to call upon "such numbers" of the militia as he considered necessary, and two days later the Governor proclaimed San Francisco to be in a state of insurrection.

At this point General Wool reneged on his promise of arms. There was an angry conference at Benicia in which Justice Terry's opposition to the vigilantes was so extreme that it alienated Sherman. Response to the call to militia duty had been sparse, and Sherman was unwilling to command men whom he could not arm. Moreover, he was a partner in a San Francisco banking firm which was threatened with bankruptcy as the result of a boycott by vigilante merchants. He resigned as militia commander, and was succeeded by Volney E. Howard, a former attorney general of Texas.

Justice Terry, a close friend of Howard and like him a former Texan, now became the chief adviser of the Law and Order faction, taking time out from his regular judicial duties. He unearthed a statute requiring the Federal government to furnish a certain allotment of arms to the state militia, and General Wool released 113 muskets. When this shipment was dispatched to San Francisco in a small schooner, the vigilantes intercepted it. On June 21, J. R. Maloney, one of the militiamen who had been in charge of the shipment, gave an account of the affair to a group of Law and Order men including Judge Terry. Vigilante policeman Sterling A. Hopkins, who had served as hangman in the execution of Cora and Casey, tried to arrest Maloney, obviously in order to prevent him from testifying against the vigilantes on a piracy charge. In the ensuing scuffle a vigilante accidentally fired a pistol, and Justice Terry stabbed Hopkins with a bowie knife. When Terry sought refuge in a militia armory, a large body of vigilantes forced their way into the building and arrested him. Shortly afterward they confiscated the last of the arms remaining in possession of militia units anywhere in the city.

As one of its members put it, the vigilance committee had organized to hunt coyotes, but in Supreme Court Justice Terry it had a grizzly bear by the tail. Nevertheless it conducted a trial, in which Terry brilliantly conducted his own defense. Fortunately, Hopkins did not die. Though Terry was "convicted" of assault with intent to kill, he was released on August 7 after a bitter disagreement among the vigilance leaders.

The next day the executive committee decided that although it would remain in existence, the vigilance committee as a whole should disband. It did so after a great parade of 6,000 armed men on August 18. Fort Gunnybags was kept open for several months as a museum, and attracted large crowds. There, after the hangings of Cora and Casey, the alleged murderers Brace and Hetherington had also been tried and hanged; Francis Murray, alias "Yankee" Sullivan, ex-pugilist and accused ballot-box stuffer, had committed suicide in his cell; and 30 men had been sentenced to deportation with orders not to return to San Francisco on pain of death. It was claimed that several hundred other bad characters had left the city in fear of the vigilantes.

The San Francisco Committee of Vigilance of 1856 was, as Josiah Royce described it, "a Business Man's Revolution." It was an application of private enterprise to the administration of justice. In the elections of November 1856 its leaders also drew up a ticket of candidates which swept every city office. Under this "people's reform" regime in 1857 the cost of the city-and-county government was reduced to one-sixth of the previous year's figure. Some schools had to be closed, but the prime objective of drastic tax reduction was temporarily accomplished. The philosophy of the vigilante leadership clearly reflected a set of attitudes characteristic of most early California businessmen and some later ones—their dislike and distrust of government and of public officeholders, their resentment of taxation, and their contempt for politicians as an inferior class. These feelings were peculiarly accentuated in a new community in which all business was highly speculative, and in which so many men—businessmen and politicians alike—were hoping to make large fortunes quickly. Naturally most of the officeholders, politicians, and lawyers were on the Law and Order side, and shared Terry's contempt for the vigilance leaders as "sour flour and pork merchants." There was some tendency for the Southern Chivalry Democrats to be Law and Order men and to despise the vigilantes as Yankee shopkeepers, but the Northern antislavery politician David Broderick was equally hostile to the vigilance committee.

The charges that the city government had been corrupt and inefficient had some basis, but the vigilance movement brought no permanent reform in these conditions. The charges that the legally constituted courts had been corrupt were in general not true, so far as the judges were concerned, and the abuses of the jury system were mainly the result of the general evasion of jury duty by otherwise respectable citizens. As for vigilante jurisprudence, its record of violations of due process was appalling.

The leaders of the vigilance committees would have served California far better if they had confined their activities to legal methods and to genuine reforms. It is doubtful that they accomplished anything whatever of real value, and they left a vicious, dangerous, and persistent tradition of contempt for the normal processes of government.

Filibusters. Somewhat related to the spirit of vigilantism was the spirit of those Californians of the 1850s who took international law into their own hands, in violation of the United States laws against filibustering. Filibusters were attempts by private adventurers to seize foreign territory by force and intrigue. Again the Spanish had furnished the word for it—*filibustero* was the

Fort Gunnybags. From a contemporary letter sheet. (Courtesy of the California Historical Society)

Spanish equivalent of "freebooter." There was a rash of such schemes, directed against Hawaii, northern Mexico, and Central America. Some of them were extravagantly praised by several California newspapers, mainly proslavery ones, as continuations of Manifest Destiny and extensions of American institutions.

None other than Sam Brannan led a filibustering expedition to Hawaii in the fall of 1851. His redwood house in San Francisco, built with Mormon funds and by donated Mormon labor, had been burned, and he had quarreled with his wife as well as with his colleagues in the vigilance committee. With a party of 24 men in the ship *Game Cock,* he landed at Honolulu on November 15, ostensibly to persuade King Kamehameha III to cede some islands to him for a colonizing venture. Hawaiian officials asserted with good reason that Brannan planned to make himself governor-general of the islands. They raised a defense force of pikemen, and Brannan returned somewhat ignominiously to San Francisco.

During the decade there were several disastrous filibustering expeditions to Sonora, most of them organized with varying degrees of secret connivance on the part of Mexican politicians and the government of Napoleon III, and involving groups of Frenchmen who had failed to find gold in California. But the most famous of all the California filibusters was William Walker, a shy and homely but intensely ambitious little man, weighing about 100 pounds, who became known to some, especially to himself, as "the gray-eyed man of destiny." Born in Tennessee, he came to California in 1850. Having failed at medicine, law, and journalism, Walker organized an armed expedition to Lower California in 1853, and proclaimed a republic, with himself as president, at La Paz on November 3. Early the following year he "annexed" neighboring Sonora, on paper, but the hostility of the Mexicans and of the United States government brought his party to the verge of starvation and forced him to surrender to American troops at the border and to face trial in a Federal court at San Francisco. There a sympathetic jury acquitted him.

Walker had grandiose plans to unite all Central America into a single military empire under his leadership and to develop its agriculture by reintroducing Negro slavery. In 1855 he led an expedition to Nicaragua, but a coalition of neighboring republics drove him out after much bloodshed. In an attempt to return in 1860 he was arrested by a British naval force and shot by a Honduran firing squad. Many American Southerners assumed that his motives were patriotic, and that he planned ultimate annexation of Central America by the United States, though he himself repeatedly denied that he had any such intention. His chief motive was his desire for personal prestige, wealth, and power.

SELECTED BIBLIOGRAPHY

The tone of most historical treatments of the vigilantes was set by three important and influential accounts, all written about the same time. Charles H. Shinn, in his *Mining Camps, a Study in American Frontier Government* (1885), accepted very uncritically the reminiscences of the participants whom he interviewed. Josiah Royce, *California, from the Conquest in 1846 to the Second Vigilance Committee in San Francisco, a Study of American Character* (1886; new edition, 1948), was more critical of the miners, but praised the San Francisco committees. Hubert Howe Bancroft, *Popular Tribunals* (two volumes, 1887), defended some of the rural tribunals and was positively worshipful of the urban ones; his views reflected the feelings of most San Francisco businessmen, of whom Bancroft was one.

Mary Floyd Williams edited the *Papers of the San Francisco Committee of Vigilance of 1851* (1919). Her *History of the San Francisco Committee of Vigilance of 1851* (1921) is scholarly in details but generally very admiring. George R. Stewart, *Committee of Vigilance, Revolution in San Francisco, 1851* (1964), is also sympathetic. Stanton A. Coblentz, *Villains and Vigilantes: the Story of James King of William and Pioneer Justice in California* (1936), is lively but flimsy, and gives insufficient attention to the numerous villains who were vigilantes. The highly laudatory spirit of *"The Lion of the Vigilantes," William T. Coleman and the Life of Old San Francisco* (1939), by James A. B. Scherer, is well suggested by its title, taken from Robert Louis Stevenson.

The few early published criticisms of the vigilantes include the anonymous *Judges and Criminals... History of the Vigilance Committee of San Francisco* (1858); James O'Meara, *The Vigilance Committee of 1856, by a Pioneer California Journalist* (1887); William Tecumseh Sherman's *Memoirs* (two volumes, 1875); and his "Unpublished Letters," *Century Magazine*, XLIII (December 1891), 296–309, which should be compared with Coleman's article in the November issue. Accounts by O'Meara, Sherman, and Coleman, are reprinted in Doyce B. Nunis, Jr., editor, *The San Francisco Vigilance Committee of 1856: Three Views* (1971), with an excellent historical introduction. See also Dwight L. Clarke, *William Tecumseh Sherman: Gold Rush Banker* (1969). Isaac J. Wistar, an associate of E. D. Baker in the defense of Cora, denounced the vigilantes in his *Autobiography* (two volumes, 1914). Some understanding of "The Law and Order View of the San Francisco Vigilance Committee of 1856" may be gained from the correspondence of Governor J. Neely Johnson, arranged for publication by Herbert G. Florcken, *California Historical Society Quarterly*, XIV (December 1935), 350–374, and XV (March, June, and September 1936), 70–87, 143–162, 247–265.

Critical treatments of vigilantism are in Ethel May Tinneman, "The Opposition to the San Francisco Vigilance Committee of 1856," M.A. thesis, University of California, Berkeley (1941); William H. Ellison, *A Self-governing Dominion, California, 1849–1860* (1950); A. Russell Buchanan, *David S. Terry of California, Dueling Judge* (1959); and John W. Caughey, *Their Majesties, the Mob* (1960), its title taken from one of the letters of Dame Shirley.

Two recent interpretations, in sharp contrast with each other (Brown's critical, Olmsted's favorable), are Richard Maxwell Brown, "The American Vigilante Tradition," in *The History of Violence in America* (1969), edited by Hugh D. Graham and Ted R. Gurr, and Brown's "Pivot of American Vigilantism: The San Francisco Vigilance Committee of 1856," in *Reflections of Western Historians* (1969), edited by John A. Carroll; and Roger Olmsted, "San Francisco and the Vigilante Style," *The American West*, VII (January and March 1970).

On filibustering, see Rufus K. Wyllys, *The French in Sonora, 1850–1854* (1932); Andrew F. Rolle, "California Filibustering and the Hawaiian Kingdom," *Pacific Historical Review*, XIX (August 1950), 251–264; William O. Scroggs, *Filibusters and Financiers* (1916); and William Walker's own account of *The War in Nicaragua* (1860).

Chapter XIII

LAND-TITLE TROUBLES

AMONG THE CIRCUMSTANCES that made for demoralization, lawlessness, and violence in early American California, one of the most important was the confused condition of the ownership of land. Not until 1851 did the United States government determine its general policy toward the confirmation of titles to the vast lands that had been granted under Mexico, and after the determination of the policy many more years were required to secure actual approval of claims. In the meantime the titles remained in dispute, and the development of the state was held back accordingly.

Problems of the Mexican grants. American laws required that land titles be defined exactly and clearly, and by American standards the Mexican system was incredibly lax and vague. In California, not even the relatively loose requirements of Mexican law had been effectively or consistently observed. Land had been abundant and of very little value, and Mexican-Californian officialdom was somewhat lackadaisical and frequently disrupted by sudden changes of personnel. The authorities failed to provide the grantees with adequate evidence of their titles, or to keep adequate records in the archives. Maps, when there were any, were absurdly sketchy, for professional surveyors were seldom available. The whole of the Pomona Valley, for example, was breezily described as "the place being vacant which is known by the name of [Rancho] San José, distant some six leagues, more or less, from the Ex-Mission of San Gabriel, a map of which place we will lay before your Excellency as soon as possible." The frequent use of the expression "a little more or less" (*poco más ó menos*) after any measure of distance was typical of the Mexican grant system. There were several legal requirements, such as that a grant had to have been approved by the territorial assembly and to have been occupied; very seldom, however, had all of the requirements been fulfilled.

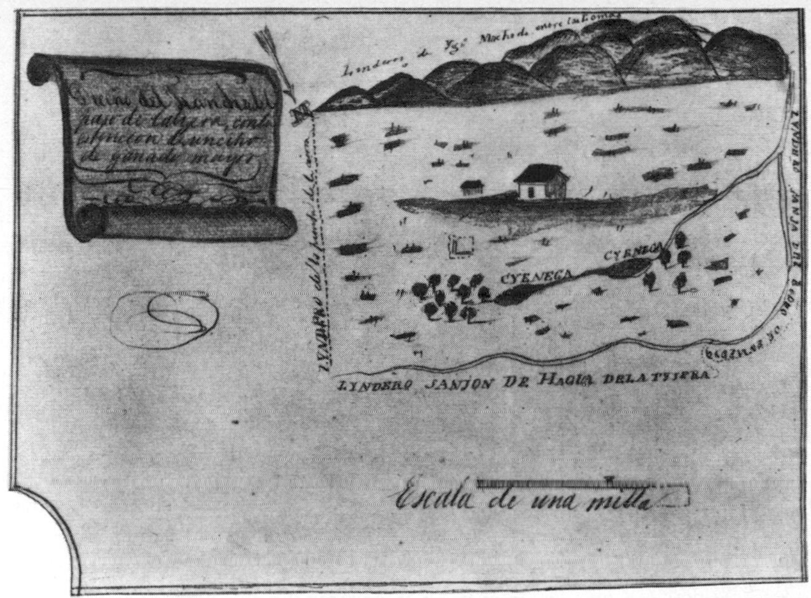

Rancho La Ciénega as described by Vicente Sanchez in a petition to Governor Micheltorena in 1843: "Bounded on the south by the rancho of Don Ignacio Machado, on the north by the water ditch de la Tijera, on the east by La Punta de la Ciénega, and on the west by the water ditch del Rodeo de Medio." (*Robert H. Becker,* Diseños of California Ranchos: Maps of Thirty-Seven Land Grants, 1822–1846, *San Francisco, 1964, No.* 33)

Map of Rancho La Ciénega superimposed on a map of a portion of the present city of Los Angeles. (Courtesy of the Bancroft Library)

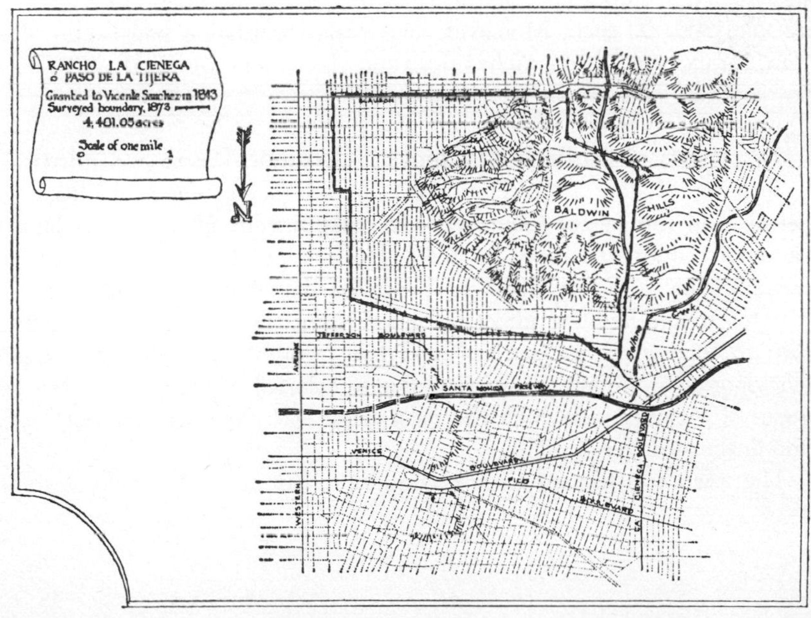

There were more than 500 ranchos in Alta California in 1846, but more than 800 claims were filed in the American courts, many of them covering portions of ranchos. The claims covered nearly all the valley lands of the coastal region as far north as the Russian River, and a number of large tracts in the Sacramento and northern San Joaquin Valleys.

The treaty of Guadalupe Hidalgo promised that "property of every kind" belonging to Mexicans in the ceded territories should be "inviolably respected"; but American settlers generally believed that all the lands in California were now, or ought to be, United States public lands by right of conquest. Under the preemption system, made general by the act of 1841, Americans were accustomed to occupy tracts on the Federal public lands before they were surveyed and opened to settlement, and then to be permitted to buy the land at the minimum price.

In Oregon, Congress made a gift of a 640-acre homestead to every settler who arrived before 1850, and although this special provision was not extended to the California settlers, many of them felt that they were entitled to something of the sort and would eventually receive it. They could not believe that a few hundred Mexican grantees would be permitted to monopolize some 13 million acres of land, without fences or boundary markers, little if any of it visibly improved and much of it entirely unoccupied. Most of the claims did not represent lands that had been long in the possession of old California families as their homes. In fact a majority of the grants were dated within the last five years before the American conquest, and it was accurately suspected that some of those claimed to have been made under Governors Micheltorena and Pico had been signed by them after the forced expirations of their terms of office, and antedated. There were many multiple grants. The various claims of the Pico family totaled 532,000 acres, and those of the De la Guerra and Carrillo families, more than 300,000 each. Moreover, large-scale speculation had begun. Thomas Larkin, for example, had purchased several claims totaling nearly 200,000 acres.

The reports of Halleck and Jones. Governor Mason had instructed his secretary of state, Capt. Henry W. Halleck (later General Halleck, Union Chief of Staff during the Civil War) to make a study of California land titles. In a report completed early in 1849, Halleck pointed out that most of the Mexican claims were imperfect, and asserted that many of them were fraudulent. This report had the effect of encouraging the views of those who were known to themselves as "settlers" and less favorably described as "squatters." Their vigorous opinions produced not only colorful argumentation but several episodes of violence, of which the most tragic was the "squatter riot" at Sacramento in the summer of 1850.

The town was located on land granted to Sutter by Alvarado, a grant that

The dark areas on the map show the grants that were later confirmed by the United States. From W. W. Robinson, Land in California, University of California Press, Berkeley, California, 1948.

would eventually be upheld. Several thousand settlers, refusing to recognize the validity of this title, had squatted on vacant lots owned by purchasers from Sutter. After sheriff's deputies began to destroy the squatters' houses and fences, there was a meeting to collect money for a legal defense fund. James McClatchy, later the founder of the city's leading journalistic family, told this meeting that "If the speculators want to fight, I am for giving them battle. . . . Let us put up all the fences pulled down and also put up [hang] all the men who pull them down." He was arrested for trying to carry out at least a part of his threat. On August 13, when an armed band moved to rescue McClatchy from the riverboat that served as a jail, Mayor Harden Bigelow gathered a crowd of citizens, and in a clash at 4th and J Streets the city assessor and three squatters were killed and the mayor was wounded. The next day another battle led to the death of Sheriff Joseph McKinney and several others on both sides.

In the meantime the Secretary of the Interior had appointed a brilliant young attorney, William Carey Jones, to make another investigation. Jones had married a sister of Jessie Benton Frémont, and the views of California land titles that he embodied in his report in March 1850 coincided with the opinions of his father-in-law, Senator Benton, and also with those of John C. Frémont, his brother-in-law and client, who had had the good fortune to purchase the only Mexican grant on which large amounts of gold were subsequently discovered. The Jones report maintained that the grants were mostly "perfect titles . . . and those which were not perfect—that is, which lack some formality, or some *evidence* of completeness, have the same *equity* as those which are perfect, and were or would have been equally respected under the government which has passed away." Thus Jones recommended a very liberal policy toward the Mexican grants. Naturally the claimants praised this report and the settlers denounced it.

The act of 1851 and the Land Commission. The act that determined the policy of the United States toward the land claims in California was introduced by Senator William M. Gwin, chief political spokesman for the American settlers. His bill provided for the appointment by the President of a board of three commissioners. This board was to decide the validity of all claims to land under Mexican titles. All the lands of the rejected claims were to be regarded as public lands. Both the claimant and the United States had the right of appeal to the Federal district court and then to the United States Supreme Court.

In general this resembled the plan which the Federal government had worked out over the previous half century in dealing with the large Spanish grants in Louisiana and Missouri. For many years Senator Benton had argued that this system made far too stringent demands upon those who sought to establish title to lands previously granted under Spain in the territories of the Louisiana Purchase. Benton considered the system not only as unjust to the grantees, but also as a source of unnecessary and dangerous public confusion and excessive litigation in the whole matter of land ownership. He had advocated the settlers' theory of their rights to form a provisional government in California, but in the land question Benton championed the cause of the Mexican grantees. His position in the Senate debates was weakened by charges that he was favoring his sons-in-law, Frémont and Jones; but his views were entirely consistent with the position he had long taken on similar land problems in his own state of Missouri.

Benton maintained that the proposed plan would have the effect of confiscating the lands of the grantees in California, and thus of violating the treaty with Mexico. Every title, he said, would be treated as a fraud against the United States until its holder had established it in three different courts, one of them the Supreme Court, located 3,000 miles away. Benton offered his own proposal, under which the confirmation of titles would have been quick and easy. A recorder would simply have accepted registration of each claim without challenge, unless, with the aid of the United States district attorney, he found definite evidence of fraud; only in such cases would litigation be required. But this plan was rejected, and the Gwin bill became law in March 1851.

The land commission held its hearings from January 1852 to March 1856. All its sessions were held in San Francisco except for one brief term at Los Angeles. Of the more than 800 cases presented to it, all but a few were appealed to the district court, and 99 were appealed to the Supreme Court. Ultimately 604 claims, involving nearly nine million acres, were confirmed, while 209 claims, involving about four million acres, were rejected. Some of the cases dragged on in the courts for several decades, and the *average* length of time required to secure evidence of ownership was *17 years* from the time of submitting a claim to the board.

By the time a grant was confirmed, its original holder was usually bankrupt. Even before 1851 most of the grantees had been in financial straits from such troubles as droughts, taxes, extravagant living, careless management, and disputes among heirs. The litigation required for an American title under the system established by the Gwin act was long and ruinously expensive. Although the alleged excessiveness of the lawyers' fees has often been exaggerated, there were dozens of instances in which the grantee was ruined while his attorney became rich, especially by taking part of the fees in land, holding the land as a speculation, and ultimately winning the case. Such legal experts as William Carey Jones, the members of the firm of Halleck, Peachy, and Billings, and the lawyer-historian Theodore H. Hittell built up large fortunes in this way. If the grantee tried to sell part of his land to pay the costs of litigation, he could get only a low price because he did not yet have a secure title. Mortgages, to which most of the grantees had to resort, were available only at catastrophic rates of compound interest ranging as high as 8 percent a month in the early 1850s.

If a grantee finally managed to establish his title in court, he often found his land occupied by settlers who refused to get off. Squatters were so numerous that their votes were a strong factor in politics. In 1852 Senator Gwin introduced a bill which would have permitted squatters to settle on 80-acre tracts of otherwise unoccupied land in Mexican grants. If the grant was later confirmed, the grantee would be compensated with 80 acres of public land elsewhere. This measure failed of adoption in Congress, but it was a good example of the settlers' demands. Another example was a state law adopted in 1856 requiring grant holders to pay squatters for their improvements or to sell them the land at its appraised value. Although this law was by no means as unreasonable as it has often been said to be, the state supreme court ruled it unconstitutional in 1857.

The most important effect of land-title troubles on the history of California was not in the hardships of the Mexican grantees, but rather in the damage done to the early development of American agriculture in the state. John S.

Hittell estimated that during the 1850s a quarter of a million Americans who would otherwise have settled in California did not do so because of the insecurity of land titles; including their families, the net loss to California was probably a full million potential residents.

Some crucial cases. Most of the early cases argued before the land commission were carefully chosen by the claimants' attorneys because the defects in the titles were relatively minor, and it seemed reasonable to approve the claims in spite of them. For example, the law had forbidden private land grants within 10 leagues of the coast, but the Mexican authorities had generally ignored this provision. Or, some of the important documents of a grant were missing but there was a long record of occupancy. The commission, in its earliest decisions, confirmed a number of such claims and thus set precedents for liberal interpretation, and for deciding the cases on "broad principles of equity."

During the first several years, much to the disgust of the settlers, the Federal courts also tended to view the claims in what the Supreme Court called a "large and liberal spirit." Judicial liberality toward the grantholder was particularly striking in the case of Frémont's claim to Las Mariposas, the only Mexican grant in the Mother Lode region. Consisting of 10 square leagues, a sizable part of the present Mariposa County, this grant had been made to Juan B. Alvarado by Governor Micheltorena in 1844. Far from having fulfilled the requirement of occupancy, Alvarado had not even seen the place when in 1847 he sold it to Frémont, through Larkin, for $3,000. Gold was discovered on it in the spring of 1849—so much gold, in fact, that it became known as the "ten-million-dollar" grant. The district court ruled the claim invalid on the ground that the original recipient of the grant had never fulfilled a single one of the several conditions attached to it. The Supreme Court, however, in a majority opinion delivered by Chief Justice Roger B. Taney, confirmed Frémont's claim, and a patent was issued to him in February 1856, a few months before he became the first Republican nominee for the Presidency.

Among its many defects, Las Mariposas was an example of the "floating" grant, that is, one in which the total area was stated but the boundaries were not specified. When the official survey was made, the boundaries were swung about in such a way as to include three rich mining districts that Frémont had not previously claimed. Several lives were then lost in attempts to evict miners who had been working in these districts. Throughout the state, settlers who had occupied what they supposed to be public lands, or lands in grants that they believed to be invalid, raised bitter protests that the Supreme Court had set unjust and dangerous precedents merely for the sake of special favor to Frémont.

In San Francisco, titles were at least as chaotic as in any other part of the state. The pueblo grant of four square leagues was not confirmed until 1866, and there were several conflicting claims of private grants, widely and correctly believed to be fraudulent but covering large parts of the area of the city. In this situation squatterism was inevitable and rampant, and many a fortune in San Francisco real estate was founded on "shot-gun titles." Squatters fortified the lots they occupied, and one of them tried to fence off Union Square. Landowners had to hire private policemen; some men, employed by land speculators to keep forcible possession of lots, made a living in this way for as much as 20 years after the gold rush. There were no "squatter riots" on the scale of the ones in Sacramento, but there were many fights, some of them fatal. Many lots were sold by the municipal authorities and the titles later upheld; but in several districts to the west and south of the center of town, city ordinances eventually had to recognize possession as the law.

Several fantastic claims were at first confirmed by the land commission and later detected as fraudulent. In the early years the United States district attorney for Northern California was overwhelmed with work, while the services of many brilliant lawyers were available to the claimants. Moreover, Federal law made no provision for the punishment of fraud in the fabrication of claims. But when Jeremiah S. Black became United States Attorney General in 1857 he secured the passage of such a law, and appointed Edwin M. Stanton, later Lincoln's Secretary of War, as special counsel for the government.

Among the suspicious claims that cried out for more critical scrutiny than they had yet received, the worst and most audacious were those of a certain José Yves Limantour, a Frenchman who had engaged in coastal trade in California in the time of Governor Micheltorena. Originally, Limantour had presented eight claims totaling more than half a million acres, said to have been granted in 1843, mainly in payment for goods delivered and services rendered to the Mexican officials. In 1856 the land commission approved two of these alleged grants. One included the islands of Yerba Buena, Alcatraz, and the Farallons, as well as Point Tiburon. The other, vastly more important, consisted of four square leagues and covered most of the land of San Francisco south of California Street. When Stanton examined the seals on the Limantour documents in 1858, he noticed that the wingspread of the Mexican eagle varied slightly from the standard measurement. Further investigation established that the seals were counterfeit and the documents fabricated; that although the signatures of Micheltorena were his own, he had written them in Mexico City in 1852 and predated the documents to 1843; and that the supporting oral testimony of two of his former subordinates had been purchased and perjured. Judge Ogden Hoffman denounced and rejected the claims in the district court. Limantour hastily left the country, taking with him a fortune in quitclaims that he had managed to collect in the two years since the favorable decision of the land commission.

Stanton's investigations also led to the ultimate rejection of the Santillán claim to three square leagues, the entire area around the San Francisco mission. This claim rested on a forged document and perjured witnesses, and on the remarkably weak and suspicious assertion that it had been made in February 1846 to a poor parish priest, Prudencio Santillán, in return for his paying the mission debts; nor was there any explanation of why Santillán was supposed to have kept his grant a secret for years afterward. Sometimes known as the Bolton and Barron claim, it had been purchased by a syndicate of Philadelphia investors who sought for many years to recover from Congress the large sum of money they had paid for it.

Through the efforts of Edwin Stanton and others in California, and of Jeremiah Black and his aides in Washington, D.C., other large-scale frauds were exposed. One of these, the Luco claim in Solano county, covered 50 square leagues or nearly a quarter of a million acres. In the single year of 1859 the Supreme Court rejected claims containing nearly two and a half million acres. Judge Hoffman charged from the district court bench, and Attorney General Black reported to Congress, that the production of fabricated land-grant documents had become an organized industry and that ex-Governors Micheltorena and Pico and several officials who had served under them had become professional forgers and perjurers. William Carey Jones, however, denounced Black's report as "reckless and mischievous."

The entire cities of Oakland, Berkeley, and Alameda were built on the land of a single grant, the Rancho San Antonio, conveyed to Sergeant Luís Peralta in 1820 as a reward for long service in the Spanish army in Northern California. Don Luís divided the ranch among his four sons in 1842. For years after 1846 Vicente Peralta stubbornly insisted that he wished no town to be built on his land, and refused to sell parts of it for that purpose. Consequently in 1850 the original street plan of Oakland was laid out as a squatter enterprise. The Peralta grant was recognized in the courts, and several decades passed before the taints of squatterism were finally cleared from Oakland titles. It is not surprising that in the 20th century the services of title insurance companies have been more widely required and used in California than in any other state.

Los Angeles anticipated its later expansive tendencies by claiming that its pueblo grant had been four leagues square rather than four square leagues. This claim, which would have given the municipality 16 square leagues, was finally reduced to the usual four.

Many writers have blamed the act of 1851 for the tragic difficulties of early American land problems in California, and Bancroft went so far as to assert that it would have been practically impossible to have devised a worse plan for dealing with them. Yet, even with the advantages of hindsight, no one has convincingly suggested a better one. Henry George and others maintained that the government should have confirmed the small claims after brief examination, and tested only the large and suspicious ones in the courts. When a large claim was declared valid, George thought the claimant should have been allowed only a small part of it, and the government should have bought the remainder from him at the low prices prevailing in 1848. Most of the area of the large grants would then have become public land. But this would have been a high-handed violation of the treaty, and irreconcilable with any system of law then prevailing in the United States.

SELECTED BIBLIOGRAPHY

Ogden Hoffman, *Report of Land Cases Determined in the United States District Court of the Northern District of California* (1862), and the "specimen cases" in Hubert Howe Bancroft, *History of California*, volume VI (1888), 548–560, were excellent descriptions. The district court records are now in the Bancroft Library. See also Robert H. Becker, *Diseños of California Ranchos* (1964), and *Designs on the Land* (1969).

Most 19th-century writers were very critical of the American government's policies toward the Mexican grants. These included Bancroft and his staff; Theodore H. Hittell, *History of California*, volume III (1898); John S. Hittell, *The Resources of California* (1863 and later editions); Josiah Royce, "The Squatter Riot of '50 in Sacramento," *The Overland Monthly*, VI (September 1885), 225–246, and his *California, . . . a Study of American Character* (1886); and Henry George, *Our Land Policy, National and State* (1874).

Joseph Ellison, *California and the Nation, 1850–1869* (1927); W. W. Robinson, *Land in California* (1948); and William H. Ellison, *A Self-governing Dominion; California, 1849–1860* (1950), included well-balanced treatments of the Mexican-grant problems. Paul W. Gates, in "The Adjudication of Spanish-Mexican Land Claims in California," *Huntington Library Quarterly*, XXI (May 1958), 213–236, and "California's Embattled Settlers," *California Historical Society Quarterly*, XLI (June 1962), 99–130, concluded that it was the settlers, rather than the grantees, who were most unfairly treated. See also his "Pre-Henry George Land Warfare in California," *California Historical Society Quarterly*, XLVI (June 1967), 121–148, "The Suscol Principle, Preemption, and California Latifundia," *Pacific Historical Review*, XXXIX (November 1970), 453–472, and "The California Land Act of 1851," *California Historical Quarterly*, L (December 1971), 395–430.

Chapter XIV

RACIAL OPPRESSION

IN THE YEARS after the gold rush a large majority of the American citizens of California, whether they had come from Northern or Southern states, cherished a fixed belief in the innate superiority of "whites" over other races. They also believed that Protestant Christians were better people than the followers of other religious faiths, and that persons of Anglo-American nativity were innately superior to those of other national origins.

Of the fears, the hatreds, and the various kinds of intolerance that accompanied this set of opinions, the deepest were probably associated with the idea of racial superiority. In part, this was because that idea was very closely associated with economic group interest; equally important, however, were the essentially irrational aspects of racial fears and hatreds.

Treatment of Mexican miners. As Americans poured into the mining districts of California in 1849 and 1850, they found themselves in competition with substantial numbers of foreigners. The most numerous of these were Mexicans from the state of Sonora, as the naming of one of the largest towns in the southern mines attested. Feelings of hostility left over from the Mexican War were intensified because many of the Sonorans were experienced miners, skillful in locating good claims, while others were peons brought to California in labor gangs to work the claims of their wealthier Mexican masters. Americans feared that foreigners were removing too much of the readily available gold, and that there would soon be none left. Mining-camp codes, enforced by vigilance committees and soon ratified by the state legislature, excluded Mexicans and Orientals from many of the diggings.

Further evidence of antiforeign sentiment appeared when the California legislature of 1850 enacted a foreign miners' license tax. Introduced by Senator Thomas Jefferson Green, the act required miners who were not citizens of the United States to pay a fee of $20 a month. This levy was so high that the

Mexicans, upon whom most of the burden would fall, were unable or unwilling to pay it, and a mass meeting in the town of Sonora announced their refusal. Hundreds of armed American miners, including many veterans wearing their old Mexican War uniforms, then gathered at Sonora to aid the collectors of the tax and to prevent Mexicans from mining without a license.

At this time there were about fifteen thousand Mexicans in the "southern mines"—Calaveras, Tuolumne, and Mariposa Counties. Under the pressures of the tax and of threats of violence, about ten thousand left the region in the summer of 1850, most of them to return to Mexico. Although the treaty of Guadalupe Hidalgo provided that Mexican citizens of California who chose to remain there for a year became American citizens automatically, many Americans, in ignorance or defiance of this provision, lumped all "Mexicans" together, and many native Californians were driven from the mines along with the Mexican nationals, in fear of their lives and with bitterness in their hearts. Their protests had little or no political effect. On the other hand, the protests of American merchants in the mining districts, who had lost so many customers, were strong enough to carry considerable weight in the legislature, especially when it became clear that the nearly prohibitive tax was bringing in only a small amount of revenue. The tax was repealed in 1851, but it was soon re-enacted in more moderate form.

In the troubles at Sonora in 1850 several hundred Frenchmen had been involved on the side of the Mexicans, to such a degree that the episode was sometimes called "the French Revolution." Mob violence between French and American miners was again narrowly averted in the summer of 1851 near Mokelumne Hill. The earliest discrimination by American Californians against foreigners, however, was directed mainly against Mexicans and other Spanish Americans. Beginning in 1852, the prime target of xenophobia became the Chinese, who had replaced the Mexicans as the most numerous and the most obviously "alien" of the various foreign groups. The California Indians, not easily classified as foreigners, were in a separate and peculiar category.

Early discrimination against the Chinese. At the end of 1849 only a few hundred Chinese had come to seek the gold of California. In 1851, however, the outbreak of the great Taiping Rebellion against the Manchu dynasty plunged China into 15 years of civil war and general disorder that further deepened the poverty of most of its people. For more than two centuries, periods of extraordinary economic depression had induced many thousands of Chinese to emigrate, particularly from South China to several parts of Southeast Asia. Now rumors of easy wealth brought a great stream of Chinese emigrants to "the Golden Mountains," their name for California. Nearly all of them, like most of the American Argonauts, were young men who dreamed of acquiring a fortune and returning home to enjoy it with the families they had left behind. But whereas most of those Americans who were disappointed in this hope eventually reconciled themselves to becoming permanent residents of California, the Chinese tended to cling for the rest of their lives to the dream of returning to their homeland, even though pitifully few of them were ever able to do so. Having no desire to become a part of a foreign country, most of the early Chinese immigrants remained alien by their own choice as much as by that of the Americans.

Even worse than the discrimination that the Chinese suffered at American hands was their oppression by creditors and other exploiters among their own countrymen. Following a pattern long established in Chinese overseas migration, impoverished young men from Canton, Hong Kong, or the neighboring rural areas made contracts for the payment of their passage under the "credit-ticket" system. In California their labor was sold, through Chinese subcontractors, to Chinese mining companies which paid them very low wages. The American miners permitted these companies to acquire and to work only the claims which they themselves had abandoned, or those which had never contained enough gold to produce a sizable profit. The hapless Chinese workers were kept in a state of debt bondage enforced by a Chinese creditor-employer network. This system operated without reference to American courts or other legal authorities, and was reenforced by various types of associations. The most important of these were the district companies, based on the several districts of Southeastern China from which nearly all of the California Chinese had come.

Indentured servitude, in which men labored for a period of years to repay the cost of their passage, was nothing new in American history. Indentured servants from England had made up more than half of the white population of several of the thirteen English colonies on the Atlantic seaboard in the 17th century and the first half of the 18th. As one observer put it, the progenitor of many a proud American family had originally come to colonial America because his person could be advantageously exchanged there for a quantity of tobacco or sassafras root. But most of the Chinese immigrants, harried both by Americans and by greedy and powerful men of their own race, found it far more difficult to rise out of debt bondage and extreme poverty.

In 1852 the number of Chinese in California rose to about twenty-five thousand. Concentrated in the mining regions and in San Francisco, they were now by far the largest of the foreign minorities. They formed a tenth of the state's population other than Indians, and nearly a third of the population in several of the mining counties. An outburst of agitation against them began when a bill was introduced in the state senate to legalize the enforcement in California of labor contracts made in China. Throughout the mining camps there was such a rash of mass meetings and resolutions denouncing this "coolie bill" that the measure was decisively defeated. Later in the legislative session of 1852 the foreign miners' license tax was reenacted with the clear understanding that it would be enforced primarily upon the Chinese. The tax was set at $3 per month, later raised to $4.

Much to the irritation of the white miners, but greatly to the benefit of the state treasury, the tax failed to discourage the Chinese, who paid it willingly in the hope that it would reconcile the whites to their continued presence in the mines. Until 1870 when the state supreme court belatedly declared it unconstitutional, this tax, paid by the Chinese almost exclusively, brought in nearly a fourth of the state's entire revenue, even though thieving tax collectors, dissatisfied with the commissions allowed them, often let the Chinese miner off with a payment of $2 if he agreed not to demand a receipt. In addition, many Chinese were victimized by Americans impersonating tax collectors.

The Chinese almost always considered it useless and unwise to try to defend themselves against any action, even including violence and robbery, directed against them by Americans. This was true even before a peculiar decision of the state supreme court rendered them still more helpless. A state law of 1850 forbade Negroes and Indians to testify in court, either "in favor of, or against a white man." In *People v. Hall* in 1854, Chief Justice Hugh C. Murray (who was 29 years old) pronounced the doctrine that the Chinese were legally Indians, since both were probably descended from the same Asiatic ancestors. Thus nonwhites (and whites also) were denied legal protection from any outrage at the hands of a white man if the only witnesses were Chinese, or Negro, or Indian. This ban against giving evidence was removed from Negroes in 1863, but Chinese and Indians remained under it until 1872, when it was dropped from the California code in deference to the Federal Civil Rights Act.

In the meantime another legal weapon against the Chinese had been found in the Federal law which had provided since 1790 that only "free white persons" could be naturalized. This provision was a deep flaw in the application of American ideas of democracy. As for the Chinese immigrants in particular, it happened that most of them had no desire for the privilege of American naturalization. Hence they would not have suffered greatly from the denial of it, if that denial had not come to be used in a remarkable number of California laws as an excuse for other forms of discrimination. This shabby device would continue to be employed for nearly a hundred years. Turned primarily against land ownership by Japanese immigrants in California in the 20th century, its use would end only when discrimination on the ground of race as such was finally stricken from the Federal naturalization statutes in 1952. In California, state laws directed against "aliens ineligible to citizenship," as a euphemism for aliens of nonwhite ancestry, began to appear in 1855 when the legislature sought to impose a head tax of $50 on all immigrants "who cannot become citizens." This was soon declared unconstitutional because the state could not tax immigration; but another state law of 1855 made ineligibility for citizenship the main definition of those to whom the foreign miners' license tax applied, and thus ensured the enforcement of the tax more specifically against the Chinese. The latter law remained in effect for many years.

Fortunately, the Chinese were a people who had developed a remarkable combination of fatalism and adaptability, during many centuries of oppression in China itself. Their sufferings, and those of all the other racial minorities, were overshadowed by the disasters that befell the California Indians.

The "Indian question." Since the 1820s the Federal government had followed a "removal policy" as its general solution of "the Indian problem." A "permanent Indian frontier" had been created along the eastern edge of the Great Plains. That region, which extended from Texas to the Canadian border, was then regarded as a "Great American Desert" where white men would never want to live. By a long series of treaties the Indian "nations" or tribes of the Eastern and Central parts of the country had been induced to move west of this line to new lands which the American government promised to reserve for them in perpetuity. But this process had scarcely been completed when in the 1840s the extension of the American boundary to the Pacific made the line obsolete.

In California, where it was no longer possible to remove the Indians to lands farther west, many American settlers argued that the only solution was to remove them from the face of the earth. Governor Burnett told the legislature that a "war of extermination will continue to be waged between the races until the Indian race becomes extinct," and that it was "beyond the power or wisdom of man" to avert the "inevitable destiny of this race." Among the American Californians this was the predominating view, and the overwhelming barbarousness of it was at the root of the tragic futility of all the attempts to solve the "Indian question."

Units loosely organized as state militia went on ineffectual and expensive Indian-hunting expeditions in 1850. In 1851 Governor John McDougal asserted in a letter to President Millard Fillmore that 100,000 Indian warriors were in a state of armed rebellion, and the following year one of California's United States Senators, John B. Weller, claimed that only a "master spirit" was needed to "confederate the tribes in a bloody and devastating war."

These statements were fantastically false. By this time there were less than 100,000 Indians of all ages and both sexes left in the whole state, and because of their inability to understand each others' dialects, and their lack of tribal organization, they were no more capable of "confederating" for war or for any other purpose than they had ever been. Yet the most terrifying assertions about them were widely believed in California.

The state's politicians demanded that the Federal government provide the funds to pay the expenses of campaigns conducted against the Indians by state militia volunteers. This, at first, the Federal authorities refused to do. Gen. Persifor F. Smith complained that the pay of a private in the latest Indian campaign of the California militia was equal to the salary of any officer in the Regular Army, except his own. Secretary of War C. M. Conrad wrote to Governor McDougal that the pay of California's volunteer Indian-fighters was "exorbitant and beyond anything ever known in this country"; that "in a population like that of California, where there are so many ardent young men, the love of adventure with some and the high pay with others" offered "inducement to perpetual collisions with the Indians"; and that this abuse was "as injurious to the State" as it was "revolting to humanity." Secretary Conrad maintained that the troubles resulted far more often from the aggressive behavior of the whites than from that of the Indians, and that there was no genuine need for a perpetual war between them.

The policies of the Federal government toward the California Indians, though very different from the policies of the state, were equally unsuccessful in providing any effective solution. In 1850 Congress passed an act authorizing three Indian agents or commissioners to negotiate a series of treaties. The commissioners were Redick McKee of Virginia, George W. Barbour of Kentucky, and Dr. Oliver M. Wozencraft, a practicing physician from Louisiana, who had been a member of the constitutional convention at Monterey. Like Governor Burnett, who had lived in Tennessee and Missouri before coming to Oregon and California, the three commissioners were Southerners. But unlike Burnett, they were men of some humanitarian feelings, and they were shocked and alarmed by the belligerent attitude of the state government.

Placing their hope of insuring peace in the idea of segregating the Indians from the whites as completely as possible, the commissioners negotiated 18 treaties affecting 139 tribes or bands. These treaties would have removed the Indians from the mining districts and other areas of white settlement and concentrated them on large reservations totaling 11,700 square miles, or 7,488,000 acres. This was about 7½ percent of the entire land area of the state. Moreover, although Congress had appropriated only $50,000 for the work of the commissioners, they let contracts totaling nearly a million dollars for provisions and beef cattle for the reservations, on the theory that, as they reported to Washington, "it is *cheaper* to feed the whole flock for a *year* than to fight them for a *week*."

Obviously, the Federal commissioners overreached themselves, and their plan was unworkable. Only a small fraction of the California Indians moved even temporarily to their proposed reservations. The Federal government could neither have persuaded nor forced the American settlers to respect the boundaries of such large areas of potentially valuable land, and in the state legislature hostility to the treaties became intense. It was argued that Indians had no right to any land at all; that not even Mexico had recognized such a right on the part of the "wild" Indians of California; that removal to the reservations would deprive the towns and ranches in Southern California of their Indian laborers; and that the government ought to have continued its previously established policy of removing the Indians entirely outside the boundaries of states.

That the last two of these arguments were contradictory, and that they both appeared in the same list of state senate resolutions in denunciation of the treaties, suggest the irrational aspects of the state of feeling that prevailed. California's United States Senators, Gwin and Weller, opposed the treaties so vigorously that the Senate rejected all of them when they came up for ratification in 1852.

Beale and the reservation system. There was widespread fear that the rejection of the treaties would lead the Indians to outbreaks of violence. Thus in 1853, as a palliative, Congress adopted a much more modest plan suggested by Edward F. Beale, the new superintendent of Indian affairs for California. Beale recommended a system of smaller reservations that would also serve as military posts for the United States Army. The Indians would be taught to engage in agriculture and handicrafts, much in the manner of the Spanish missions though without the religious emphasis. Ultimately, it was hoped, the Indians on these reservations might become self-sustaining. Five such establishments, of 25,000 acres each, were authorized under the act of 1853. The first, at Tejon in the Tehachapi foothills, attracted about twenty-five hundred Indians. Other reservations were soon established, notably the Nome Lackee in Colusa County, the Klamath on the Klamath River, and the Mendocino on the Pacific Coast.

Beale pushed his experiment with enthusiasm and vigor, but it had scarcely begun when he was removed from office, in 1854, partly because of his inefficiency in business matters and partly through the efforts of political enemies. The Office of Indian Affairs in Washington was peculiarly vulnerable to the abuses of the spoils system, and its personnel rotated with every new administration. In general, Beale's successors and their subordinates were incompetent and venal political appointees. In 1858 a Federal investigator reported that the reservations were a lamentable failure—mere almshouses for a trifling number of Indians.

Unsuccessful as this pitiful system was, however, the Federal government failed to devise a better one, and Beale's plan became the model for Federal Indian reservations all over the West for many decades afterward. In 1870, Indian agents began to be appointed on the recommendation of Christian churches, and the California Indians were placed under the care of the Methodists. But little or no improvement was possible within the limitations of the small-reservation system.

The Indian "wars." The two decades after the gold rush produced dozens of wretched episodes that can best be described as massacres, the great majority of them perpetrated on the Indians by the whites. Many of these "punitive expeditions" were financed by the state government, and during the 1850s more than a million dollars' worth of state bonds was issued to pay the expenses of local volunteer campaigns for "the suppression of Indian hostilities." The Federal government, overcoming its earlier reluctance, reimbursed the state for most of these expenditures under congressional appropriation acts of 1854 and 1861, although Federal auditors disallowed some of the most obviously exaggerated claims. In this dreary tale of legalized and subsidized murder, the Mariposa campaign and the "Modoc War" stand out as relatively colorful incidents.

In 1851 the Mariposa Battalion under James D. Savage, pursuing a band of Yosemites and Chowchillas under Chief Tenieya, rediscovered the Yosemite Valley, whose earlier discovery by Joseph Reddeford Walker's party had never been widely known. The Yosemites did not risk a battle with the Savage expedition, and in general very few of the California Indians offered any effective resistance to the military and quasi-military campaigns against them. The main exceptions came in the mountainous northern part of the state.

The most famous conflict in that region occurred after a band of Modocs left the reservation which they had been forced to share with the Oregon Klamaths, and returned without permission to their former country on Lost River. The conflict could have been prevented by allowing the Modocs to occupy a bit of land which was of very little value to the whites, and which would have been only a tiny fragment of the lands that had once been Modoc territory.

In 1873 a force of 400 soldiers, mostly of the Regular Army, drove the Modocs to take refuge in the lava beds. There, although heavily outnumbered and fighting only with old muzzle-loaders and pistols against rifles and artillery, the Modocs fortified themselves so well that they inflicted many casualties on the Americans while suffering very few of their own. At a peace conference where they were offered no better terms than a return to the reservation in Oregon, their chief Kientepoos ("Captain Jack") was goaded by some of his warriors into a plot in which they treacherously murdered Gen. E. R. S. Canby and a Methodist missionary, Dr. Eleazar Thomas, and wounded Indian Agent A. B. Meacham. Ultimately the Modocs were defeated and Captain Jack was hanged, but not until the war had cost the lives of about 75 Americans, and half a million dollars.

Decline of the Indian population. Under Spain and Mexico there had been no more than a few dozen Spaniards, a few thousand Mexican Californians, and a few hundred Americans in California—and they had occupied only parts of it. Nevertheless the aboriginal population had dropped from more than 275,000 in 1769 to about 100,000 in 1846. Epidemics had been the largest factor in this decline.

With the coming of hundreds of thousands of Americans, the Indian death rate was tragically accelerated. By 1870 there were only about 30,000 Indians left. In 1900 there were less than 16,000. Disease continued to take the largest toll, probably accounting for about 60 percent of the deaths during the second half of the 19th century. As the incoming tide of Americans drove the Indians from the food-producing areas, starvation and malnutrition probably added about 30 percent of the death toll. Less than 10 percent resulted from purely physical assault, through formal military campaigns, informal expeditions, and various other forms of homicide.

Many of the surviving Indians could get food only by stealing it from the whites, and this led to constant and violent retaliation. To a limited extent the Indian could also obtain food by working for the white man, particularly in Southern California, and the Americans adopted various regulations which continued the Mexican system of Indian peonage. Under a military order of 1847 and an act of the state legislature in 1850, any unemployed Indian could be declared a vagrant and forced to labor on public works, while those not needed for this purpose could be auctioned off to the highest bidder as indentured servants. The flourishing illegal business of kidnaping Indians, especially children, for sale as household and farm servants, was continued. A white man could mistreat and even murder an Indian with virtual impunity. J. Ross Browne wrote that "If ever an Indian was fully and honestly paid for his labor by a white settler, it was not my luck to hear of it." The treatment of Indian laborers was in general so oppressive that it contributed more to their extinction than to their support, and particularly in agriculture, the feeling that the landowner had a right to a supply of cheap labor drawn from the people of some supposedly inferior race set an evil precedent for future generations.

As for the alternative of assimilating the Indians into the general population, this was made impossible in the early American period not only by the prejudices of the whites against the Indians but also by the deep and hopeless resentment which the Indians felt against the whites.

The "free" Negroes. Although the efforts of Governor Burnett to secure legislation excluding free Negroes were no more successful than the similar efforts in the constitutional convention, the coming of "persons of color" was effectively discouraged in less direct ways, and in the late 1850s there were only about twenty-five hundred of them in California. Several state laws, such as the ban against their testimony in legal proceedings, infringed their civil rights and treated them as an inferior people. In 1852 the state adopted a harsh fugitive slave law reflecting the odious Federal statute that had been a part of the compromise under which it was admitted to the Union. Only one actual fugitive slave is known to have reached California; but the law was enforced against a number of Negroes whose masters had brought them there and later wished to return them to the South. The last and most famous of these cases, that of Archy Lee, was tried in 1858. Peter H. Burnett was then on the state supreme court. With the concurrence of the ex-Texan Justice David S. Terry, he ruled that although the master had forfeited his right to the slave by bringing him to a free state after its admission to the Union, and by remaining for a substantial time, an exception should be made in this instance because the master was young and in poor health, and in need of his slave's services. This decision was widely ridiculed, and Lee was freed shortly afterward by a United States commissioner in San Francisco.

SELECTED BIBLIOGRAPHY

Aspects of public policy toward racial minorities are dealt with in R. F. Heizer and A. F. Almquist, *The Other Californians* (1971); Lucile Eaves, *A History of California Labor Legislation* (1910); and William C. Fankhauser, *A Financial History of California* (1913), on the foreign miners' license tax. On the Mexicans, see Leonard M. Pitt, *The Decline of the Californios: A Social History of the Spanish-Speaking Californians, 1846–1890* (1966); and R. H. Morefield, "Mexicans in the California Mines, 1848–53," *California Historical Society Quarterly*, XXXV (1956), 37–46. On the Chinese, see Gunther Barth, *Bitter Strength* (1964); S. C. Miller, *The Unwelcome Immigrant* (1970); A. P. Saxton, *The Indispensable Enemy* (1971); D. V. DuFault, "The Chinese in the Mining Camps," *Southern California Quarterly*, XLI (1959), 155–170; Mary R. Coolidge, *Chinese Immigration* (1909); Elmer C. Sandmeyer, *The Anti-Chinese Movement in California* (1939); Rodman W. Paul, "The Origin of the Chinese Issue in California," *Mississippi Valley Historical Review*, XXV (1938), 181–196; and Stanford M. Lyman, *The Asian in the West* (1970).

Good accounts of the treatment of the Indians are in Joseph Ellison's *California and the Nation* and William H. Ellison's *A Self-governing Dominion*; Benjamin D. Wilson's report in John W. Caughey, editor, *The Indians of Southern California in 1852* (1952); J. Ross Browne, *The Indians of California* (1864; 1944); Alban W. Hoopes, *Indian Affairs and Their Administration, with Special Reference to the Far West, 1849–1860* (1932); Stephen Bonsal, *Edward Fitzgerald Beale* (1912); Keith A. Murray, *The Modocs and Their War* (1959); and Erwin N. Thompson, *Modoc War: Its History and Topography* (1971). *The Conflict between the California Indian and White Civilization*, part III, *The American Invasion, 1848–1870* (1943), by Sherbourne F. Cook, deals with the decline in numbers.

Some of the difficulties of the Negroes are described by Clyde A. Duniway, "Slavery in California after 1848," American Historical Association, *Annual Report . . . for the year 1905* (1906 part I); William E. Franklin, "The Archy Case," *Pacific Historical Review*, XXXII (1963), 137–154; Rudolph M. Lapp, *Archy Lee* (1969), "Negro Rights Activities in Gold Rush California," *California Historical Society Quarterly*, XLV (1966), 3–20, "The Negro in Gold Rush California," *Journal of Negro History*, XLIX (1964), 81–98; and J. A. Fisher, "The Struggle for Negro Testimony," *Southern California Quarterly*, LI (1969), 313–324.

Chapter XV

FRONTIER POLITICS

AS WE HAVE SEEN, most Californians of the 1850s were too busy searching for sudden private wealth to take a responsible interest in public affairs. Except for outbursts of privately organized "vigilance," they tended to leave the public business to a class of politicians who were themselves a rather peculiarly selected group of entrepreneurs. Theodore H. Hittell estimated that a tenth of the '49ers were politicians who had failed in "the states." A large majority of these were Democrats, unemployed because of the Whig triumph in the election of the war hero Gen. Zachary Taylor in 1848. This, coupled with the fact that the Whig party would soon be destroyed by its North-South split over slavery, ensured the Democratic domination of California politics until the coming of the Civil War. Under the constitution of 1849, elections of governors and other state officials were held every two years, in the odd-numbered years. The Democrats won virtually every important election in California in the 1850s except the state elections of 1855, which they lost to the Know-Nothings largely because of the bitter rivalry between the two main Democratic leaders—one of the most sensationally destructive rivalries in American political history.

The feud between Broderick and Gwin. Apart from the Democratic label, the chief resemblance between David C. Broderick of Tammany Hall and William M. Gwin of Tennessee was that both came to California in 1849 with the announced intention of being elected to the United States Senate. Broderick, who was only 29 at the time of his arrival at San Francisco, had received very little formal education. Gwin, 15 years older, had the advantages of formal training in both law and medicine and also of years of acquaintance with several of the country's leading statesmen. Gwin was cool, dignified, and gracious, while Broderick was hotheaded, humorless, stubborn, and domineering.

Born in the District of Columbia, the son of an immigrant Irish stonemason, Broderick as a boy had seen his father at work on the ornamentation of the Senate chamber, and had resolved that some day he would return to speak there. The family moved to New York City, where Broderick became a saloonkeeper, a ward boss for Tammany Hall, and an unsuccessful candidate for Congress. Col. J. D. Stevenson, late of the New York Volunteers, invited him to San Francisco, where Stevenson and other former members of the disbanded regiment, and of Tammany Hall, helped Broderick to form the nucleus of a Democratic political machine on the Tammany model, with special attention to the use of volunteer firefighting companies as political clubs. Broderick also began the development of a personal fortune by joining a partnership in a private mint, which, for the public convenience, manufactured coins with face values of $5 and $10 and actual gold content of $4 and $8. Even more profitable were his speculations in San Francisco waterfront lots; these speculations were greatly facilitated by the influence he acquired over city and state legislation. He became the first major political boss of San Francisco, and soon gained control of the Democratic party machinery throughout the state.

Broderick entered the state senate in 1850. The next year, when Lieutenant Governor John McDougal became Governor on the resignation of Peter H. Burnett, Broderick was elected to replace McDougal as the senate's presiding officer. By forming an alliance with John Bigler, the speaker of the assembly, and by securing Bigler's election as Governor in 1851 and again in 1853, Broderick gained control of the state patronage. He then felt ready to try to replace Gwin in the United States Senate. This, however, was a most formidable undertaking. California Democrats of Southern origin, ridiculed by their opponents as the "Chivalry" or "Shiv" faction, almost unanimously preferred Gwin to Broderick, while by no means could all of Broderick's "Northern" or "Tammany" wing of the party be depended upon to support him against Gwin. As senior United States Senator, Gwin controlled the Federal patronage. Moreover, because California was still an isolated frontier state, it regarded its own interests as far more important than any national issues, and Gwin did much for California in securing Federal legislation in its favor. Although the state was still dissatisfied with its treatment at the hands of the Federal government, Gwin was in a much better position to advance its interests in Washington than Broderick would be. Gwin introduced several bills for a transcontinental railroad, and although these failed of adoption, he was successful with other important measures. As chairman of the Senate Committee on Naval Affairs, he introduced the bill to create the navy yard at Mare Island. Another of his bills provided for the San Francisco branch of the Federal mint—an enormous improvement over Broderick's private mint.

In 1854 Broderick conceived the daring but unsuccessful scheme of trying to compel the state legislature of that year to elect him as Gwin's successor, even though the election would not normally have been held until a year later. In the legislative session of 1855, a deadlock between Gwin and Broderick prevented the election of either, or of anyone else. Consequently one of the United States senatorships remained vacant for two years, and the California Democrats were so bitterly divided that the pseudo-patriotic, nativist, self-styled "American" party, otherwise known as the Know-Nothings, gained control of the state government.

The organized political nativism of the 1850s had its roots in various secret societies like the Order of the Star Spangled Banner. A local chapter of this national fraternity was founded in San Francisco by Lt. Sam Roberts, also the founder of the Hounds. The Know-Nothing Order, nationally consolidated in 1852 out of several secret bodies, was first organized in California in May 1854. It took its name from the fact that originally it required its members to answer all questions by saying that they knew nothing about it; but it soon came partially into the open as a political movement and in the middle 1850s elected governors and legislatures in several states. The Whig party died in 1854, and the Republican party, born in the same year, was not yet strong enough to replace the Whigs.

The Know-Nothing movement seemed, for a time, to offer an escape from the frightening national divisions over the slavery issue, by promising to unite Americans against foreigners. As a national organization it was hostile to Roman Catholics because it assumed them to be under allegiance to a foreign power; most of its members, as pious Protestants, were also especially hostile to German immigrants, many of whom were freethinking and radical refugees from the suppression of the revolutions of 1848. In California, however, the nativist American movement was much influenced by the special conditions of the local hostility to foreign miners; in particular, racial antipathies were more important than religious or nationalistic ones, and there was much denunciation of the Chinese, while anti-Catholicism was soft-pedaled. In California, as elsewhere, the appearance of candidates on the Know-Nothing ticket was almost entirely opportunistic. Under Governor J. Neely Johnson the party offered no serious program of state legislation, nativist or otherwise.

By the time of the national campaign of 1856 the Democrats had recovered enough unity to ensure the state's electoral votes for James Buchanan. Frémont, the first presidential nominee of the new Republican party, made a better showing nationally than he did in California where he ran not only far behind Buchanan but even far behind the Know-Nothing candidate, ex-President Millard Fillmore. Frémont's personal popularity in California had been steadily declining since 1851, when, instead of fulfilling his duties as a Senator in Washington during the second session of the Thirty-first Congress, he had been in San Jose, lobbying unsuccessfully for reelection by the state legislature. "Thus it was," as Bancroft would remark, "throughout [Frémont's] entire career—himself first and always." The troubles in connection with his vast gold-bearing land grant also damaged Frémont's popularity with miners and squatters.

The ambition of Broderick for a United States senatorship grew steadily more obsessive through repeated frustrations. At last, in 1857, he achieved his goal. Both of the Senate seats were to be filled, Gwin's having been vacant for two years. By the unscrupulous use of every trick which his fertile imagination could conceive, Broderick induced the legislature to elect him to the full six-year term, succeeding John B. Weller, who was to be consoled with a term as Governor. Broderick forced Gwin to be content with the four-year senatorial term, and under the threat to deny him even that, he compelled Gwin to write a letter promising to make no recommendations for the Federal patronage. When President Buchanan learned what Broderick had done, he strongly disapproved of it, and although Gwin, keeping his promise, made no recommendations for Federal appointments, Buchanan appointed followers of Gwin to the positions in the customs house, the branch mint, and the Indian agencies in California, and gave none of these appointments to Broderick's supporters.

Broderick was furious. In his one important speech in the United States Senate, and in many speeches after his return to California, he denounced Buchanan and Gwin in terms of the most violent personal vituperation. He did this, he said, not because he had been denied the Federal patronage, but rather because he was opposed to Buchanan's policy of encouraging the formation of a proslavery government in the territory of Kansas, and because he had discovered that the Buchanan administration was corrupt. The depth and genuineness of Broderick's convictions on any matter of principle, however, must be very seriously questioned. The extent to which he was willing to injure his party and his friends in order to gratify his personal hatreds became so obvious that it shocked and alienated a number of his former supporters.

In the state elections of 1859 the Gwin group, now known as the Lecompton Democrats because they favored the admission of Kansas to statehood under the proslavery Lecompton constitution, won a sweeping victory over the Broderick men, who had to divide the anti-Lecompton vote with the Republicans. At this time the growth of the Republican party in California was impeded by the charge that it was friendly to the Negro, although its campaign orators denied this charge, and sought to prove that the epithet of "Black Republicans" was undeserved. Leland Stanford, the unsuccessful Republican candidate for governor in 1859, said, in accepting the nomination, that his party stood for "the cause of the white man—the cause of free labor."

During the campaign, Chief Justice David S. Terry, a candidate for renomination to the state supreme court, made a speech in which he aligned himself with the Lecompton Democrats—hardly surprising in view of his background and his strongly pro-Southern opinions. Broderick, while at breakfast in a hotel dining room in San Francisco, read a newspaper account of Terry's speech, and was overheard in an outburst of angry denunciation. He had supported Terry in his troubles with the vigilance committee of 1856, and this was how he was repaid. Whereas he had believed Terry to be the only honest member of the supreme court, it was now clear that the "d——d miserable wretch" was as corrupt as the other members. Terry waited for an apology until the end of the campaign. He had failed to win renomination, and only a few weeks remained in his term. On election day he resigned from the supreme court and shortly afterward challenged Broderick to a duel. This they fought on September 13, 1859, in a ravine near the ocean, just across the line in San Mateo County. Broderick nervously pulled the trigger of his pistol too soon, and his bullet went wild, but Terry's shot struck his opponent in the breast.

Admirers of Broderick came to believe that his dying words were: "They have killed me because I was opposed to a corrupt administration and the extension of slavery." Whether Broderick made this particular statement is doubtful, and in any case it was not an accurate description of the cause of the duel; but the popular orator Edward D. Baker quoted it in a funeral eulogy and thus launched a myth that ultimately transformed Broderick into a kind of Pacific Coast Lincoln.

Movements for state division and for a Pacific Republic. The early historians who believed that Broderick's opposition to the territorial expansion of slavery, rather than his desire for political power, was his most significant motive, were probably committing an error of emphasis. The same historians tended to see a proslavery conspiracy in the demands of Southern California for separation from the rest of the state during the 1850s. This was simply and completely an error of fact, like the notion that the proposal for larger state boundaries in the constitutional convention of 1849 was a proslavery plot. It was true that the southern counties of California repeatedly sought permission to secede from the northern ones, but the slavery question did not have anything to do with these efforts except that many imagined that it did. The real cause of the movement was the grievance of Southern California against too much taxation and too little representation.

The fears expressed by the Southern California delegates in the convention of 1849, to the effect that their part of the state would have to pay an unfair share of taxes, proved to have been extremely well founded. In 1852 Governor McDougal conceded that the six cow counties of Southern California, with a population of 6,000, paid $42,000 in property taxes, while the 12 mining counties, with a population of nearly 120,000, paid only $21,000. A state law exempted from taxation all mining claims on "United States lands," where the great majority of the claims were located. This was one of the innumerable statutes of the 1850s that conferred special favors on the mining interests. The transient population of the mining areas was counted in apportioning legislative districts, but 9 out of 10 miners neglected to pay their poll taxes. Many thousands of these delinquents could have afforded to pay, and their neglect to do so was essentially an indication of their indifference to the general welfare of the state.

The proposal of the southern counties was that they be reorganized as a territory since as yet they had only about one-tenth of the 60,000 population ordinarily necessary for separate statehood. Governor McDougal gave his support to a Southern Californian project for a convention that would include this proposal in a revised state constitution. The *San Francisco Daily Alta California* charged, and the *Los Angeles Star* indignantly denied, that the movement had a proslavery aspect. In 1852 a bill for a constitutional convention passed the assembly but died in the senate.

Gradually the justice of Southern California's grievance became recognized throughout the state, and in 1859 the legislature approved a plan introduced by Assemblyman Andrés Pico. This provided that the part of California south of 35°45′ (the northern boundary of San Luis Obispo County) should become the territory of Colorado. The voters of that region also approved the plan, but coming as it did on the eve of the Civil War it had no chance of passage in the national capital. Most members of Congress, ignorant of affairs on the remote Pacific Coast, could not be dissuaded from the belief that the measure was another dangerous aggravation of the slavery issue.

When the withdrawal of the South from the Union became an increasing threat, and then a fact, and when the Southern states formed their own Confederacy, the idea of a Pacific Republic received serious discussion. It was not new. Alvarado, Hastings, and the Bear Flaggers had dreamed of it in their various ways. California's remoteness from Mexico had almost made the dream a reality at the time of Alvarado's revolution of 1836, and California was even farther from the more settled parts of the United States than it had been from the center of Mexico. Throughout the 1850s, whenever there was discontent with Federal neglect of California, and particularly with each new defeat of a transcontinental railroad bill, there had been talk of a Western secession.

In his annual message in 1860, Governor Weller predicted that California "will not go with the South or the North, but here on the shores of the Pacific [will] found a mighty republic which may in the end prove the greatest of all." Senators Gwin and Latham and Representative Burch made similar predictions. In an editorial on the secession of South Carolina, the *Alameda Gazette* said that neither a Southerner nor a Northerner in California could be expected to take up arms against the "land of his nativity," and that a Western republic was the only solution. The *San Francisco Herald* and several other papers argued in the same vein. But the idea of a Pacific Republic never had wide popular support, and it received much less attention after the attack on Fort Sumter. The fact that the South was the first to resort to arms strengthened the unionist sympathies of many who had hoped that war could be avoided. The legislature passed a resolution pledging California's loyalty to the United States. There were 5 negative votes in the senate and 12 in the assembly.

California and the Civil War. The amount of pro-Confederate sentiment in California was grossly exaggerated during the war—by those who felt and cherished it, by those who feared it, and by those who for their own political and personal reasons wished to make it appear greater than it was. Most histories have reflected the contemporary exaggeration. Actually, less than 7 percent of the population of California in 1860 had come from the seceded states. There were many from the North who remained lukewarm in their support of the dreadful and distant conflict, and there were many from both the North and the South who detested it as fratricidal slaughter. But once the war had begun, there was never any genuine danger that California would desert the Union cause. Pro-Confederate opinion and activities were more colorful than significant.

The elections and the trends in party politics gave ample evidence that California was safe for the Union. In the state campaigns of 1861 the Republicans and the Union Democrats repudiated the right of secession and pledged the support of California for the war, and their candidates, running on these strongly unionist platforms, polled together more than two-thirds of the votes. The Breckinridge Democrats favored the preservation of the Union on a basis of compromise with the Southern states, and opposed the policy of coercing them. In the previous year this same Democratic split had given the California electoral votes to Lincoln by only a very narrow plurality over the two Democratic candidates, Senators Douglas of Illinois and Breckinridge of Kentucky. In the California elections of 1861 the continuing Democratic schism enabled the Republicans to elect their first governor, Leland Stanford, by a substantial plurality. By 1864, although the Democrats were reunited in support of the Union, the Republicans had been very successful in branding all Democrats as disloyal, and consequently a large majority of Californians voted for the reelection of Lincoln. The Republicans called themselves the Union party from 1863 to 1867.

There were many rumors of pro-Southern plots. One such rumor was that the assignment of Gen. Albert Sidney Johnston to command the Federal Military Department of the Pacific, late in 1860, was part of a conspiracy planned by Senator Gwin in which General Johnston would turn over both his army and the state of California to the Confederacy at the outbreak of war. The charge was baseless. In April 1861, after the secession of his home state of Texas, General Johnston resigned his Federal commission, but he scrupulously carried out his duties as a Union officer until his replacement arrived to take over the command at San Francisco. Later one of the ablest of the Confederate generals, he was killed in action in the battle of Shiloh.

Disloyal conspiracies did exist in California, but they were on a small scale. There were clandestine pro-Confederate societies like the Knights of the Golden Circle, the Knights of the Columbian Star, and the Committee of Thirty, but they had only a fraction of the membership that wild rumor attributed to them. There were various dreams of seizing Federal arsenals and gold shipments, and there was one romantic but futile attempt to put a conspiracy into actual operation. A group including Asbury Harpending, a young firebrand from Kentucky who had made a fortune in the California gold mines, secretly armed the small schooner *Chapman* at San Francisco in the hope of capturing a Pacific Mail steamer to use as a privateer under a Confederate letter of marque. Federal authorities knew of the plot almost from its beginning, and they seized the *Chapman* as she was weighing anchor.

A few editors of small newspapers were openly pro-Confederate. The most outspoken of these was Lovick P. Hall, a native of Mississippi who had edited proslavery papers in Oregon and California. In 1862 he established the *Equal Rights Expositor* in Visalia, because there were said to be more Confederates there than in any other town of its size outside the Confederacy. In the columns of the *Expositor,* Hall justified secession and maintained with eloquent logic that the Federal government had no legal or moral right to coerce the Southern states. He also denounced President Lincoln as an idiot, despot, liar, traitor, and murderer. Gen. George Wright, in command of the Department of the Pacific, excluded the paper from the mails along with the *Stockton Argus,* the *San Jose Tribune,* and several others; but Hall's admirers in Visalia kept the *Expositor* alive by special subscriptions, and the ban was lifted after three months. When its Thanksgiving edition ridiculed the Union armies and gave thanks for the Union military disasters of 1862, Hall was placed under military arrest. He was freed the same day after taking an oath of loyalty to the Constitution of the United States, but this did not change his editorial policies, because he said that they had always represented the true meaning of the Constitution. Early in March 1863 he published an editorial referring in particularly scurrilous language to the men who had volunteered for Federal military service. That was the *Expositor*'s last issue. Acting on their own initiative, a band of soldiers from a neighboring military post broke into its office, smashed its press, and threw its type into the street.

There were other cases of wartime interference with freedom of thought and expression. Rev. William A. Scott, pastor of the Calvary Presbyterian Church in San Francisco, after invoking equal blessings upon both Presidents, Lincoln and Davis, was burned in effigy and forced by mob demonstrations to leave the state, though he returned after the war. Because of the wartime suspension of the writ of habeas corpus, there were several arbitrary arrests of civilians by military authorities on charges of disloyal utterances. Innumerable citizens made accusations of disloyalty against their neighbors, mostly based on personal grudges. General Wright, however, was not an alarmist. He refused "to believe that it is my special duty to arrest every man or woman whose sentiments do not coincide exactly with the Government," and this comparatively moderate attitude led to demands from ultraloyalists that he be replaced by a more zealous commander.

The Republicans, as a part of their appeal to the unionist majority of the voters, were strong advocates of loyalty oaths. "National life," said a Republican campaign appeal in 1862, "should be maintained and perpetuated . . . by the ramification of test oaths into all departments of society—mechanical, mercantile, agricultural, and professional." This sweeping objective was not achieved, but in 1863 California did adopt a law requiring special loyalty oaths of the participants in court proceedings. James H. Hardy, a state district court judge, had been impeached and removed from office for using "seditious and Treasonable language" in public toasts, and although chronic drunkenness was his more serious offense, the case was alleged to prove that the California courts were centers of disloyalty. Under the act of 1863, a defendant in a civil suit could charge that the plaintiff was disloyal, and if the plaintiff did not sign a specified oath the court was required to dismiss the suit. This law also required all attorneys to sign the oath or suffer a fine and disbarment. In *Cohen v. Wright,* a test case involving a suit for the collection of a small debt, the state supreme court upheld the constitutionality of this measure; but in the recodification of the state's laws in 1872 it was eliminated along with other obsolete statutes.

Since it was never necessary for anyone to "save California for the Union," it is absurd to say that anyone did; but this honor has been variously claimed for Rev. Thomas Starr King, Col. Edward D. Baker, Governor Stanford, and others. King was a much beloved Unitarian minister, called to San Francisco from Boston in 1860. He was a captivating orator, and in several lecture tours he spoke for the Union and particularly for contributions to the work of the Sanitary Commission, the "Red Cross of the Civil War." Partly as a result of his efforts, California contributed more than a fourth of the amount that the Commission received in the entire country. His death from diphtheria in 1864 was officially mourned throughout the state.

Colonel Baker was a close personal friend of Abraham Lincoln, whom he had first known when they were young lawyers in Springfield, Illinois. In the late 1850s Baker was one of the leading organizers of the Republican party in California. In 1860 the Republicans of the new state of Oregon invited him to come there as their leader, and in the fall elected him United States Senator. He had the honor of introducing Lincoln on the occasion of his inaugural address in 1861, and he became the President's chief advisor on matters concerning the Pacific Coast. Impulsively he accepted the command of a regiment of Pennsylvania Volunteers made up in part of men who had returned to Pennsylvania from California or Oregon. He was killed while leading his regiment at Ball's Bluff in October 1861.

California's military participation in the Civil War was very limited. The Federal government did not favor the use of California volunteers in the main theaters of the war because their transportation was too expensive, and the draft was never enforced in California for the same reason. Gen. Don Andrés Pico, victor of San Pasqual and signer of the Treaty of Cahuenga with Frémont, was deeply hurt by the rejection of his offer to raise a regiment of native Californian cavalry. About 500 young Californians, including several native ones, offered their services to Massachusetts if that state would pay the cost of their organization and transportation. It did so, and the "California Battalion," as part of the 2d Massachusetts Cavalry, took part in more than 50 engagements, mainly in Virginia. About 16,000 volunteers enlisted in California during the war, but they were used mainly for local garrison duty, for guarding the overland mail routes or for policing Indians in the Northwest. A "California Column" was sent to New Mexico in 1862 to repel a Confederate invasion of the territory, but the enemy withdrew before a battle could be fought, and many members of the column left it to join the mining rush to Bill Williams Fork.

SELECTED BIBLIOGRAPHY

The party politics of the era may be traced in Winfield J. Davis, *History of Political Conventions in California, 1849–1892* (1893). Earl Pomeroy, "California, 1846–1860: Politics of a Representative Frontier State," *California Historical Society Quarterly*, XXXII (December 1953), 291–302, is a valuable commentary. Gwin's version is in William H. Ellison, editor, "Memoirs of Hon. William M. Gwin," *California Historical Society Quarterly*, XIX (March, June, September, and December 1940). James O'Meara, *Broderick and Gwin* (1881), was realistic and balanced. Bancroft, following the lead of E. D. Baker's funeral oration, made Broderick a hero and martyr. Jeremiah Lynch, *A Senator of the Fifties, David C. Broderick of California* (1911), was also eulogistic. Donald E. Hargis, "The Issues in the Broderick-Gwin Debates of 1859," *California Historical Society Quarterly*, XXXII (December 1953), 313–325, maintained that principles of national politics were substantially important in the feud; L. E. Fredman, "Broderick: a Reassessment," *Pacific Historical Review*, XXX (February 1961), 39–46, concluded otherwise. Lately Thomas, *Between Two Empires . . . William McKendree Gwin* (1969), and David A. Williams, *David C. Broderick: a Political Portrait* (1969), make a pair of biographies. See also A. Russell Buchanan, *David S. Terry . . ., Dueling Judge* (1956). A case of often-confused identity was clarified in an article on Governor John McDougal, by H. Brett Melendy, *Pacific Historical Review*, XXIX (August 1960), 231–244, and an article on United States Senator James A. McDougall, by A. Russell Buchanan, *California Historical Society Quarterly*, XV (September 1936), 199–212. On the "American" party, see Peyton Hurt, "The Rise and Fall of the 'Know Nothings' in California," *California Historical Society Quarterly*, IX (March and June 1930), 16–49, 99–128.

The state division movement is well covered in William H. Ellison, *A Self-governing Dominion*, and the Pacific Republic idea in Joseph Ellison, *California and the Nation*. The latter also has a good chapter on "Loyalty and Disloyalty."

Politics before, during, and after the war are described in Theodore H. Hittell, *History of California* volume IV (1898); George T. Clark, Leland *Stanford* (1931); Norman E. Tutorow, *Leland Stanford, Man of Many Careers* (1970); Robert H. Becker, editor, *Some Reflections of an Early California Governor* (1959), on the administration of Frederick F. Low, 1863–

1867; *Memoirs of Cornelius Cole* (1908); and Catherine Coffin Phillips, *Cornelius Cole, California Pioneer and United States Senator* (1929). See also Royce D. Delmatier, Clarence F. McIntosh, and Earl G. Waters, editors, *The Rumble of California Politics, 1848–1970* (1970), chapters 1 and 2; and H. Brett Melendy and Benjamin F. Gilbert, *The Governors of California* (1965).

Benjamin F. Gilbert, "California and the Civil War, a Bibliographical Essay," *California Historical Society Quarterly*, XL (December 1961), 289–307, is very useful. See also his "The Confederate Minority in California," *California Historical Society Quarterly*, XX (June 1941), 154–170. Asbury Harpending's account of his conspiracy is included in his memoir, *The Great Diamond Hoax* (1913, 1958). On L. P. Hall and his *Expositor*, consult Ralph S. Kuykendall, "A California State Rights Editor," *Grizzly Bear*, XXIV (January 1919), 3–4. Other civil liberties problems are described in Frank M. Stewart, "Impeachment of Judge James H. Hardy," *Southern California Law Review*, XXVIII (December 1954), 61–69, and Harold M. Hyman, "New Light on *Cohen v. Wright:* California's First Loyalty Oath Case," *Pacific Historical Review*, XXVIII (May 1959), 131–140. On California contributions to the war effort, see Milton H. Shutes, *Lincoln and California* (1943); Russell M. Posner, "Thomas Starr King and the Mercy Million," *California Historical Society Quarterly*, XLIII (December 1964), 291–308; Aurora Hunt, *The Army of the Pacific* (1951); and Oscar Lewis, *The War in the Far West* (1961). E. R. Kennedy, *The Contest for California in 1861: How Colonel E. D. Baker Saved the Pacific States to the Union* (1912), may be cited as an example of the exaggerations in many writings on this period.

Chapter XVI

CULTURE AND ANARCHY

THE SOCIETY that the gold rush produced in California was not the typical society of the older American agrarian frontier. Rather, the California mining districts and the towns that served them became, in the words of Franklin Walker, "the acme of all frontiers, the most concentrated of quickly flourishing societies," whose people "lived through a condensed version of the world's economic growth." A metropolitan and cosmopolitan city sprang up at San Francisco, a city that telescoped half a century's growth into a year, as Bayard Taylor put it, and within five years was a financial rival of New York and, in some respects, a cultural rival of Boston. The fact that California became rich even before it became a state, and the fact that San Francisco's per capita wealth, though far from being evenly distributed, was suddenly the highest in the nation, meant that there were many who could afford the good things of life. The demand was primarily for material luxuries, but it included cultural satisfactions as well, for the gold rush had drawn a remarkable number of educated men. Moreover, the great distance from the Eastern sources of cultural amenities had a hothouse effect on their local production.

On the other hand, the new culture, being so precocious, was inevitably awkward and crude. The new Californians themselves were predominantly youthful, and overwhelmingly male. Half the '49ers were between the ages of 20 and 30, and a man of 45 was likely to be described as "the old gentleman." The female contingent, one-twelfth of the population of California according to the census of 1850, would increase only to one-third in 1880 and would not equal the number of males until about 1900. A society made up so largely of young men without women was sure to be peculiarly rough and boisterous.

Newspapers and literary magazines. The most immediate demand of most Americans for the printed word, after, perhaps, their Bibles, was in the form of the newspaper, and the attempt to meet this need had begun soon after the American occupation. The first issue of California's first newspaper, the weekly *Californian,* appeared at Monterey on August 15, 1846, about five weeks after Commodore Sloat's landing. To publish it, the naval chaplain Walter Colton went into partnership with the tall frontiersman Robert Semple, whom Colton described as "true with the rifle, ready with his pen and quick at the type case." In a dusty storeroom they found a battered Ramage press, made in Boston many years earlier. Agustín V. Zamorano, a Mexican official, had imported it to Monterey in 1834, and it had been used intermittently, mainly for proclamations by the governors. "The press was old enough to be preserved as a curiosity," Colton recalled, and "the types were all rusty and all in pi. It was only by scouring that the letters could be made to show their faces." There was a barrel of ink but no paper, and the early issues came out on sheets intended for cigar wrappings, about 12 inches by 8 inches.

Half in English and half in Spanish, the *Californian* appeared each week until May of 1847 when Semple moved it to San Francisco and sold it. Its first rival, established by Sam Brannan, was the weekly *California Star,* which had been appearing regularly at San Francisco since January 9, 1847. It was printed in a loft above a grist mill. In its planning it actually antedated the *Californian,* for it was with the intention of publishing the *Star* that Brannan had brought a printing press from New York.

At that stage in the development of California journalism, it was not surprising that four months passed between the great gold discovery and the recognition of its importance by the two tiny newspapers, and that Edward C. Kemble, the young editor of the *Star* in 1848, missed one of the greatest news stories of the century and had to spend the rest of his life trying to explain his oversight. After the suspension of the two little San Francisco weeklies during the early months of the gold mania, Kemble became the owner of both of them. The result of this merger was the *Alta California.* First published under that title in January 1849, it became the first California daily a year later, and survived for 41 years more. In many respects it was the most important of all of California's early newspapers.

There were soon literally hundreds of newspapers. Throughout the mining districts almost every boom town had its paper, some with such names as the *Nevada City Miner's Spy Glass* and the *Downieville Old Oaken Bucket* (though in picturesqueness of title none could match *Satan's Bassoon,* published briefly in San Francisco). As Kemble wrote in his history of California newspapers to 1858, the press seemed to be a lichen that flourished among the rocks. Most of the mining-district papers, of course, were ephemeral, partly because of the mobility of their subscribers. A town might be almost depopulated by the rumor of a better strike in some other valley, which led to the story that in order to get rid of miners who made a nuisance of themselves by digging up the golden streets in Heaven, Saint Peter once started a rumor of a rich strike in Hell.

The gold that poured into San Francisco multiplied the wealth of "the city" in many other forms. John Russ of Stevenson's regiment bought two town lots in Yerba Buena for $30 in 1847 and sold them a decade later for enough to build the Russ House, the city's largest hotel. No one made a fortune in journalism in this period, but that was largely because so many tried. In the 10 years after the gold discovery 132 periodicals were started in San Francisco alone, and the total number of their proprietors, editors, and reporters was more than 1,000. Though most of these papers survived less than a year, their total per capita circulation and their variety were greater than in New York, London, or anywhere else. They were printed in six different languages, represented eight religious denominations and seven political parties, and, as Kemble said, "devoted themselves to the interests of religion, politics, morals, law, medicine, literature, commerce, agriculture, news and slander." In 1859 there were 12 San Francisco dailies, most notably the *Alta*, the *Herald*, the *Call*, and the *Bulletin*.

Poetry, short stories, and other literary pieces often appeared in the early newspapers, for no other frontier has ever inspired so many of its people to write. The scenes of California, and the experiences of getting there and living there, were so often extraordinary and dramatic that they cried out for description. A literary weekly, the *Golden Era*, flourished from the first day of its publication in 1852 and soon had more subscribers than any other paper on the Pacific Coast. Much of its success was due to the enthusiasm of one of its young editors, Rollin M. Daggett, who traveled through the mining districts to sell subscriptions and also wrote many of the sketches describing the miners' life. Though it paid nothing for poetry and only $5 a column for prose, nearly every writer who achieved any reputation in early American California found in it his opportunity for literary apprenticeship. Bret Harte worked on its staff, first as a typesetter and then as a columnist, and it was in the *Era* that he published his first successful story, "M'liss."

The tone of the *Golden Era* was informal to the point of breeziness, and this gave it a popular appeal that enabled it to outlast a number of competitors, including several that aspired to higher literary levels. One of these was *Hutchings's Illustrated California Magazine*, published for five years beginning in 1856. Its founder, James M. Hutchings, was an Englishman who had worked in the mines before establishing himself as a writer with his *Miner's Ten Commandments* (leading off with "Thou shalt have no other claim than one"). Printed on a single sheet, this new decalogue sold nearly 100,000 copies. Hutchings asserted that the intelligence and good taste of the reading public of California, and particularly of the mining population, had been underrated, and that his magazine would correct this error. Illustrated with woodcuts, it is best known for early writings in praise of California's mountain scenery, with which its publisher was so entranced that he spent his later years as the first hotel-keeper in the Yosemite Valley.

Writers of the '50s. The literary conventions of the time required the use of pen names, and in California's first decade of American statehood the most important pseudonyms were those of Dame Shirley; John Phoenix, alias Squibob; Old Block; and Yellow Bird.

Of all the nearly innumerable accounts of life in the mining camps of the gold rush period, the best were the letters written by a remarkably observant young woman, Louisa Amelia Knapp Smith Clapp, who signed herself "Dame Shirley." Her husband, Dr. Fayette Clapp, practiced medicine in 1851 and 1852 at Rich Bar and then at Indian Bar on the north fork of the Feather River, and while living with him there she wrote 23 letters to her sister in the East. "I take pains to describe things as I see them," she wrote, "hoping that thus you will obtain an idea of life in the mines *as it is.*" During much of her sojourn she was the only woman in camp, and she invited her sister to imagine spending a winter in a place where there were "no fresh books, no shopping, calling, nor gossiping little tea-drinkings . . . no latest fashions, no daily mail (we have an express once a month), no promenades, no rides or drives; no vegetables but potatoes and onions, no milk, no eggs, no *nothing.*" When the gold began to play out, and fear, hate, and brutality became chronic, a lynching and incidents of persecution and expulsion of Mexicans evoked some of her most vivid and sensitive passages. Yet, taken as a whole, her experiences in the diggings were so fascinating that when the camp broke up she left it with regret.

The "Shirley letters" were first published in 1854 in *The Pioneer,* a lively but unfortunately short-lived San Francisco literary monthly. This same journal also served to popularize the writings of the first of the far-western humorists, Lt. George H. Derby of the U.S. Army topographical engineers, otherwise known as "John Phoenix." Derby was a brilliant young West Pointer who had graduated seventh in a class of 59, in spite of the difficulty he usually found in taking anything seriously. It was said, for example, that he answered an examination question on what to do if besieged in a fort with provisions running low, by saying that he would abandon the fort and besiege the enemy. Assigned to duty in California, he wrote some humorous sketches for the *Alta* under his alternate pseudonym of "Squibob" ("a Hebrew word, signifying 'There you go, with your eye out' "); but his first really important literary opportunity came when he was sent to San Diego in 1853 to build a dam on the San Diego River. His boredom with the sleepy little town ended when his friend Judge John J. Ames, editor of the weekly *San Diego Herald,* the Democratic organ in the district, went north to solicit more funds from the state Democratic campaign chest. "Phoenix," left in charge of the paper for several weeks, burlesqued everything in its news and editorial columns, and among other delightful outrages switched its political support to the Whigs. Then he described editorially, and in advance, the fight that might be expected to occur when the powerfully built and vengeful Ames should return to San Diego: "We held [him] down over the press by our nose (which we had inserted between his teeth for that purpose)," and "while our hair was engaged in holding one of his hands," struck off a fair copy of the *Herald's* advertisements on the back of his shirt. Actually, Ames appreciated this most famous joke of early California as much as anyone did, and a few years later he edited the first collection of his friend's *Phoenixiana* in book form. Almost as important as Derby's own writings, in the history of American humor, were the many stories that were told about him, one being that before introducing his bride to his mother he told each that the other was deaf, and then let them shout at each other for half an hour.

Alonzo Delano, or "Old Block," also wrote many humorous sketches, collected into a book called *Chips from the Old Block,* which sold nearly 15,000 copies in California. He was famous for his prodigious nose; in fact he once asked a passing stranger to brush a mosquito from the end of that protuberance, because "You are nearer to it than I am." For Eastern readers, on the other hand, he wrote one of the most realistic accounts of the gold rush, *Life on the Plains and among the Diggings.*

It is significant that the best writers of the Far West in these years of hazard and hardship were people who had suffered intense personal tragedies in their earlier lives. Shirley was an orphan, Phoenix's father was an eccentric who deserted the family, and Old Block's wife died young, leaving him to care for two invalid children. That Phoenix and Block were humorists may be explained in considerable part by the fact that men often laugh because they are afraid they will cry. Mark Twain would write, in his old age, that "Everything human is pathetic. The secret source of humor is not joy but sorrow."

Tragedy also haunted the life of John Rollin Ridge, or Yellow Bird. That he was half Indian might not in itself have made his life too difficult, for his father was a wealthy Cherokee chief who married the daughter of the principal of the private academy in Connecticut where he had received his education. But when their son John was 12 years old he witnessed the bloody knife-murder of his father by a group of Cherokees who hated him for signing the treaty under which they had given up their lands in Georgia and moved across the Mississippi. A decade later Ridge appeared in gold rush San Francisco and began to write poems under the name of Yellow Bird, a literal translation of his Indian name.

Ridge's main literary achievement was the creation of California's greatest legend, in his book called *The Life and Adventures of Joaquín Murieta, Celebrated California Bandit,* published in 1854. Bandits flourished in the early '50s. Many of them were Mexicans, and some of these probably considered that they had been driven to lives of crime by mistreatment at the hands of Americans. Of the many cattle thefts and other robberies committed in various parts of the state, some of the most notorious were attributed to five men, all known as "Joaquín," though they had five different surnames, one of which was Murieta. In 1853 the state legislature passed an act authorizing Capt. Harry Love, a former Texan, to recruit a band of mounted rangers at state expense for the capture of any or all of the five Joaquíns; Governor Bigler, about to seek reelection, personally offered $1,000 reward for any of them. The rangers returned from their forays with a head pickled in a jar of alcohol, and collected the reward, although there was no reliable identification, and one of the rangers later boasted in a saloon that one pickled head was as good as another.

Such was the vague and dubious factual background from which John Rollin Ridge constructed his narrative. One of the threads he wove into it was the Robin Hood legend. Another thread was obviously suggested by one of the Shirley letters, describing the whipping of a Mexican by the vigilance committee of Indian Bar, and the victim's oath of deadly vengeance against his tormentors. This man now became "Joaquín Murieta"; and as "Joaquín" carried out his oath of revenge, always with his knife, Yellow Bird may have been vicariously avenging himself against the murderers of his father. Through Joaquín's guerrilla attacks upon the *gringos,* Ridge may also have vicariously redressed some of the grievances of his own people.

Bret Harte. Francis Brett Harte, who was known as "Frank" to his family and friends, had been sending poems to the papers under the name of "Bret" for several years before he came to California as a boy of 17, in 1854, to live with his mother and his stepfather in Oakland. Legend has exaggerated his subsequent personal experience and knowledge of the California mining camps, just as his famous stories created a bizarre and romanticized picture of mining life which came to be accepted as more genuine than the reality. On the other hand, it is not true that, as Josiah Royce later asserted, Harte was never anywhere near the mines. He taught school for a few months in a Sierra mining town which was probably La Grange, and which probably became the village of Smith's Pocket in "M'liss." He may have prospected for a short time, very amateurishly and unsuccessfully, and there is some evidence that for a "brief, delightful hour" early in 1857 he was an expressman on some little local stagecoach line. But the novels of Dickens, which Harte had read and reread voraciously during his adolescent years, seem to have had as much influence on his writing as any actual experiences and observations of his own. He once said that his inspiration to write stories using the mining camps as his main locale came when he read the pamphlet called *The Idle and Industrious Miner,* composed of Hogarthian drawings by Charles Nahl, with accompanying verses attributed to Old Block.

10 THE IDLE AND INDUSTRIOUS MINER.

URN to the other loitering friend
Yet on a drunken spree—
His tools neglected, and his face
[illegible]
The bottle is his chief delight,
No care disturbs his brain,
He smokes, and chews, and yawns, and drinks,
And wakes and drinks again;
Or when he leaves his cabin walls
To dig an hour or so,
Ill luck attends him,—so he thinks,—
Wherever he may go.
Forever armed with some excuse
He deems his cause is good,
Till want assails him at his door
And drives him forth for food.

THE IDLE AND INDUSTRIOUS MINER. 9

EQUITED toil! Eureka! Look!
And read within those eyes
Their speaking luster, as they dwell
Upon the glittering prize!
The vein is struck! ah, noble heart!
A thrill of joy is thine!—
A purer and a better thrill
Than that produced by wine.
A thousand thoughts of home, and bliss
Reserved for coming years
Have swiftly flashed across thy soul
And melted thee to tears—
Tears—not of grief, or vain regrets,
For thou art still a man—
But, thinking of thy poverty
And gazing in the pan!

2

"The Idle and Industrious Miner." Drawings by Charles Nahl, verse by "Old Block," Alonzo Delano. (Courtesy of the Henry E. Huntington Library and Art Gallery)

Having followed a married sister to the town of Union, now Arcata, Harte became the printer's devil and then the junior editor of the town's weekly paper, the *Northern Californian.* In February 1860, when he was 23, his senior editor took a trip to San Francisco, and the effect on Harte's career was quite as important as the effect of the comparable experience in the life of John Phoenix, though the outcome was very different. While Harte was in charge of the paper, a gang of local scoundrels sneaked into the Indian village on Gunther's Island in Humboldt Bay one morning before dawn and perpetrated the most contemptible racist massacre in the history of the state. With hatchets and axes they killed 60 Indians, mostly women and children, for no better reason than that some other tribe a hundred miles back in the mountains had been causing trouble. Harte bitterly denounced the murders in an article headed "Indiscriminate Massacre of Indians—Women and Children Butchered."

Threats against his life soon became so menacing that he left Arcata by steamer for San Francisco, but he had already demonstrated his personal courage beyond question. Thus his experience of the most brutal realities of the frontier, though short, was by no means insignificant.

In San Francisco, not long after this episode, Jessie Benton Frémont read some of Harte's work in the *Golden Era,* invited him to her home, and introduced him to her literary and political friends. Becoming active in Republican circles, he wrote many unionist poems and worked vigorously for the unionist cause in close friendship and cooperation with Edward Dickinson Baker and Thomas Starr King. Later Jessie Frémont used her influence to get him a Federal patronage appointment as a clerk in the surveyor-general's office, and then a better position in the branch mint. These jobs allowed him time for writing while assuring him of an income. For several years his poems and stories about California were mostly romantic tales of Spanish colonial days. Father José, searching for new mission sites, met Satan, in "A Legend of Monte del Diablo"; the ghosts of Drake's sailors appeared in "The Legend of Devil's Point." "The Lost Galleon," which also furnished the title for the first collection of Harte's work in book form, was a poem about a Manila galleon that was doomed to sail for 300 years in search of the saint's day that it had lost at the international dateline.

The writing that gave Harte an enduring place in the history of literature was done in less than three years while he served as the first editor and the most important contributor of *The Overland Monthly,* founded in 1868 by the San Francisco bookseller and publisher Anton Roman. Up to this time Harte had regarded the American period in California with a kind of genteel contempt. In one of his early articles he had called the 1850s "a hard, ugly, unwashed, vulgar, and lawless era." Roman seems to have persuaded him in 1868, however, that the time had come to enshrine the gold rush in romantic fiction, and for the early issues of *The Overland* Harte wrote his best stories. "The Luck of Roaring Camp" concerned the death of the camp prostitute in childbirth and the adoption of the baby by the miners. In "The Outcasts of Poker Flat" a gambler and a prostitute sacrificed their own lives in attempts to save their companions, trapped by a snowstorm. In "Tennessee's Partner," after a miner had gone to the dogs and been hanged for robbery (Harte called the lynching a "weak and foolish deed"), his partner claimed the body for burial and soon afterward died of grief and loneliness.

Harte's most famous poem, usually known as "The Heathen Chinee" though its original title was "Plain Language from Truthful James," appeared in *The Overland* in 1870, and hilariously told how a pair of gamblers were outcheated in a card game by the bland and wily Ah Sin. Harte was unhappy when this poem, which he regarded as a trifling little burlesque, became the most widely known of all his writings; and because he detested racial persecution he was further troubled when the climactic line, "We are ruined by

Chinese cheap labor," had the serious side effect of popularizing an anti-Chinese slogan. Unintentionally, he had made a major contribution to the anti-Oriental stereotype in America.

The editors of *The Atlantic Monthly* lured Harte to the East Coast in 1871 with a large advance against future writings. For the rest of his life his work was largely repetitious and of poorer quality. His most successful theme, redemption through self-sacrifice, became almost a trademark of his later stories. American editors tired of them, but in England there seemed to be an insatiable demand for "more like 'The Luck,'" and it was in England that he lived and wrote during his last years. "I grind out the old tunes on the old organ," he told his wife, "and gather up the coppers." His tragicomic, sentimental, whimsical characters were obviously Dickensian, but he succeeded brilliantly in adapting the formula to California gold rush scenes. His work was also important for the great impetus it gave to the use of local color in American fiction generally.

Mark Twain. The greatest and the most original literary product of the American West was undoubtedly Mark Twain. Although his writing career began in Virginia City, Nevada, that beginning is a part of the literary history of California, just as the whole history of the Comstock Lode was closely interwoven with the economic and social history of San Francisco.

Samuel L. Clemens came to Nevada in 1861, at the age of 25. His brother Orion was secretary to the Nevada territorial governor, and Sam was secretary to Orion. In this capacity he had neither salary nor duties, but he was badly in need of some new field of adventure. The outbreak of the Civil War had put an end to steamboating on the Mississippi River, and two miserable weeks in a home guard unit at Hannibal had given him a permanent detestation of war, even though the unit had seen no action and was not even entirely sure which side it was on. After trying his hand at mining, in which he was enthusiastic but unsuccessful, he became a reporter for the Virginia City *Territorial Enterprise* in 1862. Early in the following year he began to sign his articles with what would later be the best known of all American pseudonyms, "Mark Twain," a riverboat leadsman's term meaning two fathoms deep.

The *Territorial Enterprise* was an offshoot of the San Francisco *Golden Era.* As San Francisco provided most of the financing for the operation of the Comstock silver mines, so it also furnished most of the early Comstock writers. But the journalistic atmosphere of Virginia City was even freer than that of the larger metropolis. It specialized in burlesques and hoaxes, and in this school Mark Twain learned the writing trade. The most popular of his early scoops, for example, purported to be an account of the discovery of a petrified man—petrified in the stance of thumbing his nose at posterity. In 1864 he moved to San Francisco, met Bret Harte, and wrote sketches for the *Era.* He spent a visit to the Mother Lode country mainly in loafing in a saloon at Angel's Camp, listening to tall tales. One of these grew into the story of the celebrated jumping frog of Calaveras County, so larcenously deprived of the laurels of victory when it was weighted down with a belly full of birdshot. Published in a New York paper, and promptly reprinted in newspapers all over the country, this story made him nationally famous.

In 1867 the *Alta California* sent him on a cruise to the Mediterranean and the Holy Land with a party of culture-hungry American tourists. Two years later he gathered his reports to the *Alta* into *The Innocents Abroad.* Except for a brief visit to San Francisco to arrange for the release of copyright so that this volume could be published in New York, he never returned to California, and instead made his home in Hartford, Connecticut. He had had enough of life in the wild West; but in 1872, before turning to other literary themes, he published *Roughing It,* an autobiographical narrative of his Western experiences, full of such episodes as his visit to Mono Lake, where, he alleged, it got so cold that the only way to serve a brandy toddy was to chop it off and wrap it in a paper.

Joaquin Miller and other poets. The factual details of the life of Cincinnatus H. Miller are often difficult to determine because of the romantic imaginativeness of much of his autobiographical writing. For example, scholars still dispute whether his middle name was actually Hiner or Heine. It is probable that he was born in Indiana in 1837, that the family moved to Oregon in 1852, and that he ran away to California in 1854 when he was 17. But whereas, according to his own version, while living near Mount Shasta he loved an Indian princess who saved his life, another account of the same circumstances had it that he cohabited with a squaw who helped him break out of jail when he was arrested for borrowing a horse. In any case, his Indian mistress bore him a daughter named Cali-Shasta.

During the early part of the Civil War, Miller edited a pacifist newspaper in Oregon. In 1863 he came to San Francisco with plans for a writing career combined with a honeymoon. His bride was the daughter of a fisherman on the southern Oregon coast. She shared Miller's admiration for Byron, and wrote poems under the name of Minnie Myrtle. The young couple failed to make a living by writing in San Francisco, and their marriage ended in separation. Miller explained that Byron had never amounted to anything as a poet until after he left his wife.

Back in Oregon, Miller became a country lawyer and a judge, with no more equipment, it is said, than one law book and two six-shooters. In 1869 he published a long and very bad poem, "Joaquin," further glorifying the Murieta legend, and describing the bandit's sweetheart as a lineal descendant of Montezuma. Miller's friends, in affection, and his critics, in derision, began to call him "Joaquin," and he adopted this as his pen name. In 1870 he went to England, where he was soon accepted with enthusiasm as "the poet of the Sierras." Always a skillful showman, and quite willing to take advantage of the need of many Englishmen to regard Americans as eccentric and uncouth, he appeared in London in a red shirt, high boots, and broad sombrero, trying to look as much as possible as if he had stepped straight out of Roaring Camp. Occasionally he went so far as to smoke two cigars at once, or, on being introduced to a debutante in a Mayfair drawing room, to express his appreciation of her charms by getting down and biting her on the ankle, evoking squeals of delight. His poems were always melodramatic and often erotic. Their crudities (he once rhymed "Goethe" with "teeth") were accepted as proof of their genuine frontier origin.

In 1886 he bought a tract of land called "The Hights" (as he usually spelled it), on the hills above Oakland, on which he planted thousands of trees and built monuments to Moses, Frémont, and Browning, along with a funeral pyre for himself. There, for more than a quarter of a century, he was a California landmark, and his hospitality was a joy to droves of clubwomen.

Some of Miller's poems were not entirely without literary merit. This is the most that can reasonably be said for them, but they were probably as important as the poetic efforts of any of his contemporaries on the Pacific Coast, even though aspiring poets were very numerous. When Bret Harte compiled an anthology of California poetry in 1866, there were so many outraged protests from poets whose work had not been included that he felt compelled to bring out another volume.

Many of the aspirants were ladies, and the most talented of these was Ina Coolbrith. She had had a miserable early life, which she seldom talked about. Born Josephine Smith, she was the daughter of a younger brother of the Prophet of the Mormon church. Her father died when she was a child, and her mother left the church when the Prophet announced the doctrine of polygamy. Ina suffered through an unhappy early marriage and a deeply distressing divorce in Los Angeles, and came to San Francisco about 1865. Harte engaged her as one of his coeditors of *The Overland Monthly,* and she became a good friend of several of California's male writers, though the thought of remarriage was too painful for her to consider. Her gentle verses were an escape from sadness through pleasure in such things as flowers, birds, and the wind. For more than 20 years she was a librarian in the Oakland public library, and some of the happiest moments of her life began when a ragged boy named Jack London asked her whether she could suggest anything for him to read. She was also a foster mother, in the more literal sense, to Joaquin Miller's daughter Cali-Shasta, and to two nieces.

Quite a different sort of poetess was Adah Isaacs Menken, who bared her emotions in her passionate poems as she bared her body on the stage, in flesh-colored tights and strapped onto the back of a horse, in a more or less dramatized version of Byron's "Mazeppa."

Churches and schools. Many a Yankee, about to depart for the goldfields, had listened to a special sermon in which he was exhorted to "Take your Bible in one hand and your New England civilization in the other" and bring light to California. The first Protestant congregation in San Francisco had been organized in November 1848, when it was necessary to include Methodists, Baptists, Presbyterians, Congregationalists, Episcopalians, and Mormons in a community church in order to pay the salary of one chaplain, Timothy Dwight Hunt. "There was sweet pleasure in our unity in diversity," Hunt recalled, with a twinge of regret that the unity could not endure. As wealth rapidly increased, and the city's population gradually became a little more settled, eight major Protestant denominations were soon going their separate ways to Heaven. By 1852 San Francisco had at least 30 churches, including 22 Protestant, 6 Roman Catholic and 2 Hebrew. William Speer, a Presbyterian missionary formerly stationed in Canton, worked heroically but with limited success to convert the Chinese in San Francisco. Throughout the mining-camp towns, earnest evangelists were spreading the gospel, though unfortunately their ministrations were usually least successful with those most obviously in need of redemption.

The Roman Catholic Church in California, which had fallen into utter decay during the last years under Mexico, experienced a remarkable development as a result of the gold rush. In 1846 there were only 13 priests in the whole of Alta California, most of them almost starving. By the early '50s there were more than 100, and their work was being very generously supported. In 1852 it became appropriate to appoint the first archbishop of San Francisco, Joseph S. Alemany.

In contrast with the earnest concern for religious education on the part of the churches, the state government failed miserably to make adequate provision for public schools. Governor Burnett's first message to the legislature in December 1849 did not even mention the subject of education. Not until 1851 did the legislature pass a law authorizing local communities to establish public schools at their own expense, and not until the following year did it provide any state financial support, even though the state was receiving the larger share of the taxes on real property. California's first public high schools, in San Francisco and Sacramento, were not established until 1856. Superintendent of Public Instruction Andrew Jackson Moulder reported that in the five years before 1858 California had spent $754,000 on its prisons, and little more than a third of that amount for public education—an expenditure of nearly $2,000 for each convict, and $9 for each child. Scarcely more than a fourth of the children of school age were attending public schools, usually for less than six months of the year.

By 1866, largely through the efforts of John Swett as state superintendent, several new laws had been passed. Thus for white children, though not yet for others, something like a decent public elementary school system had been established, though only in the larger towns. Such was the limited state of educational progress a full 20 years after the American occupation of California. In the meantime the gross dereliction on the part of the state government, reflecting the selfishness and irresponsibility of the majority of its citizens and their elected representatives, had afforded a special opportunity for the private efforts of a devoted few. Various private schools and academies came into existence, most of them church supported. Though it is doubtful that real collegiate instruction began before the '60s, the College of the Pacific, a Methodist enterprise, established in San Jose but relocated to Stockton, was chartered in 1851, and the University of Santa Clara traces its origin to a college established by the Jesuits in the same year. In 1855 a group of New England Congregationalist and Presbyterian college men secured a charter of incorporation for the College of California in Oakland. The state would take over this private college in 1868, and convert it into the University of California.

SELECTED BIBLIOGRAPHY

Any account of the subject of this chapter must be indebted to Franklin Walker's excellent volume, *San Francisco's Literary Frontier* (1939). Also useful is the chapter on "Culture and Anarchy on the Pacific Coast: the Age of Gold," in Louis B. Wright's *Culture on the Moving Frontier* (1955).

A History of California Newspapers, 1846–1858, by Edward C. Kemble, first published as an extensive supplement to the *Sacramento Union* of December 25, 1858, and edited by Helen Harding Bretnor (1962), is still the basic work on the rowdy and individualistic journalism of its period. *The Annals of San Francisco* (1854), by Frank Soulé, John H. Gihon, and James Nisbet, is a historical treasurehouse drawn almost entirely from the newspapers. See also John P. Young, *Journalism in California* (1915); John Bruce, *Gaudy Century* (1948); Emerson Daggett, editor, *Frontier Journalism* (volume II, 1939), in the WPA *History of Journalism in San Francisco;* John D. Carter, "The San Francisco *Bulletin,* 1855–1865," Ph.D. thesis, University of California, Berkeley (1941); and William B. Rice, *The Los Angeles Star, 1851–1864; the Beginnings of Journalism in Southern California* (1947). F. P. Weisenburger, *Idol of the West* (1966), is a biography of Rollin M. Daggett.

The best edition of *The Shirley Letters from the California Mines* is by Carl I. Wheat (1949); see also Rodman W. Paul, "In Search of

'Dame Shirley,'" *Pacific Historical Review,* XXXIII (May 1964), 127–146. George R. Stewart, *John Phoenix, Esq.: The Veritable Squibob* (1937), is an engaging biography. The remarkable spread of the Joaquín Murieta legend may be traced in Joseph Henry Jackson, *Bad Company* (1949), and in Luis Monguió, "Lust for Riches: A Spanish Nineteenth Century Novel of the Gold Rush and Its Sources," *California Historical Society Quarterly,* XXVII (September 1948), 237–248. A later version, Walter Noble Burns's *The Robin Hood of El Dorado* (1932), was also cinematized under the same title.

George R. Stewart, *Bret Harte, Argonaut and Exile* (1931), is thorough and critical. See also Richard O'Connor, *Bret Harte, a Biography* (1966). Materials on Mark Twain's Western period include Edgar M. Branch, *The Literary Apprenticeship of Mark Twain* (1950); Ivan Benson, *Mark Twain's Western Years* (1938); Henry Nash Smith, editor, *Mark Twain of the Enterprise* (1957); and Bernard Taper, editor, *Mark Twain's San Francisco* (1963). Martin S. Peterson, *Joaquin Miller, Literary Frontiersman* (1937), deals with the poet's life, work, and literary reputation. See also M. M. Marberry, *Splendid Poseur: Joaquin Miller—American Poet* (1953).

On the churches, see William W. Ferrier, *Pioneer Church Beginnings and Educational Movements in California* (1927); William Hanchett, "The Question of Religion and the Taming of California, 1849–1854," *California Historical Society Quarterly,* XXXII (March and June 1953) 49–56, 119–144; John B. McGloin, "The California Catholic Church in Transition, 1846–1850," *California Historical Society Quarterly,* XLII (March 1963), 39–48, and *California's First Archbishop: The Life of Joseph Sadoc Alemany, O. P., 1814–1888* (1966); and Francis J. Weber, *California's Reluctant Prelate: The Life and Times of Right Reverend Thaddeus Amat, C. M. (1811–1878)* (1964), a biography of the first bishop of Los Angeles. On the schools, W. W. Ferrier, *Ninety Years of Education in California, 1846–1936* (1937); John Swett, *History of the Public School System of California* (1876), and his *Public Education in California* (1911); David F. Ferris, *Judge Marvin and the Founding of the California Public School System* (1962); James E. Myers, "The Educational Work of Andrew Jackson Moulder," Ph.D. thesis, University of California, Berkeley (1961); and Nicholas C. Polos, "A Yankee Patriot: John Swett, the Horace Mann of the Pacific," *History of Education Quarterly,* IV (March 1964), 17–32.

Chapter XVII

A FRONTIER ECONOMY

EARLY IN 1848 California's population other than Indians was less than 15,000. According to the Federal census of 1850 it was about 93,000, but this census had a number of notorious defects, the most glaring of which was that all the returns for San Francisco, Contra Costa, and Santa Clara Counties were lost. The state took its own census in 1852, and counted 223,856. For 1860 the regular census figure was more than 380,000, and for 1870 more than 560,000. Since the small proportion of women made California's birth rate lower than its death rate, immigration was obviously responsible for the remarkable growth in population. And in these years the search for economic opportunity was by far the most important force in bringing newcomers to California.

Throughout the period between the gold rush of '49 and the completion of the transcontinental railroad 20 years later, the mining of precious metal continued to dominate the economy; for although the gold output gradually declined after the peak years of the early '50s, the rich silver mines of the Comstock Lode in western Nevada began to produce enormous new wealth in 1859, and the development of the Comstock was essentially a California enterprise.

Gold mining. "The miners are beginning to discover," said the *Alta California* in the autumn of 1851, "that they are engaged in a science and a profession, and not in a mere adventure." Within a few years the gold in the beds and banks of the streams, or in surface outcroppings of quartz, was inevitably depleted. Rich deposits of the metal lay far below the surface, in solid rock or deep in the gravelly hillsides, but to mine them it was necessary to use engineering techniques that demanded heavy equipment and substantial amounts of capital.

In extracting gold from solid rock, through processes variously described as quartz, vein, or lode mining, the auriferous rock taken from a mine shaft or tunnel had to be crushed to a fine powder. After an assortment of ingenious contraptions recently manufactured in the East and in England had proved worthless, better results were obtained with more traditional devices, of which the most important was the stamp mill. Dating at least as far back as the 16th century in Europe, this was essentially a large mechanized version of the mortar and pestle.

Another machine important in quartz mining was a mule-powered contrivance developed in Spanish America and called an *arrastre,* usually anglicized as "arrastra." A mule, plodding around a circular track, moved a horizontal shaft extending from a central post that served as a pivot, and heavy abrasive stones attached to the shaft were thus dragged over the gold-bearing material.

It was difficult to grind the ore fine enough, and often less than half the gold actually contained in the crushed rock could be separated from it by quicksilver amalgamation. Part of the loss occurred because some of the gold was encased in metallic sulphides on which the mercury would not act. After about 1860, treatment of the heated mixture by chlorine gas to break down the sulphides, through a process invented in Germany several years earlier, increased the yield considerably. Sometimes the pulverized rock, mixed with water, was made to flow over coarse blankets so that fine particles of gold were caught in the cloth. The legend of the Golden Fleece had probably originated in the application of this method to sheepskin in ancient times.

Another major source of gold lay in the "Tertiary gravels." During the Tertiary geologic era a great river flowed through the region of the northern mines, laying down an immense bed of gravel containing scattered flakes of gold. Later when the whole region was thrust up to become part of the Sierra Nevada, new rivers—the Feather, the Yuba, the Bear, and the American—began to flow transversely through the bed of the older one. Much of that bed, however, was now on hilltops and hillsides, which had since been gradually covered over with debris. When the gravel hills were first discovered, attempts to mine them took the form of shafts and tunnels called "coyote holes." But working in these burrows, on hands and knees, by candlelight and in fetid air, was miserable and dangerous. The solution came with the introduction of hydraulic mining, in which an entire hillside could be washed loose by directing powerful streams of water against it.

In March 1853, near Nevada City, a former sailmaker named Anthony Chabot constructed a canvas hose, and a former tinsmith named Eli Miller made a tapered nozzle of sheet iron. Thus "hydraulicking" was born. As the stream placers gave out and the river-mining communities declined, hydraulic towns like Dutch Flat, Iowa Hill, and Gold Run sprang up and flourished. In 1861 the development of the "crinoline hose," of double-strength canvas bound with iron hoops, made it possible to throw a stream of water several hundred feet. Large amounts of water, accumulated at points considerably

Hydraulicking. (Courtesy of the Bancroft Library)

higher than the nozzle of the hose, had to be supplied through ditches and wooden flumes, and thousands of miles of these were constructed.

Part of the financing required by the expensive quartz and hydraulic operations came from joint-stock companies organized by working miners; but for men of small capital the chances for profit steadily declined. Many of those who remained in the industry were employed by increasingly large corporations, which tended to hire Americans as specialists in management and the handling of equipment and machinery, while employing Chinese and Mexicans for less-skilled labor. According to John S. Hittell, about 100,000 men were still engaged in gold mining in California in 1861, but by 1873 there were less than 30,000, of whom three-fifths were Chinese.

Whatever techniques might be devised, the supply of gold was not inexhaustible. After setting a record of more than 80 million dollars for 1852, the state's gold production decreased year by year until 1865, when it was less than 18 million. At that point it became stabilized, continuing to average about 17 million a year until the turn of the century.

The beginnings of banking. Few of the citizens of California in the early American period understood the nature and importance of banks as institutions for the lending and investment of money in business and industrial enterprise. To most Californians, as to most Americans in the years since the disastrous nationwide panic of 1837, "bank" was a hated word, for it seemed to mean primarily a corporation enjoying the legal privilege of printing and issuing notes that circulated as paper money.

This privilege had, indeed, been much abused in the older states. Most of the paper money in circulation throughout the country had been issued by hundreds of separate banking corporations chartered by special acts of state legislatures, acts that were always obtained by favoritism and often by outright bribery. The notes of these so-called "state banks" were unregulated either by government or by specie reserves, and many men had been swindled by receiving payment in such depreciated paper.

William M. Gwin was one of these, and in the tradition of Jacksonian democracy he had led the crusade against paper money in the California constitutional convention of 1849. The result was a provision similar to those included in nearly every other new state constitution adopted between the panic of 1837 and the Civil War: "The Legislature shall have no power to pass any act granting any charter for banking purposes." Other kinds of corporations might be formed under general laws providing for the formation of such bodies; but the legislature could create no corporation of any sort by special act, except for municipalities. "Associations" might "be formed under general laws, for the deposit of gold and silver," but "no such association shall make, issue, or put in circulation any bill, check, ticket, certificate, promissory note, or other paper, or the paper of any bank, to circulate as money."

In "the states" as a whole the inadequacy of the general money supply continued to require the use of state bank notes for many years, in spite of the general distrust and dislike of them. During the Civil War the Federal government resorted to extensive issues of legal tender notes, or "greenbacks." In California, however, the presence of gold in great quantities made possible its use as the dominant medium of exchange, and a desire to emphasize the utility of the state's most special product reinforced the preference for "hard money" and the scorn for paper. For many decades even large financial transactions in California were likely to be conducted in piles of gold coins, especially the $20 gold pieces known as double eagles.

Thus the state's constitutional ban against the issuance of bank notes as paper money caused relatively little trouble. But the sweeping constitutional fiat that seemed to deny legal recognition to any bank, organized for any purpose whatever, was unrealistic. In a growing economy the need for savings, lending, and investment institutions was so great that their existence was inevitable. The main effect of the state's provisions against chartering banks was simply to confine the banking business to entirely private concerns, operated by individuals, associations, or partnerships, without any particular legal sanction and, worse yet, without any public regulation. Some of the banking was also done by California branches of Eastern firms. A sounder policy for the state would have been to encourage the development of banks as corporations, with boards of directors elected annually by the stockholders; to require that the capital stock be paid in before the doors could be opened for business; to require monthly statements of all transactions; and to authorize inspection of the books by bank examiners at any time. One of James King of William's most vigorous journalistic crusades, based on his own unhappy experiences in early California banking, was for a state constitutional amendment that would have permitted the accomplishment of these purposes by law.

As it was, anyone who could make friends and attract deposits could enter the banking profession. In the early mining camps the arrangements were often very simple. At the "bank" of G. D. Dickenson at Mokelumne Hill, according to Ira B. Cross, "the vault . . . was an excavation a yard square, under the bed occupied by himself and Mrs. Dickenson; its compartments were buckskin bags, and the time-lock was a revolver of large caliber." Saloonkeepers often doubled as bankers. For many years after the gold rush a great deal of the banking was done as a sideline by firms engaged in other businesses, notably express companies, real estate brokers, and merchandizers of all sorts. In the smaller towns, sideline banking long continued to be important. As late as 1890, for example, the Cloverdale Banking and Commercial Company would be listed as "bankers and dealers in hardware and agricultural implements."

Under the circumstances, the wonder is that banking failures and defalcations were not more frequent than they were. In the early '50s, flush times and fantastic rates of interest made the lending of money immediately profitable. But a panic began in 1855, touched off by the collapse of Page, Bacon & Company, the San Francisco branch of a St. Louis express and banking concern. Partly because the drop in the state's gold output had already contracted the money market, the panic spread quickly, bringing ruin to several of the most respected banking agencies. Of the other large firms that combined banking with the express business, Adams & Company had been weakened by ruthless competition from Wells, Fargo, the Western branch of the powerful American Express. When Adams & Company went down in the California panic of 1855, there was such a run on the offices of Wells, Fargo that even this giant of early Western finance had to resort to a temporary suspension of payments. Economic revival came slowly, until the great treasure of the Comstock Lode brought a new era of financial growth.

The first Comstock silver boom, 1859–1864. Between the Washoe and Carson Valleys, a little less than 40 miles due east of Donner Pass and about 20 miles east of the California state line, stood a barren-looking mountain known in the 1850s as Sun Peak. Deep in the mountain, and coming to the surface on its eastern side, lay the world's richest deposits of silver, mixed with lesser deposits of gold. Four hundred million dollars' worth of the two metals, largely silver, would be taken from this great lode before its permanent decline in the early 1880s, and for a time the city that mushroomed around the entrances to the mine shafts would be larger than any in the Far West except San Francisco and Salt Lake City.

Beginning as early as 1850, placers in a canyon at the base of the mountain yielded moderate amounts of gold, but the flakes were hard to separate from a wretched "blue stuff." This the prospectors threw aside, cursing it because it clogged the riffle bars in their gold-rockers. The first men to establish that the "blue stuff" was silver ore, and to discover some of the outcroppings of the lode, far up near the head of the canyon, were Ethan Allen Grosch and Hoseah Ballou Grosch, sons of a Pennsylvania minister.

In 1857 one of the Grosch brothers died of an accidental wound and the other in a mountain blizzard, and their secret was temporarily lost. But a sheepherder and prospector named Henry Tompkins Paige Comstock, known as "Old Pancake" from his chief article of diet, had learned enough from the Grosches to suspect that they had made some great strike. His frantic efforts to locate it for himself were unsuccessful, and in 1859 the lode was discovered anew by the Irish prospectors Patrick McLaughlin and Peter O'Riley. Comstock was in no sense the real discoverer, but by means of bluster and bluff he was able to fool McLaughlin, O'Riley, and the other miners then in the district into believing that he had established some sort of title to the land. Thus for no better reason than his capacity for bragging and deceit, his name became immortalized in the name of the lode.

Another local prospector was James Fennimore, a drunken teamster, who had fled from a murder charge in California and changed his name to Finney and who was known in the Washoe region as "Old Virginia" from his habit of boasting about the state of his birth. One night, the story goes, he fell and broke a whisky bottle. Rising unsteadily to his knees, he said "I baptize this ground Virginia Town." For a time the place was known as Virginia, and later as Virginia City.

The circumstances of the naming of the Comstock Lode and of its local metropolis are not inappropriate to the general tenor of their history—a fantastic narrative in which the dissolute, selfish, and dishonest aspects of human nature were all too apparent. These qualities, on the other hand, were alloyed with considerable amounts of ingenuity, courage, and hard work.

Interest continued to center in the gold content of the lode until July 1859, when some ore samples taken over the Sierra to Nevada City were assayed at nearly $3,200 a ton in silver, and about half as much in gold. Soon the great rush of '59ers from California to Washoe was on, reversing the direction of the rush of '49. Sun Peak was renamed Mount Davidson, after Donald Davidson of San Francisco, who purchased Comstock ores and sent them to England for reduction in the early days before large-scale reduction processes were developed at Virginia City.

To the amazement of the Comstock miners, one of the hardest problems came from the unprecedented size of the veins. Removal of the ore created chambers too vast to be supported by any known method of timbering, and disastrous cave-ins threatened to shut down one of the richest mines until a young German engineer, Philip Deidesheimer, saved the situation by inventing the process of "square sets." These were made of timbers 4 to 6 feet long framed together in a series of interlocked cribs resembling a honeycomb. They could be built to any height or width, and in later years they made possible the creation of caverns hundreds of feet from wall to wall and from floor to dome. To help support the roof of such a chamber, some of the cribs were filled with waste rock to form pillars so strong that where they were used no lives were ever lost in cave-ins.

The Comstock soon demanded large aggregations of capital for its mines and ore-processing mills, and San Francisco bankers, along with thousands of small investors, rushed to outbid each other for shares in the bonanza. Virginia City saloons provided not only whisky but great quantities of oysters and champagne, and tickets to see such visiting luminaries as Adah Isaacs Menken were sold for as much as $100.

Several mines, especially the Ophir, the Gould & Curry, the Mexican, and the Savage, paid huge returns for several years. But there were many fraudulent sales of stock in properties with no real access to the lode, and the richer mines became entangled in a maze of litigation. In 1864, when a number of the largest ones had run into borrasca and were levying assessments on their stockholders instead of paying dividends, the inflated market for silver stocks collapsed and their total value shrank by more than half. The Comstock had come to the end of its first boom, though it was destined for another and larger one a few years later.

Agriculture. As in several other parts of the American Far West, cattle ranching was second to mining in the economic life of the frontier period. But agriculture in the sense of the cultivation of the soil, as distinct from grazing, was far less important. The California missions had once produced a variety of grains and fruits for local consumption; but after the missions were secularized these activities had almost disappeared except for a little grape growing for the purpose of making wine or brandy. Cultivation can barely be said to have existed at all in California during the last years under Mexico, and even after the gold rush its advance was slow and sparse. The insecurity of land titles, the lure of quicker wealth in other activities, and the unfamiliarity of such peculiar farming conditions as the rainless summers, all served to retard agricultural development. The food supply of the Argonauts was largely imported; the main exception was California beef, salted or driven to the mining camps on the hoof.

In 1846 there had been about 400,000 cattle in Alta California, worth about $4 a head. At the end of 1849 the price reached $500 a head at Sacramento, and for years afterward it was more than $50. Large herds were driven overland from the lower Mississippi Valley and the Southwest, thus increasing the stock and, to a degree, improving the breeds. Most of the native Californian rancheros, though suddenly and temporarily prosperous, were ruined by land litigation, interest, taxes, and inexperience in business and financial matters, and lost their ranches to Americans or Europeans.

In 1860 the number of cattle in the state was more than 3 million. But two years of disastrous drought, from 1862 to 1864, nearly wiped out the herds and the industry. The great drought marked the transition from the "age of grass" to an age of grain, and wheat now replaced beef as the state's most important agricultural product. In the early years the growing of wheat was largely concentrated in the Sacramento Valley, where Sutter had begun to raise it.

Fruit and vegetable production in the early American era were significant mainly in confirming some of the extraordinary potentialities of California soils and climate, and thus foreshadowing the tremendous developments of the future. One of the most important pioneers in the dissemination of knowledge in this field was not a farmer, but a Yankee merchant who became the state's leading agricultural publicist and lobbyist. This was James Lloyd LaFayette Warren, who came to Sacramento from Boston in 1849, engaged in general merchandizing, and then specialized in seeds, nursery stock, and agricultural implements. For an agriculture passing through a difficult infancy as the stepchild of mining and ranching, Warren became a kind of godfather. He sponsored the exhibitions that grew directly into the California state fair. In 1854, acting as a one-man agricultural pressure group and taking advantage of the provision in the state constitution that "The Legislature shall encourage, by all suitable means, the promotion of intellectual, scientific, moral, and agricultural improvement," Warren secured the establishment of the State Agricultural Society and even a small annual appropriation for it. He also founded the *California Farmer*, the state's first agricultural periodical. Like most of the agricultural journals of the time in the older states, the *Farmer* could be kept alive financially because it was published as an adjunct to a profitable mercantile business which it incidentally served to advertise.

In the 1860s, and especially after the decline of the cattle industry, the legislature appropriated state funds for bounty payments to farmers who would risk experimentation with a variety of crops, including flax, hemp, cotton, tobacco, hops, raw silk, tea, coffee, indigo, rice, and sugar from sorghum and cane. None of these crops enjoyed any permanent commercial success in this period, though some of them, especially cotton and rice, were to be important in the 20th century. For a few seasons the production of raw silk became a craze; but most of the feverish investment in mulberry trees and silkworms was carried on by speculators interested solely in collecting the bounties, and when the legislature repealed the bounty offer in 1870 the silk boom collapsed.

The shift from cattle raising to cultivation was significantly apparent in the state's laws concerning fences. The act of 1852 made it impossible for a farmer to obtain compensation for damage to his crops by a neighboring rancher's cattle unless the crops were enclosed by a "lawful fence"—and the costs of fencing were very high. By contrast, the "no fence" act of 1872 placed the full responsibility for such damages on the cattleman, whose political influence had thus obviously fallen behind that of the farmer.

Early manufactures. The needs of the miners for great quantities of lumber made sawmills the foremost branch of manufacturing in the early period of statehood. As we have seen, wooden sluices and flumes were indispensable in the more advanced stages of placer and hydraulic mining, as were heavy timbers in the underground operations of the quartz and silver mines. Moreover, construction in the towns was generally of wood, and fencing in the rural areas was almost entirely so, for barbed wire did not appear until the 1870s. To meet these demands a raw material of splendid quality and supposedly inexhaustible quantity was available in the redwoods, the world's largest known trees. In 1860 Mendocino County produced 35 million feet of lumber, mostly redwood, and Humboldt and Santa Cruz Counties milled 30 and 10 million feet, respectively. There were also many sawmills in the Sierra Nevada, where they had the advantage of being located nearer the mines, though the forests were mainly of pine and other lesser woods.

Flour milling grew and flourished along with the increasing production of wheat. The development of mills for the making of coarse woolen cloth was similarly interrelated with the spread of sheep raising, while tanneries and the making of heavy leather goods were encouraged by the plentiful supply of cowhides. Another important infant industry was the making of wagons and carriages, in which the outstanding pioneer shops were those of John Studebaker at Placerville and Phineas Banning at Wilmington. Claus Spreckels and William T. Coleman emerged as leaders in the refining of sugar cane from the Pacific islands. In iron manufactures the leading establishment was the Union Iron Works at San Francisco, founded as early as 1849. The iron, however, had to be imported; the absence of any important deposits of either iron or coal in California, along with shortages of labor and capital, and the lack of a regional population large enough to make an adequate market, were among the serious deterrents to the growth of manufacturing in the state.

Transportation. Before the railroads came, the movement of freight and passengers by water was considerably easier than their movement by land. Consequently the first major arteries of inland trade and transportation in American California were the routes of the paddlewheel steamers on San Francisco Bay and on the larger rivers of the Central Valley—between San

Francisco and the most important commercial towns of the interior, Sacramento, Stockton, and Marysville. After dozens of small companies had entered the business, operating hundreds of steamboats, overcompetition and rate wars led in 1854 to the consolidation of most of them into the California Steam Navigation Company, which came to enjoy a virtual monopoly of the bay and river traffic. On land, the development of stagecoach lines soon replaced the "pack mule express," and in 1854 the consolidation in steamboating was paralleled by the integration of five-sixths of the local stage lines into the California Stage Company, which could then offer regular service, especially throughout the more settled parts of Northern California, over routes totaling more than 1,500 miles.

The Overland California Mail act, passed by Congress in 1857, provided subsidies in the form of mail contracts and thus made possible the opening of overland stagecoach service between St. Louis and San Francisco in the following year. Postmaster General Aaron Brown, a Tennessean, chose a southern route through El Paso, Tucson, and Los Angeles, and awarded the contract to the Overland Mail Company headed by John Butterfield of New York, one of the organizers of the American Express Company. Butterfield was a brilliant administrator who was able to establish within 12 months a stage line 2,800 miles long, employing nearly 1,000 men, and providing 24-day service between San Francisco and the Mississippi River. After the outbreak of the Civil War in 1861, the Overland Mail was shifted to the central route by way of Salt Lake City. In the meantime there had been spectacular but unsuccessful experiments with camel caravans over the southern route and with the Pony Express over the central one. The Pony Express, though highly colorful, failed to make any substantial profits during its 18 months of operation, and came to an end with the opening of the transcontinental telegraph line in October 1861.

SELECTED BIBLIOGRAPHY

Doris M. Wright, "The Making of Cosmopolitan California . . . 1848–1870," *California Historical Society Quarterly*, XIX–XX (December 1940 and March 1941), 323–343, 65–79, is a detailed study of the varied components in the growth of population. Georges Sabagh, "A Critical Analysis of California Population Statistics . . . 1850–1870," M.A. thesis, University of California, Berkeley (1943), points out the defects of the census figures.

Gold mining in the '50s and '60s is described in Rodman W. Paul, *California Gold* (1947), and John W. Caughey, *Gold Is the Cornerstone* (1948). The rise of the hydraulic method is the subject of the first chapter of Robert L. Kelley, *Gold vs. Grain* (1959).

Ira B. Cross, in *Financing an Empire: History of Banking in California* (four volumes, 1927), and in "Californians and Hard Money,"

California Folklore Quarterly, IV (July 1945), 270–277, treats these complex matters with clarity.

The most widely read account of the early years of the Comstock Lode was in Mark Twain's *Roughing It*. More serious treatments include Dan De Quille (William Wright), *The Big Bonanza* (1876, 1947); Eliot Lord, *Comstock Mines and Miners* (1883); Charles H. Shinn, *The Story of the Mine* (1896); C. B. Glasscock, *The Big Bonanza* (1931); George D. Lyman, *The Saga of the Comstock* (1934); and Grant H. Smith, *History of the Comstock Lode* (1943). California and Nevada mining are placed in broader context in Rodman W. Paul, *Mining Frontiers of the Far West, 1848–1880* (1963).

On cattle ranching, see Robert G. Cleland, *The Cattle on a Thousand Hills* (1941); John W. Caughey, "Don Benito Wilson," *Huntington Library Quarterly*, II (April 1939), 285–300; and James M. Jensen, "Cattle Drives from the Ranchos to the Gold Fields of California," *Arizona and the West*, II (Winter 1960), 341–352. On American pioneer agriculture in the state: Frank Adams, "The Historical Background," in *California Agriculture* (1946), edited by Claude B. Hutchison; Robert G. Cleland and Osgood Hardy, *The March of Industry* (1929); John S. Hittell, *Resources of California* (1863, 1874, etc.); Titus F. Cronise, *The Natural Wealth of California* (1868); Iris H. Wilson, *William Wolfskill* (1965); Walton Bean, "James Warren and the Beginnings of Agricultural Institutions in California," *Pacific Historical Review*, XIII (December 1944), 361–375; Paul W. Gates, editor, *California Ranchos and Farms, 1846–1862* (1967); and Nelson Klose, "California's Experimentation in Sericulture," *Pacific Historical Review*, XXX (August 1961), 213–228.

The economic material in the *History of California*, volume VII, 1860–1890, by Frances Fuller Victor and William Nemos (*Bancroft's Works*, volume XXIV, 1890), is fairly comprehensive, though undigested. A valuable study of lumbering is H. Brett Melendy, "One Hundred Years of the Redwood Lumber Industry, 1850–1950," Ph.D. thesis, Stanford University (1952).

On transportation within the state, see Jerry MacMullen, *Paddlewheel Days in California* (1944); Ernest A. Wiltsee, *The Pioneer Miner and the Pack Mule Express* (1931); William and George H. Banning, *Six Horses* (1930); and Oscar O. Winther, *Express and Stagecoach Days in California* (1936). On the overland operations: LeRoy R. Hafen, *The Overland Mail, 1849–1869* (1926); Roscoe P. and Margaret B. Conkling, *The Butterfield Overland Mail, 1857–1869* (three volumes, 1948); Edward Hungerford, *Wells, Fargo: Advancing the American Frontier* (1949); J. V. Frederick, *Ben Holladay, the Stagecoach King* (1940); W. Turrentine Jackson, *Wagon Roads West* (1952), and "Wells Fargo Staging over the Sierra," *California Historical Society Quarterly*, XLIX (June 1970), 99–134; Harlan D. Fowler, *Camels to California* (1950); and Raymond W. Settle and Mary Settle, *Saddle and Spurs: the Pony Express Saga* (1955).

Chapter XVIII

BUILDING THE CENTRAL PACIFIC RAILROAD

FOR 20 YEARS after the gold rush, Americans in California felt extremely remote from the people of the older states, as indeed they were. For many, the dream of a transcontinental railroad symbolized all sorts of hopes for better things—for an end to feelings of isolation and alienation, and for a new age of unlimited economic prosperity. Californians, in short, came to expect much more from the railroad than it could possibly have brought them, even if the conditions under which it came into being and was subsequently managed had been far more nearly ideal than they were.

Early proposals. In the older parts of the country, talk of a transcontinental railroad had begun at least as early as 1832. The first proposal to receive a serious hearing came in 1845 from Asa Whitney, a New York merchant who had made a large fortune in trade with China, and saw a Pacific Railroad as a great new artery of American and European trade with the Orient. Whitney laid before Congress a scheme for a railroad from Lake Michigan to the Pacific at the mouth of the Columbia River. Before the American acquisition of California and the subsequent gold discovery, most congressmen still regarded the whole idea of a Pacific railroad as visionary and absurd, and the few who were sympathetic toward it were divided on whether to have it built by a private corporation with government subsidies, or by the government itself.

Throughout the 1850s, with the intensification of sectional bitterness, Southerners feared that a northern or central railroad would develop new free states, and argued that a southern route, which did not have to cross the great barriers of the Rockies and the Sierra Nevada, could be built much more economically and quickly. Northerners, on the other hand, were adamant against a railroad that would aid the expansion of slaveholding.

Congress could agree only on a provision for surveys of all the possible routes. These surveys, published in 1855 in 13 fat volumes of *Pacific Railroad Reports,* concluded only that five different transcontinental routes were feasible.

Judah and the conception of the Central Pacific. Credit for the specific plan that led to the building of the first transcontinental railroad belongs mainly to Theodore D. Judah, a brilliant young construction engineer. Born in Connecticut and trained at the Rensselaer Polytechnic Institute at Troy, New York, Judah in his 20s had established a reputation as an engineering genius through such feats as the building of the Niagara Gorge Railroad. In 1854, when he was 28, the promoters of the Sacramento Valley Railroad brought him to California to build their line from Sacramento to Folsom, the first railroad on the Pacific Coast.

Judah soon became so fanatically devoted to the idea of a central route for the first transcontinental that a number of his listeners questioned his sanity on the subject, particularly those who had had the experience of crossing the Sierra Nevada. But the idea, with its promise of an end to California's isolation, became increasingly popular, and in 1859 the state legislature approved a Pacific Railroad Convention of the sort that had been used to drum up interest in railroad projects in other regions of the country. When this body met in San Francisco it delegated Judah to carry its views to Washington, D.C.; but although he lobbied skillfully and impressively, the sectional deadlock still prevented action.

In 1860 Judah made an intensive search for the best crossing of the Sierra. Daniel W. Strong, a druggist in the prosperous hydraulic mining town of Dutch Flat, pointed out that Dutch Flat was located on a natural ramp, a long and unbroken ridge extending upward toward Emigrant Gap and Donner Pass. Judah observed that because the slope of this ridge was so gradual and continuous, it would be possible for a railroad to reach the summit elevation of about 7,000 feet in a distance of little more than 70 miles from the valley floor with a maximum grade of only 105 feet to a mile. Tremendously excited by this discovery, Judah sat at the counter of Strong's drugstore and drew up tentative articles of association for the Central Pacific Railroad of California.

Judah, Strong, and a number of citizens of Dutch Flat and the neighboring towns were able to muster about a third of the money that would have to be paid down in order to form a corporation. Full of confidence, Judah hurried to San Francisco to secure the remainder; but to his disappointment and disgust not one of the large capitalists in the city would invest in the project. Until Congress acted, they said, construction of the railroad could not begin, and they estimated that after its beginning 12 to 20 years would pass before its completion. Their money was bringing large and immediate returns in far safer enterprises.

Enter the four "associates." In his appeals to the San Francisco financiers Judah had made the tactical error of including an appeal to their public spirit and long-range vision. He turned next to the merchants of Sacramento, and with them he made no such blunder. Instead he planned his arguments in order to put all the emphasis on the possibilities of large and early returns on very modest initial investments: with a concrete proposal before it, Congress would offer cash subsidies that would pay for the construction; operating income need not wait for completion of the transcontinental line, or even of the line within California; the profitable freighting business between Sacramento and the Comstock was then passing mainly over the Sacramento Valley Railroad and thence by wagon road through Placerville and over Johnson's Pass, south of Lake Tahoe; this trade could very soon be captured for the Dutch Flat route, simply by building a good wagon road over Donner Pass to connect with the head of construction of the Central Pacific as it advanced into the mountains.

One evening in the autumn of 1860, in a room over the hardware store of Huntington & Hopkins in Sacramento, a group of merchants assembled to hear Judah's plea. Among those present were Collis P. Huntington, Leland Stanford, Charles Crocker, and Mark Hopkins. Since these men were destined to be the "Big Four," the "Railroad Kings" of California and of most of the American Far West, and thus to acquire not only fantastic wealth but also enormous economic and political power, their backgrounds are of considerable interest.

All of them had been born poor, and though all were prosperous by 1860, none, as yet, was rich. Collis P. Huntington, the son of a miserly tinker in a small town in Connecticut, had become self-supporting at the age of 14, and a successful traveling salesman a year later. At 21 he was operating his own store at Oneonta, New York. In 1849, with a capital of $1,200, he joined the gold rush. Buying and selling food and other supplies while waiting for steamer connections in Panama, he tripled his capital. In California, one day's work in the mines convinced him that mining was not his occupation, and instead he opened a store in Sacramento. Leland Stanford, son of an innkeeper in rural New York, had studied law in an office in Albany and practiced in Wisconsin before coming to California to enter the grocery business in partnership with his brothers. He had been the unsuccessful Republican candidate for state treasurer in 1857 and for governor in 1859. Charles Crocker had been a peddler, iron maker, and gold miner, and was now a Sacramento dry goods merchant. Mark Hopkins, Huntington's partner in the hardware business, was a shrewd and industrious storekeeper, the quietest and least aggressive member of the group; like the rest of them, however, he could be extraordinarily stubborn when he wished to be.

These four—"the associates," as they soon began to call themselves—were tentatively interested in Judah's plan, but cautious. In the spring of 1861, how-

Mark Hopkins, Collis P. Huntington, Theodore Judah, Leland Stanford, Charles Crocker. (Courtesy of the Bancroft Library)

ever, the outbreak of the Civil War convinced them that Congress would soon approve the project and subsidize it, and on June 28 the Central Pacific Railroad of California was formally incorporated. Stanford, who had again received the Republican nomination for Governor, was elected president of the company, Huntington vice-president, and Hopkins treasurer.

Judah was one of the directors, and the chief engineer. He was not yet aware of the extent to which he had now lost control of the enterprise, or of the difficulties he would soon have with the company's officers. His contributions to the project had thus far been much greater than theirs in every sense except the financial, and their original financial investment was almost incredibly small. The state's railroad incorporation law required stock subscriptions of $1,000 per mile of track proposed, in this case $115,000 for 115 miles of track between Sacramento and the state line; but only 10 percent of this amount had to be paid down. Huntington, Stanford, Crocker, Hopkins, and Judah each subscribed for 150 shares of stock at $100 a share; other individuals, most of whom would soon drop out, subscribed for 830 shares more, a total of 1,580 shares. But since only 10 percent was paid down, the company started with a mere $15,800 in cash.

In sworn statements made in a legal document filed a few months later, the not yet very big four reported that their combined personal assets, mostly tied up in their business firms, totaled about $100,000. This figure is interesting and significant in comparison with the personal fortunes totaling about $200,000,000 which they would ultimately gain from Theodore Judah's project.

Federal and state support. Judah's next contribution was to secure the indispensable aid of the Federal government. In the fall of 1861 he traveled to Washington in the company of the new Congressman Aaron A. Sargent, who agreed to sponsor the cause of the Central Pacific in the House of Representatives. Through Senator James A. McDougall of California, Judah also guided the drafting of the corresponding measure in the Senate. Moreover, he was made clerk of the key railroad committees of both houses, and was thus in an ideal position to provide arguments for the project at every point in the debates.

In more recent years, for Congress to permit a lobbyist to hold such a position would be grossly improper. In that era, however, the concept of conflict of interest had scarcely begun to develop in the government service. Besides, Judah was no ordinary lobbyist. He was obviously the man who had more concrete knowledge of the project under consideration than did any other man in the country at the time, and he had little difficulty in persuading Congress that the project was one of extraordinary importance. He described it as a military necessity in a war that would continue for many years. A railroad would strengthen the bonds that held the Far West in the Union, and would hasten the flow of much-needed gold from California, and silver from Nevada. The withdrawal of the Southern Senators and Representatives from Congress had removed the main opposition to a central route, and Judah's surveys gave assurance that a route directly across the Sierra was entirely feasible.

The result was the Pacific Railroad Act of 1862, which President Lincoln signed on July 1. It was amended two years later to make its terms more generous to the railroads, and thus one can conveniently summarize the acts of 1862 and 1864 together. The Central Pacific, a California corporation, was to build eastward from Sacramento. The Union Pacific, a corporation chartered by Congress, was to build westward from Omaha, Nebraska. The federal government would furnish very extensive loans and land grants to both of these companies.

The loans were in the form of United States 6-percent 30-year bonds, to be issued at the basic rate of $16,000 per mile of track. In the Sierra Nevada and the Rocky Mountains, however, the amount would be $48,000 per mile; for the region between the Sierra and the Rockies it would be $32,000. As security the act of 1862 gave the government a first mortgage on all property of the railroads. This was changed to a second mortgage in 1864 to enable the companies to market their own bonds more effectively by offering the first-mortgage lien to private investors. But it is entirely clear that the government still expected its loans to be repaid—in spite of the later arguments of the railroads in their efforts to escape this obligation.

In addition to loans, United States public lands were granted to the railroad companies in alternate sections, checkerboard fashion, on both sides of the right of way. The practice of making huge gifts of Federal land to encourage the development of railroads had been in use since 1850, when Senator Stephen A. Douglas had secured the first such grant for the benefit of the Illinois Central. Under the act of 1864, the Central Pacific and the Union Pacific were given 10 alternate sections (square miles) on each side of the line—that is, half of the land in a strip totaling 40 miles in width. Most of this land would have little or no value until the railroad was built through it, but its value would then be much increased. The purpose of retaining ownership of the alternate sections for the government was to allow the public treasury to share in the benefits of this increase, and at the same time to provide some check on the prices which the railroads could eventually have demanded if they had been allowed a monopoly on all the lands in the 40-mile strip.

Leland Stanford was elected Governor of California in September 1861, and took office in January 1862. He did not scruple to advance his own interests as president of the Central Pacific Railroad by using all his influence as Governor. In 1863 he induced the state to add further subsidies to those promised by the Federal government. The legislature also authorized several counties to issue bonds enabling them to subscribe for large amounts of Central Pacific stock. The constitutionality of some of this legislation was disputed, but in general the state courts upheld it. When a vacancy occurred in the state supreme court, Governor Stanford appointed Charles Crocker's brother, Edwin B. Crocker, to the unexpired term. The new judge was also the Central Pacific's chief legal counsel, and he did not resign from that position while he was serving as a supreme court justice.

Difficulties, and the death of Judah. Actual construction of the railroad began on January 8, 1863, after Governor and President Stanford had thrown the first shovelful of earth in the presence of a crowd assembled near the levee at the foot of K Street in Sacramento. But in spite of the enormous support already promised by the Federal government, a tangle of troubles held back the early progress of construction and threatened the very life of the project. Costs were heavy. Iron rails and locomotives had to be bought in the East at wartime prices and transported to Sacramento by sea at wartime freight rates. Cash was short, for each 40-mile unit of construction had to be completed before the Federal subsidy on it was forthcoming, and interests hostile to the railroad did everything they could to discourage private investors from lending it money. The Pacific Mail Steamship Company, the California Steam Navigation Company, Wells, Fargo & Company, the California Stage Company, and the Sacramento Valley Railroad, as well as all the California bankers who had money invested in one or more of these enterprises, naturally anticipated that the building of the Central Pacific would injure them, and they joined in denouncing it. A pamphlet called *The Great Dutch Flat Swindle* charged that the promoters were not genuinely interested in a transcontinental railroad at all, but merely in the profits of a wagon road to Washoe, and in the collection of subsidies.

The Central Pacific's own chief engineer had reason to know that these charges were not entirely unfounded as they applied to the motives of the "associates" at this time. Feeling that his own personal honor was involved, Judah was now bitterly at odds with the four men who were in control. The differences were those between a man primarily interested in the construction of a great railroad, and four men primarily concerned with making enormous profits. When these four awarded the construction contracts to Charles Crocker and Company, a dummy concern owned by themselves, Judah protested as strongly as he could. At last he broke with them completely. In October 1863 he sailed for New York, having accepted $100,000 for his interest in the Central Pacific, but taking with him options to buy out Huntington, Stanford, Crocker, and Hopkins for $100,000 each if he could persuade the Vanderbilts or other Eastern capitalists to back him.

At this point the Sacramento four were discouraged, and willing, as Charles Crocker put it, to "take a clean shirt and get out." But Judah contracted yellow fever in Panama, and died on November 2, shortly after his arrival in New York. His death was a major tragedy. If he had lived and if his hopes for a reorganization of the Central Pacific under his own leadership had been fulfilled, the history of California might have been very different.

In order to begin collecting the larger subsidies for building in the Sierra Nevada, the Big Four maintained that the "western base" of the mountains was located only 7 miles east of Sacramento. On the plea that without the higher initial subsidies the whole project might have to be abandoned—and with the aid of some ingenious testimony by the California state geologist and the state surveyor general—the Federal government was persuaded to accept this remarkable claim, and the base of the Sierra Nevada was thus moved a considerable distance westward into the Sacramento Valley. The Big Four were now men who could move mountains. They felt no gratitude toward Judah, and did not even name a crossroads station in his honor. When at last something like a suitable monument to Judah was erected at Sacramento in 1930, the initiative came not from the railroad's management but from the American Society of Civil Engineers.

Solving the problems of construction. By 1865 the initial shortage of cash had been overcome. Federal, state, and county subsidies had built up the Central Pacific's treasury, and freight and passenger revenues began to come in with the completion of the early sections of track. Moreover, the money paid out for construction was being paid to Charles Crocker and Company on terms that assured very generous profits to that company's backers, the Big Four. At the outset Crocker knew nothing whatever about the building of a railroad. But in view of the remarkable profits to be gained from that activity, under contracts made without the inconvenience of competitive bidding, he was more than willing to learn.

A shortage of labor now replaced the shortage of cash as the most chronic problem holding back the rate of construction. California white workers demanded high wages, and many of them accepted jobs only in order to get a free ride for part of the way to the Washoe mines; then they would work on the railroad only long enough to earn the price of a stage ticket for the remainder of the distance to Virginia City. In desperation Stanford suggested an experiment with Chinese laborers, even though in his inaugural address as Governor in 1862 he had vigorously denounced the immigration of Asiatics. J. H. Strobridge, superintendent of construction under Crocker, ridiculed the idea on the ground that men whose average weight was only about 110 pounds would be useless for such heavy labor. But Charles Crocker was not so sure, and he decided to give the Chinese a trial. The first experiment, with a crew of 50 Chinese in 1865, was so phenomenally successful that agents were soon recruiting them by the thousands, first in California and then in South China. At the peak of its construction work, the Central Pacific would employ more than 10,000 Chinese laborers, largely brought from China for the purpose.

Labor unions in San Francisco protested, but as the railroad advanced into the mountains and construction continued throughout the year, white workers lost all interest in jobs that required the performance of hard and dangerous labor under the conditions of winter in the Sierra. The Chinese, on the other hand, would work under any conditions at all, for long hours and at low wages, and they made only one brief effort to strike. Near Cisco in July 1867 about thirty-five hundred of them demanded a 12-hour day and $40 a month instead of $30. They gave up even these modest demands when the company threatened to discharge them. Crocker was becoming a hard-driving manager of men. Roaring up and down the line "like a bull," as he put it, he constantly urged

Coolies in wicker baskets working on the Central Pacific Railroad. From a painting by Jake Lee. (Courtesy of Kem Lee Studio, San Francisco, and the Bancroft Library)

the Chinese to greater efforts. Astonishing quantities of earth were moved with no more equipment than wheelbarrows and one-horse dump carts.

With its labor problem solved, the Central Pacific next confronted some of the world's most extraordinary physical obstacles to the building of a railroad. To get around "Cape Horn," a huge and almost vertical cliff, Chinese workmen were suspended along its granite face in wicker baskets, chipping away at the rock with hammers and chisels to create a ledge. Much greater were the difficulties in the building of Summit Tunnel, which had to be drilled through a quarter of a mile of granite so hard that blasts of the black powder then in use merely spurted back through the drill holes. Experiments with the new liquid explosive called nitroglycerin produced too many casualties through premature explosions, and the causes were hard to determine because these accidents usually obliterated not only the evidence but the witnesses. Strobridge himself lost an eye when he chanced to be too close to such an explosion. The steam-powered drill had recently been invented, and Stanford purchased one and sent it up the railhead. But Strobridge refused to use it, even though Stanford furiously pointed out that the daily progress of the Union Pacific was being measured in miles, and that of the Central Pacific in inches. Summit Tunnel

Chinese workmen replacing a trestle with earth fill. (Courtesy of the Bancroft Library)

took more than a year to complete, beginning in the summer of 1866. It was the last major tunnel in the world to be built with hand tools. On the other hand, the construction of 37 miles of snowsheds did much to redeem the Central Pacific from the charge of backwardness and lack of imagination in methods of mountain railroad building.

Charles Crocker and Company did nearly all of the original construction work between Sacramento and the Nevada line. To build the remainder of the road the Big Four organized a new corporation in 1867. This was the Contract and Finance Company, in which Huntington, Stanford, Crocker, and Hopkins were practically the only stockholders. In fairness to them it must be said that the Central Pacific was not the only railroad in this period whose chief stockholders were following the practice of letting contracts to themselves. The Union Pacific, for example, was doing the same thing through its dummy, the Crédit Mobilier. Because the books of Charles Crocker and Company and the Contract and Finance Company mysteriously disappeared, it has never been possible to determine exactly how large their profits were. But from evidence gathered in later investigations by the Federal government, the Big Four probably received twice as much as they had to pay out for the actual costs of construction.

As the tracks advanced across Nevada and into Utah a spectacular race developed between Crocker's Chinese and the Union Pacific's Irish Americans. At its climax, "Crocker's pets" established the record of 10 miles of track laid in a single day; and although the Union Pacific's chief construction engineer, Grenville M. Dodge, pointed out that "they took a week preparing for it, and embedded all their ties beforehand," he could not entirely conceal his admiration. Before Congress fully realized that it had neglected to specify the point where the two railroads should meet, they were building side by side, both anxious to garner the subsidy for every possible mile.

Promontory, Utah, was finally designated as the meeting point, and there in a famous and colorful ceremony on May 10, 1869, the joining of the rails officially took place. Telegraphers reported each step, over wires kept open throughout the nation. A polished laurel tie was laid down, the last rail was put in place, and several spikes were presented, including one of Comstock silver and two of California gold. A telegraph line was attached to the last spike, and another to a silver sledgehammer. Stanford swung and missed, but a telegrapher simulated the blow with his key, and church bells, fire bells, factory whistles, and cannon announced the news in cities all over the country. Exactly a century after the founding of the first Spanish settlement in Alta California in 1769, iron rails linked American California to her sister states.

SELECTED BIBLIOGRAPHY

The apparently deliberate destruction of many of the most significant documents by officials of the Central Pacific and its subsidiary companies, and the destruction of the entire central depository of records of the Southern Pacific by the San Francisco earthquake and fire of 1906, have placed most unfortunate limits on detailed historical knowledge of the building and development of "the railroad." Nevertheless, several important works have been written. Oscar Lewis, *The Big Four* (1938), is highly readable. Carl I. Wheat, "A Sketch of the Life of Theodore D. Judah," *California Historical Society Quarterly*, IV (September 1925), 219–271, is more than a mere sketch. Stuart Daggett, *Chapters on the History of the Southern Pacific* (1922), is an intensely critical study by a professor of transportation economics. Wesley S. Griswold, *A Work of Giants: Building the First Transcontinental Railroad* (1963), and Robert West Howard, *The Great Iron Trail: the Story of the First Transcontinental Railroad* (1963), are useful accounts of the construction of both the Central Pacific and the Union Pacific. See also Harry J. Carman and Charles H. Muller, "The Contract and Finance Company and the Central Pacific Railroad," *Mississippi Valley Historical Review*, XIV (December 1927), 326–341.

George T. Clark, *Leland Stanford* (1931), Norman E. Tutorow, *Leland Stanford: Man of Many Careers* (1970), and David S. Lavender, *The Great Persuader* (1970), on C. P. Huntington, are sympathetic biographies. Cerinda W. Evans, *Collis Potter Huntington* (two volumes, 1954), is extremely, earnestly, and naively apologistic.

Chapter XIX

THE "TERRIBLE SEVENTIES"

BY A CRUEL PARADOX, the completion of the first transcontinental railroad not only failed to bring California the expected surge of prosperity, but marked instead the beginning of a deep and general depression that continued through the whole of the next decade. A frustrated and embittered populace blamed its disappointments and sufferings on the railroad and on the Chinese. Thus the difficulties of a long period of economic distress were aggravated by racial antagonism and political upheaval.

The onset of depression. One of the many unexpected and unfavorable effects that the completion of the Pacific railroad had on the economy of California was that it suddenly exposed her merchants and manufacturers to intense competition from those of the Eastern cities. Until 1869 the bulk of the commerce of California and of most other parts of the Far West had come by water to San Francisco. Now the San Francisco merchants, already overstocked in anticipation of new demand, instead found the market glutted with new goods shipped in by rail. Months before the opening of the transcontinental, hundreds of agents of the mercantile houses of Chicago, in particular, had invaded the Far West, busily writing orders and capturing the customers of San Francisco firms. As for the hope that the goods exchanged between Europe and the Orient would be transshipped by rail across North America and thus help to enrich California's great seaport, most of that trade now passed instead through the Suez Canal, opened in the same year as the Pacific railroad.

California speculators had so far inflated the prices of land in anticipation of a boom that the actual completion of the Central Pacific caused a reaction and a decline in real estate values, rather than an advance. Though the railroad brought in thousands of new residents, most of them came seeking a prosperity they had not yet found; few could afford to buy land at high prices, and many could not have afforded it at any price.

After many years of labor shortage there was now an oversupply, and chronic unemployment. In 1868 various labor organizations had been strong enough to secure the passage of a state law providing for an 8-hour day in public works contracts, and unions had been able to persuade many private employers to agree to the same policy. But in order to roll back this advance on the part of labor, certain employers in San Francisco established a "California Labor and Employment Exchange" and an "Immigrant Aid Association," through which they carried on a nationwide propaganda campaign designed to bring as many new workers as possible to California and thus to weaken labor's bargaining power. At the same time, Chinese immigration increased sharply, encouraged by the Burlingame Treaty of 1868, and the completion of the railroad released about twelve thousand Chinese construction workers, nearly all of whom drifted back to crowd the California labor market.

When the panic of 1873 struck the national economy as a whole, it intensified the depression that had begun in California four years earlier.

Transportation monopoly. When the first transcontinental railroad was opened, the Big Four did not believe that freight and passenger revenues would ever provide the large and guaranteed profits that they had received from construction subsidies. Acting on this same belief, the directors of the Union Pacific sold their stock in that enterprise as soon as its original construction was finished. The Big Four, too, made efforts to retire from railroading with the fortunes they had already accumulated. For several reasons, however, they did not carry out their plans to dispose of their interests in the Central Pacific. The original reason was that they could find no buyers on terms they regarded as favorable. But there were other and more positive factors, which reconciled them to continuing in the railroad business. There were more land grants to be had, from further construction within California and from a new transcontinental line to be built on the southern route. Even more important, there was the prospect of being able to control rates and ensure profits by establishing throughout most of the Far West a monopoly—of unprecedented degree and scope—over transportation, the life's blood of the regional economy.

To ensure its control over the main seaport area the Central Pacific put together a network of local rail lines around San Francisco Bay, and also gained virtually complete domination of the bay's strategic waterfronts.

In 1852 the ownership of all of the waterfront and tidelands of Oakland had been granted to that infant community by the state. Oakland, in turn, had promptly granted the whole of these lands to one of its leading citizens, Horace W. Carpentier, in return for his promise to build three wharves and a schoolhouse. In 1868 Carpentier offered the railroad a controlling interest in the waterfront if it would make Oakland its main terminus on the east side of the bay.

Ownership of the lands then passed to the Oakland Waterfront Company, a new corporation in which Carpentier and Leland Stanford were the main stockholders. Not until the early 20th century would the monopoly of Oakland's waterfront be broken.

San Francisco, though it put up a bitter fight, was hardly more successful in escaping from decades of railroad domination. Most of its tidelands had remained under state ownership. In 1868, at the suggestion of ex-Governor Stanford, a state senate committee recommended that several miles of the San Francisco waterfront, including all of it that was suitable for railroad terminal facilities, be sold at nominal prices to corporations controlled by the Big Four. The *Bulletin* led other newspapers in denouncing this proposal as a breathtaking outrage, and the railroad had to be content with a mere 60 acres. But this was enough for a terminal; the Central Pacific had other means of assuring that no competing railroad would approach San Francisco for a long time to come, and it had already established political control of the state board of harbor commissioners.

While they were completing their stranglehold on the bay, the Big Four were also making plans to capture the rest of California. They bought out the promoters of the California and Oregon Railroad, and began construction of the "Shasta Route," extending up the Sacramento Valley and eventually to Portland. A line to run southward from the San Francisco Bay region through the coastal counties to Los Angeles and San Diego had been proposed in 1865, as the announced purpose of a Southern Pacific Railroad Company incorporated by a group of San Francisco capitalists. It was widely suspected that the Big Four were the real founders of this company, but this was never proved, and more reliable evidence indicates that they acquired control of it in the late '60s. In the meantime, in 1866, Congress had provided for the first southern transcontinental railroad, and authorized the Southern Pacific to build its western link. Thus by gaining control of the original Southern Pacific Railroad Company, the chief owners of the Central Pacific not only gained control of Southern California but also guaranteed themselves a long period of freedom from competition with another transcontinental route.

In 1870 the Big Four were ready to begin construction of the line to Southern California—the contracts, of course, being awarded to the Contract and Finance Company. They had already decided not to build along the coast, but rather through the San Joaquin Valley, because the usable lands in the coastal counties were under private ownership, while the San Joaquin Valley was still largely government land where the railroad could locate its grants along its right of way.

In its dealings with cities and towns the railroad was equally ruthless in putting its own interests ahead of the public's. Los Angeles, though it had only about six thousand people, was the largest town in Southern California, and already had rail connections with the coast at San Pedro and Santa Monica. Crocker threatened to ruin Los Angeles by leaving it off the main line, unless it would make the Southern Pacific a present of the Los Angeles and San Pedro Railroad, and pay a further subsidy of $600,000. In an effort to make San Bernardino an example of what could happen to towns that resisted this kind of extortion, the Southern Pacific built its division point a few miles away, thus creating the new town of Colton. For similar reasons the Central Pacific had created the "spite towns" of Lathrop, near Stockton, and Goshen, near Visalia.

For a time in the early '70s, there was a threat of competition from the Texas and Pacific under Thomas A. Scott, who was also president of the Pennsylvania Railroad. Largely through effective lobbying at Washington, however, Huntington was able to frustrate Scott's hopes of building from Texas to San Diego. The Southern Pacific itself gained full domination of the first southern transcontinental line, and by 1882 its own "Sunset Route" extended all the way from Southern California to New Orleans.

For many years the Big Four sought to maintain the fiction that the Central Pacific, the Southern Pacific, and a number of smaller lines were under separate control, but the newspapers and the public became well aware that "the railroad" was a single entity. They began to call it "the Octopus," and to think of its tracks as tentacles reaching from Oregon to Louisiana. Officially, the name Southern Pacific emerged as the name of the whole system in 1884, when the Southern Pacific Company of Kentucky was incorporated and took a lease on all property of the Central Pacific. Kentucky was chosen for the legal corporate headquarters of the system, not because the Big Four had plans for operating there, but simply because the railroad incorporation laws of that state were among the laxest in the Union.

Monopoly of California rails would not have provided so effective a monopoly of transportation if there had been extensive competition by water. But in 1869 the Big Four bought the California Steam Navigation Company, and with it the control of the bulk of the river traffic. As for ocean commerce, they first made a series of rate-fixing agreements with the Pacific Mail Steamship Company, and then, in 1874, organized their own steamship line, the Occidental and Oriental. By 1880 they had so weakened the formerly dominant Pacific Mail that they were able to control it also.

In no other region of the United States did a railroad enjoy such a degree of freedom from competition. Thus entrenched, the Big Four were free to adopt a system of setting freight rates according to the highest charge that the traffic would bear without completely bankrupting the shipper and thus depriving the railroad of his future business. The railroad could also favor one shipper and ruin another by quoting different rates for the same service. Often its agents would demand to examine the shipper's books, and then set the rate according to what they thought he could afford to pay. No railroad system in the world had a greater variety of rates—some high, some low, some published, some secret.

The more modern idea is that an impartial public regulatory body should

"The Curse of California." A cartoon from a San Francisco weekly magazine, The Wasp, *August 19, 1882. (Courtesy of the Bancroft Library)*

determine freight and passenger rates that give the railroad a fair profit, according to the costs of providing the transportation. The Big Four regarded such notions as radical and dangerous nonsense. They firmly believed that in selling transportation they should act just as they would in selling anything else. When Huntington had sold shovels, or when Stanford had sold barrels of flour, in the Sacramento of the '50s, they had charged as much as they could get. As late as 1900, Collis P. Huntington would still operate the Southern Pacific according to the ethical principles and the economic and social ideas of a Yankee trader in the gold rush.

The railroad's power to make or break almost anyone engaged in agriculture, mining, manufacturing, or commerce, through its discriminatory freight rates, was effectively used in interrelation with the development of its control over politics. Through its rates it could reward its friends and punish its enemies. If a politician did not have economic interests of his own which could be favored or ruined by rate manipulation, his constituents did. The railroad also corrupted politics in a variety of other ways, and at all levels of government, Federal, state, and local. Money was paid to politicians under an assortment of disguises. If an office holder or candidate was a lawyer, he might receive a secret fee or salary for unspecified "legal services." If not, there were contributions for "campaign expenses." The Southern Pacific developed a political machine far more powerful than any other in the state. California's government, as well as its economy, became a prisoner of "the railroad."

Land monopoly. Further public resentment against the railroad grew out of the fact that it had become by far the largest private landowner in the state. Railroads that became parts of the Southern Pacific system received from the Federal government a total of 11,588,000 acres in California, about one-fifth of all the land that is now in private ownership. These railroad land grants, added to various other factors, made the ownership of California's arable land more concentrated than in any other part of the nation. "Land monopoly" was a burning issue.

We have already noticed the problems of land tenure that were left over from the Mexican grant system, and that had the effect of concentrating so much land in the coastal region in large units owned by American speculators. Mexican grants totaling 8,850,000 acres had been confirmed in the American courts. True, the rest of the land in the state had become part of the United States public domain, and the general policy of the Federal government, under such laws as the Pre-emption Act of 1841 and the Homestead Act of 1862, encouraged the ownership of this land in small farm units. But in California the operation of that policy was almost entirely thwarted. Both before and after the railroad land-grant acts of the 1860s, public lands that were usable generally passed into the hands of large holders and speculators. If land was fertile or potentially fertile, and located where transportation facilities would make it possible to market its produce, such land was usually engrossed by speculators before a genuine homesteader had a chance to file on it. Several million acres in California were ultimately patented as homesteads, but an appalling proportion of these were dummy entries, by men surreptitiously hired to turn them over to large holders for speculation, grazing, or lumbering.

According to the theory pronounced in 1893 by Frederick Jackson Turner, then a young professor of American history at the University of Wisconsin, "the existence of an area of free land, its continuous recession, and the advance of American settlement westward, explain American development." This "Turner hypothesis" was an oversimplification and exaggeration even as applied to the upper Mississippi Valley, the region Turner knew best. As applied to the development of California, the Turner theory of the significance of the frontier is worse than worthless.

The Homestead Act did not put an end to cash sales at auction of public lands that had more than minimum value. This was particularly true of arable public lands within the limits of railroad land grants. The government's retention of the alternate sections in checkerboard pattern often failed to help the early settler, for these lands were withdrawn from entry when the railroad grant was made, and by the time they were surveyed and opened the settler typically found himself outbid by the speculator.

Government surveyors, private surveyors working under government contracts, and officials of the Federal and state land offices, acquired advance knowledge of the lands and used this knowledge for speculation on their own behalf or in collusion with others. Many of the most successful California land brokers, such as Benson and Hyde, were also surveying contractors, who thus laid the foundations of their prosperous careers. Along with cash, speculators used millions of dollars' worth of scrip, particularly the agricultural college scrip which they purchased from the states, to whom the Federal government had issued it under the Morrill Land Grant College Act of 1862. In the late '60s and early '70s the biggest of the California speculators, or "land prospectors," was William S. Chapman, who amassed holdings of more than a million acres, though he later lost his fortune in an overambitious canal project.

The Federal government granted more than 8 million acres of land to the state—2 million acres as "swamp and overflow" land under the act of 1850, and more than 6 million acres for educational purposes. The state's disposition of these lands was careless, improvident, and in many cases riddled with fraud. Lands in California that had the appearance of swamps in the rainy season might actually be among the richest lands; but they were sold, mostly to large operators, at $1.25 per acre, which was refunded to the purchaser if he swore that he had spent a like amount in reclamation.

The possibilities for building up huge land holdings were spectacularly illustrated in the story of Henry Miller, who became the state's leading cattle baron. Born Heinrich Alfred Kreiser, he had arrived in New York from Germany at 19, in 1847, with no resources except his boyhood training in the care of livestock and the cutting of meat. In 1849, with the savings from his wages as a butcher's helper, he bought a ticket to California from a friend who had changed his mind about going there, and because the ticket was marked "not transferable," he took his friend's name, Henry Miller. Within a few years he was important enough to have the change made official by a special act of the California legislature.

From operating a butcher shop in San Francisco, Miller quickly branched out, buying cattle and then buying lands for pasturage. In the northern San Joaquin Valley, for example, he was so skillful in acquiring "swamp and overflow" lands that eventually he owned both banks of the San Joaquin River in a solid strip more than 100 miles long, from the area west of Modesto to the region of Madera. Through water monopoly he was able to control much of the

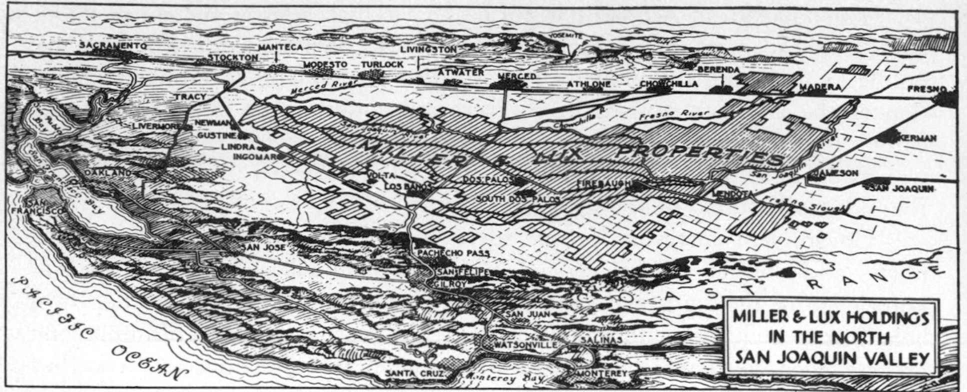

Miller and Lux Holdings in the North San Joaquin Valley. From Wallace Smith, Garden of the Sun. (*Courtesy of the Bancroft Library*)

land surrounding his own. More sagacious than William S. Chapman, he ultimately acquired many of Chapman's holdings. He formed an effective partnership with Charles Lux, a tall Alsatian who was somewhat more polished than Miller and had a slightly better command of English, and who often represented the firm's interests in San Francisco while Miller was looking after its ranches in the interior. Ultimately Miller & Lux owned more than a million acres in California, Nevada, and Oregon, and Miller liked to boast that he could ride from Mexico to Oregon and sleep every night in a ranch house of his own.

The engrossment of arable land in advance of agricultural settlement and development was a chronic problem in California, and would long have remained so, even if it had not been increased and complicated by the railroad land grants. In general, the question of the wisdom and necessity of granting public lands to railroads in the American West has remained highly debatable. The legal purpose of the grants was to aid the construction of the lines; but the railroads derived their returns from them after the lines were built—often many years afterward. In California, in particular, the grants clearly proved to have been an unwise and unsound policy. They added greatly to the wealth and power of the owners of the Southern Pacific at a time when their wealth and power had already become far too great for the public good.

The expansion of the railroad network in the 1870s did have the desirable effect of encouraging the spread of agricultural settlement in the great Central Valley, but it also created a special set of land-tenure problems. Some of these may be seen in poignantly human terms in the tragic experiences of the settlers of the district of Mussel Slough, near Hanford in what is now Kings County.

The Southern Pacific had published a number of pamphlets inviting settlers to occupy lands within the limits of its grant in the southern counties of the

San Joaquin Valley. The railroad had not yet acquired full legal ownership of these lands from the Federal government, but its pamphlets promised that as soon as it did so the settler would be assured the right to buy the land he had occupied. Prices were predicted in vague and misleading terms, such as "from $2.50 upward" per acre; but it was very clearly stated that the prices would not include the value of the settler's improvements. Mussel Slough, which carried part of the waters of the Kings River into Tulare Lake, offered possibilities for irrigation, and between 1872 and 1875 the settlers pooled their labor and constructed an elaborate system of irrigation works.

Congress repeatedly failed to appropriate enough money for the effective administration of the land offices, and this delayed the sale of the lands for many years. In 1878, after the railroad had at last acquired the titles, it addressed a letter to each settler informing him of the price of the land he occupied and that it was now for sale "to anyone." These prices ranged from $17 to $40 per acre, and the settlers charged that they included the value of their improvements, in violation of the railroad's published promises. But the Federal courts upheld the railroad's contention that it was violating no specific legal contract. The settlers tried to negotiate a compromise price scale, and here, as in a number of other matters, there is some evidence that Stanford would have liked to compromise in the interest of public relations and goodwill. But Huntington was adamant. His demand for "what the land is worth" resembled his demand for what the traffic would bear.

Walter J. Crow and Mills D. Hart now purchased occupied lands from the Southern Pacific at about $25 per acre. The settlers charged that Crow and Hart, whom they described as "Buzzard and Gizzard," were dummy purchasers hired by the railroad, although this assumption was based only on the fact that they were willing to pay the railroad's price for the land. The two men were not complete newcomers to the region, as several accounts have mistakenly assumed; Crow's family were themselves pioneer settlers of the San Joaquin Valley, and his grandfather was the founder of Crow's Landing, west of Modesto.

On the morning of May 11, 1880, United States Marshal Alonzo W. Poole, acting under Federal court orders from San Francisco, drove out in a buggy with Crow and Hart, to put them in possession of the lands they had purchased and to evict the occupants. When a group of more than 20 settlers appeared, mounted and armed, the result was the "battle of Mussel Slough," at a point about 5 miles northwest of Hanford. The marshal did not participate in the shooting, and it is impossible to determine who fired first. Seven men were killed, including Crow and Hart. Later five of the settlers were convicted of resisting a Federal officer, and served eight-month sentences in the jail at San Jose. But since public opinion was generally to the effect that the railroad had cruelly deceived and robbed the settlers, the prisoners were widely regarded as heroes rather than convicts. More than any other single development, the tragedy at Mussel Slough dramatized the intense popular resentment against large landholders in general and the railroad in particular.

The Comstock and overspeculation. During the 1870s the mining industry proved to be as great a disappointment as the railroad. In this period the Comstock Lode experienced its greatest boom. It produced about three times as much silver as in the previous decade, because of the unparalleled richness of the ore at the deeper levels. Yet the effect on California was not to relieve the depressed conditions of the '70s but to make them worse. The capital of the region, badly needed in other fields, became concentrated in the speculative market for Nevada mining stocks, and the gyrations of these stocks on the San Francisco exchange infected the public with a gambling mania that became one of the most unhappy characteristics of the times. The new bonanza created enormous fortunes for a few men, who controlled the richest mines and thus had inside knowledge to use in manipulating the stock market—but by this process they impoverished thousands of other investors. The "bonanza kings" also engaged in a number of spectacular struggles with each other, in which the investing public and the general welfare usually suffered.

The first group to attain a degree of power that justified the title of "Kings of the Comstock" were certain officials of the Bank of California, who became known as the "Bank ring," or "Ralston's ring." A state law of 1862 had permitted the incorporation of banks, with inadequate legal regulation, and under this law William Chapman Ralston had organized the Bank of California in San Francisco in 1864, just as the first Comstock boom was ending. Most of the mines were in borrasca, and several of them were flooded. Many of the owners were in financial difficulties, and William Sharon, whom Ralston had chosen as the bank's agent in Virginia City, tempted them with comparatively low interest rates into heavy borrowing. Then, after a series of foreclosures, the bank came into control of a major portion of the mines and mills. These were consolidated under Sharon's management, and new machinery installed; deeper deposits of rich ore were discovered, and millions of dollars began to pour into the vaults of the bank and the personal accounts of its officials.

With so much of the Comstock's silver behind it, the Bank of California now became and remained for several years the most highly regarded financial institution in the Far West, and William Chapman Ralston was generally recognized as the leading citizen of San Francisco. Toward that city, in his own mind, his relationship became that of Lorenzo de Medici to Florence, or King Ludwig II of Bavaria to Munich. San Francisco must become the finest city in the world, and California the most prosperous region. He sponsored and controlled a panoply of enterprises—carriage, watch, and furniture factories, woolen mills, foundries, and sugar refineries, a theater, and urban and rural real estate. In his villa at Belmont he provided lavish hospitality for every famous personage who came to San Francisco. For the distinguished tourist in California an invitation to Belmont became more essential than a trip to Yosemite. When Ambassador Anson Burlingame passed through on his way to China, Ralston named a townsite after him and sold him one of its most attractive lots for a future home.

It is interesting to compare the occasion when Ralston had the opportunity to have a town named after himself. The directors of the Central Pacific, in the process of creating a new community on their line in the northern San Joaquin Valley, offered to name it Ralston, partly in gratitude for a loan he had once made to Stanford. Ralston politely declined the honor—but the railroad directors insisted on bestowing it upon him less directly. They named the town Modesto. The idea that modesty was actually one of Ralston's prominent traits can only be regarded, as the directors regarded it, with some hilarity. They were well aware that it was San Francisco, and not a raw new village, which he wished to be considered as his monument.

About the time of the organization of the Bank of California, in 1864, a self-trained mining engineer named Adolph Sutro conceived a brilliant and daring plan for a revolutionary method of mining the Comstock Lode. This was to build a tunnel 4 miles long, beginning at a point near the Carson River and extending into the heart of Mount Davidson to strike the center of the lode at a depth of about 1,650 feet, directly under Virginia City. At that time the mines had reached levels of only about 500 feet, but many geologists believed that the lode was a true fissure vein, thousands of feet deep. A tunnel, Sutro thought, was the only effective solution. The mines were often flooded when they tapped great underground reservoirs of scalding water, which had to be pumped to the surface. The miners had to work in air that was indescribably foul, and at temperatures that often exceeded 120°. Pumping, artificial ventilation, and the hoisting of ore and earth upward were accomplished with expensive equipment that constantly wore out. Sutro's tunnel would drain the water by gravity, and provide a natural circulation of air for ventilation and cooling. It would permit the removal of ore in cars rolled down a gentle slope, to mills economically located near the tunnel's mouth and powered by the flow of the river.

In historical perspective it is clear that from nearly every viewpoint of economy and safety this was a magnificent plan, and that if all parties had cooperated to bring it to an early completion the lives of hundreds of miners would have been saved, along with tens of millions of dollars. But Ralston and Sharon, though enthusiastic about the project at first, soon determined to oppose it, not because they believed that it would not work but rather because they feared it would work too well—for Sutro's benefit, not theirs. If the mines became dependent on the use of his tunnel, then Sutro, not Ralston and Sharon, would rule the Comstock. Other capitalists, following the lead of the mighty Bank of California, refused to invest in the tunnel or to lend money to its promoter.

Sutro was a firm believer in private enterprise; during the Civil War Mark Twain quoted him as saying that the Federal government had "fooled away two or three years trying to capture Richmond, whereas if they had let the job by contract to some sensible business man, the thing would have been accomplished and forgotten long ago." As for the Sutro tunnel, however, 15 years elapsed between its conception and its completion. The Nevada legislature granted a franchise but no subsidies. Congress made a small land grant, but constant pressure from Sutro's powerful enemies blocked congressional approval of his perennial requests for a government loan. Sharon denounced Sutro, a Prussian immigrant of Jewish ancestry, as an "Assyrian carpetbagger," and asked whether it was the man or his tunnel which should be known as "the Great Bore." As part of a campaign to prove the tunnel unnecessary, Ralston and Sharon built a railroad to connect Virginia City with their own ore-reduction mills on the Carson River.

Not even a beginning was made in the actual construction of the Sutro tunnel until the autumn of 1869, and then only with limited capital subscribed by the Comstock's working miners, who thus expressed their resentment against the ruling financiers. In August a terrible fire in the Yellow Jacket mine had killed 42 men. Sutro made a powerful speech to a mass meeting of angry miners, with pictures showing how his tunnel would have enabled the men to escape. His denunciation of the selfish motives of those who opposed his project received thunderous support from the audience, and soon afterward the miners' union voted to invest all its available funds in the Sutro Tunnel Company. Later some Scottish bankers invested in the project, but its capital remained inadequate and its progress slow.

In the meantime the supremacy of Ralston and Sharon was being challenged from another quarter, by the rising fortunes of a group of four Irishmen who would eventually be the wealthiest of the Comstock's kings. John W. Mackay, James G. Fair, James C. Flood, and William S. O'Brien had all been sons of poor Irish immigrants. Mackay and Fair achieved their first successes as Comstock mine superintendents. Flood and O'Brien began their careers as partners in the ownership of a San Francisco saloon, where for several years they had the benefit of informative conversation with the leading stockbrokers who were their best customers. Then, having established a stock brokerage firm of their own, they met Mackay and Fair, with whom they formed a remarkably effective combination. Mackay and Fair were experts on the mines; Flood and O'Brien knew the San Francisco stock market. With inside information, shrewd guesses, and good luck, their fortunes increased steadily, and in 1873 they struck the "big bonanza," the very "heart of the Comstock," underlying a group of neglected mines which they had bought up and merged under the name of the Consolidated Virginia.

Ralston, whose preeminence was thus threatened, had been overextending himself in imaginative but unsound investments, such as silk mills, a large tobacco plantation near Gilroy, and even a salted "diamond mine," in which two "honest old prospectors" swindled him out of several hundred thousand dollars. In 1872 he began construction of the Palace Hotel, intended to be the largest and most lavish in the world. With its tier on tier balconies around a central garden court, it required three years to complete, and cost nearly 7 million dollars. The Palace was a larger luxury hotel than the city could then support, and for many years most of its hundreds of rooms were usually unoccupied.

In the attempt to replenish his wealth, dangerously depleted by such prodigal ventures, Ralston resorted to a desperate gamble. Believing that the Consolidated Virginia's big bonanza must extend into the property of the neighboring Ophir, he set out to gain control of the Ophir by buying up a majority of its stock. This drove prices on the San Francisco exchange to ridiculous and unprecedented heights. Elias Jackson Baldwin, then the Ophir's largest stockholder, sold out to Ralston at the very peak, and was known ever after as "Lucky" Baldwin. In January 1875, information that the great bonanza did not actually extend to the Ophir led to the collapse of its stock.

Ralston was now irretrievably ruined, but he managed to conceal the fact for a few months more. His last hope was in the Spring Valley Water Company, which he had developed earlier as the main supplier of water for San Francisco. He now proposed to enlarge the company's facilities and sell them to the city, at an extremely large profit for himself; but the *Bulletin* and the *Call* attacked the scheme as corrupt and extortionate, and the mayor announced that he would veto it. On August 26, 1875, a run on the Bank of California forced Ralston to close the bank's doors. Next morning the directors asked for and received his resignation; then he went for his accustomed swim in the waters of the bay, from which his body was recovered a few hours later. Whether he died by accident or suicide is unknown.

Ralston's more conservative associates in the Bank of California, such as Darius Ogden Mills, had refused to participate in many of his more dubious investments. They were able to salvage their own fortunes and to reopen the bank within a few weeks. Sharon, strangely enough, profited heavily from Ralston's downfall, and although Ralston's own unbridled extravagance was certainly a major cause of his ruin, the prevailing opinion in San Francisco came to be that Sharon, whom Ralston had trusted implicitly, had secretly plotted the destruction of his friend by giving him misleading advice.

That Sharon had been deeply envious of Ralston there can be little doubt. Ralston was a large, handsome, and athletic man, while Sharon, though always foppishly dressed, was small and of unattractive appearance. After Ralston's death Sharon acquired a remarkable number of what had been his late friend's most cherished possessions, notably the mansion at Belmont and the Palace Hotel.

The "Irish four," also, made Ralston's calamity their own opportunity. Mackay, Fair, Flood, and O'Brien took over several of the bank's mines and mills, consolidated them with their own combine, and established a degree of control over the Comstock that exceeded anything the "Bank ring" had achieved.

Not content with the profits of mining the greatest silver strikes of all time, they took full advantage of their power to "milk" the stock market. A suit by an outraged minority stockholder provided documentation of some of their methods; periodically they sold their stocks at the highest levels, then bought them back at low prices after deliberately giving out bearish information to break the market, thus ruining many of the smaller holders. They also did everything they could to obstruct the completion of Sutro's tunnel, just as Ralston and Sharon had done, and for similar reasons. By the time the tunnel was completed, in 1879, the richest ore bodies had already been exhausted and the great days of the Comstock were over.

SELECTED BIBLIOGRAPHY

"The Terrible Seventies" was the title of a chapter in Gertrude Atherton's *California, an Intimate History* (1914).

The volumes by Oscar Lewis and Stuart Daggett, cited for the previous chapter, are also useful here. See also Henry George, "What the Railroad Will Bring Us," *The Overland Monthly,* I (October 1868), 297–304; and John H. Kemble, "The Big Four at Sea; the History of the Occidental and Oriental Steamship Company," *Huntington Library Quarterly,* III (April 1940), 339–358.

On land monopoly, see chapter 6, "California Latifundia," in Carey McWilliams, *California: the Great Exception* (1949). Paul W. Gates, "The Homestead Law in an Incongruous Land System," *American Historical Review,* XLI (July 1936), 652–681, is reprinted, along with a number of other significant articles, in *The Public Lands* (1963), edited by Vernon Carstensen. Gates, "California's Agricultural College Lands," *Pacific Historical Review,* XXX (May 1961), 103–122, shows the extent to which the Morrill Act facilitated land speculation. The largest speculator's defense of his own activities may be found in "Henry George Reexamined: William S. Chapman's Views on Land Speculation in Nineteenth Century California," by Gerald D. Nash, in *Agricultural History,* XXXIII (July 1959), 133–137. Edward F. Treadwell, *The Cattle King* (1931), is a laudatory "dramatized biography" of Henry Miller by a Miller & Lux attorney. James L. Brown, *The Mussel Slough Tragedy* (1958), is a balanced account, as is the chapter on the same subject in Wallace Smith, *Garden of the Sun; a History of the San Joaquin Valley, 1772–1939* (1939).

George D. Lyman, *Ralston's Ring; California Plunders the Comstock Lode* (1937), covers the period from 1864 to 1875. See also the works by Eliot Lord, C. B. Glasscock, and Grant H. Smith, cited for Chapter XVII; and Robert E. Stewart, Jr., and Mary F. Stewart, *Adolph Sutro, a Biography* (1962). Oscar Lewis, *Silver Kings; the Lives and Times of Mackay, Fair, Flood, and O'Brien* (1947), deals largely with their personal lives and those of their families.

Chapter XX

POLITICAL TURMOIL AND A NEW CONSTITUTION

The increase of anti-Chinese sentiment. During most of the 1860s, when jobs were plentiful in California, the flow of Chinese immigration was slight; indeed, there were years in the middle '60s in which the Chinese who returned from California to China actually outnumbered those who came. At the end of that decade, however, when the beginning of a long period of hard times and unemployment coincided with a renewed upsurge of Oriental immigration, many Californians and particularly workingmen demanded ever stronger measures designed not merely to exclude any further Chinese immigrants but to drive out as many as possible of those who had already arrived. At the same time, to their great disgust, the proponents of these demands were confronted by a number of recent actions of the Federal government—the Burlingame Treaty, the Fourteenth Amendment, and the civil rights act—which positively encouraged Chinese immigration and blocked various efforts of state and local authorities to discourage it.

Anson Burlingame was a brilliant Massachusetts lawyer and congressman who served as American minister to China under Presidents Lincoln, Johnson, and Grant. As an enlightened Boston Republican of the Civil War and Reconstruction periods, he prided himself on freedom from race prejudice. As American minister, he formed a strong admiration for the Chinese, and a strong sympathy for the Chinese imperial government in its difficulties with foreign powers and merchants. The Burlingame Treaty of 1868 provided for the right of free immigration. The United States Senate agreed to it with only one amendment, which continued the denial of the right of naturalization.

The Fourteenth Amendment to the Federal constitution, ratified in the same year, forbade any state to "deprive any person of life, liberty, or property, without due process of law," or to "deny to any person within its jurisdiction the equal protection of the laws." The Federal civil rights act of 1870 prohibited discrimination in the courts, and discriminatory taxes against any particular group of immigrants.

Under these measures the Federal courts struck down most of the varied and ingenious anti-Chinese weapons in the arsenals of California state and municipal law. For example, in 1870 when the flow of new arrivals had made the tenements of San Francisco's Chinatown even more than usually overcrowded, a new ordinance made it a misdemeanor to maintain or occupy any sleeping room with less than 500 cubic feet of air per person. But the attempt to enforce this provision soon overcrowded the jails to such a degree that the city was grossly violating its own ordinance. In an effort to force the Chinese to choose the payment of fines rather than the serving of jail terms, the board of supervisors passed another measure requiring that the hair of every male prisoner in the jail be cut to within an inch of his scalp, thus inflicting what was for many of the Chinese the extreme indignity of the loss of the queue. Mayor William Alvord courageously vetoed this cruel and devious proposal, but it was later adopted, and remained in effect for several years before the Federal courts declared it an unconstitutional discrimination.

In this decision, and in some of the most important of the other opinions that invalidated various anti-Chinese statutes, Justice Stephen J. Field of the United States Supreme Court wrote masterpieces of refined but scathing sarcasm. Field had particularly disliked the racist proclivities of his fellow Californians since the day when he had tried and failed to prevent the hanging of Juanita at Downieville in 1851.

Much of the anti-Chinese feeling was based on essentially irrational fears, directed against an alien people who worshiped strange gods, ate strange foods, and were thought to suffer from strange diseases. But there were more substantial grounds for the Californian fear of the "Yellow Peril," in the enormous numbers of the Chinese who might swarm into the state if they were freely permitted to do so, and in the fact that their willingness to accept low wages tended to depress the wages of American workers. It is significant that Irish Americans were in the vanguard of most of the attacks on the Chinese. A generation earlier, when large numbers of Irish had migrated to the United States after the potato famine of the 1840s, it was they who had been denounced as a menace to the living standards of American labor. Now they could enjoy the position of being the denouncers. In the 1870s the Irish and the Chinese were the two largest foreign-born groups in California, each forming more than a tenth of the population of the state. In San Francisco more than a fifth of the population was Chinese, while the Irish formed almost as large a proportion. The Irish, being white and thus eligible for naturalized citizenship, now formed a large bloc of voters, while the immigrant Chinese had no votes.

"Anti-coolie clubs" joined with labor unions and "eight hour leagues" in organizing anti-Chinese parades and other public demonstrations in San Francisco. "Coolie" was a word around which a great deal of emotion and confusion revolved. It was not, as most Americans assumed, a word of Chinese origin, or a word peculiarly descriptive of a Chinese labor system. Its probable derivation was from *kuli*, meaning "muscle" in Tamil, a language of the Coromandel Coast of southern India. The British, using it to mean a hired unskilled laborer or servant, introduced the word into China, where it was approximated by two Chinese characters meaning "bitter strength." In the middle of the 19th century a flourishing traffic in the importation of laborers from China into Cuba and South America became known as the "coolie trade." Many of these laborers had been kidnaped, and were held under "labor contracts" that amounted to slavery; consequently the American, British, and Chinese governments made the vicious traffic illegal and sought to stamp it out.

It was often charged that the bulk of Chinese immigration to California was a part of this same infamous "coolie system," enforced by the Chinese Six Companies in San Francisco. On the other hand, these companies earnestly denied that any Chinese had come to California involuntarily, and earnestly asserted that their own purposes in helping their countrymen to find jobs were wholly benevolent. The truth was somewhere between these two opposite claims. It was true that the Six Companies performed many of the functions of benevolent fraternal societies. But even if they did not enforce any particular labor contracts and even though the "credit ticket" system theoretically permitted the immigrant to choose his own job, the enforcement of that system by the companies nevertheless involved a degree and kind of exploitation and debt peonage that deepened and prolonged the poverty of most of the immigrants involved.

The strongest defenders of the Chinese, apart from Christian missionary groups, were California employers, whose most common argument was that the Chinese did no harm to American labor because they performed only the hard or menial tasks that white workers did not want and would not take, such as the reclaiming of tule swamps, seasonal agricultural labor, domestic service, or laundering. But opponents of Chinese immigration argued that the Chinese were monopolizing a number of such occupations because their availability as cheap labor had depressed the wages paid in them. Moreover the Chinese were being employed in a growing list of industries in which they were clearly and sharply in competition with whites, especially the manufacturing of shoes, shirts, underwear, cigars, and tinware. And when Chinese began to be not merely workers in such factories but also owners of them, thus threatening to put white manufacturers out of business, a number of white employers suddenly became as anti-Chinese as the white workers had ever been.

There were several outbreaks of mob violence. The worst occurred in Los Angeles on the evening of October 24, 1871, after a white man had been killed in the course of a police attempt to intervene in a dispute between two Chinese companies. With complete impunity a mob of about five hundred men looted and burned the local Chinatown and killed 18 or 19 Chinese, leaving 15 of them hanging from makeshift gallows. Lesser incidents occurred sporadically throughout the 1870s in towns all the way from Chico to San Diego. California newspapers deplored these outbreaks, largely on the ground that they gave California a bad name in the Eastern states and made Eastern newspapers unsympathetic toward California's demands for Chinese exclusion.

The Workingmen's Party of California. Unemployment, discontent with economic, social, and political conditions in general, and the idea that the Chinese were the prime cause of all difficulties, combined to bring about a crisis of unrest in San Francisco in the summer and fall of 1877. The number of Chinese immigrants arriving at San Francisco in the previous year, more than 22,000, had broken all records, and the resulting situation may be compared not to a melting pot but to a pressure cooker. A severe drought in the winter of 1876–1877 had sharply reduced both agricultural production and the hydraulic mining of gold. Moreover, the final decline of the Comstock Lode had begun. Even the Consolidated Virginia, richest of all the Comstock mines, suspended dividend payments in January 1877, and the values of stocks in the leading mines, mostly owned in San Francisco, shrank by 150 million dollars within a few months.

For several years the unemployed of the whole state had flocked into "the city," where they gathered on street corners and vacant lots to discuss their grievances and to grow bitter at the lavish displays of wealth by some of their more fortunate fellow citizens. In the evening of July 23, 1877, there was a mass meeting on the "sand lots" in front of the San Francisco city hall. The reasons for this particular meeting had nothing to do with the anti-Chinese movement. Rather, it was called to express sympathy with the workers in the great railroad strike against reduction of wages, then going on in the Eastern states, and to protest against the use of troops in the recent labor riots in Pittsburgh. The call for the meeting at San Francisco on July 23 came from officials of the Workingmen's Party of the United States, recently created in New York and Chicago. This Marxist organization, which would soon change its name to the Socialist Labor Party, should not be confused with the Workingmen's Party of California, which was not yet in existence. In contrast with the latter organization, the Workingmen's Party of the United States was not anti-Chinese, because of its Marxian socialist belief in the international and universal brotherhood of the working classes.

The meeting itself was entirely orderly, but before it was over an anti-coolie club with a band and banners pushed its way into the crowd and called for a resolution against the Chinese. After this demand had been refused, a mob of hoodlums left the outskirts of the meeting, gathered recruits, and wrecked or burned a score of Chinese laundries.

The next day a meeting of businessmen organized a Committee of Public

Safety, with William T. Coleman, the head of the vigilance committee of 1856, as president. Nearly six thousand men enrolled in this "merchants' militia" within a few hours, and the Federal authorities responded to Coleman's requests for aid by sending five armed naval vessels from Mare Island to San Francisco and placing 1,700 rifles from the Benicia arsenal at his personal disposal. Fearing the consequences of the use of firearms, however, Coleman did not issue all of the rifles, and armed most of his force with hickory pick handles.

In the evening of July 25 a mob tried to burn the docks of the Pacific Mail Steamship Company. Some such action had been suggested periodically for years, because the Pacific Mail was said to be the largest importer of "coolies." There was much resentment because the Federal government, instead of acting to prevent the immigration of Chinese, was using public funds to subsidize the steamship companies that brought them. The "pick handle brigade," and the police, were able to disperse the mob and prevent the burning of the docks, but a neighboring lumberyard was burned, and in the melee four men were killed and a number wounded. This marked the end of the rioting, and a few days later the Committee of Public Safety was almost entirely disbanded. Some of the money that had been subscribed for it by frightened property owners was given to the city government for the hiring of 150 special policemen.

From these events many of the city's thousands of unemployed formed the impression that the forces of government were in alliance with the propertied classes against the "workingmen." Thus they were prepared to welcome the idea of a new workingmen's party that would try to end this injustice by gaining control of the government. Oddly enough, the man who now emerged as the leader of such a movement, a young Irish American named Denis Kearney, was the proprietor of a small business and had himself been a member of the pick handle brigade. A really adequate explanation of his motives is probably impossible; but he soon acquired a large following, mainly through his emotional and melodramatic style of oratory.

Kearney had been born in the county of Cork in Ireland, had received no formal education at all, and at the age of 11, after the death of his father, had been sent to sea as a cabin boy. In the next 10 years he rose to the rank of first mate, then settled in San Francisco and worked as a drayman. With hard work, thrift, and temperate habits he saved enough to establish a small draying concern of his own. Though self-taught, he was far from illiterate, and was one of the most vigorous speakers at the local Lyceum of Self-Culture. The views he expressed there were often both extreme and inconsistent, for his temperance in such things as liquor and tobacco did not extend to opinions or the expression of them. His maritime experiences had given him the power to command men, and when the Workingmen's Party of California took form, between August and October of 1877, he began as its secretary but soon became its "president." This was a highly unusual title in an American political party, and one apparently suggested by Coleman's title of "president" of the Committee of Public Safety, also an extraordinary organization.

To audiences gathered on the sand lots, Kearney said that the workingmen had as much right as the property owners to be armed and to form militia companies, and to emphasize his point he shouted that "every workingman should have a musket."

In the evening of October 29 Kearney held one of the most dramatic and successful of his meetings. He gathered more than a thousand of his followers at the top of Nob Hill where Crocker, Stanford, and Hopkins had built their mansions, and where Crocker had built his famous "spite fence." Crocker had wished to occupy the entire block between California and Sacramento Streets, but a man who owned one small lot with a house on it had refused to sell. Crocker had then surrounded the lot on three sides with a board fence 40 feet high, almost entirely shutting out the view and the sunshine from the little home. Pointing to the fence, Kearney cried that if it was not soon taken down the workingmen should tear it down. Then he went on to other remarks about the outrages committed by large capitalists, the corruption of incumbent politicians, and the need for his new political party.

Fearing that Kearney's speeches would lead to more riots like those of July, the city government hastily adopted an ordinance against addressing any meeting of more than 25 persons in language suggesting violence or destruction of property. This promptly became known as the "gag law," and served mainly to increase the pressure of the discontent that it sought to repress. Under this ordinance Kearney was arrested, but in his trial in January 1878 he was acquitted on the ground that no violence had actually resulted from his words. In fact, Kearney's speeches and the hope of successful political action through his new party seem to have offered a kind of safety valve. His speeches were generally extemporaneous, and accounts of them differed widely. For example, he was charged with having said that his followers should hold a Thanksgiving Day parade if they had to march "up to their knees in blood"; but it was established in court that he had said not "blood" but "mud." The *Chronicle* and the *Call,* which were then engaged in a circulation war for dominance of the morning field, often made his speeches sound more incendiary than they were. By giving a maximum of sensational publicity to his movement, the newspapers presented it with thousands of new recruits. These were attracted most of all by Kearney's denunciations of the Chinese. Whatever else he may have said, it is certain that he formed the habit of ending his speeches with: "And whatever happens, the Chinese must go!"

The constitution of 1879. Demands for a new state constitution had been heard periodically since the 1850s, and had increased in volume as the great depression of the '70s lengthened and deepened. After several defeats at the polls, the calling of a new constitutional convention was finally approved by the voters in the state elections of September 5, 1877. At that time the Work-

Denis Kearney addressing the Workingmen's party on Nob Hill, October 29, 1877. (Courtesy of the Bancroft Library)

ingmen's Party of California was still only in its inceptive stage in San Francisco. By the following April, however, when the legislature passed an enabling act setting the elections of delegates to the convention for June 19, 1878, the party under Kearney's leadership was sufficiently well organized to nominate a full ticket of delegates in every part of the state. Fear that the workingmen might actually control the convention became so great among conservatives that in most districts the Republican and Democratic nominations were fused, under the label of "Non-partisan."

The convention which was elected in June of 1878 and which met at Sacramento in September was more than three times as large as the Monterey convention of 1849, with 152 delegates as compared with 48. It was in session nearly six months, as compared with six weeks. In place of an imitative, short, and concise document, it produced one that was much more original, extraordinarily long, and extremely detailed. Yet California's second constitutional convention achieved remarkably little net improvement over the first, and virtually every hope of effective reform was ultimately disappointed.

The original bill for an enabling act had provided for 120 delegates, 3 from each of the 40 state senatorial districts; but conservative forces in the legislature had added a provision for 32 delegates at large, 8 from each of the 4 congressional districts. Non-partisans were elected to every one of these additional 32 seats. Altogether, of the 152 delegates 78 were Non-partisans, 51 Workingmen, 11 Republicans, 10 Democrats, and 2 Independents. Of the Workingmen, 30 were from San Francisco, and thus the Workingmen carried the city but not the state. By occupation, 57 delegates were lawyers, mostly conservatives; 39 were farmers; 8 were merchants; and the others were scattered over a wide range reflecting the diverse skilled trades of the San Francisco workingmen.

The conservative delegates, including some of the shrewdest lawyers and politicians in the state, could have controlled the convention easily had it not been that some of the reforms demanded by the workingmen were also demanded by the farmers, and that on the issues where these two groups could unite they commanded a majority. In Los Angeles County two delegates had even been elected on a joint farmer-workingman ticket.

The economic and political discontent of the farmers in the '70s was expressed largely through the Granger movement, or the Patrons of Husbandry. Founded in Washington, D.C., in 1867 as a social and educational organization for farmers and their wives, with local lodge units known as Granges, the movement became so active in politics after the national panic of 1873 that it gained control of several legislatures in the Middle West and secured the passage of state laws for the regulation of railroad rates. More than a fourth of the delegates in the California convention were in effect representatives of the Granger movement, though they had no separate party denomination and included men elected under all five of the official labels.

Railroad regulation was one objective that attracted not only the joint support of workingmen and farmers but the support of many business organizations as well. A law of 1876 had defined and prohibited extortion and unjust discrimination in rates and had created a state board of three transportation commissioners. The railroad executives had rendered this body powerless simply by refusing to make reports to it, and the legislature of 1878 had reduced the membership to one commissioner, who did nothing more than gather statistics. In an effort to make regulation a reality, the new constitution provided for a state railroad commission of three members elected to four-year terms, with power to establish rates and to set fines and imprisonments for violations.

The farmers also demanded changes in the tax structure, to decrease their excessive tax burden. With the help of the workingmen they secured a provision that the mortgage holder must pay the tax on his portion of the equity in a farm. In the hope of fairer assessments of taxes on land, which had fallen very heavily on the farmers and very lightly on the railroad under the system of independent county assessors, a state board of equalization was created.

Corporations and especially banks were the targets of much invective in the convention. Dr. Charles C. O'Donnell, a San Francisco physician who was one of the most vociferous of the Workingmen delegates, defined a corporation as "a corrupt combination of individuals, formed together for the purpose of escaping individual responsibility for their acts." Defenders of the corporate system were also articulate, but they were unable to prevent the inclusion of a number of provisions that sought to increase the accountability of bank and other corporation directors and stockholders.

The anti-Chinese article was long, elaborate, and emotional. It authorized the legislature to protect the state from "aliens, who are, or may become . . . dangerous or detrimental"; it forbade the employment of Chinese by corporations, or on public works "except in punishment for crime," and it denounced and prohibited "Asiatic coolieism" as "a form of human slavery."

Many of the delegates to the constitutional convention regarded themselves as more truly the representatives of "the people" than were the members of the legislature, in whom they had very little confidence. They wrote into the constitution of the state a mass of details that would normally have been left to legislative action. The result was almost the longest written constitution in the world, several times as long as the Constitution of the United States; it was ultimately exceeded in length and verbosity only by the constitutions of Louisiana and India.

Virtually no one was entirely satisfied with the convention's massive product, and the public debate over its ratification was confused. Conservatives denounced it as communistic and malicious. Workingmen, on the other hand, were angered because it did so little that was directly in the interest of labor. The provision that "eight hours shall constitute a legal day's work on all public works" added nothing whatever to the law of 1868, which had proved to be merely a recommendation without any provision for enforcement. The strongest sentiment for ratification came from the farming areas, where the Grangers cherished dreams of lower freight rates and lower taxes. On May 7, 1879, the new constitution was adopted by a majority of less than 11,000 out of a total vote of 145,000.

The frustration of reform. The general failure of the constitution of 1879 to produce major improvements in the state's government was most glaringly exemplified in the story of the railroad commission. The first elected members were Charles J. Beerstecher, a San Francisco lawyer who had been one of the Workingmen's party delegates in the convention; Joseph S. Cone of Red Bluff, a wealthy farmer; and George B. Stoneman, a future Democratic Governor of the state and the only member of the commission who made a serious attempt to carry out his duties, or even to examine the railroad companies' books. These he found incomprehensible, and he had no authority to employ an expert.

Instead of establishing new rates, the commission generally adopted the existing ones, except for a lowering of freight rates on certain agricultural products of the northern Sacramento Valley, where Cone's farm was located. A legislative investigation revealed that Beerstecher suddenly acquired a fortune for which he could not account, and that Cone was permitted to buy lands which he then sold to the treasurer of the Southern Pacific at a profit of $100,000. Largely by means of such corrupt methods, the railroad's power to control the state would continue to exceed the state's power to regulate the railroad for three decades more.

The constitutional requirement that the creditor rather than the debtor must pay the tax on the mortgaged portion of property was soon easily and almost universally evaded by raising the interest to a rate large enough to include the tax. Equally disappointing to the farmers was the general ineffectiveness of the state board of equalization. The railroad was usually able to escape from higher assessments by contesting them in the courts.

The Workingmen's party began to disintegrate soon after it reached the zenith of its power in the elections of September 3, 1879, in which the Workingmen elected the chief justice of the supreme court, 5 of the 6 associate justices, 11 senators, and 16 assemblymen. In addition they elected the Rev. Isaac S. Kalloch, a Baptist minister and sensational pulpit orator, as mayor of San Francisco. His administration, however, was stormy, unsuccessful, and discredited. In the course of a long-continued exchange of personal insults, Kalloch was shot and wounded by Charles de Young, publisher of the *Chronicle*. Kalloch's son later shot and killed de Young, and was acquitted of murder. Kearney himself was constantly involved in dissensions with other leaders or would-be leaders of the movement. Within a year after the adoption of the new constitution the Workingmen's party had virtually disappeared.

The constitution, though without substantial reason, was given some of the credit for the upturn in economic conditions in California in 1880, and the return of prosperity reduced the intensity of demands for political and social change.

Chinese exclusion. Another development that reduced public discontent in California was the surrender of the Federal government to the state's demands for a ban on Chinese immigration. This occurred because the anti-Chinese vote in California actually came to hold the balance of power between the parties in national as well as in state politics. Within the state, no party won the governorship in more than two consecutive elections during the half century from 1849 to 1899, and often the majorities were less than 1,000 votes. Chinese immigration to the United States was so concentrated on the Pacific Coast that the other states could not understand California's concern about the problem; but it became clear that her electoral votes, along with those of Washington and Oregon, could swing the Presidency to the party that made the stronger promises to exclude the Chinese.

The presidential elections of 1876 and 1888 were so close that the majorities in the electoral college went to the candidates who had received the minorities of the popular votes; and the popular majorities for James A. Garfield in 1880 and Grover Cleveland in 1884 were less than 25,000. In this situation the national Republican and Democratic platforms began to rival each other in echoing Californian anti-Chinese slogans.

Though the Federal courts nullified the main provisions of the California constitution with respect to the Chinese, new treaties with China permitted Congress to provide for their exclusion. The Federal law of 1882 prohibited

Chinese immigration for 10 years; in 1892 this was extended for 10 years more; and in 1902 the ban was made permanent.

SELECTED BIBLIOGRAPHY

Mary Roberts Coolidge, *Chinese Immigration* (1909), the work of a sociologist very sympathetic to the Chinese, tended to assume that unreasoning race prejudice and political opportunism were the only real causes of opposition to Chinese immigration. Elmer C. Sandmeyer, *The Anti-Chinese Movement in California* (1939), presented a more balanced view. Important records of testimony taken in 1876 are the *Report of the Joint Special Committee to Investigate Chinese Immigration*, 44th Congress, 2d Session (1877), and the report of the special committee of the California state senate on *Chinese Immigration; Its Social, Moral, and Political Effect* (1878). Gunther Barth, *Bitter Strength*, cited in Chapter XIV, is also important here. Other studies include Stuart C. Miller, *The Unwelcome Immigrant: The American Image of the Chinese, 1785–1882* (1970); and Ping Chiu, *Chinese Labor in California, 1850–1880: An Economic Study* (1963), a defense of the Chinese which generally coincides with the employers' arguments. On the Los Angeles riot of 1871, consult the articles by Paul M. De Falla, *Historical Society of Southern California Quarterly*, XLII (March and June 1960), 57–88, 161–185, and William R. Locklear, *Historical Society of Southern California Quarterly*, XLII (September 1960), 239–256.

Alexander P. Saxton, *The Indispensable Enemy: Labor and the Anti-Chinese Movement in California* (1971), throws new light not only on the movement in general but also on its interrelations with the rise of organized labor. See also Stanford M. Lyman, *The Asian in the West* (1970).

A good account of the Workingmen's movement is Ralph Kauer, "The Workingmen's Party of California," *Pacific Historical Review*, XIII (September 1944), 278–291. Important contemporary treatment included J. C. Stedman and R. A. Leonard, *The Workingmen's Party of California* (1878), an impassioned defense of Kearney and of the party; and Henry George, "The Kearney Agitation in California," *Popular Science Monthly*, XVII (August 1880), 433–453. The chapter on "Kearneyism in California" in James Bryce, *The American Commonwealth*, volume II (1893; new edition, 1910), was very critical. Valuable accounts may be found in Ira B. Cross, *A History of the Labor Movement in California* (1935); Cross's edition of the autobiography of *Frank B. Roney: Irish Rebel and California Labor Leader* (1931); Lucile Eaves, *A History of California Labor Legislation* (1910); and Winfield J. Davis, *History of Political Conventions in California, 1849–1892* (1893).

Davis's work is also useful on the history of the constitutional convention, of which the *Debates and Proceedings* were published in three volumes (1880). The best study is Carl B. Swisher, *Motivation and Political Technique in the California Constitutional Convention, 1878–1879* (1930). See also Dudley T. Moorehead, "Sectionalism and the California Constitution of 1879," *Pacific Historical Review*, XII (September 1943), 287–294.

Chapter XXI

CULTURE AND OLIGARCHY: LITERATURE

For a state whose population was still a little less than 2 percent of the national total at the turn of the century, California was producing a remarkable proportion of the country's most significant writing. Nearly all the state's major writers reflected in their various ways the growing pains of a disorderly and prematurely adolescent society, dominated by a few men with great fortunes.

Henry George. In the writings of Henry George, California made a striking contribution to the history of ideas. George's theories grew directly out of his personal observation of the California social environment in the late 1860s and the 1870s, and his beliefs were the responses of a sensitive man to conditions and problems that were then more particularly apparent in California than in any other part of the world. He concluded that monopoly in land, above all, had given oligarchical power to such men as the Big Four, "who a few years ago were selling coal-oil or retailing dry goods, but who now count their fortunes by the scores of millions." George's denunciation of the "unearned increment" from the increase in the value of land, and his remedy, a single tax that would confiscate private land ownership, formed a major chapter in the history of native American radicalism.

George was born in 1839 in Philadelphia; as he put it in his first notable public address, he drew his "first breath almost within the shadow of Independence Hall." His formal education ended early, and throughout his life he insisted that formal education had little importance or value. He worked for several years as a printer before he came to San Francisco at the age of 19. There he was soon married, and his efforts to keep his wife and children from outright starvation gave him a burning personal knowledge of the meaning of poverty. His writing career began with a series of jobs as reporter and editor for newspapers in San Francisco, Oakland, and Sacramento. John Nugent, who was making an effort to revive the *San Francisco Herald,* sent George to the East Coast in the hope of breaking the monopoly of the Associated Press over telegraphic news. On the sidewalks of New York, where George was struck by "the shocking contrast between monstrous wealth and debasing want," he felt a call to seek an understanding of this paradoxical and baffling condition, and to do something to ameliorate it. A year later, back in California, an answer suddenly occurred to him.

One day in 1870, when he was editing the *Oakland Transcript,* he sought relaxation in a ride through the foothills overlooking the bay. A passing teamster told him that the land they were crossing, part of a large unused tract, was being held for a price of $1,000 per acre. "Like a flash it came upon me," he recalled in later years; here was the answer to the enigma of why progress had its twin in poverty, of why when wealth increased, poverty increased with it. As land values rose with the growth of population, the man who worked the land had to pay too much for the privilege. The noblest form of labor, the production of food, was robbed to pay a huge unearned increment to the land speculator.

George denounced the railroad as the state's largest private landowner and as the beneficiary of vast subsidies in both land and cash. In a pamphlet on *The Subsidy Question* (1871), he turned *laissez-faire* theories against big business, reversing the usual line of argument. Since the publication of Darwin's *Origin of Species* in 1859, followed by Herbert Spencer's efforts to apply the Darwinian theory of natural selection to the evolution of social institutions, it had become the fashion to indulge in pseudoscientific attempts to transfer Darwin's ideas directly from biology to sociology, economics, and politics. Thus social Darwinist defenders of private business argued that government regulation was a dangerous tinkering with the process of natural selection and the survival of the fittest in free competition. But George pointed out that the railroad, which dominated business in California, had grown not by free competition but by monopoly; that it had been built mainly with government money; and that subsidies were a tremendous form of governmental intervention in the workings of a free economy.

In 1871, also, George published *Our Land and Land Policy,* a pamphlet of about a hundred pages in which he first outlined his general doctrine. Stressing the enormous withdrawals of public lands as grants to the railroads, he proposed that the ownership of these and all other lands should be returned to the people, by means of a single massive tax on land that would equal its rental value and thus have the effect of appropriating its ownership and income to the government. George argued that the earning power of all wealth consisted of wages, interest, and rent; that with the increasing productive power of labor and capital, rent tended to increase even more; and that this forced down both wages and interest. An end to private rent and to speculation in land would bring an end of industrial depressions and the maldistribution of wealth, would free business from all other forms of taxation, and indeed would cure virtually all the ills of society.

George opposed the ratifying of the new California constitution. It provided in article XVII, section 2 that "The holding of large tracts of land, uncultivated and unimproved, by individuals or corporations is against the public interest and should be discouraged," but this provision went on to say "by all means not inconsistent with the rights of private property." The last clause, George felt, would block the only reform that was truly essential. In his view, "private property in land is robbery."

George's doctrine appeared in elaborated form in 1879, in his *Progress and Poverty,* which became one of the phenomenal bestsellers of all time. By the turn of the century there were more than 5 million copies of his writings in circulation, and their influence abroad, particularly in England, was at least as great as in the United States. In 1886 George was nearly elected mayor of New York in a three-cornered race in which he received more votes than did Theodore Roosevelt. Both the devotion of his own followers and the tolerance accorded his ideas by the majority who disagreed with them were remarkable. He wrote with a personal sincerity and an intense love of mankind which no one could doubt, and he popularized what had been well called the dismal science of economics in words that often had not only the qualities of poetry but the fervor of religion. The single tax, he wrote, would bring "the Golden Age . . ., the culmination of Christianity—the city of God with its walls of jasper and its gates of pearl."

By later standards some of his ideas were illiberal. One of his early editorials justified lynching; he was opposed to labor organization and to strikes because he was sure he had a better solution; and he was extremely hostile to the Chinese, whom he considered a threat to free labor more dangerous than the Negro slave trade had ever been. On the other hand, he criticized the Kearneyites for overemphasizing Chinese exclusion and thus losing sight of the need for more fundamental social change. George's own dogma, of course, was open to the criticism that it exaggerated a single factor and offered a simple remedy.

The single tax was a naïve and emotional panacea. It has never been put into practice anywhere, partly because there have been too many landowners. Yet the idea and the man who advanced it still command respect for their part in stimulating popular thought about the problems of society.

Ambrose Bierce. Another major literary product of California journalism was Ambrose Gwinett ("Almighty God") Bierce, also known as "Bitter Bierce" and "The Wickedest Man in San Francisco." Though quite as vigorous as Henry George in criticizing things as they were, Bierce claimed to despise reform and reformers—one of the many paradoxes that characterized his personality.

The son of Marcus Aurelius Bierce, an unprosperous farmer who fathered 13 children and gave every one of them a name beginning with "A," Ambrose was born near Horse Cave Creek in a backwoods portion of southeastern Ohio. He was the tenth of the 13 children, and the last of them to survive through infancy. Though the family moved to a slightly better farming location in Indiana when he was four years old, the economic and emotional hardships of his early life contributed much to his permanent embitterment. In Bierce's parody the saccharine opening lines of "The Old Oaken Bucket,"

> How dear to this heart are the scenes of my childhood,
> When fond recollection presents them to view . . . ,

were soured into

> With what anguish of mind I remember my childhood,
> Recalled in the light of a knowledge since gained;
> The malarious farm, the wet, fungus-grown wildwood,
> The chills then contracted that since have remained.

Bierce welcomed the Civil War as an escape from his family, but four years of bloody action interrupted by only two furloughs, one of them necessitated by an almost fatal wound in the head, did nothing to sweeten his temperament. After the war he came to the Far West to take a commission in the Regular Army, then changed his mind because of the slowness of promotion in peacetime. In 1868 he was hired to take over the writing of a column called "The Town Crier" in the *San Francisco News Letter,* published by Frederick Marriott, an Englishman who was prosperously gratifying the Western reader's taste for satire, scandal, and the macabre. Bierce was ideally qualified for this kind of assignment, and his success in it encouraged him to write in the same ironic vein for the rest of his life.

In 1872 Bierce married Mollie Day, the beautiful daughter of a wealthy San Francisco family, and the bride's father paid for a honeymoon trip to England. Bierce remained there for four years, and would have liked to remain permanently. "America," he wrote, "is but a faint and stammering imitation of England." His first three books, collections of sketches from his columns under such titles as *Cobwebs from an Empty Skull,* were published in London. But his wife was so intensely homesick that she returned to San Francisco, and eventually persuaded him to join her. He returned with the greatest resentment and reluctance, and with the announcement of an intention "to purify journalism in this town by instructing such writers as it is worth while to instruct, and assassinating those it is not." He accomplished this purpose so well that he became the much-feared literary dictator of the Pacific Coast with his columns in the San Francisco *Argonaut,* then in the *Wasp,* and finally, after 1887, in young William Randolph Hearst's *Examiner.* He quarreled perennially with all his employers, beginning with the publisher of the *Argonaut,* for whom he suggested an epitaph: "Here lies Frank Pixley—as usual." "A rattlesnake," Bierce once wrote, "came home to its brood about to die—I have been bitten by the editor of a partisan journal, it said."

Bierce's short stories have often been compared to those of Edgar Allen Poe; but where Poe often resorted to the supernatural, the weird events in Bierce's narratives always had some sardonic but ostensibly rational explanation at the end. His best stories were those collected in *Tales of Soldiers and Civilians,* later published as *In the Midst of Life.* In "A Horseman in the Sky," for example, a Union soldier shot a mounted Confederate officer who had been observing the Union troop movements from the top of a cliff. Horse and rider dropped a great distance through the air like a falling equestrian statue. The rider was the soldier's own father, whom he had recognized but had been required by the circumstances to kill; the theme of parenticide frequently recurred in Bierce's writing.

Bierce's own experiences as a husband and father were disastrous and tragic failures. Toward women, who both frightened and enchanted him, he was outwardly contemptuous and patronizing. Two women writers were among his most perceptive critics. Gertrude Atherton, who sought his advice, said that his scorn for almost all novels grew out of his inability to write a novel of his own. Mary Austin's opinion was that he was "a man secretly embittered by failure to achieve direct creation," and that in his need for worshipful young protégés he was "seeking to make good in some other's gift what he had missed."

In *The Devil's Dictionary,* Bierce defined "BIRTH, n." as "The first and direst of all disasters," and he often argued that suicide was not only a right but almost a duty. His protégés, the poets George Sterling and Herman Scheffauer, both killed themselves in later years. And although the circumstances of Bierce's own demise have remained a mystery, it is clear that in 1913 when he planned to join the army of Pancho Villa as an "observer" he was seeking a death which he did not quite wish to inflict by his own hand. "Goodbye," he wrote to his niece, "if you hear of my being stood up against a Mexican stone wall and shot to rags please know that I think it a pretty good way to depart this life. It beats old age, disease, or falling down the cellar stairs. To be a Gringo in Mexico—ah, that is euthanasia!"

Bierce was a deeply tortured man, and he was never fully aware of the causes of his misery. For example, he made many efforts to find a climate that would relieve his lifelong sufferings from asthma; but he could not consider the possibility that the ailment was aggravated and partly caused by a form of interior weeping, from fear and pain too deep for outward tears.

Frank Norris. In contrast with Bierce, who regarded childhood as a disaster and the rest of life as not much better, Frank Norris attributed to his childhood much of his great talent for storytelling and much of his great enthusiasm for both real and fictional experience. The gifted novelist, Norris once wrote, was the man who retained the dramatizing imagination of a boy.

Benjamin Franklin Norris, Jr., was born in Chicago in 1870, of able and energetic parents. His father was a successful and wealthy jeweler who wanted his oldest son to join him in business, while his mother, who had been a successful actress before her marriage, wanted her sons to have artistic careers. When Frank was 14 the family moved to San Francisco, to a mansion on Sacramento Street west of Van Ness Avenue. At 17 he was sent to Paris to study art; but when he began to write stories instead, his father maintained that he was wasting his time and summoned him home. At 20 he enrolled in the University of California; but because he could not or would not pass the mathematics requirement, apparently as a part of his resistance to any preparation for business, he spent his four years at Berkeley as a special student and failed to graduate with his class in 1894. Having disliked the stylistic conformity which his English professors at Berkeley demanded, he spent a fifth collegiate year in a creative writing course at Harvard, where he worked on two stories of San Francisco, *McTeague* and *Vandover and the Brute.*

McTeague was much influenced by the works of Emile Zola, but it was the first important contribution to naturalism by an American writer and in this sense it was a pioneer novel, opening the way to modern American literature. Its hero was a charlatan dentist, and the story began in his office at Polk and California Streets, in a neighborhood which was only a few blocks from Norris's home, and which the novel described in vivid detail. McTeague married Trina, a girl who had won $5,000 in a lottery; but her cousin and jilted suitor took revenge by informing the authorities that the dentist was practicing without a license. Then the novel became a study of human degeneration, Trina's into miserliness and McTeague's into sadistic brutality. At last the ex-dentist murdered his wife, and her cousin pursued him into Death Valley where the two men died handcuffed together.

Vandover and the Brute had the same basic theme—a man's deterioration into the beast within him. A talented young artist, the story goes, neglected his gift and gave way to what Norris regarded as his own most dangerous vices, idleness and dissipation. In the end, Vandover's downward path went so far that he actually became a victim of lycanthropy, the delusion that he was a wolf.

Norris soon discovered that the naturalism of these works was too undiluted to permit the publication of either of them as a first novel at a time when the American reading public still demanded that fictional realism be highly romanticized. In search of further training and experience as a writer he joined the editorial staff of the San Francisco *Wave*. This journal had originated at Del Monte as an effort by Ben Truman of the Southern Pacific's publicity bureau to popularize the railroad's new luxury hotel. Transferred to San Francisco in a new format with the subtitle "A Weekly for Those in the Swim," the *Wave* was doing a remarkable job of surviving in competition with the *Overland* and the *Argonaut.* Norris's next novel, a rousing sea story called *Moran of the Lady Letty,* in which Moran was the first name of the hard-bitten heroine, was deliberately constructed as a potboiler and brought out serially in the *Wave* in the hope that some New York publisher might recognize its popular appeal. The hope was fulfilled. S. S. McClure, who kept an eye on the San Francisco journals for new writers, telegraphed an offer to publish *Moran* as a book and to employ Norris as a regular writer both of magazine short stories and of further novels. The publication of *McTeague* followed a few months later, in 1899, though *Vandover* would not be published until 12 years after its author's death.

Much encouraged by McClure's discovery of his work and promise, Norris conceived one of the most ambitious projects in the history of American literature, a trilogy to be called the "Epic of the Wheat." The first part would describe the growing of the wheat in California, the second its distribution by the board of trade or "pit" in Chicago, and the third its consumption in a famine-stricken village in Europe. Each of the three novels would have a central episode based on an actual occurrence, and the first, *The Octopus, a Story of California,* would center upon the battle of Mussel Slough. But Norris was not concerned with precise accuracy of historical detail; his intention was to tell the truth in what he regarded as a larger sense, including the greatest possible element of dramatic impact. Although in the course of his research he did apparently visit the town of Tulare, the Bonneville of *The Octopus,* he spent much more time on a 10,000-acre wheat ranch near Hollister, so that the locale described in the novel was not actually that of the San Joaquin Valley in 1880 but rather of a coastal valley in 1899, and the wheat growers were not the small farmers of the actual episode, but large ranchers. Consolidating his Californiana, Norris also transplanted a mission and a sleepy old Mexican town, based on San Juan Bautista, across the Coast Range and into a story in which they had had no actual part.

The Octopus also included a number of more basic inconsistencies. As a "novel with a purpose" it departed from Norris's goal of naturalistic objectivity and became in many of its passages a propagandistic tract for reform of the Trusts; it foreshadowed the Muckrakers, and indeed Norris was perceptibly influenced by the writers whom he met in the offices of *McClure's Magazine* and who would soon launch the Muckraking movement itself. Theodore Roosevelt read *The Octopus* as a tract, and remarked to a friend that apparently "conditions were worse in California than elsewhere." Another major contradiction was that in a novel which portrayed the ruin of the farmers and the victory of the railroad as a triumph of overwhelming and unmitigated evil, crying out for social reform, Norris introduced an allegory purporting to show the inevitable triumph of good in the forces of Nature, making efforts for reform unnecessary. Angèle, an innocent young girl, was raped and died in childbirth, but her child grew into a young woman as ideal as herself; so also the seeds of the wheat, corrupting in the earth, produced the beautiful, glorious bounty of the grain. Most critics have regarded this particular part of the story as a literary failure. Although *The Octopus* was a work of greater social and historical interest than

McTeague, as a piece of writing it was less carefully constructed and less finished. Yet it was and will remain one of the most important of American novels.

Although his stories contained many descriptions of dissolute conduct, Norris was a prude, with a desperate fear of anything sensual, and although he often wrote mystical praises of "the People," the lower and lower-middle classes, he was a snob, with strong biases of both class and race. He was anti-Oriental and anti-Semitic, and an admirer of Kipling's Anglo-Saxonism as well as of his literary style. Like most major writers, Norris was as contradictory and complicated as life itself, and he loved life to a degree that made his early death, at 32, of appendicitis, peculiarly sad. The trilogy was unfinished. *The Pit,* based on an actual attempt to corner the wheat market at Chicago, had degenerated into a conventional love story, and was appearing serially in the *Saturday Evening Post* at the time of his fatal illness. He had not begun the writing of *The Wolf,* which would have been the title of the third volume.

Jack London. Few men have risen to success through greater difficulties than did Jack London. He was an unwanted and illegitimate child, born in San Francisco in 1876, presumably the son of William H. Chaney, an itinerant Irish astrologer who denied paternity and whom he never saw. His mother secured a name for him by marrying John London, a kindly widower who gave his stepson what little feeling of stability there was in his earliest years. The boy grew up on the Oakland waterfront. At 15 he was an oyster pirate; at 17 he went to sea on one of the last seal-hunting voyages out of San Francisco Bay; and at 18, in 1894, he traveled to the East Coast and back as a hobo, with the excuse of being a member of the California contingent of Coxey's Army of unemployed. One of his hobo acquaintances introduced him to the *Communist Manifesto,* and his left-wing socialist opinions solidified after he returned to Oakland and experienced a series of cruelly hard and low-paying jobs, in which he worked for 60 hours a week in a jute mill, in a hand laundry, and at shoveling coal. For years he signed many of his personal letters "Yours for the Revolution."

After a few months at Oakland High School and a semester at the University of California, he joined the Klondike gold rush in 1897 and spent a year and a half in Alaska, where he discovered no gold but a great deal of material for the stories through which he hoped to make a living. His first publisher, the *Overland Monthly,* offered him $5 for a story of 5,000 words, and when even this small payment was slow in coming, he visited the office of the magazine and collected the amount in small change from the pockets of the assistant editor and the business manager, by threat of physical violence. But success came soon afterward. In 1900 S. S. McClure discovered London, as he had discovered Norris, and published London's first book, a collection of stories called

Son of the Wolf. Within a few years London was the highest-paid, best-known, and most popular writer in the world, displacing his hero Rudyard Kipling in the possession of these honors.

The Call of the Wild (1903), the most famous of London's many stories of the Far North, concerned a dog that was kidnaped in California and taken to Alaska where he reverted to savagery and ran with a wolf pack. There were several partly autobiographical novels, including *Martin Eden* (1909), and *John Barleycorn* (1913). And there were several novels or other works of socialist propaganda, the most important of which was *The Iron Heel* (1907). This story was especially striking in that it predicted the rise of fascism. On the whole, however, London's social and political ideas were little more than a jumble of Darwin, Spencer, Marx, and Nietzsche, and often his impressions of their works were based more on conversations with men who had read them than on the works themselves.

As his attempt to cross Marx's proletarianism with Nietzsche's Superman suggests, London's professions of socialism were out of tune with his own strongest feelings. His best writing was concerned not with hopes of an idealized collectivist society, but rather with the opposite theme of the triumph of some individual man or beast over more ordinary members of the respective species in some contest of wild and primordial violence. London's racism, moreover, was more extreme than either Kipling's or Norris's.

London was too emotionally insecure to be capable of happy marriage or of any other stable personal relationship. His second wife, Charmian Kittredge, lived in mortal terror that some other woman would take him away from her as easily as she had seduced him from his first wife, Bessie Maddern. Hoping to find security in a magnificent house, London spent more than $90,000 on a mansion of stone near Glen Ellen, but on the night before he was to have moved into it the interior of the house was destroyed by fire. There could be no doubt that the fire had been set deliberately, and the loss was intensified by the pain of speculating on the identity of the person who had hated him enough to do such a devilish thing to him. The alcoholism that had endangered his health for many years became progressively worse, and in 1916, at 40, in great pain from uremia, he ended his life, perhaps inadvertently, with an overdose of morphine. His career had symbolized the elemental power of humanity to struggle against tragedy and heartbreak, a struggle that was no less admirable because in his case the odds were too heavy to be overcome.

Poetry. In the second generation of American California, as in the first, no truly major poets appeared; but Joaquin Miller continued to bubble cheerfully on his hilltop; and George Sterling and Edwin Markham wrote poems of uneven quality but considerable fame.

George Sterling was descended from two old and distinguished families of

Sag Harbor, New York. As a young man he came to Oakland to be the secretary of his mother's brother, Frank C. Havens, who was about to become a millionaire in interurban railway and real estate development. But Sterling's urge to poetry interfered with his application to business, as did his friendship with Jack London, with whom he engaged in a sort of rake's progress through the San Francisco saloons. At the age of 22 Sterling met Ambrose Bierce, and fell so deeply under his influence that until Bierce's death 20 years later nearly every poem Sterling wrote was submitted to the master for criticism and correction.

Some have concluded that Sterling would never have become any sort of poet without the stimulation of Bierce's interest in him; but it is at least equally reasonable to maintain that Bierce's dominance over the whole of Sterling's early work was a tragedy, and that without that incubus Sterling would have been a much better poet than he was. Sterling's reputation remained merely local until 1907, when Bierce persuaded the editors of Hearst's *Cosmopolitan Magazine* to publish Sterling's "A Wine of Wizardry" along with an assurance by Bierce that it was one of the greatest works of literature ever written. The poem began with the quotation of some lines from one of Bierce's own poems, and the transparent egotism in Bierce's praise of it so irritated Eastern critics that they reacted with merciless ridicule. As a result, no volume of Sterling's poetry could find an Eastern publisher until long after Bierce's death.

Among Sterling's most memorable verses were the lyrics describing scenes at Carmel, where he made his home in 1908, and where his talent made him the leading figure in the artists' colony that was forming on the beautiful shores of Carmel Bay. In these years, before hard drinking made him fat and flabby, he bore a strong facial resemblance to Dante, of which he was not unaware.

His most often quoted lines, from "The City by the Sea," portrayed San Francisco, his "cool, grey city of love":

At the end of our streets is sunrise;
At the end of our streets are spars;
At the end of our streets is sunset;
At the end of our streets—the stars.

These lines, however, were far from representative of the style of his longer and more ambitious poems, which were marred by the use of archaic and otherwise unfamiliar names and by an addiction to "poetic diction." Such words as "ne'er" "afar," "thine," "'tis," and "'neath" alienated the poetic intelligentsia, while his love of obscure fantasy and his philosophy of pessimistic escapism alienated the more conventional reader. Several of the weakest and most artificial parts of Sterling's work were those that most reflected Bierce's influence. *Selected Poems* (1923) included most of Sterling's best verse.

In contrast with the Bohemianism of Sterling, Edwin Markham, an Oakland schoolteacher, was earnestly concerned for the reform of society. In 1898 Markham's poem "The Man with the Hoe," written after seeing Millet's painting, was read at a literary gathering that included Bailey Millard, then Sunday editor of William Randolph Hearst's *San Francisco Examiner.* Soon afterward the poem was published in the *Examiner* with much fanfare, after a campaign of preliminary advertising. The painting that had inspired it was owned by the Crocker family, and since they had graciously permitted the public to view it they were outraged when it was used as the basis for a piece of socialistic propaganda.

The poet Presley in Frank Norris's *The Octopus* was a composite character based in part upon Markham and in part upon Norris himself. Collis P. Huntington, who also appeared quite recognizably in *The Octopus,* had apparently made a considerable impression on Norris in an interview, by his comment that the painting was a better work of art than the poem that was written about it. But Huntington greatly weakened the force of this observation by offering a prize for another poem—one that would "answer" Markham.

Edward Rowland Sill, like Richard Henry Dana, was a New Englander who made a sea voyage to California for his health. A number of his poems and essays grew out of his walks in the Berkeley hills and on the Marin peninsula, and his poem "The Hermitage" described the feelings of a man who went to live alone on the slopes of Mt. Tamalpais. In the '70s and early '80s Sill was a professor of English at the University of California.

Historiography. Well before the end of the 19th century, California witnessed the carrying out of a truly remarkable project for the writing of its history, a project which in its unbounded ambitiousness was characteristic of the state itself. One day in 1859 Hubert Howe Bancroft, the most successful bookseller in San Francisco and in the whole of the West, happened to place together all the items in his store that dealt with the Pacific Coast. Such was the nucleus of the incomparable Bancroft Library. From collecting books, and later manuscripts, Bancroft progressed to the idea of bringing together the history that was in them. Calculating at one point that it would take him 400 years to read the whole of his collection, let alone to write a history from it, and being of a practical turn of mind, he employed a staff of assistants when the actual research and writing project began in 1871. The ablest of these was Henry L. Oak, a young graduate of Dartmouth College who was originally employed as librarian and who had no more formal training as a historian or experience as a writer than did Bancroft himself.

Few things even in California have grown as the Bancroft project grew. *Bancroft's Works,* published between 1882 and 1890, filled 39 fat and closely packed volumes. The native races of the Pacific States received five volumes, Central America three, and Mexico six; on California there were seven general chronological volumes and four others on special subjects; and the rest of the set covered the other parts of western North America. Bancroft himself was substantially the author of about one-fourth of these books. The others were written, as well as researched, by his assistants.

In all these *Works,* however, Bancroft most unwisely and unfortunately represented himself as the sole author; the assistants received no credit except in the 39th volume, called *Literary Industries,* in which Bancroft described the process of authorship in a most inadequate and misleading way. In the process of marketing the mammoth series, also, Bancroft resorted to devices that were highly questionable, though he himself did not consider them so. He secured a great claque of favorable reviews for the early volumes by making personal calls on dozens of famous authors in the East, and many purchasers whom his canvassers signed up at the beginning were not told what a large number of volumes they were contracting to buy. Finally, when the *Works* were followed in the early 1890's by the *Chronicles of the Builders of the Commonwealth,* originally projected as the "Chronicles of the Kings," and when it became known that in these enormously expensive vanity publications the length and tone of each biography was determined by the number of thousands of dollars subscribed by the biographee, there was a blast of public criticism that damaged Bancroft's reputation.

It came to be the general impression that what Collis P. Huntington was to California's economy, Hubert Howe Bancroft was to its historiography. They were, indeed, men of very similar outlook. For example, both felt that labor unions and the income tax were communistic devices by which those who did not accumulate anything were trying to obtain some of the savings of those who did. Huntington subscribed a large sum for the glowing 110-page biography of him that appeared in the *Chronicles of the Builders.* On the other hand, the biography of Leland Stanford, which had been fully prepared for publication, was omitted from the set because Stanford refused to make payment. When the *Works* had first begun to appear, Stanford had generously subscribed for 40 sets, under the impression that a full set would consist of five or six volumes. But after receiving and paying for 40 copies of each volume of the *Works* through the 23d, he canceled his subscription in an acid letter.

The five volumes on the general history of California to 1848 were written by Henry L. Oak. As a whole they were superior to the two volumes on the period 1848 to 1890, written mainly by two of Bancroft's other assistants, William Nemos and Frances Fuller Victor. And a comparison of Oak's writings with the volumes on California that were actually written by Bancroft (*California Pastoral, California Inter Pocula,* and *Popular Tribunals*), makes it clear that Oak was a better historian than his employer. Much in Oak's early volumes was ill-organized, overdetailed, and tedious; but especially in his volume on the period of the "conquest," 1846 to 1848, there were many passages of shrewd analysis and brilliant narrative. Bancroft's own historical style was florid, windy, and pontifical.

The great value of Bancroft's services to the history of western North

America lay not in his own contributions as a writer, but in the collection of materials and in the basic organization of a vast research project. These latter services were enormous and unique, and if he had tried to do much more of the research and writing himself the huge enterprise could never have been completed.

The failure to give credit to his writers was another matter. The explanation was that Bancroft was a businessman who regarded the *Works* as a product to be manufactured and sold. In *Literary Industries* he wrote: "Magnanimity . . . cuts no very great figure in business ethics. It seems that the good gold of commercial morals must have a reasonable alloy to make it wear. A certain amount of cold-blooded calculation, not to say downright meanness, is essential to business success." To Bancroft the idea of acknowledging or identifying the volumes or parts of the *Works* that were written by individual employees of his firm seemed to him as inappropriate as if the volumes had been packages containing any other commercial product. When Oak, having become a brooding invalid after 20 years of hard and anonymous labor, wrote an ineffectual protest, Bancroft replied: "I doubt that authors are in the habit of giving their employees any credit at all."

In making this statement Bancroft was quite unaware of its impropriety and irrelevance. Why later historians have failed to give proper credit to Oak for the authorship of the best volumes in the Bancroft history of California is harder to explain.

When the wealthy land-title lawyer Theodore H. Hittell wrote his own *History of California,* which was published in four volumes between 1885 and 1897, the extreme public criticisms of a number of Bancroft's methods had misled Hittell into supposing that there could be no value in any of *Bancroft's Works,* and he refused to consult them. Hittell's history was a good one; it could have been still better if he had not made this unfortunate misjudgment. John S. Hittell, brother of Theodore, was also an important pioneer of California historiography, especially in the documentation of the state's resources and economic development.

Not long after Josiah Royce had become a junior member of the philosophy department at Harvard, the publisher of a projected series of volumes on "American Commonwealths" selected him, as one of the most promising young men who had come to the East out of California, to write a volume on his native state. Royce obtained permission to use the Bancroft library, already far the largest and best collection of sources in the West. He also received much helpful advice from Oak. Royce's *California, from the Conquest in 1846 to the Second Vigilance Committee in San Francisco, a Study of American Character* (1886) took the form of an effort to establish the validity of the Hegelian dialectic of order and disorder, authority and freedom. In his later years at Harvard, Royce went on to become one of the leading American defenders of philosophical idealism.

SELECTED BIBLIOGRAPHY

The most essential sources for the study of writers are of course their own writings, many of which have been cited in the course of the chapter.

Charles A. Barker, *Henry George* (1955), is the standard work; the earlier biography by Henry George, Jr. (two volumes 1911) retains some interest. The best treatment of Bierce is Paul Fatout, *Ambrose Bierce, the Devil's Lexicographer* (1951); the biography by Carey McWilliams (1929) is lively but uncritical. Important writings on Frank Norris include the biography by Franklin Walker (1932); the studies by Ernest L. Marchand (1942), Warren French (1962), and Donald Pizer (1966); and Robert D. Lundy, "The Making of *McTeague* and *The Octopus*," Ph.D. thesis, University of California, Berkeley (1956). On the treatment of the battle of Mussel Slough by Norris and others, see the articles by Irving McKee, *Pacific Historical Review*, XVII (February 1948), 19–28, and James Lorin Brown, *ibid.*, XXVI (November 1957), 373–376. Joan London, *Jack London and His Times* (1939); Irving Stone, *Jack London: Sailor on Horseback* (1938); and Richard O'Connor, *Jack London* (1964), are biographies.

Lionel Stevenson, "George Sterling's Place in Modern Poetry," *University of California Chronicle*, XXXI (October 1929) 404–421, was a generous estimate. On Sill, consult Alfred R. Ferguson, *Edward Rowland Sill: the Twilight Poet* (1955).

On historiography see John W. Caughey, *Hubert Howe Bancroft* (1946); Harry Clark, "The Production, Publication, and Sale of the *Works* of Hubert Howe Bancroft," Ph.D. thesis, University of California, Berkeley (1969); Earl Pomeroy, "Josiah Royce, Historian in Search of Community," *Pacific Historical Review*, XL (February 1971), 1–20; Robert W. Righter, "Theodore H. Hittell and Hubert H. Bancroft," *California Historical Quarterly*, L (June 1971), 101–110; and Claude R. Petty, "John S. Hittell and the Gospel of California," *Pacific Historical Review*, XXIV (February 1955), 1–16.

Robert Louis Stevenson left some lively vignettes of Monterey and San Francisco and a charming memoir of the countryside where he spent his honeymoon on the slopes of Mount St. Helena, *The Silverado Squatters* (1883). James D. Hart, editor, *From Scotland to Silverado* (1966), includes all of Stevenson's writings about his trip to California.

Much information on both major and minor literary figures may be found in Gertrude Atherton, *Adventures of a Novelist* (1932); Mary Austin, *Earth Horizon* (1932); Franklin Walker, *San Francisco's Literary Frontier* (1939), *A Literary History of Southern California* (1950), and *The Seacoast of Bohemia* (1966); and Lawrence Clark Powell, *California Classics; the Creative Literature of the Golden State* (1971).

Chapter XXII

CULTURE AND OLIGARCHY: JOURNALISM, THE ARTS, AND EDUCATION

Lords of the press. In the later decades of the 19th century and the early years of the 20th, journalism in California's metropolis of San Francisco differed from that of the frontier days in that there came to be a smaller number of larger newspapers, owned and controlled by a few wealthy men.

Of the major San Francisco dailies destined to survive into the 20th century the oldest were the *Evening Bulletin,* founded in 1855, and the *Morning Call,* which dated from 1856. But these were ultimately outstripped in circulation and influence by two morning papers: the *Examiner,* which began as the weekly *Democratic Press* in 1863; and the *Chronicle,* founded as the *Daily Dramatic Chronicle* in 1865 by the brothers Charles and M. H. de Young.

One of the most striking developments in the whole colorful history of American newspapers was the rise of William Randolph Hearst, who was born in San Francisco in 1863, and took over the ownership and control of the *Examiner* in 1887, when he was less than 24 years old. George Hearst, his father, had bought the paper a few years earlier to advance his political ambitions. The elder Hearst was a self-trained mining engineer who had risen from poverty to a great fortune. Beginning with a tiny investment in the Ophir mine in Virginia City, he had gone on to develop the Homestake mine in South Dakota and the Anaconda silver and copper mines in Montana, and to expand his wealth still further with several huge ranches. In January 1887 a Democratic majority in the California legislature elected him to the United States Senate, and it was on March 4, the day he took his seat in Washington, that he made the gift of the *San Francisco Examiner* to his son.

A few months earlier, William Randolph Hearst had been expelled

Senator George Hearst. (Courtesy of the San Francisco Examiner)

from Harvard at the end of his junior year for indulging in an obscene expression of contempt for his professors. Since then he had worked as a reporter for Joseph Pulitzer's *New York World* in order to study Pulitzer's methods. These he would soon apply to the moribund little *Examiner* with many elaborations of his own and with spectacular results. If the *Examiner* had not passed from the elder to the younger Hearst, it might have suffered the fate of the *Alta,* which died in 1891, having spent its last years as the property and the political pawn of another Western mining-fortune Senator, James G. Fair of Nevada. But young Hearst quickly expanded the *Examiner* from four pages to eight, banished advertising from the front page in favor of headlines followed by sensational stories of crime and corruption, and brought in many special features for the reader's amusement. The term "yellow journalism" had its origin when Hearst hired away from Pulitzer the cartoonist of a popular early comic strip called "the Yellow Kid."

The originality of many of Hearst's methods has been exaggerated both by his critics and by his admirers. Not only Pulitzer and his *New York World,* but James Gordon Bennett half a century earlier in the *New York Herald,* had exploited the circulation-building possibilities of crime news and crusades for political reform. Nor was sensationalism anything new in the journalism of San Francisco; indeed, it was essentially the general brashness of early American California that was operating in the person of this scion of the new wealth of the Western mining frontier.

Hearst invested heavily in new printing equipment, especially for printing illustrations, and he went to unusual lengths with the "arranged story." If the news that actually happened was not lively enough, Hearst manufactured news that was. At the *Examiner's* expense a young couple were married in a balloon, and even, according to the *Examiner,* spent their honeymoon there—"up in the clouds." The real secret of Hearst's success was in his genius for spectacular entertainment. "The public," he wrote in an editorial in 1896, "is even more fond of entertainment than it is of information," and this philosophy of journalism became increasingly important in later years when he acquired an unprecedented number of newspapers in many cities, including the largest cities in the country. He maintained extraordinarily close control over the news and editorial policies of all his papers, and thus he had a greater influence on what was printed and read in America than any other man before or since.

No other California newspaperman acquired national influence comparable to Hearst's, but within the state there were several figures of regional importance.

In Sacramento the history of the *Bee* became synonymous with that of the McClatchy family, from the time when James McClatchy became editor in 1857, the year the *Bee* was founded. McClatchy had come from Ireland as a boy, and he brought an Irishman's hatred of land monopoly to his leadership of the squatters in the gold rush period and then to the *Bee's* editorial columns. At his death in 1883 the control of the paper passed to his son Charles ("C.K."), who was its fighting editor for nearly 50 years.

In Los Angeles, Harrison Gray Otis operated the *Times* from 1882 until his death in 1917. His influence on the institutional and cultural development of Southern California, and particularly on its labor problems, was so great that his career will be treated mainly in those contexts in later chapters.

Another outstanding personality was that of Fremont Older, editor of the *San Francisco Bulletin* from 1895. Unlike most of the other major figures in the journalistic world of the period, Older was not a publisher engaged in building up a large fortune, but lived on an editor's salary and achieved his remarkable influence unaided and unhampered by personal wealth. His career will be described as a part of the struggle for political reform in San Francisco.

The arts and architecture. As in most other times and places that have produced any considerable flourishing of art, there were many painters who, as the San Francisco critic Porter Garnett once remarked, were able to "represent" California but not to "present" or "express" it—painters who were mechanically deft but not creative, and whose work thus bore "no closer relation to art than good handwriting has to literature." There were also, however, some artists of a higher order.

The outstanding painter of pioneer life in California was Charles Christian Nahl. Born into a family that had achieved artistic distinction in Germany for

"Sunday Morning in the Mines." A painting by Charles Nahl. (Courtesy of the E. B. Crocker Art Gallery, Sacramento)

six generations, Nahl came to California with his half brother Hugo in 1850 and was soon the leading producer of lithographs for letter sheets, the famous souvenir stationery on which the miners wrote home the news from the goldfields. After Judge E. B. Crocker became his patron in 1867, Nahl was able to devote the greater part of his time to his work in oils, and a number of his paintings were included in the Crocker Art Gallery in Sacramento. Probably the best of these, and certainly the best known, was his "Sunday Morning in the Mines," which appears badly overcrowded with figures and detail in small reproductions but less so in the original, a canvas 9 feet long and 6 feet high.

Thomas A. Ayres became famous as the first artist to portray the Yosemite. James H. Hutchings, having read a newspaper account of the expedition of Maj. James D. Savage in 1851, and wisely anticipating that pictures of such spectacular scenery would strengthen the appeal of his forthcoming illustrated magazine, employed Ayres in 1855 to accompany him and others in the first tourist party ever to enter the valley. In 5 days Ayres produced five drawings, one of which, "The High Falls," has scarcely been excelled among the thousands of later efforts.

Albert Bierstadt and Thomas Hill were among the many who later painted the Yosemite and other California landscapes. The most intriguing work of Hill, however, was his attempt to provide the ultimate commemoration of the transcontinental railroad in his "Driving the Last Spike." Leland Stanford had

Yosemite Falls. A charcoal sketch by Thomas Ayres. (From the Honeyman Collection, Bancroft Library)

commissioned this painting and promised $50,000 for it; such, at least, was Hill's impression. But after the artist had spent 4 years at work on the huge and elaborate canvas, Stanford refused to buy it and denied that he had ordered it. His most vocal objection was that some 70 officials of the Union and Central Pacific Railroads were in the massive picture, very few of whom had actually been present at the scene; even Judah, who had died six years previously, was included. In somewhat the same mood in which he broke relations with Hubert Howe Bancroft, Stanford stood foursquare against contractual imposture, and in favor of historical accuracy. It was also true, however, that relatives of Charles Crocker strongly objected to the prominent position occupied by Stanford at the center of Hill's picture, and that Stanford's repudiation of the painting tended to restore the peace in the railroad family.

Scottish-born William Keith, whose active career extended from the 1860s until his death in 1911, attained greater prestige than any other California artist. His early paintings of the Sierra country were done with almost photographic

"Driving the Last Spike." A painting by Thomas Hill. (Courtesy of the Bancroft Library)

Scene at Promontory, Utah, May 10, 1869. Note the contrast with Hill's idealized painting. (Courtesy of the Bancroft Library)

realism; but his maturity and his success came when, much to the disappointment of his close friend John Muir, he turned from the high mountains to pastoral landscapes of the foothills, done with a highly mystical quality. In his later years Keith often painted from memory in his studio in San Francisco. His home was in Berkeley, and some of his best paintings were of scenes among the great oaks on the University of California campus.

Much encouragement to younger California artists came from the San Francisco Art Association, founded in 1871, and, in the South, from the California Art Club, with William Wendt as its leading spirit. Wendt came to Los Angeles in 1908 and was soon the outstanding landscape painter of Southern California, best known for his "Land of Heart's Desire." The work of Charles F. Lummis in the development of the Southwest Museum at Los Angeles was of more enduring value than any of his extensive writings.

The best California sculptor of the period was probably Ralph Stackpole, whose busts of several well-known San Franciscans were excellent portraits in stone. Greater popular acclaim, however, went to the attitudinized athletic figures by Douglas Tilden, such as the five men operating an antique drill press in the sculpture created for the "Mechanics' Monument" at Market and Bush Streets in San Francisco.

In the field of music, San Francisco had heard its first grand opera as early as February 12, 1851, when the Pellegrini opera troupe presented Bellini's *La Sonnambula* at the Adelphi Theater. But throughout the 19th century, traveling performers from the East continued to outshine the local talent, both in music and in drama.

In architecture, regional developments were somewhat more distinctive. On the other hand, "California mission architecture" has as much interest for the history of mythmaking as for the history of architecture. Charming legends to the contrary, the roof tiles were not shaped on the thighs of Indian women; the designs for the California mission buildings added nothing to the older Mexican models; and the missions had had no effects on the miserably crude architecture of the California presidios, pueblos, and ranchos. As for the so-called "Monterey colonial" style, introduced by Thomas Larkin in the 1830s, it was adapted from buildings he had seen in Massachusetts and North Carolina, and nothing about it was either Spanish-colonial or Mexican-republican except the use of adobe as the handiest material for the walls. What would pass in the 20th century as "mission" and "Monterey colonial" influences were mainly products of fond imagination.

The availability of redwood in the American period gave San Francisco in the late 19th century a larger proportion of wood frame residential buildings than any other city in the nation. Redwood became so common that there were many attempts to use paint to disguise it as stone, and the wooden house of David D. Colton on Nob Hill was even painted to simulate an Italian marble palace. Even so, the Colton house was a less offensive monument to conspicuous and meretricious waste than were the neighboring mansions of Crocker, Stan-

Post card showing California Street cable car and Nob Hill mansions. (Courtesy of the Bancroft Library)

The Hopkins mansion on San Francisco's Nob Hill. (Courtesy of the Bancroft Library)

ford, and the rest. Beauty was regarded as deriving from ornamentation rather than from any genuine architectural function, and there was a profusion of jigsaw carpentry on porches and of ironwork on mansard roofs. In the construction of public buildings the era is notorious for the tendency of architects to try to build monuments to themselves rather than to design structures that would effectively serve the purposes for which they were intended.

Schools, colleges, and universities. The development of a sense of public responsibility for education in California in the 19th century was slow, lagging far behind the growth of the state's economic resources and population. Not until 1874, when the legislature passed "an act to enforce the educational rights of children," did the state adopt compulsory education, and even then, although it applied only to the elementary level, the law was bitterly opposed on the grounds that it was un-American, that it interfered with the liberty of parents, and that it was an arrogation of new power by the government. As for public secondary education, there were only 16 high schools in the state in 1879, and several of them were wiped out by the provision of the new constitution that denied state tax funds to high schools on the ground that the primary and grammar schools were still inadequately supported—which was all too true. Some wealthy and influential men denounced any measure requiring them to pay taxes for the education of other people's children. Opposition came, Edward Rowland Sill complained, "from the aristocrat, who is very willing that the intelligence as well as the wealth of his family shall rise conspicuous over the common herd below; . . . from the demagogue, whose trade depends on the existence of an unlettered and pliable constituency; [and] from bitter sectarians."

In its provisions for elementary school textbooks California was somewhat more enterprising. In 1875, as a result of charges of corruption and collusion between local school board members and booksellers, an act of the legislature forbade excessively frequent changes in the books required. And by a constitutional amendment approved by the voters in 1884, California became the first state to provide that a uniform series of elementary school textbooks approved by the state board of education should be published by the state printing office. At first these books were sold, though at a very considerable saving in price; beginning in 1912, by state constitutional amendment, they would be distributed free.

Slow development of high schools made it inevitable that the growth of an effective demand for colleges would be even slower. For many years after colleges were opened they would have to maintain "preparatory departments," in which most of their very limited numbers of students were enrolled.

Twenty years elapsed between the enthusiastic predictions of Robert Semple in the constitutional convention at Monterey and the actual opening of the University of California, with 38 students, in the fall of 1869. In the meantime, the private enterprise of religious leaders had taken the responsibility for lighting the torch of higher education. Even before the Monterey convention adjourned in the fall of 1849 a group of Congregational and Presbyterian ministers had held a meeting in San Francisco to plan a New England-style college in California, to be organized and maintained "under the spirit and influence of the Christian religion," though interdenominational, and not under the control of any one sect. This project first took shape as the Contra Costa Academy, a "family boarding school for boys," opened in Oakland in 1853. The institution was incorporated as the College of California in 1855, though it continued to function only as a preparatory school until 1860, when it enrolled its first freshman class. In the history of higher education, as this example indicates, chronology is not an exact science, for there is often a lack of agreement as to which step constituted the "founding" of a college.

Had it not been for the Morrill Act of 1862, in which the Federal government offered land-grant endowments to the states for agricultural colleges, California would have delayed even longer than it did in establishing a state university. It was in order to secure the Federal land-grant endowment that the California legislature in 1866 issued a charter for an "Agricultural, Mining, and Mechanic Arts College."

Fortunately the attitude of the sponsors of the interdenominational College of California toward state higher education was in refreshing contrast to the fear and hostility that still marked the attitudes of most officials of private colleges throughout America, especially those organized under religious auspices. The trustees of the College of California offered to turn over their entire property to the state, to be merged with the proposed agricultural college into a state university. That the private college was dangerously mired in debt was a factor in the trustees' decision; but their offer included a magnificant tract of land north of Oakland, to which they had acquired title and to which they had planned to move their own institution. There they had already laid out the adjoining town lots and named the future community for Bishop George Berkeley, the Irish philosopher whose hopes of founding a college in colonial New England had once led him to write a poem "On the Prospect of Planting Arts and Learning in America," a poem including the words "Westward the course of empire takes its way. . . ."

When it became likely that the state would accept the offer from the College of California, John W. Dwinelle, a scholarly land-title lawyer and one of the college's trustees, was elected to the state legislature and introduced the bill that became the charter of the University of California on March 23, 1868, superseding the agricultural college's charter adopted two years earlier.

Throughout the 19th century it was difficult to attract eminent scholars to the faculty of any institution in the Far West, including the University of California. Daniel Coit Gilman remained as president for only three years before Johns Hopkins lured him back to the East. But a few able men did come to stay. Joseph LeConte, biologist and philosopher, won admiration with his writings and lectures on "evolutional idealism," in which he reconciled Darwinian theory with belief in God. Eugene W. Hilgard began the process of building the college of agriculture into a great institution of applied scientific research.

Through his ability to convince the farmers of the practical value of that research, he succeeded in quieting some of their chronic suspicions that the Morrill Act endowment was being frittered away on a merely literary college. In 1899 the regents brought Benjamin Ide Wheeler to the presidency from a professorship of Greek at Cornell, and for nearly 20 years, in the heyday of the "strong president" system in American higher education, Wheeler was the university's benevolent despot. During this period Henry Morse Stephens popularized history not only to a generation of students but also in many public lectures throughout the state, and Charles Mills Gayley and his "great books" course, which preceded the more famous enterprise at the University of Chicago by 30 years, drew classes so large that they sometimes had to be held outdoors in the Greek Theater, a gift of William Randolph Hearst.

Leland Stanford, from the time of his rise to affluence, periodically contemplated the making of some generous gift to the people of California. In 1882 he hinted strongly that he intended to do something for the struggling young state university, and Republican Governor George C. Perkins nominated him to fill an unexpired term on its board of regents. But early the next year the state senate, now controlled by the Democrats, indicated that it would not confirm the appointment, and at Stanford's own request his name was withdrawn.

No one knows whether this episode had any decisive influence on Stanford's action in founding a new private university instead of making a gift to the existing public one. The more directly relevant facts were that Leland Stanford and Jane Lathrop Stanford had been childless for the first 18 years of their marriage, until the birth of Leland, Junior; that their son occupied a very central place in their lives; and that in 1885, when he was less than 16 years old, he died. Within the same year, the parents who had lost their only child founded a university which would bear his name, and in which, as they put it, the children of California would become the foster children of their love. For the Leland Stanford Junior University they promised not only their large and beautiful stock farm at Palo Alto, as a campus, but also the bulk of their fortune.

During their long and careful search for a president, Daniel Coit Gilman told them of a distinguished biologist, David Starr Jordan, then president of Indiana University. Although Jordan had recently stated the opinion that the future of American higher education lay with the state universities, he agreed to come to Stanford, and he set it on its course toward the point at which loyal alumni would describe Stanford as "the Harvard of the West"—and Harvard as "the Stanford of the East."

At the outset there were many expressions of doubt that California needed or could successfully maintain two universities within 50 miles of each other. But in 1891, when Stanford opened, the enrollment was 559 (including a young man named Herbert Hoover), and there were nearly twice as many at Berkeley. Ten years later the enrollments at both institutions had more than doubled, and nearly 10 percent were graduate students.

The 1890s were a turning point; ever since then the active demand for higher educational facilities in California has exceeded the supply. One vital factor was the state law of 1891, which authorized the establishment of a high school by approval of the voters of any city or incorporated town of more than 1,500 people, and of a union high school by any two or more districts, the curricula to be such as to prepare the students for the university.

Of the colleges founded by the various Protestant denominations, the majority began as "church controlled" and were later described as "church related and supported"; several of them eventually became independent. The University of the Pacific, begun by the Methodists as an academy at San Jose in 1851, was moved to Santa Clara, and ultimately reestablished at Stockton in 1924. The Methodists also founded the University of Southern California, in 1879. Occidental College was established by the Presbyterians in 1887, and Pomona College by the Congregationalists in the same year. The Quakers founded Whittier College in 1901, and the Baptists established Redlands in 1909.

Of the Catholic institutions, the Jesuit Universities of Santa Clara and San Francisco date from schools opened in the 1850s, and St. Vincent's College, in Los Angeles, chartered in 1869, became Loyola University. St. Mary's College, growing out of a school established by Archbishop Alemany in San Francisco in 1863, was placed under the administration of the Christian Brothers, moved to Oakland, and relocated in 1928 in Moraga Valley.

Most of the institutions other than the Catholic ones were coeducational. The oldest women's college in the West was opened as a young ladies' seminary in Oakland in 1871, by Dr. and Mrs. Cyrus T. Mills, and chartered as Mills College in 1885, on a nonsectarian basis.

SELECTED BIBLIOGRAPHY

Journalism in California (1915), by John P. Young, managing editor of the *San Francisco Chronicle* for more than 40 years, was originally written to celebrate the 50th anniversary of that newspaper. John Roberts Bruce, *Gaudy Century; the Story of San Francisco's Hundred Years of Robust Journalism* (1948), is gaudier and less useful on the later than on the early period. The *History of Journalism in San Francisco* (seven volumes, 1939–1941, mimeographed), by the California Writers' Program of the WPA, though not actually a general history of its subject and not always accurate in details, includes much information on a number of special aspects. Of the several biographies of Hearst, those by Cora B. Older (1936) and John K. Winkler (1928, 1955), were almost as indulgent toward their subject as were his own parents; Edmond D. Coblentz, *William Randolph Hearst, a Portrait in His Own Words* (1952), is a useful anthology; the best general treatment to date is W. A. Swanberg, *Citizen Hearst* (1961), its title suggested by Orson Welles's remarkable film, "Citizen Kane" (1940). James R. Wotherspoon, "The San Francisco *Argonaut,* 1877–

1907," Ph.D. thesis, University of California, Berkeley (1962), deals with the most important of the weeklies. Robert Davenport, "San Francisco Journalism in the Time of Fremont Older," Ph.D. thesis, University of California, Los Angeles (1969), is valuable, as are Fremont Older, *My Own Story* (1926), and Jerome A. Hart, *In Our Second Century* (1931). On Los Angeles journalism see Richard Connelly Miller, "Otis and His *Times*," Ph.D. thesis, University of California, Berkeley (1961); Edwin Bingham, *Charles F. Lummis, Editor of the Southwest* (1955); and the autobiography of *William Andrew Spalding, Los Angeles Newspaperman* (1961), edited by Robert V. Hine.

Art in California (1916), including essays by Bruce Porter, Porter Garnet, Bernard Maybeck, and others, was an illustrated survey of California painting, sculpture, and architecture as represented at the Panama-Pacific International Exposition. The *Monographs* of the California Art Research Project (20 volumes, mimeographed, 1937) include accounts of about fifty California artists, mostly painters, who made their residence chiefly in San Francisco; though far from being an adequate history of art in California, this series was an interesting preliminary effort in that direction. Other useful works include the *California Centennials Exhibition of Art* (1949); Carl O. Borg and Millard Sheets, *Cross, Sword, and Gold Pan* (1936); "Thomas A. Ayres, Artist-Argonaut of California," *California Historical Society Quarterly*, XX (September 1941), 275–279, by Jeanne S. Van Nostrand; "Charles Christian Nahl, the Painter of California Pioneer Life," *California Historical Society Quarterly*, XV (December 1936), 295–305, by Eugen Neuhaus, himself a distinguished painter and teacher of art; and, also by Neuhaus, *William Keith, the Man and the Artist* (1938), and *History and Ideals of American Art* (1931). Brother Fidelis Cornelius, *Keith, Old Master of California* (two volumes, 1942–1956), includes hundreds of reproductions.

Edmond M. Gagey, *The San Francisco Stage, a History* (1950), is based on annals compiled by the Research Department of the San Francisco Federal Theatre. Constance Rourke, *Troupers of the Gold Coast* (1928), is concerned mainly with Lotta Crabtree.

Harold Kirker, *California's Architectural Frontier: Style and Tradition in the Nineteenth Century* (1960), is an important social history. See also Porter Garnett, *Stately Homes of California* (1915).

William Warren Ferrier, *Ninety Years of Education in California, 1846–1936* (1937), is valuable for the early decades, though less so for the period after 1900. Verne A. Stadtman, *The University of California, 1868–1968* (1970), is an excellent centennial history. Other centennial publications of the state university are cited below for Chapter XXXVI. On the rise of Stanford University, see Edward M. Burns, *David Starr Jordan, Prophet of Freedom* (1953); and Jordan's own prolific writings, such as *California and the Californians* (1907), and *The Days of a Man* (two volumes, 1922). Joseph Dorfman, *Thorstein Veblen and His America* (1934), and R. L. Duffus, *The Innocents at Cedro* (1944), describe Veblen's years at Stanford.

Chapter XXIII

ECONOMIC GROWTH

THE INCREASE of wealth in California in the late 19th century and the early 20th was substantial, but it was far from being an orderly process. Neither the people of California nor those of the United States had yet learned to exert any significant degree of control over the violent fluctuations of the regional and national economies. The '80s were relatively prosperous, but the panic of 1893 led to another depression so severe that the growth of California's population in the '90s was a mere 22.4 percent—the lowest rate for any decade between the 1830s and the 1930s.

The turn of the century, however, coincided with the beginning of a new cycle in which the growth of Northern California was impressive and that of Southern California truly phenomenal.

The wheat bonanza. The droughts that had ruined the cattle industry in the early 1860s were followed by a series of rainy winters, and beginning with the crop year 1866–1867 the generous rainfall made possible a full discovery of the potentialities of the Sacramento and San Joaquin Valleys for the growing of wheat without irrigation. It was an ideal crop for the wide, flat valley lands in a time of distant markets and a sparse rural population with limited capital, and for about 30 years, from the early 1860s until the panic of 1893, wheat was California's largest and most profitable agricultural commodity.

The largest wheat grower in the state was Dr. Hugh J. Glenn, who had a medical degree from the University of Missouri, but who occupied himself after 1867 with buying land on credit until he had 55,000 acres, extending for 20 miles along the west bank of the Sacramento River, where he ultimately produced more than half a million bushels a year. His mammoth wheat ranch was in Colusa County; in 1891, after his death, his achievements were memorialized in the creation of Glenn County. The title of "Wheat King" was disputed between Dr. Glenn and Isaac Friedlander, who was also a large landowner but whose greatest importance was as middleman. Friedlander speculated in the chartering of ships to carry California wheat to its most important market at Liverpool, and by repeatedly cornering the available shipping he built up a great fortune, until he overextended himself and went into bankruptcy.

Wheat ranching was a highly speculative enterprise. It also became increasingly mechanized, and one of the most significant aspects of the age of wheat in the great Central Valley of California lay in its contributions to the development of agricultural machinery. The old walking plow, known as the "foot burner," with its single plowshare, was replaced by the "Stockton gang plow," which had several shares attached to a beam, moved on wheels, and was adjustable in width and depth. In the scene made famous in Frank Norris's *Octopus,* there were 35 such plows in echelon formation, each with five plowshares and drawn by 10 horses. At the Glenn Ranch plowing was often done with as many as a hundred gang plows at once, each drawn by an eight-mule team. The Central Valley also produced new machines for planting, pulverizing the earth, and spreading it over the seed in one operation, as well as improvements of the earlier machines to combine the cutting and threshing of the grain. The flat lands and dry summers of the valley made it possible to use the largest steam-powered "combined harvesters" in the world, machines so large and heavy that they required 36 horses to move them. The need for mechanical motive power led directly to the invention of the tractor, first used in the San Joaquin Valley with steam power in 1886. Later Benjamin Holt of Stockton and others would adapt the tractor to the internal combustion engine and develop the "caterpillar" track.

The dry farming of wheat had the peculiar disadvantages of a one-crop agricultural economy. It was a kind of soil mining, ruthlessly carried on year after year without fertilizer or rotation, and inevitably the soil was exhausted and the yields declined. The average farm was large, bleak, and ugly. Fruit and vegetables came only from cans, purchased along with other food supplies at the grocery store in town. Wheat as a dominant crop began to decline in the middle 1880s under competition from the Mississippi Valley and from Russia, and it collapsed in the depression of the '90s. The spread of irrigation had also begun to make wheat less profitable than other California farm products.

Wines. The growing of grapes and the manufacture of the fermented juice into wine had their beginnings in California at the missions, for sacramental purposes and for the personal use of the mission fathers; but though the vines were hardy, the mission grapes and the processes of manufacture were of poor quality. Commercial production also began in Southern California. Jean Louis Vignes, a most appropriately named vintner from the region of Bordeaux, brought cuttings from France to a vineyard on the site of the Los Angeles Union Station in the early 1830s, and William Wolfskill established another vineyard nearby a few years later.

After the discovery of gold the center of grape and wine production shifted to the valleys around San Francisco Bay; and in the 1850s the Hungarian exile Agoston Haraszthy began the work that made him the father of the modern California wine industry, especially at his Buena Vista estate in the Sonoma Valley, purchased in 1857. In 1861 the state legislature appointed him a commissioner to report on means of improving the industry, and in this capacity he toured the wine regions of Europe and returned with 200,000 cuttings and rooted vines, representing 1,400 varieties. In the meantime the success of the cooperative community at Anaheim, a German wine colony 26 miles southeast of Los Angeles, founded in 1857, had also become an important factor in the industry's growth.

In the 1870s and 1880s the California vineyards were nearly wiped out by the phylloxera, a tiny insect species resembling plant lice or aphids, and the ravages of this pest were brought under control only by discovering resistant stocks and by gradually replanting the vineyards with them. In spite of this and other temporary setbacks the industry flourished, largely by a process of fusing a great number of varieties of European vines and winemaking skills. Vineyards spread through the Sonoma, Napa, Santa Clara, and Livermore Valleys. The climate and soils of the Central Valley were also found to be highly favorable, particularly for dessert wines, table grapes, and raisins; and ultimately the greatest of all concentrations of vineyards in California would be in Fresno County. In 1900 California produced 19 million gallons of wine, more than 80 percent of the nation's output.

The citrus industry. Like the mission grape, the mission orange was not of very good quality. It was thick-skinned, pithy, and often sour. William Wolfskill and a few others operated orange groves in the Los Angeles area in the 1850s and 1860s with mission stock and a few slightly better varieties from Hawaii and Sicily, but production was small and the market even smaller. The more significant beginnings of the California orange industry came with three new developments of the 1870s. These were the discovery that oranges grew better on lands that were slightly higher and out of the coastal fog belt, the introduction of the navel orange from Brazil, and the advent of the railroad.

In 1870 J. W. North and his associates purchased the lands of a defunct silk colony on the Rancho Jurupa near what would soon be the town of Riverside, began an irrigation canal from the Santa Ana River, and planted orange groves. Three years later, Luther C. Tibbetts and his wife Eliza, members of the Riverside group, obtained two of the dozen budded trees which the first American Protestant missionary at Bahia, Brazil, had sent to the Department of Agriculture at Washington. Within a remarkably short time the large, sweet, seedless Bahia navels were in production in the groves of the Tibbetts and others under the name of "Riverside navels." But the growers who established a number of new communities in emulation of Riverside, and with stock obtained from it, did not wish to contribute to its advertising; they again changed the popular name, this time to the "Washington navel." Substantial rail shipments to St. Louis and Chicago were under way before the end of the '70s, and in the next decade, with the development of refrigerator cars, rail shipments were increased in volume and extended to the Atlantic Coast. The great citrus belt of Southern California was in process of rapid formation.

The menace of the cottony cushion scale, a pest introduced from Australia in 1868, was overcome 23 years later by the introduction of its natural enemy, the Australian ladybird beetle. Use of the summer-ripening Valencia orange, along with the winter-ripening Brazilian navels, made possible a year-round output. Moreover the Valencias flourished nearer the coast, and with their increasing introduction in the early 20th century the citrus belt extended from Santa Barbara to San Diego and from Pasadena to Riverside. Southern California became responsible for more than two-thirds of the nation's production of oranges and more than 90 percent of its lemons.

The early development of the marketing of citrus fruits involved many difficulties, of which some were peculiar to the industry and the region and others were general problems of American agricultural marketing under the primitive and chaotic conditions of the time. The period from 1869 to the end of the century was one of serious decline in American agricultural prices because of expanding production, deflated currency, and the farmer's weak position in bargaining. He seldom had enough information about the market to know what a fair price would be, and speculators took every possible advantage of his ignorance. The markets for citrus fruits and other California specialty crops were from 2,000 to 3,000 miles away, and they were developing only gradually. With many growers and packers sending haphazard shipments, prices were so erratic that the commission merchants demanded the use of the consignment system, under which the growers bore all the risk. Sometimes the anxious shipper of a carload of fruit would receive nothing but a bill and the information that the arrival of other shipments on the same day had so glutted the market that the price received was insufficient to pay the freight and handling charges. It was often suspected and frequently established that the commission handlers reported the Eastern prices falsely, and California citrus growers formed the opinion that the commission merchant was a greater menace to their prosperity than frost or the cottony cushion scale. The answer was the cooperative marketing organization, in which the California fruit growers eventually achieved a stunning success.

In the 1870s the efforts of the wheat farmers to use the Granges as marketing and purchasing cooperatives had been dismal failures, largely because of visionary ideas and lack of business experience. A typical Granger resolution had said that the farmers did not hate the middlemen, but simply considered them unnecessary. Actually, of course, the marketing function was a highly specialized one, requiring great skill, knowledge, and diligence. The successful cooperative had to find and employ men who could bring a high degree of organization into the marketing process.

In an effort to combat the speculators who controlled the citrus market in the early years, an Orange Growers' Protective Union of Southern California was formed in 1885. The middlemen succeeded in crushing this effort by forming combinations of their own, dividing the territory into districts and refusing to buy at all except on the harshest terms. Then, however, the middlemen became so autocratic that the desperate growers were forced into stronger attempts to form cooperatives and to do their own packing and marketing. Another Orange Growers' Union was formed in 1891, and reorganized as the Southern California Fruit Exchange in 1893. After oranges had begun to be grown in important quantities as far north as Oroville and Chico, Central California growers joined the organization, and in 1905 the new name of California Fruit Growers' Exchange reflected this broadened membership. The organization was so successful that its brand name, "Sunkist," finally became almost synonymous with "California oranges and lemons" in popular usage, and in 1952 its name was officially changed to Sunkist Growers, Inc.

The nonprofit methods of the grower-owned cooperative exposed it to specious charges of being anticapitalistic. As the cooperative system took root in several other fields of agriculture, including deciduous fruits, raisins, walnuts, and dairy and poultry products, many of the private middlemen frantically denounced the whole cooperative marketing idea as sheer communism. On the other hand, one of the ablest leaders of the California Fruit Growers' Exchange, Charles C. Teague of Santa Paula, described it as a "federated democracy." The growers were organized in local packing associations; these elected the directors of district exchanges, who in turn elected the directors of the central board.

The democracy, of course, extended only to the "growers," not to the unorganized and disfranchised people who did the physical work. The citrus industry was built on cheap alien labor, first mainly Chinese and later Japanese and Mexican.

The remarkable economic achievements of the citrus growers were due in part to the fact that many of them were "gentlemen farmers," men who had acquired considerable capital before they were attracted to California to enter this particular industry. They called themselves "growers" to dissociate themselves from the rustic clumsiness and ignorance which they felt to be implied by the word "farmer." In later decades California agriculture in general would become so successfully commercialized that the word "agriculture" itself would begin to be replaced by the new term "agribusiness."

Booms in real estate. Through the 1870s the main movement of population into California was confined to its north central parts. From the next decade onward, however, Southern California grew at a more rapid rate than did the North.

The first Southern California real estate boom, a very modest one, occurred between 1868 and 1876. After the droughts that wiped out the livestock of the region, Abel Stearns narrowly escaped the sale of his 200,000 acres of land in the San Gabriel and Santa Ana valleys for $4,000 in delinquent taxes. He was saved from utter financial ruin when a group of San Francisco capitalists led by Sam Brannan purchased his ranches and began in 1868 to subdivide them into 40-acre tracts. Having bought the land at distress prices, the Brannan syndicate netted more than $2,000,000 from this investment.

Along with the spread of the citrus industry, a special factor in this early boom was the "health rush" to Southern California which began about 1870. That the climate of the area was helpful in curing tuberculosis was actually a sad delusion, but the physicians of the time encouraged thousands of invalids and their families to believe it, and Southern California newspaper editors and other boosters proclaimed its truth. By 1900, after medical theory had generally abandoned the idea, its influence declined, though a myriad of other health fads continued to flourish.

On the other hand, not all the claims for the health-giving effects of the climate, and especially for its year-round mildness and greater incidence of sunshine, could be discredited. David Starr Jordan pronounced with the scientific authority of a recognized biologist and educator that "California college girls, of the same age, are larger by almost every dimension than are the college girls of Massachusetts. They are taller, broader-shouldered, thicker-chested (with ten cubic inches more lung capacity), have larger biceps and calves, and a superiority of tested strength." This description was not inappropriate to the young ladies of a state which had received its name from that of a legendary land ruled by Amazons.

The superior potential of California for agriculture was also widely advertised, though the reports of squashes and melons so large they had to be picked on horseback led to counterpropaganda from other parts of the country to the effect that California farmers spent more time in exaggeration than in cultivation. A newspaper editor in Jackson, Mississippi, wrote that "California is a state of mind—exaltation is in the atmosphere. Birds of gorgeous plumage flit through the trees but they have no song. Flowers astound in size, gorgeous color, and infinite variety, but they have little perfume." If this writer had also asserted that the grapes, though beautiful, were sour, it could scarcely have been more obvious that envy was mixed with his derision.

The Southern Pacific Railroad had a vast amount of land to sell, and it took a leading part in the great campaign of advertising California. The railroad's publicity bureau had a number of able popular writers on its payroll, and in a flood of books, both fiction and nonfiction, and of magazine articles and stories, they described California's charms and embellished its romantic heritage. It was the Southern Pacific that began the publication of the phenomenally popular *Sunset,* a magazine of Western travel and living.

Many independent writers contributed to this flood of publicity. The transplanted New Englander Charles F. Lummis, founder and editor of the monthly magazine *Land of Sunshine,* later renamed *Out West,* went so far in romanticizing Southern California's past and present that for a time he was the leading cultural chauvinist of the region. Throughout the country the lure of California was becoming so strong that there was an eager market for almost anything that was written or said about it, even though some of the excesses of boosterism sometimes repelled the more sensitive. For example, tourist Mina Halsey, in her memoir called *A Tenderfoot in Southern California,* reported hearing the assurance that "if the Pilgrim fathers had landed on the Pacific Coast instead of the Atlantic, little old New York wouldn't be on the map."

When the Santa Fe reached Los Angeles in 1885, it began a rate war with the Southern Pacific. For a brief time a ticket from Kansas City to Los Angeles could be bought for one dollar, and the low rates, along with the attendant advertising, launched Southern California as a major tourist attraction and contributed to the real estate boom that reached a climax in 1887. Real estate sales in Los Angeles County exceeded 200 million dollars during that year, subdivisions sprang up in deserts, and the classic story of the Mississippi Bubble was surpassed in the record of incredible paper profits—and sudden crash. In the long run, however, no amount of greedy and excessive speculation could destroy the inevitable rise of California real estate values, as lands were settled and brought into profitable use.

The Southern Pacific also played a part in the advertising of California agricultural products, particularly oranges, as a highly successful method of increasing both the railroad's freight business and its land sales at the same time. In 1907 the California Fruit Growers' Exchange, in spite of its constant and bitter denunciations of the Southern Pacific's freight rates, made an agreement with the railroad for a joint advertising experiment which used Iowa as a laboratory, billboarding that state with the slogan, "Oranges for Health—California for Wealth." The results led the exchange to adopt a large and permanent program of advertising in the same vein; and during the next 7 years orange acreage in California increased by more than 70 percent, mostly in the southern part of the state.

In the early 20th century, however, the great growth of Southern California became increasingly urban rather than rural. In 1920 the population of the Los Angeles metropolitan area was five times as large as in 1900. During the same period the urban population of the San Francisco Bay area did not quite double, and thus by 1920 the populations of the two metropolitan regions were approximately equal, at about a million each.

Water and land. The peculiar importance of water in the economy of California and the peculiar patterns of its seasonal and regional distribution have made it not only a vital but a perpetually controversial factor in the state's history. Two of the major controversies came to a head in the 1880s, one a struggle of Sacramento Valley against the hydraulic mining industry, and the other a battle of farmers against "water monopolists" over the control of water for irrigation. Both quarrels were so bitter and destructive that they could be settled only when *laissez faire* gave way to the intervention of government.

Since the 1850s the hydraulickers had been dumping floods of mud, sand, and gravel into the Yuba, Bear, American, and Feather Rivers. Farms were buried by mining debris; Marysville, Yuba City, and other towns were repeatedly flooded; and the rivers, eventually including most of the Sacramento itself, were rendered unnavigable. After many inconclusive legal skirmishes, a decision of the United States circuit court in 1884 outlawed the dumping of debris into rivers, but the hydraulickers had been producing 10 million dollars' worth of gold a year, and they did not give up easily. Clandestine operations continued, harried by the "spies" of the farmers' Anti-Debris Association. After many tempestuous and inconclusive wrangles in the state legislature, a Federal law of 1893, introduced by Congressman Anthony J. Caminetti of Amador County, finally solved the problem by creating a Federal regulatory agency, the California Debris Commission.

The development of irrigation in California in the 19th century was slow, in large part because early state policy not only failed to prevent the monopolization of water rights but actually encouraged it. California water law was extremely confused and inadequate during nearly the whole first 40 years of statehood. In 1850 the first legislature simplified its tasks by adopting the common law of England for California. Members of the legislature were not particularly aware that this system included the doctrine of water law known as "riparian rights," an expression derived from the Latin *ripa,* the bank of a river, and signifying that the owner of land bordering a stream had full rights to a reasonable use of water while the owners of land not contiguous to the stream had no rights to it. Even while the first legislature was in session, the customs and regulations of the mining camps were crystallizing into an opposing system based on the doctrine of "prior appropriation," which had been used for centuries in Spain, France, and Italy, countries which, like most of California, were considerably drier than England. This concept gave the first user of water the unrestrained right to divert it from the stream and to sell this right to others.

In California the conflicting interests of the advocates of these two legal doctrines led them to fight each other to a political standstill, and consequently California lagged behind almost every other state in the American Southwest in adopting a coherent system of water law giving clear preference to the doctrine of appropriation.

Of the innumerable court battles during this long period of confusion, the most important was fought between two giants, the Miller and Lux Land and Cattle Company and the firm of James B. Haggin and Lloyd Tevis, over water rights in the San Joaquin Valley. Miller and Lux were among the state's most hated water monopolists because of their success in making strategic acquisitions of riverbank lands with an eye to riparian rights. In spite of their assertions that they were cattlemen and not land speculators, they used their riparian rights in a variety of antisocial ways. They forced landowners to sell out to them; they accumulated enormous underdeveloped and unused holdings; and they delayed the process of subdivision and resale to insure huge speculative profits for themselves. To the land holdings that gave them control of much of the San Joaquin River area they had added a 50-mile stretch along the Kern. Haggin and Tevis acquired rights of appropriation farther up the Kern with the intention of diverting water through irrigation canals to lands at some distance from the river. The state supreme court ruled in *Lux v. Haggin* in 1886 that the riparian rights of Miller and Lux made such appropriation illegal.

This decision was reached only by a bare majority, and after one of the judges had reversed himself. Moreover it was hotly denounced as a triumph of the English common law over American common sense, and as a victory for monopoly and speculation over the farmer and agricultural progress. Its intense unpopularity contributed to the calling of a stormy special session of the legislature in the summer of 1886, and finally to the passage of an important new law in the next regular session.

This was the Wright Irrigation Act of 1887, which authorized the establishment of irrigation districts, special units of local government to be formed by more than 50 persons or by a majority of the landowners in the area. These districts were to have the power of eminent domain, the power to overcome riparian rights by condemnation suits, and the right to sell bonds to finance the purchase of water rights and the construction of dams, canals, and other irrigation works. The bill's author was C. C. Wright, state senator from Modesto, where unsuccessful efforts to form such a district had been going on for some time. Within the year following the passage of the law 10 irrigation districts covering more than a million acres were in existence, most notably those in the regions of Modesto and Turlock. The early projects developed under this law had great difficuties—economic, engineering, legal, and political. Most of the larger landowners opposed them, and state supervision was as yet inadequate. But by 1911, when the 50th district was formed, the system had clearly established its vital role in the creation of California's modern agriculture.

The most colorful figure in the history of California irrigation development was Canadian-born George Chaffee, a self-educated engineering genius. After studying irrigation at Riverside, Chaffee created the highly successful communities of Etiwanda and Ontario in the 1880s. There he developed the idea of mutual water companies with one share of water company stock attached to each acre of land; built the first commercial hydroelectric plant in California and the first electrically lighted house west of the Rockies; and founded a college.

The greatest of all Chaffee's accomplishments, however, was his development of irrigation in the lower Colorado River area. As early as 1853 Dr. Oliver M. Wozencraft, then a Federal Indian agent for Southern California, had formed a plan to use the waters of the lower Colorado for irrigation, but he had been unable to put it into effect. The region was one of the dreariest desert wastes in the world, though the soil potential was extraordinary. In 1896 the California Development Company was organized, and in 1900 it secured Chaffee's services. Below the Mexican border he found some ancient dry watercourses through which very economical canals could be built, and within a year he had completed a 70-mile canal through Mexican territory, entering California at the twin border townsites which he called Mexicali and Calexico.

One of his greatest inspirations was a new name for the Colorado Desert: the Imperial Valley. This dramatic change of name did much to change the image that had repelled settlers from the area. They began to move into it in substantial numbers, and the desert did in fact begin to turn into a kind of agricultural empire.

Chaffee left the company in 1905. Not long afterward his successors built a risky bypass canal around the diversion head gate. After torrential rains the river burst through at this weak point and poured northwestward into the Imperial Valley, turning the dry Salton Sink into the Salton Sea, covering 40 miles of the Southern Pacific's roadbed, and threatening eventually to inundate the whole region. The Federal government did not intervene because the break was in Mexican territory, and the flooding continued unchecked for nearly two years. The Southern Pacific, after taking the opportunity to acquire control of the California Development Company, finally brought the flood under control in 1907 by dumping thousands of carloads of rock and gravel, and the development of the Imperial Valley was resumed.

Electric railways and urbanization. The years before and after the turn of the century were the era of the street and interurban electric railway—a development that played a vital part in the urbanization and particularly in the suburbanization of American society. The building of electric railway lines tremendously facilitated the growth of metropolitan areas by making it possible for those who worked in the center of a city to live in its outskirts or suburbs in more comfortable homes built on less expensive land. Few workers were willing to spend more than a total of an hour a day in commuting; therefore in the horse-and-buggy and horsecar era the practical maximum size of a city was little more than 12 square miles, that is, the area within a radius of 2 miles, the distance that could be traveled in 30 minutes. The trolley car, which could travel at least 5 miles in the same length of time, made it possible for the main residential area of a city to be nearly seven times as large as before—nearly 80 square miles. The interurban electric railway also did much to increase mobility, and tended to consolidate neighboring towns into a single metropolis.

The cable car had provided a colorful interlude. It was invented in San Francisco by Andrew S. Hallidie, a manufacturer of wire rope, and after the first cable line was built in 1873, on Clay Street, the idea spread to other cities. But the electric trolley introduced in Richmond, Virginia, in 1888, was obviously so much more efficient and economical even on steep hills that cable lines soon disappeared everywhere except in San Francisco, where a few were long retained, largely as tourist attractions and for reasons of local nostalgia.

Street and interurban electric railways reached the height of their importance between the 1890s and the beginning of the automobile age in 1919. The chief opportunities for profits for the promoters of these lines came not from operating revenues but from simultaneous speculation in the real estate which a new line could make suddenly and enormously more valuable.

San Francisco, "the city" of American California's first half century, was confined to a mere thumbnail of land only 7 miles square, at the tip of a peninsula. Most of the space eventually to be occupied by the metropolis of the San Francisco Bay Region was in the East Bay. These facts made a strong impression on Francis Marion "Borax" Smith, a capitalist of large imagination. In 1893, Smith began to reinvest the fortune that he had acquired in the borax business in Death Valley in a great scheme to consolidate and expand the street railway lines of the East Bay cities into the Key System, and to connect this network with San Francisco by an expanded and consolidated ferry service. In 1895, in association with Frank C. Havens of Oakland, Smith also formed the Realty Syndicate for the purpose of speculating in as much real estate as possible. Later he also formed a vast holding company designed to monopolize not only local transportation but all the other local public utilities as well. This brought him into collision with several powerful interests such as the Southern Pacific Railroad and the Pacific Gas and Electric Company. Havens, fearing that Smith was beginning to suffer from delusions of grandeur, withdrew from the syndicate in 1910, and Smith's financial empire collapsed soon afterward.

Among other miscalculations, Borax Smith had failed to realize that the greater growth of urban California in the 20th century would occur in the warmer climate of the southern part of the state. Henry Edwards Huntington perceived this more accurately.

Henry was the nephew of Collis P. Huntington, who had no son, and who hoped that his nephew would succeed him in the leadership of the Southern Pacific Railroad. This dynastic plan was strengthened when Collis arranged the marriage of Henry to a sister of Collis's adopted daughter. After serving an apprenticeship in the management of several of his uncle's smaller enterprises in the East and South, Henry Huntington came to California in 1892. On his way to San Francisco he stopped at Los Angeles, was entertained at the San Marino Ranch near Pasadena, and formed such a favorable impression of Southern California that he later bought the San Marino property and there, eventually, made his home. In San Francisco in the '90s he became vice-president of the Southern Pacific, but after the death of his uncle in 1900 the hopes for his succession to the presidency of the railroad were frustrated when Edward H. Harriman of New York, who already controlled the Union Pacific, gained control of the Southern Pacific as well. This virtual merger continued until 1913, when the Federal government dissolved it.

Henry Huntington faced the new century by moving most of his own investments and operations to Southern California. For several years part of his attention had been devoted to street railway companies in both San Francisco and Los Angeles. But now, after selling his Southern Pacific stock to Harriman, he disposed of his interests in the Market Street and other San Francisco lines to a new syndicate of trolley promoters called the United Railroads. In 1902 he invested most of his funds in a consolidation and expansion of the street and interurban railways of the region in and around Los Angeles under the name of the Pacific Electric Railway Company.

Within a few years the Pacific Electric and its big red cars welded 42 incorporated cities within a 35-mile radius of Los Angeles into the fastest-growing body in America. The P.E. became far the largest network of its kind, with more cars than any five other interurban electric systems, and its transportation of freight as well as passengers cut so heavily into the business of the Southern Pacific in the region that after many efforts Harriman finally succeeded in buying Huntington out, at an enormous price, in 1910.

In less than a decade Huntington became wealthier than his uncle had ever been, mainly by buying great tracts of land in Southern California just before announcing that new branches of the Pacific Electric would be built through them. He had separated from his first wife in the year his uncle died. He was divorced in 1906, and a few years later married his uncle's widow, thus consolidating the entire family fortune. After 1910 he retired from the more active aspects of business and devoted himself to filling his mansion at San Marino with his collection of manuscripts and rare books in the fields of English, colonial and Southwestern American literature and history. After his death in 1927 this was opened to scholars as the Huntington Library. The magnificent grounds of his estate, and his great collection of paintings, were opened to the public.

Henry Huntington shaped the system of transportation which, along with other forces, launched the entire region from Santa Monica to Redlands, and from San Fernando to Santa Ana, on the road to becoming the great City of Southern California.

SELECTED BIBLIOGRAPHY

Various aspects of economic development are treated in Robert G. Cleland and Osgood Hardy, *The March of Industry* (1929); Claude B. Hutchison, editor, *California Agriculture* (1946); and Gerald D. Nash, *State Government and Economic Development: A History of Administrative Policies in California, 1849–1933* (1964).

Accounts of wheat ranching are in Wallace Smith, *Garden of the Sun: a History of the San Joaquin Valley—1772–1939* (1939); and Joseph A. McGowan, *History of the Sacramento Valley*, volumes I and II (1961). On marketing problems see Rodman W. Paul, "The Great California Grain War; the Granger Challenges the Wheat King," *Pacific Historical Review*, XXVII (November 1958), 331–350, and "The Wheat Trade between California and the United Kingdom," *Mississippi Valley Historical Review*, XLV (December 1958), 391–412.

On wine production, Vincent P. Carosso, *The California Wine Industry, 1830–1895; a Study of the Formative Years* (1951), may be pictorially supplemented by *The Story of Wine in California* (1962), with text by M. F. K. Fisher, photographs by Max Yavno, and a foreword by Maynard Amerine; and by Joan M. Donohue, "Agostin Harasthy: A Study in Creativity," *California Historical Society Quarterly*, XLVIII (June 1969), 153–163.

The rise of the citrus and related industries and of cooperative marketing can be traced in Walter Reuther, H. J. Webber, and L. D. Batchelor, editors, *The Citrus Industry* (1967); Rahno Mabel MacCurdy, *The History of the California Fruit Growers' Exchange* (1925); Erich O. Kraemer and Henry E. Erdman, *History of Coöperation in the Marketing of Fresh Deciduous Fruits* (1933); H. E. Erdman, "The Development and Significance of California Coöperatives, 1900–1915," *Agricultural History*, XXXII (July 1958), 179–184; Charles C. Teague, *Fifty Years a Rancher* (1944); and a novel, Sidney H. Burchell, *Jacob Peek, Orange Grower; a Tale of Southern California* (1915).

On real estate booms and the rise of Southern California, see Remi A. Nadeau, *City-makers . . ., 1868–1876* (1948); John E. Baur, *Health Seekers of Southern California* (1959); Glenn S. Dumke, *The Boom of the Eighties in Southern California* (1944); T. S. Van Dyke, *Millionaires of a Day* (1890), a genial satire; Harris Newmark, *Sixty Years in Southern California* (1916); James M. Guinn, *A History of California and . . . of Los Angeles and Environs* (three volumes, 1915); W. W. Robinson, *Ranchos become Cities* (1939); Richard F. Pourade, *The Glory Years* (1964), volume IV of his *History of San Diego*; Carey McWilliams, *Southern California Country* (1946); and Franklin Walker, *Literary History of Southern California* (1950). Examples of the promotional literature include Charles Nordhoff, *California for Health,*

Pleasure, and Residence (1872); Ben C. Truman, *Homes and Happiness in the Golden State* (1883); and Charles Dudley Warner, *Our Italy* (1891). Frank L. Beach, "The Transformation of California, 1900–1920," Ph.D. thesis, University of California, Berkeley (1963), analyzes the great acceleration of the westward movement from the older states to California in the early 20th century. See also Warren Thompson, *Growth and Changes in California's Population* (1955).

Irrigation developments are described in Frank Adams, *Life of George Chaffey* (1928); Frederick D. Kershner, "George Chaffee and the Irrigation Frontier," *Agricultural History*, XXVII (October 1953), 115–122; William Smythe, *The Conquest of Arid America* (1905), a good example of the messianic tone of much writing on the subject; and David O. Woodbury, *The Colorado Conquest* (1941). The early Imperial Valley was the locale of Harold Bell Wright's bestselling novel, *The Winning of Barbara Worth* (1911).

George W. Hilton, *The Cable Car in America* (1971), traces its rise and decline. On the great era of street and interurban electric railways, see John Anderson Miller, *Fares, Please: From Horse Cars to Streamliners* (1940); George H. Hilton and John F. Due, *The Electric Interurban Railways in America* (1960); William D. Middleton, *The Interurban Era* (1961); Spencer Crump, *Ride the Big Red Cars; How Trolleys Helped Build Southern California* (1962); Laurence R. Veysey, "The Pacific Electric Railway Company" (1953, typescript on microfilm, Bancroft Library); and Robert M. Fogelson, *The Fragmented Metropolis: Los Angeles, 1850–1930* (1967).

John E. Pomfret, *The Henry E. Huntington Library and Art Gallery* (1969), begins with a good sketch of Huntington's career.

Chapter XXIV

LABOR AND CAPITAL

Backgrounds of the California labor movement. Organized relationships between workers and employers in California began to enter their modern phase in San Francisco in the 1880s. There had been labor unions in the city since the early '50s but none of them had been large, and most had been short-lived. The first large-scale labor movement in the state, the Workingmen's party of 1877 to 1880, had contributed very little to the development of modern labor organization. Kearney was ignorant of the principles of trade unionism. His followers came mainly from the ranks of the unorganized and the unemployed, and with minor exceptions the Workingmen's party received no support from the few small unions then in existence in California. The Workingmen's party put its faith entirely in political action, and in that sphere its chief accomplishment was its role in the movement that led to the exclusion of the Chinese by Federal law. California legislation in the interest of labor remained very limited. A state bureau of labor statistics was established in 1883; but laws providing on paper for the mechanics' lien and for an 8-hour day on government work lacked provisions essential for their enforcement.

Throughout the country attempts at effective labor organization suffered from labor's chronic disunity and confusion of aims. One great dispute was over the question of whether labor should avoid organized political action and confine itself to "pure and simple" or "bread and butter" unionism, that is, to collective bargaining with employers for strictly economic goals. Another basic disagreement concerned the form of organization. The oldest and most conservative plan was that of craft unionism, in which each skilled trade in a city had its own local union, reaching out toward federation with other locals in the same craft on a state and national basis, and also toward city, state, and national federations of the unions of the various crafts. This idea produced the body that would ultimately evolve into American labor's most important one. Founded in a small convention at Pittsburgh in 1881, it was reorganized under the name of the American Federation of Labor in 1886.

The Noble Order of the Knights of Labor, on the other hand, stood for a single national union capable of including men of all crafts or of none. It advocated producers' cooperatives, to be owned by the workers and to take over as many industries as possible, and at times it allied itself with the Greenback Labor party, a movement that combined currency inflation and socialism in proposals to convert the national debt into ready money, which would be lent to workers' cooperatives so that they could put private manufacturers out of business.

To the left of the Knights of Labor and the Greenbackers were the Marxians, not yet clearly divided on the issue of peaceful socialism versus communist violence; the anarchists, advocates of the abolition of government; and the syndicalists, who believed that a mighty labor organization should in effect become the government.

Among these alternatives, American labor made an overwhelming choice in favor of craft unionism—collective bargaining for higher wages, shorter hours, and other improved conditions, with political action limited to objectives closely related to these. In other words, American labor decided to seek a fairer share of the benefits of the private system of economic enterprise rather than a replacement of that system by socialized public ownership of the means of production. While British labor moved toward a new political party, based directly on the trade unions and advocating nationalization of ownership by peaceful means and through the democratic process, American organized labor in general rejected not only socialism but also the idea of forming any major political party of its own. This happened essentially because the per capita resources of the United States and the relative opportunity for the individual to rise in society were greater than in England or in any other country.

The rise of unions in San Francisco. It is true that some of the most important leaders of the labor movement in San Francisco in the 1880s were socialists. In 1881 Frank Roney, a member of the Iron Moulders' Union and a former Irish revolutionary, became president of the San Francisco Trades Assembly, then the only citywide federation of unions. And a year later Burnette G. Haskell began a lively career as a radical labor organizer.

Haskell was a native Californian, the son of a wealthy pioneer family. Though trained as a lawyer, he was too erratic and visionary to be happy or successful in a routine law practice, and instead became the editor of *Truth*, a small weekly paper that his father had founded. One evening in 1882, in search of news, he attended a meeting of the Trades Assembly. Until then he had taken no interest in labor's problems, but from that time onward he threw himself into the cause of socialism. It was typical of him that he tried to reconcile socialism and anarchism, an effort in which, needless to say, he failed. The International Workmen's Association which he organized in San Francisco in 1882 should not be confused, though it often has been, with two other organizations: the International Workingmen's Association, or "First International" or "red international," formed by Karl Marx and others in England in 1864 and dissolved in 1876; and the International Working People's Association, or "black international," formed by anarchist followers of Bakunin in London in 1881.

Haskell also took part in the organization of new labor unions in several trades, and in several of the smaller Northern California cities as well as in San Francisco. By far the most enduring contribution of his life was his leadership in the founding of the Coast Seamen's Union.

San Francisco's position as the leading seaport of the Pacific Coast made it inevitable that the labor problems of the waterfront would play a central part in the history of the city's labor relations as a whole. Moreover, working conditions in the maritime industry were peculiarly atrocious before the development of effective unions. Other men had the legal right to quit work, but for the sailor this was "desertion," and under United States law until 1915 it led to arrest and imprisonment. Until 1898 corporal punishment was permitted at sea for "justifiable cause" as interpreted by the captain of the ship, under the theory formulated in a court decision of 1806 that "the simple and somewhat rude character of seamen" required extraordinary discipline. Flogging had been abolished by Federal law in 1850 after a long campaign led by Richard Henry Dana and others, but this had merely meant that other forms of physical torture were substituted; the officer corps of the merchant marine continued to be a refuge for sadists—"bucko mates." The food was vile, and the sleeping quarters were cramped and ill-ventilated "dogholes."

The chief method of hiring seamen which prevailed throughout the world in the 19th century was the infamous crimping system. The "crimps," keepers of sailors' boarding houses on the waterfront, served also as the main employment agencies. While in port the sailor lived on credit advances from the crimp for food, clothing, and liquor, until the crimp arranged his next voyage. No sailor could get a ship in any other way, and no master could get a crew except by negotiating with the crimp to pay the sailor's wage advance. The master often had to pay the crimp an additional fee, known as "blood money" because drugged and slugged men were frequently shanghaied aboard covered with blood.

Union organization to escape from such conditions began in the coasting trade because the sailors in it were a relatively homogeneous group, more often in port and more likely to be acquainted with each other than were the "deepwater" sailors. In particular, the Pacific Coast lumber schooners were specialized vessels, and their crews had to be skilled in handling lumber as well as in seamanship. It was a group of such men whom Burnette Haskell persuaded to organize the Coast Seamen's Union in 1885.

In the same year Haskell formed the Kaweah colony, a utopian cooperative enterprise for timber cutting in what would later be Sequoia National Park. On the theory that this scheme would provide employment for seamen out of work, Haskell gained the support of many union members for the colony, and even the investment of some of the union's funds. The Kaweah experiment was unsuccessful, however, and the seamen, perceiving that Haskell was eccentric and undependable, rejected his leadership and with it the socialistic influence in their union. Instead, after merging with a separate union of steamship sailors to form the Sailors' Union of the Pacific in 1891, the coast sailors found their greatest leader for decades to come in Andrew Furuseth, a man who was proud of the sailor's craft and devoted to the philosophy and methods of craft unionism. Furuseth, more than any other individual, was ultimately responsible for the reforms of the La Follette Seamen's Act of 1915, which abolished imprisonment for desertion, regulated working conditions, and finally broke the power of the crimps.

In their dark and difficult early years in the 1880s and 1890s, however, the main achievement of the sailors' unions was in mere survival. Their strikes led the employers to form a Shipowners' Association which, in periods of crisis, temporarily established central hiring offices. These would have been an improvement over the crimping system except that they introduced a new evil, the hiring hall controlled by the employers and run primarily for the purpose of weeding out union men.

In many other industries, also, harsh working conditions still prevailed in the late 19th century. San Francisco bakers, for example, worked from 12 to 18 hours a day for 7 days a week, except Sundays when they worked 6 hours; they were compelled to board at "homes" provided by the employers. Conditions showed the greatest improvements in the few occupations in which the bulk of the workers were unionized before 1900, notably the building trades. The carpenters and other building trades unions tended to regard themselves as a skilled aristocracy of labor. In the 1890s their separate federation, the Building Trades Council, seceded from the main citywide body, the San Francisco Labor Council, and even held separate Labor Day parades, marching in opposite directions on Market Street. In general, only a small minority of wage earners were union members, and in many occupations there were no unions at all. Formal agreements between employers and unions were rare, and in most cases the employer set the terms and could change them without notice.

In the relatively prosperous years of the early 20th century, unionism in San Francisco made a remarkable surge forward. There was a great increase in membership, and new unions were successfully established in a number of occupations that had been considered unorganizable in other communities. The often-repeated statement that San Francisco in this period became "the first closed-shop city in the United States" was an exaggeration, however, for except in the building trades the closed-shop contract under which the employer agreed to hire only members of the union was actually adopted in very few instances;

indeed most bargaining agreements were still entirely informal. But in comparison with other American cities, San Francisco did become a stronghold of unionism about 1900, and remained so until the early 1920s.

In the summer of 1901 the teamsters joined with the sailors and the longshoremen in a waterfront strike that tied up the port for several weeks. Violence between strikers on the one hand and strikebreakers and the police on the other led to hundreds of injuries and four deaths. Again, as in 1877 when the apparent use of the police on the side of the business community had led the "workingmen" to form a new political party, so in 1901 the assignment of the police to protect strikebreakers led to the organization of the new Union Labor Party of San Francisco. For a time that party actually gained control of the city government. During its first six years of existence, however, it was controlled by an opportunistic and corrupt political boss, Abraham Ruef, and thus it became significant mainly for its part in the extreme corruption of California party politics, which would at last produce major attempts at political reform in the city and the state.

Triumph of the open shop in Los Angeles. In the same turn-of-the-century period when the idea of the closed shop was coming as near to acceptance in San Francisco as anywhere else in America, Los Angeles was becoming the country's leading citadel of the open shop, the precisely opposite principle, under which employers not only refused to make agreements requiring union membership of their employees but even refused to bargain with unions at all.

This remarkable polarization of institutional patterns in the two cities was one of the many extreme contrasts between them. The population of the "cow counties," as Southern California was long derisively described in the North, remained relatively sparse and rural before 1900, and because industry was still on a trifling scale in Los Angeles several decades after it had begun to flourish in San Francisco, unions in Los Angeles were less deeply rooted. But of all the factors impeding union growth in Southern California the most remarkable and effective was the personality of Harrison Gray Otis, publisher of the *Los Angeles Times*. With a great fortune built on a highly profitable newspaper and on vast real estate investments in California and Mexico, Otis made himself the leader of the most intransigent group of organized employers to be found anywhere in the United States.

He was named for that earlier Harrison Gray Otis, a distant relative, who had been one of the most distinguished political leaders of New England, and although the two Harrison Gray Otises flourished at opposite ends of the 19th century as well as of the country, their social philosophies were remarkably alike. The Massachusetts Senator had been a leader of the Federalists, whom one of their associates described as the party of "the wise, the good, and the rich." The Southern California publisher, three generations later, was equally convinced that men of wealth, in their wisdom and genius, were the only men to be trusted with economic or political power.

A related part of Otis's thinking was the result of his military experiences, as a young officer in an Ohio regiment during the Civil War and later as a general in the California National Guard. The military plan of social organization impressed him as an excellent system. The good soldier never struck and never boycotted. This feeling provided much of the emotional force behind Otis's crusade for the open shop, which he rationalized as "industrial freedom"—the freedom of the worker not to join a union and the freedom of the employer to discharge him if he did. Otis often said that he favored the "closed shop," by what he regarded as the only proper definition of it: closed to union members.

In 1890 Otis precipitated the first major conflict between employers and unions in Los Angeles, with the intention of destroying the printers' union, the oldest union in the city. Printers, as Otis pointed out, were the only workers in Southern California who were still getting boomtime wages. The boom of the '80s having collapsed, a wage cut was in order. But instead of negotiating a new agreement Otis announced a 20-percent cut, locked his union printers out, and refused to discuss a compromise. Before doing this he had formed an association with the publishers of the other three Los Angeles dailies, and had arranged to bring in nonunion printers from San Diego and elsewhere. He paid these strikebreakers the previous union wages—until the strike collapsed. Other unions helped the printers by contributing funds and by joining in a boycott of the *Times* and its advertisers. This boycott was a failure, but it tended to solidify the Los Angeles labor movement for the years of struggle that lay ahead.

The businessmen who were most antagonistic to unions formed an Employers' Association under the leadership of Otis and A. Hamburger, proprietor of the People's Store and one of Otis's largest advertisers. They also established an Independent Labor Bureau to carry on a wide campaign of advertising in the East, promising jobs at high wages for nonunion workers. The Merchants' and Manufacturers' Association of Los Angeles, originally formed in the 1890s to promote commercial and industrial enterprise, was at first outwardly neutral in Otis's war with the unions. But in 1903 the M. and M. announced that it would unite with employers injured by boycotts, which it branded as "un-American, unjust, unwarranted, and illegal." Soon afterward, however, it launched a boycott policy of its own—against employers who negotiated with unions. Bank loans were withheld and orders were transferred to other companies. The M. and M.'s boycott was more effective than any that union labor ever attempted.

At this time the drive for the open shop was becoming a national movement. A major slogan of this movement was "The Right to Work," the title of a widely discussed article by Ray Stannard Baker in *McClure's Magazine* for

January 1903, expressing sympathy for the "scab" miners in the recent Pennsylvania coal strike. The National Association of Manufacturers declared against recognition of labor unions in 1903, and its president founded a Citizens' Industrial Association of America. This body, in turn, fostered local Citizens' Alliances in which the public was invited to join with employers in fighting organized labor. Herbert George, a professional promoter, organized a Citizens' Alliance in Denver which played a major part in smashing the miners' union in the Colorado coalfields. George was then brought to Los Angeles, where he soon recruited the country's largest per capita Citizens' Alliance membership, with heavy financial support from Otis, Henry E. Huntington, and others.

Labor was not entirely without allies in the struggle for the support of public opinion. Edward W. Scripps's *Los Angeles Record,* an evening daily, was a voice for organized labor and against Otis from its founding in 1895. And in 1903 William Randolph Hearst, then a Democrat seeking labor's support for his ambition to be President of the United States, established the *Los Angeles Examiner* as a morning daily in direct competition with the *Times.* In an editorial in the first issue the *Examiner* promised to "support with its whole power the proposition that labor is justified in demanding a fair share of the wealth it produces." By 1906, however, Hearst's paper had begun to recede from its original prolabor stand, and the unions became disillusioned with him.

The struggle reached a crisis in 1910, when organized labor took the offensive in a drive for effective unionization of the Los Angeles metal trades. In the spring the metal trades employers of San Francisco agreed to an 8-hour day but warned that they could not long continue it unless their competitors in Los Angeles were unionized and forced to accept the same terms. Consequently, union organizers and funds from San Francisco suddenly strengthened the metal trades unions of Los Angeles to such a degree that they were able to begin a strike of 1,500 workers on June 1, 1910, the largest strike the city had ever witnessed. The employers refused to negotiate, and the battle attracted national attention because the whole future of the open shop was clearly at stake in the city where it was strongest. The *Times* outdid itself in denouncing the assault on "the cradle of industrial freedom," and organized labor and its sympathizers throughout the country denounced the *Times* as the nation's leading symbol of union smashing.

Before dawn on the morning of October 1, while the strike was still in full swing, a tremendous explosion destroyed the *Times* building, killed 20 men, and injured 17 others. Immediately the open-shop forces attributed this "crime of the century," as the *Times* called it, to a dynamite bomb planted by union labor's agents. Labor's partisans, on the other hand, charged that the cause was a leaking gas main, typical of the "fire-trap" in which Otis had compelled his employees to work. Unhappily the truth was that a dynamite bomb had been used and that certain individual union officials were guilty of planning the outrage.

The tragedy of the *Times* was a part of a nationwide struggle between the International Association of Bridge and Structural Iron Workers and the National Erectors' Association, a group which included most of the large employers in the field, and which was dominated by United States Steel, the largest corporation in the country. In 1906 the National Erectors' Association began a belligerent campaign to destroy the power of the Iron Workers, and succeeded in establishing the open shop throughout the industry in all large cities except Chicago and San Francisco. Driven to desperation, the union's national leaders secretly resorted to terrorism, and over a period of several years dozens of non-union construction projects in a number of cities were damaged by explosions of dynamite, though until the *Times* bombing none of these had resulted in loss of life.

William J. Burns, head of a private detective agency, was already investigating some of the lesser incidents when he was employed by the mayor of Los Angeles to investigate the *Times* disaster. In April 1911 Burns arrested Ortie McManigal, a professional dynamiter, who confessed his own part in the bombing campaign and described its planning by officials of the union at their national headquarters in Indianapolis. Union secretary John J. McNamara, his brother James B. McNamara, and McManigal were then brought to Los Angeles to be tried for complicity in the bombing of the *Times*.

Samuel Gompers, president of the American Federation of Labor, staked his prestige and that of the A.F. of L. on the belief that the charges against the McNamara brothers were a frame-up, and Clarence Darrow, one of the country's ablest trial lawyers, was employed for the defense. In 1907 Darrow had secured the acquittal of three officials of the Western Federation of Miners who were charged with hiring a dynamiter to murder a former Governor of Idaho. That American courts and communities were capable of the hysterical punishment of scapegoats had been apparent in the Haymarket Square bombing in Chicago in 1886. For that crime, four men had been convicted and executed essentially because they were anarchists, even though no shred of evidence connected them with the person who threw the bomb.

But on December 1, 1911, the millions of Americans who had believed the McNamara brothers to be the innocent victims of an employer conspiracy were stunned by their confession of guilt. The evidence against them was overwhelming, and Darrow advised his clients to plead guilty in order to save their lives.

Lincoln Steffens had conducted personal negotiations with Darrow, the prosecution, the judge, the mayor, labor, employers, Otis, and various other newspaper publishers and community leaders. Steffens saw the *Times* disaster as a proof of the dangerousness, the cruelty, and the futility of extremism in industrial relations. He proposed that the agreement to save the McNamaras from the death penalty be followed by a great series of peace conferences to end the warfare between capital and labor in the United States. But Steffens alone seems to have taken this idea seriously. Instead, the McNamaras' confession demoralized American labor, emboldened employers, and intensified the bitterness between the two sides. In Los Angeles the result was 30 more years of dominance for the open shop.

Agricultural labor: Unorganized and disfranchised. Historically, the family farm has been the institution most typical of American agriculture. Only a fourth of those gainfully employed in farming in the United States have been wage workers, and these have been "hired men" attached more or less permanently to one farm and living with the family that owned it. In California, however, more than two-thirds of the total number of persons engaged in agriculture have been wage laborers, the majority of them alien, nonwhite, and migratory. California's "peculiar institution," comparable in some ways to Southern Negro slavery, has been seasonal migratory agricultural labor in which the worker lacked the protection offered in other fields by labor unions and by the right to vote.

Several circumstances contributed to this situation: the persistence of large units of land ownership in California; specialization in a particular seasonal crop, as opposed to the year-round operations of the "general farm" more common in the Middle West; and the availability, in each successive generation, of some new supply of cheap labor drawn from some supposedly inferior race—first the Indians, then the Chinese, and later the Japanese, Hindustanis, Mexicans, and Filipinos.

Union organization would have been peculiarly difficult under these circumstances, even if the agricultural employers had not been violently opposed to it. California trade unions were not merely indifferent to the welfare of alien nonwhite workers, but sternly hostile to their presence in the United States. Groups of migratory laborers, white or nonwhite, usually disbanded at the end of the local harvest season, and wages were too low to have permitted the payment of union dues. Even the minority who were citizens of the United States were seldom in any one place long enough to qualify as voters, and because agricultural employers had great influence in the election and reelection of county supervisors and sheriffs, while migratory workers had no such influence, local lawmaking and law enforcement weighed heavily on the employer's side.

In the 1880s the majority of seasonal and casual laborers in California agriculture were Chinese, whom the large growers regarded as an ideal labor force. Many of the Chinese immigrants were skilled and experienced farmers with much to teach their American employers about agricultural efficiency. But the exclusion act of 1882 and a steady drift of Chinese from the rural areas to the cities and towns began to deplete this source of labor supply. Moreover, during the depression after the panic of 1893, unemployed whites from the cities, seeking work as "fruit tramps," participated in riots that drove thousands of Chinese laborers from the fields. A few Negroes were brought from the Southern states, but agricultural wages were so low that they soon found better pay in unskilled labor or domestic service in the cities.

For about a decade, beginning in the late 1890s, the growers found another temporary solution in the Japanese, particularly as field workers in the sugar-beet industry that sprang up after the Dingley tariff of 1897 put a heavy duty on imported sugar. But the Gentlemen's Agreement of 1907 restricted Japanese immigration, and moreover the Japanese were quick to escape from the role of cheap and docile laborers. Through clubs or associations with members of their own race as "secretaries," they began to engage in collective bargaining, and to the pained surprise of the growers they conducted the first successful strikes in the history of California agriculture. When they began to acquire land, by purchase or lease, white farmers soon joined with city labor unions in anti-Japanese agitation. In the second decade of the century the growers turned to the Hindustanis, especially for labor in the Imperial Valley, and to the Mexicans, particularly during and after World War I.

The I.W.W. Not even a serious attempt to organize a conventional labor union among California agricultural workers was made until 1903, when a Fruit Workers' Union affiliated with the A.F. of L. was formed at San Jose. Its existence was brief. The growers dealt with it by ignoring it, and it attracted little attention of any sort except for a few contemptuous newspaper editorials. By default, the attempt to organize the migratory workers fell into the hands of the new and radical movement called the Industrial Workers of the World.

The I.W.W. was an anarcho-syndicalist organization formed in Chicago in 1905. The preamble of its constitution denounced craft unionism and called instead for "one great union" made up largely of unskilled workers. The I.W.W. did not exclude any worker because of race, and it condemned the A.F. of L. for practicing racial discrimination. For the "conservative motto, 'A fair day's wage for a fair day's work,'" the I.W.W. manifesto substituted the "revolutionary watchword . . . abolition of the wage system." It spoke of "the historic mission of the working class to do away with capitalism." Sabotage, sympathetic strikes for the purpose of paralyzing an industry, and "any and all tactics that will get the results sought with the least expenditure of time and energy" were regarded as justified.

The doctrine of the I.W.W. was a counsel of despair that could appeal only to men whose condition seemed utterly hopeless. Its numerical strength, which was never large, was often absurdly exaggerated by the newspapers, and the remarkable degree of notoriety it achieved was very largely the result of the frightened manner in which many employers and public authorities reacted to it.

One tactic of the I.W.W. was the demand for the right of free speech, and through the clumsiness of police and other officials in allowing themselves to be placed in the position of denying this right, the I.W.W. attracted wide public sympathy. Street-corner gatherings to hear political or religious exhortations were then common occurrences in American cities; they have since passed from the American scene partly because of formal action against them and partly because of the onset of the automobile age. In the early 20th century many cities adopted ordinances against street speaking, which were enforced against political radicals but not against such meetings as those of the Salvation Army.

In 1910, when the I.W.W. launched a drive to organize farm laborers in the region of Fresno, several of its members were arrested for speaking on the streets of the town. More than a hundred other members than arrived on freight trains for the purpose of filling the jail, where they attracted so much outraged attention by the mass singing of radical songs that police and firemen resorted to drenching them with firehoses. A mob burned the organization tent and talked of storming the jail to lynch the prisoners. Chester H. Rowell, progressive editor of the *Fresno Republican,* excoriated the I.W.W. but also denounced the methods being used against it. Instead of giving way to hysterical repression, he advised, Fresno should undercut the I.W.W. by encouraging the growth of normal labor unions, and by following the example of Porterville, where the threat of a similar I.W.W. "invasion" had been dissolved by the simple announcement that there would be no arrests for street speaking. In Fresno, after a stalemate of several months, a compromise freed the men from jail and permitted them to speak in designated areas of the city.

Another and greater "free speech fight" occurred in 1912 in San Diego, following the adoption of an ordinance that forbade street-corner speaking in the downtown district. This ordinance had been approved after Harrison Gray Otis made a speech to a group of San Diego businessmen recommending strong measures to suppress radical propaganda. Dozens of the "Wobblies"—a nickname which Otis was the first to use in print—then came from other parts of the state to repeat their strategy of overflowing the jails. Businessmen formed a vigilance committee, and some of its members inflicted cruel beatings on a number of Wobblies without interference from the police and with open encouragement from the San Diego newspapers, the *Union* and the *Tribune*, both owned by the beet-sugar capitalist, John D. Spreckels. Only the police and the vigilantes, not the I.W.W., resorted to violence; the *San Francisco Bulletin* and also the official report of Harris Weinstock, whom Governor Hiram Johnson had appointed to investigate the disturbances, asked whether it was the "radicals" or the self-styled "good citizens" who had acted as the real anarchists and who had done more to violate the principles of the Constitution of the United States.

In its efforts to organize farm labor the I.W.W. developed methods specially adapted to the conditions of the migratory workers. Giving up the idea of local organizations with permanent dues-paying members, the Wobblies traveled about among the seasonal labor camps, formed temporary organizations "on the job," and asked either very small dues or none at all. These tactics were employed among the workers involved in the tragic incident known as the "Wheatland Riot" of August 3, 1913, which occurred on the Durst Ranch near the town of Wheatland in Yuba County a few miles southeast of Marysville.

Ralph Durst, one of the state's largest employers of migratory labor, had collected a surplus of workers for the hop-picking season through alluring advertisements in newspapers in several parts of California and southern Oregon. Needing about 1,500 workers, he advertised for 2,700, and attracted 2,800, mostly aliens. Conditions in his work camp were barbaric. As housing, a few tents were available for rental, but most of the workers built their own rude shelters of gunnysacks and poles, or slept in the open. For 2,800 men, women, and children there were eight outdoor toilets, which also had to serve as the only garbage disposal facilities. The temperature was more than 100° in the shade. Durst not only refused to provide drinking water in the fields, but refused the workers permission to rent a water wagon and haul it themselves; a cousin of Durst's had a concession to sell "lemonade," made with citric acid. The "bonus" wage that had been advertised turned out to be nothing more than a device for holding back part of the worker's wages if he left before the end of the picking season.

A mass meeting elected a committee to demand better conditions, with Richard Ford, a member of the I.W.W. better known as "Blackie" Ford, as spokesman. Durst slapped Ford, and the next day, August 3, a posse arrived from Marysville to arrest the agitators. Ford was then addressing another mass meeting, and a deputy fired a shot in the air "to sober the mob." This led to a general melee in which the district attorney, a deputy sheriff, and two workers were killed and many were injured. Governor Johnson sent five companies of the national guard to Wheatland, and in a trial at Marysville early in 1914, Ford and Herman Suhr, another I.W.W. member, were convicted of second degree murder on the theory that by leading the strike that resulted in the shooting they were guilty of conspiracy to murder the district attorney. Durst, who was as responsible for the tragedy as any other individual, received no punishment except for some acid criticism from such newspaper editors as Fremont Older and C. K. McClatchy.

SELECTED BIBLIOGRAPHY

Ira B. Cross made basic contributions in his *History of the Labor Movement in California* (1935), and his edition of the autobiography of *Frank B. Roney, Irish Rebel and California Labor Leader* (1931). David F. Selvin, *Sky Full of Storm* (1966), is a survey of the history of union organization in California. See also Alexander P. Saxton, *The Indispensable Enemy: Labor and the Anti-Chinese Movement in California* (1971); and

Philip Taft, *Labor Politics American Style: The California State Federation of Labor* (1968).

Aspects of the rise of unionism in San Francisco are treated in Lucille Eaves, *A History of California Labor Legislation with an Introductory Sketch of the San Francisco Labor Movement* (1910); Robert E. L. Knight, *Industrial Relations in the San Francisco Bay Area, 1900–1918* (1960); Paul S. Taylor, *The Sailors' Union of the Pacific* (1923); Hyman G. Weintraub, *Andrew Furuseth: Emancipator of the Seamen* (1959); William M. Camp, *San Francisco: Port of Gold* (1947); Richard H. Dillon, *Shanghaiing Days* (1961); Frederick L. Ryan, *Industrial Relations in the San Francisco Building Trades* (1936); and Bernard C. Cronin, *Father Yorke and the Labor Movement in San Francisco, 1900–1910* (1943).

Grace H. Stimson, *Rise of the Labor Movement in Los Angeles* (1955), and its sequel, Louis B. Perry and Richard S. Perry, *A History of the Los Angeles Labor Movement, 1911–1941* (1963), formed the first inclusive account of the history of organized labor in any large American city. Richard C. Miller, "Otis and His *Times*," Ph.D. thesis, University of California, Berkeley (1961), is penetrating and critical. For the *Times'* viewpoint see *The Forty-year War for a Free City: A History of the Open Shop in Los Angeles*, a special supplement issued in pamphlet form, reprinting a series of articles in the *Times* beginning October 1, 1929. On the McNamara case see also William J. Burns, *The Masked War* (1913); Louis Adamic, *Dynamite* (1931); Clarence Darrow, *The Story of My Life* (1932); *The Autobiography of Lincoln Steffens* (1931); and Graham Adams, Jr., *The Age of Industrial Violence, 1910–1915* (1966).

Important works on agricultural labor in this period include Carey McWilliams, *Factories in the Field* (1939); Varden Fuller, "The Supply of Agricultural Labor as a Factor in the Evolution of Farm Organization in California," Ph.D. thesis, University of California, Berkeley (1939), published in United States Congress, Senate, Committee on Education and Labor, *Violations of Free Speech and Rights of Labor. Hearings . . .*, part 54 (1940); and Paul S. Taylor, "Foundations of California Rural Society," *California Historical Society Quarterly*, XXIV (September 1945), 193–228.

Hyman Weintraub, "The I.W.W. in California, 1905–1931," M.A. thesis University of California, Los Angeles (1947), is the most detailed account of its subject. Others may be found in Ione E. Wilson, "The I.W.W. in California with Special Reference to Migratory Labor," M.A. thesis, University of California, Berkeley (1946); Woodrow C. Whitten, "The Wheatland Episode," *Pacific Historical Review*, XVII (February, 1948), 37–42; Paul F. Brissenden, *The I.W.W., a Study of American Syndicalism* (1919, 1957); and Carleton H. Parker, *The Casual Laborer in America* (1920). General accounts of the I.W.W. are Patrick Renshaw, *The Wobblies* (1967); Melvyn Dubofsky, *We Shall Be All* (1969); and Joseph R. Conlin, *Bread and Roses Too: Studies of the Wobblies* (1969).

Mitchell Slobodek, *A Selective Bibliography of California Labor History* (1964), is thorough and well annotated.

Chapter XXV

POLITICS IN THE ERA OF RAILROAD DOMINATION

THE LAST THIRD of the 19th century was an age of unparalleled corruption in American public life. As the English historian Philip Guedalla once put it, the names of several presidents of railroads were of greater importance in that era of American history than the names of several presidents of the United States. The leaders of huge corporations dominated not only the American economy but American politics as well, and they tended not only to despise the politicians, many of whom they easily corrupted, but also to feel contempt for government itself.

In that period it was said that the Standard Oil Company had done everything to the legislature of Pennsylvania except to refine it; but in no state was politics more subservient to big business than in California, for in no other state did a single corporation enjoy a greater degree of dominance in the economy. In California the Southern Pacific represented the greatest accumulation of wealth. It was the largest landowner and the largest employer of labor. Its rail system was the longest in the nation, extending from Portland to New Orleans and from Ogden to San Francisco. The building of the Santa Fe to Los Angeles in the '80s brought some temporary competition in Southern California, but this was soon nullified by rate agreements, and the Southern Pacific acquired partial control of the Santa Fe by buying stock.

In the '90s a group of San Francisco capitalists including Adolph Sutro, Claus and John D. Spreckels, and James D. Phelan built a "People's Railroad" through the San Joaquin Valley, but they were soon coerced into selling it to the Santa Fe. Not until 1910, when George J. Gould's Western Pacific reached Oakland, did the Southern Pacific begin to meet serious economic competition. By coincidence, that was also the year in which its stranglehold on the state's politics was broken at last.

As we have already observed, when the state government of California began its attempts to regulate the Southern Pacific in the 1870s, the railroad responded by intensifying its control of the state government. The more corrupt methods by which the railroad intervened in politics were kept as secret as possible; but the workings of the Southern Pacific's "invisible government" could not always be kept invisible, and they were starkly revealed in such episodes as the publication of the "Colton letters" and the "Dear Pard" letters, the struggle of Los Angeles for a free harbor, and the railroad's attempt to escape from the payment of its debt to the United States.

The Colton letters. For four years before his sudden death in 1878, David D. Colton had been the confidential manager of the railroad's political interests in California, while Collis P. Huntington was serving the same function in Washington, D.C. Colton liked to be known as "General," though this title was more political than military, since it dated merely from a term as a brigadier in the state militia; he had never seen active military duty. Having received his early training as a young political lieutenant of David C. Broderick, Colton was highly skilled in the shadier methods of influencing politicians. He amassed a fortune by performing this type of confidential service in exchange for opportunities to share in the profits of enterprises which would benefit from the special political privileges he could obtain.

Colton first attracted the attention of the Big Four by establishing a friendship with Charles Crocker, his neighbor on Nob Hill. Though Stanford and Hopkins disliked and distrusted Colton, Collis P. Huntington saw the potential value of his special talents, and persuaded the others to approve an agreement in 1874 under which Colton was permitted to acquire a large amount of railroad stock on credit. The new associate often used the expression "we five" in his letters to Huntington, though some of the newspapers described the group more accurately as "the Big Four and a Half."

When Colton died, his widow received only a little more than half a million dollars in the settlement of his estate. Not long afterward when some of the details of the estate of Mark Hopkins were made public and Mrs. Colton noticed that some of Hopkins's shares of stock were quoted as having a far higher cash value than she had been allowed for her husband's identical shares, she concluded that the railroad leaders had cheated her. When they coldly refused a more favorable settlement and countered with charges that her husband had embezzled railroad funds, she sued them for 4 million dollars. In 1883, in the course of the trial, her attorneys suddenly introduced as evidence several hundred letters that had been exchanged between Colton and Huntington in the years between 1874 and 1878.

In extraordinarily explicit detail these letters revealed Colton's activities in influencing the elections, reelections, and votes of members of the California legislature and the California congressional delegation, and Huntington's similar activities with members of Congress in the East. There were innumerable references to payments of money without vouchers, and discussions of the amounts which particular legislators and legislative measures might be expected to cost. In one letter, for example, Huntington had written that "It costs money to fix things. . . . I believe with $200,000 I can pass our bill, but that it is not worth this much to us." In another instance he wrote that "the boys are very hungry, and it will cost us considerable to be saved."

The state supreme court, in the case of *Ellen M. Colton v. Leland Stanford et al.*, refused to award Mrs. Colton a larger settlement, on the ground that she had formally signed and accepted the railroad's original terms. But the damage to the Southern Pacific's reputation was far greater than the value of the widow's highest demands, and in view of this fact many observers wondered why the associates had not settled the matter out of court. The explanation was that Ellen Colton had given them no warning that she had the damaging letters before she made them public. Huntington supposed that Colton had destroyed his copies of the letters, as he had instructed him to do.

For decades afterward the railroad's opponents could and did cite these letters whenever they wished to denounce the Southern Pacific for corrupting politics. Moreover, a widespread public reaction was that the Big Four were men who would defraud a partner's widow—a pattern of conduct that shocked some men to whom the payment of money for the votes of politicians seemed not only a less serious moral offense but a customary and inevitable method of conducting business.

The Huntington–Stanford feud. Collis P. Huntington's contempt for men who sought public office, which was extremely apparent throughout his letters to Colton, bore a significant relation to his feelings toward Leland Stanford. For many years Huntington had resented the degree to which Stanford received the lion's share of public attention while he, Huntington, did most of the hard work of managing the railroad's affairs. In 1885, when Stanford secured election to the United States Senate, Huntington was deeply angered. The honor had been promised, as a new term, to former Senator Aaron A. Sargent, a close friend of Huntington's who had rendered many years of faithful service to the railroad's interests in both houses of Congress.

When the founding of a memorial university was announced, Huntington felt that Stanford's vanity had become completely unendurable, and he made plans to deflate it. At an annual meeting of stockholders in 1890 Huntington announced that he would support Stanford's election to a second term as Senator only on condition that he himself be elected to the presidency of the railroad, which Stanford had held for 30 years. Then, after assuming the presidency, Huntington publicly stated that unlike his predecessor he would never "use this great corporation to advance my personal ambition at the expense of its owners, or put my hands in the treasury to defeat the people's choice, and thereby put myself into positions that should be filled by others."

Enemies of the Southern Pacific had often charged that large amounts of railroad money were spent to secure Stanford's election and reelection as United States Senator by the California legislature. Now the charge was directly corroborated by the president of the railroad itself. Huntington threw his open denunciation in Stanford's face with no more warning than either of them had had from Ellen Colton. In fact, Huntington deliberately violated a promise, given as one of the conditions of the change of presidency, that there would be no such public attack. In the next few hours Stanford's friends saw him age 10 years, and his death, in 1893, was undoubtedly hastened by Huntington's carefully laid plan to destroy him.

Beginning in 1892, and continuing for several years afterward, Stanford's former private secretary, J. M. Bassett, published in the *San Francisco Report* at weekly intervals a series of letters which he addressed to Huntington. These letters, opening with the salutation "Dear Pard," were at least partly intended to injure Huntington as Stanford had been injured. They were filled with charges of the wholesale corruption of national, state, and local officials by the railroad; and though they had little effect in penetrating the thick skin of Collis P. Huntington, they added significantly to a growing mass of public evidence.

Los Angeles fights for a free harbor. In another of his early actions as the new president of the Southern Pacific, Huntington reversed Stanford's policy toward the location of a modern deep-water harbor for Los Angeles. Senator Stanford had been supporting proposals for Federal aid in the construction of a breakwater at San Pedro. Huntington decided that the harbor must be built at Santa Monica, because he was able to purchase enough land there to ensure that the Southern Pacific could dominate the harbor by preventing any competing railroad from gaining access to it.

Huntington saw no reason that the railroad should have less control over the future port of Los Angeles than it had long exerted over the port of San Francisco, where for more than 40 years, as Governor Hiram Johnson would tell the legislature in 1913, the Southern Pacific through its control of the state harbor commission "practically owned and operated the waterfront, and used it as a private piece of business property for the advancement of its own political and business interests." But Los Angeles, though it had only 50,000 people in the early '90s, felt the stirrings of its future growth and power, and determined to fight for a harbor that would be at least relatively free of Southern Pacific control.

The roadstead at San Pedro, described by Richard Henry Dana, had served the Los Angeles area as its most common anchorage in the days of the hide and tallow trade. In 1870, largely through the efforts of Phineas Banning, Congress made the first of a series of appropriations for a modest harbor development by which Wilmington Creek, an estuary just north and east of San Pedro, eventually to be known as the inner harbor, was enabled to accommodate small coastwise vessels. In 1891 a board of Army engineers appointed with the approval of Senator Stanford reported that San Pedro Bay was the best site in the region for the construction of a breakwater and thus for the creation of a great harbor adequate for the largest oceangoing ships. But the next year, while an appropriation for this purpose was under consideration by the Senate Commerce Committee, Huntington notified the committee's chairman through a telegram sent in the name of the Southern Pacific's chief engineer that because of the alleged difficulty of driving piles into the rocky bottom at San Pedro the railroad would build its own wharf at Santa Monica.

Most of the Southern Pacific's interests at Santa Monica had been acquired from the previous promoter of that district, Senator John P. Jones of Nevada. Jones had expected his mines in the region of Death Valley and the Panamint Mountains to produce more silver than the Comstock Lode. As a part of that dream he had bought up the Santa Monica shoreline to develop it as a point of exportation for his anticipated masses of silver, and had built a railroad between Los Angeles and Santa Monica Bay. When the silver failed to materialize, the Southern Pacific took over much of Jones's Santa Monica real estate, and bought his railroad for a fraction of its cost after ruining it in a rate war.

When Huntington served blunt notice that he would use all his influence in Congress to block any appropriation for the San Pedro project, Los Angeles rebelled, and its Chamber of Commerce was able to enlist some powerful allies in the fight. Harrison Gray Otis and the *Times*; the St. Louis capitalists who had built a Terminal Railroad from Los Angeles to San Pedro; and Democratic United States Senator Stephen M. White, a Los Angeles attorney, joined the rebellion. Joseph Pulitzer's *New York World* inquired, "Is this a government for the people, or a government by Mr. Huntington, for Mr. Huntington? The question may as well be settled in the Santa Monica–San Pedro controversy as anywhere." Huntington's supporters in Congress argued that the government should not spend money for a harbor at San Pedro when "private enterprise"—that is, Mr. Huntington—was willing to undertake the cost of construction nearby; but it was well known that Huntington expected to persuade Congress to pay for a still larger breakwater at Santa Monica.

In 1896 Congress passed an appropriation for whatever site a new board of engineers should approve. When this report again favored San Pedro, Huntington secured two more years of delay through the influence of the Secretary of War, Russell A. Alger. But at last, in April 1899, the first bargeload of rock was dumped to begin construction of the breakwater at San Pedro. In later years the people of the Los Angeles Harbor District would join with the Federal government, private interests, and the city of Long Beach in providing funds; the breakwater would be extended eastward to protect the combined harbor of San Pedro and Long Beach; and Los Angeles would become one of the world's great seaports, as well as one of its great cities.

The funding bill. The original construction of the Central Pacific had been made possible by Federal loans of nearly 28 million dollars payable in 30 years. No payment of interest was required until the full maturity of the loans, and simple interest at 6 percent added more than 50 million dollars to the total obligation that was legally payable by the year 1899. In the 1870s, though the Big Four began to vote themselves huge dividends, they set aside nothing for the ultimate payment of the railroad's debt to the government and instead propounded a long series of ingenious and specious arguments for its cancellation.

Under a law proposed by Senator Thurman of Ohio in 1878, Congress required the Central Pacific to create a sinking fund of 25 percent of the net earnings of the parts of its rail network that had been built with Federal aid. Huntington, in a letter to Colton, described the legislators who voted for the Thurman Act as "communists," and Colton replied that "this Congress is simply a band of robbers." But the railroad, by manipulating both traffic and bookkeeping so as to credit as little as possible of the net earnings to the original "bond-aided" portions of the lines and as much as possible to other parts of the system, kept the sinking fund to a small fraction of its total debt to the government. And in the '90s Huntington advanced a series of proposals for a funding plan to delay payment for 50 or 100 years, at the extremely low interest rate of one-half of 1 percent. In California this aroused more opposition than any other measure in the long history of public resentment against the railroad, and Adolph Sutro and William Randolph Hearst led a chorus of denunciation of it as a plot to escape the debt entirely.

Adolph Sutro had sold all his stock in his Comstock tunnel as soon as it was completed. With the million dollars salvaged from that venture, he had moved to San Francisco, and there, by buying land whenever the local market for it reached the bottom of one of its periodic depressions, had become the owner of one-twelfth of the city's entire area. Seal Rocks, the Cliff House, the gardens of his home, and other adjoining portions of his great estate were opened to the public as a park. When the Market Street Railway company, a Southern Pacific subsidiary, took over the trolley line to this park and refused to continue a low round-trip fare, Sutro built his own parallel line and declared himself the defender of the people against the greed of the Octopus.

In 1894 Sutro was elected mayor of San Francisco on the Populist ticket. The Populist movement, the radical third party that originated among the farmers of the Middle West, was at the height of its influence during the aftermath of the panic of 1893. Sutro won the Populist nomination and the election, partly because his many philanthropies had made him a popular figure, but also because he organized a series of mass meetings to denounce Huntington's funding plan. At these meetings Sutro promised to urge the state of Kentucky to repeal the charter of the Southern Pacific Company.

William Randolph Hearst also threw the full weight of the *San Francisco Examiner* into the battle against the funding plan, and in 1894 the *Examiner* obtained more than 200,000 signatures on petitions against it. In 1896, when the crucial vote in Congress was approaching, Hearst sent Ambrose Bierce and the cartoonist Homer Davenport to Washington, D.C. For more than 20 years Bierce's opinions of the Southern Pacific leadership had been typified by his frequent printed references to "£eland $tanford," and his articles on the funding bill were as merciless as anything in his long career of journalistic mayhem. His most effective dispatch reported a conversation on the steps of the national capitol in which Huntington asked him to name his price for stopping his attacks, and Bierce replied that his price was the railroad's full debt to the government, payable to the United States Treasury. At the same time, Davenport was making Huntington the villain of some of his most famous cartoons.

In the face of Huntington's claim that failure to adopt his funding plan would bankrupt the whole Southern Pacific system and that no one would then be willing to buy it, the rebellious California legislature, elected in the depression year of 1896, adopted a resolution urging the Federal government not only to foreclose but to assume the ownership and operation of the railroad if necessary. When the funding bill was finally voted down in Congress in January 1897, popular opinion in California was so overjoyed that Democratic Governor James H. Budd proclaimed Saturday, January 16, a public holiday in celebration. Two years later a compromise agreement was reached, and under its terms the railroad completed the payment of its entire debt to the Federal government by 1909.

The Southern Pacific machine. The Los Angeles harbor fight and the funding battle were almost the only major political defeats that the railroad suffered before 1910. These two defeats occurred during the hard times of the '90s, when public discontent was at a maximum, and they were in considerable part the results of personality conflicts in which the increasing tactlessness and ruthlessness of the aging Collis P. Huntington infuriated other large operators and made them his fanatical enemies. Moreover, these two issues involved the national government. In purely state and local matters, attempts to break the grip of the railroad's political machine brought only a long succession of humiliating failures for nearly half a century.

In 1862, when a state constitutional amendment increased the term of the

Governor from 2 years to 4, it was argued that the longer term would attract better men to the gubernatorial office. But it failed to do so, largely because the corrupting influence of the railroad in state politics had already begun, and steadily continued to grow.

By the 1890s the head of the railroad's political department, who was also its chief legal counsel, had become a much more important official than the Governor; in fact he usually had the power to name the Governor, or any other public officer in California. Under his direction there was a railroad political manager in every county in the state. This manager might be the Republican boss in a Republican county, or the Democratic boss in a Democratic county; in important or doubtful counties he was merely the railroad boss, with whom both Republican and Democratic bosses had to deal. Candidates for state, county, and city offices were nominated by party conventions. There was no effective legal regulation of the party primaries in which the delegates to these conventions were elected. State law still regarded the political party as a kind of private enterprise, or private club, and this made it easy for party bosses to control primaries and conventions by a luxuriant assortment of corrupt methods without risking prosecution for election frauds.

A system of political alliance with the other public utility corporations was another factor in the railroad's power over local political bosses. The railroad itself was then the only statewide public utility, but the political interests of local street railway, gas, light, and telephone companies were similar to its own, if on a smaller scale. The railroad and other public utilities were the private business corporations that could profit most directly from special favors granted by state and local government agencies, and consequently they joined in furnishing the bulk of the money that corrupted state and local politics. This alliance came to be known in California as "the associated villainies."

To place all the blame upon the railroad and other utility corporations, however, ignores the fact that they could not have corrupted the state if so many of its citizens had not been corruptible. Leland Stanford's biographer, George T. Clark, argued that such charges must be false because "in Edmund Burke's notable phrase, 'I do not know the method of drawing up an indictment against an whole people.'" Actually, of course, it was neither possible nor necessary for the railroad to corrupt everyone. Influence over a few thousand strategically placed individuals was sufficient.

When a lawyer who was not already on the railroad's payroll was elected to the state legislature he was likely to receive a letter from the law department of the Southern Pacific stating that the railroad wished to retain an outstanding attorney from his region, during a period which happened to coincide with that of the coming session at Sacramento. A retainer fee was enclosed, and the privileged nature of the attorney-client relationship protected the secrecy of the transaction.

Of all the agencies of state government, the railroad was most careful to control the bank commission, which it allowed to be created ostensibly as a reform measure in 1878. A banker who gave aid and comfort to the railroad's enemies could suddenly find himself in disastrous trouble with this board of commissioners. Consequently, a businessman or a farmer who displeased the railroad by denouncing its rates, or by voting against its candidates while serving as a delegate to a party convention, or by opposing its measures while serving as a member of the legislature, would suddenly find himself unable to obtain further loans from his bank.

Another effective form of influence was the free pass. It cost relatively little, and it reached men who would have resisted more obvious forms of bribery. Instead of being considered a bribe, the railroad pass was a status symbol. The man who held it felt himself allied with the successful and powerful leaders of society against the ignorant and envious rabble. The constitution of 1879 specifically forbade free passes for state officeholders, but the provision was never enforced.

Many of the smaller newspapers were subsidized not only with advertising contracts but with regular and secret monthly stipends. Larger publishers such as Harrison Gray Otis, M. H. de Young, and John D. Spreckels were far too wealthy to be influenced by trifling financial considerations. But each of these three men had perennial hopes of going to the United States Senate, and though they often joined in attacks on the railroad, there were also many occasions when each of them tempered his criticism of the Southern Pacific because of his own political ambitions.

Not even the courts were immune from the railroad's influence. Justices of the Federal and state supreme courts traveled on passes. Most of the judges of the Federal district and circuit courts in San Francisco were appointed at the instance of California senators who spoke with the railroad's voice. Justice Stephen J. Field, great and brilliant "craftsman of the law," was a personal associate of the Big Four, owed his position in the United States Supreme Court to their influence, and rendered them invaluable service by writing many of the opinions through which the highest court long protected the railroad and other corporations from effective government regulation.

As for the judiciary at the state level, as J. M. Bassett reminded Huntington in one of the "Dear Pard" letters in 1895, there were few superior courts in California "in which a citizen may bring an action against you in full confidence that he will be fairly and impartially dealt with." Along with machine control over the election of judges, one of the regular duties of a county boss was to provide the railroad with secret annotated lists of veniremen to aid its attorneys in impaneling sympathetic juries.

William F. Herrin. Among the important sources of the railroad's power was its ability to enlist the most talented lawyers in its service. One such man was William F. Herrin, who headed the Southern Pacific's legal and political departments from 1893 to 1910. It was under Herrin that the railroad's political machine in California reached its highest level of efficiency.

Herrin was a product of pioneer life. Born on a farm in Oregon, he worked his way through a small college and a small law school, and within a few years after beginning his practice in San Francisco had become the chief attorney for the Sharon Estate, Miller & Lux, and the Spring Valley Water Company. In 1889 he won a national reputation when, as special counsel, he aided a United States attorney in defending a Federal Marshal, David Neagle, against a murder charge.

This case grew out of the earlier and equally sensational legal battle in which Sarah Althea Hill had claimed that she was the legal wife of Senator William Sharon under the terms of a "contract marriage," and that she was thus entitled to a large part of his enormous fortune. During the court proceedings Sharon died, and his alleged widow married one of her attorneys, David S. Terry, former chief justice of the California supreme court, who had killed Senator Broderick in their famous duel. United States Justice Stephen J. Field, while on Federal circuit court duty in San Francisco, ruled that Mrs. Terry had not been Sharon's wife and had no valid claim on the Sharon estate. Both the Terrys had brought weapons into the courtroom, and both of them threatened Field's life.

At the time of Justice Field's next visit to California, United States Marshal Neagle was assigned as his bodyguard, and when, in a railway station in Lathrop, Terry approached Field and struck him, Neagle shot Terry dead. *In re Neagle* became one of the great cases in the history of American Federal-state relations. Because Neagle was a Federal officer who had presumably acted in line of duty, the United States government wished to protect him from prosecution for murder under the laws of California. But no Federal law authorized either his assignment as bodyguard or his action in killing Terry; the United States Supreme Court ruled that these had been "fairly and properly inferable" from the Constitution. It was one of the broadest interpretations yet given to the implied powers of the national government.

Herrin was the attorney who contributed most to the preparation of the case for Neagle, in the circuit court proceedings at San Francisco. At the same time, he was also distinguishing himself more privately in his capacity as attorney for Henry Miller, by persuading the railroad to grant special secret rates and rebates on Miller's shipments of cattle and wheat. Collis P. Huntington, deeply impressed with Herrin's talents, chose him, as he had once chosen David D. Colton, to be the railroad's western political manager.

From his office in the Southern Pacific's headquarters at Fourth and Townsend streets in San Francisco, Herrin not only directed all of the company's manifold political activities, but grappled with all of its complex legal problems as well. Responsibility for either of these related functions would have been an enormous task for any man; but not even the severest critics of Herrin's methods and objectives ever questioned his ability. Franklin Hichborn, the freelance journalist and lifelong reform crusader who provided the best newspaper coverage of California party conventions, elections, and legislative sessions for several decades, often described Herrin's influence as a fountainhead of political corruption; but he also described him as "perhaps the ablest man I ever met."

Comparison of Herrin with David D. Colton suggests the evolution that occurred between the railroad's first generation and its second, in the development of its political techniques.

Failure of 19th-century reform movements. A significant factor in the perpetuation of the railroad's control of California was the often-repeated argument of railroad apologists that reasonable men should put their abilities to work, and find their rewards, within the established order of things. For example, a lieutenant governor once advised an assembly of students at the University of California to be "performers," not "reformers," in politics.

The effectiveness of such appeals was closely related to the widespread sense of futility that followed the many disheartening failures of reform. The railroad always devoted special care to its efforts to gain control of reform movements. Of the hundreds of men elected to office on platforms denouncing the railroad, so many were later found to have been brought under its influence that reform campaigns in general came to be regarded with apathy and cynicism.

A classic example was Newton Booth, a Republican who was elected Governor in 1871 on a platform opposing further state and local subsidies to the railroad. In the panic year of 1873, insurgent Republicans with strong support from the Granger movement put forward a third party called the Independent Taxpayers, and gained a majority in the state legislature in a three-cornered race with the regular Republicans and the Democrats. The Independent Taxpayers' movement in California was nicknamed the "Dolly Varden" party, a derisive term originally applied to the Liberal Republican party in national politics in 1872 because of the absurdly heterogeneous character of its following. A current fashion in women's dresses and hats was called the Dolly Varden, after an attractively dressed heroine in Dickens's *Barnaby Rudge*. Widely variegated combinations and colors, worn by all sorts of women, were passed off as being the original and genuine fashion.

Governor Booth assumed the leadership of the Independent Taxpayers' reform party of California, and echoed its promises to force the railroad's fares and freight rates down and its tax payments up. But somehow nothing substantial was done toward accomplishing these objectives. Instead Booth used his following in the legislature to secure his own election to the United States Senate. A few months later he was listed in one of Huntington's secret letters to Colton as among the railroad's most important friends. The Dolly Varden nickname took on an added connotation; Dickens's original Dolly was a coquette, and so, politically speaking, was Newton Booth.

Usually the railroad placed more reliance on Republican candidates and office holders than upon Democrats, but the Democratic party failed dismally to provide an effective vehicle for reform. The railroad was quite willing to make use of Democrats whenever they happened to have a better chance of election, and it often supported the candidates and machines of both parties at once. There was a confusing and almost total lack of clear and genuine issues between the two major parties; even in national politics they differed consistently only on the tariff, and as the 19th century wore on, much political discussion was bogged down in the dreary absurdities of "free silver."

The California Democrats also suffered from a shortage of inspiring leadership. Senator George Hearst was no reformer, and he was in close political alliance with Chris Buckley, the Democratic boss of San Francisco, who often received money from the railroad and from anyone else who was willing to pay. Senator Stephen M. White, whose father had been a Workingmen's candidate for Governor, opposed the railroad only when it was politically safe and expedient to do so. James H. Budd, the Democratic Governor elected in 1894, could accomplish little in the face of Republican majorities in the legislature.

The economic distress of the 1890s intensified a growing belief that both major parties were morally bankrupt, and this led to a new flourishing of support for third-party movements. The Nationalist party had a brief but striking career in 1890. Formed by enthusiastic readers of Edward Bellamy's utopian romance, *Looking Backward, 2000–1887,* this movement advocated a gradualist, nonviolent Christian socialism. But its appeal was mainly to urban discontent, and nearly all its following in California was in San Francisco and Los Angeles. It was overshadowed by the rise of the People's or Populist party. The Populist movement was based mainly on the increasingly bitter discontent of the farmers, but it hoped to gain support from city workers as well.

At the heart of Populism was a deep distrust of political parties, and a firm belief that no important reform could be accomplished until control of the machinery of government was taken out of the hands of party bosses and party conventions and given to the people. Thus the most enduring contribution of the Populists in California was the spread of public interest in their demands for the direct primary, the initiative, the referendum, and the recall. A few years later this part of the Populist program would form the core of the California Progressive movement.

One of the weaknesses of Populism was its devotion to a bizarre conspiracy theory. According to the advocates of this notion, the "demonetization of silver" or "crime of 1873" had been a sinister plot of international financiers and their politician hirelings for the purpose of robbing the farmers. American farmers did have a genuine grievance in the deflationary and grossly inadequate national currency system of the period, which tended to depress farm prices. But the idea that the free and unlimited coinage of silver would cure all the ills of agriculture and of the rest of the economy was a sad delusion, and it weakened the force of the sounder reform demands of the Populists, such as government controls over railroads and trusts, an income tax, unemployment relief, farm benefit programs, women's suffrage, and child labor laws. Moreover, when the national Democratic party espoused free silver in 1896 the Populists as a third party were virtually ruined.

Another weakness of the essentially agrarian radicalism of the Populist movement was the failure of its appeal to urban labor. City workers had little interest in monetary changes that would inflate the cost of food. Moreover the farmer was essentially an employer—in California often an employer of Orientals.

SELECTED BIBLIOGRAPHY

Aspects of the railroad's political activities are described in Daggett, *Chapters on the History of the Southern Pacific*; Lewis, *The Big Four*; the chapter on politics in Treadwell, *The Cattle King*; Ralph N. Traxler, "Collis P. Huntington and the Texas and Pacific Railroad Land Grants," *New Mexico Historical Review*, XXIV (April 1959), 117–133; and Jack W. Bates, "The Southern Pacific Railroad in California Politics," M.A. thesis, University of the Pacific (1942).

Important works on state politics are Winfield J. Davis, *History of Political Conventions in California, 1849–1892* (1893); and Theodore H. Hittell, *History of California, Volume IV* (1898), mainly a history of gubernatorial administrations from 1849 to 1887.

Biographical treatments include Edith Dobie, *The Political Career of Stephen Mallory White, a Study of Party Activities under the Convention System* (1927); Curtis E. Grassman, "Prologue to Progressivism: Senator Stephen M. White and the California Reform Impulse, 1875–1905," Ph.D. thesis, University of California, Los Angeles (1970); Carl B. Swisher, *Stephen J. Field, Craftsman of the Law* (1930); Oscar T. Shuck, *History of the Bench and Bar of California* (1901); and J. Edward Johnson, *History of the Supreme Court Justices of California, Volume I, 1850–1900* (1963).

On the harbor fight, see Charles Dwight Willard, *The Free Harbor Contest at Los Angeles* (1899); Ella A. Ludwig, *History of the Harbor District of Los Angeles* (1928); and Clarence H. Matson, *Building a World Gateway; the Story of Los Angeles Harbor* (1945).

Most of the railroad's arguments for cancellation of its debt were brought together by its counsel Creed Haymond in *The Central Pacific Railroad and the United States* (three parts, 1887–1889).

The first volume of the memoirs of Franklin Hichborn, "California Politics, 1891–1939" (reproduced typewriting, copies in several libraries including that of the University of California, Los Angeles), provides many insights into the structure and functioning of the Southern Pacific machine. Alexander Callow, Jr., "San Francisco's Blind Boss," *Pacific Historical Review*, XXV

(August 1956), 261–280, describes machine politics in the 1880s and early 1890s, as exemplified in the career of Christopher A. Buckley.

Attempts at state regulation are discussed in Gerald D. Nash, "The California Railroad Commission, 1876–1911," *Southern California Quarterly*, XLIV (December 1962), 287–306; and Ward M. McAfee, "Local Interests and Railroad Regulation in California during the Granger Decade," and "A Constitutional History of Railroad Rate Regulation in California, 1879–1911," *Pacific Historical Review*, XXXVII (February and August 1968), 51–66, 265–279.

On the case of Sarah Althea Hill and William Sharon, see Robert H. Kroninger, *Sarah and the Senator* (1964); and Gary L. Roberts, "In Pursuit of Duty," *The American West*, VII (September 1970), 27–33, 62–63, on Neagle's shooting of Terry.

Donald E. Walters, "Populism in California, 1889–1900," Ph.D. thesis, University of California, Berkeley (1952), stresses the contributions of the Populist program to the later and more successful Progressive movement. See also Walters, "The Feud between California Populist T. V. Cator and Democrats James Maguire and James Barry," *Pacific Historical Review*, XXVII (August 1958), 281–298; Eric F. Petersen, "The End of an Era: California's Gubernatorial Election of 1894," in the same journal, XXXVIII (May 1969), 141–156; and David B. Griffiths, "Anti-Monopoly Movements in California, 1873–1898," *Southern California Quarterly*, LII (June 1970), 93–121.

Chapter XXVI

THE ROOTS OF REFORM

Boss Ruef and the Union Labor party. For several decades before the great earthquake and fire of 1906, about a fourth of the people of California lived in San Francisco. Among the sources of the prevailing corruption in California's politics, the deep-seated habit of corruption in the government of its major city was second only to the malign influence of the railroad. There was far too much truth in the statement of the *San Francisco Call,* in 1887, that "To hold one of the principal city offices for two years is equivalent to obtaining a large fortune."

Throughout the United States, as Lord Bryce remarked in *The American Commonwealth,* the government of cities was a conspicuous failure of American democracy. This had been true in varying degrees since the early days of New York's Tammany Hall under Aaron Burr, but the problem had become worse in the age of industrialization and urbanization between the Civil War and the rise of the Progressive movement in the early 20th century. Cities, corporations, and labor unions grew so rapidly that government and law could not keep up with them. One result was an increase in the importance of the city boss, as an extralegal figure who could furnish a bridge between the lagging institutions of politics and the urgent demands of the expanding conglomerations of economic power. The boss served as a broker in a corrupt system of alliances between big business and politics that menaced democracy in cities throughout the nation.

Cosmopolitan San Francisco might have been expected to produce as the most famous of its bosses a figure as colorful and out of the ordinary as the city itself. Abraham Ruef was the only son of a moderately wealthy San Francisco family of French Jewish origin. He was a man of unusual culture and brilliant intelligence, heightened by a good university and legal education. After graduating in the middle 1880s from the University of California in Berkeley and from its law school in San Francisco, he entered politics as an idealistic young reformer. But his ideals began to decline when he attended his first Republican county convention, an experience that impressed him with the apparently hopeless realities of machine rule. Surrendering to opportunism, and relegating his ideals to campaign speeches and the writing of party platforms, he became the Republican subboss for the district in the northern part of the city then known as the Latin Quarter. Skillfully he articulated his political influence with his law practice and investments in real estate, and schemed to increase his power and wealth. An opportunity came in 1901.

At the turn of the century the mayor of San Francisco was the reform Democrat James D. Phelan, the most politically promising leader among the very large number of San Franciscans of Irish Catholic descent. A son of one of the city's leading bankers, Phelan was also a millionaire banker in his own right, and as a public officeholder he was above the temptations to corruption that afflicted men of lesser integrity and inferior financial independence. Ordinarily he held fairly liberal views on a number of economic and social issues, including the rights of organized labor. But during the great strike in the summer of 1901 his wealthy friends persuaded him to order city policemen to ride on the drays beside "scab" teamsters, thus using the police themselves as virtual strikebreakers.

This led to an angry outcry that if the power of government was thus to be used for the destruction of unions, then union men must enter politics and elect a government of their own; with this intention a group calling itself the Union Labor Party of San Francisco was organized in September. The philosophy and strategy of American craft unionism were generally opposed to any such movement, and not a single important official of any of the larger San Francisco unions would associate himself with the new party. It might have died at birth had it not acquired a foster father: Abraham Ruef perceived that he could use it for his own purposes, though he had no genuine interest whatever in labor unions except his interest in their members' votes for candidates he controlled.

Because Mayor Phelan had angered conservatives by refusing to call for state troops to put down the strike, almost as much as he had angered labor by his use of city policemen, his renomination was impossible. The Democratic and Republican nominees for mayor were colorless men. For the Union Labor candidacy, on the other hand, Ruef found a man with a remarkable combination of political assets. His friend Eugene E. Schmitz, president of the musicians' union, was a native San Franciscan of German-Irish descent and Roman Catholic faith. As yet he was little known except as a violinist and as the director of the orchestra in a fashionable theater; but he was a tall, handsome, distinguished-looking, commanding figure of a man, and also a model husband and father. "The psychology of the mass of voters," Ruef told Schmitz, "is like that of a crowd of small boys," to whom such qualities had a deep emotional appeal.

The enthusiastic political following that soon rallied to Schmitz was an impressive demonstration of Ruef's knowledge of politics as an applied social science. The many votes that were drawn essentially by Schmitz's appearance, and by the sound of his voice, were merged with the votes of labor union members, German Americans, and Irish-American Catholics, along with the votes that Ruef could deliver from his Republican machine in his own district. Schmitz was elected mayor in 1901, 1903, and 1905.

In the first two of these elections the Union Labor ticket gained only a few seats in the 18-member board of supervisors, the legislative branch of the city-and-county government. But in 1905, to Ruef's own surprise, every one of his 18 Union Labor nominees for the board of supervisors was elected. Voting machines were used for the first time, and nearly all of Schmitz's admirers, fearing to invalidate their votes among the complicated battery of levers, took the easy course of pulling down one lever for the straight party ticket.

The more important and responsible union leaders still refused to accept the "labor" party's nominations, and Ruef had selected the nominees hastily and carelessly, under the impression that they had no chance to win. Most of the new city fathers were obscure men who knew little about the nature of their office except the popular belief that supervisors customarily received bribes. They suspected, quite accurately, that Ruef received large payments from public utility corporations. In vain he pointed out to them that as a lawyer who held no public office he could quite legally receive such payments as attorney's fees, but that payments to them, as public officials, would be bribery. The new supervisors concluded that although this fine distinction might be law, it was not justice. They demanded that Ruef share his fees with them if he expected them to vote for the measures his corporate clients desired.

Several transactions of this kind were carried out in 1906. For example, the United Railroads of San Francisco, the largest street railway company, asked for a special ordinance permitting it to convert all its remaining cable car lines to overhead electric trolleys. The company paid an attorney's fee of $200,000 to Ruef; he divided $85,000 among the supervisors, and the ordinance was passed. The Pacific Gas and Electric Company paid Ruef $20,000; of this sum he paid $13,250 to the supervisors, and thereby persuaded them not to make a drastic reduction in the gas rate. There were other corrupt arrangements involving telephone and water companies.

The San Francisco graft prosecution. Such instances of corruption were by no means unprecedented, either in San Francisco or in other large American cities of the time. What was really extraordinary about them was that through some very unusual circumstances they became known to the public in complete detail. For the year 1906 also brought two crucial events in San Francisco's history. One was the disastrous earthquake and fire, in April, and the other, in October, was the announcement of the beginning of what turned out to be the most persistent graft prosecution in the history of any city in the United States.

The earthquake which rocked San Francisco at 5:14 in the morning of April 18 was so severe that it caused a number of deaths and injuries within the first few moments. But San Franciscans, anxious to counteract the idea that a similar catastrophe could ever destroy their city again, have always correctly insisted that the greatest damage was done not by the earthquake—over which man had no conceivable control—but rather by the subsequent fire, whose recurrence a better-planned water system could render impossible. The initial shock, which started more than 50 separate fires almost immediately by breaking gas connections and chimneys and overturning stoves, also shattered most of the flimsy water mains and left the firemen helpless. The fires, merging into one vast, continuous conflagration and raging for three days and two nights, destroyed the greater part of the city; 452 lives were lost.

The painful difficulties of the struggle to build a new city on the ruins of the old made San Franciscans less tolerant of corruption in their city government, and prepared them to welcome the announcement of an investigation which a small group of reformers had begun to plan, in close secrecy, before the earthquake.

The originator of this plan was Fremont Older, editor of the *San Francisco Bulletin*. Older secured a promise of cooperation from the district attorney, William H. Langdon. But the ordinary budget and staff of the district attorney's office could not have provided for the kind of investigation that was necessary, and Older induced the reform-minded millionaire capitalist Rudolph Spreckels, one of the sons of Claus Spreckels, the "sugar king," to pledge his financial support. Rudolph Spreckels ultimately contributed nearly $250,000 to the prosecution fund, mostly for hiring special detectives. Ex-Mayor Phelan also contributed. Older persuaded President Theodore Roosevelt to lend the services of the Federal government's ablest special prosecutor, Francis J. Heney, and also of its star detective, William J. Burns, who was then head of the Secret Service of the Treasury Department. The Heney-Burns team was just concluding a remarkably successful prosecution of land frauds in Oregon, where their work led to the conviction and imprisonment of a United States Senator and several other prominent men. Langdon now appointed Heney assistant district attorney of San Francisco.

The prosecution's first major move was to secure indictments charging that Ruef and Schmitz had extorted money from the proprietors of several French restaurants under the threat of blocking the renewals of their liquor licenses. The term "French restaurant" then had a special connotation in San Francisco. On the first floor there was a conventional restaurant serving excellent food at moderate prices; but on the second floor there were private supper bedrooms, and the upper floors were houses of prostitution.

San Francisco after the earthquake. The dome is that of the ruined City Hall (Courtesy of the Bancroft Library)

The charge that the boss and the mayor had taken money from these establishments was a charge of reprehensible but relatively petty graft, and based as yet on limited evidence. The real breakthrough came when Burns trapped one of the supervisors, Thomas Lonergan, into taking a planted bribe. Heney then offered Lonergan immunity from all prosecution in return for a complete disclosure of every bribery in which he and his colleagues had participated. The other supervisors, confronted with Lonergan's testimony, were also granted immunity and also made complete confessions. With this overwhelming mass of evidence Heney then obtained a full confession from Ruef himself, after promising not to prosecute him if he would testify against the "higher-ups"—the corporation executives who had made the payments to him as their "attorney." Heney then secured indictments for bribery against Patrick Calhoun, president of the United Railroads, nationally known financier, and grandson of the great statesman John C. Calhoun; against Tirey L. Ford, chief counsel of the United Railroads and former attorney general of California; and against several of the highest executives of the gas and telephone companies.

Heney's strategy was based in part on the ideas of his close friend Lincoln Steffens, the nation's leading journalistic authority on municipal corruption. Both Steffens and Heney had been born in San Francisco, and they shared a deep interest in the future of the city and the state. Steffens's boyhood home was the house in Sacramento that had since become the Governor's mansion.

Steffens had written a famous series of articles originally published in *McClure's* and brought together in 1904 in his book called *The Shame of the Cities*. The more important source of the massive graft system in America, Steffens concluded, was not the weak little politician who took bribes, but the wealthy and powerful captain of industry who paid them. "The typical businessman," Steffens had written, "is a bad citizen. If he is a 'big businessman' he is twice as bad. I found him buying boodlers in St. Louis, defending grafters in Minneapolis, sharing with bosses in Philadelphia, originating corruption in Pittsburgh, deploring reform and fighting good government with corruption funds in New York. He is a self-righteous fraud . . . and it would be a great boon if he would neglect politics."

By 1906, however, Steffens had come to feel that because the blame for corruption was shared by so many, the punishment of individuals was useless and inappropriate. Instead he advocated that after the full shock of publicity of the mass of offenses in San Francisco, there should be a general amnesty, so that all could join in the building of a sounder social fabric.

Heney, on the other hand, had no faith in this particular aspect of Steffens's views. Rather, Heney believed that only the exemplary punishment of the greatest offenders could accomplish anything of permanent value. He confided to Steffens that if he should succeed in convicting the general counsel and the president of the United Railroads, Ford and Calhoun, he would then reach for the top and try to send to prison, for bribery, not only the general counsel of the Southern Pacific, William F. Herrin, but also its president, the mighty Edward H. Harriman himself.

But the prosecution fell far short of these objectives. In a series of long trials of Ford and Calhoun, in which thousands of veniremen were examined and rejected in the attempt to find supposedly impartial jurors, the results were either hung juries or acquittals. To convict the United Railroads executives of bribery, Ruef would have had to testify that they had paid him his attorney's fee in full knowledge that he would use part of the money to bribe public officeholders. Ruef refused to give such testimony. He pointed out to Heney and Burns that among three men as well versed in law as Ford, Calhoun, and Ruef himself the open mention of bribes would have been incredibly clumsy, and Ruef publicly charged that Heney and Burns, in trying to compel him to testify otherwise, were trying to suborn perjury.

In bitter anger and frustration, Heney revoked the immunity agreement he had made with Ruef and brought him to trial for the trolley bribery. The result was that of all the defendants, Ruef alone was ultimately forced to serve a term in the state prison at San Quentin.

Mayor Schmitz was convicted of extortion in one of the French restaurant cases in June 1907 and automatically removed from office; but his conviction was invalidated by the higher courts. In the opinion of the district court of appeals, several of the trial judge's rulings had denied the defendant his legal rights, and the state supreme court, though it did not comment on this particular contention, did sustain another of the appellate court's rulings: that extortion, under the law, was the obtaining of money under a threat to do an *unlawful* injury. The act which the mayor was alleged to have threatened—blocking the renewal of the liquor license of a house of prostitution—would have been an injury that was not only lawful but actually a part of his duties as mayor. The testimony of Ruef was the only direct evidence that Schmitz had received money, either in the French restaurant matter or in the bribery cases.

San Francisco businessmen had enthusiastically supported the prosecution at its beginning, when it had appeared to be directed against corrupt politicians, especially "Union Labor" politicians. But when these men were promised immunity as a reward for furnishing the evidence on which a number of the city's best-known business executives were indicted, the San Francisco business community's enthusiasm for the prosecution rapidly cooled. In the city elections of 1909 the prosecution was voted out of office in favor of an administration that would discontinue the graft cases. Heney, running for district attorney, was badly defeated by Charles M. Fickert, a former Stanford football hero.

The Good Government movement in Los Angeles. Many San Franciscans liked to regard their city as pleasure-loving and even as romantically wicked. P. H. McCarthy, president of the San Francisco Building Trades Council and Union Labor nominee for mayor in 1909, was elected on his promise to replace the graft prosecution with a campaign to make San Francisco "the Paris of America." By contrast, Los Angeles regarded itself as a highly moral community in these years before the advent of Hollywood. Saloons were closed on Sundays, and there were more churches than in any other city of comparable size in the United States. The Southern Pacific machine dominated Los Angeles politics, but opposition to it was building up in almost every sector of political opinion from the right to the left.

Charles Dwight Willard, secretary of the Los Angeles Chamber of Commerce, had been one of the most effective leaders in the fight against the railroad's control of the harbor. So had Harrison Gray Otis, leader of the city's conservative employers.

In Otis's view no general political or social plan could possibly contribute as much to the growth, improvement, and prosperity of the community as did the leadership of vigorous individuals like himself. Therefore, as he saw it, the general welfare required that there be no unnecessary restraints upon such men in the free exercise of their talents for acquiring the wealth that was their incentive and reward. But the railroad had become just such a restraint upon free enterprise, and Otis opposed its bureaucratic power almost as much as he feared and detested labor unions, or even socialism.

As distinct from the conservatives, like Otis, who had a chronic distrust of government and feared that any political change would open the door to unionism and radicalism, there were various groups of reformers who placed their faith in the improvement and strengthening of government. These groups were divided into political and moral reformers on the one hand, and social and economic reformers on the other.

The political and moral reformers included prominent businessmen, lawyers, and journalists who shared the conservatives' belief in the supreme importance of business enterprise, but also believed that much could be accomplished by bringing "business efficiency" and "business integrity" into politics. Many such men were attracted to the "good government" clubs that were being organized in Los Angeles and other American cities, on the model of a similar organization in Boston.

The social and economic reformers tended to distrust not only the conservatives but the good government leaders as well. They believed that government should not merely become more honest and more efficient, but that it should be used to effect deeper and broader improvements in the workings of society. They included not only socialists, but also earnest and devout men and women who had been impressed by the writings of Henry George and Edward Bellamy or by the social gospel then being preached in many churches. To an extraordinary degree, union labor in Los Angeles had also been driven into alliance with such groups, as a result of the extreme tactics of Otis and his associates.

In the face of this diversity among the opponents of the railroad machine in Los Angeles, it was very difficult to assemble a coalition strong enough to put through any important reform program. That this was accomplished was largely a result of the remarkable personal qualities of Dr. John Randolph Haynes. Since his arrival in 1887 with doctorates in both medicine and philosophy from the University of Pennsylvania, Haynes had combined the most successful medical practice in Los Angeles with the building of a large fortune in real estate—a combination of achievements that won the respect of some of the most conservative businessmen and led them to retain their trust in him even though at one point he had also organized the city's first Christian Socialist club. His socialism was not very strong; he opposed strikes and boycotts, and favored private property. He was the personal physician of several leading businessmen, including Otis himself.

Dr. Haynes believed that if political democracy could be established, social democracy would follow, and poverty and injustice could ultimately be abolished. Largely through his charm and his prestige, and through a Direct Legislation League that was essentially his personal organization, Los Angeles was persuaded to adopt the initiative, the referendum, and the recall in its new charter of 1903.

This was the first provision for the recall in any governmental unit in the world, and the first adoption of the initiative and the referendum by a city. In 1904, moreover, Los Angeles put the recall to use for the first time in history.

A Good Government League, in which Dr. Haynes was prominent, organized a successful campaign to recall City Councilman J. R. Davenport for voting to award the public printing contracts to the *Los Angeles Times* when several other bids had been much lower.

This episode ended any possibility of support from Otis for the political reformers, and thereafter the *Times* never spoke of the Good Government League except to denounce and ridicule its leaders as "the Goo-Goos." But the opposition of the *Times* served to increase the support for reform on the part of Otis's newspaper rival and personal enemy, Edwin T. Earl, publisher of the *Los Angeles Express*. Earl was not only a publisher, but also the state's largest lemon grower, and consequently an opponent of the Southern Pacific, whose freight rates on lemons were among its most notoriously piratical exactions.

In the spring of 1906 Earl hired a young journalist named Edward A. Dickson and authorized him to begin a series of editorials in the *Express* denouncing the railroad machine for its control of the Los Angeles city council. Soon afterward Dickson joined with three young lawyers, Meyer Lissner, Russ Avery, and Marshall Stimson, in organizing a Non-Partisan Committee of One Hundred, and in the city election of 1906 the reform candidates nominated by this group won almost every important office except the mayoralty.

The Lincoln-Roosevelt League. The composition and the political orientation of the Los Angeles Non-Partisan Committee of 1906 had special significance because the men who organized it were also to play an important part, in the following year, in the original organization of the statewide reform movement known as the Lincoln-Roosevelt Republican League.

All the leaders and nearly all the members of the Los Angeles "Non-Partisan" group were in fact Republicans. They favored political and moral as distinct from social and economic reform; neither Dr. Haynes, nor any other community leader strongly identified with "social reform" ideas, nor any representative of organized labor, was included in the Los Angeles Non-Partisan Committee. The purpose of its original meeting in July 1906, as described by its temporary secretary, Meyer Lissner, was "to bring together the businessmen who are interested in good government." The leaders of this group were far from agreeing with Lincoln Steffens that the businessman as such was the source of political corruption. Rather, as reformers like Dickson and Lissner saw it, the corruptionist executives and minions of the Southern Pacific were traitors not only to the ideals of American government but to the ideals of American business itself; good men, who embodied these ideals, should drive the traitors from political power; leadership by "the businessmen who are interested in good government" was the country's best and indeed its only hope.

For decades most businessmen had been Republicans, while city workingmen had usually been Democrats. In the early 20th century, reform-minded

Republicans in California were deeply concerned lest the Democrats gain leadership of the reform movement in general and thus capture the state government. Indeed, reform Democrats would almost certainly have won the governorship both in 1902 and in 1906 had their chances not been sabotaged by the ambitious machinations of William Randolph Hearst in his attempts to gain the Democratic nomination for the Presidency. In 1902 Hearst had refused to support Franklin K. Lane of San Francisco, the Democratic candidate for Governor of California, because he feared Lane as a potential rival for Democratic leadership. This had caused Lane's defeat by the Republican candidate, Dr. George C. Pardee of Oakland, in a close election.

Governor Pardee had made some reform proposals which, though very limited and generally unsuccessful, were enough to cause the railroad to oppose his renomination, and the Republican state convention at Santa Cruz in September 1906 made it even more obvious than usual that the California Republican party machinery was subservient to the railroad and its allies. Abe Ruef, who had just reached the height of his power, controlled every member of the large San Francisco delegation and could thus choose the nominee for Governor. To secure the nomination of the railroad's candidate, James N. Gillett, William F. Herrin gave Ruef $14,000 "to pay the expenses of the delegates." On the evening after the convention adjourned there was a testimonial banquet at which a photograph was taken, showing Ruef seated at the center of a long table with Gillett standing behind him, his hand on Ruef's shoulder in a gesture of affectionate gratitude. Justices of the state supreme and appellate courts, indebted to Ruef for their renominations, were included in the group, along with such machine stalwarts as Walter Parker, Herrin's lieutenant in Los Angeles. For years afterward this picture was widely reprinted with such captions as "The Shame of California" and "Herrin's Cabinet."

The announcement of the beginning of the San Francisco graft prosecution in October 1906, discrediting Ruef and the nominees of the Santa Cruz convention along with him, gave the Democrats an extraordinary opportunity to win the governorship and most of the other state offices. They had a strong antirailroad platform, and their candidate for Governor, Theodore A. Bell, was a vigorous young man with a good reform record as district attorney of Napa County. Once more, however, Hearst ruined the chances of the California Democrats. In an effort to show the national Democratic party that it could not do without him, Hearst in 1906 was sponsoring a third-party movement called the Independence League, in New York, California, and a few other states. The league's ticket in California, with San Francisco district attorney William H. Langdon as the candidate for Governor, took enough votes from Bell and the Democrats to give the election to Gillett and the Republicans.

In December 1906 Dr. Haynes again displayed his talent for encouraging broad coalition among reformers by organizing a dinner at the California Club in Los Angeles with Lincoln Steffens as the principal speaker and Dickson and

"The Shame of California." Photograph from the San Francisco Call, *September 10, 1906. Abe Ruef is seated in the center. The future governor, James N. Gillett, stands behind him. Justice Frederick W. Henshaw of the State Supreme Court stands at the far left; Congressman Joseph R. Knowland at the far right.*

Lissner among the guests. Steffens made it clear that he was no longer inclined to blame corruption upon all businessmen as a class, and he urged the Los Angeles reformers to extend to the state level the efforts that had brought important successes in the recent city elections.

A few weeks later Dickson went to Sacramento as correspondent for the *Los Angeles Express* at the session of the state legislature beginning in January 1907, and the accident that assigned adjoining desks in the press row to Dickson and to Chester H. Rowell, editor of the *Fresno Morning Republican,* became one of the most important circumstances leading to the movement that would free the Republican party and the state government from the Southern Pacific Railroad.

Rowell was destined to be the outstanding intellectual leader of that movement. He was the son of Jonathan H. Rowell, a Republican congressman from central Illinois. When his father was chairman of the House committee on elections, Chester Rowell had served as clerk of that committee and thus had gained some valuable insights into the workings of practical politics. His early ambition, however, had been a professorship of philosophy, and with this intention he had done graduate work at the University of Michigan, and at two German universities, Halle and Berlin. Finding himself unable to support a wife on the salary of a college instructor, he had taken the editorship of the Fresno paper owned by his uncle.

Dickson and Rowell had never met before; but as they exchanged impressions of the 1907 legislature, which was hardly less subservient to the railroad than the Santa Cruz convention had been, the two journalists discovered that they shared a burning disgust with the condition of California politics. They agreed to join in an attempt to organize a reform movement, and sent out the call for a new organization in letters to reform-minded Republicans, especially newspaper publishers and editors, throughout the state.

A Southern California group met in Los Angeles on May 21, 1907, adopted Dickson's suggestion of the name of "Lincoln Republicans," and drew up an "emancipation proclamation," which announced as its first objective "The emancipation of the Republican Party in California from domination by the Political Bureau of the Southern Pacific Railroad Company and allied interests." Other proposals were the direct primary; the initiative, referendum, and recall; effective regulation of railroad and other utility rates; the outlawing of racetrack gambling; conservation of forests; a workmens' compensation act; a minimum wage law for women; and woman suffrage.

On August 1 a larger statewide group met in Oakland and adopted the official name of "the League of Lincoln-Roosevelt Republican Clubs." This hyphenated title was the result of a significant compromise with the desire of Francis J. Heney to change the name to "the Roosevelt League." Heney was an intense admirer of Theodore Roosevelt, and particularly of that aspect of his views which led the President to denounce as "malefactors of great wealth" such men as E. H. Harriman, head of the Southern Pacific. Roosevelt's national leadership was an important source of inspiration to progressive Republicans in California, as in other states; but at Dickson's insistence the name of Lincoln was also retained and included, to appeal to Republicans of more traditional views.

In 1908 the reformers were able to elect enough members of the legislature to make possible the enactment of a direct primary law in the 1909 session, and it became clear that in 1910, with the nominations of party candidates taken away from machine-controlled conventions and given directly to the voters, the League might gain control not only of the state Republican party organization but of the entire state government, particularly if it could find a very strong candidate for Governor to head its ticket.

At first it was supposed that the candidate would be Heney, whose leadership of the San Francisco graft prosecution was making him the state's best-known reformer. But in November 1908, early in the trial of Ruef, Heney was shot and almost fatally wounded by a man whose earlier criminal record Heney had exposed while questioning him as a prospective juror. Whether Heney would make a full recovery was uncertain for several months, and when he did return to the fray his personality was more extreme and irascible than ever. Many Republicans regarded Heney as "too radical," and particularly resented his open dislike and distrust of all businessmen. Moreover, Heney was a registered Democrat, and when he ran for district attorney of San Francisco on the Democratic ticket in 1909 and was defeated, his chances as a Republican gubernatorial candidate declined still further.

During Heney's convalescence his place was taken by Hiram W. Johnson, who had been one of his special assistants in the district attorney's office. Thus Hiram Johnson became chief prosecutor in the trial that ended in the conviction of Ruef, and thus he first attracted wide attention as a young man with a potential future as a leader of political reform.

In one of those unpredictable circumstances that are such vital ingredients in history, one obscure and demented man had made Theodore Roosevelt President of the United States by pulling the trigger of a pistol. Another, by a similar act, launched Hiram Johnson into state and national politics.

As a courtroom and platform orator, Johnson rivaled or exceeded the powers of Heney in denouncing evil and in arousing support for reform, and Johnson could appeal to a broader cross section of voters. He did not share Heney's extreme antibusiness bias, and would not alienate the votes of so many conservative Republicans; at the same time he could gain support from organized labor. Johnson had been an attorney for the San Francisco teamsters' union for eight years.

He was reluctant to run for Governor, however. His father, Grove L. Johnson, an assemblyman from Sacramento, had long been the principal leader of the Southern Pacific machine in the state legislature. Hiram had first practiced law in partnership with his father in Sacramento, and it was largely to escape their bitter quarreling over differences of political opinion that he had moved to San Francisco. There he had developed a highly lucrative legal practice and had built a delightful home at the top of Russian Hill. To give up these amenities for a return to the scene of his abrasive and torturing conflicts with his father seemed to him, and to his wife, a very poor exchange. He did not consent to run until February 1910, when Heney finally removed himself from the race and joined with Rowell and others in urging Johnson to become the League's candidate, on the ground that he was the only one who could win and thus free the state from its bondage.

In August, in the first and perhaps the most important statewide direct primary elections in California's history, Johnson won the Republican nomination for Governor, and the League won control of the Republican party. Johnson's campaign was unique, colorful, and literally hard-driving. He toured the state in an open automobile, and in the smaller towns announced his arrival by ringing a cowbell. Everywhere he stressed a single theme, his famous "promise to kick the Southern Pacific Railroad out of politics." Among his variations on the theme of the railroad's villainy, he described its practice of secretly charging bribery expenses to operating costs, and then charging still higher rates to cover the expenses. "Get us coming and going?" he cried in a speech at Los Angeles. "Why they get us every way; and we foot the bill—we pick our own pockets to bribe ourselves with our own money!" In citrus-producing areas Johnson reminded the growers how long they had struggled for tariff protection against ruinous imports of cheap foreign lemons, and how, when at last they had gained a favorable rate in the Payne-Aldrich Tariff of 1909, the railroad had promptly raised its freight rates on lemons in the exact amount of the price increase that the new tariff made possible.

Actually, in the election in November 1910, the railroad was no longer a genuine issue. The Democratic nominee for Governor, Theodore Bell, vied with Johnson in denouncing it. Moreover, he discussed a wider range of reform issues than Johnson did. Anticipating the slogans of future Democrats, Bell said that "California needs a New Deal, a Fair Deal." But unfortunately for the Democrats, and much to their disgust, William F. Herrin concluded that Bell would be the less effective and less dangerous reformer, and ordered the railroad's subbosses to support him. The support of the railroad, once so crucial in California politics, now cost Bell the votes of thousands who would not credit his outraged disavowals. It was a major factor in giving the governorship to Johnson, who received 177,191 votes to Bell's 154,835. Another factor was the substantial vote of 47,819 for the Socialist candidate, J. Stitt Wilson of Berkeley.

SELECTED BIBLIOGRAPHY

The memoirs of Abraham Ruef, "The Road I Traveled; an Autobiographic Account of My Career from University to Prison, with an Intimate Recital of the Corrupt Alliance between Big Business and Politics in San Francisco," *San Francisco Bulletin*, April 6 to September 5, 1912, were written while Ruef was in San Quentin. Other accounts are in Fremont Older, *My Own Story* (1926); Franklin Hichborn, *"The System" as Uncovered by the San Francisco Graft Prosecution* (1915); *The Autobiography of Lincoln Steffens* (1931); Walton Bean, *Boss Ruef's San Francisco* (1952); Lately Thomas, *A Debonair Scoundrel* (1962); and Robert W. Davenport, "San Francisco Journalism in the Time of Fremont Older," Ph.D. thesis, University of California, Los Angeles (1969).

On other roots of reform, Albert H. Clodius, "The Quest for Good Government in Los Angeles, 1890–1910," Ph.D. thesis, Claremont Graduate School (1953); Donald R. Culton, "Charles Dwight Willard, Los Angeles City Booster and Professional Reformer, 1888–1914," Ph.D. thesis, University of Southern California (1971); W. H. Hutchinson, *Oil, Land, and Politics* (two volumes, 1965), a biography of Senator Thomas R. Bard; and Edward F. Staniford, "Governor in the Middle," on George C. Pardee, Governor from 1903 to 1907, Ph.D. thesis, University of California, Berkeley (1955).

On the rise of the Lincoln-Roosevelt League and its triumph in 1910, see George E. Mowry, *The California Progressives* (1951); J. Gregg Layne, "The Lincoln-Roosevelt League," *Historical Society of Southern California Quarterly*, XXV (September 1943), 79–101; Irving McKee, "The Background and Early Career of Hiram Warren Johnson, 1866–1910," *Pacific Historical Review*, XIX (February 1950), 17–30; Alice M. Rose, "The Rise of California Insurgency: Origins of the League of Lincoln-Roosevelt Republican Clubs, 1900–1907," Ph.D. thesis, Stanford University (1942); Spencer C. Olin, Jr., *California's Prodigal Sons: Hiram Johnson and the Progressives, 1911–1917* (1968); and Miles C. Everett, "Chester Harvey Rowell, Pragmatic Humanist and California Progressive," Ph.D. thesis, University of California, Berkeley (1965).

Chapter XXVII

THE REPUBLICAN PROGRESSIVES IN POWER

THE MEN who organized the Lincoln-Roosevelt Republican movement, which gained control of the government of California in the elections of 1910, were primarily individualists. Most of them were young men from the urban upper middle class—lawyers, editors, or independent business enterprisers. They were highly literate, and three out of four were college educated. Eager to participate in public affairs, and finding that to do so under the old system of machine control would mean the sacrifice of their integrity, they overthrew the old system. In January 1911, in full control of both houses of the state legislature, the progressives confidently set out to establish a new order of politics in California.

The extent of public support of the state's first "progressive" legislature became clear in the special election of October 10, 1911, when the 23 of its measures that required constitutional amendments were submitted to the voters, and all but one passed. Theodore Roosevelt described the California program of 1911 as "the beginning of a new era in popular government," and as "the greatest advance ever made by any state for the benefit of its people." That assessment was not without political motivation, and it was somewhat exaggerated. For example, the reforms adopted in Wisconsin after the election of Robert M. La Follette as Governor in 1900 were at least as advanced. La Follette, however, was now a rival of Roosevelt for the national leadership of Republican progressivism, and for the Presidency, while T.R. was already looking toward Hiram Johnson as a vice-presidential running mate.

The reforms achieved in California in the single year of 1911 were remarkable, but this was partly because no other major state was more critically in need of reform.

More democracy." Ideas of morality, often related to religious affiliations, played a strong part in the feelings of many of the California progressives. In the words of editor A. J. Pillsbury, one of their leaders, they stood for "the New England conscience in government." Their view of human nature, however, was not the gloomy Calvinist conviction of man's total depravity, but rather an Emersonian optimism about man's innate capacity for good, and therefore they had a strong faith in the political abilities of "the people." One tendency in national "progressive" thought, exemplified in Herbert Croly's book, *The Promise of American Life,* in 1909, was toward a kind of elitism, which qualified its faith in the people by emphasizing the importance of the right leadership. But most of the leading California Republican progressives, though they regarded themselves as patrician reformers, also had a strong faith in democracy as against the conservative emphasis on "representative" government. Thus the heart of their reform program lay in a group of devices for increasing the power of the voters.

Foremost among these devices was a state constitutional amendment providing two methods of direct participation by the people in the lawmaking process. The initiative enabled the voters to enact laws or constitutional amendments that had presumably been blocked by legislators' unresponsiveness to popular demands; the referendum empowered the people to veto acts of the legislature. A petition signed by 8 percent of the number of voters in the last gubernatorial election could place an initiative proposal on the ballot; a referendum required 5 percent. Some of the progressives would have preferred a fixed number of signatures, perhaps 30,000. They pointed out that under the percentage system, with future increases in the state's population, the gathering of an ever-increasing number of signatures would become too difficult and expensive for reform groups, and practicable only for large special interests. But this warning, which would prove distressingly valid in later years, went unheeded in 1911. The initiative and referendum amendment was approved in the state senate with only one dissenting vote, and in the assembly with no dissenting votes at all.

The recall of public officials, the second major proposal that Governor Johnson urged upon the legislature, was much more hotly contested, especially because it included the recall of judges. The conservative minority argued that this would interfere with the impartiality of court decisions by requiring judges to "keep their ears to the ground." But Johnson replied that this was better than keeping their ears to the railroad tracks; and the recall was approved by large majorities in both houses.

Several other measures were also designed to give more power to the voters and to decrease the power of "party bosses." For example, the "party column" and the "party circle," which had encouraged voting a straight party ticket, were eliminated from the ballot. And in 1911 California became the sixth state to adopt woman suffrage.

Public utility regulation. In the regulation of railroads and other public utilities the progressives achieved their most unquestionable success. An act drafted largely by John M. Eshleman, who had been elected to the state railroad commission in 1910, gave the commission full and effective power to set rates and to end the extortionate and discriminatory practices in which the Southern Pacific had indulged with virtual impunity for so many decades. Another measure assigned to the commission the power to regulate the rates charged by all other public utilities, except those that were municipally owned. The graft prosecution in San Francisco had more than demonstrated the inadequacy of local regulation of utilities. In the state law of 1911 California acquired what was said to be the most comprehensive system of public utility regulation then in existence.

Both of these measures passed by unanimous votes in both houses. Railroad regulation, in particular, was so long overdue in 1911 that the railroad attorneys and lobbyists made almost no attempts to oppose it. After the new system had been in operation for a few months, William F. Herrin made a remarkable address to the California Bar Association in which he recalled the turmoil and the injustices of the old days, and concluded that "I think no railroad manager would agree to dispense with government regulation at the cost of returning to the old conditions."

Public morals. Much of the support for the Lincoln-Roosevelt League had come from religious and other organizations interested in suppressing the evils of drinking, gambling, and vice. When the League's "emancipation proclamation" of 1907 had promised to free the state from control by the Southern Pacific "and allied interests," many assumed that this expression referred mainly to the various public utility corporations; but in the eyes of others, it was the liquor, gambling, and prostitution contingents of the "associated villainies" which seemed the most powerful and dangerous of all. Those interests had, in fact, played a strong part in corrupt machine politics, because they feared stricter law enforcement and were politically interested in preventing it. As the "moral reformers" pointed out, Abe Ruef had been the attorney for the California Liquor Dealers' Association as well as for the United Railroads of San Francisco.

The Lincoln-Roosevelt candidate for lieutenant governor in 1910 was A. J. Wallace, a Los Angeles Methodist minister and oilman who was for many years the president of the Anti-Saloon League of California. Although Johnson privately detested his running mate, Wallace was easily elected, and received nearly as many votes as Johnson himself in almost all parts of the state except San Francisco and the wine-producing counties of the bay region.

The leaders of the temperance organizations, though many of them were actually prohibitionists, recognized that outright prohibition was still unacceptable to most of the voters. Therefore they concentrated their attack on the saloon, and argued that it was often a center of prostitution as well as of excessive drinking. Since 1874 state law had permitted local areas, at the option of their voters, to ban saloons. In 1911 the legislature passed a much stronger local-option law, based on the county supervisorial district as the unit, and eliminating various earlier legal handicaps to adoption and enforcement. In the next five years, under this legislation, more than half the districts in the state voted to close all the saloons within their borders.

Under another act of 1911, racetrack gambling was outlawed and remained so for 20 years. Still another measure made slot machines illegal, after a debate in which the decisive factor was the reading of manufacturers' catalogs explaining how easily the machines could be adjusted to guarantee the owner a heavy profit. A Red Light Abatement Act, declaring houses of prostitution to be public nuisances, was defeated in 1911 but passed in the session of 1913.

Governmental efficiency and integrity. The progressives gave California its first coherent system of supervision over state finances. This was largely the work of John Francis Neylan, a dynamic young newspaper reporter who had attracted Johnson's attention while covering the 1910 campaign for the *San Francisco Bulletin*. Neylan proposed the creation of a new agency to be called the State Board of Control, and at the age of 26 he was appointed its first chairman.

Under this board California had its first comprehensive budget and its first general inventory of state property. In 1910 there had been a state deficit of 2 million dollars; by 1917 there was a surplus of 8 million. The board exposed graft, regained embezzled money, and secured the removal of 16 corrupt officials. Under the progressives California state government was free from corruption for the first time in its history.

The progressives and labor. The progressives had a strong group consciousness, and their letters to each other often included proud references to "our sort"; but they feared and detested "class government" by any class other than themselves, and they feared the power of organized labor at least as much as the power of big business. In their view it was the state government, under enlightened progressive leadership, that could best protect and guarantee the true interests of labor, and when it had done so, the temporary evil of labor unionism would wither away. Fortunately for the unions, Governor Hiram

Johnson was more sympathetic toward organized labor than were many of the other progressive leaders, especially those from Los Angeles.

Workmen's compensation, or employers' liability for industrial accidents, was one area in which the goals and ideas of the progressives and the labor unions coincided, and new laws on this subject formed a solid achievement of labor legislation in the progressive years. Some archaic doctrines of common law had long permitted the employer to evade financial responsibility for accidental injuries or deaths of his employees in the course of their work. In 1911 a compromise plan removed these limits on the employer's legal responsibility, and created an Industrial Accident Board to administer the law; but this act included only a voluntary insurance provision. In 1913 a new and broader law made employer participation in the state-operated workmen's insurance system compulsory, except in agriculture.

The desire of the progressives to protect the interests of "the people" as a whole by curbing the power of both labor unions and employers was clearly evident in the struggle in 1911 over the Weinstock arbitration bill. Harris Weinstock, the author of this proposal, was a merchant prince of Sacramento whom the Lincoln-Roosevelt League had considered among its possible candidates for Governor. His bill would have forbidden strikes and lockouts in public utilities until after an impartial board appointed by the Governor had recommended terms of settlement. The San Francisco unions and the State Federation of Labor fought this measure bitterly, charging that it was an entering wedge for total compulsory arbitration and the ultimate abolition of the right to strike; and although all five of the Los Angeles progressive senators voted for it, the bill was finally defeated.

A similar battle in 1911 attended the defeat of an anti-injunction bill that labor unions strongly favored and that would greatly have strengthened their position in collective bargaining. Introduced by a Democratic state senator, Anthony Caminetti, this measure would not only have limited the use of court injunctions against strikes; it would also have outlawed the blacklist and the "yellow dog" contract, in which the employee agreed not to join a union; and it would have legalized secondary boycotts and peaceful picketing. This last provision would have invalidated an extreme antipicketing ordinance that the Good Government administration in Los Angeles had adopted the year before.

In the state minimum wage law for women and children, the progressives gave a degree of substance to their claim that they were better protectors of the interests of labor than were the unions themselves. Organized labor at first opposed any minimum wage laws whatever, for the same reason that it opposed compulsory arbitration—that the setting of terms by government boards might weaken and even replace union bargaining. The minimum wage, labor feared, would become the maximum. The 1911 legislature adopted an 8-hour day for women, excluding farm labor and the canning and packing industries; but it did not seriously consider a minimum wage. No state had such a law, until Massachusetts adopted the first one in 1912. Katherine Philips Edson of Los Angeles, president of the California Federation of Women's Clubs, led the movement that secured the passage of a California minimum wage law for women and children in 1913.

Records of the Bureau of Labor Statistics showed that a third of the women workers in California were being paid less than 15 cents an hour, and Mrs. Edson and other advocates of the new law argued that this condition was a menace to the women's health and morals. To the argument of some employers that they could not afford to pay higher wages, State Senator William Brown replied that if any industry in California could not pay women workers enough to support a decent standard of life the state would be better off without that industry. An Industrial Welfare Commission was to administer the act, and Governor Johnson, who had joined in pressing for passage of the law, appointed Mrs. Edson as the commission's executive officer.

In August 1913 the Wheatland riot suddenly and dramatically awakened public consciousness, and to some extent the public conscience, to the vile and disgraceful conditions in many farm labor camps. (See Chapter 24.) A state-sponsored investigation revealed that the conditions at Durst's hop ranch were typical of those inflicted on migratory workers by many other large agricultural employers throughout the state. A new Commission of Immigration and Housing, created by the legislature a few months before, assumed the authority to inspect farm labor camps, and of the 641 that it investigated in 1914, only 195 met its minimum standards, and 188 were branded as dangerously unsanitary. The next year the legislature passed a new labor camp sanitation and housing act, to be enforced by the commission. But though it made admirable efforts at enforcement, its efforts were stubbornly resisted and were never fully effective. The man who had most to do with planning this legislation, and who served as the commission's first chairman, was the distinguished social worker-businessman, Simon Lubin, a son of David Lubin, the half brother and partner of Harris Weinstock.

Another act, also a product of the Wheatland tragedy, required all employers to provide their workers with drinking water.

By later standards the labor legislation of the Johnson years was not very advanced, but it was much more than labor had ever received from Sacramento before. Several union leaders were appointed to state administrative positions: John P. McLaughlin, head of the San Francisco teamsters, became commissioner of the Bureau of Labor Statistics; Will J. French, former president of the San Francisco Labor Council, was appointed to the Industrial Accident Board; and Paul Scharrenberg, secretary of the State Federation of Labor, became a member of the Commission of Immigration and Housing. Organized labor was not unaware that the basic philosophy of the progressives was hostile to many important union goals, but the unions felt that they had a friend in Hiram Johnson, and most of their members, particularly in the working-class districts of San Francisco, continued to vote for him with enthusiasm.

The progressives and the anti-Japanese movement. An important area of agreement between organized labor and the California progressives was their shared hostility toward the Japanese. The immigration of Japanese to California had been insignificant until the late '90s, but it steadily increased in the early 20th century, and in 1905 San Francisco labor union leaders formed an Asiatic Exclusion League to combat it. Under pressure from this league the Union Labor city government announced its intention of segregating Japanese public school children along with the Chinese.

California had almost completely excluded Chinese children from its public schools until a court ruling had forbidden this practice in 1885. In San Francisco, a separate public school had then been provided for them in Chinatown. When this Chinese school was rebuilt after the earthquake and fire, its name was changed to the Oriental School, and on October 11, 1906, the Board of Education adopted an order requiring Japanese public school children to attend it.

Protests from the Japanese government led to a diplomatic crisis between Japan and the United States, and President Roosevelt ordered an investigation by his Secretary of Commerce and Labor, Victor H. Metcalf, a resident of Oakland and the only Californian in the cabinet. Metcalf reported that there had been only 93 Japanese pupils in the 23 public schools in San Francisco, and that many of them had been born in the city. However, 27 had been alien teen-agers, placed in the elementary grades because of their lack of previous schooling in English. White racists, including Sacramento Assemblyman Grove L. Johnson, declaimed upon the menace to little American schoolgirls who were seated beside older boys with evil Oriental thoughts.

Early in 1907 President Roosevelt invited Mayor Schmitz and the members of the San Francisco Board of Education to Washington, D.C., where they agreed to a compromise. Only overage pupils and those not having facility in English might be placed in separate schools, and the new regulations would apply to all children of alien birth, not to Japanese as such.

In return President Roosevelt promised limits on Japanese immigration, and negotiated the Gentlemen's Agreement in which Japan promised not to issue passports good for the continental United States to laborers, whether skilled or unskilled. But parents, wives, or children of Japanese already resident in the United States were not covered by this agreement, and through proxy marriages, arranged quite legally and in the traditional fashion by parents or other go-betweens in Japan, thousands of earlier Japanese immigrants brought "picture brides" to America. Many Californians denounced this as Oriental duplicity, criticized their own government for being duped by it, and demanded complete Japanese exclusion.

Chester Rowell, as the leading philosopher of the California Republican progressives, sought to formulate the argument for exclusion in terms of idealism tempered by realistic historical reflection. Democracy, he believed, was possible only in a homogeneous society, without extreme differences in economic and social status or even in physical appearance. If experiments in interracial democracy were to be tried anywhere, Rowell wrote, it should not be in a country with a record of spectacular failure in such efforts. The presence of Negroes in the Southern states had made democracy an empty form. America already had two great unsolved problems with the Negroes in the South and the Chinese in California, and after these experiences it should have the foresight to prevent the growth of another problem of the same kind.

Many Californians now portrayed the Japanese with the same racial stereotypes that had been used against the Chinese in earlier decades, particularly the charges that they were unassimilable and that their low standard of living depressed American wages. Soon, however, the Japanese became the object of a new complaint—that their standard of living rapidly became too high. Brought to California to replace the Chinese as cheap farm laborers, some of them escaped from this lowly status by acquiring farm land of their own. Much of this was land that they reclaimed, in the Sacramento and San Joaquin Valleys and in the San Joaquin delta. They were the first to demonstrate that rice could be grown successfully in California, and that potatoes could be grown on a commercial scale. George Shima, known as the "potato king," produced the bulk of the state's crop on his large farm in the delta region.

Bills intended to halt the expansion of the Japanese in California agriculture began to be introduced in every legislative session, and were frequently protested by the Japanese ambassador in Washington. James D. Phelan, in a statement as near to tolerance of the Japanese as he ever came, once suggested that the United States should say "diplomatically" that it regarded "the unassimilable Japanese as efficient human machines," but that "as such, they are a menace to our prosperity and happiness. Then the more sensitive citizens of Japan may find some consolation in our confession of economic inferiority." But while a wealthy urban politician might make such a statement, the small farmers of California, who feared the competition of Japanese, reacted with increased resentment and fury to the idea of making any such humiliating confession.

White supremacy and yellow peril were the doctrines of the overwhelming majority of California voters—progressives and conservatives, Republicans, Democrats, and even Socialists. The leaders of the Republican progressives, as their historian George E. Mowry has pointed out, were with very few exceptions white Anglo-Saxon Protestants of old American stock, a fact that was particularly striking in view of the generally polyglot and immigrant character of the state's population. The Irish and the southern Europeans had tended to become Democrats. Italian Americans joined Irish Americans in the front ranks of the anti-Japanese movement.

For several years State Senator Caminetti and other Democrats in the legislature embarrassed the Republican state and national administrations by repeatedly pressing for a law against Japanese land ownership. But a remarkable reversal occurred in March 1913, in the middle of that year's session of the legislature, when control of the national government passed to the Democrats, and with it the responsibility for conducting diplomatic relations with Japan. Governor Johnson and the California progressive Republicans were now free to take their turn at exploiting the anti-Japanese weapon.

Johnson did so with a particular vengeance. He hotly resented a tactic with which the Democrats had won thousands of Californian votes for Woodrow Wilson, and against the Roosevelt-Johnson national ticket, in 1912. Early in that campaign, James D. Phelan had drafted an anti-Oriental statement and persuaded Wilson to issue it as his own. A few days before the election someone circulated thousands of cards in California, quoting this statement with the wording deceptively changed to suggest that Wilson favored complete Japanese exclusion. Below this, the cards quoted Theodore Roosevelt's statement of 1906 recommending that Congress give the right of naturalization to the Japanese.

In the spring of 1913 Johnson joined with Francis J. Heney and California Attorney General Ulysses S. Webb in drafting an act which provided that aliens ineligible for American citizenship could not own land in the state, or lease it for more than three years. Under Federal law, all Orientals were ineligible for naturalization; but there had been no legal immigrants from China for 30 years, since the Federal exclusion act of 1882. Thus the new California law applied almost exclusively to Japanese aliens, without openly saying so.

The device was transparent, and Japan protested so strongly that President Wilson sent Secretary of State William Jennings Bryan to Sacramento to lobby against the bill. But Johnson easily triumphed over this "federal interference," and gleefully wrote to Theodore Roosevelt that "We have shown the Democratic doctrine of 'state's rights' to be sham and pretense, insisted upon when it is their state that is affected but denied when they represent the federal government and our state is affected."

Bryan asked that the bill be made applicable to all aliens, but this led to protests from European-owned land and mining interests. Officials of the Panama Pacific International Exposition, to be held in San Francisco, opposed the bill in fear that Japan would boycott the enterprise; but the backers of the exposition were largely Johnson's old-guard Republican opponents, and they had no influence on him. Others criticized the bill as unnecessary because the land owned or leased by Japanese was only a tiny fraction of the total acreage; but Chester Rowell replied that the "menace of Japanese ownership" was "not a present fact, but a fear of the future."

Actually, as Johnson was quite aware, the chief effects of the new law were emotional and political rather than economic. It was easily evaded. Japanese aliens transferred their land titles or leases to their American-born children, or to corporations with a majority of the stock entrusted to American-born Japanese.

Hiram Johnson's anti-Oriental views were almost as vigorous as those of his father; but his reasons for acting as the behind-the-scenes manager of what was usually called the Heney-Webb alien land bill were primarily reasons of political strategy. The legislature was determined to pass some bill of this kind, and to oppose a measure that was so popular with the state's electorate would have lost him many of his followers. Instead he won many new ones, particularly in Northern California. The alien land measure also served to distract attention from the growing disunity among the progressives and from their increasing disagreements over the nature and limits of reform.

Nonpartisanship" and cross-filing. The corruption of political parties in California by machine rule had been so extreme that the Johnson progressives blamed much of the evil on the party system itself. Consequently they tried to bring about the virtual destruction of political parties in the state. They did not quite succeed in doing this, but their efforts had the effect of ensuring that party organization, party responsibility, and the two-party system would remain extraordinarily weak in California for almost half a century to come.

The idea of nonpartisan elections was first applied at the level of city government, when the state legislature ratified a new city charter for Berkeley in 1909. Elections of judges and school officials throughout the state were made nonpartisan in 1911, and elections of county officials in 1913.

For state elections, the "cross-filing" system was adopted in an amendment of 1913, permitting a candidate to become the nominee of more than one political party for the same office. Under this provision, not only could the name of a candidate appear on the primary election ballot of more than one party, but the candidates' own party affiliations were not identified on the primary ballots.

In arguing that cross-filing was in the interest of the general welfare, the Johnson progressives were rationalizing their need to use it for their own special convenience. In 1912, when the national Progressive or "Bull Moose" party split off from the Republicans, no Progressive party was formally organized in California even though Governor Johnson was the national third party's nominee for Vice President. His followers in California remained registered as Republicans in order to keep their majority control of the state Republican organization. By doing this they were able to keep the Taft electors off the ballot, and thus Roosevelt carried the state over Wilson, though by a narrow margin. In 1913 Johnson wished to form a Progressive party in California, but many of his supporters in the legislature, elected with the Republican label, feared for their reelections if they had to forfeit it. Cross-filing was the solution. It enabled the

Progressive party of California to be formed, in December 1913, and in the following year many of the state legislators received both the Republican and the Progressive nominations.

The originators of cross-filing had not realized the full extent of its ultimate effects on the party system. These began to be apparent when one legislator was reelected in the primaries in 1914 by receiving the nominations of all five parties, the Progressives, the Republicans, the Democrats, the Prohibitionists, and the Socialists.

In 1915, having thus reduced the political party system to a shambles and finding that the results had given them firmer control of the legislature than ever before, the Johnson progressives tried to carry the nonpartisan idea to its logical conclusion. The legislature adopted an amendment providing that all state officers must be elected without party designation. But this proposal, the most extreme measure of its kind ever enacted in an American state, never went into effect. Conservative Republicans allied with Democrats to block it by turning the Progressives' own weapon, the referendum, against them. Johnson argued that state government "has become now a matter of efficient business management," which "may best be obtained without politics." Coming from as consummate a politician as Johnson this argument was highly disingenuous, and to his bitter disappointment the California voters rejected it. In a light turnout in the special referendum election of October 1915 they vetoed his "state nonpartisan elections" law. The cross-filing system, however, would remain in effect for decades, favoring incumbents, encouraging candidates to masquerade as members of parties other than their own, and enabling them to deceive thousands of ill-informed voters.

The decline of progressivism. In California, as well as in national politics, the extremely individualistic temperaments of the Progressive leaders were sources of weakness as well as of strength. They led inevitably to a series of personal quarrels that played a major part in the disintegration of the progressive movement.

The personality of Hiram Johnson bore some resemblance to that of Theodore Roosevelt, and in the early years of their association Johnson exploited this resemblance to the point of imitating Roosevelt's gestures and exclamations. Both were extraordinarily intelligent and courageous political fighters, but both also had in extraordinary degree the human failings of self-centeredness. It might have been said of Johnson, as it was said of T.R., that he disliked attending weddings and funerals because at a wedding he was not the groom and at a funeral he was not the corpse. Both men were prone to impute dishonest motives to anyone who disagreed with them, and to attribute to any rival the egotism that was characteristic of themselves. And both were masters of invective.

The Bull Moose ticket. A 1912 campaign poster. (From the Library of Congress collection)

Johnson's personal letters often included vitriolic opinions of other politicians, including his friends, and when he lost his temper with an enemy he was capable of using the most extreme language, even in a public speech. During the primary campaign of 1910, Harrison Gray Otis's *Los Angeles Times* had touched one of Johnson's most sensitive nerves by referring to his father's record of support for the railroad. Speaking in Los Angeles that evening, Johnson described Otis as "vile, infamous, degraded, and putrescent. Here he sits in senile dementia, with gangrened heart and rotting brain, grimacing at every reform and chattering in impotent rage against decency and morality."

In 1914 Johnson wished to run for the United States Senate, and had chosen John M. Eshleman to succeed him as Governor. But Francis J. Heney made it known that he would run either for Governor or for Senator, whichever of the two offices Johnson did not seek. Johnson now regarded Heney as a dangerous rival and Heney's supporters as mutineers against his own leadership. He could not break openly with Heney without a disastrous split in the Progressive party; but he solved the problem by running for Governor himself, by backing Eshleman for Lieutenant Governor, and by giving Heney virtually no support in his campaign for Senator.

The result was that James D. Phelan, the Democratic candidate, was elected Senator over the Progressive nominee, Heney, and the conservative Republican nominee, Congressman Joseph R. Knowland. In sharp contrast, the votes for Johnson for Governor and Eshleman for Lieutenant Governor were overwhelming. Johnson became the first Governor of California to be reelected since 1853. He planned to run for the other Senate seat in 1916, and then turn over the governorship to Eshleman.

In June 1916 the Progressive national convention, at Johnson's urging, again nominated Roosevelt for the Presidency. But Roosevelt declined the nomination and thus virtually scuttled the national Progressive party. Returning to the Republican fold, he announced his support for Charles Evans Hughes. In California the old-guard Republicans headed by William H. Crocker, son of Charles Crocker and leader of San Francisco's propertied aristocracy, gleefully assumed that the influence of Hiram Johnson was dead. Hughes made the same miscalculation. In his campaign visit to California in August, Hughes permitted Crocker and his associate, Francis V. Keesling, to plan all his speaking arrangements. They excluded Johnson from every platform where Hughes appeared, and did not even arrange a meeting between the two. By chance, both stopped at the Virginia Hotel in Long Beach on the afternoon of August 20, but Hughes left for Los Angeles without being informed that Johnson was in the hotel. When he learned of it, that evening, instead of telephoning Johnson personally he sent his campaign manager, accompanied by Johnson's enemy, Keesling, to make the explanation, and this irritated Johnson even more.

The California primaries were held nine days later. Johnson was still a registered Progressive, but he had cross-filed for the Republican nomination for United States Senator. To the horror of the old guard, he won the Republican nomination over their candidate, and the Johnson progressives, most of whom had now returned to the Republican party, recaptured control of the Republican state organization.

Under the circumstances, Johnson could hardly have been expected to support Hughes very enthusiastically, and he did not. Hughes lost any chance for labor votes when Crocker, a leader of open-shop forces in San Francisco, arranged a luncheon for him in a restaurant where he was served by "scab" waiters during a strike. Other votes went to Wilson because he had kept the country out of war. For these and other reasons, Hughes lost California by less than 4,000 votes, and the Presidency of the United States by losing California. But Johnson, with both Republican and Progressive nominations, won the senatorship by a margin of nearly 300,000.

Once again the California Republican progressives seemed to have triumphed. But the untimely death of Lieutenant Governor Eshleman in February

1916 had reopened the problem of succession and created further disunity. Having the power to fill the vacant lieutenant governorship by appointment, Johnson wished to choose another man whose personal loyalty to Johnson himself would be as complete as Eshleman's had been. But the Southern California leaders insisted on the appointment of Congressman William D. Stephens, a successful wholesale grocer who had been president of the Los Angeles Chamber of Commerce. Johnson regarded Stephens as "a Taft" who would betray the cause of progressivism. He was not merely something less than a thoroughgoing Johnson man; rather, Johnson charged, Stephens would belong "body and soul" to Edwin T. Earl and Edward A. Dickson, with whom Johnson's relations had become embittered.

Johnson was so reluctant to have Stephens succeed him that he delayed resigning the governorship until after the beginning of his term as Senator, and actually held both offices for two weeks in March 1917. He might have held them both for months longer if President Woodrow Wilson had not called Congress into special session in the war emergency.

Johnson had almost come to believe that he *was* the California progressive movement, and it was true that his personal leadership and popularity had been vital elements in its success. He had built up such a devoted personal following among California voters that they would keep him in the Senate until his death in 1945. But in doing everything he could to discredit Stephens, his successor as Governor, he further weakened what remained of California progressivism.

Along with these personal and factional quarrels, larger and deeper forces were also contributing to the decline of the progressive movement. Among these were the coming of the war, the consequent resurgence of conservatism, the strong antagonism toward the I.W.W., and the feeling of many Progressives that political and moral reform, the essentials of their program, had already been accomplished. There had been little economic reform beyond the minimum wage for women. The legislature had established a state conservation commission in 1911, but it was only a fact-finding body. Two years later, an act drafted by Francis J. Heney and ex-Governor Pardee had created a state water commission, but it had accomplished very little. Harris Weinstock's projects for a state agricultural marketing agency and state subsidies for farm loans and rural land settlement had been no more successful. A state health insurance plan put forward by Rowell and favored by Johnson was defeated in 1917. Conservatives branded all such measures as dangerously radical, and many business progressives agreed.

SELECTED BIBLIOGRAPHY

Mowry's *California Progressives,* Olin's *California's Prodigal Sons,* Everett's "Chester Rowell," and the second volume of Franklin Hichborn's "California Politics," all previously cited, are also of value here. Hichborn's *Story of the*

California Legislature of 1911, and its counterparts for 1913 and 1915, analyze bills and votes. Michael Rogin, "Progressivism and the California Electorate," *Journal of American History*, LV (September 1968), 297–314, analyzes public reactions. On direct government, see V. O. Key, Jr., and Winston W. Crouch, *The Initiative and Referendum in California* (1939); and Frederick L. Bird and Frances M. Ryan, *The Recall of Public Officers: a Study of the Operation of the Recall in California* (1930). On utilities, M. G. Blackford, "Business Men and the Regulation of Railroads . . . in California," *Business History Review*, XLIV (Autumn 1970), 307–319, and "The Politics of Business in California, 1890–1920," Ph.D. thesis, University of California, Berkeley (1972).

Labor measures are treated in Alexander P. Saxton, "San Francisco Labor and the Populist and Progressive Insurgencies," *Pacific Historical Review*, XXXIV (November 1965), 421–438; Gerald D. Nash, "The Influence of Labor on State Policy, 1860–1920," *California Historical Society Quarterly*, XLII (September 1963), 241–257; Norris C. Hundley, Jr., "Katherine Philips Edson and the Fight for the California Minimum Wage, 1912–1923," *Pacific Historical Review*, XXIX (August 1960), 271–286; and two Ph.D. theses, University of California, Berkeley: Earl C. Crockett, "The History of California Labor Legislation, 1910–1930" (1931); and Samuel E. Wood, "The California State Commission of Immigration and Housing" (1942).

Accounts of the anti-Japanese agitation include Roger Daniels, *The Politics of Prejudice; the Anti-Japanese Movement in California and the Struggle for Japanese Exclusion* (1962); Madelon Berkowitz, "The California Progressives and Anti-Japanese Agitation," M.A. thesis, University of California, Berkeley (1966); Thomas A. Bailey, "California, Japan, and the Alien Land Legislation of 1913," *Pacific Historical Review*, I (March 1932), 36–59; and Robert E. Hennings, "James D. Phelan and the Woodrow Wilson Anti-Oriental Statement of May 3, 1912," *California Historical Society Quarterly*, XLII (December 1963), 291–300.

The confusion that progressivism brought to the two-party system is described in A. Lincoln, "Theodore Roosevelt, Hiram Johnson, and the Vice-Presidential Nomination of 1912," *Pacific Historical Review*, XXVIII (August 1959), 267–284; and in Robert E. Hennings, "James D. Phelan and the Wilson Progressives of California," Ph.D. thesis, University of California, Berkeley (1961). The origins of cross-filing are discussed in Franklin Hichborn, "The Party, the Machine, and the Vote; the Story of Cross-filing in California Politics," *California Historical Society Quarterly*, XXXVIII (December 1959), 349–357 and XXXIX (March 1960), 19–34; James C. Findley, "Cross-filing and the Progressive Movement in California Politics," *Western Political Quarterly*, XII (September 1959), 699–711; and Robert E. Burke, "Cross-filing in California Elections, 1914–1946," M.A. thesis, University of California, Berkeley (1947).

On the campaign of 1916, see Edward A. Dickson, "How Hughes Lost California in 1916," *Congressional Record*, August 19, 1954; and F. M. Davenport, "Did Hughes Snub Johnson?" *American Political Science Review*, XLIII (April 1949), 321–332.

Chapter XXVIII

THE CONSERVATION AND USE OF NATURAL RESOURCES

NINETEENTH-CENTURY AMERICANS had regarded their country's natural resources as inexhaustible, and had exploited them with the greatest recklessness. In the progressive era, however, interest in conservation greatly increased. California's natural resources were so spectacular and the controversies over their use and development were so complicated and intense that the issues and problems of conservation inevitably became a major theme in the state's history.

The Yosemite and John Muir. One of the many tributes to the incomparable beauty of the Yosemite Valley was the fact that it was the first area in the United States to be designated by the Federal government as a park. This action was also one of the first historical landmarks in the growth of the modern sense of public responsibility for conservation in America.

One of the early advocates of a Yosemite Park was California state geologist Josiah D. Whitney, for whom Mt. Whitney was named. But the strongest impetus for the park project came from the country's leading landscape architect, Frederick Law Olmsted, who came to California during an interval between his periods of service in the development of Central Park in New York City, and became entranced with the Yosemite while temporarily engaged in the management of Frémont's Mariposa estate. In 1864, largely as a result of Olmsted's urging, Congress passed and President Lincoln signed an act granting the Yosemite Valley and the Mariposa Grove of Big Trees to the state of California. Olmsted was then appointed by the Governor as the first chairman of the Yosemite state park commission. There was no precedent for the idea of a national park, but Federal grants of land to the states for an assortment of other purposes were so frequent that the proposal for a park met little opposition. Yellowstone became the first park administered by the national government, in 1872, mainly because Wyoming and Montana were not yet states.

Almost as important in the history of the conservation idea as the Yosemite Park itself, and closely interrelated with it, was the personality of John Muir, who first came to the valley as a young man in 1868 and was never again entirely happy anywhere else. The valley and the mountains around it inspired him to a lifetime of writings and crusades which proclaimed his gospel of man's rebirth through the enjoyment of nature's beauty, and of man's obligation to preserve that beauty as a sacred trust.

Muir had been born in Scotland—"with heather in him," as he said—and had spent his boyhood on a wilderness farm in Wisconsin. Almost from infancy his father forced him to a regimen of memorizing great parts of the Bible, an influence that was very apparent in his later thinking and writing. A good example was his famous description of the Sierra as he first saw it, after he had landed at San Francisco and walked southward from Oakland to Gilroy and thence to the summit of Pacheco Pass. Across the Central Valley on a clear morning the great range "seemed not clothed with light but wholly composed of it, like the wall of some celestial city. . . . It seemed to me that the Sierra should be called, not the Nevada or Snowy Range, but the Range of Light."

After a short time in the Yosemite region, Muir wrote in his diary that "John Baptist was not more eager to get all of his fellow sinners into the Jordan than I to baptize all of mine in the beauty of God's mountains." "Climb the mountains and get their good tidings," he wrote in his first book, *The Mountains of California*. "Nature's peace will flow into you as sunshine flows into trees. The winds will blow their freshness into you and the storms their energy, while cares will drop off like autumn leaves."

In similar language Muir sent Ralph Waldo Emerson an invitation "to join me in a month's worship with Nature in the high temples of the great Sierra Crown beyond our holy Yosemite." When Emerson accepted, and came to the valley in May 1872, it was one of the supreme moments of Muir's life, though he was somewhat disappointed when the great transcendentalist, at 67, regretfully declined to join him on a camping trip, and kept to the hotels and trails.

Although Muir had studied geology and botany at the University of Wisconsin, he was not a scientist but a brilliant amateur naturalist. Yet it was he, rather than Whitney and other professional geologists of the time, who first proved that a glacier had carved the Yosemite.

Muir's essentially religious approach to nature was a blend of theism and pantheism. God, he felt, was "ensouled as a Principle in all forms of matter." Believing that evolution was not mere chance and survival of the fittest, Muir insisted that man, like nature in general, evolved by cooperation rather than competition. Thus Muir offered a philosophy of society as well as a philosophy

John Muir. From a portrait in the Yosemite Museum, Yosemite National Park. (Courtesy of the National Park Service)

of nature. As his biographer Linnie Marsh Wolfe has pointed out, his remedy for human miseries was in some respects more radical than Henry George's. Brought into his true relationship with the wilderness, man would see that he was not a separate entity but an integral part of a harmonious whole. No man had a right to subdue his fellow creatures or to appropriate and destroy their common heritage; to do so brought unbalance in nature, and loss and poverty for all.

In 1889 Muir gained an important ally in Robert Underwood Johnson, one of the editors of the *Century* magazine. On a tour of the central Sierra, Muir convinced Johnson that the Yosemite was being poorly protected under state control, and pointed out the devastation which sheep—those "hoofed locusts"—were being allowed to inflict on the mountain valleys of the region. Johnson urged Muir to carry his appeal to the people of the whole nation through articles in the *Century*.

For the next 15 years the California legislature resisted the demands of Muir and his admirers that the state return the Yosemite Valley to the Federal government. But in 1890 the eloquent writings of "great Nature's priest," as

Johnson called Muir, aroused so much national emotion that Congress set aside a large area surrounding the valley as a national forest reserve, administered by the Secretary of the Interior, who designated it as "Yosemite National Park." At the same time Congress created the Sequoia National Park, and the General Grant, which was later incorporated in Kings Canyon. The creation of Sequoia incidentally ensured the final eviction of Burnette Haskell's socialistic Kaweah colony; and the biggest *Sequoia gigantea,* which the Kaweahns had named the "Karl Marx tree," was hastily renamed the "General Sherman."

In 1892 Muir founded the Sierra Club, an organization as enthusiastically devoted to conservationist lobbying as it was to mountaineering; and at last, after many years of such pressure, the California state legislature finally approved the recession of the Yosemite Valley in 1905. A year later Congress approved the merging of the valley with the surrounding national park.

Pinchot and Roosevelt. In the eyes of John Muir and his followers, the most important of all natural resources was beauty, and the true object of the conservation movement was to preserve the beauty of the wilderness in its natural state. This school of thought came to be known as "aesthetic conservationism," or "preservationism." Sometimes allied with it but often in sharp opposition was "utilitarian" conservationism, which took form in the 1890s around the ideas of Gifford Pinchot, the pioneer of scientific forestry in America.

Born in Connecticut, Pinchot graduated from Yale, studied forestry in Germany and France, and returned to the United States to achieve spectacular success in convincing large lumber companies that they could greatly increase their long-range profits by selective logging and various other "sustained-yield" techniques of scientific forest management.

The history of the American conservation movement has often been interpreted as a moral conflict between the virtuous "people" and the evil "interests." In fact, however, a great part of American conservationism was a scientific and technological movement, often interrelated with but also distinct from the moral crusade. Many large corporate interests supported conservation, while "the people" in many parts of the West often opposed it. Some of the largest corporations in the lumber industry, including the Weyerhauser Lumber Company in the Pacific Northwest, were converted to Pinchot's ideas; and in 1898 they enthusiastically supported his appointment as chief of the Division (later the Bureau) of Forestry in the United States Department of Agriculture.

"The object of our policy," said Pinchot in one of his many speeches, "is not to preserve the forests because they are beautiful . . . or because they are refuges for the wild creatures of the wilderness." Forest reserves, in his opinion, "should be developed for commercial use rather than preserved from it."

Closely interrelated with the conservation of mountain forests was the conservation of water. As long as the soil of the mountain watersheds remained laced with living roots, it held great quantities of moisture and allowed a gradual and long-continued runoff through the streams below. Denuded by the indiscriminate cutting of timber, however, the surface soil of the mountain slopes was quickly washed away and the heavy rains and melting snow ran off in flash floods. This condition was particularly acute in Southern California, where the whole year's rainfall was sometimes limited to one or two winter cloudbursts. One of the most active conservationists in the state was William G. Kerckhoff of Los Angeles, who was both the operator of a large lumber concern and the owner of an electric light and power company. Kerckhoff became the president of the Forest and Water Society, founded in 1899 by Theodore P. Lukens of San Bernardino. This organization often joined forces with the Sierra Club in conservationist publicity and lobbying.

With Theodore Roosevelt's accession to the Presidency in September 1901, conservation gained a powerful impetus. Indeed Roosevelt was soon identifying the whole conservation movement as "my policy," and several years after he had left the White House he described conservation as the most important of all his domestic policies and his greatest contribution to reform. As a young man Roosevelt had found physical and emotional regeneration in "the strenuous life" of a ranch on the Montana-Dakota border, and his love of the outdoors was as deep and personal as that of John Muir.

Roosevelt was not, however, a preservationist, and his philosophy of conservation was much closer to Gifford Pinchot's. In May 1903, at Roosevelt's request, Muir served as his personal guide on a four-day pack trip in the Yosemite region. Muir made the mistake of giving him a blunt lecture on the need to outgrow "the boyishness of killing things," to which Roosevelt, an incurable big-game hunter, made an abashed and evasive reply.

Roosevelt once remarked that in conservation matters he placed his conscience in the keeping of Gifford Pinchot. The different viewpoints of Muir and Pinchot developed into a personal feud in which Pinchot repeatedly expressed his scorn for Muir and other "nature lovers." And when the conservation movement was dramatized in the famous White House Conference, Pinchot was able to persuade Roosevelt that Muir should not be invited.

From the time of his first annual message as President, in which he spoke of forest conservation as "an imperative business necessity," Roosevelt continuously supported proposals for huge additions to the national forest reserves, and the opponents of this policy in Congress were soon demoralized by a series of exposures of the massive and alarming extent to which timberlands on the public domain were passing into private ownership by fraud. Investigations sponsored by Secretary of the Interior Ethan Allen Hitchcock culminated in the successful prosecutions led by Francis J. Heney and William J. Burns. With the collusion of several Western senators, representatives, and judges, corrupt officials of the General Land Office had winked at innumerable dummy entries under the Federal Preemption, Homestead, and Timber and Stone acts. In the

Humboldt Bay region, for example, sailors' boarding houses had been stations for the recruitment of dummy entrymen who promptly turned over their claims to unscrupulous lumber companies or speculators for a few dollars each. Such "looters of the public domain" formed a major Western contingent of what Roosevelt called the "malefactors of great wealth." Among the worst were the partners John A. Benson and Frederick A. Hyde, two San Francisco financiers who had begun as pioneer landgrabbers in California and had then spread their operations to several other Western states.

Roosevelt's own experiences in the semiarid West had given him a firsthand knowledge of its vital need for water, and another of his early policies as President was to support the passage of the Newlands Reclamation Act of 1902. Representative (later Senator) Francis G. Newlands of Nevada was a brilliant lawyer, educated at Yale and Columbia. He had become a resident of Nevada when he went there to manage the properties he inherited from his father-in-law, Senator William Sharon. The reclamation law that he drafted provided for the use of Federal funds to build irrigation projects. Public lands within the area of these projects were to be open to entry only as homesteads of no more than 160 acres, in order to prevent speculation either by land companies or by the settlers themselves. Family farms, and not corporations, Newlands argued, should benefit from Federal irrigation.

Though Newlands was a Democrat, the theory of his law was based not on democratic political convictions but rather on his belief that the best hope for the economic development of Nevada and other parts of the Mountain West lay in the growth of a family-farm population, and that a farm of 160 acres, or even less, was quite large enough for irrigated agriculture.

The Hetch Hetchy controversy and San Francisco's water supply. The city dweller, as well as the farmer, naturally attached great importance to an assured supply of water. San Francisco was worried by its dependence on the limited nearby resources of the Spring Valley Water Company, a corporation that had been unpopular for decades, and especially since the days when William Chapman Ralston had made it a pawn in one of his last desperate schemes. In 1900 a new city charter authorized a larger and municipally owned water system. City Engineer C. E. Grunsky reported that the Hetch Hetchy Valley on the Tuolumne River in Yosemite National Park was the ideal site, superior to any of the possible alternatives.[1]

Mayor James D. Phelan applied to the Secretary of the Interior for permission to convert the Hetch Hetchy Valley into a reservoir; but the moment John Muir heard of the plan he mobilized his forces for battle, and they fought so

[1] "Hetch Hetchy" was the Miwok name of a plant; "Yosemite" was a sonorous corruption of an Indian word meaning a grizzly bear.

valiantly that the Federal government delayed its final approval of the project for 13 years.

Hetch Hetchy was about 20 miles northwest of its "sister valley," the Yosemite. Though only about half as long and half as wide as its much more famous neighbor, it bore a striking and charming resemblance to it, and was sometimes called a "Yosemite in miniature." But Hetch Hetchy was so nearly inaccessible that very few people except Muir and some other members of the Sierra Club had ever seen it. Muir called it "the Tuolumne Yosemite," and stressed the comparison with the "other Yosemite" on the Merced. Many people thought that Yosemite National Park and Yosemite Valley were the same, and telegraphed their congressmen under the impression that the San Francisco proposal would "destroy the Yosemite Valley." Muir called the flooding of Hetch Hetchy as great a sacrilege as the destruction of a cathedral, and denounced the proponents of it in the strongest terms he could think of.

James D. Phelan, an outstanding patron of the arts and the founder and leading spirit of the Association for the Improvement and Adornment of San Francisco, was outraged at the accusation that he was callously indifferent to beauty. He denounced Muir in return, and stoutly asserted that a lake, as well as a valley, could be beautiful.

Phelan and his supporters also stressed the matter of cost, and argued that while the use of Hetch Hetchy would be granted free of charge, if at all, the possible alternative sites were not only inferior and inadequate but were all controlled by private interests who wished to sell them to the city at exorbitant prices. Considerable weight was given to this argument by sensational revelations concerning the designs of the Bay Cities Water Company. This corporation, of which the San Francisco capitalist William S. Tevis was the president and main stockholder, had acquired options on certain land and water rights near Lake Tahoe, on the south fork of the American River and the north fork of the Cosumnes. It proposed to construct a water system which it would sell to the city for 10.5 million dollars, and in the summer of 1906 the Union Labor board of supervisors actually voted approval of the project. But this action was hastily reversed in the following year when the confessions of Boss Ruef and the supervisors, and other evidence obtained during the graft prosecution, revealed that the total estimated cost of the project was only 7.5 million; that of the 3 million dollars of estimated profit, the company had promised 1 million as a fee to Ruef; and that Ruef had promised to divide half of this money among the supervisors in return for their votes. This project, if it had been consummated, would have been far the largest of all Ruef's corrupt transactions.

The Federal government, sure of being denounced by someone for any action it might take in the Hetch Hetchy matter, vacillated and temporized. Each side in the controversy claimed to represent the public interest, and accused the other of representing selfish "special" interests; but the crux of the problem was the conflict between two public interests. Secretary Hitchcock rejected San Francisco's application. His successor, James R. Garfield, gave tentative approval to it, in 1908, at the urging of Pinchot and with the reluctant assent of President Roosevelt. Under President William H. Taft, however, the Hetch Hetchy issue became entangled in the famous Pinchot-Ballinger controversy, in which Pinchot accused Taft's Secretary of the Interior, Richard A. Ballinger of Oregon, of favoring private interests who wanted to gain possession of coal lands in Alaska and water-power sites on Federal lands in several Western states. Partly as a retaliation against Pinchot, Ballinger revoked the Hetch Hetchy permit. One of the innumerable paradoxes of the conservation movement was that Pinchot and Roosevelt were in the position of approving the "flooding" of a valley in a national park, while Ballinger and Taft stood with the forces of Muir and Robert U. Johnson in fighting to prevent it.

The settlement of the long struggle came at last, in 1913, essentially because it happened that President Wilson's choice for Secretary of the Interior was Franklin K. Lane, who had been city attorney of San Francisco under Mayor Phelan and had written many of the city's briefs in the fight. With the weight of the new Secretary thrown into the scales, Congress gave the final permission in an act drafted by Representative John E. Raker of California. John Muir, defeated by this shift in the sands of politics, was brokenhearted, and died a few months later.

Construction of the new water system was a vast and expensive undertaking. Costs rose sharply in the years of the war and the prosperous 1920s, and the San Francisco city engineer, M. M. O'Shaughnessy, had to present so many requests for supplemental appropriations to the board of supervisors that they began to ask him whether his initials stood for "More Money." Not until 1934 was the system in full operation, including O'Shaughnessy Dam at Hetch Hetchy; the smaller reservoirs at Lake Eleanor and Cherry Creek, to the west of it; and 155 miles of aqueduct, including a 25-mile tunnel under the Coast Range, the longest tunnel in the world at the time of its completion.

The Owens Valley–Los Angeles Aqueduct. San Francisco's chief source of water, the Tuolumne River, begins its flow at the foot of a glacier on Mt. Lyell. Only 15 miles eastward across the Sierra divide are the headwaters of the Owens River, the stream to which Los Angeles reached out for the first of the great and distant new sources of water that its phenomenal 20th-century growth began to require. The story of the Owens Valley–Los Angeles Aqueduct involved controversies even more bitter than the struggle over Hetch Hetchy.

The man who conceived the Owens Valley Aqueduct project was Fred Eaton, city engineer of Los Angeles in the '90s and its mayor from 1899 to 1901. Born in Los Angeles, Eaton had achieved his first success by working his way up to the superintendency of the city's water system when it was a mere network of open ditches from the Los Angeles River, operated by a private company.

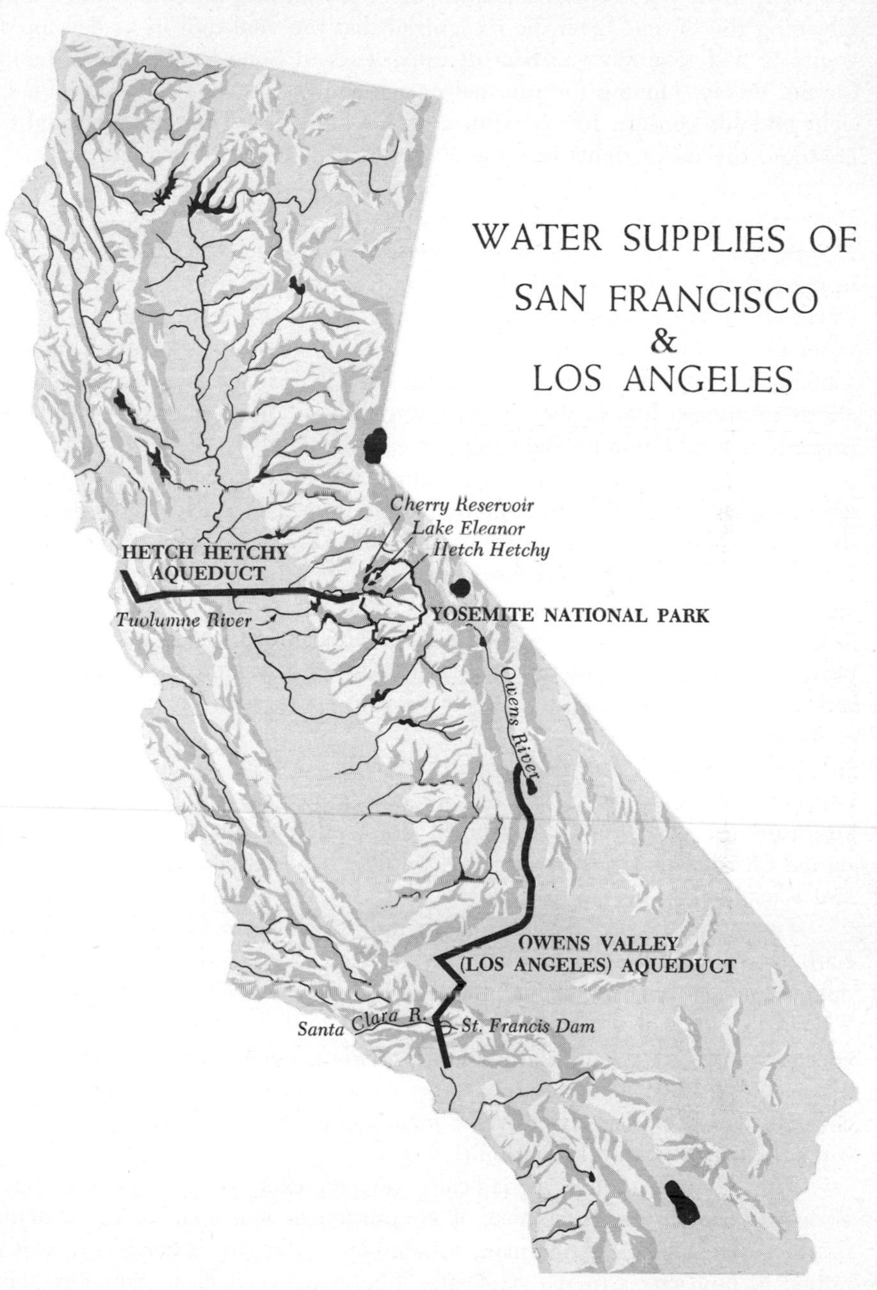
WATER SUPPLIES OF
SAN FRANCISCO
&
LOS ANGELES
Cherry Reservoir
Lake Eleanor
Hetch Hetchy
HETCH HETCHY
AQUEDUCT
Tuolumne River
YOSEMITE NATIONAL PARK
Owens River
OWENS VALLEY
(LOS ANGELES) AQUEDUCT
Santa Clara R.
St. Francis Dam

For many years Eaton spent his vacations in prospecting for a new water supply. Choosing the Owens River, he recognized that the vital unit in its development would be a storage reservoir near its upper end, in Long Valley, above the main Owens Valley. Hoping for personal enrichment as the just reward of his foresight and his concern for the future of his native city, he quietly bought the land and the water rights in Long Valley, and planned the project as a private enterprise, to sell some of the Owens River water for the irrigation of the Owens Valley itself and to sell the rest to the city of Los Angeles.

Between 1900 and 1905 the population of that city grew from 102,479 to more than 250,000. Moreover, the rainfall in these years was even less than usual, and in July 1904 Los Angeles came close to the stark terror of an actual water famine. The city engineer, William Mulholland, was a former protégé of Eaton's. For years he had responded with friendly ridicule to Eaton's confidential efforts to interest him in the remote Owens Valley. Now, however, Mulholland urgently begged Eaton to "show me this water supply."

In the meantime the United States Reclamation Service had formed a plan to irrigate the Owens Valley under the terms of the Newlands Act. When the Federal agency refused to cooperate with Eaton as a private speculator and developer, he agreed to sell his interests to the city of Los Angeles. He also agreed to act as the city's confidential agent in purchasing further lands in Owens Valley necessary for an aqueduct. This he proceeded to do, under the guise of buying lands for ranching purposes. The real purpose was to be kept secret as long as possible in order to prevent speculative increases in the price of the land.

The first public knowledge of the aqueduct project came in a long, detailed, and enthusiastic article in the *Los Angeles Times* on July 29, 1905. Not long afterward the *Los Angeles Examiner,* outraged that the *Times* had been permitted to scoop its rivals in this way, published sensational charges of collusion and conspiracy.

Two years before, a syndicate including Harrison Gray Otis, Edwin T. Earl, Henry E. Huntington, William G. Kerckhoff, and others had acquired options to buy extensive lands in the San Fernando Valley. Under the Owens Valley Aqueduct plan, now revealed, a reservoir just north of Los Angeles would be adjacent to these lands, and would provide water for their irrigation as well as for the city's domestic supply. The whole aqueduct project, the *Examiner* charged, had been conceived by the members of this San Fernando land syndicate for their own speculative profit.

This charge, though periodically revived ever since, was based on an erroneous conclusion. A number of circumstances lent color to it, particularly the fact that Moses H. Sherman, a member of the city water board, was permitted to buy shares in the syndicate. The evidence is clear, however, that in 1903 when this group of wealthy men had acquired the San Fernando land options, Eaton's dream of an aqueduct, if they had yet heard of it at all, was not the basis of their plan. Rather, they were acting on inside information from Henry E. Huntington that he was about to build a new line of the Pacific Electric into the San Fernando Valley. The same men were employing this highly profitable technique of group investment in several other prospective suburbs of Los Angeles at this same time.

In a special election in September 1905 the voters of the city overwhelmingly approved an issue of bonds for the beginning of the Owens Valley project. At the end of still another summer of frightening water shortage, the citizens of Los Angeles were in no mood to vote against a plan that promised them an adequate water supply.

The farmers and townsmen of the Owens Valley now began a bitter campaign of denunciation which they would continue for decades, charging that the aqueduct was a corrupt scheme to enrich a few of the leading capitalists of Los Angeles by seizing the water that would be needed for the agricultural development of the Owens Valley and using it to irrigate the San Fernando Valley instead. The Federal government sided with the city. President Roosevelt and Chief Forester Pinchot were persuaded that the whole future growth of Los Angeles was more important than the interests of "a few settlers in Owens Valley"; and in 1908, to prevent homestead entries in the path of the proposed aqueduct, Roosevelt ordered the extension of the Sierra National Forest eastward to include the prospective right of way, even though the only trees in the region were those planted by the settlers themselves.

Under the direction of City Engineer Mulholland the construction of the 233-mile aqueduct began in 1908 and ended five years later, at a cost within his estimate of 25 million dollars. When the first Owens River water reached the San Fernando Valley in 1913, Mulholland's engineering achievement was widely compared to the Panama Canal, and the *Los Angeles Times* called him "the Goethals of the West." Harrison Gray Otis and Edwin T. Earl, in a rare moment of agreement, joined in urging Mulholland to run for mayor, though he declined, in the salty manner of speech that was characteristic of him. He did accept an honorary doctorate from the University of California, and for a man who had arrived in Los Angeles as a young Irish immigrant, taken a job with the water company as a *zanjero,* or ditch tender, and trained himself by reading engineering textbooks at night, Mulholland seemed to have achieved as much honor, success, and happiness as a man could ask.

Unfortunately his later years were less happy. His aqueduct took its water directly out of the lower Owens River. If a year-to-year storage reservoir in Long Valley had been built when the aqueduct was constructed, or soon afterward, enough water could have been provided to meet the needs of Owens Valley, along with those of the city, for some time to come, and much bitterness could have been avoided. But Fred Eaton had demanded a price of at least 1 million dollars for his Long Valley land, and Mulholland, breaking his old friendship with Eaton, had denounced the price as too high and advised the city not to pay it. In the early 1920s a new cycle of dry years and the continuing rapid growth of Los Angeles's population led the city to siphon off virtually the entire flow of the river, and in 1924 some residents of Owens Valley began to dramatize their protests with a campaign of sabotage, which later culminated in the dynamiting of several sections of the aqueduct.

The deepest tragedy of Mulholland's career, however, was the collapse of St. Francis Dam, which he had built in San Francisquito Canyon, near Saugus, as a part of the aqueduct system. On March 13, 1928, just after midnight, this dam gave way and a wall of water rushed down the valley of the Santa Clara River, destroying much of the city of Santa Paula and killing 385 persons. In the official inquiry Mulholland testified that he had misjudged the composition of the canyon wall, that the blame was entirely his, and that he envied the dead. Mulholland then announced his retirement as chief engineer and general manager of the Los Angeles Department of Water and Power, but continued as a consultant. Later he succeeded in negotiating a compromise price for Long Valley, and a personal reconciliation, with Fred Eaton. In 1941, several years after the deaths of Eaton and Mulholland, the dam in Long Valley was completed at last, and the reservoir was named Lake Crowley, after Father John J. Crowley, a Roman Catholic priest who had worked for many years to raise the morale of the people of Owens Valley. The volume of water in the Owens River was also increased by extending a long tunnel northward to tap the streams flowing into the Mono Basin.

SELECTED BIBLIOGRAPHY

François Matthes, *The Incomparable Valley; a Geologic Interpretation of Yosemite* (1950), includes magnificent photographs and strikingly clear explanations. Hans Huth, "Yosemite: the Story of an Idea," *Sierra Club Bulletin,* XXXIII (March 1948), 47–78, deals with the origin of the state park project. Linnie March Wolfe, *Son of the Wilderness; the Life of John Muir* (1945), is an excellent biography. See also Francis P. Farquhar, *History of the Sierra Nevada* (1965).

On conservation as a national movement in this period see Samuel P. Hays, *Conservation and the Gospel of Efficiency: the Progressive Conservation Movement, 1890–1920* (1959); and Elmo R. Richardson, *The Politics of Conservation; Crusades and Controversies, 1897–1913* (1963).

Useful accounts of the Hetch Hetchy problem include Elmo R. Richardson, "The Struggle for the Valley; California's Hetch Hetchy Controversy," *California Historical Society Quarterly,* XXXVIII (September 1959), 249–258; Holway R. Jones, *John Muir and the Sierra Club: the Battle for Yosemite* (1965); M. M. O'Shaughnessy, *The Hetch Hetchy Water Supply of San Francisco* (1916); and Ray W. Taylor, *Hetch Hetchy* (1926).

The best treatments of the Owens Valley–Los Angeles Aqueduct are in

Remi A. Nadeau, *The Water Seekers* (1950), and Vincent Ostrom, *Water & Politics: a Study of Water Policies and Administration in the Development of Los Angeles* (1953). Morrow Mayo, in the chapter called "The Rape of Owens Valley" in his *Los Angeles* (1933), and Carey McWilliams, *Southern California Country* (1946), revived the syndicate-conspiracy version of the Owens Valley project, and their accounts of it are extremely unreliable; see W. W. Robinson, "Myth Making in the Los Angeles Area," *Southern California Quarterly*, XLV (March 1963), 83–94. Charles F. Outland, *Man-made Disaster* (1963), recounts the tragedy of St. Francis Dam.

Erwin Cooper, *Aqueduct Empire* (1968), is a useful history of water problems in California.

Chapter XXIX

THE TRIUMPH OF CONSERVATISM

Rise and fall of the socialist movement. In California, as well as in the United States as a whole, socialism reached its highest point during the progressive era. This not only alarmed conservatives but also gave them an opportunity to attack and weaken progressivism by linking it with socialism.

The beginnings of the organized socialist movement in the state went back to the 1880s, when Burnette G. Haskell preached a modified Marxism in San Francisco and Kaweah, and the eccentric millionaire H. Gaylord Wilshire developed a peculiarly American brand of socialism in Los Angeles.

Wilshire was an irrepressible and almost incredible figure in the history of Southern California. The son of a Cincinnati capitalist, he inherited and lost one fortune and then made and lost a series of others, in real estate, orange groves, banks, gold mines, billboards, and even a cure-all electric belt of his own invention. In the boom of the '80s he developed and subdivided the "Wilshire Tract" west of Los Angeles's Westlake Park. Harrison Gray Otis and Edwin T. Earl bought large adjoining lots and built their mansions in this subdivision, through the center of which ran a thoroughfare 120 feet wide, named Wilshire Boulevard. But with the collapse of the boom in 1888 Gaylord Wilshire became an avowed socialist, and in 1890 under the Bellamyite Nationalist label he was the first socialist in the United States to run for Congress. Next he founded *Wilshire's Magazine,* which became the country's most widely circulated socialist journal. Its motto was "Let the Nation Own the Trusts," an idea that would also play a central part in Jack London's novel, *The Iron Heel.* For a time in the '90s Wilshire lived in England and was a friend of George Bernard Shaw and the Fabian socialists.

In later years Wilshire Boulevard would be to Los Angeles more or less what the Champs Elysees was to Paris, and more than 200 enterprises from a hotel and a country club to a cleaning and dyeing company would take the name of Wilshire because it signified impeccable commercial prestige. Few if any of the proprietors or patrons of these establishments knew the identity of the original bearer of the name.

In the '90s the leadership of the California socialist movement passed from Wilshire to Job Harriman, a labor-union lawyer who came to Los Angeles for his health. Running for governor on a socialist ticket in 1898, he drew only 5,000 votes, but within a few years the extremely repressive tactics of Harrison Gray Otis and the Merchants' and Manufacturers' Association had driven so much of Los Angeles labor to socialism that Harriman repeatedly came close to being elected mayor of the city. He would almost certainly have been elected mayor in 1911 if he had not committed the socialist cause to the belief that the McNamara brothers were innocent victims of a capitalist frame-up, and if the McNamaras had not shattered this faith by confessing their guilt a few days before the city election. (See Chapter 24.) Even after that great setback Harriman came within 800 votes of being elected mayor two years later. But after this final defeat he turned from political activity to the management of a socialist cooperative experiment at Llano del Rio in the Mojave Desert region north of Los Angeles.

In the state election of 1910 more than 12 percent of the vote went to the Socialist candidate for Governor, J. Stitt Wilson, a Berkeley Methodist minister of attractive personality who described himself as a "social evangelist." In 1911 Wilson was elected mayor of Berkeley, although in his two years in that office he neither attempted nor accomplished anything radical. In 1912 he ran as the Socialist candidate for Congress against Joseph R. Knowland, the impregnable Republican leader of Oakland and dean of the California congressional delegation; although Knowland won 54 percent of the votes, Wilson drew a remarkable 40 percent, and the Democratic candidate only 6 percent.

In 1912, Socialist congressional nominees in California won 18 percent of the votes and Eugene V. Debs won nearly 12 percent of the vote for President. One Socialist assemblyman from Los Angeles was elected, and in several other districts the Socialists ran far ahead of the Democrats. The elections of 1914 produced two Socialist assemblymen and one state senator.

Though socialism called in theory for public ownership of all the means of production and distribution, the Socialists in the California legislature pressed mainly for such limited measures as the 8-hour day. They did propose a "right to work" law, using the phrase not in its later connotation of the open shop but rather to mean that every unemployed man had a right to be guaranteed a job, on state public works if necessary. This bill passed the assembly but died in the senate. Most of the actual legislative proposals of the Socialists were so moderate that they were hardly distinguishable from those advocated by the more liberal of the progressives. But conservative forces formed a Sound Government League in order to fight them, and one of the League's bulletins denounced "creeping socialism," with which conservatives lumped most progressive measures.

The rising tide of socialism in the United States in the first 15 years of the century was a general humanitarian as well as a working-class reaction to such prevailing conditions as poverty, long hours and low wages, the abuse of child labor, watered milk, and adulterated foods. The coming of World War I virtually shattered the socialist movement, not only by distracting the country's attention from these conditions but also by creating extreme disunity among the socialists themselves in their attitudes toward the war. In California such prominent Socialists as Stitt Wilson and Jack London favored the Allied cause, and resigned from the Socialist party in 1916 when it opposed American intervention.

The Mooney case. In Northern California the beginning of a long period of antilabor reaction coincided with the beginning of the war in Europe. In 1914, after several months of economic depression, an "army" of 1,500 unemployed under "General" Charles T. Kelley was driven out of Sacramento by a force of deputized citizens armed with clubs. In Stockton, after a labor campaign for the closed shop, employers formed a Merchants' and Manufacturers' Association in July 1914, imported professional strikebreakers and armed guards, and launched an open-shop drive that produced one of the bitterest labor wars in the state's history.

A similar battle might have occurred in San Francisco at the same time had it not been for the desire to avoid trouble during the Panama Pacific International Exposition. The open-shop drive of the San Francisco employers was deferred until July 1916. Then, during a longshoremen's strike, the San Francisco Chamber of Commerce called a mass meeting of 2,000 businessmen, who cheered an inflammatory address by Captain Robert Dollar, and then voted to form a Law and Order Committee in a deliberate appeal to the city's vigilante tradition.

In the summer of 1916, labor in general was opposing the military preparedness movement, while most employers favored that movement and seized the opportunity to discredit labor as unpatriotic. San Francisco business and patriotic organizations planned a great Preparedness Day parade on Market Street, in which no labor union participated. The parade was held on July 22. In the midst of it, at 2:06 in the afternoon, a bomb explosion at the corner of Steuart and Market killed 10 persons and wounded 40. Suspicion soon fell upon a radical labor agitator named Thomas J. Mooney.

For several years before the Preparedness Day bombing, Mooney had been active in San Francisco as a left-wing trade-union socialist with an aggressive personality and a genius for antagonizing people. An ironmolder by trade, he was not a union official. The description of him as a "labor leader" came from opponents of organized labor. He was interested in strike activity for the purposes of social revolution.

In 1913 the electrical workers' union had conducted a long strike against the Pacific Gas and Electric Company throughout Northern California, during which there were hundreds of depredations against the company's property, 18 of them by dynamite explosions. Warren K. Billings, a young friend of Mooney, had been arrested at Sacramento for the illegal transportation of a suitcase full of dynamite, and sentenced to two years in prison. Later in 1913 Mooney was arrested for illegal possession of explosives and charged with planning to use them to destroy the transmission line across Carquinez Straits, which would have shut off the electric light and power of most of the bay area. He was tried at Martinez, but the evidence was flimsy and he was acquitted.

In the summer of 1916 Mooney tried to organize a union among employees of the United Railroads in San Francisco. The company had not permitted union organization since 1907, when it had broken not only a strike but the carmen's union as well. Mooney's plan was to start a wildcat strike by a few of the streetcar motormen and then to stampede the others into it, but the attempt to do this, on July 14, 1916, was a fiasco. The Preparedness Day explosion occurred eight days later.

Within a few days after the explosion the police arrested Mooney, his wife Rena, and three of their associates, Warren Billings, Edward D. Nolan, and Israel Weinberg, a jitney driver. All five were arrested without evidence, warrants, or formal charges, and were denied the right of legal counsel until after they were indicted. From the time of the arrests the police and the district attorney's office dropped all further search for evidence except that which could be made to point to the defendants' guilt. Billings was tried for murder in September, convicted, and sentenced to life imprisonment. Mooney was tried in January 1917, convicted, and sentenced to hang. Later in the year Rena Mooney and Israel Weinberg were acquitted. Edward Nolan was not brought to trial.

The three main witnesses for the prosecution testified that they had seen Billings and the Mooneys at or near the scene of the crime, and that Billings was carrying a suitcase presumably containing a time bomb. Overwhelming evidence indicates that these witnesses were perjuring themselves; and it is hard to escape the conclusion that District Attorney Charles M. Fickert was aware of their perjury and encouraged it. To the witness Estelle Smith, Fickert made a promise of a parole for her uncle, who was serving a term in prison for second-degree murder. The motives of the witness Frank C. Oxman, a moderately wealthy Oregon cattle rancher, have remained unfathomable; but the witness John McDonald was obviously seeking reward money.

Charles Fickert had originally been elected district attorney of San Francisco in 1909 on his tacit promise to end the graft prosecution. He was at best an incompetent lawyer who had always been accustomed to garble or invent facts to suit his immediate purposes. In the Mooney case he did not prosecute the defendants in good faith, but because they were widely hated as radicals and because he believed that to convict them would make him Governor of California.

Again, as in the *Times* bombing a few years earlier, millions of people throughout the country believed what their social predilections made them wish to believe about the guilt or innocence of the accused. This time, however, many were afraid of being deceived by the cry of "frame-up" that had been so discredited before, and this made Fickert's work easier. The evidence against the McNamara brothers, so widely disbelieved and denounced, had turned out to be quite genuine. The evidence against Mooney and Billings, so readily believed, was fabricated.

It was apparent to many, however, that there had been an outrageous miscarriage of justice. The case took on international importance in April 1917, with a demonstration outside the American Embassy in Petrograd against the execution of a political prisoner named "Muni." President Wilson, concerned both for the interests of justice and for the American image in a war to make the world safe for democracy, asked Governor William D. Stephens to consider a commutation. The California supreme court refused to order a new trial, largely for the technical reason that the main exposure of the perjuries had occurred after the time during which a motion for a retrial was allowed.

In November 1918 Governor Stephens commuted Mooney's sentence to life imprisonment. This action was a political compromise, announced by Stephens after he had been returned to office in the gubernatorial election, after the armistice, and a few days before the date when Mooney was to have been hanged. In the antiradical hysteria of the war and postwar periods, most Californians held to a fixed belief in Mooney's guilt.

The criminal syndicalism law. Throughout the war the I.W.W. openly opposed America's participation in it, and maintained that the only just war was a class war against capitalism. Long denounced as advocates of industrial sabotage, terrorism, and violence, the Wobblies were now also branded as antipatriotic and pro-German, and often described as "Imperial Wilhelm's Warriors." They were actively involved in bitter wartime strikes, especially in the lumber industry. Late in 1918, 46 I.W.W. members were arrested in Sacramento and tried in the Federal courts as seditious conspirators. Most of them were convicted and sentenced to prison.

After the end of the war the wave of emotional antiradicalism became even greater, for the full force of public hatred was then turned upon "internal enemies." In February 1919 a five-day general strike in Seattle, organized by

Tom Mooney, interviewed by a reporter in 1933. (Courtesy of the Bancroft Library)

militant locals of the A.F. of L., was widely attributed to the I.W.W., and conservative newspapers in California cited it as proof of an imminent danger of Bolshevik revolution. In April 1919 the California legislature passed a criminal syndicalism act, although the legislature of 1917 had rejected a similar measure.

This statute defined criminal syndicalism as "any doctrine or precept advocating . . . unlawful acts of force and violence . . . as a means of accomplishing a change in industrial ownership or control, or effecting any political change." Under this law several hundred persons were prosecuted in California during the next five years.

One of the first of these trials, and by far the most famous, was that of Charlotte Anita Whitney. Before her arrest in November 1919, when she was 52 years old, Miss Whitney's career had hardly been such as to suggest that she was a dangerous criminal. Rather, she was well known as a philanthropist, social worker, and suffragist. She could trace her descent from five Mayflower pilgrims; her father had been a state senator from Alameda County; and her uncle was United States Supreme Court Justice Stephen J. Field. After graduating from Wellesley College she had worked in a settlement house in New York, and then served for many years as secretary of the Associated Charities of Oakland. She had joined the Socialist party in 1914, and during the war she was active in the pacifist movement and in the defense of Mooney and Billings.

In 1919 a number of left-wing Socialists split off to form the Communist Labor party, whose state organization was formed at a convention in Oakland. Miss Whitney, as a delegate from the Oakland Socialist local, worked for a resolution favoring only democratic and peaceful methods, but this resolution was voted down, and instead the convention ratified the national platform of the Communist Labor party. The American Communist party, which was also formed in 1919, had a platform so similar that the two organizations were later merged.

Miss Whitney's trial began in January 1920, not long after United States Attorney General A. Mitchell Palmer, who hoped to be the next Democratic candidate for President, had launched a new program of raids against "Bolshevists, anarchists, and kindred radicals." The proceedings against Miss Whitney were conducted in an atmosphere of hysterical superpatriotism, and they set a pattern for many subsequent prosecutions in which mere membership in an organization advocating violence was interpreted as sufficient evidence of criminal syndicalism under the state law. She was convicted and sentenced to 1 to 14 years in the penitentiary.

Fremont Older, one of the leading critics of the prosecution in the Mooney case, also came vigorously to the defense of Miss Whitney, and persuaded his former star reporter, John Francis Neylan, to take charge of her appeal. Neylan had studied law in his spare time, and after the end of his service as chairman of the state Board of Control had begun a highly successful law practice in San Francisco. William Randolph Hearst had employed him to negotiate the purchase of the *San Francisco Call,* had made him its publisher, and later made him general counsel of all the Hearst publications.

Neylan disagreed sharply with Miss Whitney's political views but believed that she had been unjustly convicted, and for seven years, while she remained free on bail, he fought with all the legal and political resources he could muster to keep her out of prison. The United States Supreme Court finally rendered a decision in the case in May 1927. Unanimously it upheld the conviction, and also upheld the constitutionality of the California law as being within the state's police power. Justices Holmes and Brandeis joined in a separate concurring opinion, based on the doctrine of "clear and present danger," which Holmes had formulated in *Schenck v. United States* in 1919. Miss Whitney's attorneys had failed to introduce at her trial a claim that she had done nothing to create such a danger. It was for this reason, in the opinion of the two justices, that her conviction could not be reversed on appeal.

Neylan was more successful in his fight for a pardon, which Governor Clement C. Young finally granted in June 1927. In explaining his decision the Governor made use of an argument which Neylan had also been careful to emphasize, that to imprison Miss Whitney would "revive the waning spirits of radicalism" by making her a martyr. Besides, Young concluded, she was a "lifelong friend of the unfortunate," rather than "in any true sense a 'criminal,'" and "to condemn her at sixty years of age to a felon's cell" was "absolutely unthinkable."

Upton Sinclair and others, observing sardonically that a number of obscure men had been imprisoned for offenses identical in principle with Miss Whitney's, charged that there was one law for the rich and another for the poor. Altogether, there had been 504 arrests and 264 trials under the California criminal syndicalism law, and 128 persons, mostly members of the I.W.W., had been sent to prison. Twenty-four states had adopted such laws, mostly in 1919, but in all these states except California they were dead letters after 1921. In California, active prosecutions continued until 1924, largely to discourage further attempts by the I.W.W. to organize migratory farmworkers.

Decline of organized labor. In the 1920s the business community had considerable success in branding labor unions as unpatriotic. A large segment of American public opinion believed that the unions had at best been lukewarm in their support of the war, and that they had been inclined to defend seditious radicals instead of joining in the national condemnation of them. Adding these widely held beliefs to their arsenal of weapons, employer organizations resumed their prewar battles for the open shop, and this time succeeded in establishing it even in what had previously been the union stronghold of San Francisco.

In the summer of 1921, after an unpopular and unsuccessful strike by the building trades unions, the San Francisco Chamber of Commerce created a new Industrial Association to establish and enforce "the American Plan." This expression had recently received the approval of the National Association of Manufacturers as the official name for the open shop. The drive made such remarkable headway in San Francisco that for the rest of the decade the open shop predominated even in the construction of municipal buildings. The Industrial Association maintained a "permit system" under which it withheld building materials from employers who continued to "discriminate against non-union men" by making closed-shop contracts with unions. An Impartial Wage Board, established by the association and headed by the Roman Catholic Archbishop, E. J. Hanna, very nearly replaced collective bargaining in the fixing of wage scales in the building industry. Under the philosophy of "welfare capitalism" the association also established free training schools for apprentices, employee group insurance plans, and a free employment bureau for nonunion workers. Spokesmen for the Industrial Association of San Francisco often argued that it was not a "union-busting" organization, because it forbade employers to discriminate against union members—provided they were willing to work with nonunion men.

In Los Angeles, however, employers were often more candidly eager to destroy unions entirely. The Better America Federation, a new auxiliary of the Merchants' and Manufacturers' Association, was organized in Los Angeles in May 1920 to conduct a lobbying and propaganda battle against organized labor and progressivism. Its drives for members and money made the sort of patriotic appeal that had been used to sell Liberty Bonds during the war, and indeed it made a particular effort to recruit as its publicists the men who had been the most successful bondsellers. It lobbied against higher state taxes on banks and utilities, and in favor of proposals to establish the open shop by law and to abolish all of the state regulatory boards and commissions that the progressives had created. Its propaganda sought to associate with treason and subversion anyone who disagreed with its objectives.

Throughout the '20s membership in labor unions steadily declined. In a period of prosperity and high employment, this was remarkable. The prestige of organized labor was low, and the prestige of employer organizations was correspondingly high. Many agreed with the Better America Federation in adopting as mottoes the slogan of President Warren Harding, "less government in business, more business in government," and the aphorism of President Calvin Coolidge, "the business of America is business."

Collapse of the Democratic party. During the last third of the 19th century the balance between the two major political parties had been close in California, and Democratic candidates had won five gubernatorial elections to the Republicans' four. After 1900, however, a long series of defeats began to have a cumulative effect on the Democratic party's morale. Though the state voted for Woodrow Wilson in 1916, disillusionment with his leadership set in during the war and increased still further after the armistice.

The Democratic aspirants for the governorship of California in 1918 attracted so little support that a Republican, James Rolph, Jr., the popular mayor of San Francisco, won the Democratic nomination for Governor by cross-filing. Moreover, because Rolph lost the nomination of his own party to Governor Stephens he could not legally accept the Democratic bid, and the result was that there was no Democratic candidate at all on the November ballot.

In the postwar decade the Republicans benefited from the general prosperity and from the wholesale migration to California of retired farmers and small businessmen from the Middle West. Throughout the '20s the Democrats could win no more than one of California's 11 congressional seats; cross-filing Republicans repeatedly won the Democratic nominations for six of them and were thus elected in the primaries, in which, in several cases, no Democrat even bothered to file. In 1922, of the 80 seats in the state assembly, the Democrats won only 3. In 1924 the electors pledged to the Democratic candidate for President, John W. Davis, received only 8 percent of the California vote. Through most of the decade Republicans outnumbered Democrats in California by four to one in voter's registrations.

Democratic leadership was uninspiring. James D. Phelan, who had gone to the United States Senate in 1914 as the leader of the "Wilson progressives" of California, was defeated for reelection in 1920, and the only political ideas he continued to advocate with any consistency were the ban on Japanese immigration and a loosening of the prohibition laws to permit the manufacture of wine and beer. When William G. McAdoo transferred his residence from New York to California in 1922, the California Democrats hoped that this acquisition of a leading contender for the Presidency of the United States would revive their strength. But McAdoo, who favored strong enforcement of prohibition, made his home in Los Angeles and assumed the leadership of the dry Democrats of Southern California, thus deepening the split with the Northern California wing of the party, which was decidedly wet. Early in 1924 the Los Angeles oil magnate Edward L. Doheny, under investigation for the bribery of Secretary of the Interior Albert B. Fall, let drop the fact that McAdoo was on his payroll as an attorney, and McAdoo's chances for the presidential nomination were instantly ruined even though he had no actual connection with the oil scandals. William Randolph Hearst remained a nominal Democrat through the early '20s; but after a bitter quarrel with Alfred E. Smith, Hearst became a supporter and personal admirer of President Calvin Coolidge. Will Rogers, "cowboy humorist" and political commentator of the '20s, remarked that "I am not a member of any organized political party. I'm a Democrat."

The continuing decline of Republican progressivism. Senator Hiram Johnson had abandoned the remnants of the Progressive party by 1918, and he campaigned for the Republican presidential nomination in 1920 on a platform of narrowly nationalistic and isolationist "Americanism." His irreconcilable opposition to the League of Nations so far overshadowed his interest in domestic issues that he supported the conservative lawyer Samuel M. Shortridge for the Republican nomination for United States Senator, against the distinguished progressive William Kent, largely because Shortridge opposed the League and Kent favored it.

Prohibition was another issue that confused the alignments among progressive and conservative Republicans, as well as among the Democrats. Many of the California progressives were "drys," and the disastrous failure of the prohibition experiment accelerated the general decline in the moral fervor of progressivism. Congress had submitted the Eighteenth Amendment to the states in December 1917, in the midst of the war, and California ratified it the spring of 1919, after the necessary 36 other states had already done so. It proved even less popular and less effective in California than in the rest of the country. Efforts to enforce it were concentrated against small cafés rather than against large distillers and bootleggers, and the Mexican border and the long coastline made smuggling easy. The obvious breakdown of prohibition tended to weaken all respect for law and government. One jury had to be admonished for drinking up the liquor that was the chief evidence in the trial.

The continuing crusade against the Japanese, which had never had any genuine connection with progressivism, now became a part of the new wave of superheated patriotic antiforeignism that was aiding the conservative revival throughout the country. An initiative measure adopted by a vote of three to one in 1920 repealed the provision of the law of 1913 that had permitted Japanese aliens to lease land for three years. In the Federal immigration act of 1924, California won its long fight for the complete exclusion of "aliens ineligible to citizenship." Without this clause, the quota system finally provided in the act would have permitted only 100 Japanese immigrants per year; nevertheless, Johnson and Shortridge demanded complete Japanese exclusion, and secured the support of the conservative Republican leader of the Senate, Henry Cabot Lodge. The United States had never before offered Japan so gratuitous an insult; but the Japanese ambassador's warning of "grave consequences" was interpreted in Congress as a threat, and for this reason it actually contributed to the passage of the exclusion clause.

The triumph of conservatism was most apparent in the election of Friend W. Richardson as Governor in 1922. A former state treasurer and publisher of the *Berkeley Gazette,* Richardson promised and achieved a program of "sweeping retrenchment." His "economy budget" drastically reduced appropriations, particularly for regulatory boards, humanitarian agencies, and education. "The schools," he told the legislature, "must be put on a business basis. They must not only teach but practice thrift." As heads of the various regulatory commissions, he replaced the men appointed under Johnson and Stephens with conservatives, often representatives of the business interests that the commissions had been designed to regulate.

For the election of 1926, Chester Rowell, Rudolph Spreckels, Franklin Hichborn, and others formed a Progressive Voters' League, and rallied behind the gubernatorial aspirations of Clement C. Young of Berkeley. Young, a developer of suburban real estate, had been speaker of the assembly during the progressive era and was now Lieutenant Governor. In his race for the governorship in 1926 he made his progressive followers uneasy by accepting the support of A. P. Giannini and his Bank of Italy.

Giannini's swiftly growing institution, soon to be renamed the Bank of America, was well on the way toward its goal of a system of branches to cover the whole of California. Under Governor Richardson the state authorities had yielded to the complaints of independent bankers and rival branch systems, and had tried through administrative rulings to restrict the statewide growth of branch banking. Shortly before the primary of 1926 the Bank of Italy contributed generously to the Young campaign fund, and the employees of the bank's branches throughout the state gave generously of their services as volunteer campaigners. By a narrow margin, Young won the Republican nomination from Richardson. At a time when California was almost a one-party state, this assured Young of the governorship.

As Franklin Hichborn put it, he and his fellow progressives had marveled at such a "fortunate acquisition" of support; but when Young became Governor they learned that "we were the acquisition." Early in 1927 Young's new superintendent of banks revoked the restrictions on branch banking. During the remainder of that year the branches of the Bank of Italy increased from 98 to 289.

Although Young's administration disappointed his most progressive supporters, he did reverse some of the most reactionary policies of Richardson. An act of 1929, with Young's support, made California the first state to require that every county provide old-age pensions. His most substantial achievement was a "businesslike reorganization" of the state government, which inaugurated the cabinet system in the executive branch and improved the budget system.

In the election of 1930, when the main contest was between Young and James Rolph, Jr., for the Republican nomination, Richardson had his revenge. Young was a dry and Rolph was a wet. Richardson encouraged District Attorney Buron Fitts of Los Angeles to enter the race, and thus to divide the dry vote in Southern California, so that Rolph narrowly defeated Young in the primary. With Rolph's election as Governor, Republican progressivism in California went into an even further decline.

The "Federal Plan" of reapportionment. A new system of apportioning the state senate, adopted in 1926, played a little-understood but highly important part in the successful drive of conservative business interests to consolidate their influence upon the state government.

Representation in both houses of the legislature had previously been apportioned according to population, and reapportioned, with considerable gerrymandering, every 10 years. By the early '20s, however, Los Angeles had grown so enormously that the legislators from San Francisco and Oakland joined with those from the rural Northern California counties to block any reapportionment bill that would have given the southern metropolis its full representation.

In 1926 the voters were given a choice between two initiative constitutional amendments. One provided for reapportionment in both houses on the customary basis of population. This was officially called the "All Parties" proposal, but its main support was in Los Angeles County. Its opponents always called it "the Los Angeles Plan," and thus assured its unpopularity in every other county in the state. The alternative proposal, on the other hand, bore the disingenuous but effectively persuasive label of "the Federal Plan." Based on a misleading analogy with the equal representation of the states in the upper house of

Congress, this scheme apportioned the seats in the state senate at not more than one to a county and at not more than three counties to a senatorial district.

This proposal was also advertised as coming from the "dirt farmers" of California, and the four largest agricultural organizations did support it with enthusiasm. Significantly, however, the major financial contribution in aid of its passage came from the San Francisco Chamber of Commerce, though this source was not revealed until after the election. As Franklin Hichborn observed, the plan was ideally suited to the interests of those special California farmers who labored in the tall buildings on Montgomery Street, the heart of the San Francisco financial district. Over the next several years the ingenuity of their plan became apparent in the membership of the state senate. Dirt farmers were not in evidence, and a remarkable proportion of the new senators from the rural districts turned out to be attorneys, insurance men, and others who were local representatives of corporations with headquarters in San Francisco.

California agriculture itself was becoming steadily more industrialized, and its interests more and more identified with those of the business community. The new California senate would often be described as "rural dominated." To put the matter more accurately, it became a stronghold of business conservatism, rural and urban.

SELECTED BIBLIOGRAPHY

Ralph Hancock, *Fabulous Boulevard* (1949), includes a chapter on the "Man Named Wilshire." Howard Quint, "Gaylord Wilshire and Socialism's First Congressional Campaign," *Pacific Historical Review*, XXVI (November 1957), 327–340, describes the election of 1890. On the career of Job Harriman, see Grace H. Stimson, *Rise of the Labor Movement in Los Angeles* (1955), and Robert V. Hine, *California's Utopian Colonies* (1953). J. Stitt Wilson, and the socialist movement in general, are treated in Ralph E. Shaffer, "A History of the Socialist Party of California," M.A. thesis, University of California, Berkeley (1955). See also Ira B. Cross, "Socialism in California Municipalities," *National Municipal Review*, I (1912, 611–619.

Richard H. Frost, *The Mooney Case* (1968), is far the best account. Others are in Fremont Older, *My Own Story* (1926); Curt Gentry, *Frame-Up* (1967); and the chapter on "Preparedness Day, 1916" in R. L. Duffus, *The Tower of Jewels* (1960). On newspaper opinion of the war in Europe and the preparedness movement see Richard B. Rice, "The California Press and American Neutrality, 1914 to 1917," Ph.D. thesis, University of California, Berkeley (1957); consult also Thomas G. Paterson, "California Progressives and Foreign Policy," *California Historical Society Quarterly*, XLVII (December 1968), 329–342.

Woodrow C. Whitten, *Criminal Syndicalism and the Law in California, 1919–1927* (1969), and his "The Trial of Charlotte Anita Whitney," *Pacific Historical Review*, XV (September 1946), 286–294, are objective studies of a wave of antiradical emotions. See also Ralph E. Shaffer, "Formation of the California Communist Labor Party," *Pacific Historical Review*, XXXVI (February 1967), 59–78, and "Communism in California, 1919–1924," *Science and Society*, XXXIV (Winter 1970).

The crusade for the open shop in the '20s is described in "The American Plan" a series of articles in *Pacific Industries*, I (February 1922), 15–24; David Warren Ryder, "The 'American Plan' in San Francisco," *Review of Reviews*, LXV (February 1923), 187–190, and "San Francisco's Fight for Industrial Freedom," *ibid.*, LXXVII (January 1927), 82–85; Paul Eliel, "San Francisco, a Free City," *Law and Labor*, XII (March 1930), 53, 83; and Edwin Layton, "The Better America Federation: a Case Study of Superpatriotics," *Pacific Historical Review*, XXX (May 1961), 137–148.

On the Democratic debacle, consult H. Brett Melendy, "California's Crossfiling Nightmare: the 1918 Gubernatorial Election," *Pacific Historical Review*, XXXIII (August 1964), 317–330; and Robert E. Hennings, "California Democratic Politics in the Period of Republican Ascendancy," *Pacific Historical Review*, XXXI (August 1962), 267–280.

On Hiram Johnson's drift away from progressivism, see Richard D. Batman, "The Road to the Presidency: Hoover, Johnson, and the California Republican Party, 1920–1924," Ph.D. thesis, University of Southern California (1965); and Richard Lower, "Hiram Johnson and the Progressive Denouement, 1910–1920," Ph.D. thesis, University of California, Berkeley (1969).

Political issues of the '20s are also discussed in the third and fourth volumes of Franklin Hichborn, "California Politics, 1891–1939"; Gilman M. Ostrander, *The Prohibition Movement in California, 1848–1933* (1957); Wendell E. Harmon, "The Bootlegger Era in Southern California," *Southern California Quarterly*, XXXVII (1955), 335–346; Roger Daniels, *The Politics of Prejudice* (1962); Gladys H. Waldron, "Antiforeign Movements in California, 1919–1929," Ph.D. thesis, University of California, Berkeley (1956); Russell M. Posner, "The Progressive Voters' League, 1923–1926," *California Historical Society Quarterly*, XXXVI (September 1957), 251–261, and the same writer's "State Politics and the Bank of America, 1920–1934," Ph.D. thesis, University of California, Berkeley (1956); Marquis James and Bessie R. James, *Biography of a Bank; the Story of Bank of America* (1954); and Jackson K. Putnam, "The Persistence of Progressivism in the 1920s: the Case of California," *Pacific Historical Review*, XXXV (November 1966), 395–411.

On the adoption of the "Federal Plan," see George W. Bemis, "Sectionalism and Representation in the California State Legislature, 1911–1931," Ph.D. thesis, University of California, Berkeley (1935); and Thomas S. Barclay, "Reapportionment in California," *Pacific Historical Review*, V (June 1936), 93–129.

Chapter XXX

OIL AND AUTOMOBILES

Origins of the oil industry. Though the "black gold" of California was far more valuable than the yellow gold, its rise to historical importance followed a very different trajectory. Gold production reached its height in the fifth year after it began, and then settled down for the next 80 years at about a third of the peak output of 1852. California's oil industry, on the other hand, had its first boom in the '60s, but did not begin to reach major proportions until the '90s; and its great modern expansion came in the 20th century.

For thousands of years oil had been taken from shallow pits and used for lamp fuel, caulking, internal and external medication, and a luxuriant variety of other purposes. In Mexican California, *brea* or tar was used for the roofs of adobe houses and sometimes mixed with earth for the floors.

In 1855 a local physician in the town of Titusville in northwestern Pennsylvania skimmed a little oil from a spring and sent it to Benjamin Silliman, Jr., professor of chemistry at Yale. Silliman reported that the sample could be refined into high-grade kerosene. Edwin L. Drake, a former railroad conductor, had the inspiration to drill for oil instead of merely digging for it, and to put down lengths of pipe to keep mud and water out of the drillhole. The result was the world's first commercial oil well, opened near Titusville in 1859.

California's first oil well was drilled two years later, a few miles south of Eureka. Although it produced no oil, there were forty other wells in Humboldt County by 1865, mostly in the Mattole River region, where a village was overoptimistically named Petrolia. The total output of this "field," however, was so small that it was measured in gallons rather than barrels. The more significant developments of the 1860s took place in Ventura County (part of Santa Barbara County until 1872). George S.

Gilbert, a whale oil merchant, built a small refinery on the Ojai Ranch north of Ventura in 1861. From seepage oil, Gilbert manufactured small quantities of kerosene. A few years later Thomas A. Scott, vice president of the Pennsylvania Railroad and Assistant Secretary of War in Lincoln's cabinet, sent Professor Silliman to evaluate some Western mineral properties. In the course of the same trip, in 1864, Silliman investigated the oil resources of the Ventura region.

After absorbing the glib optimism of Gilbert, Silliman wrote a number of rosy reports. "California," he predicted, "will be found to have more oil in its soil than all the whales in the Pacific Ocean." In the Ojai region "the oil is struggling to the surface at every available point and is running away down the rivers for miles." The first 10 wells drilled on the Ojai property, he estimated, would yield an annual profit of more than a million dollars.

Scott placed full faith in Silliman's judgment; Silliman's report on the oil of western Pennsylvania had led to the drilling of the Drake discovery well. Scott had made a large profit by purchasing and developing oil land near Titusville. Convinced that California's oil would far exceed Pennsylvania's, Scott headed a group of investors who bought the Ojai and several neighboring ranches and sent out the best drilling machinery then in existence.

As manager of his California properties Scott chose Thomas R. Bard, a young man from Pennsylvania. In the summer of 1865 Bard began drilling a series of wells. None of them produced oil in commercial quantities. In May 1867 Ojai Number Six became technically the first gusher in California, when it reached a depth of about 600 feet, but it flowed for only 15 minutes before it choked off. Further drilling could produce only eight barrels a day, and the oil was heavy and virtually unusable.

Silliman's California reports were quite true, and even understated, as a kind of mystical vision of the ultimate future. But as conclusions from the evidence actually before him they were fantastically exaggerated, and based on a slipshod investigation. He was unaware that California's geology, with its characteristically tilted and folded strata, would make both the finding and the extracting of oil more difficult than in Pennsylvania. Moreover the crude oil found in California in the early years was extremely heavy, asphaltic, and gummy. It made an inferior lubricant, and California kerosene, when burned for illuminating purposes, flickered, smoked, and smelled. When a sample that Silliman had analyzed was rechecked by another chemist it was discovered to have been "salted" with a well-known brand of Eastern kerosene, and when this charge was published Silliman never answered it publicly. He had received the sample from a speculator interested in promoting California oil stocks. His brother-in-law was a partner in the same speculation, and apparently Silliman preferred to allow his own reputation to suffer, rather than involve his sister in a scandal.

One of Scott's concerns, the California Petroleum Company, had an authorized capitalization of 10 million dollars, but newspaper articles charged that the company's only actual assets were 10,000 acres of ranch land worth a dollar an acre. Scott refused to finance any further search for oil on his California properties, and the state's first oil boom was over by the end of 1867.

Prospecting continued, however, notably in Pico Canyon, which was still public land and in which oil ventures were conducted under a system of mining claims patterned after those of the Mother Lode country. Pico Number One, opened in 1875, became the first commercial well in California, and Pico Number Four, opened the next year, became the well with the longest continuous production. At 600 feet, Number Four yielded 150 barrels a day, and it was still producing oil more than 90 years later.

Gradually, deeper drilling began to yield larger quantities and better grades. In 1890 Thomas R. Bard joined with Wallace L. Hardison and Lyman Stewart, who had been struggling for years as small operators, in organizing the Union Oil Company of California. Bard had turned from oil prospecting to land management in Ventura County, and had built a fortune by subdividing Thomas A. Scott's vast lands for ranching purposes, buying lands of his own, and separately leasing the ranches and the oil rights. Bard served as the first president of Union, though he soon relinquished this office, and withdrew from active participation in the company's affairs after his election to the United States Senate in 1900.

The black bonanza. Silliman's vision began to become a reality in the early 1890s, when the Union Oil Company made several substantial discoveries and laid the foundations of its future career as one of the giants of the California industry.

In 1892 Edward L. Doheny made his sensational discovery of a major oil field within the city of Los Angeles. Doheny was a prospector and lawyer who had made and lost small fortunes in gold and silver mining in New Mexico. He had never hunted oil, and had never even seen a derrick; but one day in Los Angeles, when he saw a wagonload of tarry, greasy brown dirt being hauled from an excavation to be burned as a substitute for coal in a small manufacturing plant, he realized that a mother pool of oil was feeding the pits, the oil thickening to tar as it reached the surface.

In November 1892 Doheny and his partner Charles A. Canfield leased a vacant lot near West Second Street and Glendale Boulevard and dug a shaft with pick and shovel, lifting out the dirt with a hand windlass. At a depth of 155 feet oil began to flow into the shaft, enabling them to hire a drilling rig. The flow increased rapidly, and the Los Angeles oil boom was on. Hundreds of oil wells mushroomed in front yards and back yards. For the year 1895 the total flow was more than 700,000 barrels, mostly from a strip of land about 600 feet wide and 2 miles long, which overlay a pool of great richness and depth.

Finding a market for this outpouring was an urgent problem. The answer

View of the Los Angeles city field as it appeared in 1895 with "Wells . . . as thick as the holes in a pepper box. . . ." (Courtesy of the American Petroleum Institute)

was the substitution of oil for coal. California had produced a little low-grade coal, mainly in the Mount Diablo area, but had imported most of its coal supply at great expense. Now it suddenly had a surplus of a better and much cheaper fuel. Safe and practical oil burners for locomotives were quickly developed, and by the turn of the century the railroads of the whole Southwestern United States were converting to oil. The saving in cost was matched by the relief of the passengers, for Western locomotives had burned soft coal that produced enormous quantities of smoke and cinders. The conversion of the railroads was a turning point, showing the way to the use of oil for powering ships as well as all sorts of stationary engines, and insuring California's future as a major industrial state.

In the years after Doheny's discovery of the Los Angeles City field, several other important producing areas were developed in the Southern California coastal region, notably the Santa Maria and Summerland fields in Santa Barbara County and the Fullerton, Whittier, Coyote, and Montebello fields in the Los Angeles basin. But the larger discoveries in the period between 1895 and 1920 came in the San Joaquin Valley. Great new fields were brought into production on the Kern River east of Bakersfield, and at Coalinga, McKittrick, and Midway-Sunset.

On March 15, 1910, a Union subsidiary company drilling north of Maricopa brought in one of the world's greatest gushers, Lakeview Number One. The driller, a certain "Dry Hole Charlie" Woods, was instantly renamed "Gusher Charlie." So tremendous was the blast that the derrick disappeared into the crater. Not for several weeks was the gusher brought under control, and then only by building a huge earthen dam around it, high enough to smother it in a lake of its own oil. For the next 18 months the flow varied between 15,000 and 68,000 barrels a day, a total of nearly 10 million barrels from one well. At last the casing wore out, the hole caved in, and the great gusher was dead; but the surrounding field grew into an oil empire, with its capital in the new town of Taft, named for the incumbent President.

The near-monopoly that Standard Oil had established throughout the nation in the last third of the 19th century was broken in the early 20th. As the petroleum industry entered its modern period of enormous growth, and passed from its "age of illumination" to its "age of energy," it became highly competitive, although the most important competition was among great corporations.

From the late '70s to the middle '90s Standard had dominated the market in California with oil products imported by rail from its Eastern fields and refineries. The major part of this market had been for illuminant kerosene, for which California crude was relatively worthless; but the use of kerosene declined with the advance of gas, electricity, and fuel oil. Enormous new areas of crude oil production were opening in California and in the midcontinent and gulf regions, larger than the Standard-dominated fields of Pennsylvania, Ohio, and Indiana.

In Texas, where the oil industry burst into prominence with the Spindletop gusher near Beaumont in 1901, the state government outlawed Standard's regional subsidiary, but California took no such action, and Standard moved into producing and refining operations in the Far West in 1900 when it purchased control of the Pacific Coast Oil Company. This concern had been organized in 1878 by United States Senator Charles N. Felton and Lloyd Tevis, two of San Francisco's leading venture capitalists. In 1906 it was renamed the Standard Oil Company (California). In 1911 the antitrust decision of the United States Supreme Court forced the dissolution of the Standard network into its constituent companies; but Standard of California had already become far the largest refiner on the Pacific Coast.

Another California giant was the Associated Oil Company, originally formed by a number of small producers in the San Joaquin Valley in 1901. The Southern Pacific Railroad purchased control of Associated in 1909, mainly in order to develop its own burgeoning oil interests. It continued to develop them, with great success, during a long period of litigation with the Federal government over its titles to oil-bearing lands.

In both importance and intensity this conflict rivaled the earlier struggle over the railroad's repayment of its Federal loans. From its grants dating from the 1870s the Southern Pacific owned a vast amount of land in the western San Joaquin Valley, in the very regions where some of the richest oil deposits were now being discovered. The law had excluded "mineral lands" from the grants, and although the railroad argued that petroleum was not a mineral, the United States Supreme Court, following common usage, ruled that it was. But in its other arguments the railroad was more successful. In the crucial cases, involving more than 150,000 acres, the Federal circuit court in Los Angeles ruled in 1919 that the government could not revoke the titles because it had not proven that the railroad's officials were fraudulently aware of the presence of oil when the patents were issued.

In 1919 the Southern Pacific Land Company owned more than 19 percent of all the proved oil land in California, and through its controlling interest in the Associated Oil Company the railroad produced about 18 percent of the state's oil. During the next several years, however, the Southern Pacific gradually divested itself of its direct interests in oil production and refining, and by 1928 the control of Associated had passed to the Tidewater Oil Company of New Jersey. Later it passed to Phillips 66.

In addition to Standard, Associated, and Union, the major California operators in this period included Shell; Richfield; the General Petroleum Corporation, which was purchased by the Standard Oil Company of New York, later called the Mobil Oil Corporation; the Texas Company; and Edward L. Doheny's Pan-American Petroleum Company.

The oil boom of the '20s. Three tremendous discoveries in the early '20s, all in the Los Angeles basin area, surpassed all the earlier developments and launched a boom that put oil in the forefront of California's headlong economic expansion in the "prosperity decade." Standard opened the massive new field at Huntington Beach in 1920. The next year, Union brought in the great Santa Fe Springs field south of Whittier, and Shell tapped the still greater bonanza of Signal Hill at Long Beach the richest of all the world's oil deposits in terms of barrels per acre. In 1923, these three fields together produced more than 183 million barrels of oil, out of California's total production of 263 million barrels. The value of the California crude oil produced in the decade of the '20s was more than 2½ billion dollars. This figure compares very strikingly with the value of all the gold ever mined in the state—about 2 billion dollars. California ranked first among the states in crude oil production for several years in the '20s, though it has ranked second to Texas in total cumulative output.

In 1919 about two-thirds of California's oil came from the San Joaquin Valley, and the major refineries were concentrated in the San Francisco Bay area. But in the '20s the predominance in all aspects of the oil industry quickly passed to the Los Angeles region. Exports of oil from Los Angeles harbor made it the largest oil port in the world. Petroleum refining became the state's largest manufacturing industry. In 1925 the value of oil refinery products was more than 369 million dollars. This was twice the value of the output of California's second largest branch of manufacturing, the canning and preserving of fruits and vegetables, and it was 15 percent of the entire value of all manufactured goods produced in the state.

The most infamous episode in the history of California's great oil boom of the postwar decade was the involvement of Edward L. Doheny in the scandal of the Elk Hills naval oil reserve. Doheny and other oilmen persuaded the Federal government that the best way to conserve the oil on Western public lands, against the possibility of a future war in the Pacific, was to extract the oil and store it in tanks. If left in the ground, they argued, the government's oil reserves would be less readily available, and would also be drained off by wells on adjacent private holdings. With Secretary of the Interior Albert B. Fall, an old friend and a former fellow prospector in New Mexico, Doheny arranged to lease and develop the Federal oil lands in the Elk Hills field in western Kern County. A large part of the oil was to be stored in tanks which Doheny agreed to build for the government on the West Coast and at Pearl Harbor.

Fall received a payment of $100,000 in cash, which Doheny's son brought to him in a satchel. Later Fall was convicted of taking this money as a bribe, but Doheny was acquitted of having bribed him with it. Doheny insisted that in his own view the payment had been simply a loan to an old friend to help him save his ranch from foreclosure, a loan that he would have made whether the leases were granted or not. To Fall $100,000 was a large sum but it was a trifling amount to Doheny, whose fortune exceeded 100 million. In spite of the legal determination that Doheny was innocent of criminal intent while Fall was guilty of it, the government in a civil suit won a cancellation of Doheny's leases on the ground that they had been obtained through a bribe.

By another irony, the whole Elk Hills affair was regarded at the time as less important than the scandal of the Teapot Dome reserve in Wyoming. For a similar leasing arrangement the mid-continent oil operator Harry F. Sinclair paid Fall $300,000, presumably reflecting Teapot Dome's greater richness. But that field proved to be relatively unimportant, while Elk Hills proved to be extremely rich. After the return of the Federal lands at Elk Hills to the status of a naval reserve, the government adopted a policy of taking out only enough oil to keep the wells in condition.

Beginnings of the automobile age. The vast, deep pools of oil that were discovered in the Los Angeles basin in the early '20s proved extraordinarily rich in gasoline. Thus by a most remarkable and happy coincidence huge quantities of this great source of motive power became available at the very time and in the very region where the use of the automobile was spreading more rapidly than in any other time or place in history.

In the early decades of the oil industry, gasoline had been a worse than useless byproduct of the refineries, important only because of the difficult and dangerous problem of getting rid of it. But in the automobile age, gasoline became the most valuable ingredient in a barrel of oil, and the refineries were completely redesigned to extract as much of it as possible.

Gottlieb Daimler and Carl Benz had constructed the first motor vehicle to be driven by gasoline, in Germany in 1885. The brothers Charles and Frank Duryea made the first successful gasoline-propelled motorcar in the United States at Springfield, Massachusetts in 1893, and Henry Ford and Ransome E. Olds built their first cars soon afterward.

At the turn of the century there were only about four thousand horseless carriages in America, and they were toys of the rich. Woodrow Wilson, historian and president of Princeton University, could still write as late as 1906 that "Nothing has spread socialistic feeling in this country more than the automobile. . . . They are a picture of the arrogance of wealth, with all its independence and carelessness." As Bellamy Partridge recalled, "The early motorist was constantly on the defensive. . . . In the eyes of the law he was nowhere regarded as the equal of the horse." Frightened horses were one major hazard, and their angry owners were another. The only garages were the sparsely scattered blacksmith shops, and as auto mechanics the blacksmiths were often both ill-informed and unsympathetic. Roads were vile. In 1903 the first projected transcontinental motor trip broke down at Toledo, Ohio, and it was pronounced "impossible" to reach the Pacific Coast in an automobile. A Packard disproved this soon afterward, but its cross-country journey took 61 days.

A major turning point came when Henry Ford introduced his Model T in 1908, and when one of these remarkable cars set a new record for automobile travel a year later by crossing the continent in a mere 22 days, arriving in San Francisco with New York air still in its two front tires. This achievement proved that an inexpensive car could be a good one and that long-distance travel would soon be practical. At the same time, the reports of the primitive road conditions that the Ford had encountered dramatized the need for highways that would "get the country out of the mud"; and as mass production began to bring the automobile within the average family's budget, public demand for good roads increased.

The highway movement. In 19th-century America the building and maintenance of roads was a function of county government, which had notoriously failed to perform this function either efficiently or honestly. In many counties in California the only reasonably passable roads had been those operated by toll-charging wagon-road companies, under franchises granted in defiance of a state constitutional provision. "If we want good roads," a San Diego County surveyor had said in 1862, "we must look to private enterprise. . . . Nothing less than the interest men feel in their own personal investment will induce them to do anything for a public highway."

Later the Southern Pacific used its control of county government to concentrate roadbuilding almost exclusively on feeders for its railroad lines. Some improvement came in the '80s and '90s, when bicycling became the rage and when the League of American Wheelmen became important as a better-roads lobby. Demands of farmers for passable roads increased with the establishment of rural free delivery of mail in 1894. Denunciations of glaring waste and corruption on the part of county road overseers led to the creation of a California state Bureau of Highways in 1895, but it had only research and advisory powers.

Two private organizations of motorists, the Automobile Club of Southern California with headquarters in Los Angeles and the California State Automobile Association with headquarters in San Francisco, were formed in 1900, and with many wealthy and influential men among the auto enthusiasts on their boards of directors they soon became major forces in the battle for good roads. In 1909 the California legislature authorized a bond issue of 18 million dollars for the beginning of a system of paved state highways, and the voters approved the bonds in the general election the next year.

The difficulties of this pioneering venture were formidable. As Governor Johnson informed the state highway commissioners whom he appointed in 1911, they were expected to build 50 million dollars worth of highways for 18 million. The law forbade the sale of the bonds below par, and they were not commercially saleable at par. But county boards of supervisors solved this problem by voting to purchase the state bonds, and unexpected help came from, of all sources, the Southern Pacific. To counteract the charge that it had always done everything it could to prevent the building of any roads that would compete with its own service, the railroad voluntarily reduced its freight rates on highway construction materials.

Further bond issues were approved in 1916 and 1919, with sounder provisions for their retirement from state taxes. New laws also provided better controls over the choice of routes for the connecting lateral highways, which had degenerated into a disconnected maze of special-interest roads because both the state legislature and the county authorities had been able to add local pork-barrel projects to the state system.

The California commissioners chose to build with concrete in the hope that their original roads would last for decades. Actually, their efforts at economy produced a system of highways that would have to be built over again within a few years. Their plan called for a 4-inch layer of concrete, which proved not to be thick enough, and which failed to provide adequately for varying conditions in the subsoil. The standard width was only 15 feet. Even before the introduction of trucks 8 feet wide the state highways were much too narrow, even on the straightaway. They were even more dangerous at the curves, where they were neither banked nor widened.

Private interest and enterprise had a significant part in promoting the highway movement on a national basis, as well as within the states. The Lincoln Highway Association was formed in 1912, and the next year it began construction of a graveled all-weather highway from ocean to ocean. Financial and moral support came from chambers of commerce, automobile clubs, and a variety of industrial organizations, particularly automobile manufacturers. The route of this transcontinental highway extended from New York to San Francisco Bay by way of Council Bluffs, Laramie, Salt Lake City, and Reno. Work proceeded slowly, but the whole road was marked and opened (though far from completed) in 1915, in time for Lincoln Highway Association officials to commemorate its opening with a five-car cavalcade from New York to the Panama Pacific International Exposition. The choice of San Francisco as the western terminus led to so many protests from Southern California that an "alternate route" was added, from Ely, Nevada, to Los Angeles. The Automobile Club of Southern California, volunteering for the public service of supplying thousands of direction signs from Salt Lake City westward, managed to turn a large part of the traffic in the southerly direction.

Financial support from the national government began with the Federal Highway Aid Act of 1916, but the dollar-matching grants to the states under this law were limited to rural roads suitable for the carriage of the mails, and the law actually discriminated against routes of greater significance to traffic. During the war, attempts to use the nation's roads for the transportation of soldiers and military supplies highlighted the absence of an effective national road network; and the postwar Federal Highway Act of 1921 redefined the purpose of Federal aid as the completion of an adequate national system of interstate highways.

Along with Federal grants, another great source of money was the state gasoline tax. First discovered by the Oregon legislature in 1919, this admirable form of revenue had several outstanding advantages. With obvious fairness, it apportioned the cost of highways among the users of them; service station records provided an accurate measure of use as well as a sure and inexpensive method of collection; and the tax was relatively painless because it was paid in driblets and as a part of the price of the commodity.

With ample funds for highways thus assured, the age of motorization was ready to come into full flower.

The automobile revolution. "It is probable," the President's Research Committee on Social Trends reported in 1930, "that no invention of such far-reaching importance was ever diffused with such rapidity, or so quickly exerted influences that ramified throughout the national culture." This may have been merely "probable" as an estimate of the degree to which the automobile transformed society throughout the United States in the decade after World War I. But it needs no qualification whatever as an estimate of the effects of mass motorization in California, and most of all in Southern California, where climate, scenery, and boosterism combined with low gasoline prices and increasingly good roads to make the region a motorist's paradise.

From 1920 to 1930 the population of Los Angeles County more than doubled, from less than a million to 2,208,492. The number of registered private automobiles quintupled, rising to 806,264. By 1925 the city of Los Angeles had one automobile for every three persons—more than twice the national average. Los Angeles became the most thoroughly motorized and motor-conscious city in the world.

It was also the first American metropolis whose major expansion occurred entirely within the automobile era, and the automobile intensified a process that Henry Huntington's Pacific Electric had begun–the freeing of the people of Los Angeles from the urban centralization that the limitations of the streetcar had enforced upon other great American cities. With his own car the average man could live at a considerable distance from his work, and could own his home, with lawns, flowers, and shrubbery. With the coming of the great construction boom of the '20s Los Angeles soon had a larger ratio of single-family residences and a lower population density than any other large city in the United States. The modern supermarket, designed for customers who could provide their own transportation for large quantities of groceries, was born in Los Angeles. And Realtor A. W. Ross's "Miracle Mile," on a part of Wilshire Boulevard that had been uninhabited shortly before, was probably the first large business district in the world to be created especially for the automobile age.

Tourism increased enormously in a great new wave of the American Westward Movement, and "auto camps" and "tourist cabins" sprang up. Service stations became a major new institution. The first of them has been credited to Earl B. Gilmore, whose father had bought land for a dairy farm on a part of the Hancock family's domain, once the Rancho La Brea. A substantial oil field had been opened there in 1901, near the famous pits that had held the bones of prehistoric animals mired in the tar. When Wilshire Boulevard was extended from Los Angeles to the beach at Santa Monica in 1909, Earl Gilmore was just out of Stanford. He put a tank on a farm wagon, painted it red and yellow, parked it at the corner of Wilshire Boulevard and La Brea Avenue, and sold gasoline from his father's nearby refinery, at 10 cents a gallon.

"Our forefathers," said the *Los Angeles Times* in 1926, "in their immortal independence creed set forth 'the pursuit of happiness' as an inalienable right of mankind. And how can one pursue happiness by any swifter and surer means . . . than by the use of the automobile?" Such was the spirit that dominated the prosperous '20s—for better and sometimes for worse. The motorcar contributed heavily, for example, to the deterioration of personal morals in the era of jazz, hip flasks, and flappers, for an automobile was a reasonable facsimile of a private room, readily transportable beyond the reach of chaperonage.

Quite as revolutionary as the effects of the internal combustion engine on the cities were its effects on agriculture and on rural life. The automobile put an end to the isolation of rural areas and reduced the differences in outlook between the farmer and the city dweller; the truck brought much greater flexibility to agricultural marketing; and the tractor was one of the most crucial laborsaving devices ever invented. Tractor factories had been greatly expanded during their temporary wartime conversion to military purposes, after the British government had placed huge orders with California's Holt Manufacturing Company for certain vehicles. In a successful effort to surprise the Germans on the western front, the British had circulated the information that the Holt contracts were merely for "tanks" to carry water for British troops in the deserts of Mesopotamia.

Even during the great depression of the '30s the use of the automobile continued to increase, particularly in California. Both the city workers and the agricultural migratory laborers kept their cars, even when they were unemployed and on relief.

Construction and improvement of highways steadily advanced; many a Californian had the experience of glancing down from a broad, well-engineered highway to see a fragment of the old two-lane paved road, winding, narrow, weed-grown, and coming to a dead end against the embankment of its successor —a sight that aroused a poignant sense of time and history.

SELECTED BIBLIOGRAPHY

Harold F. Williamson and Arnold R. Daum provide the best general historical account of *The American Petroleum Industry*, in two volumes subtitled *The Age of Illumination, 1859–1899* (1959) and *The Age of Energy, 1899–1959* (1963). Gerald T. White, *Formative Years in the Far West; a History of Standard Oil Company of California and Predecessors through 1919* (1962), includes excellent material on the background of the California industry as a whole. See also his *Scientists in Conflict: the Beginnings of the Oil Industry in California* (1968). Thomas R. Bard's career is the subject of W. H. Hutchinson, *Oil, Land and Politics* (two volumes, 1965); this work is more reliable on the early history of Union Oil than is the work by Earl M. Welty and Frank J. Taylor, *The Black Bonanza* (1958), the official history of the Union Oil Company of California, and its sequel, *The 76 Bonanza* (1966). On Shell, see Kendall Beaton, *Enterprise in Oil; a History of Shell in the United States* (1957). Walker A. Tompkins, *Little Giant of Signal Hill* (1967), deals with the Signal Oil and Gas Company and its founder Samuel B. Mosher. A good chapter on petroleum, and valuable production tables, are in Robert G. Cleland and Osgood Hardy, *The March of Industry* (1929). The best economic analysis of the California industry up to 1940 is Joe S. Bain, *Economics of the Pacific Coast Petroleum Industry* (three volumes, 1944–1947).

"California's Oil," *American Petroleum Institute Quarterly*, XVIII (April 1948), 3–6, is a lively popular account of developments to 1910; much of its material, however, came from Walter Stalder, "A Contribution to California Oil and Gas History," *California Oil World* (November 12, 1941). Other useful treatments are in R. P. McLaughlin and C. A. Waring, "The Petroleum Industry of California," *California State Mining Bureau Bulletin 69* (1915); Isaac F. Marcosson, *The Black Golconda; the Romance of Petroleum* (1924);

Ruth S. Knowles, *The Greatest Gamblers; the Epic of American Oil Exploration* (1959); and Richard O'Connor, *The Oil Barons* (1971). F. F. Latta, *Black Gold in the San Joaquin* (1949), has much miscellaneous information but is poorly organized. Gerald T. White, "California's Other Mineral," *Pacific Historical Review*, XXXIX (May 1970), 135–154, is one of the several articles in an issue on "The Petroleum Industry."

The best of the several histories of the automobile in America are Bellamy Partridge, *Fill 'er Up! The Story of Fifty Years of Motoring* (1952); and David L. Cohn, *Combustion on Wheels, an Informal History of the Automobile Age* (1944).

Highway development is described in Felix Riesenberg, Jr., *The Golden Road* (1962); *California Highways* (1920), by Ben Blow, manager of the Good Roads Bureau of the California State Automobile Association; Phil T. Hanna, "The Wheel and the Bell; the Story of the First Fifty Years of the Automobile Club of Southern California," *Westways*, XLII (December 1950), 41–56; Frederic L. Paxson, "The Highway Movement, 1916–1935," *American Historical Review*, LI (January 1946), 236–253; and John C. Burnham, "The Gasoline Tax and the Automobile Revolution," *Mississippi Valley Historical Review*, XLVIII (December 1961), 435–459.

On various economic and social aspects, see R. M. Fogelson, *The Fragmented Metropolis: Los Angeles, 1850–1930* (1967); Ashleigh E. Brilliant, "Social Effects of the Automobile in Southern California during the Nineteen-twenties," Ph.D. thesis, University of California, Berkeley (1964); the same writer's article on "Some Aspects of Mass Motorization in Southern California, 1919–1929," *Southern California Quarterly*, XLVII (June 1965), 191–208; Earl S. Pomeroy, *In Search of the Golden West: the Tourist in Western America* (1957); and Ernest McGaffey, "Living in the Age of Motorization," *Southern California Business*, VII (March 1928), 20–21, 34–35.

Hundreds of articles on motoring in California are cited in Anna Marie Hager and Everett G. Hager, *Cumulative Index–Westways, Touring Topics, 1909–1959* (1961).

Philip E. Pettyjohn describes "The Historical Significance of the Caterpillar Tractor," M.A. thesis, University of California, Berkeley (1959).

Chapter XXXI

THE MOVIES

"OF THE MACHINES that have changed our lives in the 20th century, only the internal combustion engine rivals the movie camera in the scope of its influence." So wrote Richard Griffith and Arthur Mayer in *The Movies*, published in 1957, and it would be hard to dispute the validity of that estimate as a judgment on the history of the first half of the 20th century—whatever may be the influence of such other devices as the nuclear bomb or the electronic computer on the second half.

The technological discoveries. The motion in "motion pictures" is of course an illusion. On the screen each successive photograph stands still for a moment, but the eye is tricked into believing that the flow of motion is continuous. As early as the second century A.D. the astronomer Ptolemy noticed the fact that the eye, upon receiving an image, retains it on the retina for a fraction of a second. In 1824 the principle of the "persistence of vision" with regard to *moving* objects was explained to the Royal Society of Great Britain by Peter Mark Roget, who is better known as the original compiler of the *Thesaurus of English Words and Phrases*. Projection of pictures on a screen was accomplished in Rome in 1640, when Athanasius Kirchener developed his "magic lantern"; pictures painted on glass and placed in front of the lantern in a darkened room appeared "magically" on the opposite wall. Louis Daguerre, a French scene painter and physicist, produced the first effective photograph in 1839.

California's contributions began in 1872, when Leland Stanford, whose interests included the breeding and racing of thoroughbred horses, made a $25,000 bet with another wealthy sportsman that a galloping horse takes all four hoofs off the ground at the same time. Stanford commissioned the San Francisco photographer Eadweard Muybridge to attempt some snapshots at a racetrack in Sacramento; but the shortest exposure then possible was one-twelfth of a second, and the pictures were much too blurred to be helpful.

In 1874 Muybridge shot and killed his wife's lover at a resort in Napa County, and although the jury acquitted him, under its own interpretation of the unwritten law, more than two years elapsed before he had sufficiently recovered his composure to return to his work. When he did so, at the racecourse on Stanford's farm at Palo Alto in 1877, the processes of photography had been so improved that a much shorter exposure was possible. With the help of John D. Isaacs, later chief engineer of the Southern Pacific, Muybridge aligned 24 cameras at 1-foot intervals along the ground beside the racetrack and used an electrically regulated timing device to trip the shutters in rapid succession as a horse galloped past. Stanford won his bet.

Muybridge's serial photographs of horses in motion stimulated the efforts of several inventors, both in Europe and in the United States. Thomas A. Edison has often received credit for the "invention of the moving picture." But it would be more accurate to say that Edison assigned his brilliant young assistant William Kennedy Laurie Dickson to investigate the subject, and that Dickson, working in the Edison laboratory in West Orange, New Jersey, coordinated the ideas of other inventors, added some of his own, and in 1889 created the first effective method of taking motion pictures on strips of celluloid.

The glass plates used in still photography were far too bulky and fragile. Edison's suggestion was the taking of pictures on an emulsion-coated cylinder that would do for the eye what his phonographic cylinder had done for the ear, and Dickson wasted several months on this impractical device. In 1889 George Eastman's photographic equipment factory at Rochester, New York, produced a method of superimposing a film of photographic chemicals on strong and flexible celluloid strips, perforated at the edges so that they could be wound on a spool. Later in the same year Dickson used these strips in a motion-picture camera, which he called the kinetograph. A sprocket wheel moved the film, with perfect regularity in starting and stopping for a fraction of a second while photographs were being registered, or, later, projected on a screen. But for several years Dickson did not make use of screen projection, and instead used only a little individual viewing machine in a box, which he called the kinetoscope.

Dickson's first moving-picture film was only 15 seconds long, and starred an Edison mechanic named Fred Ott in a spectacular performance for which he was famous around the laboratory—his sneeze. Later Dickson began to make 1-minute films using bits of vaudeville, and in 1894 some of these were shown in the first "kinetoscope parlor," a penny arcade opened in what had been a shoestore in New York City.

Edison neglected to obtain foreign patents for the Dickson motion-picture camera, and Europeans were free to imitate it or to produce machines inspired by it. In France the Lumière brothers, Auguste and Louis, devised a combined camera and projection machine that they called the *cinematographe*. Dickson's kinetoscope was a mere peep-show box into which only one person at a time could look. With screen projection the Lumières were able to open the world's first moving-picture theater, in the basement of a Paris restaurant in 1895. Edison opened the first one in the United States in a music hall in New York City the following year.

Beginnings of the art and the industry. The earliest films were brief and shaky, and their novelty soon wore off, but interest revived with the introduction of narrative. Georges Méliès, a French professional magician, produced a 15-minute version of *The Dreyfus Affair* in 1899, comprising 12 scenes from the case of the falsely accused officer, and Méliès' production of *Joan of Arc* attracted great interest in 1900. Even more popular were his many films based on pure fantasy, such as *A Trip to the Moon* (1902). He had made his first motion pictures by filming his tricks of theatrical magic. Then with delightful ingenuity he added many new tricks that the camera made possible. He discovered that by stopping the camera in the middle of a scene he could create miraculous appearances, disappearances, and transformations through double exposure, and he was the first to use the "dissolve," in which the camera was cranked back a little so that the new scene appeared to begin before the ending of the old. He also designed and painted magnificent stage settings. Méliès was the movies' first creative artist.

The first substantial American narrative film was *The Great Train Robbery,* an 8-minute western made by Edwin E. Porter, for Edison's film company, in the New Jersey countryside in 1903. This thrilling production told of a mail-train holdup, the formation of a posse, and the pursuit and killing of the desperadoes. The theme of the chase was one of the earliest of all forms of art and of entertainment, dating back to the oldest cave paintings; but what made this film even more exciting than the elemental appeal of its ancient theme was Porter's discovery that the moving picture could be an entirely new dramatic form, liberated from the narrow limits of the stage. By taking the camera outdoors "on location," and by joining together bits of film shot in different places and at different times, he pioneered the whole technique of film editing that made possible the development of the motion picture as a truly distinctive art.

A long strike of vaudeville actors in 1900 led the theater managers, for the first time, to show programs consisting solely of movies. The rental of a series of short films cost less than the wages of a series of vaudeville actors, and the theater owners discovered not only that they could make a profit with an admission charge of only 5 cents, but that a vast audience, especially of immigrants in the large cities, would flock to see even the crudest films at that modest price. Soon there were thousands of new movie houses called "nickelodeons"—a charming word, formed by combining the price of admission and the Greek word for theater.

Thus when the movies first came into mass production they were the poor man's entertainment. Not only the audiences but also the distributors and producers of the early films were drawn very largely from the ranks of men who were struggling to rise from poverty. "Respectable" businessmen and financiers shunned the infant movie industry as a possible investment. As Leo Rosten has put it, "The men who built the motion picture industry . . . were not drawn from the supposedly farsighted ranks of American business," but from "the marginal and shabby zones of enterprise, from vaudeville, nickelodeon parlors, theatrical agencies, flea circuses, petty trade." William Fox, born in Hungary, worked as a cloth sponger in New York before he opened a penny arcade, and then a nickelodeon, in Brooklyn. Jesse L. Lasky began his working life as a vaudeville cornet player in San Francisco. His brother-in-law, Samuel Goldwyn, was born Samuel Goldfish in Poland, ran away from home in Warsaw, arrived in New York alone as a steerage passenger at 13, and began work as a glove salesman. Louis B. Mayer, born in Russia, spent part of his boyhood as a rag collector in Saint John, New Brunswick. Marcus Loew and Adolph Zukor were small fur dealers before they became partners in the theater business.

All these men were deeply sensitive about their origins. Only one member of the group, Lewis J. Selznick, took public pride in his humble beginnings. Hearing of the abdication of the Czar in March 1917, he sent him a famous and fascinating cablegram: "WHEN I WAS POOR BOY IN KIEV YOUR POLICEMEN WERE NOT KIND TO ME STOP I CAME TO AMERICA AND PROSPERED STOP NOW HEAR WITH REGRET YOU ARE OUT OF JOB OVER THERE STOP FEEL NO ILL WILL . . . SO IF YOU WILL COME NEW YORK CAN GIVE YOU FINE POSITION ACTING IN PICTURES STOP SALARY NO OBJECT STOP . . . SELZNICK."

The discovery of California. At the turn of the century and for several years afterward most American films were made in New York or New Jersey. Edison and a few others controlled the American patents on cameras and projectors, but a number of "outlaw" film producers sprang up and a bitter struggle developed. William Selig, who began to make movies in Chicago, was among the many "independents" who were harrassed by Edison's lawyers. It occurred to Selig that if he made his pictures in a more remote part of the country it would be harder for Edison's subpoena servers to interfere with his operations. Late in 1907 a director and a cameraman in the employ of Selig arrived in Southern California to make the outdoor scenes of a one-reel production of *The Count of Monte Cristo,* and early in 1908 they set up a studio on Main Street in downtown Los Angeles.

Another Chicago producer, George K. Spoor, had recently organized the Essanay Film Manufacturing Company, in partnership with Gilbert M. Anderson (the "A" in Essanay). Anderson, born Max Aronson in Little Rock,

Arkansas, was a young ex-vaudevillian who had become famous as the star of *The Great Train Robbery,* and was known as Broncho Billy. Essanay was devoted largely to westerns, for which there was now an insatiable demand, and it obviously made more sense to produce westerns in the Far West than in Chicago—not to mention the relatively greater freedom from legal harrassment. In 1908 Anderson experimented with various sites in the San Francisco Bay region, and finally the canyon and ranch area near Niles, a short distance southeast of Oakland. There, during the next six years, Essanay ground out 375 one-reel westerns, one a week—all featuring the rugged, valiant, kindly cowboy Broncho Billy.

On January 1, 1909, a group of the leading manufacturers of films announced the formation of the Motion Picture Patents Company, which would often be denounced as the "movie trust." This group included the three largest American concerns, Edison, Biograph, and Vitagraph; four smaller American companies, including Selig and Essanay; and two French companies, Pathé and Méliès. All pooled their patent claims and each received a license to manufacture motion pictures. It was agreed that there would be no other licenses. The trust sought to drive other companies out of the business of making movies, and also to collect special fees from all distributors.

For several years, until the trust itself was prosecuted and dissolved as a conspiracy in restraint of trade in violation of the Sherman Act, the industry produced almost as many lawsuits as movies. Selig and Essanay, having become members of the trust, were no longer harried by legal charges of patent infringements. But a number of other companies, left outside the favored group and finding themselves more harried than ever, discovered that the Los Angeles suburb of Hollywood offered a very special advantage as a location for independent producers. It was fairly close to the international boundary. When process servers and confiscators of cameras appeared, the precious equipment and filmstocks could be hastily packed into automobiles and rushed to safety across the Mexican border.

The environs of Los Angeles also had other and more permanent advantages for moviemaking, and these appealed to members of the trust as well as to independents. There were sunshine and mild weather. And within a few miles of the studios there were outdoor scenes that would substitute for almost any locale a plot might call for—from the Sahara Desert to the French Riviera, the Khyber Pass, Sherwood Forest, the Kentucky hills, rural New England, or the battlefield of Gettysburg. Early in 1910 D. W. Griffith brought a company of Biograph players to Los Angeles, where he used San Gabriel Mission for scenes in *The Thread of Destiny: a Story of the Old Southwest,* and a few weeks later he achieved striking new camera effects by photographing the Southern California countryside from great distances in a production of *Ramona.*

Eventually the phrase "a Hollywood production" became an even more familiar and valuable asset in the advertising of movies than was the brand name

"Sunkist" in the advertising of oranges. Even more than the orange groves, the movies increased Southern California's romantic appeal to tourists and new residents and became a major factor in its burgeoning growth.

Stars and directors. The trust fight contributed not only to the rise of Hollywood but also to two other important developments in the history of American movies—the making of longer and better pictures and the invention of the star system.

Most of the men who controlled the trust and its patents were opposed to any improvements in the films their companies produced. Who, they asked, would pay the price of better films? They argued that the profits came from a mass audience of poor people, that if the price of admission was more than a nickel the industry would perish, and that the mass audience was not intelligent enough to sit through any one picture if it was longer than a single reel, or about 12 minutes.

But much longer films were being made in Europe, and independent American exhibitors began to import them as a part of their war with the trust. The breakthrough came in 1913, when the Italian film *Quo Vadis* ran for 22 weeks in New York, in a legitimate theater, with an admission price of a dollar. The first of the Biblical-spectacle pictures, it was a nine-reeler that held the audience for nearly two hours. In December 1913 the independent producer Jesse L. Lasky and his director Cecil B. deMille made the first American feature-length movie, *The Squaw Man,* in five reels.

Movie patrons had begun to favor certain players by 1910, but the companies in the trust would not advertise the names of actors and actresses lest they demand higher salaries. It was the independents who discovered that they could achieve an unbroken succession of hits by featuring personalities so consistently attractive that the patrons would line up at the box offices no matter what the quality of the films. Carl Laemmle, head of Independent Motion Pictures (IMP), launched the star system in 1910 by luring a pretty young heroine away from Biograph and publicizing her as "Florence Lawrence, the IMP girl," whereas she had previously been known only as the anonymous "Biograph girl."

Within a few years, salaries of featured players leaped from a maximum of $15 a day to an average of $1,500 a week—even though unkind critics in New York might say of one star that she had "two expressions—joy and indigestion," or of another that her performances ran "the gamut of emotions from A to B." To the movie audiences the stars were figures of personified desire, or symbols of the great moving forces of comedy or tragedy. Gladys Smith, a girl from Canada, became better known as Mary Pickford, or America's Sweetheart, in which capacity she received $500,000 a year by 1915. Young Charles Chaplin, after a miserable childhood in the London streets, became the best-known comedian in the world soon after he came to America. William S. Hart, who actually knew something of "the West" because he had grown up in Montana, was a considerable improvement over the synthetic cowboy Broncho Billy as the leading hero of the western, even though Hart's role as the good badman became almost as standardized as Billy's performances.

Movie audiences, centering their attention on the stars, have never developed an appreciation of the role of the director, but within the industry the vital importance of his function soon came to be recognized. The director fuses the script, the actors, the cameramen, and the technicans into a single pattern, a motion picture. Ultimately his conception determines what the story is, what it means, and how it is told.

David Wark Griffith was the first great American director, and his film *The Birth of a Nation* was in the technological sense the first great American motion picture. But it was also a racist distortion of American history, and because it was more widely shown and left a deeper emotional imprint on its audiences than almost any other film before or since, it stands as a classic example of both the enormous potential power of the art of the cinema and the possibilities for misuse of that power.

Griffith was a Kentuckian, the son of Brig. Gen. Jacob W. (Thunder Jake") Griffith of the Confederate Army, who had taught him all the articles of faith that made up the great "plantation illusion" of the Old South. In 1905 Thomas Dixon, a Baptist minister from North Carolina, had published *The Clansman,* a novel dedicated to his uncle, a "Grand Titan of the Invisible Empire Ku Klux Klan." The novel described that organization as "led by the reincarnated souls of the Clansmen of Old Scotland," and asserted that its achievements in the American South after the Civil War had formed "one of the most dramatic chapters in the history of the Aryan race."

When Dixon's novel of the Reconstruction became a bestseller, he rewrote it as a successful stage play. D. W. Griffith then turned it into a 3-hour motion picture, adding much background material on the causes and events of the Civil War as interpreted by Southerners like Dixon and himself. The film stereotyped the Negroes as an inferior race, made up of two groups—either fawning "good darkies" who would rather have remained in slavery, or vicious renegades. After the first showings of the film in February 1915, under its original title of *The Clansman,* Dixon enthusiastically suggested that it should be called nothing less than *The Birth of a Nation*. Griffith agreed. An "Epilogue" explained that "the establishment of the South in its rightful place [by the Ku Klux Klan] is the birth of a new nation."

After a special showing of the film at the White House, President Wilson was reported to have said that "it is like writing history with lightning, and my one regret is that it is all so terribly true." Wilson was himself a Southerner by birth and early education, and it was during his Presidency that lunchrooms, drinking fountains, and lavatories in government buildings in the District of Columbia were racially segregated for the first time since the Civil War. But if

President Wilson could see nothing wrong with *The Birth of a Nation,* there were many Americans who could; in the face of a great outcry from critics of the film, Wilson publicly disavowed his endorsement of it.

There were many demands that the picture be suppressed on the ground that it was a piece of dangerous and cruel propaganda for bigotry, but these denunciations merely gave it additional advertising. It remained at one theater in New York for 44 consecutive weeks, a record that would not be matched until the showing of *The Covered Wagon* in 1923. By 1930 more than 100 million people had seen *The Birth of a Nation,* and by 1948 it had grossed nearly 50 million dollars. It did more to fasten racial stereotypes on the American mind than anything since *Uncle Tom's Cabin,* and it was partly responsible for the great revival of the Ku Klux Klan that reached its height in the 1920s.

Griffith never understood the attacks on his masterpiece. Instead he resented and resisted them as violations of free speech, and launched a crusade to defend the "freedom of the movies" against attacks by "intolerant" people. Becoming obsessed with this theme, he produced in 1916 a vast epic called *Intolerance,* which was meant to demonstrate the tragic effects of "censorships by the public will" in four episodes of history. They were the fall of Babylon to Cyrus of Persia, the story of Christ, the massacre of the Huguenots, and a contemporary story of a corrupt orphanage.

The walls of Babylon rose to a height of 300 feet on the Griffith lot on Sunset Boulevard, and $250,000 was spent on the scenes of Belshazzar's feast alone. In the rough, *Intolerance* ran to 300,000 feet or about 70 hours of film. It was edited to 3½ hours, not including intermissions. But it mystified its audiences, and never recovered the enormous cost of its production.

A film of special significance in the cultural history of California was *Greed* (1923), based on Frank Norris's novel *McTeague, a Story of San Francisco,* and directed by Erich von Stroheim. Like Griffith's *Intolerance,* von Stroheim's *Greed* was extravagantly produced and became a financial disaster that led to the decline of its director's career. The novel so fascinated von Stroheim that he filmed it not merely chapter by chapter but line by line, and not on artificial sets but in actual rooms and streets in San Francisco and actual places in Death Valley. After he had spent six months in reducing its enormous bulk, the film was still more than 4 hours long. When he refused to edit it further or to permit anyone but himself to edit it, the Metro-Goldwyn-Mayer executives took it out of his hands and turned it over to a cutter, who reduced it from 24 reels to 11 and filled in the gaps with long subtitles. Von Stroheim refused to look at it again, though even in this mutilated form it was one of the greatest of all motion pictures.

The movies and social change. Gradually the movies escaped from their earlier status as an essentially lower-class form of entertainment and began to make a very successful appeal to the middle classes. In the 1920s—the golden

The Fox Theater in San Francisco, a movie palace built in 1929. It was demolished in 1964 to make way for a 32-story building. (Courtesy of the National General Corporation)

or rather the most heavily gilded age of the motion picture—theater owners in all the larger cities erected huge movie palaces, with lavish ornamentation and regiments of uniformed ushers.

The movies both reflected and accelerated the prevailing trends toward the urbanization of American attitudes and mores. Before 1917 more than half the films made in the United States had portrayed rural scenes and praised the simple values of rural life. But a survey made in the '20s revealed that even rural audiences had begun to react unfavorably to films with rustic themes and characters, a trend that the theatrical trade paper *Variety* reported under the famous headline "STIX NIX HIX PIX."

Cecil B. deMille, the leading director for Paramount Pictures, both anticipated and helped to create the shift in moral attitudes that occurred in the war and postwar years. Between 1918 and 1921, in such pictures as *Forbidden Fruit, Male and Female, Why Change Your Wife?* and *For Better or For Worse,* deMille showed movie audiences in intimate detail the things that they should not do, and though these films came around to defending the institution of marriage in the final scenes, they also portrayed human weakness very sympathetically.

Some of Hollywood's most famous stars began to set unfortunate examples of flamboyant misconduct in their personal lives, and there were three major scandals. In 1921 Roscoe ("Fatty") Arbuckle, a plumber's helper who had become a popular comedian, was tried for manslaughter in connection with the death of a starlet in the course of a drunken party in a hotel suite in San Francisco, and though Arbuckle was not convicted, the circumstances were lurid and disgraceful. A few months later two female stars, Mary Miles Minter and Mabel Normand, were implicated in the unsolved murder of the director William Desmond Taylor; and the handsome matinee idol Wallace Reid was revealed as a drug addict.

Before these scandals had run their course, the leaders of the industry persuaded Will H. Hays of Indiana to leave his position as Postmaster General in President Harding's cabinet and become the "czar of the movies," with power to draw up a new moral code. The plan of movie self-censorship that emanated from the "Hays Office" decreed that evil must never be made attractive and that it must always be punished. The chief result was a series of films that were ostensibly exhortations to repentance and reform, but still managed to include a great deal of sex and violence. DeMille, in particular, was highly successful in adapting to the Hays Office format in his productions of *The Ten Commandments* (1923) and *The King of Kings* (1927).

As the movies became big business, five major and three lesser companies emerged to dominate the film-producing industry. The "big five" were Loew's (including Metro-Goldwyn-Mayer as its production subsidiary); Warner Brothers; Paramount; Radio-Keith-Orpheum (RKO); and 20th Century-Fox. The "little three" were Columbia, Universal, and United Artists.

In the 1930s Louis B. Mayer became the highest salaried business executive in America and the most powerful man in Hollywood. Like most of Hollywood's other leaders, he had been a theater executive before he became a film producer. His first great financial success had come when he secured the New England distribution rights for *The Birth of a Nation.* Mayer and the other "money men" who became the rulers of the film industry were always intensely aware that they were engaged in the business of manufacturing commercial entertainment rather than in the creation of art. Directors and writers protested frequently but almost always ineffectually, and writers who valued their independence generally stayed away from Hollywood. Some, like William Saroyan, came there briefly and left in disgust; but others came, stayed, and adapted. Clifford Odets, after the success on Broadway of his inflammatory anticapitalist play, *Waiting for Lefty,* came from New York to Hollywood on a huge salary to turn out conventional movie scripts, prompting Hollywood sophisticates to ask, "Odets, where is thy sting?"

The introduction of the "talkies" had pulled the industry out of a temporary slump in 1927, and throughout the great depression of the '30s it remained more prosperous than most other industries because the public craving for its chief product—escape—was greater than ever. In 1941 there were more moving-picture theaters than banks in the United States. Attendance reached an all-time peak in 1945; but the great period of the movies ended soon after World War II, with the beginning of the rise of television.

If the automobile had done much to break up the American family, the television set did just as much to bring it together again, though on a very passive basis. In desperation Hollywood resorted to three-dimensional photography and to larger and larger screens—anything to escape that small screen in the living room, and bring people out of their homes and back into the theaters. But television had come to stay, and Hollywood would never be the same.

SELECTED BIBLIOGRAPHY

Major contributions to the general history of motion pictures include Terry Ramsaye, *A Million and One Nights: a History of the Motion Picture through 1925* (two volumes, 1926); Benjamin B. Hampton, *A History of the Movies* (1931); Lewis Jacobs, *The Rise of the American Film, a Critical History* (1939); Richard Griffith and Arthur Mayer, *The Movies; the Sixty-Year Story of the World of Hollywood and Its Effect on America, from Pre-Nickelodeon Days to the Present* (1957, 1971); Arthur Knight, *The Liveliest Art* (1957); and A. R. Fulton, *Motion Pictures: the Development of an Art from Silent Films to the Age of Television* (1960).

Leo C. Rosten, *Hollywood; the Movie Colony; the Movie Makers* (1939), is a survey of the industry as it was in the late 1930s, written with the aid of a team of social scientists. Hortense Powdermaker, *Hollywood, the Dream Factory* (1950), is an anthropologist's view.

With a few exceptions, the contributions of individuals and of companies have been very unsatisfactorily studied. The exceptions include Bosley Crowther, *The Lion's Share* (1957), a history of Metro-Goldwyn-Mayer, and the same writer's *Hollywood Rajah, the Life and Times of Louis B. Mayer* (1960); Gordon Hendricks, *The Edison Motion Picture Myth* (1961), which gives proper credit to William K. L. Dickson for the development of the "Edison" camera; Everett Carter, "Cultural History Written with Lightning: the Significance of *The Birth of a Nation*," *American Quarterly*, XII (Fall 1960), 347–357; Charles Chaplin, *My Autobiography* (1964); and Joel W. Finler, *Stroheim* (1968).

On censorship, see Raymond Moley, *The Hays Office* (1945); and Ruth A. Inglis, *Freedom of the Movies* (1947).

Chapter XXXII

WATER, POWER, AND POLITICS

Origins of the Boulder Canyon project. George Chaffee's Imperial Canal and William Mulholland's Owens Valley Aqueduct were temporary and inadequate answers to Southern California's insatiable thirst. Seeking flood control and increased irrigation for the Imperial Valley and water for the coastal cities, Southern California turned its attention to a vast project for the development of the Colorado River.

That remarkable stream drains an area of about 250,000 square miles. Rising in the Rockies of northern Colorado, it flows nearly 1,500 miles to the Gulf of California. In the agelong process of carving the world's most spectacular canyons, it becomes loaded with reddish silt and thus takes on the color that led the Spaniards to name it the *Rio Colorado* or Red River.

The distinguished geologist John Wesley Powell was the first man to explore the whole length of the main river, in 1869, as the leader of an expedition that managed to survive a trip through the rapids in large rowboats.

In 1904 Powell's nephew Arthur Powell Davis, an engineer for the United States Reclamation Service, conceived a broad proposal for the development of the lower Colorado under the unified control of the Federal government, with a great dam to store the floods and to serve as the heart of the project. The first strong public support for this plan came from the people of the Imperial Valley, who lived in terror of floods. They had not forgotten the catastrophe that began in 1905, when the river burst into the Imperial Canal and created the Salton Sea before it was finally checked in 1907. With the river's constant siltation demanding higher and higher levees, another disaster seemed inevitable without some bold new method of flood control such as the high dam that Arthur Powell Davis suggested.

The settlers of the valley had many reasons to be dissatisfied with the Imperial Canal, and particularly with the fact that its source and the first 50 miles of its flow were in Mexican territory. The Mexican government, instead of contributing to the efforts at flood control, levied duties on the American materials imported for that purpose. It also required that half of the canal's water be reserved for the irrigation of Mexican lands, and it held down the price of the water used south of the border, so that a much higher price had to be charged on the American side.

The Imperial Canal was owned by the Southern Pacific Railroad, which had first acquired control of it through a loan to the California Development Company and had then bought the entire system at a receiver's sale. In 1911 the voters of the Imperial Valley formed the Imperial Irrigation District—the largest of its kind—and approved a bond issue to buy the canal from the Southern Pacific. Soon afterward they began to agitate for an all-American canal, to be built north of the border.

Early in 1922, Secretary of the Interior Fall joined with Arthur Powell Davis, who had become the Director of the Reclamation Service, in recommending an enlarged version of Davis's earlier plan. Soon afterward the proposals in the Fall-Davis report were introduced in Congress in the form of the Swing-Johnson bill. Phil Swing, who had served for several years as chief counsel of the Imperial Irrigation District and had then been elected to Congress, sponsored the bill in the House, and Hiram Johnson gave it his powerful support in the Senate. Six years later it was finally approved as the Boulder Canyon Project Act, but only after a long and bitter struggle in both houses.

Under this plan the Federal government was to construct a dam in or near Boulder Canyon, a plant for generating hydroelectric power in connection with the dam, and an all-American canal just north of the Mexican border from the river to the Imperial Valley. Leasing of the power to public and private agencies in the region would repay the government for the cost of building the dam, and the Imperial Irrigation District would ultimately repay the cost of building the canal.

The city of Los Angeles soon joined with the Imperial Valley in ardent support of the Boulder Canyon project. A few months after the introduction of the first Swing-Johnson bill, William Mulholland warned Los Angeles that its growth was outstripping its supply of water from the Owens Valley. He called for the building of a much larger aqueduct as soon as possible, with the Colorado River as its source. Federal construction of the proposed high dam between Nevada and Arizona would greatly increase the feasibility and greatly lower the cost of a municipal aqueduct reservoir farther downstream.

On the other hand, the Federal project aroused tremendous opposition. The first difficulty to be surmounted was a wrangle among the seven states in the Colorado River area. The upper-basin states of Wyoming, Colorado, Utah, and New Mexico complained that all the benefits would go to the lower-basin states, Arizona, Nevada, and California, whose development would be so stimulated that they would gain an unfair share of the water under the laws of prior appropriation. In November 1922 Secretary of Commerce Herbert Hoover persuaded representatives of all seven states to agree to the Colorado River Compact, assuring the upper basin of a permanent claim to about half the flow of the river.

Six of the state legislatures ratified the compact, but the legislature of Arizona balked. That state demanded a share of the revenue from hydroelectric power, and a share of the water which the other states, especially California, considered excessive. Arizona then began an opposition to the Boulder Canyon project that continued for years, and a quarrel with California that continued for decades.

Further opposition came from the American owners of irrigated lands in Mexico, of whom the most notable was Harry Chandler, the son-in-law, heir, and successor of Harrison Gray Otis. Chandler headed a syndicate that owned 862,000 acres of land in Lower California, mainly in the region of the Imperial Canal. Not surprisingly, he and his *Los Angeles Times* denounced the Swing-Johnson bill as a socialistic menace to free American enterprise. But as Phil Swing remarked, Chandler was "building Boulder Dam by his opposition to it." The project was very popular in Southern California, and Chandler's motives were very obvious, as William Randolph Hearst's *Los Angeles Examiner* often pointed out.

Public or private power? Of all the sources of opposition to the Boulder Canyon project, however, the most formidable were the private power companies, not only in the Southwest but throughout the country. The struggle of private power and light interests against Federal development of the lower Colorado can be understood only in connection with their simultaneous battle to keep the government from "entering the power business" in the Tennessee Valley. During the first World War the government had constructed Wilson Dam, at Muscle Shoals on the Tennessee River in northern Alabama, to provide power for wartime nitrate production. In the 1920s Senator George W. Norris of Nebraska sponsored a bill to create a public corporation that would expand the government's existing facilities in order to develop and sell power and light, in competition with the private utility companies in the region. In 1928 President Coolidge vetoed the Norris bill as socialistic. President Hoover opposed it on the same ground, and the creation of the Tennessee Valley Authority had to await the coming of the New Deal.

For the Boulder Canyon project, on the other hand, the Swing-Johnson bill offered a compromise under which the Federal government would not act as the distributor of the power, but would lease it to private or municipal corporations, which would build their own transmission lines. Nevertheless the private companies fought the measure, largely for two reasons. The huge project would reduce the price of power in the Southwest by increasing the supply of it; and much of the power would go to the municipally owned electric system of the city of Los Angeles, thus encouraging its continuing growth at the expense of private companies, and giving aid and comfort to the "public power movement" in general.

That public ownership and distribution of electric power had come into existence in Los Angeles, a city as passionately committed to private enterprise as any community in the United States, is one of the many striking paradoxes of California history. It was even more remarkable in view of the fact that in Northern California the private Pacific Gas and Electric Company achieved an almost complete monopoly over the distribution of power and light. In 1925, after a long controversy, the San Francisco board of supervisors turned over the power from Hetch Hetchy to the P.G. and E. This arrangement was carried out even though Congress in a section of the Raker Act of 1913 had flatly forbidden the city to dispose of the power to any private company. Moreover, San Francisco made an almost incredibly bad bargain. The P.G. and E. paid the city $2,400,000 a year for the Hetch Hetchy power, and then retailed the same power for $9,000,000 a year. Nevertheless, in a long series of elections San Francisco's voters perennially failed to provide the necessary majorities for the bonds that would have financed a city-owned electrical distribution system.

In sharp contrast, the City of Los Angeles Bureau of Power and Light gradually crowded out and bought out the distribution systems of the Southern California Edison Company, Henry E. Huntington's Pacific Light and Power Company, and the Los Angeles Gas and Electric Corporation, in a process that those companies regarded as not merely creeping but galloping socialism.

"Socialized" ownership and distribution of electricity in Los Angeles had its origin in the Owens Valley water project. Chief Engineer Mulholland had pointed out that in order to ensure its ability to pay for the Owens Valley Aqueduct the city would have to sell not only the water but also the highly valuable by-product, power. He had also believed that the city must sell directly to the consumer, because it could not afford to share the revenues with private companies.

As usual, the voters of Los Angeles religiously followed Mulholland's advice, and overwhelmingly approved the necessary bonds. The bond election of 1910 provided for the building of a municipally owned generating system, and in 1914 the voters authorized the city to buy the private distribution systems. When some of the private companies resisted for a time and others announced that they would hold out to the bitter end, the city built its own competing distribution system and ultimately forced them all to sell. By the late 1930s, with a great new supply of power from the Colorado added to the supply obtained from Owens Valley, Los Angeles had a single, complete, integrated, municipal power and light system, furnishing cheap electricity to every consumer in the city.

Oddly enough, Job Harriman and his socialist followers had opposed the entire Owens Valley project on the theory that it was a plot for the further enrichment of a syndicate of land speculators. Thus for a time the socialists of Los Angeles had found themselves in a strange alliance with the private power companies against a public enterprise. In any case it was not socialistic doctrine that induced Los Angeles to adopt public power. The reasons were pragmatic, not dogmatic. Arid Los Angeles desperately needed water, which had to be brought from great distances at great cost. The sale of power would help to pay the enormous cost of the water.

Los Angeles had very little sympathy with the arguments of the private power companies against the Boulder Canyon project. The city had been hearing and rejecting very similar contentions for many years.

The liveliest of the congressional debates on the Swing-Johnson bill took place in February 1927, when it came so near to passage in the Senate that its opponents resorted to a filibuster. Senator Lawrence C. Phipps of Colorado, who had interests in several electric companies, joined with the Arizona senators and others in keeping the bill from coming to a vote. But the filibuster also served to focus national attention on the issue, and Hiram Johnson countered the arguments against the project with oratory as vigorous and colorful as any he had ever directed against the Southern Pacific. Vice President Charles G. Dawes, who presided over the spectacular battle in the Senate, noted in his memoirs that he had never seen a man "more faithful and effective in a hard fight than Johnson has been in this one."

Secretary of Commerce Herbert Hoover, as a Californian and a rival of Hiram Johnson for leadership of the Republican party both in California and in national politics, could hardly have opposed the Boulder Canyon project; and although he was deeply troubled by the charge that in building a great powerplant the Federal government would be dealing a heavy blow to a leading American private industry, he could see no other way to pay for the dam. Hoover's election to the Presidency, and the knowledge that he favored the project, finally ended the long battle over its adoption, and the Swing-Johnson bill became law on December 21, 1928.

Hoover Dam. In its final form the Boulder Canyon Project Act of 1928 provided that the principal dam might be built either in Boulder Canyon or a few miles downstream in Black Canyon. The government's engineers chose Black Canyon. Thus the name of "Boulder Dam," unofficially used during the years of debate on the project, became inaccurate. The official choice of a name for a Federal dam was a time-honored prerogative of the Secretary of the

Interior. Dr. Ray Lyman Wilbur, who held that office under President Hoover, chose the name that seemed to him in every way most eminently suitable—Hoover Dam.

But Harold L. Ickes succeeded Dr. Wilbur when the mighty structure was about half finished, and to the confusion of cartographers and the fury of Republicans the self-styled Old Curmudgeon of the New Deal was determined "to give Boulder dam its original and proper name, which my predecessor in office attempted feloniously to take from it." When Ickes asked Attorney General Homer S. Cummings for help in this undertaking, Cummings made a tactful effort to dissuade him. The Attorney General noted that the name of "Hoover Dam" appeared in the several statutes appropriating money for its construction. It would be best, he advised, to regard the whole matter of the name as "water over the Hoover (Boulder) Dam."

Ickes was unimpressed by Cummings's interpretation of the law, and unamused by his levity. President Franklin D. Roosevelt sided with Ickes, and it was as "Boulder Dam" that Roosevelt officially dedicated the structure, on September 30, 1935. In 1947 the Republican Eightieth Congress passed a bill to restore the name of "Hoover Dam," and President Truman signed the bill into law. Nevertheless, usage has sometimes continued to vary with partisan preference—or merely with confused recollection.

When it was finished, and for many years afterward, the dam was the highest and largest in the world. The project was so great that neither the government nor any one private contractor was willing to undertake its construction alone. The successful bid came from several Western engineering firms newly allied for the purpose. Felix Kahn of San Francisco suggested the name of the new group: "Six Companies, Inc.," after "the famous tribunal to which the Chinese tongs in San Francisco had submitted their differences in preference to warring with hatchet-men." Henry J. Kaiser was made chairman of the board of directors, and Frank Crowe was general superintendent of construction.

One of the participants, Frank Waters, was a man with a talent for writing as well as for engineering, and in his book on *The Colorado* he described some of the problems the Six Companies faced: ". . . sheer canyon walls so high that they distorted perspective; the lack of even a sand bar for initial footage; the desert on each side without housing or transportation facilities; and greatest of all, the terrific current of the silt-choked river." When bonding companies at first refused to touch the project because they considered the working conditions unendurable, a fully air-conditioned model city was built to house 5,000 workers. To divert the river from the construction site, four bypass tunnels had to be built through the canyon walls, two on each side. Each of these tunnels was a mile long and 50 feet in diameter with a 3-foot concrete lining. Before any concrete could be poured for the foundation of the dam, the riverbed had to be cleaned down to the bare rock. Then it had to be kept clean and dry during the whole period of construction.

When the dam first began to rise it did not resemble a dam at all, but a jumble of wooden boxes. If the concrete had been poured into a single block, the structure would have taken 125 years to cool and the expansion would have split it apart. An ammonia refrigeration plant had to be built, and 662 miles of tubing, carrying water just above the freezing point, had to be run between and through the huge concrete blocks.

As the dam neared completion it was still honeycombed with narrow galleries. Men walked a quarter of a mile through the base of it. To its crest, they rode a small elevator to the height of a 60-story building. As Waters recalled, it was "a labyrinth of cold passages; the dark interior of a great pyramid; the heart of a stone mountain; the depths of a mine. . . . Then the tubing was removed, the corridors were pumped full of concrete, and the dam was sealed."

At its base was the world's largest powerhouse to date, containing the world's largest turbines and generators. They began to operate on September 11, 1936, when President Roosevelt pushed a golden key.

Behind the dam was the world's largest reservoir, Lake Mead, named for Dr. Elwood Mead, the Commissioner of Reclamation. Its capacity was 30 million acre-feet, or nearly 10 trillion gallons. Vast as the reservoir was, however, engineers soberly pointed out that it was doomed to impermanence. They warned that the Colorado, often described as "a little too thick to drink and a little too thin to plow," would fill Lake Mead with silt within 300 years, and that over the next 30 centuries the whole process would have to be repeated 10 times, at each of the 10 other possible sites.

There were few—particularly among the thousands who soon discovered Lake Mead as a pleasure resort—who felt any serious share in the engineers' concern with the long-range prospect. But the river's great cargo of silt was also the cause of some other and much more immediate problems. Even though enormous quantities of sediment were deposited in Lake Mead, it was necessary to build huge settling basins at the headworks of the new All-American Canal, 300 miles downstream, to keep the silt from choking the Imperial Valley's irrigation systems. And unusually elaborate filtering plants were required in preparing the water for industrial and domestic use in the cities.

The Colorado River Aqueduct. In 1923 Los Angeles and several neighboring communities had begun to plan the formation of a metropolitan water district for the purpose of building the world's longest and largest domestic water supply line from the Colorado River to the coastal basin. In the discussion of water projects in Southern California it had become impossible to avoid the constant repetition of the phrase "the world's largest."

The early difficulties of another metropolitan district, the East Bay Municipal Utility District formed by Oakland and its neighbors to bring water from the Mokelumne River, had made it clear that the existing state legislation was

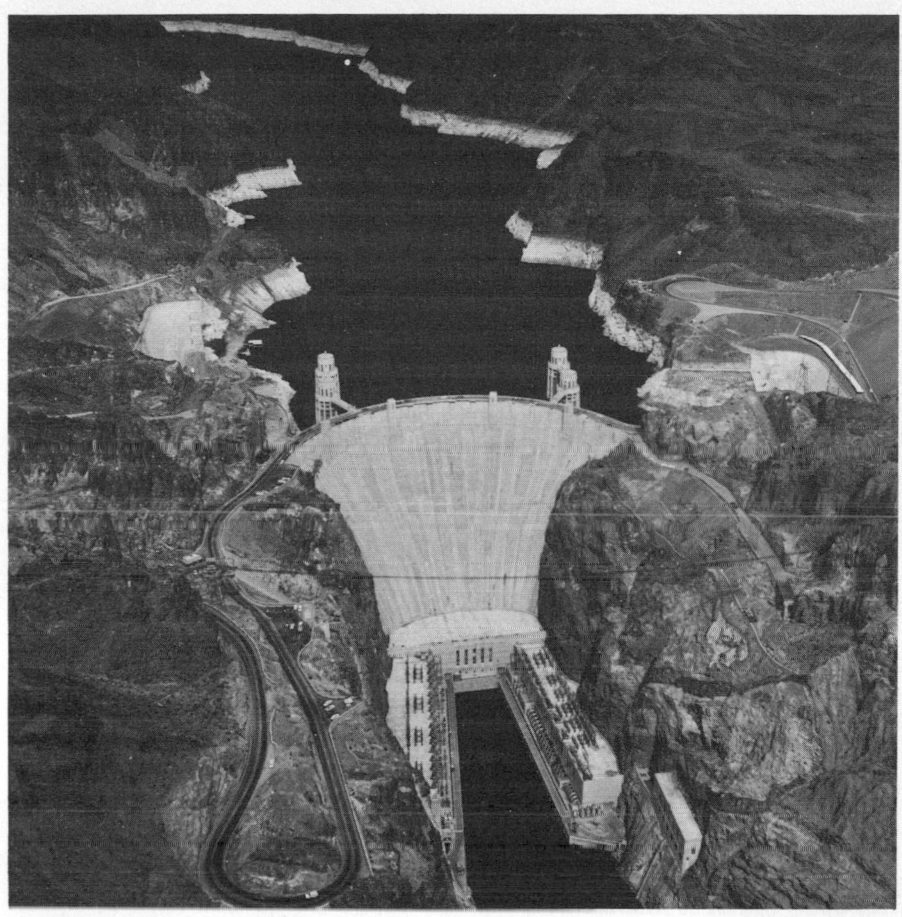

Hoover Dam (Photo by E. E. Hertzog. Courtesy of the United States Bureau of Reclamation)

faulty and inadequate. William B. Mathews, chief counsel for the Los Angeles Department of Water and Power, and James H. Howard, city attorney of Pasadena, joined in drafting a new state law. Lobbyists for the private utilities secured its defeat in 1925, but a number of Southern California legislators who opposed the bill were defeated in the next election, and in the 1927 session it passed unanimously in the senate and by a vote of 63 to 2 in the assembly.

This act became the charter of the Metropolitan Water District of Southern California. Officially organized in 1928, the district originally included Los Angeles and 10 nearby cities. Many others later joined. Los Angeles itself had already grown from its original pueblo area of 4 square leagues, or 28 square miles, to an area of more than 400 square miles, through many piecemeal annexations in which the need for water and the success of Los Angeles in acquiring it had been the prime factors.

The 220 million dollar bond issue for the great aqueduct came before the district's voters on September 29, 1931. Among its many supporters was Secretary Ray Lyman Wilbur, who had known the meaning of water to Southern California since his boyhood in Riverside. "Babylon fell," Wilbur told a Los Angeles audience, "not because of too much sin but because of too little water."

In bringing people to California, he pointed out, water was more important than railroads had ever been.

Though the concern of most of the voters was with water for domestic use, its role in the region's industrial development was equally vital. In 1919, for example, the Goodyear Tire and Rubber Company had become the first major industrial concern to locate a branch plant in Los Angeles because the city could promise the 8 million gallons of water a day that the plant would need. The company had rejected both San Francisco and San Diego because of the slower development of their water projects. In the crucial petroleum industry, 77,000 gallons of water were needed to refine 100 barrels of oil. Later improvements in equipment would enable refineries to recover much of the water and use it repeatedly. But in 1930 the Union Oil Company plant at Long Beach was still using more water than all the rest of the city.

With such compelling arguments in its favor, the huge bond issue passed by more than five to one, even though the market for municipal bonds had been steadily declining since the great crash of 1929 and was now practically nonexistent. The Reconstruction Finance Corporation, created by Congress in 1932, came to the rescue of the project and ultimately bought almost the entire issue.

The source of the Colorado River Aqueduct was to be at Parker Dam, about 150 miles below Hoover Dam. Work proceeded steadily except for two episodes in which Governor B. B. Moeur of Arizona added considerable drama and publicity to his state's perennial legal battle over the use of the river. In March 1934 Governor Moeur sent a National Guard detachment to the site of Parker Dam with orders to keep all workmen away from the Arizona shore. When the guardsmen found the land approaches inconvenient, they borrowed a ferryboat, the *Julia B.*, whose more humdrum duty had been to provide ferry service between Parker, Arizona, and Earp, California. Flying the Arizona flag, the *Julia B.* spent a glorious day at the damsite, and patriotic citizens of Tucson and Phoenix wired their congressman, demanding that the battleship *Arizona* be sent up the river to reinforce the "Arizona navy." Again in November Governor Moeur called out the National Guard to "repel the threatened invasion of the sovereignty and territory of the State of Arizona," and this time the construction work on Parker Dam was held up for several weeks.

The dam was finished on schedule in 1938, however, and in 1941 the aqueduct began to deliver water to the coastal cities. Its length, not including the distributing system, was 242 miles, from the Colorado to the main reservoir at Lake Mathews near Riverside.

San Diego remained outside the Metropolitan Water District for several years, partly because it hoped to get water from a branch of the All-American Canal. The city had often shown desperate ingenuity in its long struggle with its water problem. In December 1915 in the midst of a particularly serious drought it had even signed a contract with a professional rainmaker, Charles M. Hatfield. Promising to fill the Morena reservoir for a fee of $10,000, Hatfield built a number of "evaporating tanks," presumably to send up fumes from some combination of chemicals that remained his professional secret. A few weeks later a cloudburst overflowed the reservoir, washed out a smaller dam below it, and flooded a part of the town. The city council refused to pay Hatfield his fee; they pointed out that he had contracted to fill the reservoir, not to flood the community.

The growth of San Diego during World War II finally compelled the city and its neighbors to form a subgroup of the Metropolitan Water District of Southern California, and in 1945 construction work began on the first of two branch lines from the Colorado River Aqueduct to the San Diego region.

The Central Valley Project. Proposals for a large government project to aid the advance of irrigation in the great Central Valley were made as early as the 1870s, 60 years before such a plan was finally approved. A Federal commission under Lt. Col. B. S. Alexander recommended a system of canals in 1873, and William Hammond Hall, the first state engineer of California, began a series of detailed studies in 1878. But strong support for the idea did not begin to crystalize until 1920, when Col. Robert Bradford Marshall, chief geographer of the United States Geological Survey but acting in a private capacity, offered the state of California a broad and challenging plan. In its largest features, this was a proposal "to turn the Sacramento River into the San Joaquin Valley" through great canals, and to regulate the flow of the upper Sacramento with a high dam near Redding.

In the legislature of 1921 several progressive state senators sponsored a California Water and Power Act. On the subject of electric power, the "Marshall plan" was vague; it said only that "the sale of . . . power at fair rates" would repay much of the cost of the water developments. The proposed Water and Power Act, however, would have committed the state government to public distribution of the power produced by state-financed water projects. The bill passed the state senate by a vote of 28 to 1; but in the assembly it died in committee, largely as a result of the efforts of the Pacific Gas and Electric Company. The P.G. and E. was a consolidation of more than 400 smaller corporations. It had annexed virtually all the power and light companies of Northern and Central California.

CENTRAL VALLEY
&
COLORADO RIVER
PROJECTS
Metropolitan Water District
of Southern California
CVP power lines
Dams
Shasta Dam
Keswick Dam
Redding
Oroville
Sacramento
DELTA CROSS CHANNEL
CONTRA
COSTA CANAL
Tracy
DELTA-MENDOTA
CANAL
MADERA CANAL
Millerton Lake
Friant Dam
Fresno
FRIANT-KERN CANAL
Bakersfield
Lake Mead
Hoover Dam
Colorado
Davis Dam
River
Lake Havasu
Parker Dam
Lake Mathews
COLORADO RIVER
AQUEDUCT
COACHELLA
BRANCH CANAL
SAN DIEGO AQUEDUCT
Salton Sea
Imperial
Dam
ALL-AMERICAN CANAL
IMPERIAL CANAL

In 1922 the proponents of the state Water and Power Act succeeded in placing the measure on the ballot as an initiative constitutional amendment and spent $160,000 on their campaign in its favor. Most of this money came from Rudolph Spreckels and three other "millionaire progressives," John Randolph Haynes, William Kent, and James D. Phelan. Spreckels hired Franklin Hichborn to manage the campaign. Other active proponents included Louis Bartlett, mayor of Berkeley; Horace Porter, mayor of Riverside; and Clyde L. Seavey, city manager of Sacramento. The measure was defeated, however, and a state senate investigation later revealed that the power interests had spent more than $500,000 in their campaign against it.

This was far the largest sum yet expended in an initiative campaign in California. More than half of it came from the Pacific Gas and Electric Company, and was spent by the Greater California League. The Greater California League was Eustace Cullinan, a San Francisco attorney for the P.G. and E. South of the Tehachapis the Southern California Edison Company spent about $150,000 through a similar front called the People's Economy League. The use of such dummy organizations by the private utilities was not new. In the Hetch Hetchy fight, for example, a "Nature Lovers' Society" had so irritated William Kent that he denounced it as consisting of "nature fakers."

The proposed state Water and Power Act was again brought forward and again defeated in 1924 and 1926, and the embattled P.G. and E. dug in for a political war of unlimited duration. Of the many "community relations" techniques that it perfected, one gained special notoriety. This was a "practical incentive" plan designed to gain the "friendship and cooperation" of bankers, as explained in a letter from the P.G. and E.'s president, A. F. Hockenbeamer, to an Eastern utility executive who wished to know the secrets of the company's political success. "We have at this time accounts with 230 country banks scattered all over our territory," Hockenbeamer wrote, "and while our policy keeps an average of around a million and a half dollars tied up in balances in these country depositaries, we believe it is well worth while. . . . Incidentally, we require no interest on these deposits." This letter was subsequently made public during an investigation of utility companies by the Federal Trade Commission.

As a compromise, the 1929 legislature authorized the state engineer's office to study all the water resources of California and prepare a coordinated plan for their conservation, development, and use. The P.G. and E. offered little opposition to this measure. Studies made at public expense could be very helpful to the company's planning of its own hydroelectric projects, and the P.G. and E. had repeatedly demonstrated its political ability to keep the state government out of the power business. Construction of dams at state expense could also be greatly to the P.G. and E.'s advantage—if, as the company then expected, it could control the distribution of all the electric power that these dams would produce.

The "State Water Plan" was presented to the legislature early in 1931. Later in the same session a major obstacle was removed through the adoption of a "counties of origin" measure. This protected the Northern California counties, as the Colorado River Compact had protected the upper-Colorado-basin states, against damage to their ultimate development by future appropriation of too much of "their" water for the more arid regions.

The plan of 1931 was a comprehensive proposal to develop the water resources of the state as a whole, but it recommended a group of interrelated developments in the Central Valley as the ones most urgently needed. In 1933 the legislature embodied this recommendation in the California Central Valley Project Act. When this measure first passed the assembly, it made no provision for public power; but the little group of veteran progressive Republicans in the state senate managed to secure an amendment providing for public construction of generating plants and even of transmission lines, and the act was finally approved in this form. This was remarkable, in view of the bitter objections of the powerful P.G. and E. and the general conservatism of most of the legislators and of Governor James Rolph. But the clinching argument was that California's economy lay prostrate in the grip of the depression and that the Central Valley Project could act as an emergency rescue measure. The state at that time had no real hope of being able to pay for the project, and the only hope lay in persuading the Federal government to assume the cost. The chances of this would be much greater if the project conformed to the United States reclamation laws. Those laws gave strong preference to public agencies over private ones in the distribution of electric power from federally financed water developments.

Immediately after the passage of the Central Valley measure, the P.G. and E. began a campaign to nullify it through a referendum sponsored by one of its attorneys, Fred G. Athearn, who claimed to be acting only as a disinterested citizen. Soft-pedaling the power issue, Athearn attacked the Central Valley program as a whole. By bringing new lands under irrigation, he argued, the plan would increase the already disastrous surpluses of agricultural commodities. Moreover, it was unfair to the people of Southern California, who would receive no benefits but would have to pay taxes for a project located entirely in the northern and central parts of the state.

Supporters of the plan replied that without it many of the lands already being cultivated would have to be abandoned because of the continuing depletion of underground water through pumping. They also pointed out that the economic importance of the San Joaquin Valley to the Los Angeles area was great, and would become still greater; but in the special election of December 1933, Los Angeles County voted two to one for repeal of the Central Valley Act. Los Angeles had recently been assured of its own supply of water from the Colorado, and though it had fought hard for its own public power system, it cared little about the water and power problems of Northern California.

The voters of the state as a whole, however, upheld the Central Valley Act by a small majority, and in 1935 the Federal Bureau of Reclamation assumed responsibility for the project. Construction began in 1937.

The original Central Valley Project, authorized in the 1930s and regarded as the first phase of a much larger program, came into operation as a coordinated system in the 1950s. Its main features were three dams, five canals, and two power transmission lines.

The most impressive unit was Shasta Dam, impounding the waters of the Sacramento, McCloud, and Pit Rivers in Shasta Lake. Keswick Dam, 9 miles downstream on the Sacramento, was designed to serve both as a regulating afterbay and for the generation of additional power. Friant Dam was built on the San Joaquin River, 20 miles northeast of Fresno.

From a point just below Friant Dam the Friant-Kern Canal extended 160 miles southeastward to the region of Bakersfield. The Madera Canal ran 37 miles northwestward from Friant Dam. On the west side of the valley the Delta-Mendota Canal carried Sacramento River water 120 miles south to the Mendota pool at the great bend of the San Joaquin River, to replace water formerly taken from the San Joaquin. The Contra Costa Canal, 58 miles long, brought fresh water from the delta to agricultural, industrial, and urban users between Antioch and Martinez, and the Delta Cross Channel carried Sacramento River water to the intake of the Delta-Mendota Canal.

Through all the years when the dams and canals were being built, the Pacific Gas and Electric Company managed to block every congressional appropriation for government-owned transmission lines. When the generating plant at Shasta Dam began to produce power in 1944, Secretary of the Interior Ickes had no choice but to negotiate a 5-year agreement for the sale of all of this power to the P.G. and E.

Repeatedly the company's officials asserted before congressional committees that the Bureau of Reclamation had a "grandiose scheme" for "the socialization of the power industry in northern and central California." As the Southern Pacific Railroad had done a few decades earlier, the P.G. and E. denounced governmental infringement upon free enterprise, although in both cases it was really monopoly, not free enterprise, which the corporation was fighting to preserve.

At last, through a series of agreements beginning in 1951, the P.G. and E. and the Federal authorities solved the problem by entering into an uneasy partnership. The Bureau of Reclamation continued to sell power to the P.G. and E.; the company agreed, for the first time, to permit the use of its lines for the delivery of Federal power from Shasta Dam to the Sacramento Municipal Utility District; and the Bureau of Reclamation was finally able to build its two long-projected transmission lines from Shasta and Keswick Dams to its own plant at Tracy for use in pumping water through the Delta-Mendota and Contra Costa Canals.

Even more controversial than the power question was another issue that also involved the Federal reclamation laws. Ever since the Newlands Act of 1902 it had been the government's policy to limit the amount of water that any one owner of land could obtain from a Federal reclamation project. The maximum was enough water to irrigate 160 acres, or 320 acres in the case of a married couple.

In California, very little was said publicly about this limitation until 1944, and the large landowners indulged in much wishful thinking to the effect that it would never actually be applied to the Central Valley Project. Then, however, the Secretary of the Interior began to comply with the Federal laws that required him to negotiate contracts with irrigation districts, and to include the 160-acre limit in these contracts.

The large landowners of California, including many powerful corporations, now launched a campaign to have the acreage limit set aside. They formed a political coalition with the P.G. and E., supporting that company on power issues in return for its support of their viewpoint on the acreage matter, and this formidable alliance mounted a concerted attack on the Bureau of Reclamation and the Department of the Interior.

In the years of intense debate that followed, much confusion resulted from a popular misconception of the facts. This was the widespread and entirely erroneous belief that the 160-acre limitation restricted "the amount of land a man could own." What the Federal laws actually did was to restrict the amount of federally subsidized water that any one landowner could buy. In 1951, for example, the average price of the best grade of irrigation water from the Central Valley Project was about $2.50 per acre-foot, while the average price for the same grade of water from other sources was $6.77 per acre-foot.

Another misconception was that the owner of land in excess of 160 acres could receive no "project water" at all unless he contracted to sell the "excess" land. The truth was that the larger owner was free to buy cheap Federal water for a 160-acre *portion* of his land. He could irrigate the rest of it with "commercial" or "non-project" water. Or he *could* buy Federal water for the larger acreage. It was only if he chose the latter alternative that he was required to sign a contract to sell the "excess" acres within a certain period of years, at prices that would not allow him an unfair profit from the increase in land values resulting from the Federal project.

Congress repeatedly declined to repeal the 160-acre limitation, and the large Central Valley landholders sought relief in the courts. In 1957 the supreme court of California ruled in their favor by a majority of four to three, in the test case of the Ivanhoe Irrigation District. The acreage provision in the Federal reclamation laws, in the opinion of the majority of the California justices, was unconstitutional. "It is an unlawful discrimination," they argued, "to limit the extent of the right of an owner of real property to the use and enjoyment of his property right, including the water right which may be attached thereto, on the sole basis of the amount of property he owns."

But in 1958 the United States Supreme Court unanimously reversed this judgment. The claim of discrimination, said the highest court, "overlooks the purpose for which the project was designed." That purpose was "to benefit people, not land," and to distribute the benefits "in accordance with the greatest good of the greatest number of individuals. The limitation insures that this enormous expenditure will not go in disproportionate share to a few individuals with large land holdings. Moreover, it prevents the use of the federal reclamation service for speculative purposes. In short, the excess acreage provision acts as a ceiling, imposed equally upon all participants, on the federal subsidy that is being bestowed."

The most significant effect of this decision was to convince most of the political leaders of California that the massive water projects of the 1960s and after must be built with state rather than Federal funds, so that the larger units of land could obtain cheap, publicly subsidized water.

SELECTED BIBLIOGRAPHY

Paul L. Kleinsorge, *The Boulder Canyon Project; Historical and Legal Aspects* (1941), is a thorough study by an economist. Beverly B. Moeller, *Phil Swing and Boulder Dam* (1971), and Donald C. Swain, *Federal Conservation Policy, 1921–1933* (1963), discuss the national political problems. Less formal accounts of the battles over the development of the lower Colorado are in the second half of Remi A. Nadeau, *The Water Seekers* (1950), and the final chapters of David O. Woodbury, *The Colorado Conquest* (1941). Also useful are Norris Hundley, *Dividing the Waters: A Century of Controversy between the United States and Mexico* (1966); John U. Terrell, *War for the Colorado River* (two volumes, 1965); and Erwin Cooper, *Aqueduct Empire* (1968).

Frank Waters, *The Colorado* (1946), is particularly notable for its vivid descriptions of the building of what was then the world's largest dam. Important source books are Ray Lyman Wilbur and Elwood Mead, *The Construction of Hoover Dam* (1933), and Ray Lyman Wilbur and Northcutt Ely, *Hoover Dam Documents* (second edition, 1948).

Vincent Ostrom, *Water & Politics: a Study of Water Policies and Administration in the Development of Los Angeles* (1953); and Nelson S. Van Valen, "Power Politics: the Struggle for Municipal Ownership of Electrical Utilities in Los Angeles, 1905–1937," Ph.D. thesis, Claremont Graduate School (1964), deal with the city's adoption of public power as well as with the development of the Metropolitan Water District and the building of the Colorado River Aqueduct. On the rejection of public power in San Francisco, see Florence R. Monroy, "Water and Power in San Francisco since 1900; a Study in Municipal Government," M.A. thesis, University of California, Berkeley (1944). John W. Noble, *Its Name was M. U. D.* (1970), is a history of the East Bay Municipal Utility District.

Useful works on the Central Valley Project are Arthur D. Angel, "Political and Administrative Aspects of the Central Valley Project of California," mimeographed Ph.D. thesis, University of California, Los Angeles (1944); Marion Clawson, *The Effect of the Central Valley Project on the Agricultural and*

Industrial Economy and on the Social Character of California (1945); Mary Montgomery and Marion Clawson, *History of Legislation and Policy Formation of the Central Valley Project* (1946); Robert de Roos, *The Thirsty Land* (1948); "The Central Valley Project and Related Problems," an edition of the *California Law Review*, XXXVIII (October 1950); Hugh G. Hansen, *Central Valley Project: Federal or State?* (1955); Clair Engle, *Central Valley Project Documents* (two parts, 1956); and three Ph.D. theses, University of California, Berkeley: Jack T. Casey, "Legislative History of the Central Valley Project" (1949); Alten B. Davis, "The Excess Land Law in the Central Valley of California" (1962); and Charles E. Coate, "Water, Power, and Politics in the Central Valley Project" (1969).

Charles M. Coleman, *P. G. and E. of California; the Centennial Story of Pacific Gas and Electric Company, 1852–1952* (1952), refers to the company's political activities only in very general and favorable terms. More detailed information, and a more critical view of the political methods of the P.G. and E. and other private utility corporations, may be found in Carl D. Thompson, *Confessions of the Power Trust* (1932), based on the hearings of the Federal Trade Commission.

Most of the arguments against the 160-acre limit were collected and elaborated in Sheridan Downey, *They Would Rule the Valley* (1947), "they" being the United States Bureau of Reclamation. The opposite viewpoint is well summarized in Paul S. Taylor, "Excess Land Law: Pressure versus Principle," *California Law Review*, XLVII (August 1959), 499–541.

Chapter XXXIII

THE GREAT DEPRESSION AND POLITICS

THE PROSPERITY of the 1920s was not well distributed. Proportionally, too much of the national income was in dividends and interest and too little in wages, and therefore America's capacity to produce exceeded its capacity to consume. During the '20s American individualism had too often degenerated into irresponsibility and greed. One manifestation of this trend was the urge to get rich quickly and easily by gambling in the stock market. As banks, investment trusts, and millions of individual speculators crowded into the market with borrowed money, they bid up the prices of corporation stocks to levels that were further and further beyond any meaningful relation to the value of the companies' properties, or to their actual profits from the production of goods and services. Paper values of stocks came to represent a fantastic attempt to take in advance the income not merely of the future but of the hereafter. The result was the great crash of October 1929, which marked the beginning of the worst and longest depression in American history.

In California, the number of freight-car loadings in 1933 was less than half of what it had been in 1928, and the number of building permits was less than one-ninth of the peak figure of 1925. The depression spread from Wall Street to San Francisco's Montgomery Street, and then to many a small town's Main Street. California farm income sank in 1932 to scarcely more than half of what it had been in 1929, and there were thousands of mortgage foreclosures. With the spread of mass unemployment in both city and country, the number of Californians dependent upon public relief in 1934 was more than 1,250,000—about one-fifth of the whole population of the state. But no mere statistics can convey the real meaning of the great depression. Its meaning was in the suffering, anxiety, and grief of the millions whose lives it blighted.

In California politics, reaction to this disaster came slowly at first. Then it became extreme and frantic. But through the whole decade of depression that followed the crash, politics and government in California remained confused, demoralized, and ineffectual.

"Sunny Jim." The choice of a governor in 1930, the first year of the depression, represented politics as usual or rather worse than usual. James Rolph, Jr., had been mayor of San Francisco for 19 years, since his first election in 1911. His early career as mayor was quite creditable, but in 1918 he lost the fortune that he had made in the shipping business and his health and efficiency began to decline. During the '20s he still commanded great popular affection, mainly because of the convivial folksiness of his innumerable appearances as the city's official host, greeter, and master of ceremonies. More and more often he was in a state of cheerful insobriety. In that "era of wonderful nonsense" he seemed a highly successful large-city mayor. But to make him Governor, and expect him to cope with an emergency on the scale of the great depression, was rather as if the state of New York had promoted Mayor Jimmy Walker to the governorship.

Rolph's most important policy as Governor was his opposition to tax reform. His views on taxation were those of the most conservative wing of the business community, and he was heavily in debt to one of San Francisco's leading bankers, who was also one of his closest political advisers.

For many years, corporations and individuals with large incomes had been highly successful in evading taxation. In order to provide state support for the public schools, which were in a financial crisis because of the shrinkage of local tax revenues, the legislature of 1933 adopted a sales tax, with Rolph's approval. But when the legislature also passed an income tax measure, Rolph vetoed it. The burden of the sales tax fell heavily on the poor, and the inclusion of food among the items subject to the tax was especially resented. Corner grocers, ringing up small sales, bitterly reminded their customers that they must add "a penny for Jimmy."

In a desperate and deluded attempt to regain his popularity, Rolph made the worst mistake of his career. He openly abetted and defended a lynching.

There had been more lynchings in California than in any state outside the South, and more lynchings of white men than in any state whatever. Most of the California cases occurred in the early decades of the American period; but 59 men were lynched in California between 1875 and 1934—an average of one a year. Fifty of these were white, six were Indians, and three were Chinese; in contrast with the situation in the South, the California lynching victims were generally white men accused of murder rather than Negroes accused of sexual assault.

Throughout the country, in the early 1930s, there was a wave of kidnapings, including that of the Lindbergh baby in 1932. At San Jose, on November 26, 1933, two men who had confessed the kidnaping and murder of the son of a wealthy local merchant were being held in the county jail. When there was talk of mob action, Governor Rolph made a public "promise" that he would never call out the National Guard "to protect those two fellows." A few hours later, with this open incitement from the Governor, a mob broke into the jail, beat the sheriff unconscious, and hanged the two prisoners to trees in a nearby park.

Rolph then asserted in another public statement that "This is the best lesson California has ever given the country." He promised to pardon anyone who might be arrested for "the good job," and added that he would like to release all convicted kidnapers from the state prisons into the hands of "those fine, patriotic San Jose citizens who know how to handle such a situation." The lynchers, Rolph theorized, were men with "pioneer blood in their veins," who "were probably reminded of the metage of justice by the vigilantes in the early days of San Francisco's history."

As the *New York Times* remarked in a scathing editorial, Judge Lynch had always been a shadowy, unidentified figure. Now there was an actual and visible Governor Lynch.

In 1934 Rolph began another of his picturesque election campaigns. In burnished leather boots and a red sash he inaugurated every fiesta, parade, and rodeo, and even participated in milking contests to demonstrate his simple, human rusticity. But he collapsed during a precampaign tour, and died on June 2. Lieutenant Governor Frank Merriam, a Long Beach real estate man, succeeded him as Governor.

Social messiahs. Californians in the early 1930s were desperately searching for new leadership. It was increasingly clear that they could expect no help from the administrations of President Hoover and Governor Rolph, and the depression was growing steadily worse.

The sufferings of old people were especially severe. Thousands of them had come from other parts of the country to retire in Los Angeles or its suburbs. In the '20s, when they had been able to live fairly comfortably before they lost their savings in the depression, most of them had been conservative in their economic and political ideas, and their interest in colorful leaders had been directed mainly toward religious evangelists. One of these was Sister Aimee Semple McPherson, who preached the "Four Square Gospel" with spectacular showmanship at her Angelus Temple and over her own radio station. Another was the Reverend Robert P. Shuler, who operated a rival station. In 1926 the Reverend Mr. Shuler had led the outcry against Sister Aimee when that some-

Governor James Rolph, Jr. (Courtesy of Wide World Photos)

what tarnished angel was accused of having spent an illicit vacation in Carmel with her choir director during the time when she claimed to have been kidnaped and held for ransom in Mexico.

During the early '30s Sister Aimee's following declined, not merely because of her personal indiscretions but because interest was shifting from religious to economic and political evangelism. "Bob" Shuler, who had been an active force in Los Angeles politics for years, maintained his influence by announcing the formation of the Commonwealth party, a new political movement under his leadership.

Technocracy, which advocated a new society based on scientific management, aroused so much enthusiasm in Los Angeles that chief Technocrat Howard Scott moved his headquarters there from the East. In 1933 a group of unemployed businessmen broke off from the Technocratic persuasion to establish the Utopian Society. The Utopians drew an overflow crowd for a pageant in the Hollywood Bowl, a spectacle that resembled some of Mrs. McPherson's pro-

Aimee Semple McPherson leading a group of her followers in prayer at a "Holy Ghost Rally." (Courtesy of the Bancroft Library)

ductions at Angelus Temple except that it dramatized the triumph not of Good over Evil but of Abundance over Scarcity.

The founder of a much larger and more enduring new movement was Dr. Francis E. Townsend, an unemployed physician of Long Beach. Unsuccessful in private practice and in attempts to sell real estate, he had been saved from poverty during the first three years of the depression by a job with the city health department as one of four doctors caring for welfare cases. But in 1933 the city discontinued its health services program, and at the age of 66, having worked hard all his life, he was facing destitution. During the next few months he formulated the Townsend Plan, and backed it with an organization called Old Age Revolving Pensions, Ltd. All Americans over 60 were to receive pensions of $200 a month, all of which they must spend within 30 days. The money would come from a Federal sales tax. This plan, according to Dr. Townsend and his followers, would not only provide a decent living for old people but would also bring general prosperity by restoring "the proper circulation of money."

Though the heart of the movement remained in Southern California, Townsend Clubs sprang up all over the nation, and soon had a membership of about one and a half million "senior citizens." Their delegates assembled in regional and later in national conventions, where they sang "Onward Townsend Soldiers." To hundreds of thousands of old people the Townsend Clubs brought new hope, new friendships, and a renewed interest in life. The movement quickly became a powerful force in both state and national politics.

Labor strife. In the agonies of the depression California's long tradition of social violence was reborn in new and bitter struggles between labor and employers.

California labor problems had always been at their worst in agriculture, partly because the growers had always been able to block the development of collective bargaining. When the depression turned most of the farm regions into economic disaster areas, labor relations became worse than ever before. Agricultural workers, ill-fed or unfed, had to suffer the peculiar misery of watching food crops rot because they could not be sold for enough to pay the costs of harvesting and marketing.

Again, as in the days of the I.W.W., the wretched conditions of the migratory agricultural workers and the complete absence of conventional labor unions opened the door to the most extreme radicals, and the radicals played into the hands of the employers. The Cannery and Agricultural Workers' Industrial Union, which became active in 1933, was avowedly an arm of the Communist party, and was openly eager to hasten the disintegration of the capitalist system in agriculture. It provided the leadership for the strikes of the grape pickers at Lodi and the cotton pickers in the southern San Joaquin Valley in 1933, and the vegetable pickers in the Imperial Valley in 1934. Employer-vigilante groups, sometimes deputized by county sheriffs, did not hesitate to use violence in crushing these strikes, and the "union" was dissolved when its Communist leaders were arrested and convicted under the state criminal syndicalism law.

The National Industrial Recovery Act of 1933, in its famous section 7a, recognized the right of employees "to organize and bargain collectively through representatives of their own choosing." The New Deal's efforts to extend this right to agricultural labor were halfhearted and unsuccessful. But in the San Francisco Bay region, where organized labor had once been strong, the unions took courage from the new Federal law and set out to regain the power they had lost in the 1920s. When the employers resisted, the struggle became even more violent than in the agricultural regions. Class conflict went to such extremes that police and National Guardsmen were used to break a strike on the San Francisco waterfront, and in retaliation nearly all the unions in the bay region joined in a general strike in sympathy with the demands of the maritime workers.

The employers in the San Francisco shipping industry had destroyed the power of the International Longshoremen's Association in the bay area by breaking its strike in 1919. They had used the presence of I.W.W.'s and other radicals in several maritime unions as an excuse to destroy unionism itself. From 1919 until 1934 the only longshoremen's union in the San Francisco Bay area was the employer-controlled "Blue Book" union. Hiring was done under the "shape-up" system. The men gathered on the docks each day, and an employer-controlled hiring boss chose the ones who would get the day's work. There was no attempt at decasualization, and the system was riddled with bribery, favoritism, and blacklisting.

A new local of the International Longshoremen's Association was formed in San Francisco in the summer of 1933, and soon won practically all the men away from the employer-controlled union. Within the new local of the I.L.A. a working longshoreman named Harry R. Bridges led a militant group that persuaded the union to adopt its demands. These included union-controlled hiring halls; better wages and working conditions with extra pay for overtime; and coastwide bargaining, so that the facilities of one port could not be used to break a strike in another, and so that companies in other ports could not undercut the San Francisco wage level.

To a group of employers who had enjoyed virtual freedom from any union demands at all for more than a decade, this program seemed "revolutionary." The employers charged that Bridges was a Communist.

Bridges had been born in Australia, and as a youthful member of a seamen's union had participated in the Australian general strike of 1917. He often said that his ideas were those of militant trade unionism, and that he had held these opinions before the Communist party came into existence. He did believe in cooperation between the trade unions and the Communists, especially in labor disputes. In later years the United States government would make long and elaborate efforts to deport him on the ground that Bridges himself was or had been a Communist, but he always denied the charge, and the government never proved it.

The longshoremen in all the Pacific Coast ports went on strike on May 9, 1934, and several seafaring unions struck soon afterward. The San Francisco Chamber of Commerce and the San Francisco Industrial Association held a joint meeting and made plans to support the Waterfront Employers' Union in an attempt to open the port with strikebreakers, on the ground that the West Coast district of the International Longshoremen's Association was "in the hands of a group of Communists." The business community was confident that it could again break the longshore strike and destroy the union on the radicalism issue, as it had done in 1919.

On the morning of "Bloody Thursday," July 5, 1934, 1,000 San Francisco policemen tried to clear 5,000 pickets from the Embarcadero, the main waterfront street, to enable strikebreakers to work. Pistols were fired on both sides. Sixty-four people were injured (thirty-one of them shot), and two strikers were killed. Governor Frank F. Merriam sent in the National Guard although Mayor

Angelo Rossi had not asked for it. Seventeen hundred guardsmen with fixed bayonets occupied the waterfront.

To this all-out attempt at "opening the port," organized labor responded by closing down most of the economic activity of most of the bay region. Virtually every union in San Francisco and Alameda Counties joined in the general strike which began in the morning of Monday, July 16.

William Randolph Hearst, who was in England, sent instructions to John Francis Neylan, his chief counsel, to form a committee of the major bay area newspaper publishers and to unite them in a strategy of denouncing the general strike as Communist-inspired. News reports, as well as headlines and editorials, gave the impression that the strike was a part of the same Communist conspiracy that had caused all of the recent troubles in agriculture. Bands of vigilantes, with explicit encouragement from the newspapers and from Governor Merriam, and with no interference from the police, broke into several Communist party offices in San Francisco and Oakland, smashed the furniture, and beat up anyone they found on the premises.

In the midst of the strike Gen. Hugh S. Johnson, administrator of the NRA,[1] happened to arrive in the region to deliver an address at the University of California in Berkeley. In a conference that lasted almost all night, Neylan convinced Johnson that the general strike was "revolutionary," and Johnson expressed this opinion in his speech the next day.

Although this charge was essentially untrue, one development in the general strike gave a color of truth to it. Trucks delivering food and other essential supplies carried placards with the words "By Permission of the Strike Committee." In effect, the general strike committee temporarily usurped the licensing function of the state and local governments.

The general strike was called off at the end of its fourth day, Thursday, July 19. It had alienated majority public opinion to such a degree that American labor has never attempted a repetition of it. But if the general strike was largely a failure, so was the intransigent effort of the San Francisco employers to retain the open shop. Federal officials, including President Franklin D. Roosevelt, were now determined to settle the basic issues by a Federal arbitration that would compel the employers to accept the full meaning and spirit of section 7a. John Francis Neylan, though jubilant over the success of his role in the "breaking" of the general strike, had always believed in collective bargaining, and now

[1] The National Recovery Administration. In the early years of the depression so many new Federal agencies began to be created that the newspapers saved space by printing their initials without periods. This gave rise to the usage by which the initials of organizations created in earlier years have often continued to be printed in the old style (for example, A.F. of L.), while those created since the early 1930s are printed in the new style (for example, CIO, the Congress of Industrial Organizations, established in 1935). After their merger in 1955, they became AFL-CIO. Note, however, the persistence of a striking example of the old usage: T.R. but FDR.

used his influence in persuading the waterfront employers to accept unconditional arbitration. The Federal board's ruling, announced on October 12, provided for hiring halls and gave the longshoremen's union virtually complete control of them. This was the demand that Bridges had emphasized most, and the ruling so increased his prestige that he was later made the head of the whole Pacific Coast district of the I.L.A. For years afterward the maritime employers were bitter at what they regarded as a triumph for radicalism, accomplished through Federal intervention.

Upton Sinclair and EPIC. At the beginning of the state political campaigns of 1934 it seemed highly probable that California would elect its first Democratic Governor in the 20th century. The blame for the depression had fallen heavily on the Republicans. In the presidential election of 1932 President Hoover had lost not only his home state of California but even his home county of Santa Clara, and Democrat William G. McAdoo had been elected United States Senator from California in the Roosevelt avalanche.

But except for the uninspiring McAdoo the California Democrats were virtually leaderless. Even in national politics, the Democratic party as it had been in the 1920s had offered no real alternative to the conservatism of the Republicans. If James M. Cox had been elected President instead of Warren G. Harding in 1920, the Wall Street lawyer John W. Davis instead of Calvin Coolidge in 1924, and Alfred E. Smith instead of Herbert Hoover in 1928, the great crash would have come just as soon and the depression would have been just as severe. As for the Democratic candidates for the governorship of California from 1922 through 1930, they had been so obscure that most voters had now forgotten even their names.

George Creel, whom President Roosevelt appointed as the San Francisco regional director of the NRA in the summer of 1933, emerged as the leading spokesman of the New Deal in California. Creel had been chairman of the United States Committee on Public Information during World War I. He had lived in California only since 1926, had taken little part in state political affairs, and did not particularly want to run for governor, but Northern California Democrats persuaded him to enter the race. Some Southern California Democrats were grooming Culbert L. Olson, a liberal Los Angeles attorney. Creel, Olson, or almost any other reasonably presentable New Dealer could probably have been elected governor of California in 1934. But Upton Sinclair, who had been the Socialist candidate for the governorship in 1926 and 1930, threw the whole campaign into a turmoil by announcing in September 1933 that he was changing his party registration and would run for Governor as a Democrat.

Sinclair had been the country's best-known pamphleteer and propaganda novelist since 1906, when he had published *The Jungle,* a melodramatic story of the heartbreaking conditions of life among the immigrant packinghouse workers of Chicago. The book was a sensational bestseller—not, as Sinclair had intended, because it aroused public sympathy for the workers, and indignation against the economic and social evils of the beef trust, but because it exposed the frightfully unsanitary conditions in the preparation of meat. When he was given widespread credit for the passage of the first Federal Pure Food and Drug Act the following year, he remarked that he had "aimed at the public's heart, and by accident hit it in the stomach."

Sinclair moved to California in 1915, and made his home in Altadena, a suburb of Los Angeles. In the middle of the waterfront strike at San Pedro in 1923 he was arrested for trying to read the Constitution of the United States to a meeting of strikers on a vacant lot, and this episode led him to found the Southern California branch of the American Civil Liberties Union.

By 1933 he had written 47 books (about half of his ultimate output), and there was hardly an aspect of capitalistic society in America that had not received unfavorable attention in one or another of his writings. On the other hand, he regarded Marx as a rigid doctrinaire. His own brand of socialism was of the romantic, Americanized sort that had produced the 19th-century utopian colonies.

It was characteristic of Sinclair that when he decided to run for Governor as a Democrat he began his campaign by writing a utopian novel about it. *I, Governor of California, and How I Ended Poverty: a True Story of the Future* (1933), was an imaginative history of California from 1933 to 1938. In lively fiction it told how Sinclair was elected Governor after a campaign of unprecedented bitterness, and how he then put all the unemployed to work in state-aided cooperative enterprises.

Through this catchy, quasi-literary device Sinclair set forth his program to End Poverty in California (EPIC). If the voters should decide to let him make his novel come true, a California Authority for Land (CAL) would purchase all the farms that were sold for taxes, and establish cooperative agricultural colonies on them, with cooperative stores for the members. A California Authority for Production (CAP) would acquire thousands of factories that had been idle or only partially in use. And a California Authority for Money (CAM) would issue bonds to finance the purchases of the lands and factories, and scrip to serve as the medium of exchange among the members of the cooperatives.

Instead of the New Deal policy of curtailing production in order to raise prices, Sinclair advocated "production for use." As for the effects of EPIC on the parts of the economy that would remain in private ownership, Sinclair vacillated, in different passages in his book and in various statements during his subsequent campaign. Sometimes he described EPIC as "production for use under capitalism," and the cooperatives as merely an autonomous economic system within the capitalistic order. But at other times his enthusiastic belief in the superiority of socialism showed through. "Private industry began to crumble," he wrote in *I, Governor,* "and as quickly as any productive enterprise failed, it was made over into a public institution."

The Communist party denounced Sinclair as a "social fascist"—its current term for anyone who advocated compromise with capitalism. The Socialist party of California also repudiated him, in somewhat milder language. But he was, in fact, a Socialist who was temporarily doing his best to turn himself into a left-wing liberal Democrat because he would have a serious chance of election under the Democratic label.

The national Democratic administration regarded Sinclair's candidacy as extremely unfortunate and unwelcome. The goal of the New Deal was not to undermine the capitalist system, but to save that system by reforming it. In California, however, the Democrats had never recovered from the temporary success of the Republican progressives in making themselves the party of reform. After many years of disastrous weakness the Democrats of California had no candidate strong enough to stop a Socialist pamphleteer from capturing their party. Not even a statement from President Roosevelt opposing Sinclair could have prevented him from defeating Creel for the Democratic nomination. Under these circumstances the President adopted a policy of making no public comment whatever about the campaign in California.

The depression was still raging, and thousands of men still lived in terror of being unable to provide food for their families. Wherever Sinclair went such men crowded around him to wring his hand and promise him their support. In August 1934 he won the nomination with the highest vote that a Democratic candidate for Governor had ever received in a California primary. More than two-thirds of his total vote came from Southern California. Fifty-four percent of it came from Los Angeles County, where unemployment and other forms of economic hardship were even worse than in the state as a whole.

In the Republican primary the extremely conservative Governor Merriam won by a plurality over three relatively progressive candidates. As George Creel remarked, this left the voters of California with "a choice between epilepsy and catalepsy. Sinclair has a fantastic, impossible plan, and Merriam is as modern as the dinosaur age."

The California Republicans, now thoroughly frightened, organized an attack against Sinclair on a scale so elaborate and intensive that it marked the beginning of a whole new era in the history of American political campaign techniques. Louis B. Mayer, head of Metro-Goldwyn-Mayer studios and chairman of the Republican state central committee, mobilized the resources of the public relations, advertising, and movie industries.

Sinclair's own writings over the previous 30 years provided his opponents with much of their ammunition. He had denounced and antagonized a remarkable number of groups and institutions: the clergy, in his book *The Profits of Religion;* American colleges and universities and their governing boards, presidents, and professors, in *The Goose Step;* public schools and schoolteachers, in

The Goslings; and the press, in *The Brass Check.* But his opponents did not content themselves with reprinting passages from the most abrasive parts of these works; they also indulged in outright fabrications and distortions, to suggest falsely that Sinclair was an atheist, a Communist, and a believer in free love. In a faked newsreel a group of "tramps," who were actually movie extras made up for the part, were shown debarking from a freight train and telling an interviewer that they were the first of an army of hoboes from the East who were on their way to California because they had heard that as soon as Sinclair was elected there would be a general sharing of the wealth.

Sinclair lost the support of Dr. Townsend and his followers by criticizing the Old Age Revolving Pensions plan as "a mere money scheme," and by proposing pensions of $50 a month instead of the Townsend plan's $200. Merriam, on the other hand, won an endorsement from Townsend by promising to recommend his plan to the national Congress. At the urging of the public relations experts who had taken over his campaign, Merriam also made a strong bid for Democratic votes by declaring that he was "heartily in accord with President Roosevelt's policies."

In the November election Merriam won with a vote of 1,138,620 to 879,557 for Sinclair. A vote of 302,519 went to Raymond L. Haight, a Los Angeles Republican lawyer and state corporation commissioner who had won the nominations of the Commonwealth and Progressive parties.

From Merriam to Olson. Governor Merriam realized and acknowledged that he could not have been elected without the support of many relatively conservative New Deal Democrats, and in 1935 he signed a number of bills that brought the state into conformity with some of the New Deal's policies and measures. The most active Democratic leader in the legislature was Culbert L. Olson, who had been elected state senator from Los Angeles County as a supporter of Sinclair. Though the senate was still predominantly conservative, Olson secured its approval of new laws which repealed the sales tax on food and established a moderate state income tax. Another measure slightly increased the provisions for assistance to the indigent aged, reflecting the provisions of the new Federal Social Security Act.

In the presidential election of 1936 California backed President Roosevelt by a majority that was consistent with the general proportions of his triumph throughout the country—he also carried every other state in the Union, except Maine and Vermont. His Republican opponent, Governor Alfred M. Landon, was known as "the Kansas Coolidge" because he had balanced the budget of his own state and was thought to favor an attempt at balancing the Federal budget as well. This goal could not have been accomplished without slashing Federal appropriations. To the millions of Americans who were dependent on Federal money for relief or old age pensions, and to their millions of relatives, this idea was intensely unwelcome.

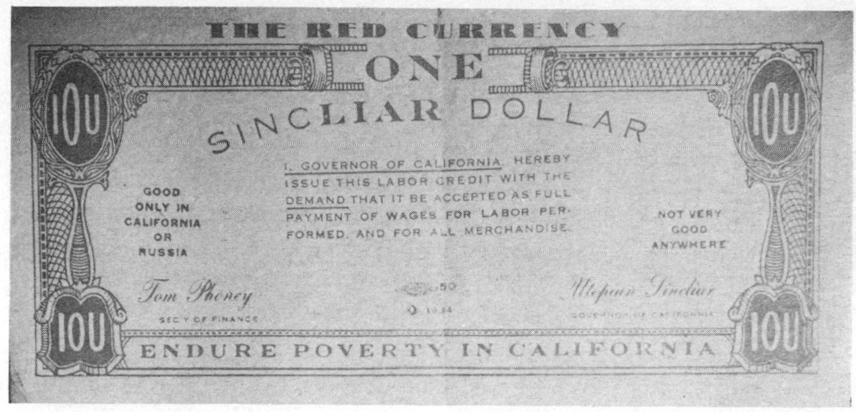

An item of campaign material in 1934. (From the collection of Raymond W. Hillman)

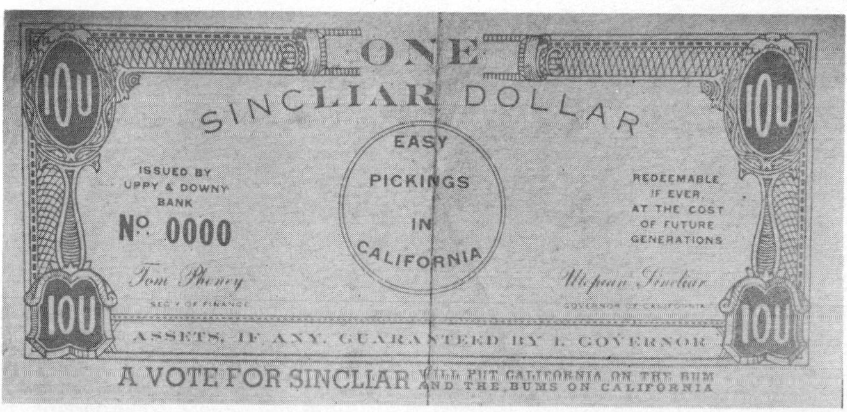

In the opinion of this huge bloc of voters, Federal and state funds for relief and pensions needed to be increased, not lowered. In the New Deal's Social Security Act of 1935, and in the corresponding Old Age Security program which California adopted in the same year, the use of the word "security" was a gross exaggeration of the benefits actually provided for old people. For state-sponsored old age pensions the Federal government contributed four-fifths of the first $25 per month, and half of any further amount up to $55. California set its maximum figure at $35, which was higher than in many other states. But to receive this maximum pension old people had to be not only without income but without relatives who could contribute to their support.

These provisions were not only inadequate, but they required humiliating investigations of personal finances and family relationships. At the same time, hopes for the Townsend Plan were waning because Congress had rejected it in favor of the Social Security Act. The way was open for a new pension scheme for the state of California alone, and the result was the aberration known as Ham 'n Eggs.

Robert Noble, a Los Angeles radio commentator, formed an organization called California Revolving Pensions, and summarized its plan with the slogan "Twenty-five Dollars Every Monday Morning." Noble entrusted some of his advertising to an agency operated by the brothers Willis and Lawrence Allen, whose chief client up to that time had been the manufacturer of Grey-Gone, a hair tonic. The Allen brothers then formed their own pension organization, excluding Noble. They shifted his slogan to "Thirty Dollars Every Thursday"; and one of their campaign orators hit upon the motto, "Ham 'n Eggs for California," by which the plan came to be commonly known.

In the California elections of 1938, pensions were the most important single issue. William G. McAdoo's denunciation of the Ham 'n Eggs movement cost him his seat in the United States Senate, when Sheridan Downey, who had won an endorsement from the Allen brothers by enthusiastically endorsing their plan, defeated McAdoo in the Democratic primary. Downey, a Sacramento lawyer, had been the EPIC candidate for Lieutenant Governor as Upton Sinclair's running mate in 1934 (opponents had disparaged the ticket as "Uppey and Downey").

If Governor Merriam had flirted with the Ham 'n Eggers in 1938 as he had flirted with the Townsendites in 1934, he would probably have been reelected. But he openly opposed Ham 'n Eggs, while Culbert L. Olson won the Democratic nomination and the governorship largely by avoiding a clear stand on the issue. As Initiative Proposition Number 25, the Ham 'n Eggs scheme was defeated by about 255,000 votes. But the vote in its favor, more than 1,143,000, was shockingly large, and it might have passed had it not been for the exposure, during the last days of the campaign, of some of the corrupt practices and unconscionable profits of the Allen brothers, its cynical and irresponsible promoters.

One of Olson's first acts as Governor was to carry out his campaign pledge of a pardon for Tom Mooney. Warren K. Billings, Mooney's codefendant, had also been convicted on perjured evidence, but because Billings had previously been convicted of a felony his pardon would have required a recommendation by the state supreme court. The court recommended only a commutation of sentence to time served, and this Olson granted. Billings would ultimately receive his full pardon from another Democratic Governor, Edmund G. Brown, in 1961.

At the end of his first week in office Governor Olson collapsed from exhaustion, and a month passed before he was able to resume his duties. This left the new administration without leadership at the most crucial time, and it never fully recovered from this demoralizing blow. But Olson could have accomplished little at best. Conservative Republicans still controlled the state senate, and although the Democrats had a small majority in the assembly, they were split into factions. Olson had almost no previous experience as an administrator.

Tactless and quick-tempered, he often antagonized men whose support would have been essential to his success. The main accomplishments of his governorship were a few modest reforms in the state's penal system and in its provisions for the care of the mentally ill.

Throughout the country the reformist enthusiasm of the New Deal was waning. The number of the liberal Democrats in Congress was sharply reduced in the 1938 elections, and as the war clouds gathered in Europe and Asia, President Roosevelt turned most of his attention to the problems of foreign affairs and national defense. Olson's chance of bringing a New Deal to California was both too little and too late.

SELECTED BIBLIOGRAPHY

Frank L. Kidner, *California Business Cycles* (1946), and California Emergency Relief Administration, *Economic Trends in California, 1929–1934* (1935), describe the economic effects of the depression.

On the careers and administrations of Rolph, Merriam, and Olson, see H. Brett Melendy and Benjamin F. Gilbert, *The Governors of California* (1965). Several theses written at the University of California, Berkeley, deal with the politics of the period. Robert Pitchell, "Twentieth Century California Voting Behavior" (Ph.D., 1955), analyzes the interrelations between social and economic factors and politics. Royce D. Delmatier, "The Rebirth of the Democratic Party in California, 1928–1938" (Ph.D., 1955), stresses the overwhelming votes for Roosevelt in 1932 and 1936, rather than the failure of the Democrats to unite the voters into an effective organization in the politics of the state. Ronald E. Chinn, "Democratic Party Politics in California, 1920–1956" (Ph.D., 1958), is a broader study. Warren F. Webb, "History of Lynching in California since 1875" (M.A., 1935), throws light on the historical background of the San Jose tragedy. Herman G. Goldbeck, "The Political Career of James Rolph, Jr." (M.A., 1936), concentrates on Rolph's earlier and happier years, as does Morley Segal, "James Rolph, Jr., and the Early Days of the San Francisco Municipal Railway," *California Historical Society Quarterly*, XLIII (March 1964), 3–18. See also Delmatier et al., *The Rumble of California Politics* (1970).

Arthur M. Schlesinger, Jr., *The Politics of Upheaval* (1960), includes excellent accounts of some of the major political developments in California in 1933 and 1934. Luther Whiteman and Samuel L. Lewis, *Glory Roads; the Psychological State of California* (1936), describes Technocracy, the Utopian Society, and other proposed roads to the millennium. Biographies of Aimee Semple McPherson are Nancy Barr Mavity, *Sister Aimee* (1931), and Lately Thomas, *The Vanishing Evangelist* (1959), and *Storming Heaven* (1970). On the Townsend Plan, see Francis E. Townsend, *New Horizons: an Autobiography* (1943); Abraham Holtzman, *The Townsend Movement: a Political Study* (1963); and J. D. Gaydowski, "The Genesis of the Townsend Plan," *Southern California Quarterly*, LII (December 1970), 365–382.

On the agricultural labor strikes, see Clarke A. Chambers, *California Farm Organizations . . . 1929–1941* (1952); on the general strike, David W. Mabon, "The West Coast Maritime and Sympathy Strikes of 1934," Ph.D. thesis, University of California, Berkeley (1965); Paul S. Taylor and Norman L. Gold, "San Francisco and the General Strike," *Survey Graphic*, XXIII (September 1934), 405–411; and Charles P. Larrowe, "The Great Maritime Strike of '34," *Labor History*, XI (Fall 1970), 403–451, and XII (Winter 1971), 3–37.

Sinclair's temporary capture of the Democratic party is described in Charles E. Larsen, "The Epic Campaign of 1934," *Pacific Historical Review*, XXVII (May 1958), 127–148; Clarence F. McIntosh, "Upton Sinclair and the EPIC Movement, 1933–1936," Ph.D. thesis, Stanford University (1955); *The Autobiography of Upton Sinclair* (1962); and George Creel, *Rebel at Large* (1947). Martin Zanger, "Politics of Confrontation: Upton Sinclair and the Launching of the ACLU in Southern California," *Pacific Historical Review*, XXXVIII (November 1969), describes a significant episode. See also Judson A. Grenier, "Upton Sinclair: a Remembrance," *California Historical Society Quarterly*, XLVIII (June 1969), 165–169.

An informal history of the rise of the Ham 'n Eggs movement is Winston Moore and Marian Moore, *Out of the Frying Pan* (1939). See also Carey McWilliams, "Pension Politics in California," in David Farrelly and Ivan Hinderaker, editors, *The Politics of California* (1951); and Frank A. Pinner, Paul Jacobs, and Philip Selznick, *Old Age and Political Behavior* (1959). Jackson K. Putnam, *Old-Age Politics in California: From Richardson to Reagan* (1970), is a major contribution.

An excellent study of the Olson administration is Robert E. Burke, *Olson's New Deal for California* (1953).

Chapter XXXIV

WARTIME GROWTH AND PROBLEMS

FROM 1919 TO 1941 the strongest feeling of the majority of Americans toward world affairs was their determination that the United States must never be involved in another world war. Senator Hiram Johnson of California was in the forefront of those who were called "isolationists" in this sense. But the raid on Pearl Harbor on December 7, 1941 left the American people no further choice. The Japanese attack, which came without warning and destroyed or crippled most of the American Pacific Fleet with bombs and aerial torpedoes, immediately produced more support for an all-out military and industrial effort than Americans had shown in any previous war.

The impact of Federal spending. In the period including the fiscal years from 1940 to 1946 the Federal government spent 360 billion dollars within the continental United States. Of this sum, it spent about 35 billion in the state of California. It would be almost impossible to exaggerate and it is difficult even to comprehend the full effects of these unprecedented expenditures in stimulating economic expansion. Every previous element in the state's economic history was dwarfed in comparison.

In the fiscal year ending June 30, 1930, the Federal government's total expenditures had been less than 3 billion dollars, of which it had spent only 191 million in California. In fiscal 1940, Federal spending in the state had risen to 728 million, much of it for relief and old-age pensions. But in the single wartime fiscal year 1945 the Federal government spent more than 8½ billion dollars in California alone. This was more than 10 percent of all Federal expenditures within the United States; and California's population in 1945 was only 7 percent of the nation's.

When the Nazis began the war with their invasion of Poland in September 1939, neither California nor the rest of the country had fully recovered from the depression that had begun with the crash nearly 10 full years before. The state's population had increased 21.7 percent during the depressed '30s (the lowest percentage increase recorded for any decade since American acquisition). But the total personal income of Californians in 1939 barely exceeded the 1930 figure of 5 billion dollars, and this meant that *per capita* income in 1939 had not yet climbed back to the level of 1930.

In 1945, however, the personal income of Californians was 15 billion dollars. In other words, the war and the increase in Federal spending raised total personal income in California to more than *three times* its prewar figure. This meant an enormous increase in per capita wealth, even allowing for a 30 percent inflation, and for a state population growth of 30 percent, between 1940 and 1945. Federal expenditures in California during World War II were 45 percent of the total personal income of California residents.

Federally financed activities took many forms, of which the most obvious were new or expanded military installations and new defense industries. In 1930 there had been only a handful of military installations in California, including the San Francisco Presidio; Fort Ord; the Mare Island Naval Shipyard; some naval facilities at San Diego; and March Field. By the end of the war all of these had been enormously expanded and the list had grown to include Camps Beale, Cooke, Pendleton, Roberts, and Stoneman; the Oakland Army Base and the Oakland Naval Supply Center; the Alameda Naval Air Station, the San Francisco Naval Shipyard, and the Treasure Island Naval Station; and several major air force bases—Castle, McClellan, Parks, and Travis.

Government money poured out through wage and salary payments to civilian and military personnel; investments in public and private facilities; purchases of supplies; and payments in the form of grants, subsidies, and interest. California received a disproportionate share of all these Federal expenditures at a time when they had grown enormously.

The most apparent effect on California's economy, apart from the general increase in its size, was the wartime expansion of manufacturing. Under government contracts American private industry produced a great variety of the sinews of war. In California, almost overnight, ships and airplanes became the most important of all the state's products.

Wartime shipyards. With the government providing the bulk of the capital, Henry J. Kaiser of Oakland became the chief private entrepreneur of California's wartime shipbuilding industry. Kaiser's reputation as an engineering and industrial genius had begun with the construction of Hoover and Parker Dams, and had continued to grow with his major role in the building of the San Francisco Bay Bridge and the dams at Bonneville and Grand Coulee. In order to produce his own cement, Kaiser had built Permanente, the largest cement plant in the world. Before the United States entered the war he had foreseen the wartime industrial crisis and had projected the first steel mill on the Pacific Coast, at Fontana, 50 miles east of Los Angeles.

New shipyards sprang up in 1942 at Richmond, Oakland, Sausalito, Vallejo, and San Pedro. In full operation for 24 hours a day in three shifts, they were soon building "Liberty ships" in 25 days, and in 1943 a new freighter was launched every 10 hours at one or another of the Kaiser shipyards.

At the peak of production in July 1943, civilian employment in the shipbuilding industry in California was nearly 300,000. Instead of the mass unemployment of the 1930s there was now a desperate shortage of labor. To one sign that said "Help Wanted!!! Male or Female, Young or Old, Experienced or Inexperienced," someone added "Dead or Alive!!!" Shipyard work was grimy and noisy, and there was the risk of being assigned to the "graveyard shift," from midnight to 8 A.M. But Kaiser advertised for workers in every part of the country, and in addition to the climate he offered such inducements as high wages, on-the-job training, a subsidized plan for group medical care, and exemption from the draft by virtue of employment in an essential war industry.

Since the shipyards could not afford to exclude anyone from their desperately short supply of labor, they offered extraordinary opportunities for women, members of minority races, and other groups whose previous chance for good pay in skilled occupations had been limited. But the disunity within American life was dramatically and painfully evident in the intense prejudices of male shipyard workers against women, of whites against nonwhites, and of all groups against the Negroes.

Before 1942, Negroes had formed only a tiny part of California's population. Wartime employment opportunity made them a substantial part of it, drawing hundreds of thousands of them into the state, as similar opportunities had drawn them from the South to Northern cities during World War I. Discrimination against them came from the labor unions rather than from the wartime shipyard employers. The Brotherhood of Boilermakers, for example, denied regular membership to Negroes and segregated them in an "auxiliary" in which they had to pay dues but could not vote in union elections.

The mushroom growth of the shipyards put heavy strains on the surrounding communities, and every facility from schools to sewers was stretched to the breaking point or beyond it. Thousands of families lived in "temporary" wartime housing projects that would remain as slums for decades afterward. The most severe growing pains were probably those of the cities of Richmond and Vallejo. In each, the population increased from about 20,000 in 1940 to more than 100,000 in 1945 and the nonwhite population rose from less than 2 percent to nearly 14 percent.

Throughout the state, wartime prosperity also brought strains and inconveniences. Things that had been regarded as necessities, even in the depression, were now luxuries. Meat and gasoline, for example, were tightly rationed. Civilian travel was discouraged, and signs in buses and railway cars sternly asked: "Is This Trip Necessary?"

Rise of the aircraft industry. The importance of shipbuilding was doomed to end with the war, but the wartime expansion in the manufacturing of aircraft and in the industries closely related to it became a much more enduring and ultimately a much larger factor in California's growth.

Before the 1930s, aircraft manufacturing in the United States was a small industry in which skilled craftsmen engaged in the leisurely production of custom-built planes. The more substantial factories were then in the East. Glenn L. Martin, who had established one of the first airplane factories in America in 1909, built some of his early planes in Southern California, but he later moved his operations to Cleveland and then to Baltimore. In 1916 the brothers Allen and Malcolm Loughead set up a shop in Santa Barbara in association with John K. Northrop. During World War I they got a contract to build seaplanes for the Navy, but the war ended before they could begin production. Refusing to be discouraged, the three men moved their little factory to Burbank, and dispelled the previously hopeless confusion over the pronunciation of "Loughead" by adopting "Lockheed" as their company name.

In 1920 young Donald Douglas left a job as chief engineer and vice president of Glenn L. Martin's company in Cleveland to go into business for himself in Southern California. With an initial capital of $600 Douglas set up his drafting room in the rear half of a barber shop on Pico Boulevard in Los Angeles. No banker would lend him a cent; but Bill Henry, a Los Angeles sportswriter, happened into the barber shop for a haircut, met Douglas, and insisted that he present his case to Harry Chandler, publisher of the *Times* and perpetual booster of new industry for the Los Angeles area. On the strength of an order for three Navy torpedo planes, Chandler and nine other Southern California businessmen lent Douglas a total of $15,000, and enabled him to establish a factory in an abandoned motion-picture studio in Santa Monica. That factory succeeded so well that in 1924 two Douglas-built Army planes made the first flight around the world, though they took several months to complete it.

T. Claude Ryan, a former Army flyer, established the first daily scheduled airline passenger service in the United States in 1922 between San Diego and Los Angeles, and the next year he began to manufacture planes at San Diego. There his small company achieved a national reputation by building the *Spirit of St. Louis,* in which Charles A. Lindbergh made his spectacular flight from New York to Paris in 1927.

The depression was particularly hard on the aircraft industry. In 1932 Douglas went for four months without an order and kept his workers employed at gardening and plant maintenance, while the Lockheed company, whose general manager had mortgaged his house and car to meet a payroll during the previous Christmas week, went into bankruptcy. A small Eastern group headed by Robert E. Gross then bought Lockheed from a Federal receivership for $40,000.

Even in the period between the two World Wars, more than half of the country's airplane production was done under government contract, and no company survived without a share of military orders. Nevertheless, the military air forces of the United States in the late '30s were alarmingly unprepared for war. In the words of Gen. George C. Marshall, they "consisted of a few partially equipped squadrons" whose planes "were largely obsolescent and could hardly have survived a single day of modern aerial combat." As late as 1939, the entire output of the American aircraft industry was less than 6,000 planes of all types—the full capacity of the factories then in existence. But in May 1940, when the Nazis flanked the Maginot Line and swept through Belgium into northern France, President Roosevelt called for an output of 50,000 planes a year, and although this figure was then regarded as shocking and impossible, actual production would more than double it by 1944.

The wartime expansion of aircraft manufacturing compressed 40 years of normal industrial progress into 40 months. In 1933, all the airframe factories in Southern California together employed only about one thousand people. In November 1943 they employed 280,300. Airframe plants, which made up the bulk of the aircraft industry in California, were only a part of the total process of aircraft production, but they were the largest part. They built the fuselage, wings, and tail, while the engines, propellers, and other equipment were made in separate factories. During the war much of the automobile industry in Detroit was converted to making aircraft engines; but it was the airframe plants that not only manufactured the shell of the aircraft but also assembled all the parts into the finished plane.

Aircraft accounted for nearly 60 percent of the money that the Federal government spent under prime contracts for goods manufactured in California during World War II, but the profits of the aircraft companies were small. The great bulk of the expansion was accomplished with Federal funds, through contracts under which the government guaranteed the entire cost and the companies received only a fixed fee in addition.

Four of the country's leading aircraft producers, Douglas, Lockheed, North American, and Northrop, had their main plants in the Los Angeles area, and two, Consolidated Vultee (or Convair) and Ryan, were in San Diego. Douglas enormously enlarged his factory at Santa Monica and established branches at El Segundo and Long Beach. Consolidated, which before the war had specialized in building flying boats, had been in San Diego since 1935, when its founder, Maj. Reuben H. Fleet, had moved it there from Buffalo, attracted by the climate and by a site on a publicly owned and ice-free waterfront.

Because clear, mild, and consistent weather offered great advantages for the production, testing, storage, and delivery of aircraft, climate became one of the principal factors in the location of airframe plants, and Southern California therefore received a large share of the industry's wartime expansion. That share would have been even larger than it was, had it not been for the memory of Pearl Harbor and the fear that Japanese carrier-based bombers might attack the Pacific Coast. The gigantic Douglas factory at Santa Monica was hidden under a camouflage cover, with dummy houses, streets, and trees, so that from the air and even from the ground it was almost impossible to distinguish the plant from its suburban residential surroundings.

The "relocation" of the Japanese Americans. The elaborate and expensive camouflaging of Southern California aircraft factories, though it proved unnecessary, did no great harm. But the fear of Japanese attack also led the government of the United States into a massive, tragic, and needless blunder. This was the evacuation from the West Coast of all persons of Japanese ancestry, and the imprisonment of most of them, citizens and aliens alike, without trial, behind barbed wire, under armed guard, in "relocation" camps in desert areas in the interior.

The attack on Pearl Harbor, and false rumors of sabotage and other treasonable acts by Japanese Americans, reactivated all the stereotyped racist delusions that had long formed the beliefs of many Californians about the Japanese. Since the early years of the century a number of the state's most influential newspapers, politicians, and organizations had frequently portrayed all persons of Japanese extraction as sly, sinister, ruthless, and incapable of loyalty to any country but Japan.

For the more effective dissemination of such ideas, Valentine S. McClatchy, publisher of the *Sacramento Bee,* had formed the California Joint Immigration Committee in 1921. This body coordinated the propaganda activities of four previous anti-Japanese and anti-Oriental organizations. Its members also included the secretary-treasurer of the State Federation of Labor, the master of the State Grange, the grand president of the Native Sons of the Golden West, the deputy adjutant of the California Department of the American Legion, and the attorney general of California. Attorney General Ulysses S. Webb, one of the principal authors of the state's alien land legislation, was often active in the work of the Joint Immigration Committee; and he often asserted in public speeches that persons of Japanese origin had inherent racial traits that rendered them unassimilable and untrustworthy as Americans. Earl Warren, when he succeeded Webb as attorney general of California in 1939, held similar views.

Immediately after the raid on Pearl Harbor, rumors of treacherous acts by Japanese Americans in Hawaii began to circulate both in the islands and on the mainland. Rumormongers claimed to know on the best authority that

Japanese vegetable trucks had blocked roads; or that one truck had rushed across Hickham Field and knocked the tails off a line of fighter planes; or that a huge arrow cut in a field of sugar cane the night before the raid had guided the Japanese bombers to this or that important target.

Secretary of the Navy Frank Knox, after returning from a hasty personal inspection of the disaster, held a tense press conference in Washington on December 15, 1941, in which he made the unfortunately phrased remark that "the most effective fifth-column work of the entire war was done in Hawaii, with the possible exception of Norway." What Knox apparently meant was that the Japanese consulate in Honolulu had been the center of a highly efficient professional espionage network; and this was true. But many reporters and newspaper readers assumed from Knox's remark that Japanese American residents of Hawaii had participated in espionage and sabotage—and this was false.

For the first several weeks after the Pearl Harbor raid the gradually increasing demands for some sort of mass action against the Japanese Americans on the West Coast received little support from Lt. Gen. John L. DeWitt, head of the Western Defense Command. On December 26 DeWitt telephoned from his headquarters at the San Francisco Presidio to the Provost Marshal General in Washington, to report that he had just received a visit from a representative of the Los Angeles Chamber of Commerce who demanded the internment of all the "Japanese" in the Los Angeles area, regardless of whether they were citizens of the United States. DeWitt was opposed. "I'm very doubtful that it would be a commonsense procedure," he told the Provost Marshal General. It would be "likely to alienate the loyal Japanese"; and "an American citizen, after all, is an American citizen."

A month later, however, General DeWitt changed his mind, largely as a result of the senational publicity given to the report of the Pearl Harbor investigating commission under Supreme Court Justice Owen J. Roberts. That report, published on January 25, 1942, laid the blame for the disaster mainly on the Army and Navy commanders in Hawaii, Lt. Gen. Walter C. Short and Adm. Husband E. Kimmel, respectively, and charged these two officers with "dereliction of duty" in having failed to take adequate precautions for the defense of the islands. Short and Kimmel had already been removed from their commands, but several congressional leaders now demanded that they suffer the further disgrace of being court-martialed.

The Roberts Report also asserted that the "Japanese spies on the Island of Oahu" had included not only "consular agents" but "persons having no open relations with the Japanese Foreign Service." Many Americans interpreted this statement as new and official evidence of widespread Japanese American disloyalty.

The truth was that there was not a scrap of valid evidence to connect any Japanese-American resident of Hawaii with any act of espionage or sabotage. But this would not be widely known until after the war; and the Roberts Report, at the time it was published, had an enormous and inflammatory effect on public opinion, especially in California. Moreover, no one found it more alarming than did General DeWitt, the officer most directly responsible for the defense of the West Coast.

On January 27 DeWitt had a long conference with Governor Culbert L. Olson. A few weeks before, Olson had pleaded for tolerance of the Japanese Americans, and for confidence in their loyalty. But now, DeWitt informed the War Department, the Governor had joined those who were "bringing pressure to move all the Japanese out." Attorney General Earl Warren, Mayor Fletcher Bowron of Los Angeles, and many others were making this demand, DeWitt reported, and the agitation for it came not merely from "people who are not thinking" but from "the best people of California. Since the publication of the Roberts Report they feel that they are living in the midst of a lot of enemies."

In a conference a few days later DeWitt remarked with intense emotion that "I am not going to be a second General Short."

DeWitt was now in a state of suppressed terror, brought on by fear of the disgrace that had befallen Short and Kimmel, and it was in this state of mind that he prepared a report headed "Final Recommendation . . . to the Secretary of War. . . . Subject: Evacuation of Japanese and other Subversive Persons from the Pacific Coast." Among other remarkable statements, this document asserted that "the Japanese race is an enemy race," and that "along the vital Pacific Coast over 112,000 potential enemies, of Japanese extraction, are at large today. There are indications that these are organized and ready for concerted action at a favorable opportunity. The very fact that no sabotage has taken place to date is a disturbing and confirming indication that such action will be taken."

This fantastic line of reasoning was very widely accepted. Walter Lippmann lent the great prestige of his column to it on February 12, and added that the Pacific Coast "is in imminent danger of a combined attack from within and without. . . . It may at any moment be a battlefield. Nobody's constitutional rights include the right to reside and do business on a battlefield." Lippmann wrote this column at San Francisco, after discussions with Attorney General Earl Warren and with the district attorney of Santa Barbara County. The day after it was published, the whole West Coast congressional delegation sent a letter to President Roosevelt demanding the "immediate evacuation of all persons of Japanese lineage . . . aliens and citizens alike" from "the entire strategic area" of California, Oregon, and Washington.

Secretary of War Henry L. Stimson and Assistant Secretary John J. McCloy, in a conference with President Roosevelt at the White House on February 11, had already asked the President for authorization to move Japanese-American citizens as well as aliens from "restricted areas" on the West Coast. There would "probably be repercussions," Roosevelt replied, but they must act from their judgment of military necessity. He qualified this statement only with the request to "Be as reasonable as you can," and McCloy informed DeWitt by telephone that the President had given the War Department "*carte blanche.*"

Attorney General Francis Biddle and his assistants in the Department of Justice had prepared a battery of arguments opposing the mass evacuation of American citizens as unconstitutional and the evacuation of enemy aliens as unnecessary and unwise. But before they could present these arguments the President informed Biddle that the question would be decided entirely on military grounds.

On February 19 President Roosevelt signed a most extraordinary document. This was an Executive order authorizing "the Secretary of War . . ., whenever he or any designated Commander deems such action necessary or desirable, to prescribe military areas in such places and of such extent as he or the appropriate Military Commander may determine, from which any or all persons may be excluded."

On March 2 the Western Defense Command issued its "Public Proclamation No. 1." All persons of Japanese ancestry were, in effect, *ordered* to migrate *voluntarily* from "Military Area No. 1"—the western halves of California, Oregon, and Washington and the southern half of Arizona. But this led to bitter protests from communities and states in the interior against being "used as a dumping ground" for the presumably disloyal and dangerous Japanese, and on March 27 another proclamation ordered the coast Japanese to cease voluntary migration and instead to await controlled evacuation and internment. Soon afterward this order was extended to include "Military Area No. 2"—the other halves of the West Coast states and Arizona.

There were then more than 93,000 Japanese Americans in California, 14,000 in Washington, and 4,000 in Oregon, or a total of about 112,000 in the three coastal states. Of these more than 71,000 were *Nisei* and about 41,000 *Issei.* Nisei were American-born citizens, of whom only a few hundred were more than 35 years old, while a large majority were under 21. Issei were Japanese immigrants, nearly all of whom were adults, since Japanese immigration had virtually ceased when Congress banned it in 1924. Because the Issei were Orientals they had never been eligible for naturalization, and their legal status was now that of enemy aliens. But in any case, the proclamations of the Western Defense Command generally used the word "Japanese" without making a distinction in the matter of citizenship.

During the spring of 1942, under Army supervision, nearly all the West Coast Japanese Americans were confined in improvised "assembly centers" at racetracks, fairgrounds, or livestock exhibition halls. During the summer and fall they were evacuated to more permanent "relocation" camps. There were 10 of these, located in some of the bleakest parts of the continent. Two were in California—at Manzanar in the Owens Valley, and at Tule Lake, between the lava beds region and the Oregon border. Two were in Arkansas. The rest were in Arizona, Utah, Colorado, Wyoming, and Idaho. All but the Arkansas camps were in desert regions, intensely hot in summer and bitterly cold in winter. The buildings were made of wood frame and tar paper.

These barracks cities were called "relocation centers" rather than "concentration camps," and they were under the control of a civilian agency, the War Relocation Authority. The administrators of the WRA were carefully chosen, mostly from the permanent staffs of the Federal Departments of Agriculture and the Interior, and in general they were able and understanding men who wished to allow the internees the maximum of self-government that was possible under the circumstances. But the camps were essentially prisons, surrounded by tall barbed wire fences and guarded by soldiers.

The evacuation was based upon the argument of "military necessity," but this argument was never tenable. The evidence that the Japanese contemplated an attack on the West Coast was trifling and ludicrous. In the evening of February 23, 1942, a lone Japanese submarine fired a few shells from its deck gun at an oil field near Santa Barbara, and did minor damage to a wooden pier. Thirty hours later, at about 2:30 A.M. on February 25, Army antiaircraft guns along the beach at Santa Monica fired several thousand rounds of ammunition at an object in the sky. It was later established that this was only a lost American weather balloon. General DeWitt's headquarters issued a statement that "the aircraft which caused the blackout in the Los Angeles area for several hours this morning have not been identified"; and Secretary Stimson recorded the event in his diary as "the Battle of Los Angeles." But a naval reconnaissance established that there were no Japanese aircraft carriers within range of the coast, and Secretary Knox assured the press that the whole thing was "a false alarm" touched off by "jittery nerves."

The Japanese never contemplated an invasion of the mainland of the United States, and moreover neither General DeWitt nor any other commander ever maintained that such a landing might be attempted. As for the possibility of air raids, the Japanese lost one of their carriers in the Battle of the Coral Sea, May 4–8, 1942; and in the Battle of Midway, June 4–6, they lost four more—all of the carriers they could have committed to any further action in the central Pacific, let alone in the eastern Pacific. Any possibility of an air attack on the American mainland ended with the Battle of Midway. Yet the movement of Japanese-American internees from the local "assembly centers" on the West Coast to the relocation centers in the interior took place *after* that battle.

The logic behind the claim of military necessity becomes even more puzzling when the evacuation from the West Coast is contrasted with the government's policy toward the Japanese Americans in the Hawaiian Islands. Numbering about 160,000—nearly one-third more than the number on the mainland—persons of Japanese ancestry constituted 38.5 percent of the population of Hawaii, as against 0.001 percent of the population of the continental United States, and 0.013 percent of the population of California. Not only did thousands of them live in close proximity to military and naval installations on Oahu, but they actually worked in them. Furthermore they continued to do so after Pearl Harbor, simply because they formed the bulk of the skilled labor on the island and could not have been replaced for months.

For some time before the outbreak of the war the military forces and the Federal Bureau of Investigation had made special efforts to assure the Japanese Americans of Hawaii that if they remained loyal to the United States in a war with Japan they would be fairly treated. Gen. Delos C. Emmons, who succeeded General Short, publicly renewed this pledge on December 21, 1941. Shortly afterward he learned that a Cabinet meeting in Washington had decided on a removal of all Japanese aliens from Oahu to internment camps on other islands. General Emmons protested so bitterly that this decision was reversed, and all major "Japanese relocation" plans for Hawaii were abandoned. A few months later an Army spokesman explained to the Honolulu press that "The shipping situation and the labor shortage make it a *military necessity* to keep most of the people of Japanese blood on the island." [The italics are inserted.]

It was not only the labor force of Hawaii that was dependent on the Japanese Americans at the outbreak of the war. The two Hawaiian National Guard regiments that shared in the task of guarding the islands included many men of Japanese descent. They were not withdrawn from the Guard regiments until May 1942, when sufficient replacements had finally arrived from the West Coast. Then they were formed into the 100th Infantry Battalion. Later, mainland Japanese Americans recruited from relocation camps were enlisted in the all-Nisei 442d Regimental Combat Team. Their units distinguished themselves and suffered heavy losses in the invasion of Italy in the autumn of 1943. The 442d became the most-decorated regiment in the annals of the American Army.

In the words of the official history of *The United States Army in World War II*, "little support for the argument that military necessity required a mass evacuation of the Japanese can be found in contemporary evidence." Instead, in defense of the Army, its official history makes the remarkable suggestion "that the cooperation of the white population of the Pacific states in the national defense effort could not have been . . . assured" if the government and the military had not bowed to "formidable pressure" from West Coast civilians for Japanese-American removal.

On the other hand, the United States Supreme Court in upholding the evacuation maintained that the Army had acted from military necessity, and that in time of war it was not the prerogative of any civilians, even the members of that court itself, to attempt to evaluate the decisions of military men on military matters. With remarkable inconsistency, the Court neglected to recall the judgments that Justice Roberts had pronounced upon the actions of General Short and Admiral Kimmel.

In the Hirabayashi case in 1943 and the Korematsu and Endo cases in 1944, the Supreme Court drastically weakened the constitutional rights of all

Americans in wartime by condoning a massive injustice that had been inflicted on a particular group of Americans because of their race. As Justice Frank Murphy put it in his dissent in the case of Korematsu, the majority of the Court upheld the government and the military in an action that went "over the . . . brink of constitutional power and . . . into the ugly abyss of racism."

Justice Roberts, also dissenting, said that while a temporary or emergency exclusion from the West Coast might have been justified, the imprisonment of the Japanese in concentration camps, solely because of their ancestry and "without evidence or inquiry" as to their "loyalty and good disposition towards the United States," was clearly unconstitutional. And Justice Robert H. Jackson, in his separate dissent, pointed out that the principle approved by the majority decision would thereafter lie about "like a loaded weapon ready for the hand of any authority that can bring forward a plausible claim of an urgent need."

Most of the evacuees were held in the relocation camps for more than two years, until after the War Department revoked the West Coast exclusion orders in December 1944. About half of them returned to the West Coast during 1945 and 1946. In many cases their return was greeted with threats and acts of terrorism; but strong voices were also raised in their behalf. Gen. Joseph W. Stilwell, in particular, denounced the terrorists as "barfly commandos." Mary Masuda, a young woman who had spent two and a half years at the Gila River relocation center, received threats of violence from a group of vigilantes when she returned to her home at Talbert, near Santa Ana. Her brother, a war hero who had been killed in Italy, was posthumously awarded the Distinguished Service Cross. On December 8, 1945, General Stilwell presented Sergeant Masuda's medal to his sister in her home at Talbert, and this sobering incident received wide publicity.

In the postwar years many Californians gradually came to realize the enormity of the mistake that had been made. Many could accept the view of the War Relocation Authority in its final report (1946): "Since we are continually striving, with the better part of our minds, to be a united people, it becomes important for us to understand and evaluate what we did, both officially and unofficially, to this particular racial segment of our population in time of global war."

SELECTED BIBLIOGRAPHY

Sterling L. Brubaker, "The Impact of Federal Government Activities on California's Economic Growth, 1930–1956," Ph.D. thesis, University of California, Berkeley (1959), clarifies the significance of the enormous expansion in Federal spending after 1940.

On the development of California manufacturing in general, see Victor R. Fuchs, *Changes in the Location of Manufacturing in the United*

States since 1929 (1962); Forest G. Hill, "The Shaping of California's Industrial Pattern," *Proceedings of the Thirteenth Annual Conference of the Western Economic Association* (1955); and James J. Parsons, "California Manufacturing," *Geographical Review*, XXXIX (April 1949), 229–241.

Wartime Employment, Production, and Conditions of Work in Shipyards, Bureau of Labor Statistics Bulletin 824 (1945), charts the expansion of shipbuilding from 1940 to 1944. Katherine Archibald, *Wartime Shipyard: a Study in Social Disunity* (1947), is a perceptive record of the problems of group prejudice. "Richmond Took a Beating," *Fortune*, XXXI (February 1945), 262–269, is one of several articles in an issue on West Coast wartime developments. See also U.S. Congress House of Representatives Select Committee to Investigate National Defense Migration, *Hearings* (1941, 1942).

John B. Rae, *Climb to Greatness: The American Aircraft Industry, 1920–1960* (1968), is the standard short account. Others are Kenneth M. Johnson, *Aerial California* (1961), on the years before 1917; Arlene Elliott, "The Rise of Aeronautics in California, 1849–1940," *Southern California Quarterly*, LII (March 1970), 1–32; Frank J. Taylor and Lawton Wright, *Democracy's Air Arsenal* (1947); William G. Cunningham, *The Aircraft Industry, a Study in Industrial Location* (1951); *Fortune*, XXIII (March 1941), *passim*; Arthur P. Allen and Betty V. H. Schneider, *Industrial Relations in the California Aircraft Industry* (1956); and Leonard G. Levenson, "Wartime Development of the Aircraft Industry," *Monthly Labor Review*, LIX (November 1944), 909–910.

On other wartime economic developments see Wytze Gorter and George H. Hildebrand, *The Pacific Coast Maritime Shipping Industry, 1930–1948* (two volumes, 1952–1954); Ewald T. Grether, *The Steel and Steel-using Industries of California* (1946); and Nedra B. Belloc, *Wages in California; War and Postwar Changes* (1948).

Jacobus tenBroek, Edward N. Barnhart, and Floyd W. Matson, *Prejudice, War, and the Constitution* (1954); U.S. Department of the Interior, War Relocation Authority, *WRA; a Story of Human Conservation* (1946); Allan R. Bosworth, *America's Concentration Camps* (1967); and Roger Daniels, *Concentration Camps USA: Japanese Americans and World War II* (1971), are general accounts of the causes, events, and historical and legal significance of the Japanese-American evacuation.

Morton Grodzins, *Americans Betrayed; Politics and the Japanese Evacuation* (1949), stresses the influence of California pressure groups and politicians on the making of the decision. U.S. Army, Western Defense Command, *Final Report; Japanese Evacuation from the West Coast, 1942* (1943), is a distressingly unreliable and misleading apologia, written largely by Col. Karl R. Bendetsen and submitted over the signature of General DeWitt. U.S. Department of the Army, Office of Military History, *Command Decisions* (1959), edited by Kent R. Greenfield, includes a chapter by Stetson Conn on "The Decision to Evacuate the Japanese from the Pacific Coast." This adds much material drawn from the files of the War Department. An essentially similar chapter, revised in several important details, is in Conn et al., *Guarding the United States and Its Outposts* (1964), a volume in the official history of *The United States Army in World War II*.

On the Supreme Court decisions, in addition to the work by tenBroek, Barnhart, and Matson, cited above, see Edward S. Corwin, *Total War and the Constitution* (1947); Eugene V. Rostow, "The Japanese American Cases—a Disaster," *Yale Law Journal*, LIV (June 1945), 489–553; and Sidney Fine, "Mr. Justice Murphy and the Hirabayashi Case," *Pacific Historical Review*, XXXIII (May 1964), 195–210.

Alexander H. Leighton, *The Governing of Men; General Principles and Recommendations Based on Experiences at a Japanese Relocation Camp* (1945), is a psychological study. On the sociological aspects, see Dorothy S. Thomas et al., *The Spoilage* (1946), and *The Salvage* (1952); Leonard Broom and Ruth Riemer, *Removal and Return; the Socioeconomic Effects of the War on Japanese Americans* (1949), which concentrates on Los Angeles County; Mine Okubo, *Citizen 13660* (1946), an enlightening memoir; *Impounded People: Japanese Americans in the Relocation Centers*, written by Edward H. Spicer and others for the War Relocation Authority in 1946 and published in 1969; Harry H. L. Kitano, *Japanese Americans: The Evolution of a Subculture* (1969); Bill Hosokawa, *Nisei: The Quiet Americans* (1969); Audrie Girdner and Anne Loftis, *The Great Betrayal: The Evacuation of the Japanese Americans during World War II* (1969); and the California Historical Society publication *Executive Order 9066*.

Chapter XXXV

MEN OF LETTERS

Robinson Jeffers. California's greatest poet was born in 1887 in Pittsburgh, Pennsylvania, where his father, William Hamilton Jeffers, was a distinguished professor of Biblical literature in a Presbyterian theological seminary. At the age of 5 Robinson Jeffers began to learn Greek and Hebrew. His father was a liberal theologian who taught him to read the Bible as Oriental literature rather than divine revelation.

When the boy was 16 the family moved to Pasadena. He attended Occidental College and then began graduate work at the University of Southern California, where he fell in love with Una Call Kuster, a fellow student who was two years older than he, and who was, unfortunately, the wife of another man. Eight years later Una Kuster finally obtained a divorce, and she and Jeffers were married. They had planned to live in Europe, but the outbreak of the World War made this impractical, and besides they chanced to discover Carmel.

Jeffers immediately recognized the place where he would do his life's work. In the mountains of the Carmel coast he saw "people living amid magnificent unspoiled scenery essentially as they did in the Idyls or the Sagas, or in Homer's Ithaca. Here was life purged of its ephemeral accretions. Men were riding after cattle, or plowing the headland, hovered by white sea-gulls, as they have done for thousands of years."

As yet only a handful of artists and writers lived at Carmel, and Jeffers was able to buy several acres, nearly the whole point of land between the lovely little bay and the mouth of the river. There, with granite carried up from the beach with his own hands, he built Tor House, his home, and Hawk Tower, a separate study with an observation platform where he could watch the hills, the coast, and the sea.

In 1916 he published *Californians,* a volume of poems written in conventional poetic forms. But soon afterward he decided "to shear the rhymetassels from my verse." So instead of rhyme and metre, as one of his best critics, Frederic I. Carpenter, has put it, Jeffers developed "forms directly imitating nature: the rythms of the waves and the tides, the beat of the heart and the blood, and the verbal cadences of unconscious thought and conversational speech."

Quite as unconventional as this singular poetic style were the starkly tragic themes of the long narrative poems that began with *Tamar* (1924) and *Roan Stallion* (1925). Tamar Cauldwell, daughter of a rancher at Point Lobos, committed incest with her brother, and the whole family perished when an insane aunt set fire to the house. In *Roan Stallion* a part-Indian woman named California transferred her affections from her white husband to her horse; and when her husband was being trampled by the stallion in the corral, though she could have saved his life by killing the horse with a rifle she deliberately held her fire until after her husband was dead.

Tamar and California resembled personifications of nonhuman forces of nature, rather than individual human beings, and their stories were inspired in large part by Greek myths, which had vital importance in Jeffers's poetry and thought. The third of his long narratives, *The Tower beyond Tragedy* (1925), took place in ancient Mycenae, and retold the myth of the murder of King Agamemnon by his queen Clytemnestra, and her murder, in turn, by their children Electra and Orestes.

With the publication of these poems in the middle 1920s, the work of Jeffers immediately found a place in the upper levels of American literary reputation. George Sterling, one of the first to recognize Jeffers as a poet of far greater importance than Sterling himself, called him "our western genius," and observed that "one could pick, unerringly, a poem of his from a stack of thousands of others."

The Women at Point Sur (1927) was much less enthusiastically received. Its theme was even more shocking to most readers than the themes of the earlier narratives, though its story was told with equally compelling power and beauty of poetic form and metaphor. Barclay, a minister, after losing his son in the World War, denounced his church, became insane, went to live as a boarder on an isolated ranch, and founded a new religion in which he was God. Then he raped his own daughter. In addition, the plot included episodes of child-murder and suicide.

This poem, as Jeffers explained in one of his letters, was intended to present a psychological theory of the origin of religions in the "personal impurities" and irrational desires of their founders. But Jeffers rejected formal religions, not religion as such. "The Answer," published in *Such Counsels You Gave to Me* (1937), was one of many of his poems which made it clear that his God was in nature:

Then what is the answer? . . .
. . . the wholeness of life and things, the divine beauty
of the universe. Love that, not man
Apart from that.

As Frederic Carpenter has pointed out, "The love of California for the roan stallion . . . suggests Jeffers's idea of 'breaking out of humanity' to a love of nature in all its aspects." This same primordial human yearning had created the myth of Europa, carried away by Zeus in the form of a bull; and the name of Europa probably suggested the name of "California" for Jeffers's heroine.

Jeffers described his own philosophy as "Inhumanism," though he used the term in his own very special sense. He rejected humanism because it overemphasized the rational, the urbane, and the civilized, and because it attached too much importance to human consciousness—the characteristic of man that seemed to set him apart from nature. Jeffers's poems sought to explore the unconscious, the realm of man's "felt nature." But though he read Freud and Jung, Jeffers never sought the aid of a psychotherapist for himself, and both the poet and his wife denied that the circumstances of their own lives had anything to do with his choice of tragic themes.

It seemed, indeed, that no man could have asked more of fortune than to live with a beautiful, talented, and devoted wife in a place that looked north on Carmel Bay and south on Point Lobos, and there to write some of the most unforgettable of modern poetry. But if Jeffers had no conscious feeling of self-blame for loving the wife of another man, and taking her to live in these isolated and beautiful surroundings, the subconscious fear of punishment was there nevertheless. At least a partial awareness of it appeared in "Apology for Bad Dreams," published in the same volume with *Roan Stallion:*

This coast crying out for tragedy like all beautiful places: and
like the passionate spirit of humanity
Pain for its bread: . . . I said in my heart:
'Better invent than suffer: imagine victims
Lest your own flesh be chosen the agonist, or you
Martyr some creature to the beauty of the place.'

It seems clear that the "imagined victims" in his poems suffered horrible punishments so that Jeffers and his wife need not suffer them.

In the 1920s, as Radcliffe Squires has suggested, Jeffers's poetry "castigated a society whose feelings of guilt demanded the castigation," but "the whip seemed excessive when an economic depression descended." People felt more than sufficiently punished by their economic sufferings, and in the '30s Jeffers's popularity and reputation sharply declined. The themes of his long poems continued to be unrelentingly harsh—his trilogy of narratives, *Cawdor* (1928), *Thurso's Landing* (1932), and *Give Your Heart to the Hawks* (1933), dealt with adultery, murder, madness, and suicide. To his personal isolation at Carmel he added an intense political isolationism; and before, during, and after World War II, he was bitterly hostile to America's involvement in it.

Jeffers had no sympathy with the complaint that his poems were full of tragedy and violence. These were the themes of Sophocles and Shakespeare, he pointed out, and they were not out of place in a century in which two World Wars had killed a hundred million people, and a third threatened to exterminate all the rest.

Jeffers was a poet of the atomic age. Always deeply interested in science, he made several visits to Lick Observatory near San Jose, where his younger brother Hamilton was a member of the staff. Astronomy had an important influence on his conception of nature; and in the 1920s when T. S. Eliot supposed that the world would end not with a bang but a whimper, Jeffers was already aware that the opposite might be the case. While physicists moved toward the splitting of the atom, Jeffers conceived a vital analogy between the atomic scientist and the tragic poet. In *Roan Stallion,* in 1925, he wrote that "humanity is the atom to be split," and one of his central conceptions of his own poetry became the idea that the violent shattering of the individual human personalities of his characters, though it might be destructive, would also lead to new discoveries and to the release of tremendous new energy.

He was well aware of the risks. "The Inquisitors," published in *The Double Axe and Other Poems* (1948), described three hills in the Coast Range, squatting like giant Indians to examine the pitiful remnants of human beings after an atomic holocaust.

Jeffers died in 1962, at 75. He has not had, and is not likely to have, any successful imitators.

John Steinbeck. As clearly as Robinson Jeffers was California's most important poet, John Steinbeck might be said to be its most important novelist. Steinbeck's early writing had as distinctive a relation to the Salinas Valley and Monterey as did Jeffers's poems to the Carmel coast. Indeed Steinbeck portrayed the Salinas Valley more thoroughly than any American region has been portrayed in modern fiction, except perhaps William Faulkner's Mississippi.

Steinbeck was born in Salinas in 1902, the year Frank Norris died. He graduated from Salinas High School in 1919 and studied at Stanford University, but, like Norris at Berkeley, he never completed the requirements for a degree.

His first novel, *Cup of Gold* (1929), was an allegorical romance about Sir Henry Morgan, the pirate-governor of Jamaica. From this, Steinbeck turned to the California scene, which would provide the locales for most of his best writing. *The Pastures of Heaven* (1932) was set in a lovely, secluded, fictional valley somewhere near the Salinas Valley. Its unifying theme was the Munroe family, their thoughtless, vicious mediocrity, and the series of episodes in which they ruined the lives of their neighbors by trying to force them into conformity with the Munroes' notions of what was proper and respectable.

Steinbeck's satirizing of pretentious middle-class values was also apparent in *Tortilla Flat* (1935), which won him the beginnings of financial success and critical notice. Though several publishers had rejected this droll account of some Mexican-American idlers in Monterey on the ground that it was too frivolous for the hard times of the depression, the book sold quite well to readers who enjoyed its supposed praise of a group of irresponsible people who were living on next to nothing. Steinbeck himself had been getting along on very little. His earlier novels had brought him only a few hundred dollars in royalties, and when he was writing *Tortilla Flat* he would have been destitute if his father, who had been for several years the treasurer of Monterey County, had not provided him with a small house in Pacific Grove and an allowance of $25 a month.

But the real theme of the novel was satirical and tragic, and not a mere glorification of anarchic escapism. Steinbeck explained in a letter to the publisher that the story was based on the Malory version of the Arthurian legends. He also recorded that the first book he had owned, at the age of 9, was the Caxton edition of Thomas Malory's *Morte d'Arthur,* and that it had had more effect on him than any book except the King James version of the Bible. Allegories based on the Arthurian myths were clearly present in several of his early novels. But in *Tortilla Flat* he burlesqued the Arthurian legends, and did it more effectively though less obviously than Mark Twain did in *A Connecticut Yankee in King Arthur's Court.*

In Dubious Battle, published early in 1936, took its title from a line in Milton's *Paradise Lost,* but dealt with the intensely contemporary and controversial theme of a strike of migratory agricultural laborers, organized and led by Communists. The episodes were largely drawn from an actual strike in the cotton fields of the San Joaquin Valley two years earlier, though the "Torgas Valley" of the novel was a composite locale. It resembled the Pajaro Valley, north of Salinas, but there had been no strike there; and the crop in the novel was apples rather than cotton.

The main characters were also composites, partly drawn, like all of Steinbeck's characters, from persons he had known, including in this case two actual Communists. But the widespread charge that *In Dubious Battle* was communistic propaganda ignored the fact that its picture of the leading Communist organizer of the strike was extremely critical. Mac cared nothing for the fate of the workers, and wished only to use them for the destruction of private ownership. Steinbeck had as deep a dislike for Communism as he had for any system that subordinated the spirit and dignity of the individual to a "Cause."

The strike was not yet over at the end of the novel, but it was obviously doomed, and the battle was "dubious" not in its outcome but in the merits of both sides. Though the novel did not editorialize overtly, Steinbeck was equally critical of the radical leadership of the strike and the ruthlessness of the growers and their vigilante supporters. His most extreme contempt was reserved for the vigilantes. For once he was in full agreement with Mac: "they're the dirtiest guys in any town. . . . They like to hurt people, and they always give it a nice name, patriotism or protecting the constitution. . . . I guess they're about the worst scum in the world." In "The Vigilante," one of the Salinas Valley stories collected in Steinbeck's volume *The Long Valley* (1938), he stressed the relation between mob sadism and sexuality.

Steinbeck made an intensive personal investigation of migratory labor conditions in the middle '30s, and summarized his conclusions in a series of articles in the *San Francisco News* in October 1936, later reprinted as a pamphlet under the title *Their Blood Is Strong.* As background he sketched the history of California's importation of foreign labor, which he called "a disgraceful picture of greed and cruelty." Then he described the new agricultural labor supply, the impoverished native American migrants from the "dust bowl" area. For the solution of the desperate and dangerous problem he recommended that a new state agricultural labor board should help to allot labor and determine fair wages; and that the workers should be helped to form union organizations and to acquire small subsistence farms where they could live when there was no call for migratory labor. Finally, he insisted that vigilante terrorism, "a criminal endangering of the peace of the state," ought to be drastically punished. It was, Steinbeck pointed out, "a system of terrorism that would be unusual in the Fascist nations of the world," and its methods were being "more powerfully and more openly practiced in California than in any other place in the United States."

Of Mice and Men (1938) was a touching allegory of the life of California ranch hands. Made into a successful motion picture, it further increased Steinbeck's reputation. His masterpiece, however, was *The Grapes of Wrath,* published the following year, and narrating the experiences of the Joad family, who were evicted from their farm in the Oklahoma dust bowl, journeyed to California in an ancient automobile, and suffered the miseries of migratory laborers in the San Joaquin Valley. It was "a crime . . . that goes beyond denunciation . . . a failure that topples all our success," Steinbeck wrote, that children were being allowed to die of starvation in the midst of rotting plenty, and that "the understanding and knowledge and skill of the men who make California fruitful" were doing nothing to prevent it.

The Kern County board of supervisors banned *The Grapes of Wrath* from the public schools and libraries under its jurisdiction, and the Associated Farmers launched an unsuccessful campaign to extend the ban to other counties; but the novel won the Pulitzer Prize and was a runaway bestseller. During the next 15 years it was reprinted nearly 50 times in 16 editions in English, and translated into a dozen other languages. Darryl Zanuck of Twentieth Century-Fox made it into a film while it was still at the top of the national bestseller list. He had taken the precaution of sending private detectives to determine the accuracy of

"Migrant Mother." Dorothea Lange (Mrs. Paul S. Taylor) took this famous photograph in 1936 at Nipomo, on Highway 101 south of San Luis Obispo. The family of dust bowl refugees had just sold the tires from its car to buy food. (From the collection of the Farm Security Administration in the Library of Congress)

the novel, and they had reported that actual conditions were even worse than the ones Steinbeck described.

The financial success of *The Grapes of Wrath* enabled Steinbeck to take an extended vacation, which also served as the basis for his next book. He accompanied his friend Edward F. Ricketts, the proprietor of a laboratory of marine biology at Monterey, on an expedition to collect biological specimens in the Gulf of California, and described this experience in *The Sea of Cortez* (1941). The mysteries of biology had always fascinated Steinbeck and had given him a deep reverence for the unity of all life. He regarded human beings as essentially animals—but this view was in no sense derogatory either to the human beings or to the animals. It was a love and respect for life in all its forms. Steinbeck immortalized Ed Ricketts, who deeply shared this feeling, in the character of Doc, the hero of *Cannery Row* (1945).

East of Eden (1952) was a fascinating and powerful novel on which Steinbeck worked with intense and exhausting labor for four years. Its original title was "Salinas Valley," and he began it in order to record, for the two small sons of his second marriage, the story of his maternal ancestors, the Hamiltons, following their migration to the valley after the Civil War. But the fictional family of Adam Trask entered the story and ultimately dominated it. As the final title suggests, the novel became an allegorical reworking of the story of Cain and Abel.

In 1962 Steinbeck's name was added to those of Sinclair Lewis, Ernest Hemingway, and William Faulkner among the very small group of American novelists to win the Nobel Prize for Literature. The award was made to him, in the words of the Secretary of the Swedish Academy, "for his at one and the same time realistic and imaginative writings, distinguished as they are by a sympathetic humor and a social perception. . . . His sympathies always go out to the oppressed, the misfits, and the distressed. . . . In him we find the American temperament also . . . in his great feeling for Nature, for the tilled soil, the waste land, the mountains and the ocean coasts, all an inexhaustible source of inspiration to Steinbeck in the midst of and beyond the world of human beings."

William Saroyan and other writers. Like Steinbeck's Salinas, William Saroyan's native town of Fresno provided much of the best material for his writing career. His parents were born in Armenia, and his father, who was educated for the ministry at the American Presbyterian School in Bitlis, came to Fresno on the promise of a post as minister of an Armenian-speaking congregation, but it failed to materialize. When William was three years old his father died, leaving the family in poverty though rich in the affectionate solidarity among the surviving relatives. From the age of 7 Saroyan sold newspapers on the streets of Fresno. Later he worked as a telegraph messenger and a grape picker. He left school at 15, never received a high school diploma, and never went to college.

His first book, *The Daring Young Man on the Flying Trapeze,* consisted of 26 short stories, written at the rate of one a day in a furnished room in San Francisco in January 1934, when he was 25 years old. The title story described the thoughts and fantasies of a young writer on a day when he had nothing to eat and was completely penniless except for one penny that he found on the sidewalk.

In an autobiographical introduction to a new edition of this volume, published in 1964 with *After Thirty Years* as a prefix to the title, Saroyan recalled the spirit of this early work. "Quite simply, I believed I was a genius," he wrote. "Like my father, I was essentially a preacher. . . . I believed in everything, but most of all in the inherent grace of the unknown and unrevealed potential at the heart of everybody and everything." Part of his joy in writing was his belief "that it could bring love, and therefore meaning and balance, order and equity, to the human race."

Among literary critics, "Saroyanesque" soon became a new word meaning an impetuous and indiscriminate love for all humanity—for all sorts of people and all human situations. This decidedly included his feelings toward women. "I can enjoy a woman I don't love," he wrote, "but I prefer to love any woman I am with."

To Saroyan the vital ingredient in literary style was creative spontaneity, and he worked to establish what he called a "tradition of carelessness," or a "jump in the river and start swimming immediately" style of writing. For many years he was in almost continuous production of hundreds of short stories, often with such engaging titles as "The Celebrated Jumping State of California" and "Love, Here Is My Hat."

His most famous novel, and probably his best, was *The Human Comedy* (1943). It dealt mostly with the alternately touching and delightful experiences of two boys who were called Ulysses and Homer Macauley, but were obviously William Saroyan and his older brother, in a town that was called Ithaca, California, but was obviously Fresno.

He wrote several plays, including *My Heart's in the Highlands, The Time of Your Life,* and *Love's Old Sweet Song,* all produced in 1939, and *The Beautiful People,* produced in 1941. The theme of *My Heart's in the Highlands* was that aspiration is all-important and success quite unimportant. In *The Time of Your Life,* the characters were the habitués of a San Francisco waterfront bar, who were enabled to find their inherent virtue when a wealthy drunk gave them money to pursue their aspirations. This play won a Pulitzer Prize in 1940, but Saroyan declined to accept the $1,000 award because he believed that "any material or official patronage . . . vitiates and embarrasses art at its source." His disrespect for money was one of his most colorful characteristics. When he first began to have money in the mid-1930s he gave much of it away to old gambling acquaintances in Third Street saloons in San Francisco, and this habit so depleted his income that he took to hawking his own books on ferryboats.

Louis B. Mayer, who first brought Saroyan to Hollywood, placed a considerable strain on his ability to love all mankind. In short, Saroyan detested Mayer; and he disliked Hollywood, especially as a place to work and especially in comparison with San Francisco. But *The Human Comedy* and *The Time of Your Life* were made into successful films, in 1943 and 1948.

William Saroyan always took pride in the fact that he had become a writer without the aid of higher education. He had, he felt, made as much of his talents as if he had "gone to Harvard or Yale or Princeton," and as if he had come "from comfortable and cultivated people . . . from English, Irish, Scotch, Welsh, French, German, or other Anglo-Saxon or Nordic stock."

George R. Stewart, on the other hand, had to be content without Saroyan's creditable handicaps. Stewart was born in Pennsylvania of Anglo-Saxon parents;

went to Princeton, where he was a contemporary of Scott Fitzgerald; received a Ph.D. at Columbia; and became a professor of English in the University of California at Berkeley. His first novel was *East of the Giants* (1938), set in pre-gold rush California. *Storm* (1941) was a brilliant description of the meteorological effects of a great low-pressure area that moved from the Pacific across the continent, and of its dramatic effects on the lives of human beings. The storm itself, known as Maria, was the heroine of this novel, which popularized the meteorologists' and foresters' practice of giving storms the names of women. *Fire* (1948) was an analogous treatment of a forest fire and its results. Stewart also wrote many works of nonfiction, several of which are cited in the bibliographies of the present volume.

One of the most curious and striking facts about the history of California literature in the first two-thirds of the 20th century was that during that whole period, in spite of the large number of writers who worked in Hollywood, Los Angeles, or San Francisco, not a single really major novel was written about any of those communities, or about any of the state's other large cities. Nathanael West's *The Day of the Locust* (1939) and Budd Schulberg's *What Makes Sammy Run* (1941) were satires rather than serious attempts at novels of Hollywood; and F. Scott Fitzgerald's *The Last Tycoon* (1941) was unfinished.

Just after World II a new group of poets appeared in San Francisco. Several of them, notably Robert Duncan and William Everson, who later became a Dominican monk and adopted the name of Brother Antoninus, had been conscientious objectors during the war, and were attracted to San Francisco by the circle of pacifists and philosophical anarchists that formed there. The opposition of these poets to all government, and particularly to war, which they regarded as government at its worst, had an important influence on the intellectual atmosphere of the San Francisco Bay area for many years to come. In several articles in national magazines, Kenneth Rexroth did much to publicize "the San Francisco Renaissance" as a name for this movement, in which he was himself an active figure. The establishment of the Poetry Center at San Francisco State College, in 1953, helped to stimulate the growing regional interest in innovative and experimental poetry.

In the mid-'50s the cultural libertarianism of San Francisco attracted another group of writers, particularly from the New York area. Self-styled the "beat generation," they began to achieve notoriety in 1956 with the publication of Jack Kerouac's exuberant and formless novel *On the Road* and Allen Ginsberg's startling *Howl and Other Poems*. The "beat" writers were a different group from the poets of the "San Francisco Renaissance," though they were sometimes lumped with them. They were even more extreme in rebelling against the prevailing norms of society and government and also against the established poetic and literary forms. Kerouac announced in a television interview that "beat," a word of his own coinage, meant "beatific." When the Russians put the first Sputnik into orbit, the San Francisco columnist Herb Caen dubbed the beat generation the "beatniks," and the derisive nickname stuck.

Ginsberg's poems were first published in England, and much of their original fame resulted from their seizure by the San Francisco customs office on the ground that they were obscene. They were then published in San Francisco by Lawrence Ferlinghetti, poet and proprietor of the City Lights Bookshop, a center for many writers and artists. Ferlinghetti was tried and acquitted on a charge of publishing an obscene book, and the publicity of this trial did much to ensure and increase popular interest in the beats and their writings.

Kerouac's novels and Ferlinghetti's poems were relatively gentle and benevolent, but Ginsberg's poetry, though it had a kind of Whitmanesque power, was intensely morbid. His *Howl* consisted of one continuous sentence nearly 2,000 words long, and was filled with references to drugs, tragically unhappy sexual encounters, madness, and suicide, all blamed upon the corruption of the existing form of society. In many poems and speeches Ginsberg inveighed against materialism, technology, the war machine—"all the forces that have assaulted the individual human spirit." Though the beat writers showed flashes of strength and beauty and perceptiveness, they were often unable to distinguish between awareness of the irrational and surrender to it. At its best the movement was one of protest against social values that it saw as bankrupt; at its worst it was a cult of anti-intellectualism and self-destructiveness—a mishmash of jazz, Zen Buddhism, marijuana, and squalor. As Thomas Parkinson observed, the new American Bohemia was as socially irresponsible as the suburbia it rejected.

No less striking than the absence of outstanding novels of California city life in the 20th century was the absence of major fiction about California politics. The nearest approach was *The Ninth Wave* (1956), by Eugene Burdick, a professor of political science. But the plot and the characterizations in that novel were unconvincing—even though it might be argued that they were not much more unbelievable than some of the realities of California politics itself. As both Carey McWilliams and Frederick Bracher have pointed out, the excessive power of pressure groups and the resulting impersonality of California politics discouraged both the emergence of distinguished individual politicians and the writing of good novels about political life.

SELECTED BIBLIOGRAPHY

Robinson Jeffers had the unique honor of becoming, within less than 10 years after the publication of his first major volume of poems, the subject of an important biographical and critical study, and of a full volume of bibliography. These were Lawrence Clark Powell, *Robinson Jeffers; the Man and His Work* (1932, new editions in 1934 and 1940); and S. S. Alberts, *Bibliography of the Works of Robinson Jeffers* (1933). Later studies include Radcliffe Squires,

The Loyalties of Robinson Jeffers (1956); and Frederic I. Carpenter, *Robinson Jeffers* (1962). Melba Berry Bennett, *The Stone Mason of Tor House; the Life and Times of Robinson Jeffers* (1966), is the first full-length biography. See also *The Selected Poetry of Robinson Jeffers* (1938); George Sterling, *Robinson Jeffers, the Man and the Artist* (1926); and David Brower, editor, *Not Man Apart; Lines from Robinson Jeffers; Photographs of the Big Sur Coast* (1965).

Important treatments of Steinbeck are in E. W. Tedlock, Jr. and C. V. Wicker, editors, *Steinbeck and His Critics, a Record of Twenty-five Years; an Anthology with Introduction and Notes* (1957); Peter Lisca, *The Wide World of John Steinbeck* (1958); Warren French, *John Steinbeck* (1961), and *A Companion to THE GRAPES OF WRATH* (1963); and Joseph Fontenrose, *John Steinbeck: an Introduction and Interpretation* (1964).

Most of William Saroyan's writings fictionalize his personal experiences, but several of his books are more explicitly autobiographical. These include *The Twin Adventures: The Adventures of William Saroyan, a Diary—The Adventures of Wesley Jackson, a Novel* (1950); *The Bicycle Rider in Beverley Hills* (1952); *Here Comes, There Goes, You Know Who* (1961); *Not Dying* (1963); and *After Thirty Years: The Daring Young Man on the Flying Trapeze* (1964). See also David Kherdian, *A Bibliography of William Saroyan, 1934–1964* (1966).

Valuable commentaries on California writers are Edmund Wilson, *The Boys in the Back Room* (1941); Frederick Bracher, "California's Literary Regionalism," *American Quarterly*, VII (Fall 1955), 275–284; Lawrence C. Powell, *Land of Fiction; 32 Novels and Stories about Southern California from Ramona to The Loved One* (1952); and Powell's *California Classics; the Creative Literature of the Golden State* (1971).

A balanced collection of "beat" writings and of comments on the movement is Thomas Parkinson, *A Casebook on the Beat* (1961). David Meltzer, *The San Francisco Poets* (1971), is a series of interviews. Bruce Cook, *The Beat Generation* (1971), attempts a literary assessment.

General anthologies of California literature include John and LaRee Caughey, editors, *California Heritage* (1971); and Robert Pearsall and Ursula S. Erickson, editors, *The Californians: Writings of Their Past and Present* (two volumes, 1960). Several hundred novels about California are listed and briefly described in Alice K. Melton, *California in Fiction* (1961).

Chapter XXXVI

CULTURAL TRENDS

William Randolph Hearst and other journalists. Until his death in 1951, at 88, William Randolph Hearst continued to exert a powerful influence in California journalism and in several other aspects of California society and culture. His publishing empire, at its peak in 1932, included 26 newspapers in cities from Boston to Seattle and from Baltimore to Los Angeles. Their Sunday editions had 22.5 percent of the total national circulation. In California, he owned and controlled the *San Francisco Examiner* and *Call-Bulletin,* the *Los Angeles Examiner* and *Herald-Express,* and the *Oakland Post-Enquirer.* In total circulation of California newspapers in 1932, Hearst papers ranked first, second, third, and fifth, with Harry Chandler's *Los Angeles Times* ranking fourth. In San Francisco, the Hearst papers then had 62 percent of the daily circulation, and 72 percent on Sundays; in Los Angeles, 59 percent and 63 percent. Thus a fantastic amount of power and influence was attached to the whims of one man who had never entirely ceased to be a spoiled child.

Hearst had been one of a pair of twins. The other infant had died at birth, and Phoebe Apperson Hearst had been advised that it would be dangerous to have more children. She and her husband then ceased to live as man and wife, and she lavished her affections on her only son. In later years she remarked that "every time Willie feels badly, he goes out and buys something." When his candidate lost the New York gubernatorial election in 1926, he bought a 10th-century Spanish cloister. He had it dismantled stone by stone, crated, and shipped to California.

Among many other things, Hearst also bought a motion-picture company in order to advance the career of his constant companion, the

William Randolph Hearst, Sr. (Courtesy of the San Francisco Examiner)

actress Marion Davies. Later he formed an alliance with the much larger Metro-Goldwyn-Mayer studio, for the same reason. Miss Davies would have preferred roles as a slightly hoydenish comedienne, but her patron always imagined her as a romantic heroine, innocent and noble; he severed their connection with M.G.M. because that company denied Miss Davies the role of Elizabeth Barrett Browning in *The Barretts of Wimpole Street.*

In 1919 Hearst had begun the building of his "castle" at San Simeon, which ultimately cost at least 30 million dollars and was the most expensive and lavish residence, either private or royal, in the world. On one of the largest of his father's ranches was a 2,000-foot eminence overlooking the Pacific. There, during family camping trips and picnics in his childhood, Hearst had experienced the happiest moments of his life. He called it *La Cuesta Encantada,* The Enchanted Hill, and on its summit, with the aid of his mother's favorite architect Julia Morgan, he built three palatial guest houses and a fourth and much larger structure called *La Casa Grande.*

This central castle was never entirely finished because unaccustomed financial stringencies forced him to curtail and then to suspend its construction after 1935. Though Hearst had helped to secure the nomination and election of Franklin D. Roosevelt, he never forgave the President for recommending the New Deal's sharp increase in the graduated income tax. Hearst and his editors denounced this measure as communistic, and seriously argued that the rich were the class "least able" to pay higher taxes, if the capitalist system was to be preserved.

Even so, there were 100 rooms in the castle, many of them transported from Europe and built in, with all their paneling, ceilings, and furniture. The rooms

Hearst Castle. (Courtesy of State of California Division of Highways)

were filled with art objects and antiques, and the gardens and terraces with statuary, from Hearst's splendid personal collections; but his insatiable acquisitiveness made those collections so large that hundreds of pieces remained in dead storage in New York and elsewhere. A huge, rocky hillside was planted with hundreds of full-grown trees at enormous expense because Hearst found its bareness unpleasant. The grounds were stocked with his own private zoo.

In his will Hearst expressed the wish that his castle should go to the University of California as a memorial to his mother, who had made many gifts to the university during her lifetime, and who had served for many years as one of its regents. But the university felt that it lacked the funds to maintain the castle. Hearst's sons then persuaded the state of California to accept it as a gift in 1957. The fears that it would prove a massive and costly white elephant were not borne out. Half a million people visited it within the first two years after its opening as a state monument. Among the attractions of the place, along with its art treasures, was the chance to participate vicariously in the life of a man who had made such a determined attempt to have everything in the world that he wanted.

Even before his death, however, Hearst's newspaper chain had entered a gradual but steady decline, and by 1965 sales and consolidations had reduced the number of Hearst papers to about a third of what it had once been. In California's two principal cities the Hearst *Examiners,* after years of losing money, were forced to surrender the entire daily morning field to the *Los Angeles Times* and the *San Francisco Chronicle*.

For newspapers, as well as for nations, hereditary monarchy has always been a notoriously risky method of choosing top management personnel. Hearst's sons did not approach the journalistic pace that their father had set in his youth and his prime, and although the *Times* and the *Chronicle* were also family concerns, the accidents of their dynastic successions were more fortunate. Their founders had no sons, but they were able to pass on their power effectively through the female line.

Harry Chandler, who succeeded his father-in-law Harrison Gray Otis as publisher of the *Times* in 1917, was even more energetic than Otis himself. Harry's son Norman, who became the publisher in 1945, improved the quality of the paper in many respects. And Norman's son Otis Chandler, who succeeded his father in 1960, improved it considerably more.

The *San Francisco Chronicle* passed from M. H. de Young to his son-in-law George T. Cameron in 1925, and to de Young's grandson Charles de Young Thieriot 30 years later. Under Cameron and his general manager Paul S. Smith the *Chronicle* made a valiant though generally thankless effort to be a West Coast *New York Times*. But under Thieriot and his executive editor Scott Newhall the *Chronicle* launched a much more successful drive to out-Hearst the *Examiner* in entertainment.

The Hearst papers finally gave up the long and debilitating circulation wars with the *Times* and the *Chronicle*. The *Los Angeles Examiner*, in 1962, and the *San Francisco Examiner*, in 1965, ceased publication as morning dailies and were merged with the Hearst evening papers in both cities. In the Sunday field, a new and strange alliance produced the "*San Francisco Sunday Examiner & Chronicle*," with sections independently edited by the *Examiner* and by the *Chronicle*.

Several nationwide trends had combined to force such consolidations. From 1945 to 1965, the cost of newspaper production in large cities increased twice as fast as the income from advertising. At the same time there was an enormous increase in the number of suburban dailies. Both circulation and advertising followed the bulk of the population increase into the suburbs. By 1962, for example, there were 23 suburban daily newspapers in Los Angeles County alone. Still further competition came from television advertising and newscasting.

Though there was much fearful talk about the dangers of the trend to "monopoly" in central-city journalism, the consolidations offered opportunities for the development of stronger and better large-city newspapers.

The arts. San Francisco maintained its reputation as the cultural capital of California without effective challenge until the 1950s, when Los Angeles finally became a serious rival for cultural leadership. The flowering of new public and private facilities for the enjoyment of art and music also increased considerably in several other communities.

For many years after its founding in the middle 1920s the M. H. de Young Memorial Museum in San Francisco's Golden Gate Park remained the principal art gallery on the Pacific Coast. By 1960 its attendance exceeded 1 million persons a year, and on Sundays it often had more visitors than even the Metropolitan Museum of Art in New York City. San Franciscans were so proud of it that they voted overwhelmingly in 1961 for the bond issue that provided a new wing to house the Avery Brundage Collection of Oriental Art.

The California Palace of the Legion of Honor was established in 1924 as a memorial to the California soldiers who died in World War I. Located in Lincoln Park overlooking the Golden Gate, it attracted almost as large an attendance as "the de Young."

These two museums, though they occasionally sponsored exhibitions of contemporary art, were heavily committed to the time-tested and accepted art of the past. The San Francisco Museum of Art, on the other hand, attempted the more difficult role of educating the public in the appreciation of contemporary painting and sculpture. It performed this role without financial support from the city, except for quarters in the Veterans Memorial Building.

The University of California Art Museum at the edge of the Berkeley campus was opened in 1970. Its nucleus had been a gift from Hans Hofmann, pioneer in abstract expressionism, of $250,000 and 45 of his paintings. Half a century earlier, in Munich, Hofmann had founded the first school for the teaching of modern painting. In 1930, the University of California gave him a summer teaching post and thus rescued him from persecution by the rising Nazi movement in Germany. His gratitude for this rescue prompted his munificent gift to the university 33 years later. Though he was penniless when he emigrated to the United States, within a few years his work was being presented in annual exhibitions in New York and the sale of his paintings made him a millionaire, a remarkable achievement for an avant-garde artist.

In addition to the art departments at many of the general college and university campuses in California, specialized institutions were also important in the training of artists. The San Francisco Art Institute, founded in 1874, continued to flourish. In Los Angeles the California Institute of the Arts began to function in 1962 as a merger of the Chouinard Art School, founded in 1921, and the Los Angeles Conservatory of Music, founded in 1883.

Los Angeles in the 1960s was second only to New York as a market for art, both in the number of commercial galleries and in the number of paintings sold.

In 1965 the Los Angeles County Art Museum was installed in magnificent new quarters designed by William Pereira, on Wilshire Boulevard, atop the old La Brea tar bed, and in its first year it attracted a much larger attendance than any other museum in the West. The voters had approved large bond issues for this project, in addition to private funds raised by Edward W. Carter, a department store executive and regent of the state university.

The various components of the Los Angeles County Museum of earlier years were split into separate institutions in the new buildings opened in 1965. On the other hand, in the remarkable development of the Oakland Public Museum in the 1960s, three small museums, separately devoted to history, art, and the sciences, were brought together not only under a single administration, but within a single theme—the culture and natural history of California.

In the field of music, California's chief distinction was the rise of the San Francisco Opera Company. Founded in 1923, it was the second oldest continuous opera group in the United States, after New York's Metropolitan. In quality, it became one of the three outstanding American companies, ranking with the Metropolitan and with Chicago's Lyric.

Grand opera ideally produced is the most spectacular and multisensuous of the performing arts, but also the most expensive. William H. Crocker had proposed the building of a San Francisco opera house in 1913, under a plan in which the Crockers and other wealthy families would make subscriptions in return for the right to have boxes reserved for themselves and their heirs in perpetuity. But the project would have required municipal funds also, and Mayor Rolph felt compelled to veto an appropriation of public money because labor leaders denounced the aristocratic pretensions in Crocker's plan.

Gaetano Merola, a Neapolitan conductor, had visited San Francisco many times, had fallen in love with the city, and had wondered why it had no permanent opera company of its own. His enthusiasm and leadership were catalysts in the establishment of the company in 1923. Nine years later its history entered a second major phase with the opening of the War Memorial Opera House—the first municipally owned opera house in the nation. In 1967 the San Francisco Opera Association and the Los Angeles Music Center announced a plan for the joint production of opera in the two cities.

Among the state's symphony orchestras there was no serious attempt to rival the leadership of the San Francisco Symphony until 1919, when William Andrews Clark, Jr., who had made his fortune in mining in Montana, became the first outstanding patron of music in Southern California by endowing the Los Angeles Philharmonic. In 1922 this orchestra began to present its famous summer concerts under the stars in the new Hollywood Bowl. With 22,000 seats, the Bowl was the world's largest natural amphitheater. For the winter concert series, however, the Philharmonic was long dependent on an unsatisfactory leased auditorium. Los Angeles voters repeatedly rejected bond issues for a municipally owned center for the performing arts. But the intrepid Dorothy Buffum (Mrs. Norman) Chandler, working almost single-handed, finally secured enough private contributions to make possible a magnificent complex of buildings for music and drama at the Civic Center. The largest of these structures, the Pavilion, designed by Welton Becket, was opened in 1964.

The leading symphony orchestras in California continued to be those of San Francisco and Los Angeles; the only other all-professional groups in the state in the mid-1960s were those of Oakland, San Jose, and Santa Clara. But there were partly professional symphonies in Marin County, Sacramento, Fresno, Santa Barbara, Claremont, Long Beach, and San Diego; and there were dozens of other groups made up of talented amateurs.

The idea that the state government should support and encourage the arts began to make limited headway, in spite of many warnings of the dangers attached to governmental involvement in this area. Some were reminded of Napoleon's ill-considered remark: "Complaints have been made that we have no national literature. This is the fault of the minister of the interior." Nevertheless, in 1963 Speaker Jess M. Unruh introduced as Assembly Bill Number One a proposal to create a California Arts Commission. This body was instructed to encourage and develop local arts councils, to stimulate the touring of professional performances and exhibitions, to advise local agencies, to confer awards, and to gather information and make reports. Speaker Unruh was particularly concerned for the development of artistic and cultural resources in the smaller communities of California because he vividly recalled the cultural poverty of the small town in Texas where he had spent his own boyhood. His bill was passed. The commission was appointed by the Governor, and made its first extensive report in 1966; but the appropriations for it were trifling, especially in comparison with those made for the New York State Council on the Arts.

The California legislature's chief measure of encouragement to the cultural resources of small communities in the 1966 session was its choice of one of its own members, Assemblyman Charles B. ("Gus") Garrigus of Reedley (population 5,850), for the long-vacant office of poet laureate of California. This interesting selection followed a debate in which it was emphasized that the office carried no salary. Had fame been the principal criterion, the legislature would have had to select Allen Ginsberg—a most improbable development.

Architecture. At several periods in the 20th century California produced or attracted some of the most talented architects in America. Of these, Willis Polk, Bernard Maybeck, and John Galen Howard in the San Francisco Bay area, the Greene brothers in Pasadena, and Irving Gill in San Diego and Los Angeles had begun their work before the turn of the century, though their most notable achievements came after 1900.

Willis Polk, the son of a San Francisco architect, was trained in the offices of A. Page Brown in San Francisco and Daniel Hudson Burnham in Chicago. Polk collaborated with Brown in the design of San Francisco's Ferry Building in 1896, and assisted Burnham in 1903 in drafting the elaborate and ill-fated San Francisco master plan, of which the idea of the Civic Center was the only major feature actually adopted.

After the earthquake and fire, Polk became known as "the man who rebuilt San Francisco," an exaggerated description which he himself did not hesitate to endorse. The Chronicle Building, the Mills Building, the Pacific Union Club, and the restoration of Mission Dolores, as well as many of the finest residences in the city, were among his more famous assignments.

Most of Polk's downtown commercial buildings were of a monumental and conservative style, with much neoclassical ornamentation, but in 1918 he produced the world's first "glass skyscraper." This was the Hallidie Building on Sutter near Montgomery, appropriately named for another local pioneer, the inventor of the cable car. Polk could not entirely forego the use of decoration, in the form of lacy ironwork that contrasted oddly with the great glass facade; but his Hallidie Building was the first really outstanding architectural innovation ever attempted in San Francisco.

Polk was a diminutive man, of considerable vanity along with his considerable genius. Late in his career when someone unearthed the fact that he had never had an architect's license, he replied that he was no mere architect but "a master builder."

Bernard Maybeck, too, had his own special genius for the new as well as for the old in architecture. To Maybeck all ages were the present. He was equally interested in the industrial environment of the 20th century and in the Romanesque and Gothic structures he had admired as a student in Paris, and these interests combined to produce a remarkably freewheeling eclecticism.

In 1896, when Phoebe Apperson Hearst visited the campus of the University of California with an offer to endow a mining building as a memorial to her late husband, Maybeck was a young man holding a bread-and-butter job as a teacher of descriptive geometry. He was also the university's nearest approach to a professor of architecture, and as such he was delegated to encourage Mrs. Hearst's tentative interest in providing future buildings for the campus. To his own amazement he succeeded in persuading her to endow a lavish international architectural competition for a master plan.

Emile Benard of Paris, who won the prize, refused to come to Berkeley in order to put his own plan into practice. Instead John Galen Howard of New York was brought to Berkeley in 1901 to supervise the plan's execution. The Benard plan for the campus gradually became the Howard plan. Howard became professor of architecture and Maybeck was out of a job.

During the next few years Maybeck designed many residences in Berkeley and San Francisco, most of them immediately recognizable as "Maybecks" because of his distinctive blend of Gothic Revival with Bay Region Redwood Shingle.

His most striking design, however, was that of the Christian Science Church on Dwight Way in Berkeley, built in 1910. Maybeck's own religious feelings were as eclectic as his architectural impulses, and when a group of ladies asked him to build them a church with materials "that are what they claim to be, not imitations," he was reminded of the sincere faith of the men who had built the early Romanesque churches in southern France. They would, he was sure, have used the most modern materials obtainable. From the industrial architecture of his own time, Maybeck took asbestos panels and steel factory sash for the windows. Cast concrete and local redwood completed the list of materials. Supporting the exterior were square fluted columns of concrete. Atop each column was a large trellis of redwood beams to carry wistaria vines. With complete confidence and amazing success Maybeck intermingled Romanesque columns with the timber work of a Japanese shrine, with Gothic tracery, and with Byzantine decoration.

His most famous building was the Palace of Fine Arts, with its delightful lagoon, designed for the Panama Pacific International Exposition of 1915. Originally the architectural committee had excluded Maybeck from the planning of the fair, on the ground that he had never before designed a large structure. The committee had assigned the Palace of Fine Arts to Willis Polk, who found himself too busy with other phases of the exposition. Polk employed Maybeck as a draftsman and paid him by the hour. The resulting structure became such a beloved part of the San Francisco landscape that when its temporary materials eventually crumbled it was rebuilt in permanent form.

In Pasadena the brothers Charles and Henry Greene created the California Bungalow style, which not only dominated residential architecture in Southern California in the early 20th century but was also widely imitated in other states. "Bungalow" was originally a British-Indian corruption of the word "Bengali," and referred to a single-storied house or cottage designed for English civil servants during short terms of residence. Pasadena attracted many wealthy people who also wanted fairly simple dwellings for part-time occupancy.

In 1903 the Greene brothers designed for Arturo Bandini a "bungalow" modeled on the plan of the early California adobes, though built of redwood. The rooms were grouped around three sides of a patio or central court, enclosed on the fourth side by a wooden, flower-covered pergola. The patio was an outdoor living room, and there was great freedom of movement between the indoor and outdoor parts of the house.

The Greenes acquired so many wealthy clients that virtually all of their later houses were large and expensive. But their many imitators designed thousands of modest bungalows that were pleasant, practical, and enormously popular as homes, though they lacked the quality of the Greene brothers' fine wood craftsmanship.

The first California architect to be deeply committed to modernism was Irving Gill. Like Frank Lloyd Wright, Gill was trained as a draftsman under Louis H. Sullivan in Chicago. Sullivan's motto was that "form follows function," and chronologically, at least, he was the father of architectural modernism. Like the later modernists, Sullivan complained bitterly that the Chicago Columbian Exposition of 1893, and the classical revival that it produced, had set back the advance of modern architecture by 50 years.

Poor health brought Gill to San Diego in 1893, and there he developed a highly original style, using plaster-coated reinforced concrete walls, flat roofs, and simple windows, all with an austerely complete absence of ornament. When planning began for San Diego's Panama Pacific Exposition to be held in 1915, Gill was the city's best known architect; but the local authorities entrusted the control of the building plans for the fair to Bertram Goodhue of New York, who had written a book on Spanish colonial architecture in Mexico.

Goodhue, in his California Building and other permanent structures for the San Diego exposition, revived the rich and exuberant but also extravagant and capricious ornamentation that José Churriguera had made the dominant style of architecture in Spain and Mexico in the late 17th and early 18th centuries. Many of the mission buildings of Mexico and California had been naïve examples of that style, much modified by the lack of trained workmen. For many years after the San Diego fair there was a great vogue for the Churrigueresque in California, with the towers of Hearst's castle at San Simeon as a notable example.

Nothing could have been in more extreme contrast with the work of Irving Gill. The San Diego exposition and its revival of Churrigueresque disheartened Gill and set back the public acceptance of his ideas in much the same way that the Chicago fair and its classical revival had shattered the promising career of Louis Sullivan and stunted the progress of his work. Gill gave up his practice in San Diego and moved his office to Los Angeles, where he received only a few commissions.

Bertram Goodhue did something to redeem himself in the eyes of modernists by finding a new idiom in his design for the Los Angeles Public Library, built in 1925. This was the first public building in Los Angeles to integrate the murals and sculpture with the design of the building as a whole.

When modernism finally began to achieve genuine acceptance in California it was largely through the work of Richard Neutra, an Austrian architect who settled in Los Angeles in 1926. In Vienna, Neutra had studied under Adolf Loos, who believed that "the evolution of culture marches with the elimination of ornament from useful objects." Loos had been one of the first to realize what he called "the splendour of industry and its close connections with aesthetics." Neutra was one of the small international group, including Adolf Loos and Frank Lloyd Wright, who achieved an early realization that the machine was at the base of the new architecture, and not an evil spirit to be feared and exorcised.

Neutra and other architects of the "contemporary" or "international" style made use of many of the new materials and methods that machine production made possible. Examples were their uses of plate glass, of prefabricated structural parts, and of reinforced concrete as a self-supporting slab. Employing such modern materials and taking particular advantage of the mild climate to make the fullest use of sliding glass doors (or rather walls), Neutra designed some of the most delightful and beautiful homes, schools, and commercial buildings in Southern California.

Neutra's enthusiasm for the region was a spur to his talents. "Man loves to immigrate to the south," he wrote. "Like all Nordic barbarians we want to go to sunny Hellas, or to the land where the lemon blooms and no icy storms trouble us."

A contemporary of Neutra's, also from Vienna, was R. M. Schindler, whose distinctive features and flowing hair made him resemble Rodin's bust of Balzac. Schindler was a master of hillside planning, and of new designs for small houses, to which he gave an informal dignity that did much to bring residential architecture in Los Angeles out of a long period of provincialism.

After the middle of the century, the reasons for the existence of a distinctive regional style in California tended to disappear, as materials, methods of building, and purposes of building, though increasingly diverse, also became increasingly common to many parts of the country. With the spread of air conditioning, even the regional variations in climate became less significant. In the words of the San Francisco architect Thomas S. Creighton, a Neutra house in Wisconsin had become very much like a Neutra house in Southern California, and "the ranch house is just as applicable (or, should I say, equally inappropriate) on Long Island as in Orange County." A continued search for "regional" styles in architecture, Creighton thought, would be "as fruitless as any other copying of the work of a previous period. . . . Where architects strive for a 'local' expression, one usually finds only surface clichés and borrowed mannerisms." The need was not for some new "California style," but for new architectural concepts that would reflect new advances in American city and regional planning, and new dimensions in education, health care, penology, travel, and many other activities.

Education. In the years of headlong growth and general prosperity that followed World War II, California's public schools remained impoverished. The state spent more than 40 percent of its budget for education, and its per capita expenditures for public schools were among the highest in the country—but these figures were grossly misleading because California's school-age population grew twice as fast as its general population. Between 1950 and 1960, while the total number of people in the state was increasing by roughly 50 percent, public school enrollment grew by more than 100 percent. An unprecedentedly large proportion of the people who were migrating to California were young married couples, able and inclined to bear numerous children. The schools were chronically short of money, of classroom space, of teachers—of everything, in fact, except pupils. And no relief was in sight. By conservative estimate, the California public school enrollment of 3 million in 1960 would be doubled by 1970.

To make matters worse, California's systems of public school administration and finance were cumbersome and antiquated. In 1962 the voters took out their dissatisfactions with the public schools by electing as state superintendent of public instruction the ultraconservative polemicist Max Rafferty, a former physical education teacher. In the same year they reelected the liberal Democratic Governor Edmund G. Brown; and since the Governor appointed the state board of education, the result was a series of bitter and continuous conflicts between Superintendent Rafferty and the state board under the chairmanship of Thomas W. Braden, a strongly liberal newspaper publisher from Oceanside. The elective-superintendent system compared very unfavorably with the New York plan, in which the state board of education selected a well-qualified chief state school officer who administered a budget large enough to enable him to develop an effective state department of education.

The tax structure underlying California school finance was obsolete and inadequate. Local property taxes were approaching the saturation point, and there were vast inequalities in the amounts of taxable property in the various school districts. The bulk of state school funds went to the poorer districts, but this fell far short of removing the inequities. Even in many wealthy districts the voters often rejected school bond issues, partly because the California constitution required a two-thirds vote for such bonds. Only three other states had so high a requirement—more than half the states required only a simple majority, and in the rest the provision ranged from 55 to 60 percent.

Many economists began to suggest that the state should take over the functions of local tax assessment to insure equal treatment for all, though achievement of this reform was probably far in the future. That property tax assessments in many localities were not only inequitable but corrupt was evident in 1966 when assessment officials of San Francisco, Alameda, and San Diego Counties were convicted of systematic bribetaking.

Another reform proposal called for the consolidation of many small neighboring school districts into larger and more efficient ones; but although the need for this change was glaringly obvious, it met intense resistance from local school administrators and district board members.

The ever-increasing annual tidal waves of postwar babies that flooded into the public schools in the 1950s began to inundate the colleges and universities in the following decade. But the state was considerably more successful in providing for the enormous growth of public higher education than it was in coping with its public school problems. In addition to establishing the largest and best state university system in the country, California was also outstanding in the development of state colleges and junior colleges.

The state college system traced its origin to 1862, when a two-year normal school was established in San Francisco. This was moved to San Jose in 1870. Other such schools were later established in various parts of the state, and their programs lengthened to four years. They were promoted to the rank of "teachers' colleges" in 1921, and designated as general "state colleges" in 1935.

The beginnings of two-year junior colleges stemmed from the passage of a state law in 1907 authorizing the governing boards of city, district, or county high schools to establish post-high school courses. Fresno established the first public junior college in the United States in 1910, and California has since led all the states in the establishment and support of such institutions. By mid-century they had begun to be called "city colleges" or "community colleges," though state policy prevented them from expanding their programs to four years.

There was a *Report of a Survey of the Needs of California in Higher Education* in 1948, and a *Restudy of the Needs . . .* in 1955. Each of these sets of proposals, at the time of its publication, seemed impressively satisfactory to some and ridiculously overambitious and expensive to others; but each proved to be out of date and insufficient, even before it was printed. As projections continued to skyrocket, it seemed that new college and university campuses would be needed in almost incredible numbers. Moreover, there was no adequate system of coordinating the plans for expansion on the part of the university, the state colleges, and the junior colleges, which were engaged in sharp rivalries with each other, and often presented conflicting demands.

In 1959 the legislature authorized a survey team, made up of representatives of both public and private institutions of higher education, to prepare a master plan. This plan was then embodied in the Donohoe Higher Education Act of 1960, named for Miss Dorothy Donohoe, a member of the state assembly from Kern County. The state colleges, which had been inadequately governed by the state board of education, were placed under a state college board of trustees, generally modeled on the university's board of regents except that the terms of the appointed members were for 8 years instead of 16. A Coordinating Council for Higher Education was created, with representatives from the university, state colleges, junior colleges, and private institutions.

Under this master plan the choosing of locations for new campuses proceeded in a much better coordinated fashion than it ever had before. By 1965 there were 21 state colleges and 77 junior colleges; and the state university had 8 general campuses as well as a number of specialized installations.

Five of the state university's general campuses had been created before 1960. At Los Angeles, a normal school had become the "University of California, Southern Branch" in 1919. This had become "U.C.L.A." in 1931, and by 1950 its student body was almost as large as the one at Berkeley. Santa Barbara State College became the University of California, Santa Barbara, in 1944. In the late 1940s, colleges of letters and science were established at Davis and at Riverside, in connection with what had originally been branches of the university-wide college of agriculture. After 1960, under the master plan, new general campuses of the university were established at Santa Cruz, Irvine, and San Diego. In 1971, the legislature authorized the changing of the names of a number of the "state colleges" to "state universities."

SELECTED BIBLIOGRAPHY

W. A. Swanberg, *Citizen Hearst* (1961), is the best biography. Several of the other works previously cited in the bibliography of Chapter XXII for the earlier part of Hearst's long career are relevant for the later part of it as well. See also Rodney P. Carlisle, "The Political Ideas and Influence of William Randolph Hearst, 1928–1936," Ph.D. thesis, University of California, Berkeley (1965); and Oscar Lewis, *Fabulous San Simeon, a History of the Hearst Castle* (1958). Robert A. Rosenstone, "Manchester Boddy and the L. A. Daily News," *California Historical Society Quarterly*, XLIX (December 1970), 291–307, describes the only major liberal newspaper in Los Angeles from 1926 to 1952. William Rivers and David Rubin, *A Region's Press: Anatomy of Newspapers in the San Francisco Bay Area* (1971), is a critical analysis from a liberal viewpoint. Paul C. Smith, *Personal File* (1964), is a good memoir.

The Arts in California (1966), the first general report of the California Arts Commission, surveys the cultural and artistic resources of the state in 1965. Mel Scott, *Partnership in the Arts: Public and Private Support of Cultural Activities in the San Francisco Bay Area* (1963), and *The States and the Arts: The California Arts Commission and the Emerging Federal-State Partnership* (1971), urge greater public support. California, University, *The Cultural Arts* (1964), is the transcript of Conference II in a series on *California and the Challenge of Growth.*

Howard Swan, *History of Music in the Southwest, 1825–1950* (1952) is a social history with music as its central thread. Consult also Arthur Bloomfield, *The San Francisco Opera, 1923–1961* (1961); Ronald L. Davis, *A History of Opera in the American West* (1965); Isabel M. Jones, *Hollywood Bowl* (1936); José Rodríguez, editor, *Music and Dance in California* (1940); and Richard D. Saunders, editor, *Music and Dance in California and the West* (1948).

Esther McCoy, *Five California Architects* (1960), describes the careers of Maybeck, the two Greene brothers, Gill, and Schindler. An excellent sequel is the same author's study of *Richard Neutra* (1960). See also Judd L. Kahn, "Imperial San Francisco: History of a Vision," Ph.D. thesis, University of California, Berkeley (1971); Roger R. Olmsted and T. H. Watkins, *Here Today: San Francisco's Architectural Heritage* (1968); Oscar Lewis, *Here Lived the Californians* (1957); Harold Gilliam and Phil Palmer, *The Face of San Francisco* (1960); Esther McCoy, *Modern California Houses; Case Study Houses, 1945–1962* (1962); Frank Harris, editor, *A Guide to Contemporary Architecture in Southern California* (1951); Douglas Honnold, *Southern California Architecture, 1769–1956* (1956); W. Boesiger, editor, *Richard Neutra, Buildings and Projects* (1951), with its supplement (1959); Reyner Banham,

Los Angeles: The Architecture of Four Ecologies (1971); and Helen M. Ferris, "Irving John Gill," *Journal of San Diego History*, XVII (Fall 1971).

Material on the history and problems of the public schools may be found in Roy W. Cloud, *Education in California; Leaders, Organizations, and Accomplishments of the First Hundred Years* (1952); James C. Stone, *California's Commitment to Public Education* (1961); James C. Stone and R. Ross Hempstead, *California Education Today* (1968); Theodore L. Reller, *Problems of Public Education in the San Francisco Bay Area* (1963); and two Ph.D. theses, University of California, Berkeley: Lee S. Dolson, "Administration of the San Francisco Public Schools, 1847 to 1947" (1964), and Leighton Johnson, "Development of the Central State Agency for Public Education in California" (1951).

Arthur G. Coons, *Crises in California Higher Education* (1969), is a memoir of the creation and experience of the Coordinating Council, 1959–1968. Ernest G. Palola et al., *Higher Education by Design: The Sociology of Planning* (1970), includes a major section on the master plan. Merton E. Hill traces *The Junior College Movement in California, 1907–1948* (1949).

Verne A. Stadtman, *The University of California, 1868–1968* (1970), a valuable general history, heads the list of the state university's centennial publications. Others are *The Centennial Record* (1968), an encyclopedia of university facts edited by Stadtman; Irving Stone, editor, *There Was Light: Autobiography of a University* (1970), a collection of short memoirs; and Albert G. Pickerel and May Dornin, *The University of California: a Pictorial History* (1968).

Other institutional histories include Edith R. Mirrielees, *Stanford: The Story of a University* (1959); Manuel P. Servín and Iris H. Wilson, *Southern California and Its University* (1969); Andrew Hamilton and John B. Backson, *UCLA on the Move* (1969); Benjamin F. Gilbert, *Pioneers for One Hundred Years, San Jose State College, 1857–1957* (1957); Andrew F. Rolle, *Occidental College: The First Seventy-five Years, 1887–1962* (1962); Charles W. Cooper, *Whittier: Independent College in California; Founded by Quakers, 1887* (1967); and Mary D. McNamee, *Light in the Valley: The Story of California's College of Notre Dame* (1967).

Chapter XXXVII

REPUBLICAN ASCENDANCY

THE ROLLS of registered voters show that the great depression of the 1930s had converted California from an overwhelmingly Republican to a heavily Democratic state. In 1930 the number of Californians registered as Democrats had been only 22 percent of the two-party registration. In 1936 it had risen to 60 percent, and this three-to-two superiority of Democratic over Republican voters continued with little variation for decades afterward. Yet from 1942 until 1958 the preponderantly Democratic voters of California elected heavy majorities of Republicans to state offices.

"Nonpartisanship" favors the Republicans. More than ever before, the political conditions of the depressed '30s had identified the Republicans as the party of the "haves" and the Democrats as the party of the "have-nots." A large majority of businessmen continued to be Republicans. So did a substantial proportion of white Anglo-Saxon Protestants. The Democrats, on the other hand, drew the bulk of their following from labor, the unemployed, and ethnic and religious minority groups. Most of the huge increase in Democratic registration in the early '30s was made up of citizens who had never taken the trouble to register before, and who now did so in desperation out of a desire to vote for a government that would take a greater interest in the welfare of the less advantaged members of society.

All of this meant, however, that most Democratic voters were less educated and less informed than most Republican voters. In this situation California's peculiar cross-filing law tended to keep Republican incumbents in office. Under that law the party affiliations of candidates did not appear on the primary election ballot, but a candidate running for reelection was listed first, and identified as "Incumbent." Hundreds of thousands of Democratic voters were quite unaware that the incumbent whose name appeared on the Democratic primary ballot could be and in fact usually was a Republican. Under this system, three-fourths of the elections to state offices were usually won in the primaries by incumbents who won the nominations of both major parties. In the legislative session of 1945, for example, 36 of the 40 state senators had been elected in the primaries, and most of them were Republican incumbents.

In other respects, also, the Republicans were in a much better position than the Democrats to cope with the "nonpartisan" system (or rather the antiparty system), which the Republican progressives under Hiram Johnson had introduced. The Republicans not only had most of the experienced and successful candidates; they also had far more money for political campaigning, and they had the support of a great majority of the newspapers, including the three most influential ones, the *Los Angeles Times,* the *San Francisco Chronicle,* and the *Oakland Tribune.*

A newspaper is ordinarily a business enterprise, dependent for the bulk of its income on the advertising of other business enterprises. Consequently most newspaper publishers preferred the Republican party, with its orientation toward business interests, low taxes, and a minimum of governmental control. Remembering the preponderance of Democratic voters, however, California newspapers tended to support Republican candidates as individuals without overstressing their party affiliation. And the papers often spoke favorably of the group of conservative Democratic assemblymen who called themselves the "economy bloc."

The governorship of Earl Warren. The California Republicans also found a leader who was ideally qualified to turn the state's nonpartisan tradition to Republican advantage. Earl Warren did this so successfully that when he was elected to his second term as Governor in 1946 he won the Democratic as well as the Republican nomination, and became the only California Governor ever elected in the primary.

Warren was born in Los Angeles in 1891, and grew up in Kern City, a railroad town near Bakersfield. His father, who had come from Norway and whose name was derived from the Norwegian name "Vaare," was a master car repairman for the Southern Pacific, and later a real estate broker.

Like Hiram Johnson, his political hero, Warren studied at the University of California in Berkeley and made his early political reputation as a public prosecutor. But the personalities of the two men were very different. Johnson was emotional and volatile; Warren was calm and almost stolid. Johnson's courtroom manner, when he served as the deputy prosecutor in the trial of Abe Ruef, had been flamboyant. Warren, as district attorney of Alameda County in the 1920s and '30s, was equally effective but more judicious, and more concerned for the legal rights of the accused.

After a term as state attorney general, Warren easily defeated Culbert L.

Olson for the governorship in 1942. During the war years when California enjoyed the unprecedented blessing of a large surplus of revenue from the wartime boom, Warren became a very popular Governor. He sponsored reductions in taxes, and still was able to preserve a surplus in the treasury for the postwar expansion of such services as highways and public higher education to keep up with the state's tremendous growth.

In 1945 Warren alarmed his conservative supporters by recommending a state compulsory health insurance law. He carried a private medical and hospital insurance policy for himself, his wife, and their six children, but he also felt great concern for the tragedy that major illness could bring to less fortunate families, and he recalled from childhood his father's moving account of the loss of an uncle who had died because there was no money to pay for a doctor. Some of the more advanced Republican progressives, led by Chester Rowell, had advocated state health insurance as early as 1916, but this, along with many other social reforms, had been a casualty of World War I. Governor Olson had revived the proposal, but the opposition of the California Medical Association and the private insurance companies, in alliance with conservative interests in general, had always defeated it. The same alliance now defeated Warren's proposals also, and the experience did much to disillusion him with the conservative elements in the Republican party.

The oil and trucking lobbies disillusioned him further by their resistance to an increase in the gasoline tax, which Warren requested in 1947 in order to pay for a great expansion of state highways and freeways. Sam Collins, speaker of the assembly, permitted an oil lobbyist to use the speaker's office as a command post for the battle against the tax bill, though a compromise increase was finally agreed upon. As Warren pointed out, the oil and trucking interests were remarkably shortsighted in their opposition to the measure, since it made possible a new statewide network of freeways that increased the sale of gasoline and greatly aided the growth of the trucking industry.

In his election to an unprecedented third term as Governor of California in 1950, Warren did not quite repeat his triumph of 1946 by winning the Democratic as well as the Republican nomination in the primary, but in the general election in November he received a million votes more than the Democratic nominee, Congressman James Roosevelt of Los Angeles.

Democrats often complained that Warren represented himself as nonpartisan whenever he ran for Governor, but that in presidential years he was strictly a Republican. As temporary chairman and keynote speaker of the Republican national convention in 1944 he delivered an intensely partisan address. In 1948—the only election he ever lost—he was the Republican nominee for Vice President, as the running mate of Governor Thomas E. Dewey of New York. In 1952 Warren was an important contender for the Republican presidential nomination, which he would probably have received as the compromise candidate if the convention had not managed to break the deadlock between Senator Robert A. Taft and Gen. Dwight D. Eisenhower.

In September 1953, after the death of Chief Justice Frederick M. Vinson, President Eisenhower appointed Governor Warren as Chief Justice of the United States.

The power of special interests. Cross-filing and other antiparty laws had been designed to destroy the power of corrupt "political machines" in California. But in weakening the power and responsibility of the party organization, these laws opened the way for an extraordinary development of the interest-group machine, which filled the power vacuum. Arthur H. Samish, a lobbyist for a coalition of liquor, oil, bus, trucking, mining, banking, billboard, theatrical, racetrack, and other interests, came to have almost as much power in the 1930s and 1940s as William F. Herrin had exercised at the turn of the century.

Lobbying has often been known as "the fourth branch of government," or as "the third house" of a legislature. In fact, the lawmaking process in any democratic government would be crippled if the legislative body tried to operate without the constant flow of information from representatives of interested groups. But the corrupt use of power and especially the power of money to influence legislation and the elections of legislators has always been a menace to democracy. The California constitution of 1879 stated that "Any person who seeks to influence the vote of a member of the Legislature by bribery, promise of reward, intimidation, or any other dishonest means, shall be guilty of lobbying, which is hereby declared a felony." But no penalty was specified, and no one was ever convicted under this provision. The line between good and bad lobbying proved very hard to draw.

Arthur H. Samish, king of the California lobbyists, began his career in 1924 as "secretary-manager" of a group of small bus companies called the Motor Carriers' Association. After the repeal of the Eighteenth Amendment he organized the state's brewers, distillers, and tavernkeepers into a kind of prosaloon league, and in 1935 he made a contract with the California State Brewers' Association providing an assessment of 5 cents on every barrel of beer for a political fund to be dispensed by Samish with no accounting. In later years he often reminded his clients in the liquor industry that as a result of his efforts California had the lowest liquor taxes in the nation. He also reminded the oil companies which retained him as a lobbyist that oil severance taxes in Louisiana and Texas were about a hundred times as high as in California.

In 1938 the Sacramento grand jury employed a private detective named Howard R. Philbrick to investigate charges of attempts to bribe members of the state senate. Philbrick reported finding "ample evidence that corruption, direct and indirect, has influenced the course of legislation." Samish, Philbrick discovered, had received or controlled about $500,000 during the previous three years, and "some of his clients undoubtedly paid more in fees to Mr. Samish than they paid in state taxes for the support of all legitimate functions of state government." The basis of his method was "to acquire influence with a group of

Legislators through campaign contributions or other favors and then to sell that influence to industries concerned with legislation."

When the Philbrick Report appeared in the daily journal of the state senate on April 4, 1939, the senate ordered the issue destroyed and reprinted without the report, but Governor Culbert L. Olson ordered 15,000 copies printed at the expense of the Governor's office. Philbrick recommended legislation to require full disclosure of the financial transactions of lobbyists; but although Olson pressed for this and other reforms of lobbying, nothing was done.

Ten years later, on August 13 and 20, 1949, *Collier's* magazine published another exposé called "The Secret Boss of California." Oddly enough, Samish himself provided some of the most spectacular material for these articles in an interview with their author, Lester Velie. Forgetting, for once, the importance of secrecy in his operations, and giving way to the most arrogant braggadocio, Samish posed for a color photograph in his hotel suite at the state capital. On his knee he held a ventriloquist's dummy which he addressed as "Mr. Legislature."

The appearance of such an article and especially of such a picture in a national magazine finally compelled the California legislature to take some sort of action. Governor Earl Warren, when Velie asked him whether it was he or Samish who had more influence with the legislature, replied that "On matters that affect his clients, Artie unquestionably has more power than the governor." Warren asked for new restrictions on lobbying in a special session in December 1949, but the legislature would pass only a compromise bill that he considered inadequate. This law required lobbyists to register and to file monthly financial statements, but these statements usually proved to be so vague that they were practically meaningless.

The downfall of Samish resulted from his failure to report his income and expenditures to the Federal government. In 1953 he was convicted of income tax evasion, and later served two years in a Federal penitentiary. The state assembly reorganized its committee system in 1953 to eliminate Samish's influence. The next year one former speaker of the assembly, Charles W. Lyon, was convicted of bribery in liquor license transactions, and another former speaker, Sam Collins, was indicted, but released after two hung juries.

In addition to lobbying, which gained such a dangerous degree of influence over the California legislature, special interests also found another powerful weapon in the professional campaign management firm—a distinctive contribution of California to American politics. The "publicity" for American political campaigns had previously been handled, as Carey McWilliams put it, by "broken down politicians and alcoholic camp followers." But in the 1930s an organization called Campaigns, Inc., a remarkable partnership of two Californians, Clem Whitaker and Leone Baxter, revolutionized political campaigning by making carefully planned use of mass media and of the commercial techniques of the advertising industry. It was natural that the first full-fledged pro-

Arthur H. Samish and "Mr. Legislature." Taking photographs for Collier's, *Fred Lyon caught Samish in this remarkable pose in his suite at the Senator Hotel in Sacramento. (Courtesy of Fred Lyon)*

fessional campaign management firm in the United States should have developed in California, because of the state's lack of party organization, its constant influx of new voters, and its extraordinarily frequent use of the initiative and the referendum.

Clem Whitaker was a reporter in Sacramento at the age of 17. Within a few years he was operating his own Capitol News Bureau, furnishing syndicated news on state politics to more than 80 California papers. In 1933 he met Leone Baxter, an articulate and attractive young widow who worked for the Redding Chamber of Commerce in opposition to the Pacific Gas and Electric Company's referendum campaign against the state's Central Valley Project law. Joining forces, Whitaker and Baxter organized the countercampaign that defeated the referendum by a narrow margin. In 1934 Whitaker and Baxter managed the Republican campaign against Upton Sinclair. And though they later expressed regret at some of the shabbier devices they felt compelled to use against him, it was this campaign that firmly established their reputation. The partners were married in 1938.

For the next 20 years their support decided many of the key issues of California politics. They usually managed the campaigns for or against five or six initiative or referendum propositions in every state election. They opposed Ham 'n Eggs and reapportionment of the state senate, and worked for higher salaries for teachers, for state aid to public schools, and for the state employees' retirement system. They managed Earl Warren's first campaign for Governor, teaching him to smile and to take full advantage of the photogenic qualities of his large and happy family. But they turned against him in 1945 by taking over the campaign of the California Medical Association to brand his state health plan as "socialized medicine"; and their success led the American Medical Association to employ them in 1949 for its drive to block President Harry S. Truman's Federal health insurance proposals.

Whitaker and Baxter would accept no campaign that was not in accord with their own political views, and as their financial success increased, their views became more and more conservative. The purposes of their clients, Baxter wrote, must be consistent with "individual initiative and personal responsibility; the free operation of our economic society; reasonable freedom from government control and direction."

For the campaign against "medicare" they set up offices in Chicago and for many years administered a multimillion-dollar fund drawn largely from special compulsory assessments upon the doctor members of the A.M.A. This was the largest cause that Whitaker and Baxter had ever served, but it was not the most meritorious. Their tactics, and those of the A.M.A., created so much resentment that they ultimately did almost as much to advance as to retard the movement toward nationwide health insurance, which finally went into effect in 1966 in spite of their efforts.

The spurious issue of "loyalty." The years after World War II saw the beginning of a "cold war" between the United States and the Soviet Union, and also of a period of reaction in American domestic politics. From the defeat of Germany and Japan, Russia secured an enormous expansion of its military power, and of Communist influence, in Eastern Europe and Eastern Asia. In the United States the Republican party had considerable success in blaming these menacing developments on the policies of the Democratic national administration. By charging that the liberal Democratic leadership was "soft on Communism," the Republicans had their revenge for all the years when they had been branded unfairly but effectively as the party of depression: they now branded the Democrats unfairly but effectively as the party of treason.

In the congressional elections of 1946 the Republicans gained control of both houses of Congress, and in California seven Democratic incumbents lost their seats in the House to Republicans. One of the victorious Republicans was Richard M. Nixon of Whittier, a political newcomer who defeated Jerry Voorhis, the liberal Democrat who had represented the district for 10 years and had been one of the most effective supporters of the New Deal.

Richard Nixon would later become the first native son of California to win a major party's nomination for the Presidency of the United States. He was born in 1913, to Quaker parents at Yorba Linda in Orange County. In 1922 the family acquired a general store and gasoline station in Whittier, and there Richard and his brothers worked long hours after school. He worked his way through Whittier College, won a scholarship that enabled him to graduate with honors from the law school of Duke University, practiced law in his hometown, and served during the war as a Naval Reserve officer.

In his campaign against Voorhis in 1946 Nixon followed a strategy of innuendo which the Republican National Committee had recommended to the party's candidates. He accused his Democratic opponent of disloyalty to America, not directly but through guilt by association. He charged that Voorhis was "one of those who front for un-American elements, wittingly or otherwise, by advocating increased federal controls over the lives of the people"; that Voorhis had the endorsement of the CIO Political Action Committee; and that the CIO-PAC was Communist infiltrated.

As a member of the House Committee on Un-American Activities during his first term in Congress, Nixon rendered a service of enormous practical value to his party. He discovered convincing evidence that Alger Hiss, a Democrat who had served in the State Department during the war, had been a secret Communist during the 1930s, when he had engaged in an espionage scheme to transmit government documents to the Russians. Eventually, on January 21, 1950, Hiss was convicted of perjury for denying these charges.

Hiss had been a member, though a minor member, of the American delegation at Yalta. He had been secretary-general of the conference that had organized the United Nations at San Francisco in 1945. In 1948, when the accusations against him were made, he was president of the Carnegie Endowment for International Peace.

Republicans now argued that under the Democrats a one-time Communist spy had been able to infiltrate the upper levels of the Federal government, even the Department of State, and that therefore the Democratic party in general must be tainted with Communism. This reasoning ignored a fact that considerably weakened its validity: John Foster Dulles, the Republican party's principal adviser on foreign affairs and later Secretary of State, was chairman of the board of the Carnegie Endowment for International Peace when that board had carefully screened Hiss's record before selecting him as president. But this fact received little publicity.

It was a time of intense fear of world Communism, a fear that was increased by the explosion of the first Russian atomic bomb in 1949 and the outbreak of the Korean War in 1950. In this period many Americans were even willing to credit the wild charges of Senator Joseph R. McCarthy of Wisconsin, who made a series of speeches in which he "held in his hand a list," alleged to contain the names of some specific number of "card-carrying Communists now employed in the State Department." McCarthy could never recall the exact number from one speech to the next, and he never uncovered a single person who was or ever had been a Communist in the government service. Nixon, on the other hand, had actually uncovered one such person, according to the verdict of a jury.

In 1950 Nixon won election to the United States Senate over the Democratic nominee Congresswoman Helen Gahagan Douglas, wife of the actor Melvyn Douglas and herself a former film star. Nixon's most effective campaign weapon against Mrs. Douglas was the charge that her voting record in the House of Representatives corresponded with the Communist party line.

Nixon had chanced upon the most rapid political escalator that the times provided. In 1951, after his election as Senator, and again in 1953 after his further elevation to the Vice Presidency, nearly every Republican member of the House of Representatives applied for a seat on the House Committee on Un-American Activities.

That institution, originally founded in 1938 under the chairmanship of the conservative Democratic Representative Martin Dies of Texas, had been imitated in a number of states. The California legislature established a joint "Fact-Finding Committee on Un-American Activities" in 1941, with Jack B. Tenney of Los Angeles as chairman. Tenney was a piano player and songwriter whose first widely known achievement was the composing of a popular song called "Mexicali Rose." It was his good fortune that this song caught the fancy of Arthur H. Samish. Tenney had also studied law at night. In 1936 he was elected to the state assembly as a protégé of Samish. During the 1930s Tenney was a left-wing Democrat, but in 1939 his views shifted from the far left to the far right, after his defeat for reelection as president of the Los Angeles local of the musicians' union, which he blamed upon communist elements in the union organization. He later changed his party registration to Republican.

As chairman of California's "little Dies Committee," Tenney followed the worst practices of such investigations. He set himself up as prosecutor, judge, and jury. With the protection of legal immunity from libel, he bullied witnesses and denied them the rights of due process that they would have had in a normal legal proceeding. He bracketed the innocent with the guilty, convicted by accusation, punished by publicity, and tried to silence criticism of such methods by directing these same methods against every critic.

The reports of the Tenney Committee often included charges of communist influence in the University of California. Early in 1949 Tenney introduced a proposal for a state constitutional amendment to take from the regents and give to the legislature the power to insure the loyalty of the university's employees. The university's lobbyist and comptroller, James H. Corley, considered this a dangerous political interference in university affairs. He persuaded Tenney not to push his constitutional amendment, in return for a promise that the university itself would take some sort of action.

Troubles on the Los Angeles campus over the question of invitations to anti-capitalist speakers had already inclined most of the regents to favor some method of giving renewed emphasis to their existing policy which forbade the employment of Communists on the university staff. This feeling among the regents, along with the Corley-Tenney agreement, led to the adoption of the famous "loyalty oath," which embroiled the University of California in the bitterest controversy in the history of American higher education up to that time.

Employees of the state university, along with all officers of the state government, had long been required to take an affirmative oath to support the constitutions of the United States and of California. This was a loyalty oath in the true and proper sense. But as a supplement to it the university attorney now drafted what would be better described as a negative disclaimer of disloyalty, requiring the professor or other university employee to swear that he did "not believe in," was "not a member of," and did not "support any party or organization that believes in, advocates, or teaches the overthrow of the United States Government, by force or by any illegal or constitutional methods." This was later modified to include the words "I am not a member of the Communist party."

In March President Robert G. Sproul presented the new oath to a secret session of the regents as an emergency measure and they adopted it virtually without debate. Not until May did the faculty learn that a new special oath would become a condition of employment on July 1. Thus professors who might not wish to submit to it were given only a few weeks in which to find other positions, and the principle of academic tenure at the University of California was suddenly destroyed. The faculty rebelled. Many distinguished scholars whose loyalty was beyond question refused to sign the new oath, and the university was thrown into an uproar that continued for nearly three years.

Ironically, the state supreme court eventually ruled that Tenney's proposed constitutional amendment would have been meaningless because the legislature had always had, and the regents had never had, the authority to ensure the loyalty of university employees.

Another irony was that shortly after the proposed university oath was made public Tenney was discredited and deprived of all his power in the legislature. In June 1949 he was forced to resign the chairmanship of the "un-American activities" committee because he had begun to accuse fellow members of the legislature—and even Arthur H. Samish—of being Communist sympathizers. His accusations against two members of the assembly in 1947 had aroused so much resentment in that body that Tenney, who had been elected as the senator from Los Angeles County in 1942, was forced to introduce a resolution continuing his committee as a senate committee only, instead of a joint legislative one. In 1949 the senate threatened to discontinue the committee entirely unless Tenney resigned from it. He was replaced as chairman by Senator Hugh M. Burns of Fresno, a conservative Democrat.

In the face of the faculty rebellion against the special oath, President Sproul reversed himself and asked the regents to repeal it. But Regent John Francis Neylan led a majority of the board in refusing to do so, and in clinging to the refusal during a year of bitter debate. This was the same Neylan who had once accepted the case of Charlotte Anita Whitney and appealed her conviction for criminal syndicalism all the way to the United States Supreme Court. But during his close association with William Randolph Hearst in the 1930s, Neylan had drifted steadily to the right, and in 1950 this fighting liberal of earlier years was still fighting but no longer liberal. He was, in fact, a strong admirer of Senator McCarthy.

A negative disclaimer of seditious belief was peculiarly objectionable when it was specially required of university professors, and when it was required of anyone who had already taken, in good faith, a positive oath of loyalty. In these circumstances the requirement of a redundant negative oath signified nothing except a gratuitous suspicion that one was guilty of both sedition and perjury, and when this suspicion was directed toward scholars as a special class it was certain to be resented. But most members of the public did not understand the basis of this resentment and could see no objection to such an oath. A device more certain to create misunderstanding and hostility between the academic community and the business community could not have been imagined.

Governor Warren, as an ex officio member of the board of regents, favored repeal of the special oath. It was, he argued, not only harmful to the university and to academic freedom; it was also completely worthless. A Communist, he pointed out, "would take the oath and laugh." No one who was plotting to commit treason would cavil at mere perjury. But these arguments did not prevail. Regent Lawrence Mario Giannini, son and successor of the founder of the Bank of America, said that if the board rescinded the oath, "flags would fly in the Kremlin" in celebration, and he himself would feel compelled to "organize twentieth-century vigilantes" against the subsequent wave of communism in California. Other regents argued that "insubordination" not "disloyalty" was the issue. In August 1950, by a vote of 12 to 10 the board voted to dismiss 32 nonsigning professors. In September the academic senate at Berkeley voted to "condemn" this action of "a bare majority" of the regents. Thus for the first time in history an American university faculty adopted a formal resolution of censure against a university governing board.

Professor Edward C. Tolman, previously chairman of the Berkeley psychology department, led the nonsigners in bringing suit against the board as represented by its secretary and treasurer, Robert M. Underhill, and in 1951 a state district court of appeals ruled that the special oath violated the state constitutional provision protecting the freedom of the university against political influence. The state supreme court disagreed with this interpretation, in its final ruling in *Tolman v. Underhill* in 1952, but it also invalidated the oath and ordered the professors reinstated, on the narrower ground that the requirement of a loyalty oath was within the power of the legislature and not of the regents. The legislature, in a special session called after the beginning of the Korean War in 1950, had adopted the Levering Act requiring an elaborate nondisloyalty oath of all state employees, including those of the university, and the state supreme court upheld this requirement. In doing so it was following the current doctrines of the United States Supreme Court; but under Warren as chief justice that body became more liberal. In the 1960s, it struck down similar oath laws in several other states, and thus enabled the supreme court of California to declare the Levering oath unconstitutional, in 1967, largely on the ground that mere membership in an organization was not evidence of disloyalty. The case was *Vogel v. County of Los Angeles*; Robert Vogel was a taxpayer who sued to stop the spending of tax money on the administration of an unconstitutional requirement. A few months later, in 1968, the California criminal syndicalism act of 1919 was invalidated when the federal district court in Los Angeles in *Harris v. Younger* ruled the act unconstitutionally vague and overbroad and a violation of the guarantee of freedom of speech under the First Amendment.

Under the chairmanship of Senator Hugh M. Burns the committee on un-American activities discontinued the practice of holding public hearings. There was no notable improvement in the quality of its stereotyped annual reports, which continued for many years to be prepared by the same staff director that Tenney had employed. The committee went out of existence in 1971, after the senate's new president pro tem, James R. Mills, a liberal Democrat from San Diego, discovered that it had established "subversive" files on several senators because they had voted against its appropriations.

The governorship of Goodwin J. Knight. In October 1953, when Earl Warren left the governorship for higher office, his successor was Lieutenant Governor Goodwin J. Knight, a Republican from Los Angeles. An affable man with a husky physique, an impressive appearance, and a sonorous voice, Knight was a political campaigner by temperament and lifelong inclination. Born in Provo, Utah, in 1896, the son of a lawyer and mining engineer, he moved with the family to Los Angeles in 1904, and began his active participation in politics at the age of 13 by distributing handbills in aid of Hiram Johnson's first campaign for governor.

Knight graduated from Stanford, established a successful law practice in Los Angeles, and made a profit of nearly $500,000 on the purchase and sale of the Elephant-Eagle gold mines in Kern County. He campaigned vigorously for Governor Frank Merriam in 1934, and the next year Merriam appointed him to a superior court judgeship in Los Angeles. He served in this office for 11 years, during which he also made himself widely known by acting as moderator for "open forum" and "town hall" radio programs in both Los Angeles and San Francisco. He was elected Lieutenant Governor with the aid of Whitaker and Baxter in 1946.

Though he strenuously opposed the liberal policies of Governor Warren on such issues as state health insurance and loyalty oaths, Knight recognized that Warren's remarkable successes in gaining reelection as a Republican Governor were based on his ability to capture Democratic votes, and particularly labor votes. Therefore Knight made and kept a promise that as Governor he would veto all antilabor measures. Thus he received the formal endorsement of the California Federation of Labor, and in his campaign in 1954 he easily defeated his Democratic opponent, Richard P. Graves, who had little political experience and was virtually unknown to most of the voters.

Knight's decision to imitate the basic strategy of Governor Warren might have given him still another term at Sacramento if William F. Knowland, his staunchly conservative rival for the leadership of the California Republicans, had not shattered the party by deciding to leave the United States Senate and run for Governor in 1958 on a platform openly antagonistic to organized labor.

SELECTED BIBLIOGRAPHY

Eugene C. Lee, *California Votes* (1963), is a review and analysis of registration and voting from 1928 to 1962. William Buchanan, *Legislative Partisanship: the Deviant Case of California* (1963), includes a perceptive account of legislative politics from 1935 to 1960.

On the effects of cross-filing, in addition to the works cited for Chapter XXVII, see Dean E. McHenry, "Cross Filing of Political Candidates in California," *Annals of the American Academy of Political and Social Science*, CCXLVIII (November 1946), 226–231; Robert J. Pitchell, "The Electoral System and Voting Behavior: the Case of California's Cross-Filing," *Western Political Quarterly*, XII (June 1959), 459–484; and Dean R. Cresap, *Party Politics in the Golden State* (1954).

Earl Warren and his governorship are discussed in Leo Katcher, *Earl Warren: A Political Biography* (1967); Richard B. Harvey, *Earl Warren: Governor of California* (1969); Lloyd R. Henderson, "Earl Warren and California Politics," Ph.D. thesis, University of California, Berkeley (1965); James R. Bell, "The Executive Office of the California Governor under Earl Warren, 1943–1953," Ph.D. thesis, University of California, Berkeley (1956); Irving Stone, *Earl Warren: A Great American Story* (1948), a campaign biography; Raymond Moley, 27 *Masters of Politics* (1949); Thomas S. Barclay, "Earl Warren, So-Called Nonpartisan," in J. T. Salter, editor, *Public Men in and out of Office* (1946); and John D. Weaver, *Warren: The Man, the Court, the Era* (1967).

The most detailed treatment of lobbying activities is Elmer R. Rusco, "Machine Politics, California Model: Arthur H. Samish and the Alcoholic Beverage Industry," Ph.D. thesis, University of California, Berkeley (1960).

For the principal exposés, see Howard R. Philbrick, *Legislative Investigative Report* (1939); and Lester Velie, "The Secret Boss of California," *Collier's*, CXXIV (August 13, 1949), 11–13, 71–73, and (August 20, 1949), 12–13, 60, 62–63. Parts of the Philbrick and Velie accounts are reprinted in David Farrelly and Ivan Hinderaker, editors, *The Politics of California* (1951). Sarah J. Conwill, "Regulation of Lobbying in California," M.A. thesis, University of California, Berkeley (1959), and Edgar Lane, *Lobbying and the Law* (1964), emphasize the difficulty and ineffectiveness of state legal regulation. Arthur H. Samish and Bob Thomas, *The Secret Boss of California* (1971), is a lively memoir.

Important accounts of the rise of campaign management firms are Carey McWilliams, "Government by Whitaker and Baxter," *The Nation*, CLXXII (April 14 and 21 and May 5, 1951), 346–348, 366–369, 418–421; Stanley Kelley, Jr., *Professional Public Relations and Political Power* (1956); and Robert J. Pitchell, "The Influence of Professional Campaign Management Firms in Partisan Elections in California," *Western Political Quarterly*, XI (June 1958), 278–300. On the use of money in elections see Leonard C. Rowe and William Buchanan, "Campaign Funds in California: What the Records Reveal," *California Historical Society Quarterly*, XLI (September 1962), 195–210.

The congressional career of Jerry Voorhis from 1936 to 1946, and that of Richard Nixon from 1946 to 1952, illustrated the decline of support for New Deal viewpoints and the rising popularity of conservative Republican ones in the postwar years. On Voorhis, see the chapter by Claudius O. Johnson in J. T. Salter, *Public Men*, pp. 322–343; and Jerry Voorhis, *Confessions of a Congressman* (1947). Earl Mazo, *Richard Nixon: a Political and Personal Portrait* (1959, 1960), is moderately favorable. William Costello, *The Facts about Nixon; an Unauthorized Biography* (1960), is moderately critical. See also Richard M. Nixon, *Six Crises* (1962).

On the "loyalty" issue in California, consult Edward L. Barrett, Jr., *The Tenney Committee* (1951); David P. Gardner, *The California Oath Controversy* (1967); George R. Stewart, *The Year of the Oath* (1950); John W. Caughey, "A University in Jeopardy," *Harper's Magazine*, CCI (November 1950), 68–75, and "Farewell to California's 'Loyalty' Oath," *Pacific Historical Review*, XXXVIII (May 1969), 123–128; and R. L. Pritchard, "California Un-American Activities Investigations," *California Historical Society Quarterly*, XLIX (December 1970), 309–327.

Accounts of the political career of Governor Goodwin J. Knight are in H. Brett Melendy and Benjamin F. Gilbert, *The Governors of California* (1965); and Frank J. Taylor, "How To Run for Office," *Saturday Evening Post*, CCXXVIII (October 29, 1955), 34 ff.

Chapter XXXVIII

DEMOCRATIC REVIVAL

THE REPUBLICANS of California in 1952 held five of the six statewide executive offices that were filled by partisan elections; both of the United States senatorships; nearly two-thirds of the seats in the House of Representatives; and more than two-thirds of the seats in the state legislature. After 1958 these proportions were almost exactly reversed. Through a combination of Democratic efforts and Republican blunders, the latent Democratic majority was at last able to assert itself.

Rise of informal party organizations. A major turning point was the formation in 1953 of the California Democratic Council, a federation of local clubs made up of "amateur Democrats." The Republicans had formed such a body—the California Republican Assembly, at a low point in their party's fortunes in 1933—but the Democrats had been unable to follow suit because of the lack of comparable dedication and enthusiasm among their grass-roots volunteer workers. In 1952, however, Adlai E. Stevenson became a kind of patron saint for liberal Democrats, and hundreds of new Democratic clubs sprang up in support of his presidential candidacy. Intense disappointment at his defeat played a part in bringing these clubs together in a statewide federation the next year.

State conventions of the unofficial California Republican Assembly had contributed heavily to Republican successes by making preprimary endorsements of candidates. On the other hand, extreme confusion and division had continued to weaken the Democratic aspirants in the primaries until their party acquired its own informal nominating machinery in the state conventions of the California Democratic Council. For some years after this system was established, few candidates of either party could win nomination without the endorsement of the CRA or the CDC. Some protested that these endorsements defeated the whole purpose of the direct primary and virtually returned the nominating function to the party convention system. But the informal organizations were much more democratic and less subject to boss control than the old party conventions had been, and to the degree that they could unite each party behind one candidate, they reduced the costs of preprimary campaigning and the excessive role of money in elections.

The Democratic triumph of 1958. When Senator William F. Knowland first decided to run for Governor of California, it seemed highly probable that he would win. In 1952 he had been reelected to the United States Senate in the primaries, having won the Democratic as well as the Republican nomination, an honor that no other candidate except Hiram Johnson had ever received.

Knowland had been in the Senate since 1945, when Governor Earl Warren had taken the opportunity to reward an old friend and staunch supporter, Joseph R. Knowland, publisher of the *Oakland Tribune,* by appointing his able and promising son to the seat that Hiram Johnson's death had left vacant. Robert A. Taft was so impressed with Knowland that he made him his own successor as the leader of the Republicans in the Senate.

Knowland's strategy in running for Governor in 1958 had several aspects. As Governor he could head the large California delegation to the Republican national convention of 1960. Thus he might secure the presidential nomination for himself, or at least deny it to Vice President Richard M. Nixon, with whom he was not on friendly terms. Another objective was to reverse Governor Knight's prolabor policies by securing the passage of a state "right to work" law in California. Thus Knowland would consolidate his right to succeed his mentor, Senator Taft, as the recognized leader of the forces of conservatism in American politics. Taft's most famous achievement, the Taft-Hartley labor relations act of 1947, had permitted the states to adopt laws forbidding union-shop contracts, and during the next 10 years several nonindustrial states had passed such measures. Among the advocates of these laws the phrase "right to work," based on the idea that a worker should not have to join a union in order to hold a job, had replaced the earlier open-shop slogan, "the American plan."

Knowland anticipated that he would defeat Knight in the gubernatorial primary, in which the labor vote would be so divided between Knight and the most likely Democratic candidate, Edmund G. Brown, that Knowland might even win both nominations. But friends of Governor Knight, including Norman Chandler, publisher of the *Los Angeles Times,* upset this strategy. They joined with President Eisenhower and Vice President Nixon in persuading Knight to run for Knowland's seat in the Senate instead of fighting him for the governorship. Eisenhower was persuaded that this was necessary for party harmony. Nixon was delighted because both of his two chief rivals in his home state were about to be eliminated as serious political contenders.

Edmund G. Brown, who now emerged as the leader of the California

Democrats, was a native San Franciscan, born in 1905. When he was in the seventh grade at Fremont Grammar School a ringing patriotic speech for the sale of liberty bonds had earned him the nickname of "Patrick Henry" Brown, and he continued to be known as "Pat" throughout his later career. He graduated from the San Francisco College of Law, became district attorney of San Francisco in 1944, and was elected state attorney general in 1950.

In the campaign of 1958 organized labor achieved the greatest degree of unity that it had shown in the whole history of California politics, in support of Brown and in opposition to Knowland and the open shop. There were about 1,500,000 union members in California, and with their close relatives they constituted more than a third of the eligible voters. Many union leaders discovered that more than half of their members had not registered to vote and that an even larger proportion of them were uninformed on political issues. Labor organizations now united in persuading an unprecedented number of union members to register and to vote.

Against Initiative Proposition 18, the right to work proposal endorsed by Knowland and opposed by Brown, labor collected a campaign fund in excess of 2.5 million dollars, more than twice the total funds contributed in the proposition's favor. With the aid of the San Francisco public relations firm of Leonard B. Gross and Curtis Roberts, labor sponsored a huge campaign of billboard, television, and newspaper advertising, stressing the argument that "so-called 'right to work' means the right to work for less and less and less."

In the election of November 1958 Brown won nearly 60 percent of the votes, and Proposition 18 lost by almost exactly the same percentage. The vote for Brown was 3,140,176; for Knowland, 2,110,911. Brown carried 54 of the state's 58 counties. The Democrats won margins of 27 seats to 13 in the state senate and 47 to 33 in the assembly.

Brown's legislative program. In January 1959 the Democrats found themselves in control of both houses of the California legislature for the first time in 80 years. In his inaugural address, Governor Brown promised to follow "the path of responsible liberalism . . ., in the giant footsteps of such memorable Governors as Hughes and Roosevelt in New York, Wilson in New Jersey, La Follette in Wisconsin, Altgeld and Stevenson in Illinois, and Johnson and Warren in California."

Brown proposed a number of liberal measures, and the legislature enacted most of them. He recommended a law against racial discrimination by employers and labor unions, and the legislature responded with a fair employment practices act. Maximum payments for unemployment insurance, disability, and workmen's compensation were substantially increased. For the protection of consumers, a state office of consumer's counsel was created, with authority to act against false or misleading practices in labeling and packaging, and deceptive carrying charges on installment credit purchases. A state economic development agency was established to attract new industries and aid long-range planning.

Tax increases were adopted, to meet a deficit left over from the previous year and to enable the state government to keep up with the swift growth of the state's population by expanding its programs of highways, aid to local school districts, and crime control. At the Governor's urging the legislature authorized studies that led to a master plan for higher education and to plans for the reorganization of many state offices under centralized departments. Cross-filing in elections was abolished.

Only a few of Governor Brown's proposals failed of enactment in 1959, most notably his request for a minimum wage of $1.25 an hour for workers not covered by Federal law. Abolition of capital punishment, which he urged in 1960, was also rejected.

The California Water Plan. Probably Brown's greatest single achievement as Governor was the adoption of the huge bond issue that enabled the state to proceed with its master plan for water development.

Most of California's water was in the northern half of the state, while most of the need for water was in the southern half. The Los Angeles basin, for example, had only 0.06 percent of California's natural stream flow of water, and by the late 1950s it had about 60 percent of the state's population.

Under Governor Earl Warren, the legislature had authorized studies for a statewide water program that would ultimately be much larger than the Federal Central Valley Project. But organized labor, conservative bankers, and majority opinion in Northern California were strongly opposed to the state plan. Labor leaders argued that because the state program would not come under the Federal limitation of 160 acres on the size of farms eligible to receive publicly subsidized water, the plan would result in the "unjust enrichment" of huge landowning corporations that were already too rich and too powerful. Major beneficiaries, labor pointed out, would include the Southern Pacific, Standard Oil, the Kern County Land Company, the Los Angeles Times Corporation, and other groups that held vast tracts in the southwestern San Joaquin Valley.

In the face of this opposition Governor Knight refused to become involved in the battle. But Governor Brown believed that the water plan was indispensable for California's future growth, and he threw all his political weight behind it. In 1959, at his insistence, the legislature authorized the submission to the voters of a bond issue of $1,750,000,000. This was the largest issue of bonds ever adopted by any state for any purpose. Most of the money would be used for the Feather River Project, the first phase of a much larger long-range plan. The voters of California approved "Brown's water bonds" in November 1960, after he had urged them to do so in speeches throughout the state.

Republicans later protested against Brown's receiving so much of the credit.

They pointed out that many of the details of the plan had been worked out during the administrations of Warren and Knight. But it was Brown who was willing to stake his political career on the controversial proposal, and it was he who persuaded the legislature and the voters to adopt it.

The heart of the Feather River Project was Oroville Dam, 735 feet high, the tallest in the United States, storing a trillion gallons or 3.5 million acre-feet, and assuring a controlled flow of water to the San Joaquin delta region. From the delta, as Brown said at the groundbreaking ceremonies in October 1961, "we are going to build a river 500 miles long" in order "to correct an accident of people and geography." He was referring to the aqueduct that would carry water along the western side of the San Joaquin Valley and into Southern California.

Altogether, the California Water Plan envisioned 376 new reservoirs and a vast network of aqueducts throughout the state, to be constructed over a period of 60 years at an estimated cost of 11.8 billion dollars. In 1960 the total storage capacity of dams in California was about 20 million acre-feet. The new reservoirs to be built under the 60-year state master plan would add a capacity of 77 million acre-feet. About half of their hydroelectric power output would be used to pump the water through the aqueducts. Sales of water and power would ultimately repay the entire cost of constructing and operating the gigantic system of dams, canals, and powerplants.

Some critics of the plan, including the *San Francisco Chronicle*, argued that it might be unnecessary in view of the development of new techniques for the desalinization of sea water. The Bechtel Corporation conducted a series of studies sponsored by the Metropolitan Water District of Southern California, the Atomic Energy Commission, and the Department of the Interior. On the basis of these studies, the Metropolitan Water District signed a contract in 1966 with the Federal government for the building of a nuclear-powered water desalting plant on a man-made island off the coast of Orange County. Heat from nuclear reactors would distill the salt water by turning it to steam in a series of low-pressure chambers, and would also turn a battery of turbines to generate electricity. The costs of the water and power would not be far above those of the more conventional methods of providing them.

It seemed improbable, however, that desalinization alone would ever meet California's constantly growing demands for more water. The state was likely to need all the water and all the electric power that it could get, from all feasible sources.

Extremists, right and left. One of the key factors in California politics in the 1960s was the emergence of vividly colorful but startlingly eccentric new varieties of fanaticism at both ends of the political spectrum. On the far right, the John Birch Society became a ludicrous parody of the conservatism of the Republicans, and thus contributed substantially to their defeats in the state election of 1962 and the national election of 1964. At the other extreme, an

This Delta Pumping Plant is part of the State Water Project, and will provide the initial lift for the four billion gallons a day which will flow through the California Aqueduct. Its pumps will lift the water 244 feet up from the Sacramento-San Joaquin Delta in the giant pipes and start it south to Central, Coastal, and Southern California for use in homes, farms, and factories. The Delta Pumping Plant was dedicated on September 9, 1967, 117th anniversary of California's admission to the Union. (Courtesy of the State of California Department of Water Resources)

anarchistic student wing of the "New Left," in coalition with the "hippies," the younger counterparts of the beatniks, parodied the liberalism of the Democrats and contributed to the defeat of Governor Brown in the election of 1966.

The tendency to polarization in philosophical and political opinions has always characterized the discussion of human affairs. Medieval philosophers asserted that every man was born either a Platonist or an Aristotelian. Environment is a more probable explanation than heredity, though Gilbert and Sullivan, in the context of English party politics in the 19th century, maintained that

Every boy and every gal
That's born into the world alive
Is either a little Liberal
Or else a little Conservative.

In 20th-century American politics, especially after the 1930s, "liberalism" was the belief that government should take positive actions in the interest of the greater welfare and greater liberties of the whole people, and that it should also take negative, regulatory actions to protect the public from abuses of freedom by private business. Most American "conservatives," during the same period, regarded their doctrine as an alternative and superior theory of progress. They argued not merely for the need to conserve what was good in the past, but also for the related belief that the best way to ensure the continued progress and improvement of American society was to leave the fullest possible freedom to the operations of private enterprise. The mainstream of American politics was a constant process of compromise between these two philosophies. But to the extremists of both the radical right and the radical left, compromise was unendurable.

The John Birch Society, founded in December 1958, was named in honor of a young man from Macon, Georgia, who had been a Baptist missionary in China before World War II, and who was killed by Chinese Communists in August 1945 while serving as a captain in the American Army. The founder of the Birch Society was Robert Welch, a retired candy manufacturer who had been defeated for the Republican nomination for Lieutenant Governor of Massachusetts, and who suspected that communist infiltration of the Republican party had been responsible for his defeat. Welch and many of his followers believed that the graduated income tax, social security, the United Nations, and racial integration in the public schools were communist plots; that the fluoridation of water was a communist conspiracy to weaken the American people by slow poison; that all mental health work was a plot to brainwash Americans into communism; and that President Harry S. Truman, President Dwight D. Eisenhower, Secretary of State John Foster Dulles, and Chief Justice Earl Warren were communist agents.

Most Birchers concealed their membership, and the general public first became aware of the society's existence in January 1961, when Thomas M. Storke, veteran publisher of the *Santa Barbara News-Press*, exposed some of its activities in his newspaper. An ostensibly student-sponsored "Freedom-Club" at the University of California at Santa Barbara had been offering prizes for essays advocating the impeachment of Chief Justice Earl Warren. The *News-Press* revealed that an outsider, a Birch organizer, was directing the club and using outside funds. In 1962, Storke received a Pulitzer Prize for distinguished achievement in journalism "for calling public attention to the efforts of the semisecret John Birch Society to wage a campaign of hate and vilification."

The *Los Angeles Times* published its own attack on the Birchers in March 1961. Nevertheless, the organization continued to grow in several parts of the country, and most of all in Southern California. Wealthy businessmen and retired military officers joined it in considerable numbers. Two Republican members of the House of Representatives from Southern California, John Rousselot and Edgar Hiestand, avowed their membership in the Birch Society.

To Richard M. Nixon, who was planning to run for Governor of California in 1962, the fantastic doctrines of Robert Welch and his followers were a serious embarrassment. Nixon felt that the Birch Society was "the monkey on the elephant's back," and that if he accepted its support the result would be the best financed but most disastrous campaign in the state's political history. Therefore he publicly repudiated the Birchers and stated that there was no place in the Republican party for anyone who charged that Dwight D. Eisenhower and John Foster Dulles were communists.

Nixon could hardly have done otherwise. He was indebted to Eisenhower for two terms as Vice President, and for the Republican presidential nomination in 1960. In that year, with Eisenhower's support, Nixon had received a total popular vote that was only a tiny fraction less than John F. Kennedy's; and he had won the electoral vote of California, though by a narrow margin.

Having attempted to dissociate himself from right-wing extremism, and having thus lost some of his right-wing support, Nixon made a desperate effort to use his old issue of left-wing extremism against Governor Edmund G. Brown. But his campaign charge that Brown, a Roman Catholic, was "soft on communism," was absurdly unconvincing.

Nixon gave an irritating impression of arrogance and overconfidence that disenchanted many who had once voted for him. Many also disliked his apparent intention to serve only two years as Governor and then use the office as a stepping-stone to the Presidency in 1964. In the election on November 6, 1962, Brown defeated him by nearly 300,000 votes, although Senator Thomas H. Kuchel, a liberal Republican, was reelected by a margin of 700,000. On the morning after the election, Nixon appeared at a press conference, unshaven and distraught, and delivered a rambling attack on the press, blaming his defeat on unfair reporting of his campaign. A few weeks later he announced that he would leave California to become a partner in a law firm in New York City.

The split between the "moderates" and the right-wing extremists continued to bedevil the Republicans in 1964. In the California presidential primary the ultraconservative Senator Barry Goldwater of Arizona, who opposed medicare and social security, defeated the moderate Governor Nelson Rockefeller of New York, and at the Republican national convention in San Francisco the large California delegation, headed by ex-Senator William F. Knowland, clinched the nomination for Goldwater.

It was widely reported that at least a hundred of Goldwater's delegates were Birchers. When Rockefeller proposed a platform amendment condemning "the Ku Klux Klan, the Communist Party, and the John Birch Society," he was shouted down. On the other hand, Goldwater included in his acceptance speech a statement that "extremism in the defense of liberty is no vice," and that "moderation in the pursuit of justice is not a virtue." His supporters at the convention cheered wildly, but the words had an opposite effect on millions of voters in the television audience, and the next day Rockefeller spoke for many moderate Republicans when he called the statement "dangerous, irresponsible, and frightening." In the election in November, President Lyndon B. Johnson defeated Goldwater, both in California and in the nation as a whole, by the widest margins given to a presidential candidate since 1936.

The most effective campaign speech for Goldwater in 1964 was a widely televised fund-raising address by the screen and television actor Ronald Reagan. This speech led some conservatives to express the wish that Reagan had been the candidate instead of Goldwater, and a group of wealthy Southern California Republicans led by Henry Salvatori, head of a petroleum exploration company, formed the nucleus of a movement to make Reagan the next Governor of California.

Reagan was a convert to conservatism. As a student at a small college in Illinois, the state of his birth, he had been one of the leaders of a strike against a drastic cut in the college's budget, a strike so successful that it forced the resignation of the president who had proposed the cut. After his graduation Reagan spent five years as a radio sportscaster in Des Moines before he came to Hollywood in 1937 at the age of 26. In his interests in politics, and in the affairs of the Screen Actors Guild, of which he later became president, his views in these early years were those of a left-wing liberal Democrat. His name was once omitted from a list of supporters of Helen Gahagan Douglas because he was considered too far left. But later he became a Democrat for Eisenhower and a Democrat for Nixon, and finally changed his registration to Republican in 1962.

Reagan acquired a 305-acre ranch in the Malibu hills for the breeding of thoroughbred horses. But such tracts in the outskirts of the growing metropolitan area were turning into residential subdivisions. The rise in the value of Reagan's land, and a series of large increases in the taxes on it, coincided with a change in his political philosophy. He became strongly hostile toward taxation and toward the growth of governmental activities that required tax support. During the same period, in the 1950s and early '60s, the General Electric Company employed him to appear regularly on the television programs it sponsored, and also to make speeches to its employees and to civic groups. These addresses lauded private enterprise and were increasingly critical of government.

In the gubernatorial campaign of 1966 Reagan was remarkably successful in restoring a degree of unity among the California Republicans. He followed a policy laid down by the chairman of the party's state central committee, Dr. Gaylord Parkinson, a Southern California obstetrician. This policy was sometimes known as "Parkinson's law," or "the Eleventh Commandment": "Thou shalt not speak ill of any other Republican." When some advisers urged Reagan to repudiate the Birch Society, as Nixon had done in 1962 and as even Goldwater finally did in 1966, Reagan replied that he would not "blanket-indict" any group, and that "if a man votes for me it means that he's buying my philosophy, not that I'm buying his."

In these and other matters of campaign strategy Reagan had the help of Spencer-Roberts-Haffner, the firm that had supplanted Whitaker and Baxter as leaders in the field of campaign management. Stuart Spencer and William Roberts were Southern Californians, and Fred J. Haffner was the Northern California partner.

In 1964, when Spencer and Roberts had managed Rockefeller's campaign in the California primary, they had denounced Goldwater as an extremist. But in 1966 their studies of voter reactions revealed that, in Roberts' words, "The right-wing issue is now old hat." Although the Birchers on the far right and the beatniks on the far left seemed equally irrational and repellent to most of the voters, disorderly left-wing demonstrations at Berkeley and elsewhere were now receiving far greater attention from the news media.

The outbreak of the "Free Speech Movement" on the Berkeley campus of the University of California, in the autumn of 1964, followed a tightening of campus rules against student political activity. In a rebellion against these rules a group of students used tactics of mass civil disobedience that they had learned while participating in the civil rights movement in the South. When they led a massive sit-in in Sproul Hall, the administration building, Governor Brown ordered state and local police to intervene. In the largest mass arrest in the state's history more than 700 persons, mostly students, were dragged or carried from the building. Later, in a mass trial, 578 of them were found guilty of trespassing, and many of resisting arrest.

Other court decisions, however, had indicated that some of the university's strict rules might be unconstitutional denials of free speech. These rules were now liberalized. The Berkeley faculty passed resolutions that the university should not regulate the content of political advocacy, but should regulate the time, place, and manner of it in order to prevent interference with normal university functions. In the minds of some of the radical students, however, interference with the functioning of the university and every other institution of the establishment was a vital part of the content of their political advocacy. They failed to recognize that the right to dissent was not the right to disrupt.

During the early months of the Berkeley disturbances, when there were genuine issues of civil liberties, the Free Speech Movement had the support not only of the few hundred radicals but of many thousands of liberal idealists as well, including many of the university's best students. But later, in desperate efforts to keep "the movement" going, some of the youthful leaders of the "New Left" resorted to such ruinous tactics as contempt of court and obscenity. As their base of support narrowed, the left-wing political activists became dependent on the hippies to swell the ranks of their demonstrations. The appearance and behavior of some of these groups in front of the television news cameras produced revulsion in hundreds of thousands of voters, and Ronald Reagan took full advantage of the situation with campaign promises to clean up the Berkeley campus. Not since the public reaction against the I.W.W. during and after World War I had such a small number of left-wing extremists created so much support for political conservatism in California.

American involvement in the war in Vietnam added to the troubles of the

Democrats. Governor Brown supported the Vietnam policies of President Johnson, and when Simon Casady, president of the California Democratic Council, denounced those policies, Brown forced Casady to resign. The issue caused a disastrous split in the CDC, which had once been a major source of strength for Brown's campaigns.

Undoubtedly, however, the most decisive single factor in the California gubernatorial campaign of 1966 was the "white backlash" against Negro demands for residential desegregation and job equality. These issues shattered the coalition between organized labor and racial minority groups that had been essential to Brown's victories in 1958 and 1962. Brown had approved the passage of the Rumford Act, an open housing law, in 1963, and had denounced opponents of the law as "shock troops of bigotry." But the next year the voters overwhelmingly adopted an initiative constitutional amendment, Proposition 14, that rejected all open-housing legislation. In 1965 the tragic riot in the Negro ghetto of Watts, a suburb of Los Angeles, intensified the white reaction against the civil rights movement in general and residential integration in particular.[1]

Reagan, in his campaign speeches, repeatedly expressed his opposition to the Rumford Act but insisted that in doing so he was defending the right of private property, not indulging in racial bigotry. This stand won him the votes of many white Democrats, including many labor union members and their families. Precinct by precinct, all over the state, the vote for Reagan in 1966 was almost identical with the vote for Proposition 14 in 1964.

Reagan's attacks on the rising costs of government also won some defectors from the Democratic ranks. Brown favored monthly withholding of state income taxes, which had been adopted in most other states. Reagan opposed this measure on the ground that "people should hurt when they pay taxes," and withholding would make the payments less painful. Many members of labor unions, and of the lower and middle classes in general, had been enjoying rising incomes and were experiencing a new resentment against taxation.

In the election on November 8, 1966, Reagan defeated Brown by 3,742,913 to 2,749,174, a margin just short of a million votes. Attorney General Thomas C. Lynch was the only Democrat to win reelection to statewide office. But the Democrats retained small majorities in both houses of the legislature, and under the leadership of Speaker Jess M. Unruh they were in a position to make Reagan's administration as Governor extremely difficult.

SELECTED BIBLIOGRAPHY

The rise of informal party organizations is described in Leonard C. Rowe, *Pre-primary Endorsements in California Politics* (1962); Markell C. Baer, *Story of the California Republican Assembly* (1955); Francis Carney, *The*

[1] These problems are discussed in more detail in Chapter XL.

Rise of the Democratic Clubs in California (1958); and James Q. Wilson, *The Amateur Democrat* (1962), a discussion of club politics in New York, Chicago, and Los Angeles.

On the sweeping Democratic victory of 1958, see Totton J. Anderson, "The 1958 Election in California," *Western Political Quarterly*, XII (March 1959), 276–300; and Earl C. Behrens, "California, the New Men," chapter X in *States in Crisis: Politics in Ten American States, 1950–1962* (1964), edited by James Reichley. Melendy and Gilbert, *The Governors of California*, includes a summary of Brown's governorship through 1964. Eugene C. Lee, editor, *The California Governmental Process; Problems and Issues* (1966), and Eugene P. Dvorin and Arthur J. Misner, editors, *California Politics and Policies* (1966), are collections of writings on political problems of the '60s. Edmond Costantini, *The Democratic Leadership Corps in California* (1967), analyzes the national convention delegation of 1960.

California Water Resources Board, *Bulletin No. 3. The California Water Plan* (1957), is the basic description of the 60-year project. Sydney Kossen, "California's $2 Billion Thirst," *Harper's Magazine*, CCXXII (March 1961), 94–102, describes the Feather River Project; Dorothy C. Tompkins, *Water Plans for California: a Bibliography* (1961), is a valuable guide to source materials, especially public documents. See also David Seckler, editor, *California Water: A Study in Resource Management* (1971).

Thomas M. Storke describes his exposure of the Birch Society in *I Write for Freedom* (1963). On Brown's victory over Nixon, see Totton J. Anderson and Eugene C. Lee, "The 1962 Election in California," *Western Political Quarterly*, XVI (June 1963), 396–420. Seymour M. Lipset and Sheldon S. Wolin, editors, *The Berkeley Student Revolt: Facts and Interpretations* (1965), includes a variety of viewpoints. Max Heirich, *The Beginning: Berkeley, 1964* (1970), is sympathetic and uncritical. Ronald Reagan, *Where's the Rest of Me?* (1965), is an autobiography, as told to Richard Hubler. Totton J. Anderson and Eugene C. Lee, "The 1966 Election in California," *Western Political Quarterly*, XX (June 1967), 535–554, and Roy V. Peel, "The California Elections of 1966," in John P. Carney and William M. Alexander, editors, *California and United States Governments* (1967), 226–256, deal with Reagan's election. Curt Gentry, *The Last Days of the Late Great State of California* (1968), has irreverent but relevant comments on California politics and regions in the mid-1960s.

The careers of Brown and Reagan are analyzed in Melvin H. Bernstein, "Political Leadership in California," Ph.D. thesis, University of California, Los Angeles (1970).

Chapter XXXIX

INDUSTRIALIZED AGRICULTURE AND DISORGANIZED LABOR

Green gold. Though the processes of urbanization were continuing and accelerating, agriculture was still California's largest single industry in 1965, when the value of the state's farm products reached 3.5 billion dollars. This was more than the value of the output of any branch of manufacturing in the state—or rather of any *other* branch of "manufacturing." As Paul S. Taylor has remarked, in industrialized agriculture "the term 'farmer' no more suggests a man with a hand on the plow than 'manufacturer' now means what it once did—a maker of things by hand." California farms themselves, in the words of Carey McWilliams, had long been "factories in the field." The products of their nearest rivals, the factories making aircraft and other items of transportation equipment, had an annual value of about 3 billion dollars in 1965. The state's entire production of minerals totaled about 1.4 billion dollars, of which crude petroleum accounted for more than half.

The structure of agriculture in California was not only extraordinarily complex in itself; it was also interrelated with other industries to an extraordinary degree. The canning, packing, and processing of food and kindred products added a value of about $2,225,000,000. When all benefits to the transportation, marketing, and other related industries were added, the total income arising directly or indirectly from California agriculture was at least 13 billion dollars in 1965. One in every five jobs in the state was directly related to agriculture, though 90 percent of the students in the college of agriculture of the University of California would find employment in what the college's dean called "the non-farming segment of agriculture—everything from management of natural resources to food processing and retailing."

Among the states, California had ranked first in farm income since the 1930s, and its lead was steadily widening. Several of its climates permitted year-round growing, and favored the production of fruit and truck crops for luxury markets at seasons when other states could offer little or no competition. California's unmatched level of farm capitalization permitted the greatest use of scientific techniques, and resulted in the nation's highest level of farm productivity. One-fourth of the nation's irrigated land was in California; two-thirds of the state's cultivated land was irrigated.

California's agriculture was not only the most prosperous in the country, but far and away the most diversified. Because of the variety of its soils and climates it had 118 different types of farms, according to the United States census classification, while Pennsylvania, which ranked second in this respect, had only 25 types. Thanks in part to the genius of Luther Burbank of Santa Rosa, nearly 300 different agricultural commodities were produced in California, including all of the nation's commercial supply of almonds, artichokes, figs, nectarines, and olives; practically all of the walnuts, dates, and lemons; a third of the nation's fruit, including most of the apricots, grapes, pears, plums, and prunes; and more than a fourth of the nation's vegetables including most of the asparagus, broccoli, carrots, celery, and lettuce. California also ranked first in beef cattle, beet sugar, strawberries, tomatoes, and turkeys. It was second in cotton, and third in the production of milk.

But while California agriculture as a whole was remarkably diversified, the great majority of the farms were extremely specialized. Specialization even within a crop was common. For example, many farms produced peaches exclusively for canning or for drying, and many produced grapes only for the table or for raisins or for wine.

While total farm income in California was going steadily up, the number of farm units was going steadily down, partly because the growth of suburbs removed land from agricultural use, and partly because many small farms were consolidated into large ones. From 1940 to 1960 the number of farms in the state decreased from 133,000 to less than 100,000 while their average size increased from 230 acres to 372 acres. Of the smaller farms that remained, many were not really commercial, and were operated only on a part-time basis.

More than 70 percent of California farm income went to less than 15 percent of the farms, and most of the large farm units, which produced the bulk of the total output, were owned by large corporations. Even family farms were being incorporated to escape from inheritance taxes and litigation after the death of the owner and to secure greater access to capital. There were still thousands of commercial family farms, and many were still financially successful, particularly those producing some one intensively irrigated specialty crop. But in the general trend to consolidation, mechanization, and constantly increasing capitalization, thousands of small farmers were squeezed out. The proportion of farm residents in California dropped from 9.7 percent of the state's population in 1940 to 5.8 percent in 1950, and 2.7 percent in 1960.

Although the cultivated acreage in California was only 2.6 percent of the national total in 1965, it produced 12.3 percent of the dollar value of the nation's harvested crops. The income of commercial family farms in California was more than twice the national average, and the margin in favor of the large corporation farms was even larger. These facts provided, in themselves, an eloquent commentary on the claims of California growers that they could not afford to pay higher wages to their workers than did farmers in other parts of the United States.

The empire of agribusiness. Many forces had worked together to produce irreversible change in what Americans had once called "farming as a way of life." Successful farming had always been a business, but now it was becoming a business organized in larger and larger units. This was occurring not only through "horizontal integration" or the merging of farm units into larger ones, but also through the still more revolutionary process of "vertical integration," in which a large company operated at every level from the field to the supermarket.

The men who had pioneered in the formation of these vertically integrated and highly diversified agricultural corporations, and had set the pattern for them, were two Italian immigrants, Mark J. Fontana and Joseph Di Giorgio.

Fontana had created the California Fruit Canner's Association in 1899, and in 1916 had been instrumental in merging four large packing concerns into the California Packing Corporation, which became the world's largest canner of fruits and vegetables. CalPac was the grower as well as the packer of many of the goods that were sold under its Del Monte label. In 1965 it owned 24,000 acres of cultivated land and leased 74,000. It also contracted with hundreds of smaller growers for their crops, often before they were harvested and sometimes before they were planted. It owned 44 canneries, and its 50 warehouses were spread throughout the United States and Canada. Its sales were nearly 400 million dollars a year.

Joseph Di Giorgio had become a large grower in the southern San Joaquin Valley in the early years of the century, and had bought the marketing and shipping interests of the Earl Fruit Company in 1910. The canned goods produced by the Di Giorgio Corporation were known to consumers through its S & W label.

Another integrated "farmer" was Schenley Industries, which raised many of the grapes that went into its wines. Among the many other large owners of farmlands were the Bank of America, the Southern Pacific and Santa Fe Railroads, the Kern County Land Company, the Los Angeles Times Corporation, and the Irvine Corporation. Hunt Foods and Industries, headed by Norton

Simon, did not operate as a grower but was important as the world's largest processor and distributor of tomato products, and as a major producer of salad and cooking oils.

The backing of such large aggregations of capital facilitated the constant development of new technological advances in all of the complex operations of agribusiness. An indispensable ally in this process was the University of California's college of agriculture, an outgrowth of the Morrill Land Grant College Act, adopted a century earlier for the purpose of aiding the country's millions of small farmers.

The Federal and state funds that supported the college's tremendously successful research program were augmented by the funds of the Giannini Foundation of Agricultural Economics. Amadeo Peter Giannini, founder of the Bank of America, was also a regent of the university. His son, Lawrence Mario Giannini, succeeded him both as a regent and as head of the bank. If "L.M." in turn had had a son, both the bank and the regency would have continued to be hereditary, but since he did not, the problem was solved by the appointment of Jesse W. Tapp, president of the Bank of America, as chairman of the state board of agriculture and thus as an ex officio regent.

The impact of science and technology on California agriculture was astounding. In 1961 university agricultural engineers devised a mechanical tomato picker so efficient and gentle that when they ran a fresh egg through it the egg was deposited in the box uncracked. Soon afterward they developed a mechanical thumb that could press down on the top of each head of lettuce, decide electronically whether it was ready to be picked, and signal another part of the machine to pick it. Nine-tenths of California's cotton was being picked by machinery before the rate reached one-tenth in the Southern states. Agricultural scientists developed mechanical treeshakers for fruits and nuts. For the more delicate fruits there were machines that could lift the human picker into branches of the tree and swing him rapidly about among them.

In the American agricultural economy of 1920, one farmer had been able to grow enough food for eight persons. In 1950, one farmer could produce enough food for 15 persons; in 1965, for 30. In California the ratios were much greater, but exact figures were impossible to determine because of the peculiar difficulty of defining "a farmer."

A major factor encouraging the further advance of a mechanized, highly capitalized agriculture, concentrated in high-income-per-acre crops, was the continuing growth of the real income and purchasing power of the average American family. With this increase came ever-greater demand for fruits, vegetables, dairy products, poultry, and eggs—all California specialties.

Another pressure for crops that used land intensively was the rapidly rising value of land itself. Of California's slightly less than 100 million acres, only about 17.5 million were suitable for cultivation, and more than 13 million were being cultivated in 1965. Cities, factories, freeways, and other nonfarm uses

Cotton harvesting in the San Joaquin Valley. The plants had been defoliated by aerial spraying. (Courtesy of Agricultural Publications, University of California, Berkeley)

occupied more than 3 million acres, and would probably spread over another million acres in another 10 years. Inconveniently, the land that was most valuable for agriculture was often the land that lay directly in the paths of urban growth. Los Angeles County, for example, had been for many years the richest agricultural county in the nation; but as its suburbs spread over what had once been prime irrigated cropland, its agricultural output rapidly fell behind that of such counties as Fresno and San Joaquin.

Though living space had an inexorable priority and would continue to exercise it, there was no basis for fears of a disastrous shortage of farmland or of food. With improving techniques the yield from each acre was steadily growing, and lands once considered unsuitable would be brought into production. The California Water Plan had been devised with this in mind. But these changes were certain to be increasingly expensive, and the prospects for the small, low-cost family farmer were increasingly dim.

Farm fascism" in the 1930s. California growers had discovered very early that the cost of labor was the only one of their costs of production that they could usually keep down. And they had kept it down, with all the economic and political power at their command.

Since the early American period, as Varden Fuller has pointed out, farmland values in California had been capitalized on the basis of the availability of cheap, unorganized migratory labor, much of it alien and nonwhite—Chinese, then Japanese, and later Mexican and Filipino. Thus the historic cheap-labor surplus, by helping to keep land prices high and farm mortgages heavy, had kept the small farmer's return on his own labor to a low level, while at the same time it had maintained the profits of the large farms that employed the bulk of the hired workers.

In 1933 and 1934, when the Communist party organized a series of agricultural strikes and made a determined effort to unionize migratory farm labor, the forces of agribusiness launched an all-out countercampaign through a new organization called the Associated Farmers of California. The funds for its support came largely from the California Packing Corporation; the Southern Pacific Railroad; the Industrial Association of San Francisco; Southern Californians, Inc., a group of industrial employers; the Holly Sugar Corporation; and the Spreckels Investment Company. The Pacific Gas and Electric Company also made common cause with the large growers, because their needs for power to pump irrigation water made them some of its best customers. Most of these big-business concerns tried to keep their contributions to the Associated Farmers confidential in order to maintain the image of a "farmers' organization."

Throughout the state, units of the Associated Farmers worked in intimate cooperation with local law enforcement officials. Most county sheriffs were politically allied with agribusiness interests. In some counties, migratory workers could not be employed unless they were registered with the sheriff's office, and the Associated Farmers provided the sheriff with lists of "agitators" and "dangerous radicals" including all persons known to have been members of unions. Such men were not only denied employment but were often ordered out of the county. In Contra Costa County, for example, farm employment practices were regulated under this plan with the guidance of two men. One was the sheriff, and the other was Philip S. Bancroft, a large grower and a top official of the Associated Farmers.

When a strike threatened, growers or their managerial employees were often made special deputies, though they did not always wait for this legal authorization and often acted simply as armed vigilantes. In the strike of the A. F. of L. lettuce-packers' union at Salinas in 1936, agribusiness groups recruited a "general staff" which supplanted the sheriff and the chief of police. Col. Henry Sanborn, an Army Reserve officer and publisher of the anti-Communist journal, *The American Citizen,* was employed as "coordinator" of all antistrike forces, including the local law enforcement officers as well as a "citizens' army" armed with shotguns and pick handles. The chief of the state highway patrol and a representative of the state attorney general's office gave their approval to this arrangement.

Under the aegis of the Associated Farmers, county "major disaster" ordinances were interpreted as applying to strikes, and the organization also aided in many prosecutions not only of Communists but of almost any other agricultural strike leaders under the state criminal syndicalism law.

Among the justifications used by the embattled "farmers" in their extreme resistance to any form of labor unionism were two arguments that had some color of validity during the darkest years of the great depression in 1933 and 1934. At that time it was often true that growers could not have paid higher wages without raising the cost of production above the prices that the crops could be sold for; it was also true that the main attempts to organize migratory farm laborers were then in the hands of the Communist party, which was interested in the workers chiefly as pawns in its drive to overthrow the capitalist system. But agribusiness interests continued to repeat these arguments in later years when prices and profits had risen greatly, and when radical influence was no longer substantially involved.

In the middle and later years of the 1930s, dispossessed families from the Dust Bowl region came into California at the rate of more than 100,000 persons a year, most of them to swell the supply of migratory farm labor. People of Anglo-American stock, working in family groups, now made up the bulk of the state's migratory labor force for the first time, and as a result, the public interest in the plight of farm laborers increased somewhat, though only temporarily. Carey McWilliams's *Factories in the Field* and John Steinbeck's *The Grapes of Wrath,* both published in 1939, helped to stimulate this interest. McWilliams's book included a chapter on the activities of the Associated Farmers and their allies entitled "The Rise of Farm Fascism."

In the administration of Governor Culbert L. Olson, McWilliams was chief of the state division of immigration and housing, and in that capacity he made himself a thorn in the flesh of agribusiness by inspecting private farm labor camps and denouncing their vile conditions. The annual convention of the Associated Farmers passed a resolution describing McWilliams as "California's Agricultural Pest Number One, outranking pear blight and the boll weevil." The state legislature, under agribusiness influence, passed a bill to abolish McWilliams's position, but Governor Olson pocket-vetoed this proposed "anti-McWilliams act."

In 1939 and 1940 the La Follette Committee, a subcommittee of the United States Senate Committee on Education and Labor under the chairmanship of Senator Robert M. La Follette, Jr., of Wisconsin, held extensive and often sensational hearings in California in the course of its investigation of "violations of free speech and rights of labor." But most of its hearings and reports, though very detailed and revealing, were not published in full until after the nation had entered World War II. The committee's recommendations for reform, introduced in 1942, produced no action in Congress. The "Okies" flocked to the shipyards; Mexicans and Mexican Americans again became the majority of the California farm labor force; and the public lost what interest it had had in the whole matter. The Dies Committee was attracting more attention than the La Follette Committee, and in 1946, as the reactionary cycle swung still further, "young Bob," now an "old progressive," lost the Wisconsin Republican senatorial nomination to Joseph R. McCarthy.

The rise and fall of the bracero program. The demands of World War II produced a sudden, genuine, and desperate shortage of farm labor, and the California growers called for large numbers of workers from Mexico to make up the shortage. In 1942, under an act of Congress and an agreement with Mexico, the United States Department of Agriculture assumed the responsibility for recruiting, contracting, transporting, housing, and feeding these temporary immigrant farm workers. In a formal sense, this was the beginning of the "bracero program."

The meaning of the Spanish word *braceros* ("the strong-armed ones") bore a striking resemblance to the meaning of the Tamil word *kuli*.

There had been an informal bracero program 25 years earlier during World War I, when private labor contractors had supplied California growers with seasonal workers from Mexico. Thousands of peons had been eager for the opportunity, since the Mexican Revolution had turned hordes of them into displaced persons, much as the Taiping Rebellion had nudged thousands of destitute Chinese toward California in the 1850s.

The growers were able to persuade Congress not to include Mexico in the postwar quota system of immigration restrictions, and the surge of Mexicans into California had continued through the 1920s; but it had slowed in the depression years, and the Mexican government had then found itself forced to pay the costs of repatriating many of its impoverished nationals who could no longer obtain work in California and who were not eligible for relief there. In 1942 the Mexican government feared that this experience would be repeated, and it therefore demanded that the United States government, rather than private labor contractors, must take responsibility for the immigrant workers.

After World War II the bracero program continued in force with the enthusiastic support of California growers, though President Truman, to their irritation, removed the program from the grower-oriented Department of Agriculture and assigned it to the Department of Labor by Executive order in 1948.

More numerous than the braceros in the years after the end of World War II were the illegal "wetbacks." While their exact numbers could not be known, it was estimated that more than half a million of these illegal immigrants crossed and recrossed the international boundary each year, most of them to work in the fields of California and other states in the Southwest.

In 1951 Congress adopted the famous Public Law 78, and also gave special legislative recognition to a new agreement with Mexico. Together these measures provided the most elaborate plan of importing contract workers in which the United States had ever engaged, and although the plan was approved as a "Korean War emergency" measure, it ultimately provided the basis for continuing the bracero program until 1964, 11 years after the Korean War had ended.

Under this system, Mexican officials assembled the braceros, and the United States Department of Labor provided for their transportation to reception centers north of the border. There they were turned over to labor contractors representing the growers' associations. At the insistence of the Mexican government, there were standard contracts covering wages, hours, transportation, housing, and working conditions. The American government guaranteed the provision of emergency medical care, workmen's compensation, disability and death benefits, and burial expenses. Though such provisions were minimal, they were far superior to the benefits available to American farm laborers, who enjoyed no legal protection at all.

In 1957, the peak year, California imported 192,438 braceros. In 1960 about 100,000 of them were at work in the state at the peak season in early September, and they formed about a quarter of the seasonal farm labor force. Most of them worked on the larger farms; about 5.2 percent of the farms in California employed 60 percent of the total number of seasonal hired workers—including more than 80 percent of the braceros.

As Congress continued to grant its long series of extensions of the program, it became increasingly hard to disguise the fact that the bracero system perpetuated the tragic poverty of the American migratory laborers. It depressed wages, destroyed the bargaining power of the domestic worker, and drove away local labor. There were many incidents in which braceros were used as strikebreakers with the connivance of government officials. Ostensibly, P.L. 78 allowed the importation of braceros only when it would "not adversely affect the wages and working conditions of domestic agricultural workers"; when "sufficient domestic workers . . . [were] not available"; and when "reasonable efforts [had] been made to attract domestic workers at wages . . . comparable to those offered foreign workers." This last provision would have tended to freeze farm wages at the wretched levels of the early 1950s, even if the rest of the provisions of P.L. 78 had been effectively enforced—which they were not. In effect, the system encouraged the growers to offer the lowest possible wages and the worst possible conditions to domestic workers, not merely because this practice saved money for the growers, as it always had, but also because it reduced the "availability" of domestic laborers and thus maximized the growers' legal eligibility to hire braceros.

To employers of seasonal farmworkers, the braceros represented a supply of cheap, docile, and "dependable" labor—guaranteed to arrive and to vanish exactly when the employers wanted it to. California growers continued to rationalize such motives on the basis of race, as they had done for more than a century. Anglo-Americans, the growers constantly assured themselves and the public, simply could not perform stoop labor as well as nonwhites, who were equipped by racial heredity with stronger backs.

There was no scientific basis for this assumption, and no Californian who knew his state's history should have had to be reminded that Anglo-Americans with gold-pans had not only performed the most backbreaking form of stoop labor ever invented, but had also insisted that *only* white men were suited for it. The actual difference, of course, was in the hope of financial return. It was not that Americans could not perform stoop labor, but rather that they did not want to perform it for stoop wages.

As agribusiness clung to the braceros, public criticism slowly intensified.

Agriculture was in the untenable position of being the only private industry which maintained that the government was obligated to provide it with a labor supply, and a cheap one at that. At last, in 1963, Congress refused to approve the customary two-year extension of the bracero program, and instead ordered its termination at the end of the following year, with a few minor and tightly limited exceptions.

The growers predicted disastrous shortages of harvest labor, and warned housewives of food scarcities and drastic price increases. These predictions proved baseless; 1965 was another record year in California agricultural output, and food prices rose insignificantly or not at all. By offering somewhat better wages and working conditions, the growers were able to attract enough domestic labor and thus to refute their own perennial claims that it would be impossible to do so.

Nevertheless, the growers and their allies replaced their old slogan, "the braceros are here to stay," with "bracero, come back"—*bracero regresa!* The Bank of America announced that it would withhold crop loans unless the government would guarantee the supply of labor. Agribusiness spokesmen insisted that crops would be destroyed or left to rot because labor was not available. George Murphy, the new United States Senator from Hollywood, was driven past miles of the parked cars of domestic laborers at work in the fields, and then photographed beside a grower plowing under a single row of strawberries.

But majority opinion had at last become not merely skeptical but hostile toward the growers' claims. In *The Slaves We Rent* (1965), Truman E. Moore called the bracero program a reincarnation of the Spanish *encomienda,* and a captive-labor system as out of date in modern America as a slave ship in New York harbor.

Unionization breaks through. Though the growers often denied that their desire for braceros was in any way related to their desire to block the organization of labor unions by domestic farmworkers, the connection was inescapable, and the growers used many of the same arguments for both purposes. Most of these arguments were variations on the traditional American political theme that "farming" was "different" from all other business enterprises.

Because the harvesting of perishable crops was intensely seasonal, one argument ran, growers required a "dependable" labor force, were uniquely vulnerable to strikes, and therefore could never tolerate unions.

This contention ignored a number of facts. Canning was equally seasonal; yet it had been unionized for many years, with great advantage to the employers rather than with any undue hardship to them. The marketing of perishable crops was as dependent on transportation workers as it was on harvest and cannery workers, yet the industries involved in the transportation of food had been entirely unionized for decades.

Agricultural labor itself had been organized in Hawaii since 1945, and unionization, far from ruining the Hawaiian agribusiness economy, had been a major factor in its mounting prosperity and growth. Significantly, it was the International Longshoremen's and Warehousemen's Union that had successfully organized the Hawaiian agricultural workers.

The longshoremen had once been the victims of a casual labor system, and their successful battle against it had spectacularly demonstrated the advantages of stable employment, for the employer as well as the worker. Since the unionization of the West Coast waterfronts in the 1930s, a stable and contented work force together with the advance of automation had made possible the loading of several times as much cargo per man-hour at enormous savings to the shipping lines. In 1961 the shipping companies agreed to share these profits with the union members by negotiating with Harry Bridges' longshoremen a pioneering contract for wages as high as $10,000 a year, with retirement income and other benefits at a comparable level. Under such conditions, said Bridges, "the strike is an obsolete weapon." This was the same Bridges who had once been denounced as a menace to the national safety.

Most of the employers in the canning, trucking, railroad, and shipping industries (and, in Hawaii, even the growers) had long since tacitly conceded that union contracts were the best method of assuring a dependable labor supply. Where seasonal agricultural problems were involved, an appropriate solution was the no-strike contract, negotiated months in advance of the harvest. As for the alleged dependability of Mexican alien contract labor, on the other hand, the California growers had had to live in perpetual fear that the government would shut off the flow, as indeed it eventually did.

An often-repeated contention of California growers was that like other "American farmers" they had always maintained a personal and almost familial solicitude toward their hired hands, and that this relationship would be sacrificed in the "impersonal" process of union bargaining. Much of the public in California consisted of recent arrivals from the North Central and Northeastern parts of the nation, where this idea had once had some faint semblance of truth. Many remained unaware that it had never had any validity as applied to the typical employer-employee relationships in the agriculture of California, where wage rates were set by growers' associations much more often than by bargaining of any sort, and where hiring was usually done through labor contractors who performed the functions of company unions.

Growers also maintained that they believed in "collective bargaining," but only with men who actually worked for them, and not with labor union officials, whom they almost invariably described as "outside agitators." But this was the same claim that employers in virtually every other industry had used in earlier times in efforts to block the beginnings of unions. It ignored the fact that collective bargaining could not be genuine if workers were denied the right to choose experienced professional representatives as their bargaining agents. The truth was that most of the growers wished to continue to hire such representatives of their own—the labor contractors—while continuing to deny any effective representation to the workers.

The most genuine objection of the growers to collective bargaining was that it was sure to raise wages and to increase other costs to the farm employer. But in the long run not even this objection was valid, even on a strictly economic level. Higher wages would enable hundreds of thousands of American migrant-worker families to buy more food, and at the same time would lower the costs of relief and many of the other costs of poverty and misery.

Extreme poverty and the disorganization that accompanied it had always been a major obstacle to organizing farmworkers, who were generally regarded as too demoralized to be even potential union material. The A. F. of L. had repeatedly attempted the job and had repeatedly given it up. Paul Scharrenberg, long the official spokesman of the A. F. of L. in California, remarked in 1935 that "only fanatics are willing to live in shacks or tents and get their heads broken in the interests of migratory labor."

Clark Kerr, on the basis of his wide experience as a mediator of labor disputes, maintained as late as 1961 that "about the only time you ever get farm workers organized is when it is done by some group with an ideological inclination for more than a bona fide union purpose." He recommended wage boards to set minimum standards, as the main hope of improvement. Varden Fuller, one of the ablest students of the problem, long believed that farmworkers could never be unionized until some unprecedented awakening of public conscience impelled the Federal government to bring farm labor under the laws guaranteeing the right of collective bargaining, and after many years he nearly gave up hope that this would ever occur.

But the two largest national labor groups had merged in 1955, and four years later the organization thus formed, the AFL-CIO, returned to the offensive on the farm labor front with a new Agricultural Workers Organizing Committee. A veteran building trades union official, C. Al Green, assumed the national directorship of AWOC in 1962.

At about the same time, Cesar Chavez left a secure and comfortable job as an official of a Mexican-American community service society to begin the hard and hazardous task of organizing a new and independent union called the National Farm Workers Association, at a salary of $50 a week.

Chavez had been born near Yuma, Arizona, on a small homestead near the Colorado River. This family farm was lost through unpaid taxes in the depression of the '30s. He had worked as a migrant farm laborer from early childhood, and consequently had obtained his eight years of formal education with difficulty in nearly 40 different California public schools.

Chavez conceived the new NFWA as a labor organization that would offer its members the benefits of a credit union and other services, while it offered employers a stable and dependable work force, made up of skillful and well-organized crews of NFWA members working with no-strike contracts. He placed no hope in agricultural strikes, having seen too many disheartening examples of them.

But on September 8, 1965, AWOC members began a strike against 33 grape growers in the district around Delano in northern Kern County; and two weeks later Chavez's NFWA decided to join it.

For the first several months there seemed to be no chance whatever that the strike could win. So many strikebreakers were brought in that the grape harvest in the district was larger than in the previous year. Yet the strike continued until, in the spring and summer of 1966, it won a series of brilliant victories that set a precedent for ultimate unionization of at least the larger farms throughout California.

If the Delano strike had been attempted a few years earlier it would have met the fate of every previous attempt to organize farm labor. But now a new force was at work—the strong and increasing sympathy of a part of the white public for the civil rights of ethnic minorities in general and farm workers in particular. Neither of the unions involved in the Delano strike was segregated, but the AWOC local, under Larry Itliong as regional director, consisted mainly of Filipino Americans, while most of the members of Chavez's NFWA were Mexican Americans. The brief flicker of public sympathy for migrant workers in the late 1930s had arisen mainly because, for the first time, they were then predominantly "Nordic." In the 1960s, however, new and different manifestations of public conscience were emerging.

The NFWA had been awarded a substantial grant as a part of the Federal "war on poverty" program. Payments under this grant were deferred during the strike, with the approval and indeed at the insistence of Chavez, who often remarked that "the only way to fight poverty is with a union contract." But gifts of money and food for the strikers poured into Delano from several other labor unions, from church groups throughout California, and from many other sympathizers with the civil rights movement.

The longshoremen in the San Francisco Bay area refused to load grapes from the struck vineyards, of which the largest were owned by Schenley Industries and the Di Giorgio Corporation. Nationwide boycotts were launched against Schenley wines and liquors, against Di Giorgio's S & W canned goods, and against stores that sold them. In the spring of 1966, executives of Schenley concluded that the adverse publicity was counteracting the effects of the large sums the company spent to advertise its products. In this light, the much smaller amounts the company saved by refusing to raise wages in its vineyards were obviously a very poor economy; and on April 6, 1966, Schenley Industries made the historic announcement that it had agreed to recognize the National Farm Workers' Association as the sole bargaining representative for its fieldworkers. This was the first recognition of a farmworker's union by a major California grower.

The next day the Di Giorgio Corporation announced that it would permit its workers to decide by ballot whether they wished to be represented by a union, and if so, what union. The victorious allies, Itliong's AWOC and Chavez's NFWA, merged to form the United Farm Workers Organizing Committee. In the election on August 30, 1966, although the Di Giorgio Corporation had always insisted that its employees did not want to be unionized, its field-wokers voted 530 for UFWOC, 331 for the Teamsters Union, and 12 for no union.

Several northern California growers of wine grapes then signed contracts with the United Farm Workers, but the great majority of California producers of table grapes held out. They were encouraged by the election of Ronald Reagan, a vigorous opponent of farm unions, to the governorship in 1966. In August 1967 Chavez called for a boycott against the Giumarra Vineyards, the nation's largest table-grape producers; and in 1968 the UFW launched a national boycott of all California table grapes. This move captured the attention of the whole country and became a burning social issue. Although Governor Reagan, Senator George Murphy, and presidential candidate Richard Nixon condemned the boycott, the mayors of San Francisco, New York, Chicago, Cleveland, Honolulu, and several other large cities announced their approval of it; and it became so effective that the growers were threatened with ruin. At last, in July 1970, Giumarra and most of the other large California table-grape growers agreed to union contracts with the United Farm Workers.

Chavez's next move was against the lettuce growers of the Salinas Valley; but as soon as those growers learned that the grape producers were about to surrender, they hurriedly negotiated contracts with the Teamsters Union in order to forestall the UFW drive. One maverick Salinas lettuce grower, Bud Antle, had included his field workers in his contracts with the Teamsters since 1961. Now there was a rush to imitate him, because, said a Salinas growers' representative, "the Teamsters are a trade union. Chavez' union is a civil rights movement." Chavez denounced the Teamsters' agreements as "sweetheart contracts," and complained that the Teamsters had broken a promise to leave the organization of field workers to the UFW. He called a strike and a lettuce boycott; but the courts ruled that this was a jurisdictional strike and therefore illegal, and Chavez spent several days in jail. Labor relations in the lettuce fields remained complex and unresolved, under a long and uneasy truce.

The equal protection of the laws." Until 1966 agricultural labor was specifically excluded from the provisions of virtually every Federal and state law that protected the rights of other workers. Minimum wages, unemployment insurance, social security, collective bargaining—all were guaranteed to others and specifically denied to farm labor.

The rationalization for this was always that "farmers had special problems." The truth was that they had special political power. Agricultural employers were heavily overrepresented in Congress and in almost every state legislature, while the interests of farmworkers were almost totally unrepresented. Equally important were the stubborn apathy, ignorance, and illusions of the American public on the subject. This was a blind spot comparable to one that the British upper and middle classes had once demonstrated for more than a hundred years. When Oliver Goldsmith wrote in *The Deserted Village*

> Ill fares the land, to hastening ills a prey,
> Where wealth accumulates and men decay,

he was praised as a poet but accused of being inaccurate, oversentimental, and unpatriotic as a historian. Yet, as Carey McWilliams pointed out, when careful studies of the history of the British village laborer were made nearly a century and a half later, they vindicated Goldsmith's description.

The ending of the bracero program had been an important preliminary to reform, but only a negative one. At long last, in August and September of 1964, Congress made its first positive moves toward correcting a shameful set of conditions. The Economic Opportunity Act of 1964 included grants to agencies aiding migrant workers, and an amendment to the National Housing Act provided direct loans for construction of farm-labor housing. In September 1966 Congress took the historic step of extending the protection of a new Federal minimum-wage law to farmworkers. This was only a token beginning. While the minimum wage for most other workers was raised to $1.60 an hour, effective in 1968, the national minimum for farm labor was set at only $1, and not even this would apply to small employers. In the pioneering union contract, on the other hand, Schenley Industries had agreed to pay $1.60 an hour to its California fieldworkers.

The new Federal laws were at least an entering wedge, however, and committees both of Congress and of the California legislature worked with new vigor in studying proposals for further reforms. California needed an agricultural minimum-wage provision much higher than the national one. Laws governing union representation elections needed to be applied to agriculture. More subsidies to help provide decent housing for migrant workers were essential in order to eradicate the rural slums that were far worse than anything in the cities. For migrant workers and their families the conditions of recruitment, transportation, health, sanitation, workmen's compensation, child labor, education, and civil and political rights were disgracefully and incredibly substandard. The first steps toward reform, in the middle 1960s, were timid and halting, and through 1971 the attempts to extend the provisions of the National Labor Relations Act to farm workers remained deadlocked. This was partly because Chavez did not wish to give up the weapon of the secondary boycott, which was illegal for workers covered by the NLRA.

SELECTED BIBLIOGRAPHY

Paul N. Williams and others, "Green Gold: California's $3.5 Billion Agricultural Industry," *California*, LIV (Autumn 1964), 23–51, is an informative special report in the magazine of the California State Chamber of Commerce. California, University, *Food for Man in the Future* (1964), Proceedings of Conference III in the series on *California and the Challenge of Growth*, is a useful survey of the state's agricultural problems and prospects. Good sources of statistics are California, Economic Development Agency, *California Statistical Abstract*, and U.S. Department of Agriculture, *Agricultural Statistics*, both annual publications.

Several theses at the University of California, Berkeley, contribute to California's agricultural history. On some of the effects of mechanization, see John W. Mamer, "The Generation and Proliferation of Agricultural Hand-labor-saving Technology; a Case Study of Sugar Beets" (Ph.D., 1958); and Francis J. Smith, "The Impact of Technological Change on the Marketing of Salinas Lettuce" (Ph.D., 1961). On particular crops, see Colin C. Archibald, "History of Cotton Production in California" (M.A., 1950); Rolf W. Ordal, "History of the California Walnut Industry" (Ph.D., 1952); Elizabeth M. Riley, "History of the Almond Industry in California" (M.A., 1948). See also Charles C. Cooley, "The California Date Growing Industry, 1890–1939," *Southern California Quarterly*, XLIX (March and June 1967), 47–64, 167–192; Joseph Giovinco, "Democracy in Banking: the Bank of Italy and California's Italians," *California Historical Society Quarterly*, XLVII (September 1968), 195–218; and Hans C. Palmer, "Italian Immigration and the Development of California Agriculture," Ph.D. thesis, University of California, Berkeley (1965).

Walter Goldschmidt, *As You Sow* (1947), analyzed the social structure of Arvin, a community based on corporate agriculture, and compared it unfavorably with the social structure of Dinuba, a town in a district of family farms. Some of the subsequent attacks on the methods and conclusions of Goldschmidt's study are described in Richard S. Kirkendall, "Social Science in the Central Valley of California: an Episode," *California Historical Society Quarterly*, XLIII (September 1964), 195–218.

Varden Fuller, "The Supply of Agricultural Labor as a Factor in the Evolution of Farm Organization in California," Ph.D. thesis, University of California, Berkeley (1939), was published in United States Senate Committee on Education and Labor, *Violations of Free Speech and Rights of Labor. Hearings before a Subcommittee . . .*, part 54 (1940), pp. 19777–19898. The other parts of these hearings before the La Follette subcommittee (published 1940–1943), and also many of the parts of the subcommittee's *Report* (1942–1943), are indispensable sources for the troubled agricultural history of the 1930s. See also the *Hearings* (1940–1941) and *Reports* (1941), of the House of Representatives Select Committee to Investigate Interstate Migration of Destitute Citizens, chaired by Congressman John H. Tolan of Oakland; and Walter J. Stein, "California and the 'Dust Bowl' Migration," Ph.D. thesis, University of California, Berkeley (1969).

Other important works dealing with the state's peculiar farm labor problems are Carey McWilliams, *Factories in the Field; the Story of Migratory Farm Labor in California* (1939), and *Ill Fares the Land; Migratory Labor in the United States* (1942); Dorothea Lange and Paul S. Taylor, *An American Exodus: a Record of Human Erosion* (1939); and Lloyd S. Fisher, *The Harvest Labor Market in California* (1953).

On the use of Mexican and other immigrant labor, see Paul S. Taylor, *Mexican Labor in the United States: Imperial Valley, California* (1928); John R. Martinez, "Mexican Immigration to the United States, 1910–1930," Ph.D. thesis, University of California, Berkeley (1957); John C. Elac, "The Employment of Mexican Workers in U.S. Agriculture, 1900–1960," Ph.D. thesis, University of California, Los Angeles (1961); Charles Wollenberg, "*Huelga*, 1928 Style: The Imperial Valley Cantaloupe Workers' Strike," *Pacific Historical Review*, XXXVIII (February 1969), 45–58; James F. Rooney, "The Effects of Imported Mexican Farm Labor in a California County," *American Journal of Economics and Sociology*, XX (October 1961), 513–521, a study conducted in San Joaquin County in 1957; Leo Grebler, *Mexican Immigration to the United States–The Record and Its Implications* (1966); R. K. Das, *Hindustani Workers on the Pacific Coast* (1923); and Bruno Lasker, *Filipino Immigration to the United States* (1931).

Important studies of the bracero program are Ernesto Galarza, *Merchants of Labor: the Mexican Bracero Story* (1964); Otey M. Scruggs, "The Evolution of the Mexican Farm Labor Agreement of 1942," *Agricultural History*, XXXIV (July 1960), 140–149; Ellis W. Hawley, "The Politics of the Mexican Labor Issue, 1950–1965," *ibid.*, XL (July 1966), 157–176; N. Ray Gilmore and Gladys Gilmore, "The Bracero in California," *Pacific Historical Review*, XXXII (August 1963), 265–282; and Truman E. Moore, *The Slaves We Rent* (1965).

On the background of the farm labor union question, see Stuart M. Jamieson, *Labor Unionism in American Agriculture*, U.S. Bureau of Labor Statistics Bulletin No. 836 (1945); Alexander Morin, *The Organizability of Farm Labor in the United States* (1952); and Varden Fuller, *Labor Relations in Agriculture* (1955).

U.S. Department of Labor, *Year of Transition: Seasonal Farm Labor, 1965* (1966), is an incisive report by Secretary of Labor W. Willard Wirtz on the results of the termination of the bracero program and the needs for reform in the conditions of domestic farm labor.

On the movement led by Cesar Chavez, see Peter Matthiessen, *Sal Si Puedes: Cesar Chavez and the New American Revolution* (1969); John G. Dunne, *Delano: The Story of the California Grape Strike* (1967, 1971); and Joan London and Henry Anderson, *So Shall Ye Reap* (1970).

Chapter XL

THE SLOW RETREAT OF RACIAL INTOLERANCE

The California Indians. All the nonwhite minorities in American California suffered from various kinds of unjust discrimination, but the mistreatment of the Indians began earliest and was far the worst. Between 1846 and 1900 about one-tenth of the California Indians were victims of outright genocide, while disease and starvation killed many more. In California, as in other parts of the United States, the history of American treatment of the Indians in the 19th century was too often a sickening record of racist murder and sanctimonious fraud.

Several idealistic individuals tried to ameliorate the situation. In the early 1880s the New England authoress Helen Hunt Jackson sent copies of her book, *A Century of Dishonor,* to all the members of Congress. At Mrs. Jackson's request, Congress then made her a member of a special commission to report on the Indians of Southern California. Her fellow commissioner was Abbot Kinney, the wealthy promoter of a romantic imitation of Venice a few miles south of Los Angeles. Their report had little effect on Congress, but Mrs. Jackson's research for it aided the writing of her novel *Ramona.*

This novel was often called the *Uncle Tom's Cabin* of California, but its most enduring effect was merely to create a collection of regional myths that stimulated the tourist trade. These legends became so ingrained in the culture of Southern California that they were often mistaken for realities. In later years many who visited "Ramona's birthplace" in San Diego or the annual "Ramona Pageant" at Hemet were surprised and disappointed if they chanced to learn that *Ramona* was a novel rather than a biography.

In 1901 Charles F. Lummis organized the Sequoya League with the aid of Thomas R. Bard, David Starr Jordan, and others. Its main object was better treatment of the Indians, and its main accomplishment was an act of Congress that provided money to purchase some land near Pala for the Indians who were evicted from Warner's Ranch.

The problems of the Indians in California were different from those of most other American Indian tribes in that only a minority of the California Indians were ever placed on reservations. The treaties of the early 1850s, providing for large reservations in California, were never ratified, and most of the attempts to provide small reservations were unsuccessful. Most of the California Indians were left to survive as best they might on the fringes of American settlement. Most of them did not survive. Of those who did, the majority became agricultural laborers.

Some of the most geographically isolated of the California tribes, such as the Yahi, tried to continue their ancient manner of life and to avoid contact with white society. The country of the Yahi was in the Mill Creek region south of Mount Lassen, a district of barren hills whose chief vegetation was scrub oak and poison oak. The gold seekers of the 1850s had hunted the Yahi as if they were wild animals, and by 1870 it was supposed that they were extinct. But on August 29, 1911, a man who was apparently the last survivor of the tribe was found in a slaughterhouse near Oroville, where he had come in search of food. Professor Kroeber called him Ishi, the Yahi word for *man. Yahi* meant simply *the people.*

Professors Alfred L. Kroeber and Thomas T. Waterman of the University of California brought Ishi to the university's museum of anthropology, then in San Francisco. There the "last wild Indian in North America" lived for several years until his death. Middle-aged and in reasonably good health at the time of his "capture" by the sheriff at Oroville, Ishi caught his first cold in San Francisco, and later succumbed to tuberculosis. But in the meantime this stone-age man had adapted himself remarkably well to a 20th-century environment. Alfred Kroeber believed that Ishi had made the transition from one culture to another more effectively and more quickly than he himself could have done, and the episode became an important example of the kind of evidence that led virtually every competent anthropologist in the world to reject the idea of the biological inferiority of so-called "primitive races."

During World War I a number of Indians served in the armed forces, and in 1924, partly in recognition of that service, Congress gave American Indians the rights of citizenship in the United States and in the states of their residence. Congress also recognized that an injustice had been done to the California Indians, in particular, by the failure to ratify the reservation treaties of the early 1850s, which had promised them more than 7 million acres of land. In 1928 Congress authorized the attorney general of California to bring suit against the United States on behalf of the California Indians, to determine what financial compensation should be made to them. A special census provided by the act of

1928 enumerated 23,540 persons as living descendants of California Indians, and thus entitled to compensation. But the case dragged on until 1944, and when the Federal court of claims finally made its award it was only for a little more than 5 million dollars, or about $200 per person.

In the special case of the survivors of the Cahuilla tribe, also known as the Palm Springs Indians, the results of litigation were startlingly different. In the 1870s the Federal government had granted the odd-numbered sections of desert land in the Palm Springs area to the Southern Pacific Railroad, and the even-numbered sections, checkerboard-fashion, to the Cahuilla Indians. When Palm Springs became a booming resort town in the 1920s the surviving Cahuillas, numbering about 100, tried to persuade the Federal government to permit the leasing of some of their lands to the eager hotel promoters, but the government refused. Lee Arenas, one of the Cahuillas, managed to interest a former justice of the California supreme court, John W. Preston, in taking the case to the Supreme Court of the United States. In 1944 the Court ruled that each of the Cahuillas should receive the rental from $350,000 worth of individually allotted land, as well as a share of the income from 30,000 acres of tribal land.

The contrast between the ridiculously inadequate award by the Federal court of claims to the California Indians in 1944, and the lucrative award by the Supreme Court to the Palm Springs Indians in the same year was so striking that it helped persuade Congress to pass the Indian Claims Commission Act of 1946. This law entitled American Indians to payments from the Federal government equivalent to the original value of the lands their ancestors had once occupied. The determination of the amounts was a fantastically complex matter; but in 1965, after many years of hearings, the descendants of the California Indians finally received and voted to accept an award of a little more than 29 million dollars. This was about 45 cents an acre for 64 million acres of land, nearly two-thirds of the total area of California. Since the number of eligible descendants was then about 33,000, the practical effect was that each would ultimately receive a payment of something less than $900.

From the 1920s onward, both the United States and the state of California demonstrated awakenings of conscience in their treatment of the Indians. California abolished all legal distinctions between persons of Indian ancestry and other citizens, and although there were still instances of illegal discrimination by prejudiced individual officials, especially in local law enforcement and in county welfare policies, California led all the states in making Indians fully eligible to receive the benefits of the public schools, welfare assistance, old age and survivors payments, and other public services.

The long and tragic decline in the Indian population was reversed, and the Indians became the fastest-growing minority group. In 1965, according to the best estimates, the number of persons of Indian ancestry in California had risen to 75,000, partly through natural increase and partly through migration to California cities from reservations in other states, aided by job training and relocation programs of the Federal government. Only 7,400, or less than 10 percent of the Indians in the state, were living on the 82 Federal reservations. Only three of these, at Hoopa Valley, Fort Yuma, and Bishop, had more than 500 residents and only 18 reservations had more than 100. The smaller units, sometimes called "rancherias," were better described as group homesites.

In the nation as a whole, a much larger proportion of the American Indians not only lived on reserved tribal lands but strongly wished to remain on them, in order to preserve their community life and their cultural identity. For decades most of the American Indians had stubbornly resisted the efforts of the Federal government, under the Dawes Act of 1887, to terminate the reservation system and to push them into the "mainstream" of American life. The government had finally abandoned this coercive policy by adopting the Indian Reorganization Act of 1934, which encouraged Indians who wished to remain with their tribal communities to do so. In the 1960s, the Federal government's policy was one of aiding both the economic and social development of the tribal communities and the relocation of those individuals who wished to leave the reservations and move to the cities. But the majority, nationwide, remained deeply skeptical that they would ever be allowed to join the "mainstream of American society" as equal members. One American Indian college student remarked that "It is dishonest to use the word 'integration.' You have never wanted us to integrate, but only to conform."

On the other hand, since most of the Indians of California had never lived on reservations, they had always been under much greater pressure to seek assimilation. In gradually increasing numbers, though in widely varying degrees, some of them achieved it. In general, however, although they were the state's fastest-growing minority group, they remained the most economically depressed one. Their average family income was the lowest of all; and the rate of unemployment among American Indians in California in 1965 was more than 15 percent—three times as high as the rate for whites and 4 percent above the rate for Negroes.

The Orientals. If the worst racial persecutions in American history were those inflicted on the Indians before 1900, the most obvious and flagrant racist abuse in the United States in the 20th century was that which the Japanese Americans suffered when they were deprived of their property and placed in concentration camps during World War II. But that abuse was a temporary one and the very extremity of the blundering injustice of it ultimately helped enable the people of the United States and the people of California to learn a lesson from it.

Even during the war itself some Californians had opposed the anti-Japanese hysteria. The Pacific Coast Committee on American Principles and Fair Play, organized in December 1941 with President Robert Gordon Sproul and several members of the faculty of the University of California among its leaders, carried on a valiant campaign in defense of the rights of the Japanese Americans. The heroism of Nisei soldiers was a reproach to anti-Japanese racism. And after the end of the war the memory of Hiroshima and Nagasaki neutralized the memory of Pearl Harbor.

As the War Relocation Authority pointed out in the concluding sentence of its final report in 1946, "Although there is undoubtedly a marked xenophobic tendency in the United States, there is also a strong and stubborn potential for fair-mindedness among the American people—a potential which should be carefully studied, fostered, and brought to the highest degree of assertiveness in the interest of greater racial tolerance and a richer realization of democratic values."

Congress recognized in 1948 that the Japanese Americans were entitled to financial compensation. Families had sold their homes and businesses in frantic haste. Some had lost everything they had, and many had lost most of what they had. Claims totaling 400 million dollars were filed by 44,000 Japanese Americans, who ultimately received settlements totaling 38 million. Congress also provided for the return of confiscated bank deposits, though the legal process was difficult and recovery was slow and incomplete.

In 1952, after California's alien land law had been in effect for 39 years, the state supreme court struck it down as unconstitutional. At about the same time, Congress entirely abandoned the racial definition of "aliens ineligible for citizenship." Very few nations had ever withheld the privilege of naturalization on racial grounds, and in doing so the United States had been in the company of Nazi Germany and the Union of South Africa. In 1952 the McCarran-Walter Immigration and Nationality Act provided that "the right of a person to become a naturalized citizen of the United States shall not be denied or abridged because of race."

An important factor in turning the tide of public feeling in favor of the Japanese Americans was that they reacted to mistreatment in an extraordinary way—by establishing an unrivaled record of good citizenship. They ranked higher in education and lower in crime and juvenile delinquency than any other ethnic group in the United States, including the native whites. In 1960 they averaged 12 years of schooling, as against 11 for whites and 8.6 for Negroes. In impressive numbers they obtained advanced degrees and jobs in such professional fields as business administration, engineering, and optometry, in which skilled men were in such short supply that traditional racial barriers could be circumvented. Their record of physical and mental health was almost incredible. The average longevity of Japanese Americans was 74.5 years for men and 81.2 years for women—nearly seven years above the figures for California whites and well above the record of any other group in human history. Three Japanese traditions, the strength of the family, the belief in the value of education, and the belief in the virtue of hard work, did most to account for this unparalleled triumph over adversity.

Similar traditions also accounted for a high rate of achievement among the Chinese Americans. In average length of school attendance, for example, they surpassed the whites, although they did not quite equal the Japanese. For the Chinese Americans the educational picture in 1960 was one of extremes. A very high proportion of them had gone to college, but 40 percent had not gone beyond the eighth grade. The shortages of engineers, scientists, professors, doctors, and nurses opened thousands of professional jobs to educated Chinese Americans, and this began to occur before the end of World War II, rather than after it, as in the case of the Japanese.

During the war the Federal government began to remove its legal discriminations against the Chinese. Congress repealed the Chinese Exclusion Act in 1943, in order, as President Roosevelt put it, to "correct a historic mistake and silence the distorted Japanese propaganda." The results were more important in principle than in practice, for although China was now permitted to have an immigration quota it was so low that only about 10,000 persons were admitted under it in the next 20 years. In 1965, however, Congress abolished the national-origins quota system. Under the new law, total annual immigration remained about the same but admission was on the basis of skills or family relationships. This permitted a substantial though still a moderate increase in Chinese immigration, much of it from Hong Kong to California.

For the Filipino Americans the situation was less favorable in virtually all respects. Although unemployment was lower for Japanese and Chinese men and women than for whites, it was considerably higher for Filipinos. Because of the importation of large numbers of unmarried Filipinos as agricultural laborers, the number of Filipino-American men was three times the number of women as late as 1950, and this drastic imbalance had cruel effects on the community life, family life, and general morale of the group.

The Negroes. Of all the racial minorities, the Negroes attracted the largest share of public attention in the decades after the end of World War II. They became more active than other groups in openly protesting against racial discrimination, and their protests, both peaceful and violent, received wide coverage in the national news media.

Negroes formed about 11 percent of the total population of the United States. In California the proportion was lower but still highly significant. The major influx had begun in 1942 with the sudden demand for labor in the shipyards and other war industries, and thereafter the percentage of Negroes in the state's population, which had been only 1.8 in 1940, rose to 4.3 in 1950 and 5.6 in 1960. But their presence was even more apparent because most of them became concentrated in all-black neighborhoods in the cities of Los Angeles, San Francisco, Oakland, Berkeley, and Richmond.

As Gunnar Myrdal pointed out in *An American Dilemma* (1944), a tragic "conflict between equalitarian ideals and discriminatory practice" had characterized American treatment of the Negroes, and as a result "their situation is pathological. . . . The masses of American Negroes are destitute."

The family, which was so great a source of strength for the Japanese Americans, was tragically weaker among American Negroes. For two centuries, under the system of slavery, the law had not recognized marriages between Negro slaves, and during that period the outrages committed by white men against Negro family life had had shattering psychological effects that were not erased in a century after abolition. The ability of the Negro husband and father to protect his family and to provide for its subsistence had only partially improved, and consequently the number of men who deserted their families was far higher than in any other group.

Lack of education was another crucial factor. In 1960 more than 40 percent of California Negroes had not gone beyond the eighth grade, and this became increasingly disastrous as mechanization and automation eliminated more and more unskilled jobs.

One of the most important developments in the movement toward a better life for the Negro in America came in the decision of the United States Supreme Court in 1954, which forbade racial segregation in the public schools; it was written by Chief Justice Earl Warren for a unanimous court. Reversing the decision of the Court in *Plessy v. Ferguson* in 1896, which had permitted so-called "separate but equal" facilities, the Court now ruled that public school segregation violated the Fourteenth Amendment provision which guaranteed the equal protection of the laws. To segregate Negro children solely on the grounds of their race, said Chief Justice Warren, "generates a feeling of inferiority as to their status in the community that may affect their hearts and minds in a way unlikely ever to be undone." Warren had learned a great deal about racism from his own mistake in advocating Japanese evacuation.

Formal segregation of pupils by race had been abolished in most of the public school districts of California for many years, and the state law which permitted local districts to continue the practice had been repealed in 1946. Yet *de facto* school segregation continued and even increased, mainly because residential segregation not only continued but actually became intensified. In the problem of unequal opportunity, housing was not only as important as education but also closely interrelated with it.

California had been the first state to attempt a legal sanction for segregated housing, when the constitution of 1879 authorized cities and towns to restrict the occupany of Chinese and even to forbid their residence within the city limits. In 1890 the United States Supreme Court had struck down this provision in the case of a San Francisco ordinance purporting to define the "boundaries" of Chinatown. In 1917 the Supreme Court invalidated another racial zoning ordinance by ruling that the "separate but equal" doctrine did not apply to the ownership of real property.

Real estate interests, wishing to maintain the sanctity of all-white neighborhoods, often relied upon the right of contract. Deeds for the sale of residential property included "restrictive covenants" in which the buyer promised not to sell to anyone other than "Caucasians." But in 1948, in *Shelley v. Kraemer,* the Supreme Court refused to permit the continued enforcement of these contracts by the courts, on the ground that such enforcement constituted action by agencies of state government in denial of "equal protection." The Los Angeles Board of Realtors and the California Real Estate Association launched a campaign for a Federal constitutional amendment to reverse the Supreme Court's ruling, but this project failed.

In 1959 the heavily Democratic California legislature adopted the Unruh Civil Rights Act, named for Jess M. Unruh, the speaker of the assembly. This law forbade racial discrimination by anyone engaged in business (including real estate brokers), and permitted anyone who suffered such discrimination to recover damages in the courts. In 1963 the legislature passed the Rumford Act, named for Negro Assemblyman W. Byron Rumford of Berkeley, which declared racial discrimination in housing to be against public policy, and forbade owners of residential property including more than four units, or owners of any publicly assisted residential property, to engage in racial discrimination in its rental or sale. Enforcement was in the hands of a state commission empowered to investigate complaints, conciliate disputes, and if necessary issue cease-and-desist orders.

Not long after the passage of the Rumford "fair housing" or "open occupancy" law, the California Real Estate Association began a campaign not only against this particular act but against every form of what the association denounced as "forced housing." This led to the drafting of Initiative Proposition 14, a state constitutional amendment incorporating what the realtors' organization called "the right to sell." That remarkable document proposed to invalidate every past or future state law or local ordinance that limited the right of any person to refuse "to sell, lease, or rent any part or all of his real property . . . to such person or persons as he in his absolute discretion chooses."

In November 1964 the voters of California approved Proposition 14 by more than two to one, and thus most of the white voters demonstrated that they were bitterly opposed to residential desegregation and deeply frightened by it. They feared a loss of social status if nonwhites moved into their neighborhoods. They feared decline of property values, though several studies had shown that this did not necessarily occur and that when it did the neighborhoods were usually those where property values had already been deteriorating. The whites also feared for their personal safety, even though the Negroes who could afford to move into white neighborhoods were seldom the ones who were disposed to violence and crime. Part of this "white backlash" was essentially irrational—the cancerous terror that came with the mass delusional neurosis of racism.

The realtors, more than any other group except the Negroes, had long been aware of the extent of white opposition to integrated housing. The livelihood of most real estate brokers and salesmen depended on their commissions from the sale of residential property, and many sellers refused to deal with brokers who would not conspire with them to maintain the color line. When the California Real Estate Association canvassed its members for money to aid the passage of Proposition 14, its most cogent statement of purpose was a direct one: ". . . to save your business."

The rationalizations, however, were many. Some realtors believed and publicly argued that the demand for integrated housing was a communistic plot against property rights. But they never made clear why a white man's freedom to sell or rent his property as he chose should be greater than a Negro's freedom to buy or rent that property if he could pay for it. For anyone, the right to buy must always have preceded the "right to sell."

In the words of Prof. Richard R. B. Powell, a leading authority on the law of real property, "It is difficult for a white person fully to realize the hurt to human dignity, the deep feeling of injustice, the . . . establishment of the foundations of bitter hatred caused to a Negro when he finds that his money is not acceptable in the purchase of a home or in the rental of housing."

Realtors argued that education, not legislation, was the only effective antidote for racial prejudice. Yet their own main attempt to influence the views of their clients was a call for even more discrimination than before. They urged the white majority to use its political power in an effort to establish the privilege of race discrimination in housing as a constitutional right. In May 1966 the state supreme court struck down this effort by invalidating Proposition 14 as an unconstitutional denial of the equal protection of the laws. There were many protests that the court had "violated the will of the people." But California had a long history of racist legislation that had been adopted by large majorities of the voters, yet properly discarded by the courts. In May 1967 the United States Supreme Court finally struck down Proposition 14 as unconstitutional. The only state that had adopted such a provision was not Alabama or Mississippi, but California.

At least as important as the political and social resistance to Negro penetration of white neighborhoods was the economic discrimination that kept them in menial jobs, or kept them from getting any jobs at all, and thus held down their ability to pay for decent housing. In California, as in most other states, nearly all labor unions in fields involving skilled workers had excluded Negroes entirely until World War II. In January 1945, in *James v. Marinship Corporation*, the California supreme court had declared this practice contrary to public policy. But even when Negroes were grudgingly admitted as union members, rules of seniority continued to favor the whites, and in the craft unions in which admission was through apprenticeship, white nepotism and amitism dominated the awarding of apprentice positions.

In 1959 a new state law forbade discrimination in employment, and created a fair employment practices commission to hear complaints; but the law had little effect on the total situation. In 1966, after a riot in the Negro ghetto of

Hunter's Point in San Francisco, Mayor John F. Shelley denounced "the medieval practice" of racial discrimination in some unions, and the board of supervisors empowered the city's human rights commission to enforce a new ordinance against discriminatory hiring by any employer doing business with the city government. But the major union organizations joined in a statement which asserted, as "the position of organized labor," that no public agency had the right to intervene in arrangements between unions and employers. Thus the unions took essentially the same position with respect to jobs that the organized realtors had taken with respect to the sale and rental of housing.

The passage of Proposition 14 and the deepening of Negro unemployment were among the grievances that contributed to the massive and tragic Watts riot in Los Angeles. The number of Negroes in Los Angeles County had grown from about 25,000 before World War II to nearly 650,000 in 1965, and most of them were crowded into the southern part of the city, including the Watts district. Housing in Los Angeles, as the county commission on human relations pointed out, was more strictly segregated than in any city in the southern states. The public transportation system was so wretched that an unemployed Negro, if he lived in Watts and could not afford a car, found that to answer an advertisement for a job required an average of 3 hours of bus travel.

The riot in the "palm tree ghetto" of Watts began on the sweltering and smoggy evening of August 11, 1965. A state highway patrolman had arrested a young Negro, Marquette Frye, for drunken driving. Frye resisted arrest. When his mother and a young woman bystander became involved in the scuffle, they also were forcibly arrested, and because the two women happened to be wearing loose-fitting garments, the rumor spread that two "pregnant women" had been victims of "police brutality."

The ensuing riot lasted for several days and was brought under control only by the intervention of the National Guard. It is more precisely called the "Los Angeles riot," since the bulk of the damage occurred in the Negro residential districts to the north and northwest of Watts, over a total area of more than 11 square miles. At least 34 persons were killed, 31 of them Negroes. In terms of loss of life this did not quite equal the record of the East St. Louis riot of 1917; but in terms of property losses, amounting to more than 40 million dollars, the Los Angeles riot was the most destructive in American history. More than 600 buildings were damaged, including more than 200 completely destroyed by fire. Perhaps even greater than the physical destruction, however, was the damage to the progress of racial tolerance and understanding.

The Mexican Americans. Far the largest ethnic minority in California was the group that the census listed as of "Spanish origin," nearly all of whom, in California, were Mexican Americans. In 1970 more than 3 million of them lived in California, and they formed more than 15 percent of the state's population, as compared with 11 percent Negroes, 1 percent Japanese, and 1 percent Chinese.

In 1910, the census had enumerated only 51,000 persons of Mexican ancestry in California, but the Mexican revolution of 1910–1920 combined with World War I to begin a long process of mass immigration from Mexico to the American Southwest. By 1945, only Mexico City had a larger Mexican population than Los Angeles. The result, however, was what George I. Sánchez has called "cultural indigestion." Most of the immigrants were laborers. Barriers of prejudice and of language blocked their economic advancement and their social assimilation. In Los Angeles, they were concentrated in the eastern part of the city almost to the degree that the Negroes were concentrated in the southern part of it. World War II brought some limited progress. Paradoxically, some of this resulted from uneasy afterthoughts about two flagrant wartime episodes of Anglo-American bigotry—the "Sleepy Lagoon" murder trial and the "Zoot Suit" riots.

On August 2, 1942, on the east side of Los Angeles, the body of a Mexican-American boy with a fractured skull was found beside a germ infested old reservoir, used as a swimming hole, which the newspapers dubbed the "Sleepy Lagoon." There had been some scuffling the night before between two juvenile gangs, but there was no direct evidence of murder, and no witness. Nevertheless, 300 young Mexican Americans were arrested, 23 indicted, and 17 convicted. The defendants were brutally treated while in jail, and racial prejudice was apparent throughout the proceedings. In a pseudo-scientific report to the grand jury, a police lieutenant explained violent crime by Mexicans as a racial characteristic, and the chief of police and the sheriff endorsed the report. The bias in the trial was so blatant and so clearly symptomatic of a larger social injustice that it ultimately led to some improvement in public attitudes. This came in part from the work of a defense committee headed by Carey McWilliams and in part from the verdict of the appellate court, which threw out all the convictions and strongly rebuked the trial judge.

During this period, some young Mexican Americans were wearing the "zoot suit," originally as the proper costume for jitterbug dancing but later to attract attention, to show their emancipation from their elders, and to express their group solidarity. Much of the public believed that not only all zoot suiters but virtually all young Mexican Americans were *pachucos*, or juvenile hoodlums. On June 3, 1943, mobs of white sailors, soldiers, and civilians in downtown Los Angeles began to beat up zoot suiters and tear off their clothes, and these race riots continued for six days until the Navy declared Los Angeles off limits.

This episode, too, ultimately contributed to some reaction against group prejudice. Moreover, the experience of Mexican Americans in uniform during the war was very different from that of their zoot-suited younger brothers. Mexican Americans were not segregated in the armed forces, and many acquired a new experience of integrated living. They volunteered in greater numbers and won more Congressional Medals of Honor, proportionately, than any other ethnic group. After the war many improved their status by education under the "G.I. bill."

Most of the immigrants had brought with them the folkways of poor people from rural Mexico. For example, family ties were very strong, but this often meant that children dropped out of school at an early age to help support their relatives. Such folkways led to stereotyped conceptions of the Mexican Americans as completely passive and resistant to social change, conceptions which persisted longer in Anglo-American opinion than among the Mexican Americans themselves, except in the poorest barrios or neighborhoods. The war and postwar periods brought a degree of occupational and geographical mobility that considerably weakened caste barriers against intermarriage, equality of employment, and housing opportunities. By the end of the 1960s, Mexican Americans in California were much more heterogeneous and much more urbanized than was commonly supposed. More than 85 percent of them lived in cities. Less than 15 percent of those employed were agricultural laborers.

Yet the Mexican Americans were still a deeply disadvantaged minority, caught in a vicious circle of undereducation and underemployment. Of the Mexican Americans employed in California, about half were "semiskilled or skilled" workers, including those in the entrepreneurial and professional fields; but within almost every occupational group the earnings of the Mexican Americans were much lower than the average. The percentage of families with annual incomes below the official "poverty" level of $3,000 was nearly twice the percentage for families in general. The high school dropout rate was more than 50 percent. Many children had grown up in households where only Spanish was spoken, and although the Bilingual Education Act of 1967 provided some Federal funds to help the public schools begin to deal more effectively with the language problem, the effort was belated and progress was slow.

Mexican Americans also had great difficulty in gaining political representation. The election of Edward R. Roybal to the Los Angeles city council in 1949 broke a long tradition of Anglo exclusiveness, and although the Mexican American Political Association, formed in 1959, succeeded in getting Roybal elected to Congress in 1962, for the rest of the decade it was unable to recover his seat on the city council for another Mexican American. Representation in the state legislature in the 1960s was limited to one or two assemblymen and no state senators. There was an enthusiastic "Viva Kennedy" movement during the campaign of 1960 (partly because Kennedy was a Catholic), and in general the Mexican Americans were heavily committed to the Democratic party; but they complained that the Democrats took their support for granted, did little for their interests, and gerrymandered their districts. There was much internal disunity among them, with too many ambitious individuals unwilling to withdraw from campaigns in favor of electable candidates. There were relatively few Mexican Americans wealthy enough to contribute heavily to campaign funds, and most of them were suspicious of political activists. Jealousies between "brown" and "black" weakened the chances of effective political coalitions with the Negroes, the other large nonwhite minority. For example, when Julian Nava insisted on entering the primary for the office of state superintendent of public instruction in 1970, he almost spoiled the chances of Wilson Riles to defeat Max Rafferty and thus to become the first Negro elected to a statewide office in California.

In the late 1960s, many of the younger Mexican Americans joined a militant new crusade in search of ethnic identity, parallel with the new black consciousness but determined to be more than an imitation of it. Reviving the belief of the 19th-century philosopher José Vasconcelos that people of mixed race would inherit the earth, they called themselves *La Raza*—"the Race" or "the People." Another appellation, also embraced with defiant pride, was *Chicanos*, a shortened, corrupted form of *Mexicano* with the first syllable dropped and the "x" pronounced as "ch" in the fashion of Mexico's Chihuahua Indians. Some Chicanos pointed out that in the mythology of the Aztecs the ancestral home called *Aztlan* had included the American Southwest. Thus in a symbolic sense Chicanos could regard themselves as the rightful owners of the whole region, rather than unprivileged visitors with their only roots south of the border.

After many decades of quiet patience, Mexican Americans showed signs of becoming America's newest angry minority. They had taken virtually no part in the Los Angeles riots of 1965; but in October 1970, after a series of increasingly bitter confrontations with police and sheriff's deputies in East Los Angeles, a Chicano antiwar demonstration degenerated into a major riot in which Ruben Salazar, a *Los Angeles Times* columnist and reporter, was unintentionally killed by a tear gas grenade. He had been one of the city's best-known Mexican-American spokesmen, and one of the most important advocates of orderly social change.

"Integration" had been terribly slow and terribly limited. Impatient younger leaders of the ethnic minority groups were now insisting that even if it ever came they would not want it, and that their only hope lay in the defiant glorification of their own separateness.

SELECTED BIBLIOGRAPHY

Jack D. Forbes, *Native Americans of California and Nevada* (1969), and Frank Quinn, *Indians of California, Past and Present* (1956), provide general introductions to 20th-century developments. Kenneth M. Johnson's monograph, *K-344, or The Indians of California vs. the United States* (1966), also includes much useful information on the broader history of California Indian problems. So do Sherburne F. Cook, "Migration and Urbanization of the Indians in California," *Human Biology*, XV (February 1943), 33–45, and "Racial Fusion among the California and Nevada Indians," *Human Biology*, XV (May 1943), 153–165; and Theodora Kroeber, *Ishi in Two Worlds; a Biography of the Last Wild Indian in North America* (1962). On Federal and state legislation, see Theodore H. Haas, "The Legal Aspects of Indian Affairs from 1887 to 1957," in *American Indians and American Life*, an issue of the *Annals of the American Academy of Political and Social Science*, CCCXI (May 1957), 12–22; Chauncey S. Goodrich, "Legal Status of the California Indians," *California Law Re-*

view, XIV (January and March 1926), 83–100 and 157–187; and Ferdinand F. Fernandez, "Except a California Indian: A Study in Legal Discrimination," *Southern California Quarterly*, L (June 1968), 161–175. Material on the 1960s may be found in California, Department of Industrial Relations, Division of Fair Employment Practices, *American Indians in California: Population, Education, Employment, Income* (November 1965); California, Legislature, Senate, Interim Committee on California Indian Affairs, *Progress Report . . . on Indians in Rural and Reservation Areas* (February 1966); Joan Ablon, "Relocated Indians in the San Francisco Bay Area: Concepts of Acculturation, Success and Identity in the City," Ph.D. thesis, University of Chicago (1963); D'Arcy McNickle, "The Indian Tests the Mainstream," *The Nation*, CCIII (September 26, 1966), 275–279; and Alvin M. Josephy, Jr., editor, *Red Power: The American Indians' Fight for Freedom* (1971). Bibliographies on the California Indians are in California, Division of Beaches and Parks, *Ethnographic Report*, Numbers 1–5 (1962).

On the improvement of feeling toward the Japanese Americans, see Atlee E. Shidler, "The Fair Play Committee; a Study in the Protection of the Rights of Minority Groups," M.A. thesis, Claremont Graduate School (1952); and William Petersen, "Success Story, Japanese-American Style," *New York Times Magazine* (January 9, 1966), 20 ff. Good general studies are Yamato Ichihashi, *Japancse in the United States* (1932); and thc volumes by Harry H. L. Kitano and Bill Hosokawa, cited above for Chapter XXXIV. Works on the Chinese Americans include Shien Woo Kung, *Chinese in American Life; Some Aspects of Their History, Status, Problems, and Contributions* (1962); Rose Hum Lee, *The Chinese in the United States of America* (1960); Fred W. Riggs, *Pressures on Congress: a Study of the Repeal of Chinese Exclusion* (1950); Kian Moon Kwan, "Assimilation of the Chinese in the United States: an Exploratory Study in California," Ph.D. thesis, University of California, Berkeley (1958); Kwang-Ching Liu, *Americans and Chinese* (1963); and Betty Lee Sung, *Mountain of Gold* (1967), reprinted as *The Story of the Chinese in America* (1971).

California, Department of Industrial Relations, Division of Fair Employment Practices, *Californians of Japanese, Chinese, and Filipino Ancestry* (June 1965), contains valuable statistics. Other useful pamphlets in this series are *Negro Californians* (June 1963); *Californians of Spanish Surname* (May 1964); and *Negroes and Mexicans in South and East Los Angeles: Changes between 1960 and 1965 in Population, Employment, Income, Family Status* (July 1966).

Valuable works on the Negro migration and its problems include Edward E. France, "Some Aspects of the Migration of the Negro to the San Francisco Bay Area since 1940," Ph.D. thesis, University of California, Berkeley (1962); Lawrence B. de Graaf, "Negro Migration to Los Angeles, 1930–1950," Ph.D. thesis, University of California, Los Angeles (1962), and his "The City of Black Angels: Emergence of the Los Angeles Ghetto, 1890–1930," *Pacific Historical Review*, XXXIX (August 1970), 323–352; Jack Greenberg, *Race Relations and American Law* (1959); Luigi Laurenti, *Property Values and Race: Studies in Seven Cities* (1960); Davis McEntire, *Residence and Race; Final and Comprehensive Report to the Commission on Race and Housing* (1960);

Alfred Arvins, editor, *Open Occupancy vs. Forced Housing under the Fourteenth Amendment* (1963), a symposium by authors opposed to open-housing legislation; John H. Denton, editor, *Race and Property* (1964), a symposium presenting both sides; Thomas W. Casstevens, *Politics, Housing, and Race Relations: California's Rumford Act and Proposition 14* (1967); Raymond E. Wolfinger and Fred E. Greenstein, "The Repeal of Fair Housing in California: an Analysis of Referendum Voting," *American Political Science Review*, LXII (September 1968), 753–769; and Ray Marshall, *The Negro and Organized Labor* (1965).

On the Watts riot, see John A. McCone and others, *Violence in the City—an End or a Beginning? A Report of the Governor's Commission on the Los Angeles Riots* (December 2, 1965); Jerry Cohen and William S. Murphy, *Burn, Baby Burn! The Los Angeles Race Riot, August 1965* (1966); Robert Conot, *Rivers of Blood, Years of Darkness* (1967); Paul Bullock, editor, *Watts: The Aftermath* (1969); Nathan Cohen, editor, *The Los Angeles Riots: A Socio-psychological Study* (1970); and Joseph Boskin and Victor Pilson, "The Los Angeles Riot of 1965: A Medical Profile of an Urban Crisis," *Pacific Historical Review*, XXXIX (August 1970), 353–366.

On the Mexican Americans, a useful bibliography is the *Guide to Materials Relating to Persons of Mexican Heritage in the United States* (1969), compiled by the United States Inter-Agency Committee on Mexican-American Affairs. The most extensive general study to date is Leo Grebler, Joan W. Moore, Ralph C. Guzmán, et al., *The Mexican-American People; the Nation's Second Largest Minority* (1970), growing out of the Mexican American Study Project at the University of California, Los Angeles, and analyzing the socio-economic position of Mexican Americans in California, Texas, New Mexico, Arizona, and Colorado.

Other valuable works in the order of their appearance include *Mexicans in California* (1930), the Report of Governor C. C. Young's Mexican Fact-Finding Committee; Manuel Gamio, *Mexican Immigration to the United States* (1930), and *The Mexican Immigrant, His Life Story: Autobiographic Documents* (1931); Emory S. Bogardus, *The Mexican in the United States* (1934); Carey McWilliams, *North From Mexico* (1949); Beatrice W. Griffith, *American Me* (1948); Raúl Morín, *Among the Valiant: Mexican Americans in World War II and Korea* (1963); Ralph C. Guzmán, "Politics and Policies of the Mexican-American Community," in Eugene Dvorin and Arthur Misner, editors, *California Politics and Policies* (1966); Julian Samora, editor, *La Raza: Forgotten Americans* (1966); Fernando Penalosa, "The Changing Mexican American in Southern California," *Sociology and Social Research*, LI (July 1967), 405–417; and Manuel P. Servín, editor, *The Mexican Americans: An Awakening Minority* (1970). See also the writings of Paul S. Taylor, John R. Martinez, and others, cited for Chapter XXXIX, above.

Anthologies on racial problems in California are Roger Daniels and Spencer C. Olin, Jr., editors, *Racism in California: A Reader on the History of Oppression* (1972); George E. Frakes and Curtis B. Solberg, editors, *Minorities in California History* (1971); an issue of the *California Historical Quarterly*, L (September 1971), also reprinted as *Neither Separate nor Equal* (1971); and Charles Wollenberg, editor, *Ethnic Conflict in California History* (1970).

Chapter XLI

THE MOST POPULOUS STATE

Explosion of population. Late in 1962 California passed New York and became the most populous state in the union. Governor Edmund G. Brown proclaimed December 31st of that year a special holiday, "Population Day," though many refused to join in the celebration. Said the *San Francisco Chronicle:* "The occasion clearly calls for mourning, for a gathering up of all the inner resources to withstand this historic buffeting under which the State's once magnificent supply of elbow-room and breathing space has vanished."

Economic opportunity continued to combine with the amenities of mild climate, scenic beauty, and California's romantic reputation to attract new residents from other states at the rate of a thousand a day. These newcomers made up nearly two-thirds of a total annual population increase of more than 500,000.

Though large areas of severe poverty remained, Californians as a whole were steadily becoming more affluent as well as more numerous. In 1955 their total personal income was about 30 billion dollars. In 1965 it was nearly 60 billion dollars, the largest in the nation. In per capita income, which exceeded $3,000 in 1965, California was a close second to New York, and the gap was narrowing. A major factor was the increasing importance of industries requiring specialized, highly skilled and highly paid workers.

The aerospace industry. The greatest single element in the growth of population and wealth in California in the 1950s and 1960s was the tremendous expansion of the aerospace industry, mostly financed by the Federal government. In 1966 the Department of Defense and the National Aeronautics and Space Administration awarded contracts totaling more than 8 billion dollars to California firms. Nearly 175,000 persons were employed in the manufacture of aircraft in California, and an even larger number, about

200,000, in the manufacture of electronic equipment. Including other branches such as missiles and instruments, the aerospace industry employed nearly 500,000 Californians in 1966—about one-third of the total number employed in manufacturing, and about 7 percent of the total civilian employment in the state.

The 1950s had seen the development of a hydrogen bomb warhead small enough to be carried by an intercontinental ballistic missile, and of rockets powerful enough not only to carry the bombs but also to facilitate the peaceful exploration of space. In the military sphere, this was the period of what Winston Churchill called "the peace of mutual terror," when it became apparent that the only defense in an all-out war would be all-out retaliation. The United States found itself in a race with Russia for a supply of missiles great enough to guarantee its "security," and at the same time for the honor of being the first to place a man on the moon.

Scientific research required a large share of the Federal government's enormous expenditures in the aerospace field, and California received more than 40 percent of the billions of dollars spent under research contracts. Southern California became the nation's leading center of aerodynamic research in guided missiles, jet propulsion, and supersonic flight, partly because a large part of the aircraft industry had already been concentrated there, and partly because the empty spaces of the Mojave Desert to the north and east of Los Angeles were ideal for aerospace testing and experimentation. Another factor was the concentration of scientific talent at the California Institute of Technology in Pasadena. In Northern California, there were similar concentrations at Stanford and the University of California at Berkeley, and this played a part in the growth of vast new aerospace research and manufacturing facilities, especially at Sunnyvale and other points between San Jose and San Francisco.

Huge nonprofit organizations were created for scientific research and strategic planning, in order to minimize favoritism toward private companies, and conflicts of private interest. The most famous of the new nonprofit agencies was the RAND Corporation (from R and D, research and development). Its headquarters were established at Santa Monica. Another was the Aerospace Corporation, with headquarters in Los Angeles.

Of the major aircraft manufacturing companies, Lockheed received the largest share of government aerospace orders, but Douglas, Hughes, North American, Northrop, and others were also important. North American established its new Rocketdyne division at Canoga Park, northwest of Los Angeles. Northrop established its Nortronics division at Palos Verdes. Convair, at San Diego, became a division of General Dynamics. Aerojet-General built huge plants at Azusa and at Sacramento.

In 1964, when the last Minuteman intercontinental ballistic missile was completed and installed in its "silo," the aerospace industry experienced a temporary decline in employment, and there was much apprehension about a "precarious one-crop economy," dependent on Federal defense expenditures. Governor Brown proposed that the aerospace scientists and engineers should turn their talents to civilian uses, and that, for example, the men who had "found a way to get a moon probe off the launching pad" should turn to finding "a way to get able-bodied men off the relief rolls." At Brown's suggestion the state government commissioned a series of studies in which several aerospace corporations applied their sophisticated, computerized analytical techniques to some of the state's problems in such fields as welfare, transportation, air and water pollution, and prisons. The Lockheed Missiles & Space Company made a study of a Statewide Federated Information System, for the interchange and central indexing of information among the state, county, and city governments, through electronic data processing.

After the end of World War II, California had proved that its economy could survive huge cutbacks in military spending, and could find plenty of peaceful channels for continued growth. There was no reason to doubt that it could do so again, if military spending should again decline sharply. For example, more than 40 percent of the investment in the aerospace industry in the 1960s was for the peaceful exploration of space. There were some complaints against such large Federal outlays for this purpose. But on June 1, 1966, when Surveyor I accomplished its mission of a controlled soft landing on the moon and began to send back photographs of the moon's surface, and when the scientists of Cal Tech's Jet Propulsion Laboratory gathered before the television cameras to interpret the photographs, the effect was so dramatic that it silenced most of the criticism.

The aerospace scientists and engineers were not the only important group that contributed to the growth of what President Clark Kerr of the University of California called "the knowledge industry." Nor were the aerospace research and development agencies the only "think tanks" that found ideal locations in California. For example, the Stanford Research Institute was established at Menlo Park, the Center for the Study of Democratic Institutions at Santa Barbara, and the Center for Advanced Study in the Behavioral Sciences at Stanford University.

Megalopolis in Arcadia. The growth of population was urban (or suburban), rather than agricultural, for agriculture's growth came from mechanization, not from increases in manpower. In 1970 more than 90 percent of the people in California lived in the 14 areas that the Census Bureau listed as "metropolitan." Los Angeles-Long Beach had about 35 percent of the state's population, San Francisco-Oakland about 15 percent, and San Diego 7 percent. Anaheim-Santa Ana, Bakersfield, Fresno, Oxnard-Ventura, Sacramento, Salinas-Monterey, San Bernardino-Riverside, San Jose, Santa Barbara, Stockton, and Vallejo-Napa, with their suburbs, had risen to "metropolitan" rank. Ultimately there would be one continuous metropolitan area extending from Santa Barbara to San Bernardino to San Diego and another from Sacramento to San Jose.

Los Angeles County, the most populous county in the nation, passed the

7 million mark in 1966. As a center of industrial employment, Los Angeles had already passed Chicago and was second only to New York City. One visitor to Los Angeles, appalled by freeways and smog, said "I have seen the future, and it doesn't work." But on the whole it did work, in spite of its shortcomings and inconveniences.

While the suburban areas were doubling or tripling in population every 10 years, the central portion of Los Angeles experienced a slight decline between 1950 and 1965, and was the only one of the five major parts of the metropolitan area that did not have more than a million residents. Although the metropolis as a whole might loosely be said to have an "axis" in Wilshire Boulevard, extending from "downtown" to the ocean, it could no longer be said to have a "center" at all. Los Angeles had once been described as "a collection of suburbs in search of a city." Now it was often said that they had stopped searching. The fragmentation of the city and the newness of much of its population made for lack of unity and lack of civic consciousness. Some of the sharpest of Mayor Samuel W. Yorty's perennial battles with the city council were fought with members from the outlying districts.

The name "autopia," coined for one of the attractions at Disneyland, could well be applied to the whole megalopolis of Los Angeles. In its devotion to automobility the area acquired 1,000 miles of freeways and 10,000 miles of cars. On an average day more than 350,000 cars and trucks passed one point near the civic center, at the junction of six freeways, where the interchange resembled the mechanism of a giant watch. Nearly everyone between the ages of 15 and 85 had an automobile except the very poor. Most college students drove to and from their campuses, and the University of California at Los Angeles had to undertake the building of parking structures with a total of more than 10,000 spaces. In many residential areas pedestrians were so rare that they were objects of suspicion, and in one such district Aldous Huxley was arrested one evening when the officers in a patrol car refused to believe that he was out for a walk.

So many of the wealthier executives began to commute to their offices in helicopters that most of the newer high-rise office buildings had heliports on their roofs.

Many of the new subdivisions that sprawled over the Southern California landscape were flimsily constructed and unimaginatively planned. But a new breed of regional planners emerged, designing not merely "planned communities" but entire "environments." The most striking example was William L. Pereira's master plan for the new campus of the University of California at Irvine, and for the new community to be built around it. This was the world's largest private community development project. On the Irvine Ranch, 93,000 acres of land in Orange County, the lower tier of 40,000 acres near the coast was planned to include the campus, residential areas, electronic and other industries, and vast green stretches with ample recreation facilities. The central tier was devoted to citrus groves and pasture lands, and the upper tier, a mountain wilderness of 30,000 acres, was reserved for recreation.

The world's first four-level freeway interchange, near the Los Angeles civic center. (Courtesy of the State of California Division of Highways)

The San Francisco Bay area had a population of 3.2 million in 1960, roughly half as many people as the Los Angeles-Long Beach metropolis. In finance, San Francisco continued to be a much larger source of loans for the whole of the Far West than was Los Angeles. The bay also retained its preeminence in shipping. Its waterfront labor relations had become a model of cooperation, and what had once been a single port had become a complex of separate, related ports including those of Oakland, Alameda, Redwood City, Richmond, Sacramento, Stockton, and Antioch, as well as San Francisco. Like the central portion of Los Angeles, the city of San Francisco registered a slight decline in population in the 1950s and 1960s. But the other communities around the bay were growing steadily.

Reapportionment. With the continued growth of the metropolitan areas, especially those in Southern California, the archaic "federal" system of representation in the California state senate became more and more obviously inequitable. Los Angeles County, with a population of 6,036,771 in the 1960 census, was the most populous legislative district in the United States, yet it had the same number of votes in the state senate as the Alpine-Mono-Inyo district, with 14,294 people: one vote. A resident of Alpine, Mono, or Inyo County cast a vote worth 422 times as much as the vote of a resident of Los Angeles County. This was far the widest disparity in any state. One-quarter of the population elected three-quarters of the California state senators. A majority of the senators could be elected by 10.7 percent of the California voters.

Initiative proposals to modify the "little federal" system and reapportion the California senate were rejected at the polls in 1928, 1948, 1960, and 1962. One of the few things that most voters could remember from their courses on American history and government in high school or college was the "great compromise," under which the large and small states were equally represented in the United States Senate, while the lower house was apportioned according to population. Most voters clung to the hazy and misleading idea that what was appropriate for the Federal government must be appropriate for the states.

In the 1960s, the Federal courts intervened. The legislature of Tennessee had not reapportioned itself for more than half a century, and the United States Supreme Court ruled in *Baker v. Carr,* on March 26, 1962, that the courts could review the matter. In *Reynolds v. Sims,* on June 15, 1964, the Supreme Court pronounced a sweeping new doctrine: that one man's vote must be worth as much as another's in the election of state legislators. The equal protection clause of the Fourteenth Amendment, said the Court, required that seats in both houses of a state legislature be apportioned on a population basis. "The so-called federal analogy" was discarded as fallacious and inapplicable. Counties, the Court pointed out, were merely political subdivisions created by the state governments, not sovereign entities like the states themselves. Whether or not the people of a state had approved an apportionment based on a principle other than population was irrelevant. "A citizen's constitutional rights can hardly be infringed upon because a majority of the people choose to do so." Constitutional law, said the Court, was not a matter of majority vote.

Chief Justice Earl Warren was one of the prime movers in the adoption of the "one man, one vote" doctrine, even though as Governor of California he had been one of those who had opposed reapportionment of its state senate.

Once the Supreme Court had clarified the matter, popular opinion changed. The idea that all citizens should be represented equally in legislatures was not especially shocking to the voters, and several opinion polls indicated that they approved the new doctrine by wide margins, in California as well as in other states. The northern members of the California senate, many of whom would lose their seats, engaged in a series of desperate maneuvers in the attempt to escape reapportionment. They supported a forlorn proposal for a new amendment to the Federal constitution, and in a meeting of the state senate's judiciary committee in June of 1964, when Chairman Edwin J. Regan of Weaverville invited additional suggestions, Senator Joseph A. Rattigan of Santa Rosa asked whether a proposal for armed insurrection would be in order. But all such efforts failed, and a three-judge panel of the Federal district court of appeals ruled that the California legislature must reapportion its upper house by July 1, 1965, or the courts would do so.

When the legislature adjourned in June of that year without coming to an agreement on any of the proposed plans, Governor Brown called a special session. On October 21, 1965, that session adopted a bill sponsored by Assemblyman Don A. Allen, Sr., a Los Angeles Democrat who was chairman of the assembly committee on elections and reapportionment. Under this law there were no deviations of more than 15 percent in the populations of the new senatorial districts. Consequently in the election of 1966, under the new plan of apportionment, the control of the state senate passed to Southern California, which had elected a majority of the assemblymen since the 1930s.

In 1965, the last year under the "federal" system, a large group of state senators from Northern California revived a proposal that had been made periodically since the 1850s. This was a plan to divide the state at the Tehachapi Mountains, and this latest version of it would have included the counties of Santa Barbara and Kern within the northern state, giving only seven counties to the southern one.

But polls showed that more than two-thirds of the voters, even in the North, were opposed to any plan for state division. Moreover, the Tehachapi line had long been obsolete as a demarcation between the Northern and Southern regions of California. In the eyes of the people of "Southern California," that region had always included the counties of San Luis Obispo, Kern, and San Bernardino, and by the early 1960s, Los Angeles publications commonly spoke of the "15 counties of Southern California." Inyo and Mono had been annexed when Los Angeles gained control of their water resources. Kings and Tulare were added when more of their agricultural products began to be shipped to the South than to the North. For the same reason, the South later announced the annexation of Fresno County, though not without some objections from the North.

Conservation. Among California's many growing pains was a deep fear that overpopulation would destroy the very amenities of open space, natural beauty, and breathable air that had originally attracted so many of the newcomers to the state. Hugo M. Fisher, administrator of the California State Resources Agency, expressed this fear in a speech in 1966. "Far short of the population density that will tax our potential food supply," said Fisher, "there will be a limit to the tolerance of the human spirit—the advent of social and cultural stagnation that come from overcrowding, the disappearance of compassion and sensible morality, and the dignity of man."

In spite of several expansions of the state and national park system, it was clear that park facilities would soon be inadequate. By the mid-'60s, Yosemite Valley in the summer was full of automobiles, noisy motorcycles, and crowded camps that resembled slums. In 1962 the National Park Service began to acquire land for the Point Reyes National Seashore, which would ultimately include the 10-mile Point Reyes Beach and the land around Drake's Bay. The Sierra Club backed a plan for the purchase of 90,000 acres for a Redwood National Park; but the lumber industry countered with a plan that would have involved little more

CALIFORNIA COUNTIES
The 43 counties of 'Northern California'
The 14 counties of 'Southern California'
DISPUTED
Del Norte
Siskiyou
Modoc
Humbolt
Trinity
Shasta
Lassen
Tehama
Mendocino
Plumas
Glenn
Butte
Sutter
Sierra
Colusa
Yuba
Lake
Nevada
Placer
Napa
Sacramento
Sonoma
Yolo
El Dorado
Contra Costa
Solano
Amador
Alpine
Marin
San Joaquin
Calaveras
San Francisco
Tuolumne
Alameda
Stanislaus
San Mateo
Mariposa
Santa Clara
Santa Cruz
Merced
Madera
Mono
San Benito
Fresno
Monterey
Inyo
Kings
Tulare
San Luis Obispo
Kern
Santa Barbara
San Bernardino
Ventura
Los Angeles
Orange
Riverside
San Diego
Imperial

Half Dome, Yosemite, from the valley floor. The scene is an impressive commentary on the side effects of California's population growth. (Photo by Rondal Partridge, © 1964. Courtesy of San Francisco *magazine)*

than a transfer to the National Park Service of existing state parks in Humboldt and Del Norte Counties. Governor Ronald Reagan, as usual, sided with the viewpoint of private industry. He remarked during his campaign in 1966 that anyone who had seen one redwood tree had seen them all. Later, however, he agreed to a compromise under which the Federal government would acquire 30,500 acres of private lands, as well as the 27,500 acres in three state parks; and under this plan Congress created the Redwood National Park in 1968.

The most urgent and difficult of California's problems in the conservation of natural resources were the problems of conserving the air and of trying to stem the menacing advance of air pollution. "Smog" began to produce a sharp decrease in visibility, and painful irritations of nose and eyes, in Los Angeles in 1943, and by the 1960s this condition had become so chronic that on bad days the city vanished. When, as often happened, the air in and over the Los Angeles basin became stagnant and a temperature inversion occurred, the rays of the sun reacted photochemically with various waste products in the air to produce new and still more dangerous pollutants. The result was not merely a blight on the beauty of the region and a cause of sharp discomfort, but also a menace to health and a source of costly damage to several crops. The growing of leafy vegetables in the Los Angeles basin virtually ceased.

The San Francisco Bay area, like the Los Angeles basin, had a bowllike shape, and smog began to be a severe problem in the bay region also. Los Angeles created an air pollution control district in 1947, and the San Francisco Bay counties formed a similar district in 1955. These agencies had some success in persuading or compelling industrial plants to reduce the emission of noxious wastes, often by installing expensive equipment. Yet the smog grew steadily worse. It became apparent that the chief offender was the automobile, with its output of hydrocarbons, oxides of nitrogen, and toxic carbon monoxide.

As the number of motor vehicles steadily increased, smog began to form in the interior valleys and threatened ultimately to spread over most of the state. Even in the San Bernardino Mountains, at altitudes up to 7,000 feet, pine trees began to show signs of damage.

In 1961 the legislature passed an act that would eventually require all cars to be equipped with crankcase smog suppressors; but these devices were only partially effective. It began to appear that only the replacement of the internal combustion engine with some other form of motive power could finally solve the problem. In 1966 several major automobile manufacturers revealed the results of experiments with new types of battery-powered electric cars, but the batteries in these models were bulky and impossibly expensive, and they had to be recharged every 40 to 80 miles.

Transportation. In 1965 California had 68 cars for every 100 persons of driving age, compared with a national average of 51 cars. There were nearly 10 million registered private motor vehicles in the state, including cars, trucks, and buses, and in 1970 the number of automobiles alone was nearly 10 million.

A vast network of freeways spread over the length and breadth of California, and most communities welcomed their coming, though the engineers of the Division of Highways sometimes showed limited imagination in their design. But in San Francisco a major "freeway revolt" began in 1959 when the new Embarcadero Freeway cut off the view of the lower half of the Ferry Building as seen from Market Street. The public outcry forced the state engineers to leave the freeway half finished, instead of carrying out their plan to extend it all the way around the Embarcadero and the Marina. In 1964, when the state authorities proposed a freeway through a part of Golden Gate Park,

The Golden Gate Bridge and San Francisco. (Courtesy of the State of California Division of Highways)

the revolt flared again, after folksinger Malvina Reynolds composed a stirring protest song called "The Cement Octopus." Such intransigence made San Francisco the despair of both state and Federal highway planners, who called the city the worst highway bottleneck in America.

But while San Francisco was rebelling against freeways, it took the lead in planning an electrified rapid transit system that would have the great advantages of reducing not only traffic congestion but also air pollution from motor vehicle exhausts. In 1962 the voters of San Francisco, Alameda, and Contra Costa counties approved the formation of the Bay Area Rapid Transit District, and the building of a rail network that would connect the cities and suburbs of the East Bay with the stations of a subway under Market Street, through an earthquake-proof tunnel under the bay. BART was scheduled to carry its first passengers in 1972, with an automated, computerized operating system, no motormen or conductors, and only a single attendant on each train. It was the first all-new transit system to be built in the United States in 60 years.

In Los Angeles, on the other hand, most of the voters and taxpayers showed their determination to cling to the privilege of doing all their traveling throughout the sprawling metropolitan area in their private automobiles. The affluent majority repeatedly refused to subsidize a public rapid transit system that only the poorer minority would use. A Southern California Rapid Transit District came into existence, on paper; but for many years it could do no more than operate a fleet of traffic-bound buses, and propose a plan for exclusive express busways to parallel the freeways.

The railroads continued to prosper from the hauling of freight, but their passenger traffic steadily declined. They often begged the state public utilities commission to approve the discontinuance or drastic reduction of their passenger service, but the commission turned down most of these requests. The railroads were often accused of making their passenger trains and schedules as unattractive and inconvenient as possible, in the hope that they would eventually be permitted to discontinue entirely the unprofitable business of carrying passengers in competition with automobiles, buses, and airplanes. The problem was nationwide, and at last, the Federal government established the semipublic National Rail Passenger Corporation, also called "Amtrak," which took over the operation of the country's intercity passenger trains on May 1, 1971, eliminated more than half of them, and tried to make the remaining ones attractive and successful again.

On the other hand, California's air transportation industry doubled its volume between 1960 and 1967, and the airlane between Los Angeles and San Francisco became the most traveled in the world.

The age of television. Though transportation by automobile and airplane was constantly increasing the mobility of most Californians, they were also spending a remarkable amount of time immobilized—in front of their television sets. The effects on their general well-being were dubious. Television broadcasting in the United States had developed as a marriage between the advertising and entertainment industries, a marriage that often brought out the worst in both. Advertising was the dominant partner. The film industry had always been engaged in the manufacture of mass entertainment for the commercial purpose of selling the product at the box office. But when the process of film making merged with the business of advertising and selling almost any product whatever, commercialism sank to depths it had previously reached only in radio. Most of the "prime viewing time" was given over to violence, sex, crime, quiz programs, situation comedies, and old movies interrupted by incredibly frequent commercials. In 1961 the chairman of the Federal Communications Commission described the results as "a wasteland."

Most of the programming decisions were made by network executives in New York, under the influence of advertisers and advertising agencies.

But the manufacture of films for television was concentrated in Hollywood, as the manufacture of movies had been, and though the output of full-length movies greatly declined, the grinding out of routine television serials and commercials made Hollywood busier than it had ever been before and brought it to an unprecedented level of economic prosperity. The Screen Actors Guild reported that in 1965 about 25 percent of the earnings of its members came from motion pictures, 35 percent from television programs, and nearly 40 percent from television commercials.

Early in 1967 a Carnegie Commission Report suggested a tax on the purchase of every television set, for the support of educational television. One of the most striking passages in this report was written by E. B. White: "I think television should be the visual counterpart of our literary essay, should arouse our dreams, satisfy our hunger for beauty, take us on journeys, enable us to participate in events, present great drama and music, explore the sea and the sky and the woods and the hills. It should be our Chautauqua, our Minsky's, and our Camelot. It should restate and clarify the social dilemma and the political pickle. Once in a while it does, and you get a quick glimpse of its potential."

There was a tremendous need for improvement in the quality of television. There was also a tremendous potential for improvement. These things were also true of the general state of civilization in California.

SELECTED BIBLIOGRAPHY

The annual editions of the *California Statistical Abstract*, beginning in 1960, are very useful. On developments up to the 1950s, see Margaret S. Gordon, *Employment Expansion and Population Growth, the California Experience, 1900–1950* (1954); Davis McEntire, *The Labor Force in California . . . 1900–1950* (1952); Warren S. Thompson, *Growth and Changes in California's Population* (1955); and Edward L. Ullman, "Amenities as a Factor in Regional Growth," *Geographical Review*, XL (January 1954), 119–132. Remi Nadeau, *California: the New Society* (1963), is a lively survey. See also "California, the Nation within a Nation," a special issue of the *Saturday Review*, L (September 23, 1967).

H. O. Stekler, *The Structure and Performance of the Aerospace Industry* (1965), is the first approach to a definitive analysis of the industry as a whole.

On metropolitan growth, see Ernest A. Engelbert, editor, *Metropolitan California* (1961), a collection of papers prepared for the Governor's Commission on Metropolitan Area Problems; and California, University, *The Metropolitan Future* (1965), Proceedings of Conference V in the series on *California and the Challenge of Growth*. Valuable works on Los Angeles include Winston W. Crouch and Beatrice Dinerman, *Southern California Metropolis, a Study in Development of Government for a Metropolitan Area* (1963); and John Anson Ford, *Thirty Explosive Years in Los Angeles County* (1961), on the 1930s through the 1950s. R. G. Lillard, *Eden in Jeopardy* (1966), Christopher Rand, *Los Angeles, the Ultimate City* (1967), and Francis Carney, "The Decentralized Politics of Los Angeles," *Annals of the American Academy of Political and Social Science* (May 1964), pp. 107–121, are penetrating studies of Los Angeles in the mid-'60s. The growth and problems of other metropolitan areas are treated in Mel Scott, *The San Francisco Bay Area* (1959); Lawrence Kinnaird, *History of the Greater San Francisco Bay Region* (three volumes, 1967); Kingsley Davis and Eleanor Langlois, *Future Demographic Growth of the San Francisco Bay Area* (1963); Thomas J. Kent, Jr., *City and*

Regional Planning for the Metropolitan San Francisco Bay Area (1963); and Christian L. Larsen, *Growth and Government in Sacramento* (1966).

On reapportionment, see Don A. Allen, Sr., *Legislative Sourcebook; the California Legislature and Reapportionment, 1849–1965* (1965); and Malcolm E. Jewell, editor, *The Politics of Reapportionment* (1962).

Pleas for conservation in the '60s include Raymond F. Dasmann, *The Destruction of California* (1965); Samuel E. Wood, *California, Going, Going . . .* (1962); Samuel E. Wood and Alfred E. Heller, *The Phantom Cities of California* (1963); and California, University, *Natural Resources: Air, Land, Water* (1964), Proceedings of Conference VI in the series on *California and the Challenge of Growth*. In the same series see also *The Impact of Science* (1964), Proceedings of Conference IV, including a paper by John T. Middleton on "Smog-free Air and Its Price."

On transportation problems, see Wilfred Owen, *Cities in the Motor Age* (1959); and Lawrence Halprin, *Freeways* (1966).

Chapter XLII

WAR, RECESSION AND SOCIAL FERMENT

WAR, INFLATION, AND RECESSION. The social and psychological consequences of the Vietnam War, as well as its economic consequences, were very different from those of World War II. Pearl Harbor had united the nation, but the war in Southeast Asia became one of the most bitterly divisive issues in American history. In the years before America was plunged into World War II the country had gone to great lengths to try to avoid an inevitable involvement; but in the case of Vietnam many felt that the United States had gone far out of its way to engage in a futile conflict of which the necessity and even the morality were doubtful at best, and the costs tragic and apparently wasted. At the beginning of World War II, the American economy was still in the depression and still operating at a fraction of its productive capacity; it badly needed the injection of huge government expenditures, made psychologically and politically acceptable by unquestioned military demands. During World War II, Federal price and wage controls and huge wartime taxes kept some brakes on inflation. At the beginning of major involvement in Southeast Asia, on the other hand, the American economy was already operating close to capacity; and during the great buildup of American forces in Vietnam between 1965 and 1968, involving vast expenditures for the undeclared war, the Federal government failed to apply wartime economic controls, and avoided substantial increases in taxes. The result was a massive inflation and overheating of the economy, with dangerously high percentage rates of price increases, compounded from year to year.

In 1969, in an attempt to halt the inflation process, the Nixon administration began drastic cuts in Federal spending for the armed forces and for the space program, and the Federal Reserve Board made a series of increases in interest rates. These actions, though they failed to stop the inflation, led to the first recession in 10 years and the worst and longest one in 30 years. The stock market fell 300 points. Unemployment rose to about 5 percent nationally and to nearly 8 percent in California. Among those who held their jobs, fear of unemployment led many to reduce their spending habits.

California suffered more than the rest of the nation because so much of its manufacturing depended on Federal spending in the aerospace industry. Aerospace employment in California, which exceeded 600,000 in 1967, was down to about 400,000 in 1971, with particularly severe effects in San Diego, Orange, Los Angeles, and Santa Clara Counties, where the industry was concentrated. A large proportion of the unemployed were highly skilled engineers, scientists, and technicians.

Cutbacks in military aircraft were especially disastrous for Lockheed, the nation's largest single defense contractor. In 1971, only a Federal guarantee of a huge loan saved it from bankruptcy—a fate actually suffered by Rolls Royce, the British firm that built many of the engines for Lockheed's planes. Douglas, now merged into McDonnell-Douglas, suffered from the sharp and unexpected decline that the recession produced in commercial air passenger traffic, and the resulting decrease in the airlines' orders for large new jets. In 1971, Congress dealt the aircraft industry a heavy blow by cutting off funds for the continued development of an American supersonic transport, on the grounds that the SST would be both uneconomical and a noise polluter.

The reduction of the budget of the National Aeronautics and Space Administration from nearly 6 billion dollars in 1968 to about half that sum in 1971 was a bitter disappointment to those who had hoped that continued growth of NASA's program for the peaceful exploration of space would cushion the shocks of military retrenchment. The first landing of American astronauts on the moon in July 1969 was a dazzling and historic event, breathlessly watched on television by millions, but later flights seemed largely repetitious and in some cases unsuccessful or frighteningly hazardous. Public interest did not remain high enough to keep the expenditures for the program from being slashed.

Population slowdown. The economic recession that began in 1969 was a major factor in a sharp decrease in the rate of California's population growth. Though the state's population reached 20 million in 1970, giving it five more seats in Congress, the increase during that year was less than 1 percent. This was the lowest annual percentage increase on record, and for the first time in its entire history the state's population grew at a slower annual rate than did that of the nation as a whole. Natural increase, which had almost always formed the smaller part of the state's growth, had suddenly become far the larger part, while net migration in 1970 was only 27,000, compared with 356,000 in 1963, the peak figure of the previous decade. These were the official figures of the state Department of Finance. Some unofficial estimates maintained that 25,000 more persons actually *left* the state in 1970 than came into it. The decline in California's attraction of new residents was due in part to economic conditions, and in part to smog, overcrowding, and a kind of social and cultural malaise that afflicted the state and its image.

The slowing of population increase led to drastic scaling down of the growth projections under California's master plans for public higher education and water development. In the 1960s, it had been estimated that the University of California would enroll 250,000 students in 1985, and that the new campuses at Santa Cruz, Irvine, and San Diego would have 27,500 each. But in 1971 the official predictions were that the state university's total enrollment would reach 140,000 in 1980 and then level off for the rest of the decade, and that the three newest campuses would have only about half as many students as originally planned. It was pointed out that although the postwar baby boom had continued through the 1950s, California's birth rate had fallen considerably during the 1960s.

In 1971 the Metropolitan Water District of Southern California took the unprecedented action of reducing its estimates of future needs for water from the northern part of the state, and the California Department of Water Resources cautiously admitted that perhaps not all the many long-range developments in the state water plan would actually be required.

Concern for the environment. The drastic slowdown in population growth at the end of the 1960s coincided with the sudden emergence of a radically new system of Californian values. Throughout the state's history, the greatest numbers had been thought of as the greatest good. Now many began to denounce population growth as a menace to the quality of life and of the natural environment. For example, the San Francisco conservationist organization California Tomorrow proposed a new-resident tax on people moving into the state and a limitation of income tax exemptions to two children.

Air pollution continued to be the most obvious menace to the quality of the environment. Researchers established that an average day's breathing of the air of Los Angeles—or New York—involved an intake of toxic materials equivalent to smoking about 38 cigarettes. Smog conditions were routinely reported along with the other weather data; and in the Los Angeles schools, physical education classes and use of the playgrounds were sometimes halted because of the dangers of breathing too deeply. The Federal government created an Environmental Protection Agency; and in the Clean Air Act of 1970 Congress provided that by 1976 new cars must be equipped with devices that would reduce emissions of hydrocarbon, carbon monoxide, and nitrogen oxide by 90 percent.

The California legislature passed a series of increasingly strong antismog laws; but in 1970 a "clean air amendment" to the state constitution, Proposition 18, was defeated by an outpouring of funds from the highway lobby. The constitution provided that the state's income from a seven-cent-a-gallon gasoline tax and from auto license fees could be spent only for highway construction and maintenance. Proposition 18 would have permitted the use of 25 percent of these funds for state aid to rapid transit projects and other methods of combatting air pollution. The sponsors of this proposal, a loose coalition called "Californians Against Smog," included the League of Women Voters, the League of California Cities, the Sierra Club, the Tuberculosis and Respiratory Disease Association, and the California Medical Association. Both major candidates for governor and most candidates for the legislature endorsed the plan, and early opinion polls showed strong public support for it. But its opponents, organized as "Californians Against the Street and Road Tax Trap," built a large campaign fund mainly through contributions from oil companies and auto clubs. Outspending the supporters of the plan by 22 to 1, its opponents acknowledged expenditures of more than $350,000 for a campaign of billboard, television, radio, and newspaper advertisements, often with grossly misleading captions. Edmund G. Brown, Jr., who became secretary of state in the same election, pointed out that an unprecedentedly large amount of the money used to defeat the measure had been contributed anonymously, in violation of the state election code.

The outcry produced by the defeat of Proposition 18 in 1970 encouraged the formation of a remarkable grass-roots movement for a much more sweeping and drastic initiative measure on the presidential primary ballot in June 1972. This movement was led by Edwin Koupal, who gave up a prosperous career as an automobile dealer to work full time for conservation, and by his wife Joyce, a nurse. The Koupals had previously led an unsuccessful campaign to recall Governor Reagan. Now they organized a People's Lobby, a group of volunteers who qualified a proposed Clean Environment Act for the ballot by collecting nearly half a million signatures, mostly at tables set up in shopping centers. This initiative measure proposed to limit the lead content of gasoline, authorize the shutting down of businesses that violated air pollution standards, restrict the use of pesticides, ban construction of atomic powered generating plants for five years, and restrict tideland oil and gas operations. The California Chamber of Commerce, the first organization to take alarm at the measure, asserted that its "severe regime" would produce "an economic standstill." Organized labor also opposed the measure, and the voters rejected it as too extreme.

The growth and influence of the Sierra Club had a major part in the great growth of interest in protecting the natural environment. Under David Brower as its executive director in the 1960s, the club's membership grew from 7,000 to 77,000. Brower's love of the wilderness was so passionate that he advocated reducing the population of the United States to a hundred million. He developed a program of publishing beautiful books that argued the cause of conservation through photographs of exquisite details from the natural world, combined with the words of such writers as John Muir, Robinson Jeffers, and Henry David Thoreau; and during the 1960s people paid 10 million dollars for these books. In the field of lobbying, Brower led the successful fights to prevent the inundation of parts of the Dinosaur National Monument by a dam on the Green River in Utah, and the building of two dams on the Colorado above and below the Grand Canyon. After he purchased a famous full-page newspaper advertisement denouncing these projects, the Internal Revenue Service temporarily suspended the Sierra Club's tax-exempt status on the ground that it was engaging in political activity. Some of the club's directors felt that Brower was overreaching himself. When the Pacific Gas and Electric Company gave in to conservationist pressure and abandoned its plans for a nuclear power plant at Bodega Head on the northern California coast in favor of an alternate site at Diablo Canyon near San Luis Obispo, and when Brower denounced that site as well, a majority of the club's board of directors disagreed with him and voted to endorse the Diablo Canyon alternative. At last Brower was forced out as executive director, and in 1969 he formed the Friends of the Earth, a new group "streamlined for aggressive political and legal action" and having no tax deduction or tax exemption privileges, in order to fight without restrictions "to restore the environment" and "to preserve the remaining wilderness."

The San Francisco Bay Conservation and Development Commission (BCDC), first established by the state legislature on a trial basis in 1965 and given permanent status and greater regulatory powers in 1969, proved quite successful in its efforts to "save the bay." It virtually halted the land fills that had reduced the size of the bay by 40 percent in little more than a hundred years. The Tahoe Regional Planning Agency, jointly operated by California and Nevada and authorized by Congress in 1969, combatted the pollution of Lake Tahoe's pure blue waters by sewage and the threatened destruction of the beauty of its surroundings by excessive and hasty construction.

When an offshore well of the Union Oil Company sprang a leak early in 1969 and smeared the beaches of Santa Barbara with oil, and when two years later a pair of Standard Oil tankers collided in the fog just inside the Golden Gate, spilling a great quantity of oil into San Francisco Bay and doing considerable damage to bird and marine life, much emotional fuel was added to the environmentalist movement, though later studies indicated that little permanent damage had been done.

Drilling rig leaking oil, six miles offshore from Santa Barbara, January 30, 1969. (Courtesy of United Press International.)

The environmentalist crusade was not without its critics. Some pointed out that it made little effort to ally with labor or consumer groups, and that it catered primarily to the wealthy and the white and sought to preserve a "Wilderness for the Wasps." The word *ecology*, long a conventional scientific term for the study of the relations between organisms and their environments, suddenly became so popularized that some scientists feared its meaning was being endangered by misuse, overuse, and sloganeering. Some observers ridiculed the ecology movement's publicists as "the disaster lobby," and complained of "verbal pollution" in some of the movement's more exaggerated statements. It was pointed out that the word *smog* had been coined, not in Los Angeles, but in London in 1902, and that the pollution of the air by burning coal had been much worse in English and American cities in the 19th century than the pollution by internal combustion engines in the 20th. One group of ecological alarmists maintained that an overheating of the earth's atmosphere produced by air pollution would melt the polar icecaps, while another group threatened the opposite effect and a new ice age. But in spite of its occasional emotional excesses there was hope that the environmentalist crusade would leave a genuine and permanent heritage of concern for the quality of life.

The hippie movement. One of the most remarkable social phenomena of the second half of the 1960s was the growth of the hippie movement among the young. The hippie mystique had many aspects, including social protest and normal feelings of rebellion characteristic of adolescence. But many young adherents of the hippie movement were motivated by deep personal maladjustment and alienation. The compassionate doctors who served in the overburdened Free Medical Clinic in San Francisco's Haight-Ashbury district eventually concluded that the most typical young residents of that hippie colony had come to it because they had felt emotionally deprived and emotionally abused in their childhood homes—often economically affluent homes. Craving love, joy, and self-realization, many of them believed that such needs could be satisfied by certain drugs, especially when taken in the company of other young people with similar feelings. They often described their movement as a "subculture" or "counterculture," and sometimes quite candidly as a "drug culture." Its culture included rock music, psychedelic art, the doctrines of astrology or Krishna Consciousness, and communal social relationships analogous with those of gypsies or of certain American Indian tribes. The word *hip* has been defined as meaning "to be in the know, particularly about the drug underworld." The word *hippie* was derived by journalists from Norman Mailer's term *hipster*.

An essential factor in the spread of the hippie movement was the popularization of the new drug lysergic acid diethylamide or LSD. This drug was first synthesized by a Swiss chemist in 1938. In the early 1960s Dr. Timothy Leary, a lecturer on clinical psychology at Harvard and the holder of a Ph.D. in psychology from the University of California at Berkeley, was one of a group engaged in experiments with several drugs, including LSD, which they described as "psychedelic" or "consciousness-expanding." Their critics insisted that LSD was more accurately described as mind-distorting and hallucinogenic and that its effects on different individuals were dangerously unpredictable, a kind of "chemical Russian roulette." Colors intensified and changed, shape and spatial relations were distorted, and inanimate objects seemed to pulsate and to assume great emotional significance. To some the experience was deeply moving, exhilarating, and "self-revealing"—an experience of "cosmic oneness," or an "exploration of inner space." But to others it brought panic, bizarre and suicidal behavior, and temporary or even permanent psychosis. Leary was dismissed from the Harvard faculty in 1963 for administering the drug to an undergraduate without medical approval. He then began to proselytize its use throughout the country in writings and speeches, urging young people in particular to "tune in, turn on, and drop out with me." He formed an organization, somewhat like a religious sect, which he called the League for Spiritual Discovery. Another important propagandist for LSD was Ken Kesey, a young novelist who had studied creative writing at Stanford in the early 1960s and had first taken the drug in laboratory experiments to earn extra money, at the nearby Veterans Hospital in Menlo Park.

The formula for LSD, which Leary and others now published, is fairly simple, and quantities of it were soon manufactured by uncertified chemists in improvised laboratories. The drug was not outlawed in California until October 1966, although mere possession of marijuana had been a felony since the 1930s. The frequency of the hippies' use of LSD varied considerably, but many of them used marijuana almost every day when they could obtain it. Some of them believed that they took both drugs as a kind of religious sacrament. "Basically, man is God," said the leader of one hippie commune, "and this is one of the profound insights you have under LSD. You experience yourself as God." Episcopal Bishop James Pike, of Grace Cathedral in San Francisco, compared the hippies to the early Christians in their style of hair and dress, their visions of a beautiful life in the future, and their persecution by the established order. But the courts refused to recognize the hippie movement as a religion, or to accept a religious defense in cases involving violation of the laws against marijuana and LSD, although other court decisions had legitimized the use of peyote in the religious services of an American Indian group.

In 1966 the news media began to give the hippies massive publicity, and often described them sympathetically as "flower children" or "the love generation." In 1967 when the movement reached its peak there were probably about 200,000 full-time hippies in the nation, and as many more part-time, summer, and weekend hippies, mostly young. Millions of other Americans, young and old, were fellow travelers. The largest colony was in the Haight-Ashbury district of San Francisco, and there were others in the Telegraph Avenue area south of the university campus in Berkeley; in Los Angeles on the Sunset Strip and along Fairfax Avenue in West Hollywood; and in Greenwich Village in New York. Smaller enclaves sprang up in almost every major American city, and there were various rural communes, notably in California, New Mexico, and Colorado.

Hippie leaders maintained that they were seeking to establish a new communal freedom from individual anxieties, and to remove themselves from a decadent society full of war and oppression into a utopia of peace and love. It was more than coincidental that the years in which the hippie movement attracted its greatest following were also the years of the great expansion of American armed forces in Vietnam. Many young Americans believed that their

Hippies at Haight and Ashbury Streets, San Francisco, October 6, 1967. This ceremony commemorated the "Death of Hip," in order that it might be reborn in purer form. (*Courtesy of United Press International*)

country's participation in the war in Southeast Asia was morally indefensible, and their hatred of the war was a major factor in their feelings of alienation from the whole prevailing system of society.

The hippie movement began to decline as soon as it reached its peak in the nationally publicized "summer of love" in San Francisco in 1967. The Haight-Ashbury district became "America's first teen-age slum," and it grew so crowded that shortages of LSD and marijuana developed. This brought a shift to methamphetamines ("speed") and heroin; and as the effects of drug abuse became apparent the focus of the mass media shifted from sympathetic curiosity to alarmed hostility. The drug traffic produced a fantastic crime rate; and the young "street people" who had talked so much of peace and love became victims of frequent violence, from drug pushers, from motorcycle gangs,

Haight Street in 1971. (Courtesy of United Press International)

and from the police. Many hippies became increasingly prone to violence and vandalism themselves. A rash of assaults and murders broke out in "the Haight," and after several orgies of window smashing, the shops in the neighborhood were boarded up and the once-thronged streets nearly deserted. A young man named Charles Manson, along with his hippie "family," moved from the Haight to a ranch in southern California; and although it was entirely unfair to regard Manson as a typical hippie, the grisly murders that his group committed a few months later, in Los Angeles in 1969, had a chilling effect on the hippie image.

One element in the decline and decay of the Haight-Ashbury was the way in which various parts of the Establishment, including the news media and even the tourist industry, sought to capitalize on it. The fashion industry coopted the costumes and hairstyles of the hippies, much to the disgust of Abby Hoffman, Allen Ginsberg, and others; and the entertainment industry coopted their music. Thus while some sectors of the established order were now reacting to the hippie movement with demands for vigorous repression of it, other sectors were killing the movement with supposed kindness. It was not the first time that the private enterprise system in California had demonstrated its flexibility and ingenuity by smothering dissent with cooptation. Gaylord Wilshire and Jack London were previous examples. Very few of the later Californians who drove or shopped or went to their offices in the executive suites on Wilshire Boulevard in Los

Angeles were aware that Wilshire was a socialist and that Upton Sinclair was first converted to socialism by reading *Wilshire's Magazine*. And very few of those who dined well and expensively in the fashionable restaurants around Jack London Square in Oakland were aware that London signed hundreds of his letters "Yours for the Revolution."

The hippie movement was further weakened in December 1969 when an open-air concert at Altamont in rural Alameda County, attended by a huge crowd of hippies and other devotees of electrically amplified rock music, turned into a disaster. Promoters of the event had hired the members of a Hell's Angels motorcycle club to serve as security guards in order to keep the audience from overrunning the stage in their eagerness to get close to such idolized performers as the Rolling Stones. Noise, chaos, and irrationality dominated the scene, and a young man was stabbed to death in a scuffle with the Hell's Angels. One of the most popular rock lyrics had celebrated the emergence of the new youth culture as "the dawning of the Age of Aquarius." An observer remarked that the Age of Aquarius had ended with the flash of a knife at Altamont. The student newspaper at the University of California at Berkeley, reviewing a documentary film about the Altamont tragedy, said that "it was the end of a decade of dreams; the beginning of a decade of facing the realities of the human condition. . . . We went there with visions of getting back to the land, and we left the land a mire of every human problem from pollution to murder."

In the early 1970s the fashion industry continued to commercialize the hippie styles of dress, and this gave the impression that the movement was more widespread and more deeply rooted than it still was. The hippie movement did have significant effects on the attitudes, manners, and morals of the young, and it was a sensational challenge to the old American values of hard work, thrift, and deferred gratification. But this challenge came in such an extreme form, or in hippie jargon such a "far out" form, that it drove most Americans to become more than ever alienated from the alienated.

Black radicalism. In the meantime, the Negro civil rights movement had taken a new and radical turn. In 1966, Stokely Carmichael became the new head of the Student Nonviolent Coordinating Committee. He soon turned it into a movement of violent nonstudents, ordered all whites to get out of it, and raised the cry of "black power." In the autumn of 1966, the Black Panther Party for Self-Defense was founded in Oakland by two young black militants, Huey P. Newton and Bobby G. Seale. They had met as students at the old Grove Street campus of Merritt College, a public junior college drawing many of its students from predominantly black areas in west and north Oakland. Newton and Seale were influenced by the writings of Malcolm X and Frantz Fanon, and later by those of Marx, Lenin, Mao Tse-tung, Ho Chi Minh, and

Che Guevara. But their strongest feeling, growing out of their personal experience, was a hatred of the frequently prejudiced and cruel treatment of black people by white policemen. The black panther was originally the ballot emblem of a Negro civil rights party organized in Alabama in 1965. Newton liked the name and adopted it because, he said, the panther was reputed never to make an unprovoked attack, but to defend itself ferociously. Newton and Seale established a system of patrol cars; carrying law books and guns, they trailed police cars through the Oakland slums to protect the constitutional rights of black people.

One of the new party's first and most important converts was Eldridge Cleaver, a vigorously articulate black man who had twice been in prison. His first term, beginning when he was eighteen, had been spent in the California state prison at Soledad for possession of marijuana. After his release, burning with resentment, he had turned to the raping of white women as a symbolic act of "insurrection," intended, according to his own account, "to send waves of consternation throughout the white race." This brought him another and longer term in prison, during which he came to repudiate the act of rape and to regard his own resort to it as a symptom of the "dehumanization" that he had suffered; but he was resolved to fight by more effective means against the social system that he felt had brutalized and degraded black people like himself.

In prison Cleaver had become an admirer of the Black Muslim leader Malcolm X, who was assassinated in 1965. Early in 1967, the widow of Malcolm X made a visit to San Francisco; and Cleaver, recently released on parole, wanted to meet her. A squad of Black Panthers appeared at the airport and acted as her bodyguards while she was in the city. They wore paramilitary black uniforms and black berets, and carried guns. The sight of them was an exhilarating experience for Cleaver, and he threw himself into the cause of the new party. He became its "Minister of Information." Seale was "Chairman," and Newton was "Minister of Defense" and later "Supreme Commander."

In the spring of 1967 the California legislature was preparing to pass a gun control law directed against the Black Panthers; and on May 2, when the bill was debated, a caravan of armed Panthers drove from Oakland to Sacramento, read a manifesto on the steps of the capitol denouncing the "racist legislature," and then walked onto the floor of the assembly carrying guns. They were quickly expelled from the chamber, and Seale and others were later arrested. The sensational publicity given to the affair aroused much public alarm, and great condemnation of the Panthers, but it also gave the party wide advertising among militant young blacks and led to the organization of branches in several other parts of the country.

Intense fear and hostility between policemen and Panthers soon led to many tragic shooting affrays. On October 28, 1967, gunfire erupted after an Oakland police car stopped an automobile driven by Huey Newton. One officer

Two members of the Black Panther Party meet a police lieutenant on the steps of the state capitol in Sacramento, May 2, 1967. Earlier several members had entered the Assembly chamber and had had their guns taken away. (Courtesy of United Press International)

was killed; another policeman and Newton were wounded. On April 6, 1968, also in Oakland, there was more shooting in which two policemen were wounded, a young Panther was killed, and Eldridge Cleaver was wounded and arrested. Newton was tried in the summer of 1968 and convicted of manslaughter, but the conviction was reversed on appeal, and two later trials ended in hung juries. Cleaver was released on bail but when a higher court overruled the release, he fled to Algeria rather than return to prison.

Though their beliefs and tactics were radical, the Panthers did not share the view of several other black militant groups that all whites were evil. In part this was because of their admiration for their white attorneys, especially Charles Garry, a radical lawyer of Armenian extraction. The Panthers denounced the extreme separatism of black "cultural nationalist" groups and ridiculed their advocacy of wearing African styles of dress and studying Swahili and other aspects of African culture. In January 1969, during an argument over such issues at a meeting of the Black Students Union on the campus of UCLA, two young leaders of the Black Panther movement in Los Angeles were shot and killed by members of a "cultural nationalist" faction.

The Black Panther party was considerably weakened when a bitter quarrel developed between Cleaver, who issued periodic calls for revolutionist guerrilla warfare from his exile in Algeria, and Newton, who favored much more moderate tactics, including such programs as free breakfasts for children, a free medical clinic, and free bus transportation for relatives of prisoners on visiting days.

Campus turmoil. American college students of the 1950s had been called "the silent generation." Those who reached college age in the '50s had been born in the '30s, and when these "depression babies" became young adults they were too driven by anxiety about material success to be interested in any form of political or social dissent. Students took virtually no part, for example, in the University of California "loyalty oath" controversy.

The college students of the middle and later 1960s, on the other hand, were the great wave of postwar babies, born and reared in relative affluence, but in such numbers that they badly overcrowded the public schools and were often discontented with the crowding. Some of them discovered that their massive numbers could be a form of power.

Stirrings of student unrest in California appeared in May 1960 when a crowd of college students, protesting their exclusion from a hearing of the House Un-American Activities Committee in the San Francisco city hall, jammed the rotunda by sitting down in the balcony. The police washed them down the stairs with fire hoses and drove them from the building with clubs. At about the same time, Negro college sudents in the Southern states began to attack the racial segregation of lunch counters with the tactic of the sit-in. This tactic had been used for a short time in 1937, in a different context, by some of the relatively radical new CIO unions, in the form of the "sit-down strike" in which striking workers occupied the property of the employer; but organized labor had soon abandoned the sit-down, not only because it was ruled illegal but also because it alienated the public. In the early 1960s, however, the Federal courts ruled that the racial segregation of lunch counters was unconstitutional and therefore that those who had participated in the lunch-counter sit-ins were merely demanding their constitutional rights and could not be validly arrested.

Several students from the University of California at Berkeley had spent their summers in civil rights activities in the deep South, and in the fall of 1964 they borrowed the civil-rights tactics of mass civil disobedience for use against the university, when it tried to enforce its rules against student political activity on campus. The university was apparently unaware that some of these rules were in violation of some very recent Federal court decisions. The United States Supreme Court had said in *Edwards v. South Carolina* in 1963 that "student

The beginning of the Free Speech Movement at Berkeley, October 2, 1964. Thousands of students blockaded a police car in Sproul Plaza for about 36 hours, and many speeches were made from the roof of the car. (Courtesy University Archives, Bancroft Library)

speakers may even advocate violations of the law provided such advocacy does not constitute a clear and present danger within the meaning of the Supreme Court cases on this subject"; and that "much of the conduct that the public finds objectionable is constitutionally protected."

In this sense the student rebellion at Berkeley in 1964 was truly a "Free Speech Movement," contending for a high principle of student civil liberties by methods that were nonviolent even though they did involve a kind of mass force. But the radical young leaders of the movement, in the first flush of what seemed to them their revolutionary dawn, became overconfident. In a speech from the steps of Sproul Hall, Mario Savio promised his followers that he could protect them from going to jail or from any other form of punishment. The apparent success of the tactics of sitting-in and going limp when arrested made the young rebels feel invincible and invulnerable, physically and morally, and this intoxicated them with an illusory sense of power. The courts soon ruled, however, that occupying a university building was merely a form of illegal trespass and that going limp was merely a form of resisting arrest. Many of the student rebels believed that they were acting in the tradition of Henry David Thoreau, the father of American "civil disobedience"; they were unaware, or had wishfully forgotten, that when Thoreau broke the law because it was bad, he had insisted that he be put in the Concord jail, not only as a matter of principle but also to dramatize his cause. The I.W.W.s had deliberately filled the jails in their fights for free speech. Mahatma Gandhi, Martin Luther King, and Cesar Chavez expected to be imprisoned if they broke the law. But when hundreds of students were sentenced to jail after a mass trial in Berkeley in 1965, they were disenchanted and embittered. The sense of newness and magic began to go out of the new movement, and a sense of frustration and desperation took its place. The idea of nonviolence was soon lost in a welter of confrontation and disruption, and a drift toward violence and vandalism set in. This was a tragedy, not only for the young people themselves but for a society that cried out for improvement and badly needed the freshness of youthful idealism.

Another failing of many of the student rebels was one that made a mockery of the name of the "Free Speech Movement." They began to deny the right of free speech to anyone but themselves, by shouting down any speaker who disagreed with them. In this they were encouraged by one of their principal heroes, the neo-Marxist Herbert Marcuse, professor of philosophy at the new University of California at San Diego. In his essay on "Repressive Tolerance," published in 1965, Marcuse argued that because the idea of toleration had been cleverly perverted by the capitalist establishment to keep revolutionary dissent in harmless channels, the dissenters should no longer tolerate the expression of orthodox ideas. (This might have deserved the response of Leo Tolstoy to the question of whether there was not a valid distinction between "reactionary repression" and "revolutionary repression": if there was, said Tolstoy, it was the difference between the excrement of dogs and the excrement of cats.) In other writings Marcuse maintained that American labor was too corrupted by capitalism to bring about a revolution against it, but that an intellectual elite of university students could do so; and this was another idea that made him an idol of the young followers of what was coming to be called the New Left. That movement was not quite so new as many of its followers supposed. For example, Students for a Democratic Society (SDS), often said to have been founded in the early 1960s, was in fact an offshoot of the League for Industrial Democracy, which was directly descended from the Intercollegiate Socialist Society founded by Upton Sinclair and Jack London in 1905.

The Free Speech Movement of 1964 gave Berkeley a considerable reputation as the cradle of student revolt in America; and in the subsequent years this reputation attracted many young radicals, some of them students and others former students, to the university campus and to the parts of Berkeley and Oakland to the south of it. Protest against the escalation of the war in Vietnam and a continuing crusade against racism at home were now the major channels of youthful rebellion. In October 1965 the radical Vietnam Day Committee organized a mass march from the Berkeley campus to the Oakland Army Base, with a vague plan to blockade it, but the march was stopped by police at the Oakland city line, and in a similar attempt the next day the marchers were further demoralized when a gang of Hell's Angels launched an unexplained assault on them.

The college student radicalism of the 1960s was at first quite separate from the hippie movement, but it gradually became interrelated with it. During an unsuccessful student strike at Berkeley in December 1966, and the equally unsuccessful campaign of Jerry Rubin, a young New Left organizer, for the mayoralty of Berkeley in the spring of 1967, the student radicals began to form a working alliance with the hippies, with whom they now shared the feelings of a persecuted minority. For many of their followers, both movements became communal attempts to escape from reality. Some found escape in revolutionist fantasies and some in drugs—some in SDS, some in LSD, some in both.

A series of violent episodes began. In October 1967 a major draft riot occurred after a crowd of young radicals, trying to shut down the Oakland induction center, were routed by police who sprayed them with a temporarily blinding new chemical known as Mace. The new vogue of "student power" spread across the country. In April 1968 hundreds of students staged a sit-in at Columbia University, and when it was broken up by police, many violently resisted arrest. In August, during the Democratic national convention in Chicago, there was a violent confrontation between police and the mass of young militants who had gathered in an effort to pressure the convention into taking a stand against the Vietnam War and into nominating Senator Eugene McCarthy. The most publicized of the demonstrators were the "Youth International Party," or Yippies, one of whose leaders was Jerry Rubin, once a graduate student in sociology at the University of California at Berkeley but now a full-time revolutionist. Combining his political activities with the use of drugs, which he advocated as an aid to revolution, Rubin urged junior high school students to prepare to kill their parents and burn their school libraries.

In the autumn of 1968 the Berkeley campus returned to the limelight when radical students, taking advantage of a new university policy encouraging educational experimentation, initiated a course called "Social Analysis 139X, Dehumanization and Regeneration in the American Social Order." This course was built around the life and personality of Eldridge Cleaver, who was to give a series of "guest lectures" in it. Cleaver, then out of prison on parole, was the candidate of the Peace and Freedom party for the Presidency of the United States, and had chosen Jerry Rubin as his running mate. The university regents, who for nearly fifty years had delegated final approval of all courses to a committee of the faculty, now intervened to prevent the course from being given for credit, and a violent student strike failed to reverse this order. Cleaver led a crowd of students in Sproul Plaza in an obscene chant against Governor Reagan.

While the furor over the "Cleaver course on American racism" was still in the headlines, trouble erupted at San Francisco State College, where radical leaders of the Black Students Union demanded the creation of a black studies department run exclusively by blacks and teaching revolutionist doctrines. This was the most important of "fifteen non-negotiable demands," some of which had been added by a "Third World Liberation Front" including Latin-American and Asian-American radical students. The demands were to be backed "by any means necessary," including a long strike characterized by Maoist rhetoric, violent disruption of classes, vandalism, and personal assault. The large tactical squad of the San Francisco police, specially trained for campus riot duty, finally broke the strike with mass maneuvers and arrests.

The San Francisco State uprising was a failure, but before it was over a similar movement was launched at Berkeley, early in 1969, with a strike to demand an autonomous "Third World College." Though this demand was not granted, the campus did establish a Department of Ethnic Studies. Next came the disastrous affair of the "People's Park," in May 1969. This began when Berkeley's radical young "street people" tried to appropriate a block of university-owned land near Telegraph Avenue as a park for their own use. When the university fenced the block, a mob gathered to try to destroy the fence, and there was a riot in which sheriff's deputies responded to the throwing of rocks by firing shotguns. One young bystander, watching from a rooftop on Telegraph Avenue, was killed, and another was blinded. This tragedy frightened, enraged, and "radicalized" thousands of young people throughout the region and produced such a massive movement to "take the park" that a force of National Guardsmen was sent to protect it. A National Guard helicopter broke up a disorderly crowd on the campus by spraying the whole area with tear gas, which drifted into dozens of classrooms and even into the campus hospital.

By this time, Berkeley was only one of many American university towns with large groups of rebellious and violence-prone young people. There was repeated violence and arson at Stanford. The University of California at Santa Barbara had long been thought of as a quietly conservative campus, but in February 1970 its student residential community of Isla Vista exploded in a series of riots in which the branch of the Bank of America was burned and a student was killed when a deputy's gun discharged accidentally. Student rebellion reached a nationwide climax in May 1970 after a detachment of Ohio National

Police encircle militant students at San Francisco State College, January 23, 1969. About 380 demonstrators were arrested and taken away in patrol wagons, after many of them had hurled rocks and bottles at the police. (*Courtesy of United Press International*)

Guardsmen shot and killed four young people on the campus of Kent State University, following the burning of the ROTC building in protest against the "spreading of the war" to Cambodia. For the rest of the spring term many American campuses experienced various degrees of disruption. At Berkeley, thousands of students and a few faculty members tried to "reconstitute" the campus as a center for argumentation against the war and tried to stop all other campus activity until the war was ended.

Such extreme tactics did not end the war and only succeeded in damaging universities and colleges in the eyes of the great majority of the public. Campus rebellion now began to burn itself out, and two events of the summer of 1970 contributed to a widespread public revulsion against further violence. A bomb allegedly set off by four young ultraradicals destroyed a laboratory building at the University of Wisconsin and killed a graduate student. And an attempt by a group of black convicts to escape from a courtroom at San Rafael, California, with guns allegedly purchased by Angela Davis, resulted in several deaths including that of a judge. In the eyes of many, this tragedy at Frank Lloyd Wright's beautiful Marin County civic center had an important connection with the history of campus radicalism in California. Angela Davis was a young black radical scholar, an avowed member of the Communist party, and a student of Professor Herbert Marcuse of the University of California at San Diego. The regents of the university had recently refused to renew her appointment as an acting assistant professor of philosophy at UCLA. Nearly two years after the Marin shootout she was finally acquitted of complicity in it.

By the fall of 1970 the volcano of student rebellion had become dormant, if not extinct. By 1971 even radical students at Berkeley began to speak of "the old New Left of the 1960s," and to debate "why the movement died." New Left student radicalism had collapsed largely from its own weaknesses, excesses, and general counterproductiveness. Other factors were the gradual winding down of the Vietnam War, the extreme political reaction of taxpaying voters against the costs of educating students who had tried to close the colleges with strikes and violence, the dampening effects of tuition increases and the economic recession, and the coming of the 18-year-old vote and the growth of interest in the possibilities of "working within the system." Mass disruption on the campus was an idea whose time had come and gone.

A report of the American Council on Education, ranking the graduate school of the University of California at Berkeley as the best in the country, received very limited publicity and did little to counteract the massively hostile reaction of most California voters to the radicalism of the student New Left. One of many examples was the fate of a proposed bond issue for the university which appeared on the statewide ballot in 1970 in the wake of the attempt to "reconstitute" the campuses. Even though the bonds were clearly limited to the provision of badly needed new facilities for *medical* schools, they were decisively voted down, essentially because the name "University of California" was attached to them. Such sentiment contributed heavily to the reelection of the conservative Governor Reagan in November 1970; public opinion polls showed that many of his supporters were disappointed because state taxes had been raised in spite of his promises to reduce them; but that the most widely supported of all his policies was the firmness with which he had dealt with "campus rioters."

SELECTED BIBLIOGRAPHY

Economic and population trends may be followed in the *Economic Report of the Governor*, prepared by the state Department of Finance, and in the *California Statistical Abstract*, both annual publications.

The upsurge of concern for the environment is exemplified in William Bronson, *How to Kill a Golden State* (1968), and Harold Gilliam, *Between the Devil and the Deep Blue Bay: The Struggle to Save San Francisco Bay* (1969). Collections of material on ecology are Garrett De Bell, editor, *Environmental Handbook; Prepared for the First National Environmental Teach-in* (1970); Grant S. McConnell, editor, *Protecting Our Environment* (1970); and George E. Frakes and Curtis B. Solberg, editors, *Pollution Papers* (1971). The conservationist quarterly *Cry California*, published by California Tomorrow, was launched in 1965. Robert C. Fellmeth and others, *Power and Land in California* (1971), produced under the auspices of Ralph Nader's national organization, includes massive criticisms of water pollution and other misuses of the environment.

Lewis Yablonsky, *The Hippie Trip* (1968), is a sociological study of the hippie movement of the 1960s. It can be interestingly compared with Lawrence Lipton, *The Holy Barbarians* (1959), a sympathetic description of the beatniks of the '50s as exemplified in their colony in Venice, California. David E. Smith and John Luce, *Love Needs Care* (1971), is a thorough history of the Haight-Ashbury and the Free Medical Clinic. See also Theodore Roszak, *The Making of a Counter Culture* (1969); Nicholas Von Hoffman, *We Are the People Our Parents Warned Us Against* (1969); Joe David Brown, editor, *The Hippies* (1967); Warren Hinckle, "A Social History of the Hippies," *Ramparts* (March 1967), reprinted in Dennis Hale and Jonathan Eisen, editors, *The California Dream* (1968); and Tom Wolfe, *The Electric Kool-Aid Acid Test* (1968), on Ken Kesey's propaganda for LSD. Hippie "underground" newspapers included the *Berkeley Barb*, the San Francisco *Oracle* and its Los Angeles namesake; and the Los Angeles *Free Press*.

Important works on black radicalism in California include Eldridge Cleaver, *Soul on Ice* (1968); Bobby Seale, *Seize the Time: The Story of the Black Panther Party and Huey P. Newton* (1970); Philip S. Foner, editor, *The Black Panthers Speak* (1970); Edward J. Epstein, "The Panthers and the Police: A Pattern of Genocide?" *New Yorker,* February 13, 1971; and Theodore Draper, *The Rediscovery of Black Nationalism* (1969).

On campus rebellions, in addition to the works of Lipset, Wolin, and Heirich cited above for Chapter XXXVIII, see Michael C. Otten, *University Authority and the Student: The Berkeley Experience* (1970); John Searle, *The Campus War* (1971); Art Seidenbaum, *Confrontation on Campus* (1969); and "Law and Order on the Campus," from the *Report of the Select Committee on Campus Disturbances,* California Assembly, May 1969, in E. C. Lee and W. D. Hawley, editors, *The Challenge of California* (1970), pp. 165–174. The troubles of San Francisco State College produced a spate of memoirs, including John Summerskill, *President 7* (1971); Robert Smith, Richard Axen, and Devere Pentony, *By Any Means Necessary* (1971); Kay Boyle, *The Long Walk at San Francisco State* (1971); William Barlow and Peter Shapiro, *An End to Silence: The San Francisco State College Movement in the '60s* (1971); and Dikran Karagueuzian, *Blow It Up!* (1971).

Chapter XLIII

POLITICS IN THE REAGAN ERA

THE CREATIVE SOCIETY." The governorship of Ronald Reagan began on January 2, 1967; and he chose to take the oath of office within the first few minutes after midnight, in the capitol rotunda. His first public utterance as Governor, recorded on television, was a quip to Senator George Murphy: "Well, George, here we are on the late show again." The customary procedure would have been to combine the swearing-in with the delivery of the inaugural address, three days later, on the capitol mall. In another departure from custom, Reagan chose to receive the oath from an associate justice of the state supreme court who was a conservative, rather than from the chief justice who was a liberal. The outgoing Governor was also excluded from the proceedings.

The reasons for the extraordinary timing of the oath were never clearly explained, but there was no mystery about the central idea of the new administration, as stated in the inaugural address on January 5: "The cost of California's government is too high. It adversely affects our business climate.... We are going to squeeze and cut and trim until we reduce the cost of government." Speaking as a self-styled "citizen-politician" who had never before held a public office, Reagan thus made a powerful appeal to the popular mood of hostility toward government and taxation. For many years, he said, "you and I have been shushed like children and told there are no simple answers to complex problems which are beyond our comprehension. Well, the truth is, there are simple answers—there are just not easy ones.... The time has come to run a check to see if all the services government provides were in answer to demands or were just goodies dreamed up for our supposed betterment."

"This does not mean," he said, that "there is no part for government to play. Government has a legitimate role... in taking the lead in mobiliz-

Governor Ronald Reagan is sworn in by California Supreme Court Justice Marshall F. McComb in the specially decorated capitol rotunda shortly after midnight, January 2, 1967. Reagan's left hand is on the Bible of Father Junípero Serra, which is held by California Senate Chaplain Wilbur Choy. In the background are statues of Queen Isabella and Christopher Columbus. (Courtesy of United Press International)

ing the full and voluntary resources of the people. In California we call this partnership between the people and government the Creative Society."

This slogan had been coined early in the campaign of 1966 by one of Reagan's most enthusiastic supporters, W. Steuart McBirnie, an ultraconservative minister of Glendale who conducted a radio program called "The Voice of Americanism." Politicians, said McBirnie, "should be catalysts to harness all the resources of the private sector of the nation to solve America's problems." To "get that creative energy loaned to government, you get businessmen to volunteer as one-dollar-a-year men as during the [first World] War." During the campaign Governor Brown had denounced Reagan for adopting as the label for his own program a slogan devised by a right-wing fundamentalist. But Reagan had replied: "I'm very proud to have had the help of Dr. McBirnie.... The Creative Society is the same philosophy which I have held and expressed for the last fifteen years many times in speeches."

Reagan's conservative philosophy was not, he insisted, "a retreat into the past." Yet it had an intensely nostalgic quality. Reagan described his constituency as "the forgotten American... that fellow... working 60 hours a week to provide the advantages for his family, but being taxed heavily to take care of some other people's problems." This was remarkably reminiscent of the "forgotten man," a phrase first used as the title of a public lecture by the conservative economist William Graham Sumner in 1883 and referring to "the self-supporting and self-respecting person who has to bear the cost of all the political bungling and social quackery. There is always somebody who pays," said Sumner, "and it is always the sober, honest, industrious, economical men or women."

Reagan's political and social philosophy was a stunning reversal of the ideas of such Governors as Earl Warren and Edmund G. Brown, who had believed that government services should have a great, direct, and positive role in the state's development.

An actual reduction in the total budget of a huge and growing state, in a period of inflation, was an impossibility. Most of the state government's annual expenditures were mandated by law. The largest of the state services whose budgets could be reduced at the Governor's discretion were in the fields of state higher education and mental health, and in these sensitive areas Reagan made drastic cuts. He decided to reduce state funds for the University of California by nearly 30 percent of what the regents had asked for the coming year, although enrollments and costs were increasing; and he decreed a similar reduction in funds for the state college system. To make up part of the difference, Reagan proposed that the university and the state colleges should institute substantial tuition charges. These, he said at a press conference, "would help get rid of undesirables. Those there to agitate and not to study might think twice before they pay tuition." Reagan himself had worked to earn his way through a private college, with a substantial tuition only partly covered by an athletic scholarship. His views on tuition were in interesting contrast with those of Edmund G. Brown, who had been unable to afford to go to college at all except for night law school, but who believed all the more deeply in California's long-established policy of tuition-free public higher education.

In one of his campaign speeches, Reagan had said that he was "sick at what has happened at Berkeley. Sick at the sit-ins, the teach-ins, the walkouts. When I am elected Governor I will organize a throw-out, and Clark Kerr will head that list." Reagan was not, however, solely responsible for the dismissal of President Kerr, although it occurred at the first regents' meeting that he attended as Governor, early in 1967. Most of the regents had been dissatisfied with Kerr's handling of student disruptions since the Sproul Hall sit-in of December 1964, when Governor Brown had sent the state police into the building at the request of Berkeley Chancellor Edward W. Strong, and against Kerr's advice; Kerr had proposed instead that he and the governor should enter the building together and attempt personal negotiations with the students. The regents might have dismissed him in 1965 if Brown had not interceded to prevent it, and Reagan's accession merely tipped the balance. But the dismissal of Kerr sent shock waves throughout the national academic community, where it was angrily denounced as an anti-intellectual assault on academic freedom. Brown wrote in 1970 that he was "shocked by Reagan's attack on higher education in the state. He had done about everything destructive possible except to invite commercial lumber interests to log the beautiful groves of trees off the university campuses." President John H. Bunzel of San Jose State College, a liberal Democrat who had fought the radicals when he was head of the political science department at San Francisco State, said that "My philosophy of government is very different from that of our governor. I do not believe that government is best which does the least for higher education." Such criticisms were not confined to Reagan's partisan opponents. The Republican *Los Angeles Times* editorialized in vain against his policies toward higher education.

But most of the voters of California approved of Reagan's education policies, and he did not modify them as the years passed. This was not true of his assault on the budget of the state Department of Mental Hygiene, which became generally regarded as the greatest mistake of his first year in office, and which even Reagan later tacitly recognized as an error, to be at least partially rectified in future budgets. In March 1967, on the basis of misleading statistics and wishful thinking, Reagan announced that a decrease in the number of patients in the state hospitals would permit a reduction of 3,700 in the department's staff and a saving to the state of more than 17 million dollars. The result was a major setback in the state's progress toward adequate care of the mentally ill.

In spite of such widely publicized "economies," Reagan was forced in July 1967 to sign a record budget of more than 5 billion dollars, and tax increases of nearly 1 billion, although he was able to claim that he had cut the rate of annual increase in the state budget from 16 percent to 8 percent.

Reagan's inaugural address had also promised to "support a bipartisan effort" to lift the "archaic" 160-acre limit on irrigation water from Federal projects. To organize the attack on the limitation he appointed a Governor's Task Force headed by Burnham Enerson, water attorney for the Kern County Land Company. The task force recommended that the limit be raised to 640 acres and that water for larger units be made available at a higher price in order to "remove the subsidy," according to a formula long proposed by the late Democratic Senator Clair Engle. Senator George Murphy introduced a bill to this effect, but it failed to win approval in Congress.

Reagan and Nixon. From the time when Henry Salvatori and other wealthy conservative Republicans had formed the "Friends of Ronald Reagan" in 1965, they had made little or no secret of the fact that they were grooming him not only for the governorship of California but also for the Presidency of the United States. The phrase "the Creative Society," though it represented a political philosophy quite opposite to that of "the Great Society" and the "war on poverty" of the national Democratic administration, was also intended to suggest a presidential program. On the night of his election as governor, Reagan announced that he would head a slate of delegates pledged to him as California's favorite-son candidate for President in the Republican national convention in 1968. This was necessary, he said, to protect the party unity of California Republicans from the effects of another struggle like the Goldwater-Rockefeller contest that had divided them so bitterly in the California Republican primary of 1964.

Though Reagan insisted that he had no real presidential ambitions and would be fully concerned with his duties as Governor, he was actually a very serious presidential candidate. He was much in demand as a speaker at Republican fund-raising dinners throughout the country, particularly in the Southern states. The party had been growing rapidly there, and it was expected that the South would hold the balance of power in the next election. Though Reagan was as conservative as Goldwater, the country was in a more conservative mood than it had been in 1964, thanks largely to hostile public reaction against the riotous behavior of radicals, whom Reagan never ceased to denounce. And although his ideas and policies as Governor were often criticized as simplistic and negativistic, few observers could still question his appeal and effectiveness as a political campaigner. Television had created a whole new world of political campaigning, and Reagan was a master of that medium. Most of the critics who tried to write him off as a second rate actor who got into politics because his acting career had declined were now forced to recognize him as a highly skilled politician who had by accident spent several years as an actor.

Richard Nixon, until his strength emerged in the 1968 presidential primaries, was widely assumed to be disqualified by the stigma of his defeat for the governorship of his own state of California in 1962. Reagan had now defeated Brown, who had defeated Nixon. On the day after the 1962 election, many newspapers reported that the voters of California had "removed Richard Nixon from politics," but the reports of his political death were greatly exaggerated. For the next several years, while building up a fortune as a partner in a leading law firm in New York, Nixon also worked loyally and patiently for Republican candidates and party treasuries throughout the nation, and in the process maintained his contacts with party leaders. He worked hard for Goldwater in 1964, and in the end, four years later, Goldwater threw his support to Nixon even though his ideological preference was for Reagan.

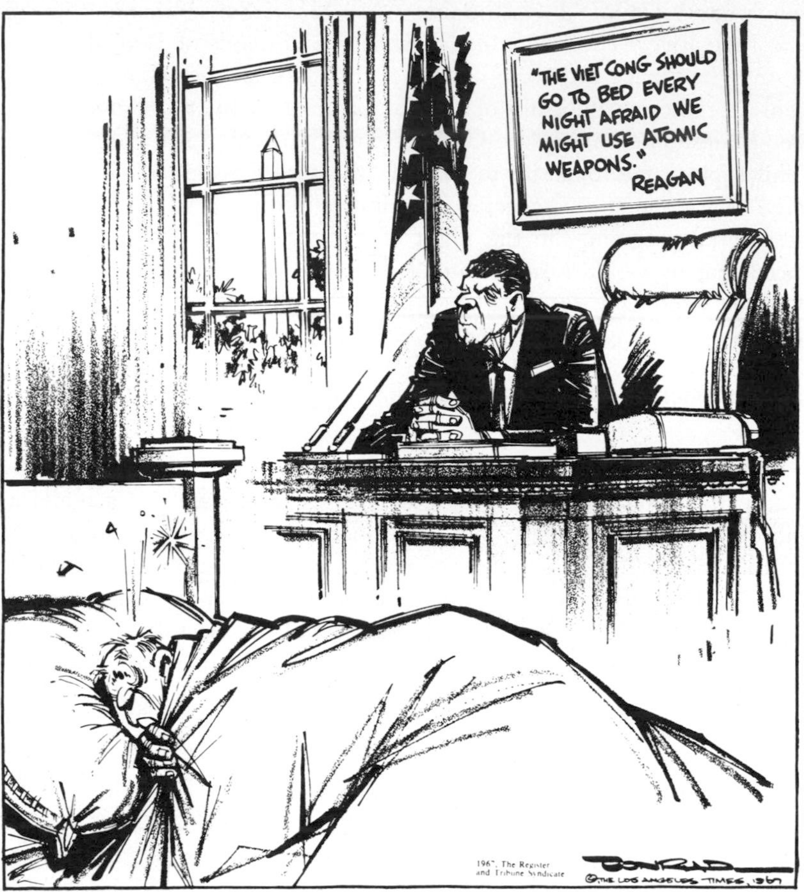

Americans should go to bed every night afraid Reagan might become President. Cartoon by Paul Conrad in the Los Angeles Times, *July 5, 1967. (Courtesy of The Register and Tribune Syndicate)*

Reagan was substantially to the right of Nixon on virtually all issues, foreign and domestic. On the war in Vietnam, Nixon had been in a sense "the original hawk," when as Vice President in the mid-1950s he had advocated American military intervention many years before it became a reality. But in 1968, recognizing the mounting disillusionment with the stalemated conflict, Nixon took a very cautious stand, claiming to have a plan for bringing the war to an early end, a plan that he would reveal after he was elected. Reagan, on the other hand, did not waver from his ultrahawkish position. He deplored the restraints placed on American military action by the fear that China might intervene in Vietnam as it had in Korea. "The Viet Cong," said Reagan, "should go to bed every night afraid we might use atomic weapons." *Los Angeles Times* cartoonist Paul Conrad responded with a cartoon captioned: "Americans should go to bed every night afraid Reagan might become President." Conrad's cartoons criticized Reagan more consistently than did the *Times*'s editorials; in this and other respects he was sometimes described as "ahead of the *Times*."

On racial issues, also, Nixon was more successful than Reagan in avoiding dangerously unambiguous stands. Reagan refused to avow any disagreement with the political views of George Wallace of Alabama, the third-party candidate who was a serious rival of both Nixon and Reagan for the support of the South.

When the Republican national convention was about to assemble at Miami Beach, Goldwater advised Reagan to release the California delegates to Nixon as soon as possible, but Reagan persisted to the last moment in the belief that he might actually be nominated himself. Some Republicans still cherished a fantastic hope that Rockefeller and Reagan might join as running mates on a "dream ticket" uniting the party's moderate and conservative wings. But Nixon could not be stopped.

The Democrats in 1968 were more badly divided than the Republicans. President Johnson's smashing victory over Senator Goldwater in 1964 had been in considerable part a result of Goldwater's open advocacy of an escalation of the war in Vietnam, but Johnson himself had since followed the tragic course of enormous military involvement, essentially, perhaps, because he could not bear to be "the first President of the United States to lose a war." Victory proved unattainable, however, and under tremendous criticism Johnson announced on March 31, 1968, that he would not run for reelection. He hoped to be succeeded by Hubert Humphrey, who as Vice President had supported him on Vietnam. In the California Democratic primary, the principal contenders were Senators Robert Kennedy and Eugene McCarthy, both strong critics of the administration's war policies. Kennedy won with a slate of delegates headed by Jess Unruh; but on the night of his California primary victory Kennedy was assassinated in Los Angeles. Humphrey won the nomination in the stormy convention at Chicago, but Unruh gave him almost no support in the subsequent campaign; and in November Nixon won the electoral votes of California by a narrow margin, as he had done in 1960. In that year, John F. Kennedy's nationwide popular vote had been only 0.17 of 1 percent larger than Nixon's—in terms of percentage the closest presidential election in American history. In 1968 Nixon's nationwide margin over Humphrey was only 0.71 of 1 percent. But however narrowly, Nixon had now become the first native Californian to be President of the United States. He soon transferred his state citizenship from New York back to California and his personal residence as a voter to a coastal mansion that would also serve as the "Western White House," at San Clemente in his native Orange County.

Plans for unity among California Republicans in 1968 had been damaged when Max Rafferty, the right-wing state superintendent of public instruction, insisted on running for the United States senatorship long held by the moderately

Robert F. Kennedy, with his wife and his principal California backer, Jess Unruh, celebrating his victory in the California primary, June 4, 1968. A few minutes later the 42-year-old Senator was brought down by an assassin's bullets. (Courtesy of United Press International)

liberal Republican Thomas Kuchel. Many Republican business leaders were aware that Kuchel's seniority and increasing influence in the Senate had great value in such matters as the allocation of government contracts to California firms. Henry Salvatori told Rafferty to stay out of the race and warned him that he would get no campaign money from Reagan's backers. Nevertheless, Rafferty entered the Republican primary and defeated Kuchel in it; but this so angered Kuchel's many admirers that they refused to vote for Rafferty in the general election, which he lost to the liberal Democrat, Alan Cranston.

Reagan, Unruh, and the elections of 1970. Governor Reagan enjoyed very little success with his legislative programs during his first term. The Democrats had narrowly retained control of both the senate and the assembly in the elections of 1966, and although the Republicans won both houses by equally narrow margins in 1968, their majorities were not solid enough to ensure passage of the governor's measures. In 1970 he campaigned vigorously for Republican candidates in many legislative districts, hoping to carry them into office on his political coattails. But although his personal charisma was strong enough to win his own re-election over Jess Unruh, his efforts to purge Democratic legislators failed dismally, and the Democrats regained both houses. Unruh could console himself with the boast that "we cut off his coattails right up to the lapels."

Unruh had become the most important leader of the California legislature in its whole history and the best-known state legislator in the United States. He had grown up in rural Kansas and Texas in a family so poor that "we bathed, when we bathed, in the horse troughs. . . . I never wore socks before I was twelve, but no one could tell the difference because my feet were so dirty." He dropped out of a small college in his first year, enlisted in the Navy, and spent World War II in the Aleutians while Ronald Reagan was making training films for the Army Air Corps in Hollywood and starring in an Irving Berlin musical called *This is the Army*, in which George Murphy played the role of Reagan's father. After the war, Unruh studied at the University of Southern California on the G.I. bill and in 1948, the year of his graduation, made the first of three unsuccessful campaigns for the state assembly. The difficulties of conducting these campaigns without significant financial backing impressed him with the fact that, as he often remarked in later years, "money is the mother's milk of politics."

In 1954 Unruh won his first election to the assembly from his district in Inglewood on the southwestern edge of Los Angeles, and his political genius soon brought him to the attention of Los Angeles financier Howard S. Ahmanson, widely regarded as the wealthiest man in the state. Ahmanson had been the largest financial backer of Governor Goodwin J. Knight, but in 1958 he foresaw the approaching Republican debacle. A pragmatist who cared nothing for partisan ideology, Ahmanson felt that California business interests would be wise to back a key man in the new legislature, and he found him in Unruh, then the chairman of the finance and insurance committee of the assembly. He had no objection to Unruh's liberal philosophy of social legislation; Ahmanson himself was once described as "too rich to be a Democrat and too liberal to be a Republican." He took charge of a pool of business contributions to campaign funds, and followed the advice of Unruh in allocating the money among Democratic candidates for the legislature.

The influence that this gave Unruh, along with his own talents for political organization, made him the most powerful figure in the legislature since the days of Arthur H. Samish. No one could assert that he was corrupt, as Samish had been; but for a time his image did become that of an arrogant political boss, and the Ahmanson-Unruh system involved Unruh, in his own words, in "the dangerous game of taking money from would-be corrupters—to elect men who would fight corruption." He was elected speaker of the assembly in 1961 and held the office until January 1969, the longest speakership in the history of California. For a time he demonstrated more arrogance than finesse. In the famous affair of "the Lockup," one night in the summer of 1963, when the 28 Republican assemblymen had prevented the necessary two-thirds approval of the budget by withholding their votes, Speaker Unruh invoked an obscure parliamentary procedure to keep them locked in the assembly chamber for nearly 23 hours. "Mr. Unruh," said the columnist Arthur Hoppe, "weighs between 200 and 400 pounds, chews cigars and opponents, and is probably the most powerful politician in California." In the early 1960s, he was often called "Big Daddy," partly because of his strong exercise of authority and partly because of his physical proportions. But Unruh was sensitive to the criticism he received and earnestly worked to counteract it. For example, he reduced his weight by 100 pounds in four months, and thereafter kept his figure trim though husky.

Unruh tremendously improved both the efficiency and the integrity of the California legislature. That body had never had a staff that would make it a match for either the lobbyists or the executive branch. Unruh pushed through a plan for a whole new corps of expert legislative assistants or consultants, and in 1966 he sponsored a constitutional amendment that raised the salaries of state legislators from $6,000 to $16,000, plus expenses, with further increases in subsequent years and with a generous retirement plan. In a survey made in 1970 by the national Citizens' Conference on State Legislatures, California's ranked as clearly the best in the country.

When Unruh decided to run for governor in 1970 he faced many handicaps. Not only was Reagan a formidable opponent whom the polls showed to have retained much of his original popularity with the voters, but also Unruh had many enemies within his own party. He had feuded with Governor Brown for years and had given him no support for a third term in 1966 because he believed Brown had virtually promised him the nomination in that year in return for support against Nixon in 1962. Unruh's failure to support Humphrey in 1968 had probably lost the state's electoral votes to Nixon, and this had angered many Democrats. The wealthiest campaign contributors backed Reagan, not only because most of them agreed with his ideology but also because he was the prospective winner; nearly three times as much money was spent on Reagan's campaign in 1970 as was spent on Unruh's. Moreover, there were few clear issues. The question of the responsibility for the absence of any substantial tax reform was so complex that the blame seemed to be about equally divided. As for the continuation of campus disorders through the spring of 1970, Unruh tried to blame Governor Reagan, as Reagan had blamed Governor Brown four years earlier, but the voters doubted Unruh's claim that he could have dealt with unruly students more effectively.

Unruh tried to cope with his chronic shortage of campaign money by using unorthodox tactics to obtain free television news coverage. For example, he staged a news conference in front of the residence of Henry Salvatori and engaged that outraged kingmaker in a sulphurous verbal confrontation. Unruh

Jess Unruh in heated discussion with Mr. and Mrs. Henry Salvatori, September 7, 1970. (Courtesy of United Press International)

denounced Reagan as the creature of wealthy men and corporate interests, but the effectiveness of this argument was somewhat weakened by the political backing that he himself had received from such interests in earlier years. When the votes for governor were counted, Reagan had 3,439,664 to Unruh's 2,938,607. The margin of 501,057 was only half as large as Reagan's margin of nearly a million votes over Brown in 1966, but it was still an impressive victory.

On the other hand, the elections for United States senator, for state superintendent of public instruction, and for the legislature were heavy setbacks for the Republicans. Early in 1970, it was revealed that during his senatorship George Murphy had secretly received a large salary and other perquisites from the Technicolor Corporation, and although he denied that this had compromised his integrity, many felt that it had. President Nixon considered it vital that Murphy's seat in the Senate, from Nixon's own state, should not go to the Democrats, especially since the other seat already had. Shortly before the election, Nixon appeared with Murphy and Reagan at San Jose, to speak for them and for other Republican candidates. A crowd of antiwar demonstrators had gathered, and it was widely reported, though also denied, that they threw rocks and other missiles that struck the President's car. There was evidence that Nixon, Murphy, and Reagan deliberately baited the demonstrators in the hope of gaining greater political advantage from their discreditable behavior. Reporters quoted Reagan as saying, "We gave them the peace sign back. That always infuriates them." Murphy's campaign managers ran a full-page newspaper advertisement headed "ANARCHY," in which they falsely accused his Democratic opponent, Congressman John Tunney, of sympathizing with such disorders, and of failing to support "law and order" in general. But such desperate tactics failed, and Tunney defeated Murphy overwhelmingly.

In the race for state superintendent, the two-term incumbent Max Rafferty was opposed by Wilson Riles, a Negro who was Rafferty's own deputy superintendent; it was to Rafferty's credit that he had appointed a substantial number of members of minority groups to offices in the state department of education. But he bore deep political scars from his disastrous campaign for the United States Senate in 1968, during which an enterprising reporter had come up with the story that Rafferty, who often denounced young opponents of the Vietnam War as draft dodgers, had walked with a cane during World War II and thrown it away on VJ day. Rafferty's personal political ambitions had made something of a mockery of the supposed nonpartisanship of the state superintendency; and Riles decisively defeated him, to become the first black man ever elected to a statewide office in California.

In 1963, state Republican leaders had formulated the "California Plan," designed to concentrate on the defeat of several Democratic assemblymen and senators in each election in order to gain solid Republican control of the legislature by 1971 and thus to control the decennial reapportionment of legislative and congressional districts, as the Democrats had done, to their great advantage, in 1961. Through the middle and late '60s the plan seemed to be on schedule, but in the crucial elections of 1970 it failed. The Democrats gained two seats in the state senate for a majority of 21 to 19, and four in the assembly for a majority of 43 to 37. In the spring and summer the Democrats had put on a highly successful voter registration drive, reviving some of the grassroots strength that they had developed in the 1950s. The declining reputations of Murphy and Rafferty hurt the whole Republican "team." And the deepening of the economic recession in the latter part of 1970 may have been the largest factor of all. Several Republican leaders maintained, probably correctly, that if the election had been held a few months earlier Reagan would have won by a million votes and his party would have held the legislature.

Welfare and taxation. During the prosperous 1960s, the proportion of Americans whose incomes were below the "poverty" level had decreased from 20 percent to 15 percent. In the same period, the proportion of the poor who received public assistance had greatly increased. Nationally, the welfare rolls doubled between 1965 and 1970. The Federal government paid about half of the cost and the states and counties the other half, and there were frequent increases in Federal matching appropriations, with many liberalizations of eligibility under the Federal welfare laws. Public assistance for the poor came to be regarded as a legal right rather than a personal disgrace. The burden fell most heavily on the taxpayers of the large cities and the urban industrial states because of the mass migration to the cities of poor blacks, and to a lesser extent poor whites, from the rural South, where they had been displaced by the mechanization of agriculture and the curtailment of agricultural production under Federal subsidies.

The existing welfare system not only failed to solve the problems of poverty but in many respects made them worse. The higher welfare payments in the urban states acted as a magnet for unschooled Southern Negroes. When they reached the cities they found themselves locked into a deepening cycle of poverty, either through a dependence on welfare or through unskilled jobs with minimum wages that kept them poor while depriving them of welfare benefits. The Los Angeles riots of August 1965 and the similar ghetto riots in several other large American cities in the summer of 1967 were in considerable part the results of this pattern of frustration and despair.

In August 1969 President Nixon proposed a new national urban policy, with massive improvements in the welfare system as its keystone. Remarkably enough, Nixon had appointed the liberal sociologist Daniel P. Moynihan of Harvard as one of his special advisers, and the new welfare plan was essentially Moynihan's work. Nixon advocated it as "the greatest single social reform in the last 40 years." He began to speak of his own administration as an "age of reform," and to talk more about reform than any Republican President since Theodore Roosevelt.

Under the current system, Nixon pointed out, "the person on welfare can often have a higher income than his neighbor who holds a low paying job." This situation "makes working people feel like fools. It makes the taxpayer furious and the welfare recipient bitter, and it inflicts the distillation of all this anger and bitterness on the children who inherit this land. It is a disgrace to the American spirit." Many a father left his wife and children because they could have a higher income on welfare but were ineligible for it if he was present in the home. "His children grow up either entirely without a father, or with a father who sneaks in and out of the house one step ahead of the welfare worker."

Under the Nixon reform proposals, welfare would be administered by the Federal government through the Social Security Administration, rather than by state and county agencies. To reduce the gross inequalities under which a family of the same size with no other income was receiving about $50 a month in Mississippi and about $300 in a few industrial states, the family would receive a minimum Federal payment of about $200 a month, which the states could supplement. To remove the incentives to unemployment or to desertion by the father, all poor families and not only those without a father would be eligible; and the family would be permitted to keep part of its earnings without any loss of welfare payments, and still more with only partial reductions in welfare. Thus not only those already on welfare but also the families of the "working poor," numbering about 2 million families or 10 million persons, would be included in the system, with the effect of nearly doubling the welfare rolls. Except for the disabled and mothers with preschool children, adult welfare recipients would have to accept employment if offered; and Federal job training, child care, and family planning services would be provided. The increased costs, amounting to many billions of dollars annually, would be borne by the Federal government, and at the same time, under a new "revenue-sharing" plan, gradually increasing amounts of Federal revenues would be turned over to the states, cities, and counties, many of which were faced with near-bankruptcy.

With amendments devised largely by Representative Wilbur Mills, Democrat of Arkansas, chairman of the House Ways and Means Committee, welfare reform bills passed the House in 1970 and 1971 but failed in the Senate; and in August 1971, when President Nixon announced an emergency anti-inflation program of freezing wages and prices, he asked that the effective dates of his national welfare proposals be deferred until 1973.

In California, Governor Reagan was also calling for welfare reform, but in his view the "reform" of welfare meant primarily the reduction of its cost. He called it "a cancer eating at our vitals," and pointed out that California, with 10 percent of the country's population, had 16 percent of the total number of persons on welfare. The economic recession intensified the cost problem by enlarging the welfare rolls while it decreased the state's revenues from income and sales taxes. Early in 1971, nearly 10 percent of the people of California were receiving public assistance, compared with less than 7 percent for the nation as a whole; 14 percent of the people of San Francisco were on relief, and 12.7 percent of the people of Los Angeles County. Because California's welfare benefits were among the highest, its costs per person were more than twice the national average.

Jess Unruh, as the Democratic candidate for Governor of California in 1970, endorsed President Nixon's welfare proposals, while Reagan, the Republican Governor, strongly opposed the Republican President's plan. The proposed concentration of authority over welfare in the Federal government was offensive to Reagan's conservative political philosophy, as was its increased cost to the taxpayers, even though the Federal budget would bear most of that cost and the state's share would be lowered. In 1971 Reagan called for massive reductions in California welfare costs, but the leaders of the Democratic majority in the legislature pointed out that hopes of removing many people from the welfare rolls by requiring them to work would be limited by the fact that only about 1 percent of the recipients were able-bodied adult males, while the mass of them were mothers, children, the blind, the disabled, or the aged. In August 1971 Reagan and the Democratic speaker of the assembly, Robert Moretti, worked out a compromise that was intended to bring reductions of about $200 million in California's total costs, mainly through tightened eligibility standards, better control of frauds, and lower maximum grants.

A companion measure, the result of a similar partisan compromise, sought to reduce the costs and tighten the administration of the state program of payments for the "medically indigent." After Congress had created the Federal system of "Medicare" for the elderly in 1965, it had also provided Federal matching grants to the states to help them pay for medical care for those too poor to afford it, whether they were on welfare or not. Nationally this system was known as "Medicaid"; California's subsidiary system, known as "MediCal," went into effect in 1966. Since his first year in office, Governor Reagan had repeatedly tried to cut MediCal payments by administrative orders, which were often ruled illegal by the courts. Several such rulings had been won by young lawyers for the California Rural Legal Assistance agency, a part of the Federal program of legal services for the poor under the Federal Office of Economic Opportunity. In 1971 Reagan exercised his legal authority to veto the annual Federal grant for the CRLA; but the national administration reinstated the grant after a special investigation which rejected Reagan's charges of illegal conduct against the agency.

When Reagan submitted his annual budget in January 1971, he insisted that the state's expenses for the next fiscal year could be met without increasing taxes, if welfare and MediCal costs were reduced, cost-of-living increases denied to state employees, and various other state expenses cut to the barest minimum. President Charles J. Hitch of the University of California complained that the governor had cut the university's budget "not merely to the bone but to the marrow." Yet in spite of these austerities Reagan was forced in December 1971 to sign a bill increasing state taxes by $500 million, largely because of declining revenues in another year of recession. The bulk of the new revenues came in the form of an income withholding tax, effective on January 1, 1972. Of the 38 states with income taxes, California had been the only one that did not provide for withholding; but Reagan had long promised never to approve it, and after signing the bill he told reporters that he had had to be "dragged kicking and screaming" to the desk where he did so. Another blow to Reagan's prestige among tax-conscious voters came when it was revealed that he had paid no state taxes on his own income for 1969 and 1970, mainly, he explained, because he had made some investments in buying a ranch in Riverside County and stocking it with cattle, which had involved large outlays and no immediate profits.

County and city governments and local school districts were in even worse financial condition than was the state, with the result that property taxes had been tremendously increased. Both Republicans and Democrats had promised tax relief for local governments and for the home owners, but this was slow in coming, partly because of the deadlock between the conservative Republican governor and the Democratic legislature over how it should be accomplished. The problem became even more complex in September 1971 when the California supreme court ruled in *Serrano v. Ivy Baker Priest* (who was the state treasurer), that the entire system of financing public schools through local property taxes was unconstitutional because it violated the equal-protection clause of the Fourteenth Amendment. The court pointed out that the wealthy school district of Beverly Hills spent $1,231 for each pupil while the poor district of Baldwin Park spent only $577.

In the early 1970s California's fiscal problems remained far from solution. The depth and complexity of the problems themselves would have made solutions difficult; the added element of frequent deadlocks between the Republican Governor and the Democratic legislature made any fully satisfactory solutions impossible.

SELECTED BIBLIOGRAPHY

Ronald Reagan, *The Creative Society* (1968), is a collection of speeches. Dissenting views may be found in Edmund G. Brown, *Reagan and Reality: The Two Californias* (1970). Useful biographical studies are Bill Boyarsky, *The Rise of Ronald Reagan* (1968); Joseph Lewis, *What Makes Reagan Run?* (1968); and Lou Cannon, *Ronnie and Jesse: A Political Odyssey* (1969), on Reagan and Unruh. Jules Witcover, *The Resurrection of Richard Nixon* (1970), and Gary Wills, *Nixon Agonistes* (1970), deal with Nixon's attainment of the Presidency.

See also Gladwin Hill, *Dancing Bear: An Inside Look at California Politics* (1968); Royce D. Delmatier et al., *The Rumble of California Politics* (1970), chapter XIII, "California and National Politics"; Frank H. Jonas and John L. Harmer, "The 1968 Election in California," *Western Political Quarterly*, XXII (September 1969), 468–474; and Totton J. Anderson and Charles G. Bell, "The 1970 Election in California," *ibid.*, XXIV (June 1971), 252–273.

The *California Journal*, beginning in January 1970, is a useful monthly digest of state government and politics.

Jacobus tenBroek, "California's Welfare Law—Origins and Development," *California Law Review*, XLV (July 1957), 241–303, and "California's Dual System of Family Law," *Stanford Law Review*, XVI (March–July 1964), 257–317 and 900–981, and XVII (April 1965), 614–682, include much historical background material and much criticism of traditional concepts and practices. See also James Leiby, "State Welfare Administration in California, 1879–1929," *Pacific Historical Review*, XLI (May 1972), 189–206.

THE PAST IS PROLOGUE

THROUGH the mid-1960s California's modern growth was a truly remarkable and historic process. Industry had flourished over the whole range of modern economic activity. Government had been a tremendous and essential catalyst, not only through Federal expenditures but also through state functions such as public higher education, water resources development, and highway building. An effective partnership between industry and government made California not only the wealthiest but also the most dynamic and promising of the states.

In the late '60s and early '70s California entered a cycle of adversity. The earlier projections of the Census Bureau, that the state's population would reach 25 million in 1975 and 40 million in the year 2000, were considerably scaled down. Yet it is reasonable to expect that California will resume its growth, at a slower rate, and it is reasonable to hope that the compensation for less growth will be more maturity. For in the truest sense the growth of a civilization should be measured in qualitative rather than quantitative terms; and in this sense the opportunities for California's future growth are greater than ever.

INDEX

AUTHORS CITED

GOVERNORS OF CALIFORNIA	EVENTS IN CALIFORNIA		EVENTS IN THE BRITISH COLONIES AND THE UNITED STATES	PRESIDENTS OF THE UNITED STATES
	Discovery of (Baja) California	1533		
	Cabrillo's discovery of San Diego Bay	1542		
	Drake's landing	1579		
	Vizcaíno at the Bay of Monterey	1602		
		1607	Founding of Jamestown, Virginia	
		1620	Landing of Pilgrims at Plymouth	
Gaspar de Portolá		1768		
	Founding of San Diego Discovery of San Francisco Bay	1769		
Pedro Fages	Founding of Monterey	1770	Boston Massacre	
Fernando Rivera y Moncada		1773		
Felipe de Neve	Ayala's exploration of San Francisco Bay	1775	Battles of Lexington and Concord	
	Founding of San Francisco	1776	Declaration of Independence	
	Founding of Los Angeles	1781		
Pedro Fages		1782		
		1783	Treaty of Paris	
	Visit of La Pérouse	1786		
		1787	Constitutional Convention	
		1789		George Washington
José Antonio Roméu		1791		
José Joaquín de Arrillaga		1792		
Diego de Borica		1794		
		1797		John Adams
José Joaquín de Arrillaga		1800		
		1801		Thomas Jefferson
		1803	Louisiana Purchase	
	Visit of Rezanov	1806		
		1809		James Madison
José Argüello		1814		
Pablo Vicente de Solá		1815		
		1817		James Monroe
Luis Argüello	End of Spanish rule	1822		
José María Echeandía		1825		John Q. Adams
	Visit of Jedediah Smith	1826		
		1829		Andrew Jackson
Manuel Victoria		1831		
Pío Pico José María Echeandía (South) Agustín V. Zamorano (North)		1832		
José Figueroa		1833		
	Secularization of the missions	1834		
José Castro		1835		
Nicolás Gutiérrez Mariano Chico Juan Bautista Alvarado	Alvarado's "revolution" makes California autonomous	1836	Independence of Texas	
		1837		Martin Van Buren
		1841		William H. Harrison, John Tyler
Manuel Micheltorena		1842		
Pío Pico		1845	Annexation of Texas	James K. Polk
José María Flores MILITARY GOVERNORS: John D. Sloat, Robert F. Stockton, John C. Fremont,	American occupation	1846	Mexican War	
Stephen W. Kearny, Richard B. Mason,		1847		
	Discovery of gold	1848		
Persifor F. Smith, Bennett Riley Peter H. Burnett, Ind. Dem.	Monterey Convention	1849		Zachary Taylor
	Admission to statehood	1850		Millard Fillmore
John McDougal, Ind. Dem.	1st Vigilance Committee in San Francisco	1851		
John Bigler, Dem.		1852		